Modern African Conflicts

Modern African Conflicts

An Encyclopedia of Civil Wars, Revolutions, and Terrorism

Timothy J. Stapleton, Editor

BLOOMSBURY ACADEMIC
NEW YORK • LONDON • OXFORD • NEW DELHI • SYDNEY

BLOOMSBURY ACADEMIC
Bloomsbury Publishing Inc
1385 Broadway, New York, NY 10018, USA
50 Bedford Square, London, WC1B 3DP, UK
29 Earlsfort Terrace, Dublin 2, Ireland

BLOOMSBURY, BLOOMSBURY ACADEMIC and the Diana logo
are trademarks of Bloomsbury Publishing Plc

First published in the United States of America by ABC-CLIO 2022
Paperback edition published by Bloomsbury Academic 2025

Copyright © Bloomsbury Publishing Inc, 2025

COVER PHOTO: ZANLA guerrilla in Zimbabwe, 1980.
(Peter Jordan/Alamy Stock Photo)

All rights reserved. No part of this publication may be reproduced or transmitted
in any form or by any means, electronic or mechanical, including photocopying,
recording, or any information storage or retrieval
system, without prior permission in writing from the publishers.

Bloomsbury Publishing Inc does not have any control over, or responsibility for,
any third-party websites referred to or in this book. All internet addresses given
in this book were correct at the time of going to press. The author and publisher
regret any inconvenience caused if addresses have changed or sites have
ceased to exist, but can accept no responsibility for any such changes.

Library of Congress Cataloging-in-Publication Data
Names: Stapleton, Timothy J. (Timothy Joseph), 1967– editor.
Title: Modern African conflicts : an encyclopedia of civil wars,
revolutions, and terrorism / Timothy J. Stapleton, editor.
Description: Santa Barbara, California : ABC-CLIO, An Imprint of ABC-CLIO, LLC, [2022] |
Includes bibliographical references and index.
Identifiers: LCCN 2022002046 (print) | LCCN 2022002047 (ebook) |
ISBN 9781440869693 (hardcover) | ISBN 9781440869709 (ebook)
Subjects: LCSH: Civil war—Africa—History—Encyclopedias. |
Revolutions—Africa—History—Encyclopedias. | Terrorism—Africa—History—Encyclopedias. |
Africa—History, Military—Encyclopedias. | Africa—Politics and government—1960–
Classification: LCC DT21.5 .M63 2022 (print) | LCC DT21.5 (ebook) |
DDC 355.0096—dc23/eng/20220208
LC record available at https://lccn.loc.gov/2022002046
LC ebook record available at https://lccn.loc.gov/2022002047

ISBN: HB: 978-1-4408-6969-3
PB: 979-8-7651-4016-1
ePDF: 978-1-4408-6970-9
eBook: 979-8-2161-1835-0

To find out more about our authors and books visit www.bloomsbury.com
and sign up for our newsletters.

Contents

Alphabetical List of Entries   vii

Topical List of Entries   xi

Introduction   xv

Timeline   xxi

A–Z Entries   1

Bibliography   367

About the Editor and Contributors   385

Index   389

Alphabetical List of Entries

Afabet, Battle of
African Armed Forces
Afwerki, Isaias
Air Power in Postcolonial African Wars
Al-Bashir, Omar (Umar) Hassan Ahmad
Algerian Civil War
Algerian War of Independence
Al-Qaeda in the Islamic Maghreb (AQIM)
Al-Shabaab
Amin, Idi
Angolan Armed Forces (FAPLA and FAA)
Angolan Conflicts
Ansar al-Sharia in Libya
Anyanya
Arab Spring
Arab-Israeli Wars
Armed Islamic Group (GIA)
Army of Islamic Salvation (AIS)
Azanian People's Liberation Army (APLA)
Barre, Mohamed Siad
Belgian Military Intervention in Africa
Bokassa, Jean-Bédel
Boko Haram
Bouteflika, Abdelaziz
Bozizé, François
British Military Involvement in Postcolonial Africa
Burundi, Civil War and Genocide
Buyoya, Pierre
Cabindan Insurgency
Cabral, Amílcar
Cameroon Conflicts
Canadian Military Involvement in Africa
Casamance Separatism
Central African Republic (CAR), Conflict in
Chad, Conflict in
Child Soldiers in Africa
Christmas War
Cold War in Africa
Congo Crisis
Congo Wars
Côte d'Ivoire Civil War
Coups and Military Regimes in Africa
Cuba and Africa
Cuito Cuanavale, Battle of
Darfur Genocide
Déby, Idriss

Democratic Republic of the Congo (DRC), Continuing Violence in
Diamonds and Conflict in Postcolonial Africa
Doe, Samuel
Dos Santos, Jose Eduardo
East African Mutiny
ECOWAS Military Interventions
Eritrea-Ethiopia War
Eritrean Liberation Front (ELF)
Eritrean People's Liberation Front (EPLF)
Eritrean War of Independence
Ethiopia: Insurgency and Interstate War
Famine in Postcolonial African Conflicts
"Five Majors" Coup, Nigeria
French Military Involvement in Postcolonial Africa
Gaddafi, Muammar
Garang, John de Mabior
Gbagbo, Laurent
Genocide in Africa
Gowon, Yakubu "Jack" Dan-Yumma
Habré, Hissène
Habyarimana, Juvénal
Haftar, Khalifa Belqasim
Hutu Power Movements
Islamic Salvation Front (FIS)
Janjaweed
Justice and Equality Movement (JEM)
Kabila, Joseph
Kabila, Laurent
Kagame, Paul
Kagera War
Kenya, Mau Mau Emergency

Kiir, Salva Mayardit
Lagu, Joseph Yanga
Liberian Civil Wars
Liberians United for Reconciliation and Democracy (LURD)
Libya, Conflicts with Egypt and the United States
Libyan Civil War, First
Libyan Civil War, Second
Lord's Resistance Army (LRA)
Machar, Riek Teny Dhurgon
Mengistu Haile Mariam
Mercenaries in African Conflicts
Micombero, Michel
Mobutu Sese Seko
Mogadishu, Battle of
Mokhtar Belmokhtar
Mondlane, Eduardo
Mozambique Civil War
Mozambique National Resistance (RENAMO)
Mugabe, Robert
Museveni, Yoweri
Namibia Independence War
Nasser, Gamal Abdel
National Front for the Liberation of Angola (FNLA)
National Liberation Front (FLN) Algeria
National Patriotic Front of Liberia (NPFL)
National Resistance Army (NRA)
National Union for the Total Independence of Angola (UNITA)
Navies in Postcolonial Africa
Neto, António Agostinho
Nigerian Civil War
Nkomo, Joshua

Nkurunziza, Pierre
Nujoma, Sam
Nyerere, Julius
Ogaden War
Ojukwu, Chukwuemeka Odumegwu
Operation Boleas: The SADC's Military Intervention into Lesotho
Operation Restore Hope
Peacekeeping in Africa
Popular Movement for the Liberation of Angola (MPLA)
Portuguese Africa, Independence Wars (Angola, Mozambique, and Guinea-Bissau)
Quifangondo, Battle of
Refugees in Postcolonial Africa
Revolutionary United Front (RUF)
Roberto, Holden Álverto
Rwanda, Civil War and Genocide
Rwandan Patriotic Front (RPF)
Sankara, Thomas
Sankoh, Foday Saybana
Savimbi, Jonas
Shaba, Zaire: Rebel Incursions and Foreign Intervention
Sierra Leone Civil War
Sirte, Battle of
Somalia Civil War
South Africa, Armed Struggle against Apartheid
South Africa's Border War
South Sudan Civil War
South West Africa People's Organization (SWAPO)
Soviet Military Involvement in Africa
Sudan Civil War, First
Sudan Civil War, Second
Sudan Liberation Army (SLA)
Sudan People's Liberation Movement/Army (SPLM/A)
Suez Crisis
Taylor, Charles McArthur Ghankay
Tigray People's Liberation Front (TPLF)
Tuareg Rebellions since 1960 (Mali and Niger)
Uganda, Insurgency in the North
Uganda's Civil War: The Bush War
Umkhonto we Sizwe (MK)
U.S. Africa Command
U.S. Military Involvement in Africa
Western Sahara, Conflict in
Women and War in Africa
Zenawi, Meles
Zimbabwe, Massacres (Gukurahundi)
Zimbabwe African National Union (ZANU)
Zimbabwe African People's Union (ZAPU)
Zimbabwe Independence War

Topical List of Entries

EVENTS

Afabet, Battle of
Algerian Civil War
Algerian War of Independence
Angolan Conflicts
Arab Spring
Arab-Israeli Wars
Burundi, Civil War and Genocide
Cabindan Insurgency
Cameroon Conflicts
Central African Republic (CAR), Conflict in
Chad, Conflict in
Christmas War
Cold War in Africa
Congo Crisis
Congo Wars
Côte d'Ivoire Civil War
Cuito Cuanavale, Battle of
Darfur Genocide
Democratic Republic of the Congo (DRC), Continuing Violence in
East African Mutiny
ECOWAS Military Interventions
Eritrea-Ethiopia War
Eritrean War of Independence
Ethiopia: Insurgency and Interstate War
"Five Majors" Coup, Nigeria
Kagera War
Kenya, Mau Mau Emergency
Liberian Civil Wars
Libya, Conflicts with Egypt and the United States
Libyan Civil War, First
Libyan Civil War, Second
Mogadishu, Battle of
Mozambique Civil War
Namibia Independence War
Nigerian Civil War
Ogaden War
Operation Boleas: The SADC's Military Intervention into Lesotho
Operation Restore Hope
Portuguese Africa, Independence Wars (Angola, Mozambique, and Guinea-Bissau)
Quifangondo, Battle of
Rwanda, Civil War and Genocide
Shaba, Zaire: Rebel Incursions and Foreign Intervention
Sierra Leone Civil War
Sirte, Battle of

Somalia Civil War
South Africa, Armed Struggle against Apartheid
South Africa's Border War
South Sudan Civil War
Sudan Civil War, First
Sudan Civil War, Second
Tuareg Rebellions since 1960 (Mali and Niger)
Uganda, Insurgency in the North
Uganda's Civil War: The Bush War
Western Sahara, Conflict in
Zimbabwe, Massacres (Gukurahundi)
Zimbabwe Independence War

IDEAS, ISSUES, AND MOVEMENTS

Air Power in Postcolonial African Wars
Belgian Military Intervention in Africa
British Military Involvement in Postcolonial Africa
Canadian Military Involvement in Africa
Casamance Separatism
Child Soldiers in Africa
Coups and Military Regimes in Africa
Cuba and Africa
Diamonds and Conflict in Postcolonial Africa
Famine in Postcolonial African Conflicts
French Military Involvement in Postcolonial Africa
Genocide in Africa
Hutu Power Movements
Justice and Equality Movement (JEM)
Peacekeeping in Africa
Refugees in Postcolonial Africa
Soviet Military Involvement in Africa
Suez Crisis
U.S. Military Involvement in Africa
Women and War in Africa

INDIVIDUALS

Afwerki, Isaias
Al-Bashir, Omar (Umar) Hassan Ahmad
Amin, Idi
Barre, Mohamed Siad
Bokassa, Jean-Bédel
Bouteflika, Abdelaziz
Bozizé, François
Buyoya, Pierre
Cabral, Amílcar
Déby, Idriss
Doe, Samuel
Dos Santos, Jose Eduardo
Gaddafi, Muammar
Garang, John de Mabior
Gbagbo, Laurent
Gowon, Yakubu "Jack" Dan-Yumma
Habré, Hissène
Habyarimana, Juvénal
Haftar, Khalifa Belqasim
Kabila, Joseph
Kabila, Laurent
Kagame, Paul
Kiir, Salva Mayardit
Lagu, Joseph Yanga
Machar, Riek Teny Dhurgon
Mengistu Haile Mariam
Micombero, Michel
Mobutu Sese Seko

Mokhtar Belmokhtar
Mondlane, Eduardo
Mugabe, Robert
Museveni, Yoweri
Nasser, Gamal Abdel
Neto, António Agostinho
Nkomo, Joshua
Nkurunziza, Pierre
Nujoma, Sam
Nyerere, Julius
Ojukwu, Chukwuemeka Odumegwu
Roberto, Holden Álverto
Sankara, Thomas
Sankoh, Foday Saybana
Savimbi, Jonas
Taylor, Charles McArthur Ghankay
Zenawi, Meles

ORGANIZATIONS

African Armed Forces
Al-Qaeda in the Islamic Maghreb (AQIM)
Al-Shabaab
Angolan Armed Forces (FAPLA and FAA)
Ansar al-Sharia in Libya
Anyanya
Armed Islamic Group (GIA)
Army of Islamic Salvation (AIS)
Azanian People's Liberation Army (APLA)
Boko Haram
Eritrean Liberation Front (ELF)
Eritrean People's Liberation Front (EPLF)
Islamic Salvation Front (FIS)
Janjaweed
Liberians United for Reconciliation and Democracy (LURD)
Lord's Resistance Army (LRA)
Mercenaries in African Conflicts
Mozambique National Resistance (RENAMO)
National Front for the Liberation of Angola (FNLA)
National Liberation Front (FLN) Algeria
National Patriotic Front of Liberia (NPFL)
National Resistance Army (NRA)
National Union for the Total Independence of Angola (UNITA)
Navies in Postcolonial Africa
Popular Movement for the Liberation of Angola (MPLA)
Revolutionary United Front (RUF)
Rwandan Patriotic Front (RPF)
South West Africa People's Organization (SWAPO)
Sudan Liberation Army (SLA)
Sudan People's Liberation Movement/ Army (SPLM/A)
Tigray People's Liberation Front (TPLF)
Umkhonto we Sizwe (MK)
U.S. Africa Command
Zimbabwe African National Union (ZANU)
Zimbabwe African People's Union (ZAPU)

Introduction

Armed conflicts represent a substantial part of African history since around 1960. Conquered by European powers during the late nineteenth and early twentieth century, most African colonies transformed into independent states during the late 1950s and 1960s. Many factors contributed to the decolonization of Africa, including the post–World War II weakness of European colonial powers, the development of a bipolar world order dominated by two officially anti-colonial superpowers (the United States and the Soviet Union), the rise of an international anti-colonial movement, including newly independent countries in Asia and the protests of African nationalists within the colonies. While most African countries gained independence through a process of negotiation between outgoing European colonial regimes and African political leaders, some parts of Africa experienced protracted anti-colonial wars. Together with the Suez Crisis of 1956 that subordinated the colonial powers to the new superpowers, anti-colonial struggles fought in Kenya, Madagascar, Cameroon, and Algeria during the 1950s informed wider British and French decolonization across the continent. However, the unwillingness of Portugal to withdraw from Angola, Mozambique, and Guinea-Bissau as well as the continuation of white settler–minority regimes in Southern Rhodesia (now Zimbabwe), South West Africa (now Namibia), and South Africa led to insurgencies in these territories that began in the 1960s and ended at various times from the 1970s to the early 1990s. Corresponding with the decolonization era, especially from around 1960, the global Cold War superimposed itself on many of these conflicts, with the United States and its Western allies providing direct or indirect support for the remaining colonial/settler states and the Soviet Union and the Eastern Bloc assisting African liberation movements.

Postcolonial African conflicts were/are either interstate wars or civil wars or sometimes both. Direct warfare between African states (interstate wars) remained uncommon in independent Africa. The Organisation of African Unity (OAU), formed in 1963 as a compromise between Pan-Africanist leaders such as Kwame Nkrumah of Ghana who wanted unification and others such as the presidents of the former French colonies who remained close to France, maintained a policy of safeguarding the borders imposed on Africa during the colonial era and inherited by the postcolonial states. In addition, impoverished African states built armed forces, including new air forces and navies but often lacked the resources to engage in protracted conventional warfare without external assistance. Nevertheless, a number of state versus state wars occurred in postcolonial Africa. Although the scale and intensity of operations varied, brief wars ranging from a few days to a few months took place between Algeria and Morocco in 1963, Libya and Egypt in 1977, Ethiopia and Somalia in 1977–1978, Tanzania and Uganda in 1978–1979, and Burkina Faso and Mali in 1985. The few protracted interstate wars, lasting several or more years, included apartheid South Africa's constant armed incursions into southern Angola from 1975 to 1988, Libya's military operations in northern Chad during the 1970s and 1980s that culminated in the 1987 "Toyota War" and the Eritrean-Ethiopian War of 1998–2000. Furthermore, Egypt played a central role among the Arab powers in the Arab-Israeli conflicts of 1948, 1956, 1967, and 1973. Africa's most complex interstate wars took place in Zaire/Democratic Republic of the Congo (DRC) in the late 1990s and early 2000s. This began with the "First Congo War" of 1996–1997 when Rwanda, Uganda, and Angola invaded Zaire (DRC) to overthrow the Mobutu regime. The situation escalated during the "Second Congo War" of 1998–2002, also called "Africa's World War," when Rwanda and Uganda invaded DRC where the new government called on direct military assistance from Angola, Namibia, and Zimbabwe.

Civil wars became the most common form of armed conflict in postcolonial Africa. Upon independence, African states inherited borders imposed by European colonial conquest, and these often ignored important factors around physical or human geography. Divided by colonial and postcolonial borders, some large African ethnic groups live in different countries such as Somalis in Somalia, Kenya, Ethiopia, and Djibouti; Bakongo in Congo-Brazzaville, Congo-Kinshasa (DRC), and Angola; and Kalanga in Botswana and Zimbabwe. In West Africa, since European invaders arrived on the coast and advanced inland, many independent states include a southern coastal and forested region inhabited by Christians and a hinterland Savannah and Sahel region inhabited by Muslims. While the physical and human geography of West Africa reflects long west-east strips such as the coastal forest and the interior Sahel, the colonial powers–imposed political borders comprise a south-north axis cutting across ethnicities, religions, and environments. Additionally, colonial rule and colonial economies created regional disparities in Africa, with some areas within a country becoming relatively prosperous and others marginalized, and the colonial powers' ethnic divide-and-rule policies exacerbated tensions. Given these factors, African states experienced a series of regional secessionist movements almost immediately after independence, with some of these conflicts continuing for many years or decades. Regional secessions led to the Congo Crisis of 1960–1963, the Nigerian Civil War of 1967–1970, the First Sudan Civil War of 1955–1972, a series of interrelated conflicts within Ethiopia from the 1960s to 1991, periodic Tuareg rebellions in northern Mali and Niger from the 1960s to the 2010s, and the crisis in Southern Cameroon that began in 2016. Lesser-known but persistent separatist conflicts in independent Africa include those in the Cabinda Enclave of Angola from 1975, the Casamance region of Senegal from 1982, and the Caprivi Strip of Namibia from 1994. Due to the many secessionist movements in postcolonial Africa, the hostility of the OAU (renamed African Union from 2002) and its member states limited their success to two cases. Eritrea gained independence from Ethiopia in 1991 in circumstances related to end of the Cold War, and South Sudan seceded from Sudan in 2011 within the context of the American-led "War on Terror." Somaliland broke away from the civil war–ravaged Republic of Somalia in 1991, but the former failed to gain international recognition. Aside from secessionist movements, regionalism and overlapping factors like ethnicity and religion influenced other civil wars in postcolonial Africa. In Uganda, southern rebels fought a northern-dominated state in the early to the mid-1980s, and northern rebels fought a predominantly southern government from the late 1980s to the mid-2000s. From the 1960s, Chad experienced a series of civil wars between governments based in the south and supported by France and rebels based in the north and backed by Libya. After Angola's 1975 independence from Portugal, the rebel group with access to the capital took power, forming a state, but faced armed opposition from other insurgent forces in the north and south. Similarly, violence between southern-based governments and northern rebel forces broke out in Côte d'Ivoire and the Central African Republic (CAR) during the 2000s. In some cases, African groups favored by the colonial rulers faced retribution and overthrow after independence. In Rwanda, where Belgian colonial officials favored the Tutsi minority, Hutu leaders overthrew the Tutsi officials in 1959, ushering in a Hutu-majoritarian republic eventually eliminated by predominantly Tutsi exiled rebels who invaded in 1990 and took over during the genocide against the Tutsi in 1994. Conversely, in Burundi, a Tutsi military regime emerged in 1965, clung to power by exterminating potential leaders among the Hutu majority in the 1972 genocide, and faced an insurgency by Hutu rebels in the 1990s and 2000s that led to political change and a predominantly Hutu government. During the late 2000s and 2010s, a combination of influence from international Islamist extremism, deep regional marginalization, and ineffective governance led to insurgencies in West Africa's Sahelian hinterland, including parts of Mali, Niger, Burkina Faso, and northeastern Nigeria. In roughly the same areas, desertification accelerated by climate change informed violence between herding and farming communities over a decreasing amount of useable land. In many of these examples, and since the decolonization era, rival African states attempted to undermine each other by backing rebel groups in each other's territories. For instance, Zaire (DRC) backed rebels in northern Angola, and Angola hosted insurgents from southern Zaire during the 1970s, and Uganda supported rebels in southern Sudan during the Second Sudan Civil War (1983–2005), and in turn, Sudan sponsored insurgents in northern Uganda.

The changing international context greatly affected wars in postcolonial Africa. From around 1960 to 1990, rival superpowers and their allies supported authoritarian regimes and various rebel groups in Africa. For instance, during the 1970s and 1980s, the United States backed the Mobutu dictatorship in Zaire and insurgents in southern Angola, while the Soviet Union supported the Angolan and Ethiopian governments and liberation fighters in southern Africa. Many African states claimed association with the nonaligned movement, though in reality, they often sided with an external Cold War power. African leaders claimed affiliation with Cold War ideologies like capitalism and communism and therefore received external support from respective superpowers in what appeared like "proxy wars," but at the same time, conflicts in postcolonial Africa always originated in local problems and competitions over power. In Africa, Cold War alliances sometimes shifted, with, for example, the Soviet Union abandoning Somalia and supporting a new regime in Ethiopia, hitherto a Western ally, during the Ogaden War of 1977–1978. The Cold War did not cause African conflicts, but it usually made them deadlier, with external powers providing many billions of dollars worth of arms and ammunition to combatants. Indeed, some of the last "proxy" battles of the waning Cold War occurred in southern Angola during the late 1980s. With the end of the Cold War and the collapse of the Soviet Union at the start of the 1990s, the context of African wars changed substantially. The fall of hitherto superpower-backed authoritarian regimes led to a spate of civil wars in parts of Africa, including in Liberia, Sierra Leone, Zaire/DRC, and Côte d'Ivoire or a continuation of civil wars such as in Angola and Sudan during the 1990s and 2000s. In the neoliberal world order, parties to conflicts in Africa could no longer rely on ideological affiliation to gain external support, and they turned increasingly to extracting valuable resources such as oil, hardwood, diamonds, or minerals associated with the emerging electronics industry to finance their efforts. Similarly, the new free market context led to a resurgence of mercenaries engaged in African conflicts though as corporatized private military contractors rather than as agents of Western powers as they had been in the 1960s. Another broad phase in African warfare began with the 2001 Islamist terrorist attacks on the United States. While its disastrous intervention in Somalia in the early 1990s made the United States hesitant to become involved in subsequent conflicts in Africa, the American-led "War on Terror" involved cultivating and supporting allies among African states. For example, Ethiopia hosted bases for American drones flying reconnaissance and bombing missions against Islamist forces in the Horn of Africa region, and the Ethiopian military invaded Somalia in 2006 to prevent Islamists from seizing power. At the same time, the spread of the global jihadist movement superimposed itself on parts of Africa, informing insurgency or continued insurgency in the Sahel, Horn, and North Africa regions and recently in northern Mozambique.

Postcolonial Africa experienced a series of direct foreign military interventions. Since around 1960, and despite changing contexts, France pursued a consistent policy of sustained and robust military action in Francophone Africa comprising former French and Belgian colonies. For example, during the Cold War era, French troops supported various regimes in Chad during that country's long civil war and conflict with Libya, and French forces pursued Islamist insurgents in Mali and Niger during the 2010s and into the 2020s. Belgium conducted several vigorous interventions in its former Congo territory (Zaire/DRC) during the 1960s and 1970s but then switched to joining multinational peace missions in Africa from the 1990s. While Britain generally avoided military action in its former colonies in Africa, the British military provided assistance to a number of postconflict African armed forces such as Zimbabwe and South Africa, consistently sent its own troops to Kenya and Botswana for training, and intervened directly in East Africa in 1964 and Sierra Leone in 2000. With the exception of the Somalia intervention in the early 1990s, the United States avoided large military operations in postcolonial Africa, supporting some French and Belgian deployments and providing weapons and training to some African militaries such as Cold War allies Morocco and Zaire. Prompted by the post-2001 "War on Terror," the United States created the Africa Command to facilitate military engagement and anti-terrorist operations on the continent. The Cold War–era Soviet Union sent military advisers and technicians to allied African states like Angola and Ethiopia, but from the 1990s, bankrupt Russia largely withdrew from Africa until the 2010s when a resurgent Moscow sent private military contractors to the CAR and Libya and planned a naval base on Sudan's Red Sea coast. Supplementing Soviet efforts, though acting independently, Cuba dispatched large military expeditionary forces to Angola and Ethiopia during the Cold War, but subsequent and dire economic problems limited the island's engagement on the continent to humanitarian concerns. While China supplied military training and equipment to some African insurgent groups and state militaries, including that of Tanzania during the Cold War, the first Chinese military base in Africa opened in Djibouti in 2017 supporting naval operations in the Indian Ocean and reflecting China's increasing economic relationship with the continent. Although some international peacekeeping operations occurred in Africa during the Cold War, most famously during the Congo Crisis, these multiplied dramatically from the 1990s, with the continent hosting some of the world's largest and longest-running UN missions in places like the DRC, CAR, Sudan, and Mali. In Africa's post–Cold War era, the African Union (AU) and African regional organizations like the Economic Community of West African States (ECOWAS) also mounted their own international interventions attempting to end conflicts.

While some postcolonial African wars involved large mechanized ground forces and deployment of air power such as in southern Angola and the Horn of Africa during the Cold War, most wars in modern Africa have been fought primarily by light infantry forces using small arms, especially the ubiquitous Soviet-designed AK-47 assault rifle. As such, most postcolonial African wars have not caused massive numbers of battlefield casualties among soldiers. Civilians have suffered the most from the continent's wars. Given the lack of precise records and limited international reporting on African conflicts, experts debate the death tolls for specific conflicts, with humanitarian activists often inflating figures to inspire international intervention and some parties to conflicts understating them to minimize their culpability in potential war crimes. In most of Africa's wars, the breakdown of food production, medical services, and living conditions has caused far more deaths than combat between armies. Another major impact of African wars on civilians has been to produce millions of internally displaced people (IDPs) within their countries and refugees fleeing across borders. In the context of protracted wars such as in Sudan, the Great Lakes region, and the Horn of Africa, people lived in refugee camps for decades in a tragic situation that still exists in many places.

Although many African wars took place within the past few decades and some remain ongoing, researchers often experience problems in finding the primary source information on them. Given the dangerous conditions and uncooperative warring parties, as well as lack of interest about Africa in the developed world, journalists have not conducted an extensive coverage of Africa's postcolonial conflicts. Official documentation remains very difficult to locate, as African governments and state armed forces were and still are obsessively secretive about military activities, usually lacking any obligation to provide their citizens with information, even long after events. Similarly, non-state actors like liberation movements and rebel groups fighting asymmetrical wars maintained secrecy to protect themselves and were not in a position to produce or preserve detailed records. Furthermore, and with some important exceptions, many scholars working on Africa avoided in-depth explorations of warfare believing that it reinforced negative stereotypes of the continent and its people. This led to a situation where historians and other scholars often know a lot around the causes, context, key events, and endings of specific postcolonial African wars but very little about the details of military engagements and the forces that fought them. Several recent academics have described much of the literature on conflict in postcolonial Africa as producing an image of "warless wars" with very little impact on the broader study of military affairs. It is much easier to find out what happened in many of Africa's colonial wars fought well over a century ago than about its postindependence conflicts.

This one-volume encyclopedia provides concise historical information on conflicts that occurred in postcolonial Africa. The entries deal with most wars fought on the continent since the 1950s and cover a selection of themes, armed groups, interventionist foreign powers, events, and leaders. Each entry ends with a short "Further Reading" list of specialized academic studies, enabling a beginning reader to explore these subjects in greater depth. That said, and given the problems related to evidence explained earlier, some African conflicts have been studied more than others, resulting in an unbalanced literature and a paucity of information on some topics.

Timothy J. Stapleton

Further Reading

Clayton, Anthony. *Frontiersmen: Warfare in Africa since 1950*. London: UCL Press, 1999.

Doron, Roy, and Charles Thomas. "Introducing the New Lens of African Military History." *Journal of African Military History* 3, no. 2 (1999): 79–92.

Reid, Richard. *Warfare in African History*. Cambridge: Cambridge University Press, 2012.

Reno, William. *Warfare in Independent Africa*. Cambridge: Cambridge University Press, 2011.

Stapleton, Timothy. *Africa: War and Conflict in the Twentieth Century*. London: Routledge, 2018.

Stapleton, Timothy. *A Military History of Africa*. Vol. 3, *The Era of Independence: From the Congo Crisis to Africa's World War, c. 1963–2012*. Santa Barbara, CA: Praeger Security International, 2013.

Williams, Paul. *War and Conflict in Africa*. Cambridge: Polity Press, 2011.

Timeline

1952–1960
Kenya Emergency

1954–1962
Algerian War of Independence

1955–1971
Insurgency in Cameroon

1955–1972
First Sudan Civil War

1956
Suez Crisis

1960–1963
Katanga Secession (Congo Crisis)

1960–1974
Independence wars in Portuguese Africa (Angola, Mozambique, and Guinea-Bissau)

1961–1990
Anti-apartheid armed struggle in South Africa

1961–1991
Independence war in Eritrea

1962
Tuareg Rebellion in Mali

1963
Creation of Organisation of African Unity (OAU)

1964
Genocide in Rwanda

1964–1965
Rebellion in eastern Congo and Kwilu

1965–1980
Zimbabwe's Independence War/Rhodesian Bush War

1966–1967
Mutinies in eastern Congo

1966–1989
War of Independence in South West Africa (Namibia)

1967
Arab-Israeli War (Six-Day War)

1967–1970
Nigerian Civil War

1968–1990
Civil war in Chad

1972
Genocide in Burundi

1973
Arab-Israeli War (Yom Kippur War)

1975–1989
Angolan Civil War (involvement of South African, Cuban, Soviet forces)

1976–1991
Western Sahara Conflict

1977–1978
Ogaden War (Somalia-Ethiopia)

1977–1978
Egypt-Libya War

1977–1978
Shaba conflicts

1977–1992
Mozambique Civil War

1978–1979
Kagera War (Tanzania-Uganda)

1978–1991
Insurgency in Tigray, Ethiopia

1981
American naval operations off Libya

1981–1986
Insurgency in southern Uganda

1981–1987
Oppression in southwestern Zimbabwe (Gukurahundi)

1981–present
Somalia Civil War

1983–2005
Second Sudan Civil War

1985
Mali-Burkina Faso (Christmas War)

1986
American naval operations off Libya

1986–2006
Insurgency in northern Uganda

1987
Libya-Chad War (Toyota War)

1988
Battle of Cuito Cuanavale in Angola—Battle of Afabet in Eritrea (then part of Ethiopia)

1989
American naval operations off Libya

1989–1997
First Liberian Civil War

1990–1993
Rwandan Patriotic Front (RPF) invasion of Rwanda

1990–1995
Tuareg rebellion in Mali and Niger

1991
Collapse of the Soviet Union

1991–2002
Sierra Leone Civil War

1991–2002
Algerian Civil War

1992–1995
United Nations and U.S. intervention in Somalia

1992–2002
Continuation of Angolan Civil War

1993
Battle of Mogadishu ("Black Hawk Down" incident)

1993–2005
Burundi Civil War

1994
Genocide in Rwanda

1996–1997
First Congo War

1998–2000
Eritrea-Ethiopia War

1998–2002
Second Congo War (Africa's World War)

1999–2003
Second Liberian Civil War

2000
British intervention in Sierra Leone

2001
Terrorist attacks on the United States

2002
OAU transforms into the African Union (AU)

2002
Launch of the International Criminal Court

2002–present
Continuing violence in the eastern DRC

2002–2011
Côte d'Ivoire Civil War

2003–present
Civil war in Western Sudan (Darfur)

2004–2007
Central African Republic Civil War

2005–2010
Civil war in Chad

2006–2009
Ethiopian intervention in Somalia's Civil War

2007
Battle of Mogadishu

2007
Arrival of African Union Mission to Somalia (AMISOM)

2007–2009
Tuareg rebellion in Mali and Niger

2009–present
Boko Haram insurgency in Nigeria

2011
First Libyan Civil War

2012–2013
M23 rebellion in the eastern DRC

2012–present
Civil war in Mali—Conflict in Sahel

2012–present
Central African Republic Civil War

2013–2020
South Sudan Civil War

2014–2020
Second Libyan Civil War

2020–present
Civil War in Ethiopia

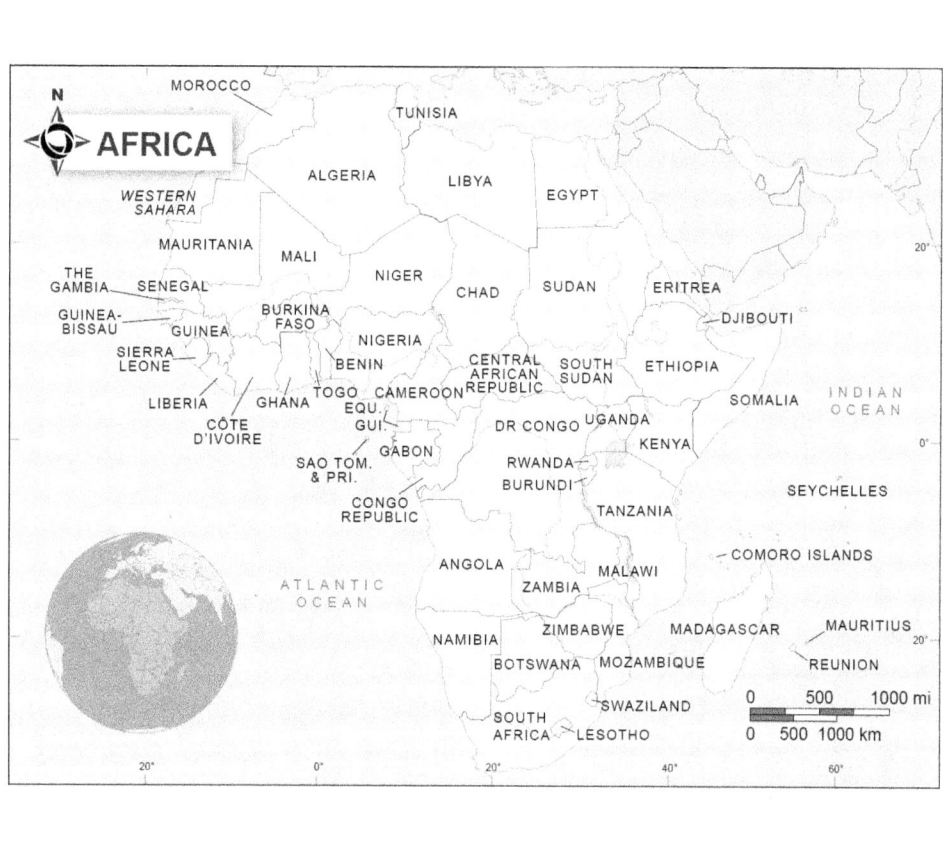

Afabet, Battle of (March 17–20, 1988)

The Battle of Afabet was a decisive clash between the Eritrean People's Liberation Front (EPLF) and the Ethiopian military during the Eritrean War of Independence. The battle was a crushing Eritrean victory, with the majority of the Ethiopian force being killed or captured while the Eritrean force suffered minimal casualties. The battle was the culmination of a longer strategy of the Eritreans to gradually weaken the Ethiopian military and then draw its formations into a decisive battle on terrain favorable to the EPLF. The Eritrean victory effectively ended Ethiopian resistance to the advance of the Eritreans and their allies and made their victory a foregone conclusion.

The roots of the Battle of Afabet lay in the previous years' Ethiopian campaigns. The Ethiopian communist government, known as the Derg, had been receiving significant military aid from the Union of Soviet Socialist Republics since the late 1970s and had largely driven the EPLF forces into their fortified mountain bases around Nacfa. However, despite a significant advantage in numbers and material, the Ethiopians failed to defeat the Eritreans in a series of massive conventional offensives launched between 1979 and 1986. Instead, the Eritreans managed to rebuild their stocks of weaponry and ammunition from their defeated foes while effectively reorganizing in their mountain bases. At the beginning of 1987, the Ethiopian military was exhausted and dealing with a proliferation of insurgent fronts, leading them to leave an understrength force in the Afabet region to try and contain the EPLF and plan a new offensive.

The EPLF took advantage of the Ethiopian Army's weakness to launch a series of attacks on the Ethiopian forces. In December 1987, the EPLF forces managed to badly defeat the Ethiopian forces and cause a rapid change of Ethiopian command. While the Ethiopians struggled to respond with an offensive of their own, the Eritreans kept up the offensive and marched their forces to the Hedai Valley, surrounding the Ethiopian garrison there on three sides and launching a coordinated attack beginning on March 17, 1988. The resultant Battle of Afabet would see the Eritreans slowly strangle and crush the trapped Ethiopian forces even as they held off Ethiopian reinforcements from the nearby Keren garrison. The majority of the Ethiopians were captured, with only a handful escaping to Keren.

The battle was a crushing blow to the Ethiopians. Their losses totaled around 15,000 trained soldiers, the vast majority of their effective troops left in the field. Their remaining forces, already trapped in various counterinsurgency operations throughout Ethiopia, now saw their morale hit a nadir. Conversely, the Eritreans had only an estimated 125 killed and 269 wounded, leaving their own forces almost entirely intact. In addition, the victory caused the Eritrean morale to soar and provided them with vast stockpiles of captured equipment. While the Ethiopian regime would fight on for another three years, the Battle of Afabet effectively made an Ethiopian victory over the EPLF an impossibility.

Charles G. Thomas

See also: Eritrean People's Liberation Front (EPLF); Eritrean War of Independence; Ethiopia: Insurgency and Interstate War; Mengistu Haile Mariam; Soviet Military Involvement in Africa.

Further Reading

Ayele, Fantahun. *The Ethiopian Army from Victory to Collapse, 1977–1991*. Evanston, IL: Northwestern University Press, 2014.

Connell, Dan. *Against All Odds: A Chronicle of the Eritrean Revolution*. Lawrenceville, NJ: Red Sea Press, 1997.

Pool, David. *From Guerrillas to Government: The Eritrean People's Liberation Front*. Athens: Ohio University Press, 2001.

Tareke, Gebru. *The Ethiopian Revolution: War in the Horn of Africa*. New Haven, CT: Yale University Press, 2009.

African Armed Forces

The experience of European colonial conquest and rule from the late nineteenth century to around the 1960s reinvented African military institutions and cultures. While some precolonial military structures survived as elements of indigenous culture, colonial states in Africa formed Western-style locally recruited armies to maintain internal security and provide soldiers for external service such as during the world wars. Upon Africa's decolonization in the late 1950s and 1960s, these colonial armies transformed into the national armed forces or defense forces of the new sovereign states. Given this context, colonial regional military commands such as Britain's Royal West African Frontier Force (RWAFF) and the King's African Rifles (KAR) in East Africa disbanded, with constituent territorial units becoming national armies with the same uniforms, weapons, organization, and sometimes, British officers. In the former French territories, which usually maintained close relations with the former colonial power, African military personnel had to decide on continuing service in the French Army or joining the new territorial forces. A few African countries that did not have colonial armies lacked militaries on independence, and new cash-strapped governments decided not to form defense forces. In the Gambia, the British had disbanded the colonial military in 1958, and the former High Commission Territories of Southern Africa—Botswana, Lesotho, and Swaziland—had never had permanent colonial forces given their proximity to white minority–ruled South Africa. Gaining independence in the 1960s, these states eventually founded their own militaries, such as Botswana in 1977, given the intensification of conflict in southern Africa and the Gambia in 1985 as part of its short-lived confederation with Senegal. While the German and then Belgian rulers of Rwanda and Burundi neglected to found locally recruited colonial armies in these territories, the Belgians created Rwandan and Burundian militaries in the late 1950s to maintain military relations with these states after their 1962 independence.

Since colonial armies constituted racially hierarchical organizations led by white European officers, African armed forces experienced a rapid process of Africanization of their officer corps during the decolonization era. During the 1950s, outgoing colonial officials initiated special programs to train the first generation of African officers, who often attended military academies in the metropole. With independence, African governments greatly accelerated the process of Africanizing their officer corps, and within a few years, European officers seconded to their armed forces had gone home. To train their officers, African armed forces founded military academies with the help of foreign partners and continued to send some officer candidates to other countries. For instance, the Ghana Military Academy, formed in 1960 with British and Canadian instructors, and the Nigerian Defence Academy, formed in 1964 with assistance from Indian officers. Nevertheless, the extremely rapid promotion of officers in the early years of Africa's independence, together with other factors involving ethnicity in politics and dire economic problems, contributed to the rise of a military coup culture in some African states.

After independence, African militaries evolved different institutional cultures stemming from state political ideologies and foreign sponsorship. Those African states that retained cordial relations, including military cooperation, with their former colonial rulers, usually adopted the Western model of professional armed forces, theoretically separate from civilian politics. They also organized along Western military lines and continued the military culture of the former colonial ruler. This category included most of the former French territories and the prominent former British colonies of Nigeria and Kenya. Given the Cold War context that lasted until the late 1980s, some African states distanced themselves from their former colonial powers and developed militaries modeled on Eastern Bloc forces. From the 1960s, socialist regimes in Guinea and Tanzania transformed inherited colonial armies into politicized party militias with assistance from the People's Republic of China. Successful revolutions, coups, and liberation movements also led to radical changes in African militaries. From the mid-1970s, revolutionary regimes in Angola and Ethiopia created large armed forces modeled and equipped along Soviet lines, given major Soviet and Cuban military assistance in the fighting of protracted conflicts. The end of wars through negotiations produced combined military structures. For example, the conventional Western-style militaries of the previous white-minority states of Zimbabwe (formerly Rhodesia) and South Africa combined, in 1980 and 1994, respectively, with demobilized guerrilla armies to found new national defense forces. While the conventional structure and Western traditions of these forces survived, especially given the influence of British advisers, political transformation meant that ex-insurgents ascended to top military command posts and the number of white personnel declined. As such, the Zimbabwe Defence Forces (ZDF) developed a veneer of Western professionalism but, in reality, functioned as a military wing of the authoritarian ruling party. Other negotiated settlements produced integrated state militaries such as in the Democratic Republic of the Congo in 2003 when state forces combined with several domestic rebel groups though some rebel factions resisted the integration process. In post–Cold War Africa, absent the ideologies of the 1960s–1980s, such military amalgamations rarely produced radical changes in military culture or organization.

Some postcolonial African militaries developed praetorian and predatory habits. Officers and sometimes noncommissioned personnel became involved in political intrigue to the detriment of their forces' military capabilities and skills. Adding to the praetorian culture, paranoid African heads of state tried to safeguard against military coups by forming special presidential guard units outside the normal command structure of the armed forces, but this usually intensified military politicization. At the same time, armed soldiers extorted and abused civilians, further undermining the credibility and image of the military. During the 1970s and 1980s, personalist dictators like Idi Amin in Uganda and Mobutu Sese Seko in Zaire (now DRC), both products of accelerated Africanization of the officer corps right after independence, failed to pay their soldiers, letting them extract wealth from oppressed civilians. Given the rising international concern over human rights from the 2000s, as well as greater Western military engagement with some African armed forces in the context of the global "War on Terror," African military authorities expressed rhetoric around protecting civilians, but their troops sometimes failed to live up to those standards. Protesting unacceptable service conditions, and in the context of political breakdown, some African soldiers staged mutinies, such as in newly independent Congo-Leopoldville in 1960, the Central African Republic in the 1990s, and Côte d'Ivoire in 2017. Illustrating the relationship between the state and the military, Africa's few stable democracies produced professional and disciplined militaries, such as in Botswana and Senegal.

Timothy J. Stapleton

See also: Air Power in Postcolonial African Wars; Amin, Idi; Angolan Conflicts; British Military Involvement in Postcolonial Africa; Canadian Military Involvement in Africa; Cold War in Africa; Coups and Military Regimes in Africa; East African Mutiny; Ethiopia: Insurgency and Interstate War; French Military Involvement in Postcolonial Africa; Mobutu Sese Seko; National Resistance Army (NRA); Navies in Postcolonial Africa; Rwandan Patriotic Front (RPF); Soviet Military Involvement in Africa; U.S. Military Involvement in Africa; Zimbabwe, Massacres (Gukurahundi).

Further Reading

Baynham, Simon. *The Military and Politics in Nkrumah's Ghana*. Boulder, CO: Westview Press, 1988.

Parsons, Timothy. *The 1964 Army Mutinies and the Making of Modern East Africa*. Westport, CT: Praeger, 2003.

Peters, Jimi. *The Nigerian Military and the State*. London: I.B. Tauris, 1997.

Prunier, Gerard. *Africa's World War: Congo, the Rwanda Genocide and the Making of a Continental Catastrophe*. Oxford: Oxford University Press, 2009.

Rupiya, Martin, ed. *Evolutions and Revolutions: A Contemporary History of Militaries in Southern Africa*. Pretoria: Institute for Security Studies, 2005.

Tareke, Gebru. *The Ethiopian Revolution: War in the Horn of Africa*. New Haven, CT: Yale University Press, 2009.

Thomas, Charles. "The Tanzanian People's Defence Force: An Exercise in Nation Building." PhD thesis, University of Texas at Austin, 2012.

Afwerki, Isaias (1946–)

The head of the former Eritrean People's Liberation Front (EPLF), Isaias Afwerki led Eritrea to independence from Ethiopia and became the new nation's first president in 1993.

Isaias was born on February 2, 1946, in Asmara, the capital of Eritrea. He became a deputy division commander of the Eritrean Liberation Front (ELF) in 1967, a post he held for three years. Several years later, he helped found the EPLF, and he led the group in the last stages of the Eritrean rebellion. The attempt to throw off Ethiopian rule began in 1962, when Ethiopia annexed the coastal region outright, and intensified in 1977. The EPLF, which had support among both Christians and Muslims, took Asmara in April 1991 and in May, defeated the last Ethiopian forces in the region.

Isaias quickly secured U.S. support of Eritrean independence and, in June 1991, announced that his movement would seek the United Nations' sponsorship of a referendum on independence, to be held within two years. He also announced that he would seek Ethiopian assistance in setting up a provisional government for Eritrea and said that stability in Ethiopia was in the best interest of the new nation.

Though Eritrea was not officially independent, it operated as an independent nation for two years under the guidance of Isaias before it was officially declared independent in May 1993 following an April 1993 referendum in which 99.8 percent of Eritrean voters endorsed independence. Shortly afterward, Isaias was elected president by the new national assembly. In February 1994, Isaias's EPLF renamed itself the People's Front for Democracy and Justice.

Eritrea continues to struggle to rebuild itself after years of economic catastrophe. Isaias has worked to build a strong nation despite the economic hardships, in part, by introducing a national service program in May 1994. Participants in the program serve for a term of 18 months, focusing on military training for the first six months and spending the remaining time learning about the country and rebuilding the agricultural sector.

Isaias also hopes to play a guiding role in African affairs, making a dramatic statement at the opening session of the Organisation of African Unity (OAU) in June 1993. He blasted the organization for its failure during the previous 30 years to achieve its objectives. Isaias told the gathered delegates that while the OAU professed support of human rights, economic development, and other worthy goals for the African continent, it had not worked seriously to realize them. He called the continent a "marginalized actor" on the world's economic and political scene and said it seemed to continually produce "the wrong manuals" for political management, economic development, and democratization.

However, Isaias's own government has not yet lived up to the goals he set out before the OAU. Eritrea remains a one-party state, and Isaias has yet to hold presidential elections that were planned for 2001. Plans for a new constitution have repeatedly been put on hold, and democratic freedoms remain out of reach. Human rights groups and a growing opposition contingent within Eritrea have charged that Isaias leads a repressive government intent on quashing dissent.

Soon after a two-year border war with Ethiopia led to a cease-fire in 2000, his government shut down all private newspapers, detained several journalists, and arrested 11 prominent government critics, all of whom had fought with Isaias in the nation's earlier war for independence from Ethiopia. These moves created a deep division among Eritreans, and by May 2003, more than a dozen opposition groups had formed an alliance intent on overthrowing Isaias through paramilitary strikes on government targets. Given the authoritarian and oppressive regime cultivated by Afwerki, including compulsory military service for youth, large numbers of Eritreans fled their country.

In 2018 Isaias began to engage in talks with Ethiopian prime minister Abiy Ahmed, who had reached out in order to improve the troubled relationship between the two countries. As a result of these talks, by July 2018 Isaias and Ahmed signed a peace agreement, officially ending the war between Eritrea and Ethiopia and reestablishing commercial and diplomatic relations. Subsequently, in 2020, Eritrean forces became involved in the conflict in Ethiopia's Tigray province fighting rebels from the Tigray People's Liberation Front (TPLF) who opposed the Ethiopian government of Abiy Ahmed.

ABC-CLIO

See also: Eritrea-Ethiopia War; Eritrean Liberation Front (ELF); Eritrean People's Liberation Front (EPLF); Eritrean War of Independence; Ethiopia: Insurgency and Interstate War. Tigray People's Liberation Front (TPLF)

Further Reading

Connell, Dan. *Against All Odds: A Chronicle of the Eritrean Revolution*. Lawrenceville, NJ: Red Sea Press, 1997.

Iyob, Ruth. *The Eritrean Struggle for Independence: Domination, Resistance, Nationalism, 1941–1993*. Cambridge: Cambridge University Press, 1997.

Kibreab, Gaim. *The Eritrean National Service: Servitude for "the Common Good" and the Youth Exodus*. Woodbridge: James Currey, 2017.

Pool, David. *From Guerrillas to Government: The Eritrean People's Liberation Front*. Athens: Ohio University Press, 2001.

Air Power in Postcolonial African Wars

From the earliest days of the use of air power in warfare, aircraft featured in conflicts fought in Africa. During their 1911 invasion of Libya, the Italian military became the first in the history of warfare to use airplanes for reconnaissance and bombing. This innovation inspired Italian army officer Giulio Douhet's ideas about the supremacy of air power, later expressed in his 1922 book *Command of the Air*. Most of the World War I campaigns fought in Africa featured limited use of military aircraft. In 1915 British airplanes directed the naval gunnery that sunk the German cruiser *Konigsberg* as it was hiding in the Rufigi River delta of German East Africa (today's Tanzania). Both sides employed aircraft, primarily for reconnaissance, during the South African invasion of German South West Africa (now Namibia) and the German-led Ottoman attacks on the British-controlled Suez Canal in Egypt. During the interwar period (1919–1939), some colonial authorities believed that air power could be used as an efficient method for controlling subject populations in Africa and the Middle East without deploying large occupation armies. As such, aircraft played a central role in colonial counterinsurgencies of the 1920s and 1930s. In 1920 Britain's newly formed Royal Air Force (RAF) used a dozen biplanes to bomb the mountain strongholds of Somali rebel leader Mohammed Abdullah Hassan, whom the British called the "Mad Mullah," ending his 20-year resistance. Britain's colonial secretary Winston Churchill famously called this operation "the cheapest war in history." In 1922, the new South African Air Force (SAAF) used air power to suppress an armed insurrection by white mine workers around Johannesburg and a rebellion by the Bondelswart community in South African–administered South West Africa. The French in Morocco and the Italians in Libya made extensive use of air power during counterinsurgency operations in the 1920s and 1930s. The Italian forces that invaded Ethiopia in 1935–1936 relied heavily on air power, utilizing around 600 aircraft for the bombing and deployment of chemical weapons. During World War II, the East African campaign of 1940–1941 and the North Africa campaign of 1940–1943 witnessed the widespread use of aircraft in various roles by all sides. The use of air power by colonial powers continued during Africa's decolonization wars of the 1950s and early 1960s. During the Mau Mau Emergency in Kenya in the 1950s, RAF aircraft flew reconnaissance, propaganda leaflet–dropping, and bombing missions. While the effectiveness of aerially bombing insurgent forest hideouts was initially questioned, it appears that RAF bombing in Kenya inflicted significant casualties on the rebels and encouraged them to abandon some areas. During Algeria's Independence War (1954–1962), the French military pioneered the use of helicopters in warfare, providing a model for American forces in Vietnam and Portuguese forces in Angola, Mozambique, and Guinea-Bissau.

The first African air forces were established during the 1920s and 1930s. As a sub-imperial power of Britain, the white minority–ruled Union of South Africa established the continent's first air force in 1920 with a gift of 113 airplanes from London. In 1935, the white-minority administration of Britain's Southern Rhodesia created a military air unit that became the Southern Rhodesian Air Force (SRAF) at the start of World War II, and at the same time, the territory hosted the British Empire Air Training Scheme (BEATS). Both the SAAF and SRAF augmented the RAF in several theaters of World War II, particularly East Africa and the Mediterranean. In the early days of South Africa's apartheid regime, which sought to position itself on the Western side of the unfolding Cold War, South African pilots flew in the Berlin Airlift of 1948–1949; a SAAF fighter squadron conducted over 12,000 sorties during the Korean War of 1950–1953; and South Africa acquired jet fighters and bombers, C-130 transport aircraft, and helicopters from Britain, Canada, and France during the 1950s and early 1960s. Reflecting the British occupation of Egypt, the Egyptian Air Force that formed in 1930 employed British aircraft and British advisers. While Egypt's technical neutrality meant that its air force did not fight in the Second World War, the Egyptian Air Force flew during the First Arab-Israeli War in 1948. Within the context of military modernization meant to protect Ethiopian independence, Emperor Haile Selassie founded the Imperial Ethiopian Air Force (IEAF) in 1929 and acquired a dozen airplanes flown by a small number of foreign and Ethiopian pilots during the early 1930s. In 1946, given the liberation of Ethiopia from Italian occupation during the Second World War, the emperor returned and reestablished the IEAF, trained and led by Swedish officers until the early 1960s. Within the Cold War context of the 1950s, Britain initially supplied aircraft to Ethiopia, but during the 1950s, the United States became the primary sponsor of the IEAF, providing pilot and technical training, F-86 Sabrejet fighters, and C-47 transport aircraft.

Most African air forces emerged during the decolonization era of the late 1950s and 1960s. Since the locally recruited colonial militaries that transformed into the national armed forces of the newly independent African states represented ground forces, new governments embarked on expensive programs to develop air power capabilities. Kwame Nkrumah, the Pan-Africanist leader of Ghana, which became the first sub-Saharan country to gain independence in 1957, believed that he needed to create a significant military force to contribute to the liberation of the rest of Africa from the remaining colonial powers and white-minority states. As a result, the Ghana Air Force (GAF) formed in 1959 with instructors from India, Israel, Britain, and Canada, and within a few years, it consisted of 900 Ghanaian personnel and 70 aircraft, including helicopters, Italian jet trainers, and Canadian bush planes. Shortly after Nigeria's independence in 1960, the Nigerian military sent personnel for pilot training in Ethiopia, Canada, and West Germany, and in 1964 the Nigerian Air Force (NAF) was established with an operational base at Kaduna and a variety of light aircraft and French helicopters. Initially, West Germany took a leading role in the NAF, providing its first commanding officer and training 500 Nigerian personnel. During the Nigerian Civil War (1967–1970), the federal military government's NAF came under a Nigerian officer and expanded dramatically with the addition of Soviet MIG-17 jet fighters, Ilyushin IL-28 jet bombers, and medium transport airplanes, many flown by foreign pilots. Given its territorial disputes with neighboring Western-backed Ethiopia, which possessed one of Africa's most potent air forces, newly independent and unified Somalia created an air force in 1964 with Soviet assistance, initially receiving MIG-17s and then, in 1976, 24 supersonic MIG-21 fighters and several Ilyushin bombers, representing the most lethal strike capability south of the Sahara. Reflecting independent Kenya's continued close alliance with former colonial power Britain, the Kenyan Air Force (KAF) was founded in 1964, just a few months after independence, and relied on British support; in the 1970s, it acquired Hunter jet aircraft from Britain and then F-5 jets from the United States. The involvement of some KAF officers in an attempted coup in 1982 led to the air element coming under army command until 1994 when it was reestablished as a distinct service. Distancing his country from Britain and reinventing the former colonial military as a militia of the ruling party, Tanzania's Julius Nyerere initially sought assistance from Canada in creating an air element for the Tanzanian People's Defence Force (TPDF) in the 1960s, but the desire for more lethal aircraft prompted him to establish closer ties with China, which trained pilots, constructed an air base, and provided MIG-17 fighters during the early 1970s. Israel, seeking to end its diplomatic isolation and cultivate military allies south of the Arab states, played a central role in founding the Ugandan Air Force in 1964, donating reconnaissance and transport aircraft and a dozen Fouga Magister jet trainers, training pilots and technicians, and constructing several air fields. At the same time, Ugandan prime minister Milton Obote tried to balance the Israeli influence by accepting Chinese and Soviet military assistance, including Soviet MIG-17s and Soviet training of air force personnel. Cold War allegiances became instrumental in shaping North African air forces. Established in 1956, the Royal Moroccan Air Force, although it initially purchased some Soviet aircraft, developed in close association with former colonial power France and the United States. During the 1970s and 1980s, as it fought rebels in Western Sahara, Morocco purchased 39 Mirage fighters, 24 Gazelle helicopter gunships, and various light aircraft from France as well as 20 F-5 fighters and 15 C-130 transports from the United States. After fighting to achieve independence from France in 1962, Algeria established an air force with strong ties to the Soviet Union, which supplied aircraft such as MiG-17 light bombers, MiG-21 interceptors, Su-7 fighter-bombers, Antonov transports and transport helicopters; provided training; and built an air base. Tensions with neighboring Morocco led to Algeria using oil revenues to upgrade its fleet of Soviet aircraft and helicopters during the late 1970s and 1980s. During the 1950s, particularly after the 1956 Suez Crisis, the Egyptian regime of Gamal Abd al-Nassar moved closer to the Soviet Union, replacing its British aircraft with Soviet models, sometimes flown by Czech or Russian pilots. By the start of 1967, on the eve of another war with Israel, the Egyptian Air Force consisted entirely of Soviet-supplied aircraft such as MIG-21 fighters and Ilyushin IL-28 and TU-16 bombers.

Although most postcolonial African wars comprised civil wars and insurgencies fought by light infantry using small arms, air power exercised a disproportionate impact on many of these events. During the Congo Crisis of the early 1960s, separatist Katanga's small air force enabled it to survive until the arrival of a United Nations air force made up of Ethiopian, Indian, and Swedish assets that quelled the secession. Subsequently, in 1964–1965, American-supplied ground attack aircraft, piloted by Cuban exiles, and Belgian airborne operations, facilitated by the U.S. Air Force, proved decisive in suppressing an Eastern Bloc–backed rebellion in eastern Congo. While the federal government's overwhelming air superiority helped it win the Nigerian Civil War, the small Biafra Air Force, including a squadron of light prop aircraft armed with rockets called the "Babies of Biafra," disrupted Nigerian oil production and prolonged the life of the separatist state. In a similar way, the illegal white supremacist regime in Rhodesia, despite international sanctions, clung to power during the 1970s' liberation war by using its air power, including airmobile reaction teams and aerial bombing of insurgent camps in neighboring Zambia and Mozambique. At the end of the 1980s, the loss of long-standing South African air superiority over the South West Africa/Angola border, given the arrival of Cuba's Soviet air defense system and more Cuban aircraft, contributed to Pretoria's decision to grant independence to Namibia, which arguably led to the eventual end of apartheid in South Africa. In 1998, at the start of "Africa's World War," also fought in the Democratic Republic of the Congo (DRC), ground attack aircraft from the Zimbabwe Air Force prevented invading Rwandan troops, who had arrived in the western Congo by hijacked airliners, from seizing the capital of Kinshasa and interdicted other Rwandan forces in the east. During the 2013 French intervention in Mali known as Operation Serval, French air power decimated Tuareg separatist and Islamist insurgents, allowing French ground forces to drive them out of towns such as Gao and Timbuktu. Air power became even more influential during the conventional and mechanized wars between Egypt and Israel. In the 1967 conflict, Israel inflicting a stunning victory on Egypt by conducting a preemptive air strike that destroyed the Egyptian Air Force on the ground, and in 1973, Egyptian ground forces enjoyed success only as long as their air defense shield kept the Israeli Air Force (IAF) at bay.

Timothy J. Stapleton

See also: African Armed Forces; Arab-Israeli Wars; Cold War in Africa; Congo Crisis; Congo Wars; Ethiopia: Insurgency and Interstate War; French Military Involvement in Postcolonial Africa; Nigerian Civil War; Western Sahara, Conflict in.

Further Reading

Becker, Dave. *On Wings of Eagles: South Africa's Military Aviation History.* Durban: Walker-Ramus, 1991.

Dorn, Walter. "The UN's First Air Force: Peacekeepers in Combat, Congo 1960–64." *Journal of Military History* 77, no. 4 (October 2013): 1399–1424.

Kilford, Christopher R. *The Other Cold War: Canadian Military Assistance in the Developing World.* Kingston: Canadian Defence Academy Press, 2010.

Lord, Dick. *From Fledgling to Eagle: The South African Air Force during the Border War.* Johannesburg: 30 Degrees South, 2008.

Mutanda, Darlington. *The Rhodesian Air Force in Zimbabwe's War of Liberation, 1966–1980.* Jefferson, NC: McFarland, 2016.

Omissi, David. *Air Power and Colonial Control: The Royal Air Force, 1919–1939.* Manchester: Manchester University Press, 1990.

Al-Bashir, Omar (Umar) Hassan Ahmad (1945–)

Bashir was born on January 1, 1945. He became the longest-serving president of Sudan from 1989 to 2019, when he was ousted from power by the Sudanese Armed Forces. Bashir's early military career started with his admission into the Sudanese Army as a cadet in the paratroopers in 1960. By 1966, he graduated from the Sudanese Military Academy in Khartoum. His meteoric rise in the army led to his appointment as paratroop commander.

On June 30, 1989, Bashir staged a bloodless coup that toppled the coalition government of Prime Minister Sadiq al-Mahdi. By October 1989, the Revolutionary Command Council (RCC) for National Salvation was created by Bashir as the ruling body in Sudan. In addition, all political parties were banned except the National Islamic Front (NIF). Government officials were also arrested, including 100 military officers. The constitution was abolished; the national assembly and trade unions were also banned.

After Bashir came to power, several attempts were made to resolve the conflict between the Khartoum government and the Sudan People's Liberation Army (SPLA). However, the regime's support for Sharia law and its imposition on the southern Sudanese compromised the possibility of a peaceful dialogue with John Garang, leader of the SPLA. Throughout the 1990s Bashir's regime consistently waged war against the SPLA in the south. Thus, the incessant war affected the social and economic life of the Sudanese, and the unpopularity of Bashir's regime, especially among the southerners, increased.

In particular, Bashir's political affiliation with the NIF, headed by Hassan Turabi, who championed for the transformation of Sudan into an Islamic state, influenced Bashir's attempts to enact Sharia law in Sudan. Thus, the southern Sudanese, displaced in Khartoum, were dehumanized by the imposition of Sharia law. Furthermore, the liberalization of trade and migration with Arab countries were some of the prominent features of Bashir's foreign policy. During this period Osama bin Laden relocated to Sudan. As a result of bin Laden's clandestine support for different terrorist groups, Khartoum condoned such groups. Eventually, sanctions were imposed on Sudan by the United States for its role in human rights abuses and for its support of terrorism.

After the September 11, 2001, terrorist attack on the United States, there was enormous international pressure on Sudan to stop supporting the operation of terrorist groups in Sudan. Concomitantly, Khartoum's alliance with the Janjaweed militia attacks against civilians in Darfur instigated the issuance of the warrant for Bashir's arrest in March 2009 by the International Criminal Court. After South Sudan's independence from Sudan in 2011, an enormous oil reserve and resulting revenues were lost by Khartoum, which worsened its economic situation. Although Bashir initiated policies to tackle this situation, his ineffectual economic and political policies, among others, caused vehement opposition, which ended his regime.

Yusuf Sholeye

See also: Coups and Military Regimes in Africa; Darfur Genocide; Garang, John de Mabior; Sudan Civil War, Second; Sudan People's Liberation Movement/Army (SPLM/A).

Further Reading

Collins, Robert O. *The History of Modern Sudan.* Cambridge: Cambridge University Press, 2008.

Kramer, Robert S., Richard Lobban, and Fluehr Lobban. *Historical Dictionary of Sudan: African Historical Dictionaries.* Lanham: Scarecrow Press, 2013.

Moorcroft, Paul. *Omar al-Bashir and Africa's Longest War.* Barnsley: Pen and Sword, 2015.

Algerian Civil War (1992–2002)

After gaining independence in 1962, Algeria was ruled by the militaristic and secular National Liberation Front (FLN), which had fought an anti-colonial war against the French during the 1950s. Under the FLN, Algeria was described as "not a state with an army, but an army with a state." At the end of the 1980s, given protest brought on by economic problems and the changing international political context related to the end of the Cold War, Algeria embarked on multiparty democratic reforms, in which the Islamic Salvation Front (FIS) gained popularity among the urban poor. In January 1992 the Algerian military, dominated by FLN officers who feared the rise of Islamists and loss of access to the country's substantial oil revenue, seized the state and annulled recent elections in which the NIS had performed well. Forcing long-serving president and former military officer Chadli Benjedid to resign, the military ruled through a series of puppet civilian presidents.

Banned by the military-dominated Algerian state, the FIS turned to guerrilla warfare, forming the Islamic Armed Movement (MIA) that operated in mountainous rural areas and the Armed Islamic Group (GIA) that focused on towns and cities. Recently returned veterans of the war against the Soviet Union in Afghanistan joined these insurgent groups, furthering Islamist extremism and militancy. In 1993 the more radical GIA declared war on the comparatively moderate FIS and MIA and targeted anyone associated with civil society or the government. On the other hand, MIA military strategy concentrated on sabotaging state infrastructure and attacking state security forces. A major rebel victory took place in March 1994 when over 1,000 Islamist prisoners orchestrated a mass escape from Tazoult prison.

As it had done with the Soviet Union during the Cold War era, Algeria's state used oil money to buy weapons from cash-strapped Russia and other former Soviet republics as well from the French defense industry. At the same time, the Algerian government dramatically enlarged its paramilitary forces from around 30,000 to around 180,000 personnel, who bore the brunt of fighting in the civil war. The strength of Algeria's conventional military dropped from a peak of 170,000 in the mid-1980s to 120,000 in 1995 with conscripts comprising about half the force. As the war unfolded, the Algerian military split into two camps, with those led by the army chief of staff General Mohamed Lamari and supported by unions and feminist groups, who sought to exterminate the rebels, and those influenced by minister of defense and eventually high council of state General Liamine Zeroual, who preferred negotiation. Following the failure of negotiations with the FIS in October 1994, however, Zeroual began to lean toward the eradication camp, promoting officers who held such views, establishing armed self-defense militias and barring journalists from reporting on the war. In February and March 1995, security forces killed between 96 and 230 Islamist prisoners during a prison riot, and the military killed several hundred insurgents in a week-long battle southwest of Algiers.

Remaining small, the extremist GIA fielded around 2,000 to 3,000 insurgents. In 1994 the GIA declared violence-plagued Algiers a liberated zone, proclaimed an Islamic caliphate, and expanded its terrorist operations to France, with the hijacking of a French airliner. In the countryside the more moderate FIS and MIA formed the Army of Islamic Salvation (AIS), condemning GIA brutality against civilians and promoting the adoption of pluralistic democracy. With the 1995 election of General Zeroual who defeated several Islamist candidates to win the presidency, thus illustrating the popular support for secularism, the GIA massacred entire villages and urban neighborhoods, seeing anyone not actively combating the Algerian state as apostates. The election results also prompted violence and assassinations within the GIA and AIS as well as large battles between these groups.

The AIS, disgusted by the massacres, declared a cease-fire with the government in September 1997 and negotiated amnesty for its members. In 1999, given the sudden resignation of Zeroual, FLN veteran leader Abdelaziz Bouteflika was elected president and initiated a program that decreased violence, by granting amnesty to insurgents who had not committed rape or murder. Many rebels returned to civilian life. By 2002 the GIA had been effectively destroyed by internal conflict and effective state military operations, facilitated by American support that began after the September 2001 Islamist attacks on the United States. The United States provided Algeria with sophisticated military equipment such as night-vision devices and froze financial assets associated with Algerian Islamists. In February 2002 Antar Zouabri, who had led the GIA since 1996, was killed in a firefight with Algerian security forces. From 2004, with Bouteflika's reelection and the death or retirement of generals who favored the eradication of insurgents, Algeria continued the amnesty program for rebels and security force members and encouraged the demobilization of hundreds more insurgents. The Salafist Group for Preaching and Combat (GSPC), which had split from the GIA in 1998 disagreeing with the massacres, continued the Islamist struggle but found its presence in Algeria increasingly untenable. As such, the GSPC withdrew south into the Sahara and across the border into Niger, Mali, and Chad, where its members ultimately became involved in local conflicts such as the Tuareg Rebellion. In 2007 the GSPC adopted the name Al-Qaeda in the Islamic Maghreb (AQIM), thereby declaring its allegiance to a wider internationalist jihadist movement. During the late 2000s and 2010s, exiled Algerian Islamists who had fought in their country's civil war became influential in the expansion of violence throughout West Africa's Sahel zone. Amid the protests of the 2011 "Arab Spring," Bouteflika canceled Algeria's almost 20-year state of emergency, and another wave of even larger demonstrations in the country in 2019 prompted the resignation of the elderly and ailing president. Although the Algerian government maintained that 150,000 people were killed during the civil war, a subsequent study accounts for 44,000 dead or missing between 1992 and 2002.

Timothy J. Stapleton

See also: Algerian War of Independence; Al-Qaeda in the Islamic Maghreb (AQIM); Arab Spring; Armed Islamic Group (GIA); Army of Islamic Salvation (AIS); Bouteflika, Abdelaziz; Islamic Salvation Front (FIS); National Liberation Front (FLN) Algeria; Tuareg Rebellions since 1960 (Mali and Niger).

Further Reading

Martinez, Luis. *The Algerian Civil War 1990–1998*. New York: Columbia University Press, 2000.

Willis, Michael. *The Islamist Challenge in Algeria: A Political History*. New York: New York University Press, 1997.

Willis, Michael. *Power and Politics in the Maghreb: Algeria, Tunisia and Morocco from Independence to the Arab Spring.* London: Hurst, 2012.

Algerian War of Independence (1954–1962)

The Algerian War of Independence was a military effort by France during 1954–1962 to maintain its hold on its last, largest, and most important colony in the face of a Muslim insurgency. France regarded the Algerian War as part of the larger Cold War and tried unsuccessfully to convince its North Atlantic Treaty Organization (NATO) partners that maintaining French control over Algeria was in the best interests of the alliance. Unsupported by its allies, France found itself increasingly isolated in diplomatic circles. Ultimately, France experienced a humiliating defeat and a colonial exodus.

For 130 years, Algeria had been at the core of the French Empire. France conquered Algiers in 1830 and expanded the territory. Algeria became the headquarters of the French Foreign Legion (at Sidi-Bel-Abbès) and home to the largest number of European settlers in the Islamic world. In 1960 there were one million Europeans (known as colons or pieds-noirs) in Algeria. Unique among French colonies, Algeria became a political component of France, as Algiers, Constantine, and Oran were departments of the French Republic and had representation in the French Chamber of Deputies.

Nonetheless, Algeria was not fully three French departments, as only the European population enjoyed full rights there. The colon and Muslim populations lived separate and unequal lives, with the Europeans controlling the bulk of the wealth. Meanwhile, the French expanded Algeria's frontiers deep into the Sahara.

The Great Depression of the 1930s affected Algeria's Muslims more than any experience since their conquest as they began to migrate from the countryside into the cities in search of work. Subsequently, the Muslim birthrate climbed dramatically because of easier access to health care facilities.

While the colons sought to preserve their status, French officials vacillated between promoting colon interests and advancing reforms for the Muslims. Pro-Muslim reform efforts ultimately failed because of political pressure from the colons and their representatives in Paris. While French political theorists debated between assimilation and autonomy for Algeria's Muslims, the Muslim majority remained largely resentful of the privileged status of the colons.

The first Muslim political organizations appeared in the 1930s, the most important of these being Ahmed Messali Hadj's Mouvement pour le Triomphe des Libertés Démocratiques (MTLD, Movement for the Victory of Democratic Liberties). World War II (1939–1945) brought opportunities for change that increasing numbers of Algerian Muslims desired. Following the Anglo-American landings in North Africa in November 1942, Muslim activists met with American envoy Robert Murphy and Free French general Henri Giraud concerning postwar freedoms but received no firm commitments. As the war in Europe was ending and the Arab League was forming, pent-up Muslim frustrations were vented in the Sétif Uprising of May 8, 1945. Muslim mobs massacred colons before colonial troops restored order, and hundreds of Muslims were killed in a colon reprisal termed a "rat hunt."

Returning Muslim veterans were shocked by what they regarded as the French government's heavy-handed actions after Sétif, and some (including veteran Ahmed Ben Bella) joined the MTLD. Ben Bella went on to form the MTLD's paramilitary branch, the Organization Speciale, and soon fled to Egypt to enlist the support of President Gamal Abdel Nasser. Pro-independence Algerian Muslims were emboldened by the Viet Minh's victory over French forces at Dien Bien Phu in Vietnam in May 1954, and when Algerian Muslim leaders met Ho Chi Minh at the Bandung Conference in April 1955, he assured them that the French could be defeated.

Ben Bella and his compatriots formed the Front de Libération Nationale (FLN, National Liberation Front) on October 10, 1954, and the FLN revolution officially began on the night of October 31 to November 1. The FLN organized its manpower into several military districts, or *wilayas*. Its goal was to end French control of Algeria and drive out or eliminate the colon population. Wilaya 4, located near Algiers, was especially important, and the FLN was particularly active in Kabylia and the Aures Mountains. The party's organization was rigidly hierarchical and tolerated no dissent. In form and style, the party resembled Soviet bloc communist parties, although it claimed to offer a noncommunist and non-Western alternative ideology, articulated by Frantz Fanon.

As France steadily increased the number of its military forces in Algeria to fight the growing insurgency, French officials sought support from NATO partners in the Algerian War, arguing that keeping Algeria French would ensure that NATO's southern flank would be safe from communism. As a part of France, Algeria was included in the original NATO Charter, but this argument fell on deaf ears in Washington.

The Arab League promoted Pan-Arabism and the image of universal Arab and Muslim support for the FLN. The French grant of independence to both Tunisia and Morocco in March 1956 further bolstered Algeria's Muslims. When France, Great Britain, and Israel invaded Egypt in the Suez Crisis of 1956, both the United States and the Soviet Union condemned the move, and the French, unable to topple Nasser, were forced to contend with an FLN supply base that they could neither attack nor eliminate.

On August 20, 1955, the FLN attacked colon civilians in the Philippeville Massacre, and colon reprisals resulted in the deaths of several thousand Muslims. In September FLN operative Saadi Yacef commenced a terrorist-style bombing campaign against colon civilians in Algiers. Meanwhile, other FLN leaders targeted governmental officials for assassination. The FLN movement faced a setback on October 22, however, when Ben Bella was captured.

Under Socialist premier Guy Mollet, in 1956 the bulk of the French Army was transferred to Algeria, and in December 1956 and January 1957, battle-tested French troops with combat experience in Indochina arrived in Algeria to restore order in the city of Algiers. Among them were General Raoul Salan (commander in chief), paratrooper division commander Brigadier General Jacques Massu, and colonels Yves Godard and Marcel Bigeard, both of whom were adept at intelligence gathering and infiltration. Massu's men made steady headway, and Saadi Yacef was captured in September 1957. The Battle of Algiers was now won. The

1966 film *The Battle of Algiers*, produced by Gillo Pontecorvo and Saadi Yacef with Algerian support, garnered international acclaim while depicting the French as brutal occupiers and revealing the murders and torture practiced by the French Army. The FLN, on the other hand, routinely murdered captured French soldiers and colon civilians.

Despite victory in Algiers in 1957, French forces were not able to quell the Algerian rebellion or gain the confidence of the colons. Some colons grew fearful that the French government was about to negotiate with the FLN, and in spring 1958 groups of colons began to hatch a plan to change the colonial government. Colon veteran Pierre Lagaillarde organized hundreds of commandos and began a revolt on May 13, 1958. Army leaders, believing that they had been sold out by the Paris government in Indochina, were determined that this would not happen in Algeria. Soon, tens of thousands of colons and Muslims arrived outside the government building in Algiers to protest French government policy. Massu quickly formed a Committee of Public Safety, and Salan assumed leadership of the body. Salan then went before the throngs of protesters.

Although the plotters would have preferred someone more frankly authoritarian, Salan called for the return to power of General Charles de Gaulle. Although de Gaulle had been out of power for more than a decade, on May 19 he announced his willingness to assume authority.

Massu was prepared to bring back de Gaulle by force if necessary, and plans were developed to dispatch paratroopers to metropolitan France from Algeria, but the military option was not required. On June 1, 1958, the French National Assembly named de Gaulle premier, technically the last premier of the Fourth Republic. The colons and the army professionals had managed to change the political leadership of the mother country.

De Gaulle visited Algeria five times between June and December 1958. At Oran on June 4, he said about France's mission in Algeria that "she is here forever." A month later, he proposed a budget allocation of 15 billion francs for Algerian housing, education, and public works, and that October he suggested an even more sweeping proposal, known as the Constantine Plan. The funding for the massive projects, however, was never forthcoming, and true Algerian reform was never realized. It was probably too late in any case for reform to impact the Muslim community.

Algeria's new military commander, General Maurice Challe, arrived in Algeria on December 12, 1958, and launched a series of attacks on FLN positions in rural Kabylia in early 1959. Muslim troops loyal to the French guided special mobile French troops called Commandos de Chasse. An aggressive set of sorties deep in Kabylia made much headway, and Challe calculated that by the end of October, his men had killed half of the FLN operatives there. A second phase of the offensive was to occur in 1960, but by then de Gaulle, who had gradually eliminated options, had decided that Algerian independence was inevitable.

De Gaulle braced his generals for the decision to let go of Algeria in late August 1959 and then addressed the nation on September 19, 1959, declaring his support for Algerian self-determination. Fearing for their future, some Ultras created the Front Nationale Français and fomented another revolt on January 24, 1960, in the so-called Barricades Week. Mayhem ensued when policemen tried to restore order, and many people were killed or wounded. Challe fled Algiers on January 28, but the next day de Gaulle, wearing his old army uniform, turned the tide via a televised address to the nation. On February 1, army units swore loyalty to the government. The revolt quickly collapsed. Early in 1961 increasingly desperate Ultras formed a terrorist group called the Secret Army Organization (OAS) that targeted colons whom they regarded as traitors.

The Generals' Putsch of April 20–26, 1961, seriously threatened de Gaulle's regime. Challe wanted a revolt limited to Algeria, but Salan and his colleagues (ground forces chief of staff General André Zeller and recently retired inspector general of the air force Edmond Jouhaud) had all prepared for a revolt in France as well. The generals had the support of many frontline officers in addition to almost two divisions of troops. The Foreign Legion arrested the colony's commander in chief, General Fernand Gambiez, and paratroopers near Rambouillet prepared to march on Paris after obtaining armored support. The coup collapsed, however, as police units managed to convince the paratroopers to depart, and army units again swore loyalty to de Gaulle.

On June 10, 1961, de Gaulle held secret meetings with FLN representatives in Paris and then on June 14 made a televised appeal for the FLN's so-called provisional government to come to Paris to negotiate an end to the war. Peace talks during June 25–29 failed to lead to resolution, but de Gaulle's mind was already made up. During his visit to Algeria in December, he was greeted by large pro-FLN Muslim rallies and anti-colon riots. The United Nations recognized Algeria's independence on December 20, and on January 8, 1962, the French public voted in favor of Algerian independence.

A massive exodus of colons was already under way. Nearly one million returned to their ancestral homelands (half of them went to France, while most of the rest went to Spain and Italy). Peace talks resumed in March at Évian, and both sides reached a settlement on May 18, 1962. The formal handover of power occurred on July 4 when the FLN's Provisional Committee took control of Algeria, and in September Ben Bella was elected Algeria's first president.

The Algerian War resulted in some 18,000 French military deaths, 3,000 colon deaths, and about 300,000 Muslim deaths. Some 30,000 colons remained behind. They were ostensibly granted equal rights in the peace treaty but instead faced official discrimination by the FLN government and the loss of much of their property. The FLN remained in power until 1989, practicing a form of socialism until changes in Soviet foreign policy necessitated changes in Algerian internal affairs.

William E. Watson

See also: Algerian Civil War; Cold War in Africa; French Military Involvement in Postcolonial Africa; National Liberation Front (FLN) Algeria; Suez Crisis.

Further Reading

Evans, Martin. *Algeria: France's Undeclared War.* Oxford: Oxford University Press, 2012.

Horne, Alistair. *A Savage War of Peace: Algeria, 1954–1962.* New York: Viking, 1977.

Kettle, Michael. *De Gaulle and Algeria, 1940–1960.* London: Quartet, 1993.

Servan-Schreiber, Jean-Jacques. *Lieutenant in Algeria.* Translated by Ronald Matthews. New York: Knopf, 1957.

Talbott, John. *The War without a Name: France in Algeria, 1954–1962*. New York: Knopf, 1980.

Watson, William E. *Tricolor and Crescent: France and the Islamic World*. Westport, CT: Praeger, 2003.

Alliance of Democratic Forces for the Liberation of Congo (AFDL)

See Congo Wars

Allied Democratic Forces (ADF)

See Congo Wars; Democratic Republic of the Congo (DRC), Continuing Violence in; Uganda, Insurgency in the North

Al-Qaeda in the Islamic Maghreb (AQIM)

AQIM is a violent extremist organization that operates in North and West Africa. Led by the Algerian jihadist Abdelmalek Droukdel, who claims to be located in the Kabylie mountain region of Algeria, most of AQIM's operations have been conducted in the Sahel with fighters and equipment located in the sanctuary of the Sahara, most notably, northern Mali. AQIM is an organization descended from the Armed Islamic Group (GIA), which was an insurgency that used terrorist tactics against the military junta that successfully overthrew the democratically elected Islamic Salvation Front, the largest Islamic opposition party in Algeria, in 1992. The GIA, like the famous popular movement and insurgency from the Algerian War of Independence against France, the National Liberation Front (FLN), moved to sanctuary areas in remote locations difficult for the government to control. Successful Algerian military counterinsurgency operations put significant pressure on the GIA. Subsequently, GIA operations became increasingly violent and oppressive against local communities in a period known as the "dark decade" in Algeria. The GIA was formed and led by a group of Algerian veterans from the Afghan-Soviet War with ties to Osama bin Laden and his then nascent global terrorist organization Al-Qaeda. For example, the GIA hijacked an Air France flight in 1994 in order to use it to crash into the Eiffel Tower in an unsuccessful precursor to the 9/11 attacks. GIA's indiscriminate violence, however, gained opprobrium from every angle, including Osama bin Laden. In response, GIA leaders formed the Salafist Group for Preaching and Combat (GSPC) in 1998, a new organization inspired more by contemporary transnational terrorism and Osama bin Laden's Al-Qaeda (AQ) franchise instead of insurgencies like the FLN, which were wars of liberation directed against colonial legacies. GSPC changed its name in 2007 to AQIM and initially continued along similar lines with support zones in the Sahara and attack zones in Algeria. The AQ name change fomented operational shifts, however, and AQIM leaders like Mokhtar Belmokhtar and Abu Zeid in the Sahara or the "Southern Zone" became more closely aligned to local Tuareg criminal rebel groups as well as gaining significant freedom of action to conduct their own activities and operations. Terrorist alliances with local Saharan groups enabled AQIM Southern Zone commanders to increase their operations and attacks outside Algeria as well as expand for-profit activities such as smuggling and kidnapping for ransom. It is likely the AQ "merger" by AQIM did not bring additional resources, which Droukdel had hoped, and AQIM, therefore, was forced to remain financially self-reliant. In 2012 these AQIM and rebel alliances enabled large-scale, complex, and combined attacks against Malian security forces, where the combined rebel force seized more than half of Mali and created an autonomous region they named Azawad. In response, France launched a military intervention named Operation Serval. Successful French military operations, along with numerous disagreements among the diverse and multifaceted fighting groups in northern Mali, resulted in an operational breakdown and fragmentation of the Southern Zone AQIM groups. While AQIM leadership nominally remained in Algeria, AQIM fighters continued to seek sanctuary in northern Mali as well as southern Libya and perhaps Niger. AQIM remains operational at present, although it is impossible to determine its precise relationship with other violent groups in the region such as Islamic State. Theories to the motives of AQIM have ranged from AQIM being an extension of the Algerian secret security services in order to justify military operations as well as support the military-industrial complex in Algiers to AQIM being merely a smuggling network that uses the guise of religion as a cover for its supposedly enormously profitable criminal activities.

Joseph Guido

See also: Algerian Civil War; French Military Involvement in Postcolonial Africa; Mokhtar Belmokhtar; Tuareg Rebellions since 1960 (Mali and Niger).

Further Reading
Botha, Anneli. *Terrorism in the Maghreb: The Transnationalisation of Domestic Terrorism.* Pretoria: Institute for Security Studies, 2008.
Guido, Joseph. *Terrorist Sanctuary in the Sahara: A Case Study.* Carlisle Barracks, PA: Strategic Studies Institute/U.S. Army War College, 2017.
Hammer, Joshua. *The Bad-Ass Librarians of Timbuktu and Their Race to Save the World's Most Precious Manuscripts.* New York: Simon & Schuster, 2016.
Keenan, Jeremy. *The Dark Sahara: America's War on Terror in Africa.* London: Pluto Press, 2009.
Keenan, Jeremy. *The Dying Sahara: US Imperialism and Terror in Africa.* London: Pluto Press, 2012.
Mokeddem, Mohamed. *Al Qaida Au Maghreb Islamique: Contrebande Au Nom De L'islam* (Al-Qaeda in the Islamic Maghreb: Smuggling in the Name of Islam). Algiers: Casbah-Editions, 2010.
Shurkin, Michael. *France's War in Mali: Lessons for an Expeditionary Army.* Santa Monica, CA: RAND, 2014.

Al-Shabaab

Originally, Al-Shabaab (literally "the youth") was the hard-line youth militia of the Islamic Courts Union (ICU), which briefly took control of Mogadishu, Kismayo, and other areas of southern Somalia in June 2006. When a combination of Ethiopian and Somalian transitional federal government (TFG) troops forced the ICU to withdraw from the capital in December 2006, Al-Shabaab reconstituted itself as an independent organization and in early 2007 initiated an insurgency in an attempt to gain control of the country. Originally led by Aden Hashi Farah Ayor, the group has used assassinations, bombings, and more recently, suicide attacks to target TFG forces, African Union Mission in Somalia (AMISOM) peacekeepers, the United Nations, and foreign nationals. The group's declared intention is to establish a caliphate in Somalia based on a strict Wahhabi interpretation of Islam.

Formally called Harakat Al-Shabaab al-Mujahideen, or Movement of Warrior Youth, the organization was led by Sheikh Ahmed Abdi Godane after U.S. air strikes killed Farah and several other commanders on May 1, 2008. Under Godane's leadership, Al-Shabaab overran Kismayo in August 2008 and by the summer of 2010 had seized most of southern and central Somalia, including much of the capital, Mogadishu. After Godane was killed by U.S. air strikes on September 1, 2014, he was replaced by Ahmad Umar, about whom little is known.

Al-Shabaab appears to be divided into three commands: the Bay and Bokol, South Central and Mogadishu, and Puntland and Somaliland. An affiliate group also exists in the Juba Valley. The group funds itself mainly through charitable donations raised in areas it controls, although there have been repeated allegations that it has diverted aid in these regions to buttress its war chest. Al-Shabaab's strength is very hard to determine with any amount of accuracy. Some sources claim it directly controls as few as 1,000 fighters, while other sources claim that it has as many as 8,000–9,000 active combatants.

Some of Al-Shabaab's most significant early attacks included a suicide car attack on an AMISOM base in Mogadishu, killing six peacekeepers (February 22, 2009); a suicide car bomb at the Medina Hotel, Beledweyne, killing 35, including TFG security minister Omar Hashi Aden (June 18, 2009); the truck bombing of an AMISOM base in Mogadishu, killing 21 peacekeepers (September 17, 2009); and a suicide attack at Hotel Shamo in Mogadishu, where a ceremony was being held for medical students, killing three TFG ministers.

In addition to these domestic attacks, there is increasing concern that Al-Shabaab has forged close links with foreign extremists, many of whom are thought to be based in Somalia and helping with the training of the group's members. Fears were further heightened in February 2010 when Al-Shabaab formally declared its organizational and operational allegiance to Al-Qaeda. More recently, Al-Shabaab is believed to have forged informal alliances with Al-Qaeda in the Islamic Maghreb (AQIM) as well as Boko Haram, the latter of which is a militant Islamist group operating chiefly in northeastern Nigeria, but also in portions of Cameroon, Chad, and Niger. In 2015, the Islamic State of Iraq and Syria (ISIS) released several recruiting videos in an attempt to entice Al-Shabaab members to join its ranks. The move was met with open hostility among Al-Shabaab's leadership, which cautioned its members not to engage with ISIS.

Moreover, it now appears that the group has made a conscious strategic decision to strike international targets. Al-Shabaab has been linked to a 2009 plot to attack the Holsworthy Barracks in Australia, efforts aimed at recruiting Americans to carry out bombings on U.S. soil, and the attempted assassination in January 2010 of Danish cartoonist Kurt Westergaard, who created controversy in the Muslim world by drawing pictures depicting Muhammad wearing a bomb in his turban. More seriously, the group claimed responsibility for the July 11, 2010, suicide bombings in Kampala, which killed 74 people and wounded another 70, as well as an attack against a bus station in Nairobi on November 31 that left three people dead and injured 39. Al-Shabaab justified the strikes as retaliation for Ugandan and Kenyan support of the AMISOM mission in Somalia. During a famine in Somalia in 2011, Al-Shabaab was accused of blocking the delivery of aid from Western relief agencies. The organization claimed responsibility for the attack on a UN compound in 2013 that killed 22 people.

In September 2013 Al-Shabaab militants assaulted an upscale suburban shopping mall in Nairobi, Kenya, resulting in the deaths of 61 civilians and six Kenyan security officers. In May 2014 the group launched an attack on a Djibouti restaurant, killing three people and wounding several others. In Garissa, Kenya, Al-Shabaab militants staged a massive assault on Garissa University College in April 2015, during which 152 people died and 72 others were wounded. Meanwhile, in February 2015 the extremist group released a video online in which it vowed to attack shopping malls in the United States and Canada; although no such attacks have yet occurred, mall operators increased security for the remainder of 2015 and into 2016. At the same time, Al-Shabaab attacks continued in Somalia, with Mogadishu the favored target.

By August 2014, Al-Shabaab had suffered a series of military reversals, as TFG and AMISOM forces gradually retook more and more territory once held by the rebel group. That same month, the Somali government announced a major military campaign to flush out remaining Al-Shabaab strongholds from the countryside. The Somali government also issued a blanket 45-day amnesty for all Al-Shabaab members in an effort to eviscerate the organization and convince members to engage in peace talks with the TFG. By 2016 a number of ranking Al-Shabaab members had turned themselves in; meanwhile, military operations against the group continued, including U.S. drone and air strikes. On March 5, 2016, U.S. warplanes bombed Al-Shabaab's Raso training camp, situated some 120 miles to the north of Somalia's capital at Mogadishu. The Pentagon indicated that an estimated 150 Al-Shabaab militants were killed in the attack.

Richard Warnes

See also: Al-Qaeda in the Islamic Maghreb (AQIM); Boko Haram; Ethiopia: Insurgency and Interstate War; Somalia Civil War; U.S. Africa Command; U.S. Military Involvement in Africa.

Further Reading

Fergusson, James. *The World's Most Dangerous Place: Inside the Outlaw State of Somalia.* Boston: Da Capo Press, 2013.

Hansen, Stig Jarle. *Al-Shabaab in Somalia: The History and Ideology of a Militant Islamist Group.* Oxford: Oxford University Press, 2013.

Maruf, Harun, and Dan Joseph. *Inside Al-Shabaab: The Secret History of Al Qaeda's Most Powerful Ally.* Bloomington: Indiana University Press, 2018.

Amin, Idi (1925–2003)

Idi Amin was the military dictator of Uganda from 1971 to 1979 who led a brutal and regionally destabilizing regime until fleeing into exile in the wake of the

Kagera War. Born in the West Nile province of Uganda in 1925, Amin was a member of the Kakwa ethnic group, a minority population that was favored by the British colonial regime as a "martial race." Amin followed many of his peers into military service, joining the King's African Rifles as a cook in 1946 before becoming a formal askari in 1947. He excelled in the colonial military, being described by his commanders as an ideal soldier, combining their desired traits of discipline, obedience, physical prowess, and a propensity for violence. Amin saw service against Somali bandits in northern Kenya and during the Kenya Emergency of the 1950s, where he provided exceptional service and was promoted to a noncommissioned officer.

The late colonial era saw Amin serving in small conflicts where he earned first a commission as an *afande*, a native warrant officer, and then as a first lieutenant in 1961. The latter promotion came as the British were beginning the process of Africanization within their military, setting Amin up as one of the senior members of the military before independence. Upon independence in 1962, he was promoted rapidly, from captain to major to deputy commander of the army in 1964. The following year Milton Obote's administration promoted him to commander of the army. This promotion was repaid through Amin's 1966 violent suppression of Obote's political rival, the kabaka of Uganda, cementing Obote's regime.

Amin used his newfound political clout to recruit heavily from his Kakwa brethren as well as other northern Ugandan groups, filling the ranks of the military with allies. With the military's loyalty now unquestioned, Amin launched a coup against Obote's floundering administration in 1971, seizing power with the tacit approval of the United States, Britain, and Israel. While initially greeted as a reformer, Amin quickly turned into a vicious authoritarian. His regime was marked by the cruel eviction of the South Asian population of Uganda, the mass imprisonment and torture of his citizens, aggression toward his neighbor in Tanzania, and multiple purges of his military as he rooted out potential rivals and tried to maintain his power base in the military.

It was this attempt to keep his military in check that led to his critical mistake. In looking for a distraction for suspected military plotters, Amin launched an invasion of Tanzania's Kagera region in October 1978. Amin had assumed the Tanzanians would not be able to muster a response, but the resultant Kagera War saw the full-scale mobilization of the Tanzanian populace and the reinvigoration of Ugandan dissidents. Amin's purge-weakened military was consistently defeated in the field despite Amin's exhortations, leading to Amin ultimately fleeing into exile in April 1979, first to Libya and then to Saudi Arabia. He would remain in exile as a guest of the Saudi royal family until his death in 2003.

Charles G. Thomas

See also: Coups and Military Regimes in Africa; Kagera War; Kenya, Mau Mau Emergency; Uganda, Insurgency in the North; Uganda's Civil War: The Bush War.

Further Reading

Amin, Idi, Barbet Schroeder, Jean-Pierre Rassam, Charles-Henri Favrod, Jean-François Chauvel, Nestor Almendros, Denise de Casabianca, et al. *Général Idi Amin Dada: Autoportrait*. 2014. http://ucsb.kanopystreaming.com/node/113004

Avirgan, Tony, and Martha Honey. *War in Uganda: The Legacy of Idi Amin*. Dar es Salaam: Tanzania Publishing House, 1983.

Decker, Alicia. *In Idi Amin's Shadow: Women, Gender and Militarism in Uganda*. Athens: Ohio University Press, 2014.

Gwyn, David, and Ali A Mazrui. *Idi Amin: Death-Light of Africa*. Boston: Little, Brown, 1977.

Kyemba, Henry. *A State of Blood: The Inside Story of Idi Amin*. Kampala: Fountain Publishers, 1997.

Angolan Armed Forces (FAPLA and FAA)

FAPLA (*Forças Armadas Populares de Libertação de Angola* or the People's Armed Forces for the Liberation of Angola) was officially formed on August 1, 1974, by the MPLA (*Movimento Popular de Libertação de Angola* or Popular Movement for the Liberation of Angola)—one of three rival political groups jockeying for position in Angola in the face of the prospect of independence from Portugal. FAPLA would exist until its successor, the FAA (*Forças Armadas Angolanas*) was formed on October 9, 1991. FAPLA consisted not only of ground forces but also air defense forces (formed on January 21, 1976, and divided into air and antiaircraft elements) and a navy (formed on July 10, 1976), supported by militia forces.

When the ground forces of FAPLA were initially established, its first combat units were formed on the basis of guerilla units—some of which had been fighting the Portuguese colonial power since the early 1960s. Guerilla units initially converted into "companies" in the new army. By the time of independence on November 11, 1975, the first nominally brigade-strength unit of FAPLA had been formed with Cuban assistance. By the end of 1975, FAPLA and Cuban forces had all but destroyed what was the MPLA's principal political and military rival at the time of independence, the U.S.-backed FNLA (*Frente Nacional de Libertação de Angola* or National Front for the Liberation of Angola), the armed wing of which was known as ELNA (*Exército de Libertação Nacional de Angola* or Army of National Liberation of Angola). The battle of Quifangondo on November 10, 1975, between FAPLA and ELNA, both with foreign allies, proved significant not only in the MPLA securing the Angolan capital, Luanda, on independence from Portugal but also as a turning point in the fortunes of the FNLA. From 1976 the MPLA government and FAPLA were left to deal with the third independence movement in the country, UNITA (*União Nacional para a Independência Total de Angola* or National Union for the Total Independence of Angola), the armed forces of which were known as FAPLA (*Forças Armadas Populares de Libertação de Angola* or People's Armed Forces for the Liberation of Angola). UNITA was backed initially by South Africa, although under the Reagan administration in the United States, from 1981 onward, it would receive growing support from the United States. In addition to the threat from UNITA, FAPLA faced the prospect of further South African military intervention in the Angolan Civil War, where the SADF (South African Defence Force) had first intervened in support of both the FNLA and UNITA in 1975.

One of the first tasks for the new Angolan government army was to establish the means to provide personnel to the armed forces who had appropriate education and skills. In July 1976 the first all-arms academy for officer training in the ground forces was opened in Huambo, with a military-political academy graduating its first political officers in March 1977. Keeping the brigade as the principal ground operational unit, by the end of 1978, FAPLA was focused on the development of 10 light infantry brigades, with Cuban assistance, that would be suited to engagement with the guerilla forces of UNITA. However, there was growing concern within FAPLA in the face of South African military incursions into Angola, ostensibly against the Angolan-backed SWAPO (South West Africa People's Organization) based in southern Angola, where SWAPO was operating from southern Angola in order to conduct operations in adjacent South African–occupied South West Africa (Namibia). Consequently, FAPLA increasingly focused on the development of mechanized forces capable of facing the SADF among other weapon systems like Soviet-supplied tanks and armored personnel carriers. Military advisers from the Soviet Union, as opposed to from Cuba, played the dominant role in overseeing the formation of such mechanized units, where by the mid-1980s, there were some 2,000 Soviet military advisers involved in the development of FAPLA. Soviet advisers also played a role in the introduction of "Landing and Storm" troops in FAPLA during the early 1980s—that is, primarily heliborne forces—able to respond more effectively to UNITA guerillas than the mechanized brigades, as well as in the creation of special forces during the mid-1980s.

One of FAPLA's key weaknesses during the early 1980s was inadequate personnel in frontline units, where despite the introduction of universal military service for 18- to 35-year-olds of both sexes, the strength of FAPLA's infantry brigades was according to a highly placed Soviet source only 50–80 percent of establishment during this period. By 1985 FAPLA's brigades were typically approaching 80 percent of list strength in terms of personnel according to the same source. The Soviet sources go on to highlight that there was also a particular absence of qualified junior officers during the same period, which was, to some extent, corrected, thanks to training offered either in Angola or in the USSR. The extent of Soviet influence over FAPLA by the mid-1980s is highlighted by the existence of such elements as Soviet-style chemical troops within FAPLA as well as the fact that FAPLA had a political system with political officers in the Soviet mold. Certainly, Soviet advisers seem to have played a significant role in the planning of FAPLA offensive operations from the mid-1980s.

Soviet-advised FAPLA mechanized forces launched a series of operations against UNITA in southern Angola during the second half of the 1980s, culminating in the Battle of Cuito Cuanavale and Cuban military intervention in 1987–1988 against the forces of UNITA spearheaded by the SADF. By this time, UNITA too had adopted increasingly regular and mechanized elements that could operate alongside the SADF. Cuban intervention in Angola in 1987–1988 proved decisive in bringing South Africa to the negotiating table over independence for what would become Namibia, where the latter was linked to the withdrawal of Cuban forces from Angola, but not the withdrawal of Soviet advisers. Nonetheless, although Soviet influence over the development of FAPLA continued until its rebirth as FAA and beyond in the form of Russian influence, after the collapse of the Soviet Union, Portugal also entered the scene as a source of expertise and advice for the Angolan Armed Forces.

Formed as part of the Angolan peace process at the start of the 1990s, FAA theoretically represented an amalgamation of former MPLA/FAPLA and UNITA/FALA elements. However, both sides lacked confidence in the transition, maintaining separate forces, and when the civil war resumed in late 1992, only around 4,000 former FALA fighters had joined an FAA meant to reach 50,000 personnel. As Angola's new state military under the MPLA government, FAA fought a long campaign against UNITA rebels during the rest of the 1990s and early 2000s. Indeed, the former UNITA fighters in FAA remained loyal to their new force, contributing significantly to its eventual success against the rebels. During this last phase of Angola's long civil war, UNITA diamond smuggling through neighboring countries prompted FAA intervention in Zaire/Democratic Republic of the Congo (DRC) and the Republic of the Congo. An FAA intervention force played a central role in deposing the Mobutu dictatorship during the First Congo War (1996–1997), transforming Zaire into DRC. In October 1997 FAA troops supported by tanks and combat aircraft left Cabinda and crossed into the Republic of the Congo, where they seized the capital and oil production facilities, deposed President Pascal Lissouba who had been receiving assistance from UNITA, and reinstalled Denis Sassou Nguesso who had maintained a cordial relationship with the Soviet Union during the latter part of the Cold War. Again, during the Second Congo War or Africa's World War (1998–2002), FAA intervention along with allies Zimbabwe and Namibia saved the Laurent Kabila regime in DRC. Among the many combatants in this conflict, and given its experience of conventional warfare in southern Angola and strong Soviet military influence during the 1980s, the FAA represented a potent mechanized force supported by helicopter gunships and ground attack aircraft that decisively defeated Rwandan and rebel Congolese light infantry at the critical early engagement at Kitona in August 1998. However, the MPLA state eventually tired of military involvement and stalemate in the DRC, with rumors circulating that it backed the assassination of Kabila in order to facilitate negotiations. In the years following the end of the Angolan Civil War in 2002, and with the continuation of compulsory military service in Angola, the 90,000-strong FAA comprised one of the largest and most powerful militaries in Southern and Central Africa.

Alexander Hill and Timothy J. Stapleton

See also: Angolan Conflicts; Congo Wars; Cuba and Africa; Namibia Independence War; National Union for the Total Independence of Angola (UNITA); Popular Movement for the Liberation of Angola (MPLA); South Africa's Border War; Soviet Military Involvement in Africa.

Further Reading

FAPLA: Baluarte da paz em Angola/FAPLA: Bulwark of Peace in Angola. Luanda: FAPLA (Departamento de Agitação e Propaganda), [between 1989 and 1991].

Junior, Miguel. *The Formation and Development of the Angolan Armed Forces.* Bloomington, IN: AuthorHouse, 2019.

Junior, Miguel. *Popular Armed Forces for the Liberation of Angola, First National Army and the War (1975–1991)*. Bloomington, IN: AuthorHouse, 2015.

Krakhmalov, S. P. *Angola i ee armiia*. Moscow: Voennoe izdatel'stvo Ministerstvo oboroni SSSR, 1980.

Leao, Ana, and Martin Rupiya. "A Military History of the Angolan Armed Forces from the 1960s Onwards—as Told by Former Combatants." In *Evolutions and Revolutions: A Contemporary History of Militaries in Southern Africa*, edited by Martin Rupiya, 7–41. Pretoria: Institute for Security Studies, 2005.

Angolan Conflicts (1975–2002)

After Portugal fought three counterinsurgency wars during the 1960s and early 1970s to retain its African colonies, a 1974 coup in Lisbon prompted Portuguese withdrawal from these territories, one of which was Angola that gained independence the next year. The Angolan independence movements that had been fighting the Portuguese and sometimes each other than engaged in a civil war that would drag on for more than a quarter century. In 1975 the groups vying for power comprised the Popular Movement for the Liberation of Angola (MPLA) around the capital of Luanda, the National Front for the Liberation of Angola (FNLA) based in the north near the border with Zaire (now the Democratic Republic of the Congo) and the National Union for the Total Independence of Angola (UNITA) located in the south. With control of the capital and indirect Cuban and Soviet military support, the MPLA quickly seized state apparatus and proclaimed itself as a government. This development worried apartheid South Africa, as an MPLA-ruled Angola would very likely offer assistance to the South West Africa People's Organization (SWAPO) insurgents fighting against the South African administration of South West Africa (SWA, now Namibia). In addition, the United States worried about the further spread of Soviet influence in Africa and Soviet access to Angolan oil. In August 1975 South African Defence Force (SADF) units in SWA crossed the Angolan border to seize the important hydroelectric infrastructure at Calueque, and South Africa began supplying and training fighters from FNLA and UNITA. Nevertheless, using armored vehicles from Cuba and the Soviet Union, MPLA undertook a successful offensive, occupying much of Angola.

In October 1975 the SADF launched an invasion of Angola titled "Operation Savannah" in support of UNITA and FNLA. At Balombo, a UNITA force augmented by some South African armored cars and land rovers fitted with missile launchers unsuccessfully attempted to halt an MPLA advance that captured the center of Nova Lisboa (Huambo) and then occupied the coast down to the SWA border and seized most southern Angolan towns. As a result, several mechanized SADF columns comprising a total of around 2,500 men and 600 vehicles advanced into Angola. Pushing back MPLA forces, the South Africans linked up with FLNA and UNITA fighters to take control of southern Angola, including centers such as Perreira de Eca, Rocadas, Sa da Bandiera (Lubango), and the port of Mocamedes (Namibe). In November, after overcoming further resistance by MPLA forces with Cuban advisers, the South Africans and their Angolan allies seized the major ports of Benguela and Lobito. The South African–led offensive succeeded because of superior firepower, aerial supply and transport, effective leadership and training, and the late rainy season that kept the ground dry and facilitated mobility.

In the north, at the same time, FNLA forces tried to break through MPLA positions at Quifangondo with a view to capturing the nearby capital of Luanda. American-funded Portuguese mercenaries, troops from Zaire, and South African heavy artillery and air power supported this FNLA offensive. In early November Fidel Castro, without consulting his Soviet allies, initiated direct military intervention in Angola flying a 650-strong Cuban special forces battalion to Luanda and sending an artillery regiment ship. On November 10, 1975, Angola's Independence Day, FNLA leader Holden Roberto dismissed warnings from his South African and Portuguese military advisers and mounted a frontal attack along the road to Quifangondo. With South African air support proving ineffective as the bombers flew high to avoid identification, the FNLA soldiers were funneled down the narrow road with swamps on both sides, where they were massacred by fire from newly arrived Cuban rocket launchers and mortars. As a result of this decisive defeat, FNLA disappeared as a significant faction in the Angolan Civil War.

South of Luanda, in mid-November, South African–led forces captured Novo Redondo, but some Cuban troops moved south to bolster MPLA units on the Queve River. Although the South Africans began flying in reinforcements at the recently captured Cela airfield, a force of SADF armored cars and UNITA fighters trying to cross a bridge near Ebo fell into a Cuban/MPLA ambush and suffered heavy casualties. This disaster, together with the start of the rainy season, delayed the South African–UNITA advance, giving the Cubans time to bring in more troops amounting to around 4000 troops by the end of the year and additional Soviet arms. In mid-December South African forces pushed north from Cela, penetrating Cuban/MPLA defenses on the Nhia River at "Bridge 14" but were quickly halted by determined Cuban troops. At the close of December, Cuban forces occupied hill positions between Quibala and Cela and resisted a South African counterattack by calling for artillery on their own position. To the east, South African and UNITA troops tried to control the economically important Benguela railway up to the border with Zaire, but it proved impossible to advance that far.

Cuban intervention, coupled with several other factors, informed a South African withdrawal from Angola. The reliance of South Africa on military personnel drawn from its white minority led to manpower shortages, with the government extending the duty of some national servicemen (conscripts) and citizen force reservists. The United States withdrew its support for the operation, given reports of the South African invasion of Angola in the Western press, including news of the capture of four South African soldiers by MPLA. In January 1976 South African forces began moving south, abandoning Cela and Novo Redondo, and by early February, 4,000–5,000 SADF troops held an 80 kilometer wide strip of Angolan territory adjacent to the SWA border. UNITA almost collapsed without South African support. Although Cuban and MPLA troops occupied Huambo, Lobito, and Benguela, their supply lines became extended, and they faced South African minefields to the south, which prompted a political solution. In late March, as a result, South Africa withdrew its forces from Angola after assurances from Angola's newly installed MPLA government to protect the Calueque-Ruacana hydroelectric project and respect the SWA border. Within white minority–ruled South Africa, news of the SADF defeat in Angola partly motivated the June 1976 mass uprising by Black youth that revived the anti-apartheid struggle.

Confirming Pretoria's fears, Angola's MPLA state permitted SWAPO to establish bases in southern Angola, therefore increasing insurgent activity across the border in northern SWA. As a result, the SADF mounted a series of cross-border operations to eliminate SWAPO infrastructure in Angola, which brought the South Africans into conflict with Cuban forces and the MPLA government military, now called the People's Armed Forces for the Liberation of Angola (FAPLA). South Africa's incursions into southern Angola ranged from small special forces commando raids to large conventional mechanized and airborne operations. In May 1978 Operation Reindeer involved an ambitious SADF battalion parachute assault 250 kilometer north of the border at Cassinga and, simultaneously, a mechanized and helicopter attack on other positions just 25 kilometers into Angola. In the subsequent international media battle over the Cassinga raid, the SADF claimed to have killed 600 armed SWAPO insurgents while SWAPO maintained that the victims comprised unarmed refugees. The operation's overland component saw use of the new SADF Ratel infantry fighting vehicles and killed 248 SWAPO fighters and captured 200 to a loss of only two South Africans. In response, SWAPO better concealed its facilities in Angola and positioned them close to protective Cuban and FAPLA forces.

From the start of the 1980s, UNITA, led by Jonas Savimbi, revived, with renewed support from South Africa and the hawkish Reagan administration in the United States. As such, UNITA seized control of southeastern Angola using the town of Mavinga as an operational base and advanced into the central region. This move denied SWAPO access to southeastern Angola and therefore restricted its infiltration of neighboring SWA to the north-central region of Ovamboland, easing South African counterinsurgency efforts. Furthermore, UNITA's comeback diverted Cuban and FAPLA forces from the SWA border, and SWAPO became obliged to send fighters to assist in the war against Savimbi's rebels. The 1980s also witnessed increased South African cross-border operations. In June 1980 South Africa mounted Operation Sceptic (also called Smoke Shell), comprising a sudden and large-scale mechanized assault on a SWAPO complex in southern Angola involving direct combat between the SADF and FAPLA and deployment of SWAPO mechanized units. The SADF, which lost 17 personnel in the fighting, captured many Soviet-made vehicles and killed 380 SWAPO and FAPLA troops. Subsequently, SWAPO withdrew its bases from the border, further hindering its infiltration of SWA, and it merged its logistical system with FAPLA. During June and July 1981, the SADF launched Operation Carnation in which it destroyed SWAPO logistical bases inside southern Angola. Operation Protea, carried out in August 1981, involved 4,000 troops organized into four battle groups, thus amounting to the largest South African mechanized operation since the Second World War, and with 138 aircraft, it also represented the largest South African air operation of the Angolan war. Protea aimed at destroying SWAPO infrastructure some 50 kilometers into south-central Angola, thus complementing South African counterinsurgency efforts in the adjacent Ovamboland of SWA. These SADF assaults killed around 1,000 SWAPO and FAPLA personnel, destroyed or captured around $250 million worth of Soviet-supplied military equipment, and apprehended a Soviet officer. Exploiting Protea's success, the SADF embarked on Operation Daisy in November 1981 with mechanized and airborne units moving into southern Angola to destroy a SWAPO complex. During 1982, South African incursions into Angola included a helicopter assault on a SWAPO staging area, killing 200 insurgents, and air strikes on SWAPO command centers that killed 345. In early 1983 SWAPO reoccupied bases around Xangongo and Ongiva, protected by a nearby FAPLA brigade, and increased insurgent infiltration into SWA. As a result, the South Africans embarked on Operation Askari in December 1983, sending four mechanized battle groups against SWAPO positions in southern Angola. At the outset of January 1984, SADF elements attacking a SWAPO position near Cuvelai clashed with a FAPLA brigade and two Cuban battalions, which withdrew after suffering 324 deaths. Twenty-one South Africans were lost in the battle.

Prompted by South African military successes in southern Angola, the negotiated 1984 Lusaka Agreement included promises by Pretoria to withdraw its forces from Angola and by the MPLA government to stop SWAPO and the Cubans from deploying along Angola's southern border with SWA. Both sides initially lived up to these pledges, but SWAPO, not a signatory to the agreement, returned to southern Angola, intensifying the insurgency in SWA and inciting a resumption of South African cross-border actions in 1985. The Lusaka Agreement also enabled FAPLA and its allies to mount offensives against UNITA. In 1985 Soviet officers in Angola planned and directed Operation Congresso II in southeast Angola involving 20,000 FAPLA troops with tanks, fighter-bombers, and helicopter gunships, and the Cubans likely provided artillery, air defense, and air support. The 30,000 lightly equipped UNITA infantry failed to stop the mechanized onslaught, and despite limited SADF assistance, including airlifts, Savimbi's fighters withdrew to Mavinga. In September's Operation Wallpaper, the SADF escalated its support for UNITA with air strikes that inflicted terrible losses on FAPLA units. Ten Soviet officers sent to salvage the now faltering offensive died when their aircraft was downed by a South African jet fighter. By the time the Soviets pulled FAPLA units back to their staging area at Cuito Cuanavale in October, the Angolan state forces had sustained 2,500 casualties and lost 32 armored vehicles, 100 trucks, and over a dozen aircraft. Around 2,000 UNITA fighters were killed or wounded.

In 1986 the Soviets dispatched 1,000 military advisers and over a billion dollars' worth of military hardware to Angola. Some 20,000 FAPLA, 7,000 SWAPO and 900 South African African National Congress (ANC) fighters assembled around Luena and Cuito Cuanavale, and in late May they renewed the offensive against UNITA. Their advance was slowed by UNITA ambushes on FAPLA supply lines, a UNITA–South African raid on the Cuito Cuanavale airfield, and South African Special Forces raids on oil storage facilities at the port of Namibe and a bridge on the Cuito River. The Soviets canceled the offensive by August.

Operation Saluting October of 1987 represented the final Soviet-led FAPLA operation against UNITA and included another $1.5 billion of Soviet equipment transported to Angola. Desperately needing a victory to bolster flagging support for the war in Cuba, Fidel Castro authorized the use of Cuban frontline troops. Soviet planners ignored warnings from South African ANC leaders, who had agents embedded in the SADF, that South Africa would intervene in Angola to save its client UNITA. Although the impending South African elections made Pretoria hesitant to act aggressively in Angola as white South African casualties could be politically sensitive to white voters, the SADF dispatched artillery and anti-tank units and organized airlifts to assist UNITA. In July 1987 four FAPLA brigades departed Cuito Cuanavale, pressing southeast toward UNITA's Mavinga stronghold. This triggered the SADF Operation Modular at the beginning of August, with mechanized forces comprising around 3,000 troops moving into southeast Angola in direct combat support of UNITA. During September, the SADF force, supported by air strikes, isolated and destroyed the FAPLA brigades as they attempted to traverse the Lomba River. In one battle at the start of October, a South African battle group surprised a FAPLA brigade constructing a bridge across the river, killing 600 Angolan troops and destroying or capturing 127 vehicles. This one-sided engagement resulted in a single South African killed and five wounded. In early October, FAPLA forces, having sustained around 4,000 casualties during the disastrous Operation Saluting October, retreated to Cuito Cuanavale. Simultaneously, the SADF reinforced its units in Angola, adding tanks and self-propelled howitzers.

The SADF pursued the fleeing FAPLA troops and besieged Cuito Cuanavale as the Soviets reduced their military presence in Angola, leaving the MPLA government to plead for more Cuban assistance. Castro took direct control of military operations in Angola and sent 3,000 Cuban troops along with tanks and artillery to Cuito Cuanavale. He also dispatched Cuba's top fighter pilots to Angola and moved another 3,500 Cuban troops into southwestern Angola to threaten the other end of the SWA border and therefore distract the South Africans. Castro pursued a plan of using military pressure to compel the South Africans to make concessions during international negotiations. Although South African president P. W. Botha instructed the SADF to destroy all FAPLA forces on the east side of the Cuito River, this never happened, as UN protests and the political sensitivity of white South African fatalities made South Africa hesitant to send in reinforcements.

At the end of 1987, a three-tier Cuban/FAPLA defense force, including tanks, artillery, multiple rocket launchers, entrenchments, and huge minefields protected Cuito Cuanavale. In January 1988 South African artillery pounded FAPLA's outer defense layer in preparation for an attack by SADF mechanized units and UNITA troops that led to tank versus tank combat. After inflicting serious losses on FAPLA, the SADF units withdrew to prepare for another assault, but this was delayed for a month, given a hepatitis outbreak. During the reprieve, Cuban reinforcements arrived at Cuito Cuanavale and the defensive ring tightened. West of the Cuito River, beyond the range of South African guns, Cuban artillery on high ground could engage anything on the battlefield. In mid-February, a joint SADF-UNITA offensive, including South African tanks, defeated the Cuito Cuanavale outer defensive ring. A near suicidal counterattack by Cuban tanks stopped the South Africans from seizing the Cuito River Bridge. While 500 FAPLA solders and 32 Cubans were killed, UNITA casualties were heavy, but only four South Africans were killed and seven wounded. In late February 1988, Castro withdrew all his forces west of the Cuito River except one FAPLA brigade and a Cuban tank battalion to guard the bridge and the adjacent area known as the "Tumpo Triangle," and they laid minefields along every approach to Cuito Cuanavale. Several more attacks by SADF mechanized units were turned back by mines, Cuban artillery, and air strikes, boosting the morale of the Cuito Cuanavale garrison. The SADF force, with only 17 out of its 28 tanks working, mounted yet another attack at the end of February, as the national service period of many of its soldiers was about to expire, but this operation was abandoned, given mines, Cuban artillery, and mechanical problems. The South Africans lost momentum during the time it took to replace the outgoing brigade with a new one that arrived in March. In late March, in the context of Operation Packer, which included South African aerial attacks on FAPLA and diversionary actions by UNITA, the newly arrived SADF brigade undertook a mechanized assault that fizzled, given the same problems as before. Realizing that it could not completely evict Cuban/FAPLA units west of the Cuito River, Pretoria withdrew the SADF from the area and planted its own minefields to discourage a counteroffensive.

After the successful defense of Cuito Cuanavale in southeast Angola, Castro sent Cuban forces to the southwest to reinforce FAPLA and SWAPO units. The air war, previously dominated by South Africa, shifted, as improved airfields in Angola enabled Cuban aircraft to fly over SWA and a Soviet-made air defense system countered South African planes over southern Angola. In April and May 1988, South African and Cuban forces clashed in southwestern Angola when the former crossed the border pursuing SWAPO insurgents. By the end of May, two full Cuban divisions comprising 12,000 men and 200 tanks, along with mixed Cuban-SWAPO mechanized battalions, occupied southwestern Angola. In June the SADF conducted Operation Excite, halting a southwest Cuban advance toward the border town of Calueque. Cuban aircraft then bombed the Calueque hydroelectric station killing 11 South African soldiers prompting the SADF to destroy a major bridge on the Cunene River and deploy a division along the south side of the border to deter an anticipated Cuban/FAPLA invasion of SWA. At this time, the number of Cuban troops in Angola reached 65,000. Worried about the domestic political repercussion of more casualties, South Africa and Cuba disengaged militarily and concluded a settlement during American-sponsored negotiations. South African forces departed from southern Angola and the entirety of SWA in 1989; the Cubans withdrew from southern Angola around the same time and left the country in 1991, and Namibia attained independence in 1990 with an elected SWAPO government.

The removal of the South African threat enabled the Angolan government to launch a major military offensive against UNITA's center of Mavinga in December 1989. However, the FAPLA advance stalled, and UNITA then mounted a counteroffensive in May and June 1990, capturing the oil port of Ambriz and advancing into central Angola. With the end of the Cold War, the United States and the weakening Soviet Union pushed their respective Angolan allies, MPLA and UNITA, to negotiate. As such, the MPLA government repudiated socialism and the one-party-state system. In May 1991 MPLA and UNITA signed the Bicesse Accords, stipulating a cease-fire, the holding of multiparty elections within a year, demobilization of the country's 150,000 combatants, and the founding of a new integrated Angolan Armed Forces (FAA), all supervised by a UN mission. However, Savimbi rejected the results of the September 1992 elections, which he lost, and this renewed violence between the MPLA government and UNITA rebels. At the start of 1993, fighting spread to 15 of Angola's 18 provinces, and UNITA mounted a national offensive, seizing many towns across the country and threatening the oi- rich Cabinda enclave. Lacking U.S. support, which had sustained it throughout the 1980s, UNITA now sustained itself by smuggling diamonds out of Angola via Zaire, where the faltering Mobutu regime clung to power. The success of an offensive by the FAA (the new name of the Angolan state military) compelled Savimbi to enter the November 1994 Lusaka Agreement in which the MPLA and UNITA promised to end their conflict and form a coalition government. Nevertheless, fighting once again resumed in 1995, with oil-rich Luanda briefly hiring mercenaries from South African–based Executive Outcomes and purchasing more arms, and the FAA invaded Zaire in 1997 to cut off UNITA diamond exports and help topple Mobutu. Angolan president Jose Eduardo dos Santos, in January 1999, declared that that only a military solution could end the conflict as UN officials left the rebel areas. As further FAA operations reduced UNITA-held territory, the MPLA government herded rural people into towns to prevent them from helping the insurgents. With Savimbi's death in a February 2002 ambush by the FAA, UNITA resumed the Lusaka peace process with around 81,000 UNITA rebels and 350,000 dependents entering demobilization camps. Angolans experienced five decades of continuous warfare beginning with the anti-colonial struggle of the 1960s and early 1970s that morphed into a Cold War proxy conflict during the late 1970s and 1980s and ended as a civil war. In 2003 Angolans faced destroyed infrastructure, agricultural production hindered by large minefields, and lack of medical care and running water. In addition, many Angolans lost limbs from mine explosions, and one-third of the country's population was internally displaced. In what some called a "negative peace," the MPLA maintained a firm grip on the Angolan state and its oil revenue.

Timothy J. Stapleton

See also: Angolan Armed Forces (FAPLA and FAA); Cuba and Africa; Cuito Cuanavale, Battle of; Diamonds and Conflict in Postcolonial Africa; Dos Santos, Jose Eduardo; National Front for the Liberation of Angola (FNLA); National Union for the Total Independence of Angola (UNITA); Neto, António Agostinho; Nujoma, Sam; Peacekeeping in Africa; Popular Movement for the Liberation of Angola (MPLA); Portuguese Africa, Independence Wars (Angola, Mozambique, and Guinea-Bissau); Quifangondo, Battle of; Roberto, Holden Álverto; Savimbi, Jonas; South West Africa People's Organization (SWAPO); Soviet Military Involvement in Africa.

Further Reading
George, Edward. *The Cuban Intervention in Angola, 1965–1991: From Che Guevara to Cuito Cuanavale*. London: Frank Cass, 2005.

Gleijeses, Piero. *Conflicting Missions: Havana, Washington and Africa, 1959–1976.* Chapel Hill: University of North Carolina Press, 2002.

Gleijeses, Piero. *Visions of Freedom: Havana, Washington, Pretoria and the Struggle for Southern Africa, 1976–1991.* Chapel Hill: University of North Carolina Press, 2013.

Pollack, Peter. *The Last Hot Battle of the Cold War: South Africa vs. Cuba in the Angolan Civil War.* Oxford: Casemate, 2013.

Scholtz, Leopold. *The SADF in the Border War, 1966–1989.* Cape Town: Tafelberg, 2013.

Weigert, Stephen. *Angola: A Modern Military History, 1961–2002.* New York: Palgrave Macmillan, 2011.

Ansar al-Sharia in Libya

A powerful Salafi militia in Libya seeking to establish an Islamic state by violence to implement Sharia law. Several militant organizations in the Middle East–North Africa region use variations of the name *Ansar* al-Sharia, meaning "supporters of Islamic law." Ansar al-Sharia (ASL) emerged after the 2011 Libyan Revolution as a variety of actors struggled violently for local and regional control. Its operations began with an extensive program of outreach, or recruitment, that included providing social services as well as preaching. This group also sent shipments of relief goods to Sudan, Syria, and Gaza, revealing a sophisticated logistics capability and possible sponsorship from Sudan and Turkey. This movement includes two prominent groups within Libya: (1) the more prominent Ansar al-Sharia in Benghazi (ASB), led by Muhammad al-Zawahi until his death in late 2014; and (2) Ansar al-Sharia in Derna (ASD), led by former Guantanamo Bay–inmate Abu Sufyan bin Qumu. While these groups took root independently in their respective locales, they cooperated when possible for their shared ends. ASL gained international notoriety after members of the two groups conducted coordinated terrorist attacks on September 11, 2012, against the U.S. diplomatic facilities in Benghazi, Libya, killing four Americans, including U.S. ambassador J. Christopher Stevens. Although the ASL later denied involvement in these attacks, witnesses identified organization members at the scenes. On November 28, 2017, a U.S. District Court jury convicted Ahmed Abu Khattala, a senior leader of ASB, for his involvement in the attack on the diplomatic compound.

In 2014, as ASL's influence began to falter, the United States and the United Kingdom designated ASB and ASD as foreign terrorist organizations. The forces of General Khalifa Haftar fought the ASL intensively. Following al-Zawahi's death in 2014, along with heavy losses in the following years that killed most of ASL's leadership and its fighters, a significant number of the remaining members reportedly defected to the Islamic State (Daesh) in Libya. On May 27, 2018, Ansar al-Sharia in Libya formally dissolved. This signifies only that most of the members shifted to the Islamic State or to Al-Qaeda in the Islamic Maghreb (AQIM).

Melvin R. Korsmo

See also: Al-Qaeda in the Islamic Maghreb (AQIM); Gaddafi, Muammar; Libyan Civil War, First; Libyan Civil War, Second.

Further Reading

Gråtrud, Henrik, and Vidar Benjamin Skretting. "*Ansar al-Sharia* in Libya: An Enduring Threat." *Perspectives on Terrorism* 11, no. 1 (February 2017): 40–53.

Zelin, Aaron Y. "The Rise and Decline of *Ansar al-Sharia* in Libya." *Current Trends in Islamist Ideology* 18 (May 2015): 104–118.

Anti-Balaka Militia

See Central African Republic (CAR), Conflict in.

Anyanya

The Anya-Nya was the southern Sudan guerrilla group that fought against the Sudan government during the First Sudanese Civil War. Anya-Nya is derived from the word *Inyanya*, the name for a deadly poisonous snake venom that is popular among the Latuko (or Latuka), Madi, and Acholi ethnic groups in southern Sudan. Anya-Nya was formed on August 19, 1963, in Kampala, the capital of Uganda. Prominent southern Sudan leaders who were in exile such as Joseph Oduho, George Akumbek, Father Saturnino Lohure, Julius Moroga, and Severino Fuli spearheaded the formation of the guerrilla group. In addition, exiled members of the Equatoria Corps among the southerners such as Joseph Lagu, who participated in the Torit mutiny of 1955, were prominent members of the Anya-Nya.

Although the guerrilla movement started in the Equatoria region, yet ethnic groups in the Bahr-el-Ghazal and the Upper Nile regions also supported the insurgent activities of the Anya-Nya against the Sudanese Army. The emergence of Anya-Nya initiated a new phase during the First Sudanese Civil War. It launched its first military offensive against the Sudanese Army on September 19, 1963, in Eastern Equatoria. From this point, politicians and military leaders in southern Sudan adopted a more aggressive approach in agitating for the secessionist agenda of the southerners. In particular, members of the Sudan African National Union (SANU) such as Joseph Oduho and Joseph Lagu used their popularity among the southerners to facilitate support for the Anya-Nya in southern Sudan and among the exiles in neighboring countries in Uganda and the Democratic Republic of the Congo.

After starting its operation in 1963, Anya-Nya main targets were police stations and military outposts. Sporadic attacks on these places provided the guerrilla group with arms and ammunition captured from security forces. Spears, bows, and arrows were also used during the Anya-Nya's hit-and-run guerrilla tactics against the Sudanese Army. Although these weapons were inferior to those of the Sudanese Army, however, the patriotism of the southerners provided the Anya-Nya with local support despite the attacks by military forces. For instance, in the Bahr-el-Ghazal region, local inhabitants were required to pay taxes in form of food and cattle in order to support the Anya-Nya. In addition, skins of crocodiles, pythons, and rhinoceroses and elephant tusks were either sold or bartered to obtain the needs of the guerrilla group.

Anya-Nya's training camps were also located in the Nyangara and Bangidi regions of the Democratic Republic of the Congo, while refugee camps in Gulu in

Northern Uganda were also used to raise funds for the guerrillas. External support from Israel also provided arms and ammunition for the Anya-Nya. Ethnic rivalry and leadership problems within the guerrilla movement weakened its ability to effectively coordinate its sociopolitical activities in the southern region.

Yusuf Sholeye

See also: Lagu, Joseph Yanga; Sudan Civil War, First.

Further Reading

Beshir, Omer Mohamed. *The Southern Sudan Conflict: Background to Conflict*. London: Hurst, 1968.

Collins, Robert O. *History of Modern Sudan*. Cambridge: Cambridge University Press, 2008.

Poggo, S. Scopas. *The First Sudanese Civil War: Africans, Arabs, and Israelis in Southern Sudan, 1955–1972*. New York: Palgrave Macmillan, 2009.

Arab Spring (2011)

The Arab Spring consisted of a series of large-scale, protracted protest demonstrations in many Arab countries, beginning in 2011, that led to the replacement of governing elites in Tunisia and Egypt, intervention by other Gulf states in Bahrain, and complex civil wars with significant external involvement in Yemen, Libya, and Syria. The scale, consequences, and apparently contagious character of these protest movements, which caught regional experts by surprise, have stimulated significant research to explain the vulnerability of states to civil discord and instability. Observers of these movements offer a number of useful conclusions regarding the motivations of protesters, the supporting structural conditions for large protest movements, and any facilitating factors.

The traditional journalistic account begins on December 17, 2010, when the video of Tarek el-Tayeb Mohamed Bouazizi setting himself on fire, in protest against government abuse and humiliation, sparked demonstrations all over Tunisia. The dramatically growing protests, ultimately called the Jasmine Revolution, forced President Zine al-Abidine Ben Ali to flee to Saudi Arabia on January 14, 2011. People in many different Arabic-speaking countries watched these events on Al Jazeera and followed the social media campaigns of activists. They noted their similar living conditions: political exclusion under highly corrupt, aged, authoritarian rulers; inflation; and high levels of unemployment, even for educated youth. On January 17, 2011, the initial Green March protests began in Oman. On January 24, 2011, Yemeni security forces arrested the well-connected and influential activist Tawakil Karman, which provoked peaceful protests that would last for a year. On January 25, 2011, protests began in Tahrir Square, Egypt. Egyptian president Hosni Mubarak resigned on February 11, 2011, after 18 days of revolution. This inspired millions of people to think that they also could remove their rulers by collective action. These events motivated protests in more countries, stimulating renewal in the "Regime Change Cascades" literature.

On February 14, 2011, both Sunni and Shi'a opposition groups occupied the Pearl Roundabout in Manama, Bahrain. Three days later, the February 17th Revolution began in Benghazi, Libya, and quickly spread. After another three days, an organized cycle of protests began in Morocco, called the February 20 Revolution. Liberals took encouragement from these events, hoping that they would lead to greater individual liberties and even the expansion of political rights. This led to the expression "The Arab Spring," an optimistic reference to the 1968 democratic opening in Czechoslovakia called the Prague Spring. However, governments raised their determination to deter and suppress any rebellion among their own residents. On March 6, 2011, Saudi Arabia deployed massive security forces against Shi'a protests in the east. On March 15, 2011, Gulf Cooperation Council troops entered Bahrain to support the king's security forces in crushing demonstrations. Three days later in Yemen, government supporters killed 52 protesters, causing major military leaders to defect to the opposition. On March 18, 2011, Syrian government forces shot five protesters in Dara'a, followed by many further provocations that eventually grew into the Syrian civil war.

In the three states where protests sparked civil war, international intervention has played a significant role. On March 19, 2011, the United States, Britain, and France led the UN-authorized Operation Odyssey Dawn assault on the forces of Muammar Gaddafi in support of the rebellion. In Syria, the government would call on Iran and Russia to support its side in the war, reinforced by Hezbollah from Lebanon. On the other side, the Gulf states and Turkey supported a variety of Islamist militias. In Yemen, a precarious, internally divided state finally collapsed under assault from competing ambitious militias and the grievances of a desperately poor population. For all its internal conflict, the Yemen Civil War gained formal international recognition when Saudi Arabia led a coalition of neighboring states to begin fighting against the Houthis.

These movements took a different character in each state, reflecting local conditions; the historical development of local civic organizing capacity; and the varying levels of political skill, legitimacy, and resources possessed by the ruling elites. In general, wealthy oil-exporting countries passed through the seasons of political passion without change. The monarchies lacking oil revenues to placate the grievances of the masses endured these conflicts by offering a small show of political opening and then restrained application of coercive suppression.

In the final analysis, for the people of many states, this protest cycle brought only calamity. In Egypt, the replacement of elites, from the June 24, 2012, election of Mohammad Morsi as president of Egypt to his overthrow in a military coup after the Tamarod rebellion of 2013, has left the people in worse conditions than when protests began. Only in Tunisia have the political parties demonstrated political maturity and the willingness to compromise. They have created a credible constitution and new political institutions, while not yet making progress on the economic grievances of the population. However, these 2011 protests have established the political agency of the people to express their grievances. Their example continues to inspire collective action, as seen in the 2019 protests in Algeria, Jordan, and Sudan.

Jonathan K. Zartman

See also: Ansar al-Sharia in Libya; Gaddafi, Muammar; Libyan Civil War, First.

Further Reading
Al-Sumait, Fahed, Nele Lenze, and Michael C. Hudson, eds. *The Arab Uprisings: Catalysts, Dynamics, and Trajectories.* Boulder, CO: Rowman & Littlefield, 2015.

Khatib, Lina, and Ellen Lust, eds. *Taking It to the Streets: The Transformation of Arab Activism*. Baltimore: Johns Hopkins University Press, 2014.

Zartman, I. William, ed. *Arab Spring: Negotiating in the Shadow of the Intifadat*. Athens: University of Georgia Press, 2015.

Arab-Israeli Wars (1948–1973)

The Arab-Israeli conflict has been going on at varying levels of intensity for more than 60 years, but its roots extend back for centuries. The current incarnation of this conflict can be traced to the establishment of the State of Israel. There are a key set of documents that were instrumental in the creation of Israel. These documents (including the Basle Declaration, the Sykes-Picot Agreement, the Balfour Declaration, the British Mandate for Palestine of 1920, and the Israelis' Proclamation of Independence in 1948) increased the tensions in the region by establishing and recognizing on a global stage the State of Israel, carved out from the lands of Palestine.

From its beginning in 1948 (which Israel considered a "rebirth" rather than an initial founding), the new Jewish state has been able to prevail over various combinations of Arab opponents. The founding members of Israel vowed that there would never be another Holocaust. They decided that the Jewish state would spend unlimited effort and money on the Israeli armed forces to prevent an Arab victory, which they believed could only end in another, final Holocaust. The Arabs, united in their opposition to Israel, remained divided along nationalist, tribal, and familial lines. Despite their tremendous advantages in geography, population, and resources, the Arabs have never been able to match Israel's military prowess, although they nearly did so in 1973.

Both the Arabs and the Israelis have received help from other nations. In the early stages, Israel received assistance from Great Britain and France in the form of diplomatic recognition and the supply of arms. It also received financial assistance from private individuals in Europe and the United States, which made possible the purchase of sophisticated technology from weapons-exporting states. The lower technological levels of military forces in the Middle East made the use of surplus equipment left over from World War II sufficient to meet the needs of the belligerents for more than a decade after the declaration of Israeli independence. After the Suez Crisis fiasco of 1956, Israel turned to the United States, which had always backed it diplomatically and now began to supply it with weapons. The Arab world reached out to the Soviet Union. This aid also helped the Soviet Union achieve its long-sought goal of a military presence in the Mediterranean.

A general overview of each of the major conflicts follows.

THE ISRAELI WAR OF INDEPENDENCE, 1948

From a population of 600,000, Israel fielded 30,000 for local defense and 15,000 as a field force. The return of personnel from World War II, particularly those who had served in the British military, as well as the existence of Jewish militias created before the war, allowed Israel to quickly field a unified command of veteran fighters. Israel quickly defeated the local Palestinian contingents. Then, in a war characterized by a series of truces followed by a series of battles, the Israel Defense Forces (IDF) grew in strength as a result of foreign volunteers and the purchase of equipment. Intervention by Egypt, Jordan, Lebanon, and Syria, with support from Iraq and Saudi Arabia, was poorly coordinated, and the Jewish forces were able to defeat them piecemeal, utilizing the advantage of interior lines to shift forces to whichever front faced the most imminent threat. The Israeli War of Independence culminated in a series of individual armistice agreements in 1949 that defined Israel's borders but never led to a treaty of peace.

THE SINAI CAMPAIGN, 1956

The Arab world was humiliated by its defeat in 1949 and formally expressed its determination never to make peace with Israel and to eradicate it as a nation. Discontent with the undeniable fact of Israel's existence led to a long series of assassinations of Arab leaders. A result of one of these assassinations was the rise to power of the charismatic Gamal Abdel Nasser in Egypt. Nasser, proclaiming his intention of destroying Israel, rearmed Egypt with massive supplies of modern equipment from Czechoslovakia, then a Soviet satellite. Nasser supported Arab revolutionary movements throughout the Arab world and gained great prestige by seizing and nationalizing the Suez Canal.

France and Great Britain reacted to this violation of the Anglo-Egyptian Treaty by planning an invasion of Egypt. Israel, already concerned about Nasser's repeated threats, was planning an invasion of its own. It readily accepted an Anglo-French invitation to participate, gaining an influx of French arms. The Anglo-French-Israeli alliance counted on the United States and the Soviet Union not intervening because of the current tensions over Hungary and Poland.

Israeli forces conquered the Sinai Peninsula in what military historians have termed "a work of art." However, muddling by the British and French leadership and the surprisingly vehement disapproval of the United States and the Soviet Union resulted in a complete fiasco. The French and British forces, late in arriving, were forced to withdraw. Israel had to give up the territory it had conquered in the Sinai Campaign in return for promises of free passage of its shipping in certain Arab waters. Curiously, Nasser, despite the overwhelming defeat of his forces at the hands of the Israelis, gained even greater stature as a result of his defiance of France and England. Israel realized through the Sinai Campaign that it could not rely on foreign assistance to achieve its own security. The machinations of the superpowers would always take precedence over any guarantees to the fledgling Jewish state. As such, Israel embarked on a massive effort to develop its own weapons industry, military education system, and compulsory service for its citizenry.

THE SIX-DAY WAR, 1967

Hostilities continued after 1956 with border clashes and a perpetuation of the long cycle of violence. Revolutions and assassinations were common, with Iraq coming under Soviet influence and a civil war breaking out in once peaceful Lebanon. During 1967 Egypt mobilized forces on Israel's borders as did Jordan and Iraq. Other Arab states sent volunteer forces to participate in Nasser's oft-threatened invasion. France cut off its supply of weapons to Israel, seeking to curry favor with the Arab nations. Israel responded with a brilliant campaign that saw the Israeli Air Force (IAF) carry out a successful surprise attack on Arab air forces on the ground, essentially destroying them in the first two days of the conflict. After that, Israeli air superiority ensured the serial defeat of Egyptian, Syrian, Jordanian, and Iraqi forces. The Arab nations accepted a cease-fire proposed by the United Nations (UN) on June 10, ending the Six-Day War. Israel had seized large amounts of Arab territory during the conflict, including the West Bank and East Jerusalem from Jordan, the Sinai Peninsula and Gaza Strip from Egypt, and the Golan Heights from Syria. While the seizures and subsequent occupations created a more defensible perimeter for Israel, they also virtually guaranteed future conflict and transformed the international perception of Israel from a state on the defensive, seeking to protect its own territory, to a regional conqueror, aggressively expanding its national borders.

THE WAR OF ATTRITION, 1967–1970

The undeclared War of Attrition did not receive much attention outside of the Middle East but was a proclamation of the Arab world's intent to reclaim all the territory it had lost during the Six-Day War. In the process, the conduct of warfare in the Middle East was totally revised, with the introduction of modern weapons, including surface-to-air missiles (SAMs), sophisticated radar defenses, and much more. Further, it introduced the Cold War directly into the Middle East, where, for the first time, the results of an Arab-Israeli conflict could escalate into a nuclear exchange between the superpowers. The Soviet Union sent thousands of personnel to teach the Egyptian forces Soviet tactics and supplied thousands of tanks, artillery, and aircraft. Israel was supplied with modern arms by the United States and built up a series of fortifications along the Suez Canal known as the Bar-Lev Line. These defenses were to serve as a trip wire to allow Israel sufficient time to call up its reserves and then defeat any Arab incursion. Israeli leaders began to assume a permanent superiority over any Arab military forces, and this arrogance led to a gradual decline in the equipment and readiness of IDF personnel.

THE YOM KIPPUR WAR, 1973

Evidence indicates that Nasser intended to invade Israel again in 1970, but a fatal heart attack in September forestalled this plan. His successor, Anwar Sadat, was widely discounted as a leader yet proved to be a man of exceptional vision. Sadat felt that all he had to do was seize some of the land that Israel had conquered in 1967 and hold it until the UN began hearings. He believed those hearings would force Israel to leave the Arab territory it occupied. He masterfully disguised his intentions, even while obtaining Syria's agreement to go to war against Israel in October 1973. To counter Israeli air superiority, so amply demonstrated in the

Six-Day War, Sadat negotiated for the construction of a massive Soviet air defense network, including radar installations, mobile command centers, and a dense concentration of surface-to-air missiles (SAMs), including man-portable weapons. Likewise, Syrian president Hafez al-Assad accepted Soviet assistance in the form of anti-tank weapons to counter Israeli armor superiority. The Israeli leaders, intoxicated by their previous successes, allowed hubris to cloud their judgment. As a result, the well-coordinated Egyptian and Syrian attack was a complete surprise and came very close to defeating Israel. The IDF just managed to hold on while the United States and the Soviet Union bristled with misunderstandings that almost escalated to a nuclear exchange. U.S. secretary of state Henry Kissinger was able to assuage Soviet fears while also mediating the armistice talks between the Arabs and Israelis. Eventually, the IDF prevailed in the Yom Kippur War (also known as the October War and the Ramadan War), but only by the narrowest margin and thanks in great part to a massive resupply effort code-named Operation Nickel Grass from the United States.

POST-1973 DEVELOPMENTS AND CONFLICTS

Since 1973, conflict has continued at varying levels, from suicide bombers to the massacre of Israeli athletes at the 1972 Munich Olympics to Israel's 1982 invasion of southern Lebanon. There have been peaceful high points as well, including the unprecedented visit by Sadat to Jerusalem in 1977; the Camp David Accords of 1978 and the subsequent Jewish withdrawal from the Sinai; and the Oslo Agreement of 1993, in which Israel and the Palestinian Authority (PA) formally recognized each other. Israel showed unusual restraint during the 1991 Persian Gulf War, when Iraqi leader Saddam Hussein authorized the firing of missiles against Israel. Diplomatic pressure from the United States, as well as the transfer of Patriot antiballistic missile (ABM) systems, convinced the Israelis to withhold retaliatory strikes. The likely consequence of any such strike would have been the disintegration of Arab participation in the coalition against Iraq, as no Arab state would deliberately side with Israel against a fellow Islamic government. On a number of occasions, the IAF has bombed neighboring territory, typically in response to missile or mortar strikes or rocket attacks on Jewish settlements within Israel. More recently, Israel launched another invasion of southern Lebanon in the summer of 2006, with the goal of eradicating guerrilla sites near the Israeli border.

In December 2008, Israel commenced a brief offensive against Hamas (a fundamentalist Palestinian group) in the Gaza Strip. The catalyst for this brief conflict was Hamas rocket fire into southern Israel, which had killed three Israeli civilians. The Israeli attack heavily damaged Gaza and resulted in some 1,400 deaths there. Thirteen Israelis also died. In July 2014 Israeli forces invaded the Gaza Strip, following a 10-day air and artillery campaign designed to destroy Hamas's tunnels and its rocket-firing capabilities. After seven weeks of heavy fighting, 2,200 Gazans (70 percent of them civilians) died, while 72 Israelis died (six of them civilians). A permanent cease-fire was reached on August 26, 2014.

Despite the lack of yet another outbreak of major, open warfare, the Arab-Israeli conflict still exists today. In particular, tensions between Israelis and

Palestinians living in the Occupied Territories and Gaza Strip have resulted in numerous acts of aggression on both sides. Many proposals for the creation of a separate Palestinian state have been advanced, but neither side has proven sufficiently willing to compromise to create a lasting peace in the region.

Walter Boyne and Paul J. Springer

See also: British Military Involvement in Postcolonial Africa; Cold War in Africa; French Military Involvement in Postcolonial Africa; Gaddafi, Muammar; Nasser, Gamal Abdel; Soviet Military Involvement in Africa; Suez Crisis; U.S. Military Involvement in Africa.

Further Reading

Aker, Frank. *October 1973: The Arab-Israeli War.* Hamden, CT: N.p., 1985.

Dunstan, Simon. *The Yom Kippur War 1973 (I): The Golan Heights and (II): The Sinai.* Oxford: Osprey Publishing, 2003.

Herzog, Chaim. *The Arab-Israeli Wars: War and Peace in the Middle East.* Updated by Shlomo Gazit. New York: Vintage Books, 2004.

McGregor, Andrew. *A Military History of Modern Egypt; from the Ottoman Conquest to the Ramadan War.* Westport, CT: Praeger Security International, 2006.

Oren, Michael B. *Six Days of War: June 1967 and the Making of the Modern Middle East.* New York: Oxford University Press, 2002.

Pollack, Kenneth. *Arabs at War: Military Effectiveness, 1948–1991.* Lincoln: University of Nebraska Press, 2002.

Armed Islamic Group (GIA)

The Armed Islamic Group (GIA) is a terrorist organization dedicated to the overthrow of the Algerian government. In 1992 after the Algerian military arrested large numbers of the Islamic Salvation Front (FIS), members and politicians, militants formed the Islamic Armed Movement (MIA), which sought to engage the government in negotiations. In contrast, a diverse collection of groups dedicated to combat, including many veterans of the war in Afghanistan, formed the Armed Islamic Group (GIA, from the French Groupe Islamique Armé). The GIA conducted a series of assassinations and attacks on journalists and intellectuals and even attacked other Islamist groups, such as the leaders of the FIS and MIA. The GIA rejected any compromise with any group or individual that did not subscribe to its exclusive Salafist ideology. At its height, the GIA attracted hundreds of new members each month and became a major force in the Algerian conflict (1991–2002). However, the Algerian government proved quite adept at capturing or killing the leaders of the GIA, which limited its effectiveness. The continued leadership changes led both to ideological splits and to even greater radicalization.

A number of massacres of civilians, including whole villages, for which observers could not attribute the guilt, created a severe war fatigue and discredited both the militant Islamist groups and the government. The high levels of total violence caused most of the civilian population to turn against the GIA. Large numbers of militants began to desert the GIA, due to the indiscriminate nature of attacks. For the same reason, a commander, Hassan Hattab, broke away from the GIA in 1998 to form the Salafist Group for Preaching and Combat (GSPC). In 2002 Algerian security forces killed the last commander of the GIA in a battle, effectively ending the GIA's existence as a terror organization. The GSPC eventually became Al-Qaeda in the Islamic Maghreb (AQIM), with many former members of the GIA, as evidence of the continuing appeal of Islamist ideology as a means of political opposition in Algeria.

Paul J. Springer

See also: Algerian Civil War; Al-Qaeda in the Islamic Maghreb (AQIM).

Further Reading

Evans, Martin, and John Phillips. *Algeria: Anger of the Dispossessed*. New Haven, CT: Yale University Press, 2007.

Filiu, Jean Pierre. *From Deep State to Islamic State: The Arab Counter-Revolution and Its Jihadi Legacy*. London: Hurst, 2015.

Le Suer, James D. *Between Terror and Democracy: Algeria since 1989*. New York: Zed Books, 2010.

Army for the Liberation of Rwanda (ALIR)

See Congo Wars; Hutu Power Movements

Army of Islamic Salvation (AIS)

The armed wing of the Islamic Salvation Front (FIS) was founded by Madani Mezrag and Ahmed Benaicha on July 18, 1994. They united several different FIS-supporting, anti-government guerrilla forces that had been fighting since the interruption of the electoral process in Algeria in 1992.

Unlike other armed Islamic groups, the Army of Islamic Salvation (AIS) considered jihad as only one of several possible means to reestablish the electoral process, which would have led to establishing a proper Islamic state. As a consequence, it adopted a long-term, guerrilla strategy, mainly against the Algerian state and its representatives, explicitly avoiding suicide bombings against masses of civilians. AIS could gain only limited popular support, mostly in the peripheral regions and among the religious middle class.

In 1995, AIS declared its support for a negotiated political solution to the conflict with the government. Between 1995 and 1996, it directly attacked the GIA. After subsequent negotiations with the Algerian authorities, in 1997 the AIS unilaterally declared a cease-fire. Mezrag declared AIS dissolved on October 1, 1997, and both Mezrag and Benaicha have offered support to the government in the fight against different armed Islamic groups. Former AIS combatants obtained amnesty in 2000, within President Bouteflika's national reconciliation policies. However, the government arrested some former AIS militants in 2013 on charges that they recruited Algerians to fight under the banner of Jabhat al-Nusra in Syria and established ties with jihadist groups in Libya and Tunisia.

Valentina Fedele

See also: Algerian Civil War; Armed Islamic Group (GIA).

Further Reading

Hafez, Mohammed M. "Armed Islamic Movements and Political Violence in Algeria." *Middle East Journal* 54, no. 4 (2000): 572–591.

Willis, Michael J. *The Islamist Challenge in Algeria: A Political History*. New York: New York University Press, 1997.

Azanian People's Liberation Army (APLA)

In the decades-long struggle to end apartheid in South Africa, various groups took divergent paths. The oldest and most famous of them was the multiracial African National Congress, which created an armed wing, *Umkhonto we Sizwe*, a.k.a., "MK," in 1961. The second most prominent group was the Pan-Africanist Congress of Azania (PAC), with Azania referring to the group's preferred name for South Africa. The PAC was an explicitly "Africanist"—or African only—organization, formed in 1959 by a number of former ANC members, most notably Robert Sobukwe and P. K. Leballo. The PAC adhered to the motto of "Africa for the Africans" and sought to create a government of Africans, by Africans, for Africans; its leaders rejected the multiracial vision of other groups. The PAC typically took a more radical and hard-line approach in its policies and actions, both in its political efforts and in the military methods of its armed wing, initially called *Poqo* ("pure" or "alone" in Xhosa) and subsequently renamed the Azanian People's Liberation Army.

Like the ANC, from which it grew, PAC leaders grew frustrated by the failure of nonviolent strategies to overcome apartheid in the 1950s. The PAC's "positive action campaign" of 1960 led to large anti-pass demonstrations throughout the country, and ultimately to the Sharpeville Massacre on March. Soon after, the government banned the PAC (as well as the ANC), which caused significant chaos in the organization, as it struggled to operate underground and from abroad and to do so while it created *Poqo* and attempted to initiate armed insurrection.

From 1961 to 1967, with support from other Africa governments such as Kwame Nkrumah's Ghana, *Poqo* asserted it was picking up the anti-imperialist struggles of its forebears. *Poqo* leaflets stated "The white people shall suffer, the black people will rule. Freedom comes after bloodshed. *Poqo* has started." Other slogans ("[W]e shall drive them into the sea" and "[T]hey must go back to Europe") may have been effective for recruitment, but they led not only to sporadic attacks on police and Black collaborators but also to murders of civilians that even some PAC leaders criticized. Thus, some military activities failed to be guided properly by official PAC ideology. Unlike the ANC's force, MK, which planned acts of violence to force the government to be a more willing negotiator, *Poqo* sought to overthrow the government via an armed uprising of the rural poor. In a 1963 press conference in Maseru, Lesotho, Leballo announced the plan for *Poqo* to initiate a "general uprising" in South Africa. The premature pronouncement, coupled with poor operational security, led to mass arrests throughout South Africa, and nothing more than local operations and other isolated acts of violence came off it. By 1967 the government had contained *Poqo*, and the PAC sought to develop a new military strategy.

By 1968, having secured funding from the OAU Liberation Committee, perhaps 200 PAC recruits were training in the Congo, Ghana, and Algeria, and that year the PAC force was renamed APLA (though the name change was neither properly explained or coordinated, internally or externally). APLA attempted to become a more formal guerrilla army, with Gerald Kondlo its first commander, a headquarters in Dar es Salaam, and bases in Tanzania and Zambia. Occasionally, APLA leaders and trainees were expelled from or dispersed within those counties. Relations with the People's Republic of China appear to have encouraged APLA to develop a new strategy for protracted guerrilla warfare, which it referred to as "people's war," hinging on the debatable assumption that South Africa had a large land-hungry peasant class. APLA attacks were to target the many isolated white farmers in the countryside. As farmers were cleared from the land—by murder and intimidation—new bases, sanctuaries, and even APLA-governed polities were to emerge. Apparently, few lieutenants, much less many rank-and-file soldiers, understood this new Maoist strategy, at least for the next decade, as APLA engaged in only sporadic, disjointed operations that made little strategic progress.

In 1978 this led to the adoption of the "New Road of Revolution," which officially guided PAC military strategy until the PAC was unbanned in 1990. APLA established arms caches in South Africa and infiltrated more soldiers into South Africa. Still, actual military operations were infrequent until the mid-1980s due to a host of internal and external problems. An internal conflict between Maoists and Marxist-Leninists proved distracting as did a violent struggle—which ultimately split the organization—to determine the successor to Sobukwe as PAC president after his death from cancer in 1978. Operations in 1978–1979 suffered again from poor operational security, as groups of insurgents were arrested. APLA also suffered from serious difficulties with the Tanzanian government, which violently occupied the main camp at Chunya and disarmed or dispersed its occupants. By 1985, APLA showed signs of having resolved its serious organizational and morale problems as recruiting increased, and it conducted more attacks over the next few years, mostly using grenades and pistols against policemen and soldiers. Still, the number of trainees and operatives remained relatively small, with most estimates suggesting 800–2,500 soldiers training abroad and approximately 120 guerrillas operating within South Africa at any given time.

In 1990 the government lifted the ban on the PAC. While PAC leaders debated whether to engage in negotiations, APLA continued the armed struggle. While much of the violence during this period resulted from fighting between the ANC and Zulu-nationalist Inkatha supporters, APLA gained notoriety by continuing attacks on whites. With a slogan of "One settler, one bullet," APLA perpetrated several violent attacks, not only against policemen, but also increasingly against civilians in farms, restaurants, clubs, hotels, and even churches. Many attacks showed sophisticated planning and skill in execution. PAC finally renounced the armed struggle in 1994, a belated rejection of violence that came after the recent APLA attacks had thrilled many young militants but also alienated masses of older voters who rejected them at the polls that year in favor of the multiracial vision of other parties, such as the ANC.

Mark E. Grotelueschen

See also: South Africa, Armed Struggle against Apartheid; Umkhonto we Sizwe (MK).

Further Reading

Kondlo, Kwandiwe. *In the Twilight of the Revolution. The Pan Africanist Congress of Azania (South Africa) 1959–1994*. Basel: Basler Afrika Bibliographien, 2009.

Lodge, Tom. "Soldiers of the Storm: A Profile of the Azanian People's Liberation Army." In *About Turn: The Transformation of the South African Military and Intelligence*, edited by Jakkie Cilliers and Markus Reichardt. Pretoria: Institute for Defence Policy, 1996.

B

Barre, Mohamed Siad (1919–1995)

Mohamed Siad Barre (born October 6, 1919, died January 2, 1995) was a Somali military commander, politician, and the president of Somalia from 1969 to 1991. Barre fled Somalia in 1991 after his government's collapse in 1991 and died in 1995.

Barre was born near Shilavo, which was a part of the Ogaden province of Ethiopia. He pretended to be born in Somalia, so he would be eligible to join the Italian colonial police in 1935. Barre remained in the military and became vice commander upon Somalia's independence in 1960. Barre soon after began to work with Soviet military advisers, and he became receptive to Marxist-Leninism.

On October 15, 1969, a police officer assassinated President Abdirashid Ali Sharmarke, which some historians believe was related to clan-related conflict. On October 21, 1969, Barre led the army in a bloodless coup of Somalia, banned all political parties, and arrested multiple senior politicians. Barre believed that absolute loyalty to a common ideal was essential for a stable state, and he attempted to unify Somalia's ethnic groups under a common socialist identity. One example of this was the implementation of a common Somali language in 1972 and a mass-literacy campaign in 1974.

These efforts were one part of his goals for "Somali-weyn," or "Greater Somalia." Greater Somalia was an idea that originated in the early twentieth century, whereby all Somali people would unify under one state. This unification included parts of modern-day Ethiopia and Djibouti. Shortly after Djibouti held referendums and seceded from Somalia in early 1977, Barre began preparations for an invasion of Ethiopia. Barre wanted control of the Ogaden because he wanted to unify the Somali majority with Somalia. Barre launched an invasion of Ethiopia in July 1977 to capture the Ogaden and incorporate it into Greater Somalia. While initially successful, the war resulted in the destruction of the Somali military. The Soviet Union also opposed Somalia during the war because Ethiopia was also a Marxist-Leninist state, and the Soviet Union saw Ethiopia as a useful ally.

Somalia became increasingly unstable in the 1980s. Multiple clan-based movements formed in the early 1980s, including the Somali National Movement. Barre used military force to suppress uprisings throughout this decade, including against civilian centers he suspected of disloyalty. This counterinsurgency campaign, however, escalated into systemic killings of Isaaq civilians from 1987 to 1989. One prominent example was the deliberate aerial bombardment of the cities of Hargeisa and Burao in 1988. These bombings resulted in tens of thousands of civilians dead, over 500,000 Somali refugees who fled into Ethiopia, and widespread condemnation of Barre's regime.

Resistance forces applied more pressure to Barre as public sentiment turned against him. Opposition forces captured Mogadishu on January 26, 1991, which forced Barre into exile. Barre initially fled to Kenya and latter to Lagos, Nigeria. Barre died on January 2, 1995, of a heart attack. Opinions remain divided within Somalia on how much people should praise his modernization programs and condemn his authoritarian practices in the late 1970s and 1980s.

Quentin Holbert

See also: Cold War in Africa; Ethiopia: Insurgency and Interstate War; Ogaden War; Somalia Civil War; Soviet Military Involvement in Africa.

Further Reading
Harper, Mary. *Getting Somalia Wrong?: Faith, War and Hope in a Shattered State.* London: Zed Books, 2012.
Schmidt, Elizabeth. *Foreign Intervention in Africa: From the Cold War to the War on Terror.* Cambridge: Cambridge University Press, 2013.
Tareke, Gebru. "The Ethiopia-Somalia War of 1977 Revisited." *International Journal of African Historical Studies* 33, no. 3 (2000): 635–667.

Belgian Military Intervention in Africa (1960–)

Despite its status as a small Western European power with a modest-sized military, Belgium intervened regularly in its former colonial territories in Africa. During the 1950s, given the Cold War context, Belgium expanded its military presence in the Congo, constructing a new air base at Kamina and stationing metropolitan Belgian troops in the colony to supplement the locally recruited army called the Force Publique. At this point Belgium developed its Para-Commando Regiment as an airmobile reaction force capable of intervening in Central Africa. Given the hasty independence of the Congo in 1960 and the lack of Congolese officers, Belgian officers continued to lead the Force Publique, prompting a mutiny among dissatisfied soldiers and triggering the "Congo Crisis." Just a few weeks after independence, a Belgian naval task force arrived, offloading Belgian troops who occupied the Congo's major towns to protect Belgian civilians, but this led to accusations that Brussels was attempting to recolonize the country. While a United Nations force replaced the Belgian troops in the Congo, Belgian officers continued to advise the re-created Congolese National Army (ANC), and Belgium provided military support for the separatist state in Katanga, including Belgian mercenaries. After the demise of secessionist Katanga, Belgium supported the central government of the Congo against leftist rebels in the east. In addition to providing military advisers for the ANC and technicians to support Congo's American-supplied aircraft, Belgium conducted two major airborne operations in eastern Congo in November 1964 that rescued Western hostages and defeated the Simba rebels. Transported by American aircraft staging out of Kamina, and in conjunction with Belgian-led ANC and mercenary ground forces, 350 Belgian paratroopers dropped on Stanleyville (now Kisangani) during Operation Dragon Rouge, and 250 jumped on Paulis (now Isiro) in Operation Dragon Noire. Belgium canceled its plans for more Dragon operations, given the international outcry about its intervention in independent Africa. Furthermore, in 1960, Belgium founded locally recruited militaries in the mandated territories of Rwanda and Burundi, sending officer candidates to the Royal Military Academy in Brussels. While local officers took command of the armed forces of Rwanda and Burundi when these countries became independent in 1962, Belgian military advisers continued to play a significant role. At the end of 1963, Belgian officers led a Rwandan military force that repelled an incursion by exiled Rwandan Tutsi rebels. Subsequently, Belgium continued to pursue defense agreements with independent Congo (Zaire from 1971) and Rwanda but not with Burundi, given the 1972 genocide of educated Hutu in that country. Despite a strained relationship with the Mobutu regime over its nationalization of Belgian businesses and Zaire's growing military relationship with France, Belgium continued to send military advisers and instructors to Zaire during the 1970s and 1980s. In May 1978, during Operation Red Bean, 1,100 Belgian paratroopers landed at Kolwezi in southern Zaire to rescue hostages taken by exiled Katangese rebels and evacuate foreigners. Although the Belgian intervention occurred simultaneous with a French parachute jump on Kolwezi, the two operations had not been coordinated. About half the Belgian force remained in southern Zaire until the arrival of a Western-backed Inter-African Force. During Operation Green Apple in February 1979, prompted by rumors of coup plots against the Mobutu regime, Belgium flew 250 paratroopers to a base at Kitona west of Kinshasa and dispatched a naval vessel to provide logistical support. The force withdrew after a few weeks.

With the end of the Cold War, a new phase of active Belgian military intervention in Africa took place during the 1990s, including participation in UN missions. Belgian and French troops deployed in Rwanda in 1990 in response to the invasion of the predominantly Tutsi Rwandan Patriotic Front (RPF). Unlike the French, the Belgians withdrew after a few weeks, ending their Operation Green Bean. In 1993, Belgium contributed a battalion to the United Nations Assistance Mission in Rwanda (UNAMIR), which monitored the peace process. However, with the killing of 10 Belgian soldiers in April 1994, at the outset of the genocide against the Tutsi, the Belgian battalion withdrew from UNAMIR, moving to the Kigali airport where a Belgian airmobile force arrived to evacuate European civilians as part of Operation Silverback, and all departed Rwanda. In 1991, a crisis brought on by the weakening of the Mobutu regime in Zaire led to a Belgian military deployment called Operation Blue Beam meant to facilitate the evacuation of Westerners. This operation also involved deployments to neighboring Congo-Brazzaville and Gabon. Around the same time, Mobutu severed his military ties with Belgium, ordering the expulsion of Belgian military advisers. In 1993, Belgian and French troops flew to Brazzaville in preparation for an operation in Kinshasa, where Zairean troops mutinied, but Mobutu refused to allow the Belgian forces into his country. Belgium also contributed to several UN missions outside its former colonial empire in Africa. A small number of Belgian military personnel and gendarmes participated in the 1989–1990 United Nations Transition Assistance Group (UNTAG) during the independence process in Namibia. In 1993, Belgian paracommandos joined the American-led international intervention in Somalia called Operation Restore Hope and the United Nations Operation in Somalia (UNOSOM).

As happened with other contingents, Belgian para-commandos faced accusations of committing atrocities against Somali civilians. During the 2000s, Belgium provided military instructors for the newly integrated militaries of the Democratic Republic of the Congo (DRC) and Burundi, and Belgian medical and communications detachments joined the European Union's 2003 Interim Emergency Multinational Force (IEMF) in northeastern DRC.

Timothy J. Stapleton

See also: Congo Crisis; Peacekeeping in Africa; Rwanda, Civil War and Genocide; Shaba, Zaire: Rebel Incursions and Foreign Intervention; Somalia Civil War.

Further Reading

Odom, Thomas. *Dragon Operations: Hostage Rescues in the Congo, 1964–65.* Fort Levenworth, KS: Combat Studies Institute, 1988.

Odom, Thomas P. *Shaba II: The French and Belgian Intervention in Zaire in 1978.* Fort Leavenworth, KS: U.S. Army Command and General Staff College, Combat Studies Institute, 1993.

Prunier, Gerard. *The Rwanda Crisis: History of a Genocide.* New York: Columbia University Press, 1995.

Rouvez, Alain. *Disconsolate Empires: French, British and Belgian Military Involvement in Post-Colonial Sub-Saharan Africa.* Lanham, MD: University Press of America, 1994.

Vanthemsche, Guy. *Belgium and the Congo, 1885–1980.* Cambridge: Cambridge University Press, 2012.

Bokassa, Jean-Bédel (1921–1996)

Jean-Bédel Bokassa was the leader of the Central African Republic from 1966 to 1979. His bizarre behavior and violent policies made him a symbol of the corrupt leadership that afflicted many postindependence African nations.

Bokassa was born in Bobangui, in the French colony of Ubangi Chari, on February 22, 1921. He was one of 12 children of a Mbaka chief in the Lobaye province. When he was six, his father was killed in a French prefecture's office. His mother committed suicide very soon thereafter. The orphaned Bokassa was educated in Roman Catholic mission schools in Bangui and Brazzaville. He considered joining the priesthood but instead opted for a career in the military.

In 1939, Bokassa enlisted in the French colonial army in the opening days of World War II. After the fall of France in 1940, he joined the Free French Forces organized by General Charles de Gaulle and was decorated for combat in France and the Congo. After the war he served the French Army in Indochina between 1946 and 1954, becoming an officer in 1949. By the time he left the French Army in 1961, he had attained the rank of captain.

The Oubangui-Chari colony achieved its independence in 1960 and became the Central African Republic. Bokassa's family played an instrumental role in the campaign to end French rule. Bokassa's uncle, Barthelemy Boganda, led the independence movement until his death in 1959. Bokassa's cousin, David Dacko, became the nation's first president. Dacko appointed Bokassa as the commander in chief of the nation's armed forces in 1963.

The new nation faced serious economic problems, which President Dacko tried to solve through a series of austerity measures. When he proposed cuts in the budget of the armed forces, however, Bokassa overthrew him on December 31, 1965, and declared himself president. Bokassa declared his intentions to return the nation to civilian rule when the economic crisis subsided. After removing all potential threats to his authority, however, he failed to relinquish his position as the nation's dictator.

Shortly after his accession to power, Bokassa began to exhibit erratic behavior. In 1970, he outlawed all strikes and demonstrations within the country. In 1971, to commemorate Mother's Day, he released all women imprisoned in the nation's jails and executed all men accused of serious crimes against women. The following year he had himself declared president for life. In 1976, he renamed his nation the Central African Empire and crowned himself Emperor Bokassa I. His coronation was celebrated with an elaborate ceremony that cost the impoverished country $30 million.

Bokassa cultivated relations with Western nations willing to supply economic assistance to his regime. France retained close relations with Bokassa despite his odd behavior because it was reliant on the Central African Republic as a supplier of uranium. Bokassa also sought aid from Libya and briefly converted to Islam to curry favor with Libyan leader Muammar Gaddafi. He returned to Christianity, however, when the aid was not forthcoming. Eventually, Bokassa's bizarre behavior embarrassed Western donors, who began withdrawing their assistance in the late 1970s.

In early 1979, Bokassa announced that all schoolchildren in the nation were required to wear expensive uniforms produced by a factory owned by one of his wives. The order inspired widespread protests. The army arrested many of the child protesters and placed them in prison, at which point they were massacred by Bokassa's own personal guard. Fed up with the emperor's bizarre and bloody rule, the French intervened militarily to depose Bokassa in September 1979. Bokassa was sent into exile in Côte d'Ivoire and replaced by Dacko, the man he had ousted 14 years earlier.

Dacko's hold on power proved tenuous, and the military removed him from power six months after he took office. Bokassa returned to the Central African Republic in 1986 and stood trial for the murder of several political opponents as well as for cannibalism and grand theft. He was convicted and sentenced to death, but his sentence was commuted to life in prison. He was granted amnesty in 1993 and died on November 3, 1996.

ABC-CLIO

See also: Central African Republic (CAR), Conflict in; Coups and Military Regimes in Africa; French Military Involvement in Postcolonial Africa; Gaddafi, Muammar.

Further Reading

Kalck, Pierre. *Historical Dictionary of the Central African Republic*. Lanham, MD: Scarecrow Press, 2005.

Titley, Brian. *Dark Age: The Political Odyssey of Emperor Bokassa*. Montreal: McGill-Queen's University Press, 1997.

Boko Haram

The conflict between the Islamist group *Jama'atul Alhul Sunnah Lidda'wati wal Jihad*, popularly known as Boko Haram, and the Nigerian government has been raging for over a decade now. With its main theater being the northeastern region of Nigeria, the conflict, which began in 2009, has killed thousands of people and displaced millions. Founded in 2002, in the Borno state capital of Maiduguri, under the leadership of Mohammed Yusuf, Boko Haram, which means "Western education is forbidden," opposes all forms of Western influence, including Nigeria's democracy, which it considers has made the country immoral and corrupt. The aim of the group's violent activities therefore is to topple Nigeria's democracy and establish an Islamic state governed by a strict form of Sharia. Religious insecurity, exploitation by Nigeria's political elites, and socioeconomic disparities between northern and southern Nigeria are the immediate causes of the emergence of Boko Haram and its resort to violence. However, the Nigerian government's counterinsurgency approach has over the years prolonged the conflict and worsened the violent crisis.

Militant religiosity in northern Nigeria began with the jihad by Usman dan Fodio in the nineteenth century. It was triggered by dan Fodio's quest to reform Islam, as he deemed it diluted due to its contact with the indigenous religious practices in the Hausa region in northern Nigeria as well as grievances over taxation by local rulers. The jihad ultimately led to the establishment of the Sokoto Caliphate, which lasted until British colonization in 1903. Similar processes took place in the Kanem-Bornu state that existed in precolonial northeastern Nigeria. In 1914, a merger between the northern and southern British territories created the present-day Nigeria. During the colonial period in northern Nigeria, the introduction of the indirect-rule system enabled the emirs of the caliphate to continue ruling their people using Sharia law while they remained accountable to the British. However, the northern Muslims saw Nigeria as a secular state rather than a religious one because they considered the British as Christian infidels. The adoption of Western democracy after gaining independence in 1960 further heightened religious opposition to the secular Nigerian state.

To many northern Muslims, Western democracy is a colonial construct based on Christian values and must be replaced with an Islamic state governed by Sharia. Mohammed Yusuf identified Western democracy and other influences to be the main causes of the corruption, immorality, and marginalization in Nigeria and situated a solution to that in the implantation of a strict form of Sharia throughout the country. This was the core message in Yusuf's preaching, which attracted followers to his cause.

Politics in Nigeria is marred by corruption, embezzlement, and misappropriation of state resources by political elites. The political elites have come to recognize their position as a means of accumulating wealth rather than serving the people. The endemic corruption, coupled with poor governance, has consequently strained the relationship between the people and the state. It is in opposition to these political troubles that Boko Haram emerged as a challenger to the Nigerian state, seeking to overthrow the country's democracy and institute Sharia law. In most of his preaching, Mohammed Yusuf was very critical of the corrupt practices and bad governance of the northern political elites. His message, therefore, resonated with the youth and unemployed who recognized him as a positive influence and hence supported his movement.

Politics in Nigeria is fragmented along ethnic and religious lines. As a result, elite politicians most often exploit ethnic and religious sentiments as a means of attaining power. In the process, most politicians engage social groups to help them amass popular support while intimidating their opponents. However, when the demands of such groups are not met by the very elites they helped, they emerge as stiff opposition to the political system and the state. Such practices among some elite politicians contributed to the emergence of Boko Haram. Ali Modu Sherrif, a member of the All Nigeria Peoples Party (ANPP) and a former governor of Borno state is believed to have engaged members of Boko Haram in his private militia called "Ecomog boys" toward his election in 2003. He is also believed to have supported the group both financially and with ammunition during its formative years. However, following his inability to implement strict Sharia law throughout Borno state as demanded by Boko Haram, the group, out of a feeling of disappointment, began resorting to extremist measures to seek the implementation of its demand while opposing the entire political system.

Another significant reason for the emergence of Boko Haram and its resort to violence is socioeconomic marginalization. Poverty, unemployment, and illiteracy are lamentably high in Nigeria's northern region compared to the south. The region also suffers from a lack of basic social amenities like schools, hospitals, and pipe-borne water. The socioeconomic marginalization of northern Nigeria is attributable to the British colonial rule and the emergence of the country's oil industry in the southeast.

The implementation of the indirect-rule system in northern Nigeria by the British colonial administrators and the subsequent barring of Christian missionaries from the region consequently resulted in the retardation of development and modernization. As industrial activities were limited to the south, so were basic social services such as transport infrastructure, Western education, good health care, pipe-borne water, and electricity. These eventually opened the south up to rapid economic growth, urbanization, and general development compared to the north.

Similarly, the development of the oil and gas sector in Nigeria has led to the neglect of the agrarian sector, which is the mainstay of the northern economy. With the continued dominance of the oil and gas sector, a majority of state resources are invested in its development at the expense of the agrarian sector, resulting in a persistent decline in agricultural outputs and the collapse of most agriculture-related factories. As the main economic activity in the northern region, these situations have over the years led to a spike in unemployment, deteriorating social amenities, a collapse of the region's economy, and an ultimate rise in poverty levels. In 2010, the southeast and southwest geopolitical zones had poverty rates of 67.0 and 59.1 percent compared to 76.3 and 77.7 percent for the northeast and northwest geopolitical zones, respectively. Again, with a national literacy average of 53 percent as of 2012, Kano, the northern region's commercial capital and Nigeria's second-biggest city, had a literacy rate of 49 percent. The northern states of Borno and Sokoto had literacy rates of 15 and 10 percent, respectively. These make the northern region not only the poorest region of the country but also the region with the worst literacy level.

It is in light of such socioeconomic marginalization of the northern region, coupled with the endemic corruption among its political elites, that Boko Haram emerged as a front seeking betterment through the establishment of an Islamic state and the implementation of Sharia throughout Nigeria.

Besides the aforementioned root causes of the emergence of Boko Haram and its conflict with the Nigerian state, further exacerbating the violent rhetoric of the group and hence prolonging the conflict, is the government's counterinsurgency approach. Although considerable efforts have been made by the government to end the conflict through negotiation, the most extensive approach adopted over the years has been the use of force toward the violent destruction of the group. This includes the declaration of a state of emergency in the states of Borno, Adamawa, Niger, and Plateau in 2011 and later in the states of Adamawa, Yobe, and Borno in 2013; the establishment and deployment of a Joint Task Force (JTF) and a Civilian Joint Task Force (CJTF); and the use of the regional joint military offensive in the form of the Multinational Joint Task Force (MNJTF).

However, this heavy-handed approach has not only failed to end the conflict but has pushed Boko Haram toward embracing a more lethal approach in its activities. This is evident in the dramatic transformation in the nature, lethality, and frequency of the group's attacks following the extrajudicial killing of Mohammed Yusuf in 2009 while in police custody. Since 2010, Boko Haram has adopted different tactical approaches. They include the use of guerilla tactics, conventional warfare, suicide bombers, improvised explosive devices (IEDs), and vehicle-borne improvised explosive devices (VBIEDs). The heavy-handed counterinsurgency by the Nigerian state has further alienated the people, thereby helping Boko Haram to win their support and sympathy for its cause. Nevertheless, disagreements within Boko Haram led to the group splitting into a separate faction called Islamic State West Africa Province (ISWA or ISWAP). While Boko Haram is often compared to other Africa's other Islamist armed groups such as Al-Shabaab in Somalia and Al-Qaeda in the Islamic Maghreb (AQIM), its specific links with these movements remain unclear.

It is indeed clear that, while the emergence of Boko Haram and its resort to violence is traceable to deep-seated religious and socioeconomic sentiments among most Nigerians, the corrupt, divisive, and contentious nature of the country's political landscape has provided the conducive grounds for such sentiments to erupt into violence. Rather than addressing the root causes of the conflict, the government's heavy-handed counterinsurgency operation has further pushed Boko Haram to assume a more radical and aggressive posture, thereby prolonging the conflict. In over a decade of violent clashes between the government and members of Boko Haram, peace is still far away.

Gershon Adela

See also: Al-Qaeda in the Islamic Maghreb (AQIM); Al-Shabaab; Cameroon Conflicts; Nigerian Civil War.

Further Reading

Anugwom, Edlyne Eze. *The Boko Haram Insurgency in Nigeria: Perspectives from Within*. Basingstoke: Palgrave Macmillan, 2019.

Comolli, Virgina. *Boko Haram: Nigeria's Islamist Insurgency*. London: Hurst, 2015.

David, Ojochenemi J., Lucky E. Asuelime, and Hakeem Onapajo. *Boko Haram: The Socio-economic drivers*. Cham: Springer International Publishing, 2015.

Mustapha, Abdul Raufu, ed. *Sects & Social Disorder: Muslim Identities & Conflict in Northern Nigeria*. Woodbridge: Boydell & Brewer, 2014.

Thurston, Alexander. *Boko Haram: The History of an African Jihadist Movement*. Princeton, NJ: Princeton University Press, 2018.

Varin, Caroline. *Boko Haram and the War on Terror*. Santa Barbara, CA: Praeger, 2016.

Bouteflika, Abdelaziz (1937–)

Algerian politician and president of Algeria from 1999 to 2019, Bouteflika was born on March 2, 1937, in Oudja, Morocco, into a family of Algerian immigrants. In 1956, he joined the armed wing of the Front de Libération Nationale (FLN) to fight in the Algerian War of Independence. After independence, he served in the cabinet of two presidents. In 1983, he was convicted of embezzling state funds from the accounts of the Algerian embassies but was given amnesty by President Benjedid, and then he spent six years abroad. In 1989, the Algerian Army brought him back to serve in the Central Committee of the FLN. In 1999, as the military's candidate, Bouteflika became president, after an election with significant irregularities.

During his presidencies, he worked hard to regain international legitimacy as well as bring internal peace. He promoted a legal amnesty program called "The Charter for Peace and National Reconciliation" of 2006. He engaged in bureaucratic struggles to overcome resistance from hard-line advocates of a purely military solution to terrorism—known as "eradicators." Through the combination of military action, with persistent negotiations and a second major amnesty program—the December 2009 Law on Civil Concord—his administration dramatically reduced the incidence of terrorist attacks. In spring 2001, excessive violence by the gendarmerie in the Kabila region provoked sharp protests by the Berber population, denouncing cultural, economic, and social exclusion. He stood for a third term in 2009 and was reelected, in spite of poor health and a mixed record. He promised reforms, and a deepening of democracy in the aftermath of the protests of 2010–2012, but apart from improving women's rights, the political changes further tightened the government's control over society and restricted political opportunity. He used General Ahmed Gaid Salah to bring the military security services (Département du Renseignement et de la Sécurité, the DRS) under civilian control, through restructuring and retirements. His administration continues to pursue massive infrastructure investments and tries to regain investor confidence and international support. After an enabling constitutional amendment, in spite of repeated, protracted hospitalizations in France, he ran for a fourth term and was reelected in 2014. The political opposition argues that the president's bad health disqualifies him from further leadership. When he announced that he would seek a fifth term, protests began on February 22, 2019, and under pressure from the army, he resigned on April 2, 2019.

Valentina Fedele

See also: Algerian Civil War; Algerian War of Independence; National Liberation Front (FLN) Algeria.

Further Reading

McDougall, James. *A History of Algeria*. Cambridge: Cambridge University Press, 2017.

Mortimer, Robert. "State and Army in Algeria: The 'Bouteflika Effect.'" *Journal of North African Studies* 11, no. 2 (June 2006): 155–171.

Tlemcani, Rachid. "Algeria under Bouteflika: Civil Strife and National Reconciliation." *Carnegie Papers* no. 7 (February 2008).

Bozizé, François (1946–)

General François Bozizé, the former president of the Central African Republic, came to power in a March 2003 coup welcomed by most citizens for its promise of economic revitalization for the country. Formerly the nation's army chief, Bozizé overthrew the embattled government of his former ally, President Ange-Félix Patassé, while Patassé was out of the country. Bozizé then proclaimed himself president and installed a new government that included both opposition leaders and supporters of Patassé. He was formally elected to the post by the country's citizens in the February 2005 general poll and reelected in January 2011. However, he was himself ousted in a coup in March 2013.

Bozizé is no stranger to coups. Like Patassé, he was a prominent member of the opposition against the dictatorship of military leader Andre Kolingba in the 1980s and early 1990s. Bozizé led a coup against Kolingba in 1983 and, as a result, was arrested and tortured by the government. He later fled to Togo, where he lived in exile until Kolingba was voted out of office in 1993. It has been reported that Bozizé and Patassé became friends and political allies during this time, since Patassé also opposed Kolingba's regime and spent more than 10 years in exile in Togo.

When Kolingba was forced to hold democratic elections in 1993, both Bozizé and Patassé ran against him. Patassé won the presidency, but the alliance between the two men continued, and Patassé named Bozizé his army chief of staff. Bozizé remained a staunch supporter of Patassé, helping to put down several attempted coups in the late 1990s.

Eventually, however, as Bozizé has noted in several speeches, he became dissatisfied with Patassé's rule. When dissident government troops attempted to overthrow Patassé in May 2001, suspicions were raised that Bozizé had been behind the action. A commission investigating the coup ordered Bozizé to answer questions, but he refused and fled to neighboring Chad with about 300 supporters.

When Bozizé returned almost two years later, he brought with him about 1,000 supporters and took over the capital, Bangui, on March 15, 2003. They met little resistance; in fact, many Bangui residents danced in the streets. With the economy in bad shape and many military personnel and government workers owed several months' worth of back pay, many said they believed that Bozizé could revive the country and put an end to government mismanagement. Although the African Union (AU) condemned the coup, on March 20 a coalition of opposition parties announced that they supported Bozizé, and the Central African Economic and Monetary Community urged the AU to do the same. On March 28, more than 100,000 citizens of the Central African Republic turned out for a massive unplanned rally to show their support, carrying signs that read "We've been freed" and "Long live liberator François Bozizé."

Bozizé is widely respected among Central Africans for being a simple man of the people. Before he fled the country in 2001, he was often seen driving around Bangui in his old, beat-up Citroen, waving to people he knew. He has also enjoyed strong support in the capital. Following the 2003 coup, Bozizé announced on national radio that he had seized power "because of the mismanagement of the country and its inability to carry out its domestic responsibilities." Speaking in the national Sangho language, he said, "This country was down in the dirt. It was pillaged. The democratic game was not being played. We have suffered greatly. . . . Now is the time for real change."

Bozizé then suspended the constitution and dissolved congress—moves that have made many international observers wary. However, he assured the country that his takeover was just "a temporary suspension of the democratic process." Bozizé named a prime minister, Abel Goumba—founder of the Patriotic Front for Progress—and a cabinet within two weeks of the coup. He promised to hold democratic elections by January 2005.

The nation's new military leader acknowledged that he faced a steep challenge in reviving the economy. Bozizé pledged to restart negotiations with the World Bank and the International Monetary Fund, both of which had previously refused loans to the Central African Republic, criticizing its monetary practices. He also promised to restructure the Central African Army and government, starting by handing out back pay to civil service workers who had gone unpaid for months at a time during a series of strikes.

Following a December 2004 nationwide referendum in which Central Africans overwhelmingly approved a new constitution, Bozizé publicly endorsed the charter, which increased the amount of power exercised by the prime minister and congress and contains a provision limiting the length of the presidential term in office to five years, with a one-time option for renewal. Citizens again turned out in large numbers for the February 2005 general poll, formally voting Bozizé into office. He was reelected in January 2011, after elections were delayed for nearly a year over problems with preparations. Patassé returned to the country in 2009 with Bozizé's permission and, though ailing with diabetes, ran against his former ally and longtime rival. Bozizé won with 66 percent of the vote, and Patassé came in second with 20 percent amid balloting widely criticized as beset by irregularities and fraud. Patassé died on April 5, 2011, in Cameroon, where he had traveled for treatment.

Bozizé faced occasional armed rebellions throughout his presidency. In December 2012, an alliance of rebel groups called Seleka took over much of the sparsely populated north of the country and advanced on Bangui. Peace negotiations were quickly arranged in Libreville, Gabon, and a power-sharing agreement with the rebels was reached. Bozizé agreed not to seek reelection in elections specified for 2016. However, in March rebel leaders accused Bozizé of not meeting terms of the agreement, and Seleka fighters were able to take over Bangui against the weak CAR army (even bolstered by 400 South African troops) on the weekend of March 23–24; Bozizé fled to Cameroon, and rebel leader Michel Djotodia declared himself president. Although the subject of an international arrest warrant related to crimes committed during his regime, Bozizé returned to CAR in 2019 intending to run for president, but a local court disqualified him based on lack of moral character.

Terri Nichols

See also: Central African Republic (CAR), Conflict in; Congo Wars; Coups and Military Regimes in Africa; French Military Involvement in Postcolonial Africa.

Further Reading
Bradshaw, Richard, and Juan Fandos-Ruis. *Historical Dictionary of the Central African Republic.* Lanham, MD: Rowman & Littlefield, 2016.
Carayannis, T., and L. Lombard, eds. *Making Sense of the Central African Republic.* London: Zed Books, 2015.
Lombard, Louisa. *State of Rebellion: Violence and Intervention in the Central African Republic.* London: Zed Books, 2016.

British Military Involvement in Postcolonial Africa

Compared to the robust military interventions conducted by France in postcolonial Francophone Africa, Britain's post-1960 military activities on the continent including in its former colonies appears much more reserved. Nevertheless, in 1964 Britain carried out a military intervention in the recently independent former British territories of East Africa. Faced with a mutiny by African troops over poor service conditions and the continued presence of British officers, the governments of Uganda, Kenya, and Tanganyika reluctantly called on military assistance from the former colonial ruler. While a British brigade based in Kenya easily put down the mutiny in that territory and Uganda, the Royal Navy transported British marines to the epicenter of the disturbance in Tanganyika, where they suppressed mutinous garrisons. As a result of the mutiny, Kenya cultivated closer relations with Britain, maintaining a British-style professional military, but Tanganyika (soon-to-be Tanzania) cut its defense relations with Britain and developed an overtly politicized military with the help of China. During the rest of the Cold War years, British military activities in Africa remained low key though still significant in some areas. In the Gambia, in 1981, a two-man British Special Air Service team cooperated with the Senegalese military to suppress a coup.

A few former British colonies cultivated particularly strong military relations with their old colonial master. In some former British colonies in Africa, such as

Nigeria, Kenya, and Malawi, British officers remained in command positions for a few years after independence until African officers gained enough training and experience to replace them. In some instances, British officers commanded elements of African national defense forces until the 1970s. Despite Britain's brutal counterinsurgency campaign in Kenya during the 1950s "Mau Mau" Emergency, postcolonial Kenya became an important British ally on the continent and a Western ally in the broader Cold War context. While the British brigade in Kenya that had provided a strategic reserve for operations in the Middle East withdrew from the country in 1964, Britain and Kenya signed a defense agreement, with the British gaining access to Kenyan training areas, airfields, and the port of Mombasa. In turn, Britain provided the Kenyan military with training and logistical services, and the constant rotation of British battalions through Kenya for training served to discourage military coups in the country. While the British government gave many millions of pounds to Kenya to develop its military capabilities, arms purchased with this money had to come from Britain, and Britain discouraged other countries including its allies from granting military assistance to Kenya. From 1963 to 1967, Britain provided Kenya with additional funding and military training to mount a counterinsurgency campaign against Somali rebels in the north called the "Shifta War." In 1977, Britain played in a key role in the establishment of the Botswana Defence Force (BDF) that countered Rhodesian and South African aggression. Britain sold arms to Botswana, and British troops regularly trained in Botswana.

In some postconflict situations in Africa, a British Military Advisory and Training Team (BMATT) provided guidance in the establishment of new state militaries, combining elements of formerly hostile forces such as in Zimbabwe in the 1980s and Namibia and South Africa in the 1990s. In 2000, Britain carried out its first serious military intervention in Africa in almost 40 years. While Operation Palliser initially involved the deployment of a British force to Sierra Leone to evacuate foreigners and deliver humanitarian aid, the expedition intervened forcefully to defeat local rebels and ultimately brought an end to the country's civil war. This intervention continued during Operation Barras, which bolstered the UN presence, and Britain became intimately involved in training a new Sierra Leone Army. These successful British operations in Sierra Leone encouraged the Tony Blair administration to launch a new but short-lived policy of robust military action that would arguably lead to the 2003 invasion of Iraq.

Timothy J. Stapleton

See also: African Armed Forces; East African Mutiny; Kenya, Mau Mau Emergency; Sierra Leone Civil War.

Further Reading

Davis, Dickie. "The British Experience in Africa and Oman." *Prism: The Journal of Complex Operations* (November 20, 2017). https://cco.ndu.edu/News/Article/1375921/12-the-british-experience-in-africa-and-oman/

Dorman, Andrew. *Blair's Successful War: British Military Intervention in Sierra Leone.* Farnham: Ashgate, 2009.

Rouvez, Alain. *Disconsolate Empires: French, British and Belgian Military Involvement in Post-Colonial Sub-Saharan Africa.* Lanham, MD: University Press of America, 1994.

Whitaker, Blake. "The 'New Model' Armies of Africa? The British Military Advisory and Training Team and the Creation of the Zimbabwe National Army." PhD thesis, Texas A&M University, 2014.

Burundi, Civil War and Genocide (1962–2008)

Upon its 1962 independence from Belgium, Burundi's constitutional monarchy attempted to balance the representation of the hitherto dominant Tutsi minority associated with the monarchy and the historically marginalized Hutu majority in government. The assassination of prime minister elect Crown Prince Louis Rwagasore on the eve of independence tainted the transition to power and set the stage for future political violence. In 1965, the assassination of the first Hutu prime minister and the king's hesitance to appoint another Hutu prime minister despite the success of Hutu candidates in an election incited Hutu army officers to attempt a coup, but this was crushed by Tutsi soldiers. In 1966, Tutsi officer Captain Michel Micombero organized a coup that toppled the monarchy, founded a republic, and developed a military controlled by Tutsi from southern Burundi. Micombero governed through a National Revolutionary Council comprising 17 military officers including 12 Tutsi. In April 1972, Burundian Hutu rebels crossed from Tanzania into southern Burundi, seizing armories and murdering several thousand Tutsi and some Hutu who refused to join them. Some of the insurgents then declared a "People's Republic," quickly crushed by a Burundian state military offensive. In turn, Zairean dictator Mobutu Sese Seko dispatched 200 of his paratroopers to secure Bujumbura airport and protect Micombero, who proclaimed martial law. Micombero's army killed over 500 of its 600 remaining Hutu military personnel. At the end of May, Burundian Tutsi soldiers and Tutsi youth militia, acting according to an obvious plan and incited by radio hate propaganda, murdered 100,000 to 200,0000 Hutu throughout the country. The genocide targeted educated Hutu and Hutu students, aiming to eradicate any possible Hutu political leadership in the country. When this mass violence stopped in late August, several hundred thousand mostly Hutu had fled to neighboring Zaire, Rwanda, and Tanzania, and almost no educated Hutu remained in Burundi.

A succession of Tutsi military regimes ruled Burundi during the 1970s and 1980s. Burundi's Tutsi leaders feared the rise of a Hutu-majoritarian republic similar to Rwanda where the Tutsis faced oppression and massacres. By 1985, the minority Tutsi comprised some 96 percent of the Burundian Armed Forces (FAB) and two-thirds of University of Bujumbura students. In 1976 Micombero, given his loss of international credibility over the 1972 genocide against the Hutu, was toppled by Colonel Jean-Baptiste Bagaza. In turn, Bagaza's restrictions on the pro-Hutu Catholic Church caused international diplomatic embarrassment, leading to the takeover of Major Pierre Buyoya in 1987. In 1980, in Tanzania, Burundian Hutu exiles led by Remy Gahutu founded the Party for the Liberation of the Hutu People (PALIPEHUTU) that aimed to overturn minority Tutsi domination in their home country. In August 1988, the murder of a Hutu family in Burundi's Kirundo province incited Hutu civilians to kill 300 Tutsi. The predominantly Tutsi army responded with an operation that massacred 20,000 Hutu and chased tens of thousands to neighboring countries. With the mass violence jeopardizing the granting of aid money from Western governments, Buyoyo appointed a state commission that ultimately resulted in the establishment of a national unity government in 1991 with 12 Hutu and 12 Tutsi ministers. The key posts of defense, foreign affairs, and the interior remained with the Tutsi who represented far less than half the population. Although the government removed discrimination against the Hutus in the education system, the Tutsi army rejected similar reforms and brutally suppressed two minor Hutu rebellions in 1991.

In the context of the democratization taking place in many parts of Africa in the 1990s, Burundi's June 1993 election resulted in a victory for the largely Hutu and restrained Front for Democracy in Burundi (FRODEBU). Nevertheless, the assassination of Burundi's new Hutu president, FRODEBU's Melchior Ndadaye, by Tutsi soldiers in October led to violence between the Hutu and Tutsi in which 50,000–100,000 people died and the crossing of many Burundian Hutu refugees into Rwanda as it was emerging from a civil war. In April 1994, Burundi's next Hutu president Cyprien Ntaryamira died in the same plane crash as Rwandan president Juvénal Habyarimana, and thousands of Rwandan Tutsi escaped the subsequent genocide in their country by fleeing into Burundi. In what has been described as a "creeping coup," Burundi's security forces and Tutsi extremists used intimidation and violence to render elected FRODEBU officials powerless. A Hutu militia called Intagoheka (those who do not sleep) began attacks on the Tutsi army in April 1994, and some FRODEBU leaders created the National Council for the Defense of Democracy (CNDD) with an armed wing called Forces for the Defense of Democracy (FDD) in June. The goal of CNDD/FDD was to achieve internationally supervised negotiations and restructure the Tutsi-dominated Burundian military. In early 1995, the FDD launched attacks on Burundi's army, particularly in the provinces of Cibitoke and Bubanza, where they set up alternative local governments and collected taxes. From March to June 1995, the army "ethnically cleansed" the capital of Bujumbura, expelling large numbers of Hutu into nearby hills and across the border into Zaire. Between July and September 1995, the older rebel group PALIPEHUTU joined the conflict, massacring Tutsi civilians in Cibitoke province and in turn inciting military retaliation against Hutu. Most of the 15,000–25,000 civilians killed during 1995 comprised Hutu murdered by the army or Tutsi militia, but the number of Tutsi civilians and soldiers killed by the rebels gradually increased. In early 1996, the small National Liberation Front (FROLINA) that had split from PALIPEHUTU attacked military outposts and Tutsi civilians in the south. In February 1996, to deprive the rebels of civilian assistance, the Burundian Army began resettling rural Hutu communities in concentration camps, which contained about 300,000 residents within six months. By mid-1996, 11 out of Burundi's 15 provinces experienced civil war, military pressure on the army increased, and FRODEBU president Sylvestre Ntibantunganya lacked any influence.

Buyoya again seized power in the July 1996 coup. While Tutsi soldiers and militia wanted the aggressive Bagaza to take charge, army officers favored the comparatively moderate Buyoya who appeared more tolerable to the international community. Simultaneously, military intervention by Rwanda's new predominantly Tutsi regime in eastern Zaire eliminated CNDD-FDD bases, leading to increased violence in Burundi's south as retreating rebels moved to Tanzania. In turn, during 1997 and early 1998, Burundi's Western provinces became the most affected by the war, as they bordered on Tanzania, now used by the rebels as a sanctuary. During 1997 the Burundian Army and rebels killed some 5,000 to 10,000 civilians and Burundi's minister of defense Colonel Firmin Sinziyoheba declared that all Hutu males of military age represented the enemy. On New Year's Eve 1997, CNDD-FDD rebels attacked Bujumbura airport and a nearby military camp.

Buyoya pursued military and diplomatic strategies to end the war. While he introduced one-year compulsory military service for secondary school and junior university students, Tutsi youth represented all those enlisted. Burundi's army increased from 13,000 troops in 1993 to 30,000 in 1996 and 45,500 in 2002. Government spending on the war amounted to half the annual budget, and the state imposed a war tax on civil servants and farmers. Facilitated by South Africa's Nelson Mandela, an August 2000 peace agreement stipulated that Buyoya would rule for 18 months followed by FRODEBU's Domitien Ndayizeye for another 18 months, but the armed wings of CNDD and PALIPEHUTU rejected the deal. The agreement also committed the parties to establish a new integrated National Defence Force (FDN) in which no group—Hutu, Tutsi, or the very small Twa minority—would have greater than 50 percent representation, with 40 percent of the officer corps coming from the CNDD-FDD. In October, 700 South African troops arrived in Burundi to protect exiled political leaders returning to participate in the peace process.

Despite the negotiations, violence continued such as in late December 2000 when the National Liberation Forces (FNL), the armed wing of PALIPEHUTU, rebels stopped a bus outside Bujumbura, divided Hutu and Tutsi passengers, and murdered 20 of the latter as well as a British aid worker. From October–December 2000, an army offensive against the FNL in Tenga Forest near Bujumbura resulted in 200 rebels and 20 soldiers killed. In February 2001 the rebels renewed attacks on the capital, prompting another army offensive involving artillery and ground attack jets in December, which according to the government, killed 500 insurgents. Burundi's peace process dragged out as officials in the neighboring Democratic Republic of the Congo (DRC, formerly, Zaire) permitted the CNDD-FDD to reestablish staging areas in the east of that country, rebel factions fought each other, and rebel leaders split between moderates and radicals. The main differences between the insurgent movements were that the CNDD-FDD possessed external bases and foreign support and advocated democratic reform while PALIPEHUTU-FNL was mostly based within Burundi and pursued a pro-Hutu/anti-Tutsi agenda. In December 2002 Pierre Nkurunziza, former university lecturer and FDD leader, agreed a cease-fire that would result in his CNDD transforming into a political party and merging its fighters with the army. Regional peace talks aimed at ending civil war and external intervention in the DRC influenced this process. With the UN unwilling to commit peacekeepers to Burundi given the continuation of violence, the African Union (AU, formerly, the

Organisation of African Unity or OAU) mounted its first peacekeeping mission in April 2003 called African Union Mission in Burundi (AMIB) with 3,300 troops mostly from South Africa, Ethiopia, and Mozambique. AMIB protected the transitional government, secured centers for the demobilization of combatants, and facilitated the return of displaced people to their homes. As planned, Ndayizeye came to power in May 2003, resulting in the signing of a formal peace agreement in Pretoria in October. However, the civil war continued, as the extremist pro-Hutu FNL of Agathon Rwasa still refused to participate in the peace process. With the new peace agreement, AMIB amalgamated into the United Nations Peace Operation in Burundi (ONUB) in June 2004, with this international force growing to 4,500 troops and 1,000 civilians by 2005 and demobilizing some 20,000 fighters. In 2005 CNDD won Burundi's first elections since 1994 resulting in Nkurunziza becoming Burundi's president. FNL agreed to the cease-fire the next year. Despite a brief battle between the army and FNL in Bujumbura in April 2008, the rebels eventually embarked on disarmament, demobilization, and reintegration and abandoned the name PALIPEHUTU, given the banning of ethnic labels in names of political parties. The process of integrating former FAB, FDD, and other armed groups into the new Burundi Defence Force began in 2005 with Belgium and the Netherlands providing some training. Later, the participation of Burundian soldiers in an African Union force fighting Islamist militants in Somalia resulted in some American assistance.

In 2010, Nkurunziza won a second presidential term as opposition leaders including former rebel Rwasa withdrew from the election over concerns of vote rigging. In 2015 violent protests broke out when Nkurunziza declared that he would exploit a loophole in the wording of the new constitution to run for a third term in office despite this being widely seen as illegal. Following a failed coup attempt by elements of the military, the president gained reelection amid international objections. Fearing the return of mass violence, tens of thousands of mainly Tutsi Burundians fled to Tanzania and Rwanda, and the Nkurunziza government accused neighboring Rwanda of sponsoring exiled Burundian rebels. Murders of state officials, military officers, and opposition leaders inspired international concern over possible massacres of the Tutsi minority, but the violence did not seem to correspond with that pattern. Nkuruniza died suddenly during the 2020 COVID-19 pandemic just before handing over the presidency to his recently elected successor and CNDD leader Evariste Ndayishimiye.

Timothy J. Stapleton

See also: Buyoya, Pierre; Congo Wars; Coups and Military Regimes in Africa; Genocide in Africa; Hutu Power Movements; Micombero, Michel; Nkurunziza, Pierre; Peacekeeping in Africa; Refugees in Postcolonial Africa; Rwanda, Civil War and Genocide.

Further Reading

Chretien, Jean-Pierre, and Jean-François Dupaquier. *Burundi 1972; Au Bord du Genocides*. Paris: Karthala, 2007.

Lemarchand, Rene. *Burundi: Ethnic Conflict and Genocide*. Cambridge: Cambridge University Press, 1994.

Lemarchand, Rene. *The Dynamics of Violence in Central Africa*. Philadelphia: University of Pennsylvania Press, 2009.

Marineau, Josiah. "Securing Peace in Burundi: External Interventions to End the Civil War, 1993–2006." In *Securing Africa: Local Crises and Foreign Interventions*, edited by Toyin Falola and Charles Thomas, 229–248. New York: Routledge, 2014.

Mwakikagile, Godfrey. *Burundi; The Hutu and the Tutsi: Cauldron of Conflict and Quest for Dynamic Compromise.* Dar es Salaam: New Africa Press, 2012.

Sommers, Marc. *Fear in Bongoland: Burundian Refugees in Urban Tanzania.* New York: Berghahn Books, 2001.

Watt, Nigel. *Burundi: The Biography of a Small African Country.* London: Hurst, 2008.

Buyoya, Pierre (1949–2020)

Major Pierre Buyoya first served as president of Burundi's Tutsi-dominated military regime from October 1987 to June 1993. During that tenure, he oversaw changes directed at increasing the political involvement of the majority Hutu people despite his being a member of the dominant but minority Tutsi ethnic group. In late July 1996, Buyoya became president once again following a coup by the Tutsi-dominated army in which the Hutu-led government of Sylvestre Ntibantunganya was overthrown. However, he stepped down in April 2003 as part of a cease-fire agreement between the government and some Hutu rebel groups.

Born in the Bururi province of Burundi in 1949, Buyoya joined the Burundian military and attended officer training at the Royal Military Academy in Brussels, Belgium. During the late 1970s and 1980s, he served as a senior member of Burundi's military regime led by other Tutsi officers from Bururi and under the banner of the Union for National Progress (UPRONA). In September 1987, he led a military coup against President Jean-Baptiste Bagaza while Bagaza was out of the country. He accused Bagaza of corruption and created the Military Committee for National Salvation, heading a regime that continued to be dominated by the Tutsi minority. Beginning in 1987, he served as president, defense minister, and chairperson of the Military Committee for National Salvation.

In 1989 in the face of challenges to his power from his own Tutsi group, as well as pressure from the majority Hutu people, Buyoya vowed to introduce laws that would pave the way for equal opportunity in the fields of education, military, and employment. In the early 1990s, in the context of democratization across Africa, he initiated a series of constitutional reforms including a "controlled" multiparty politics supported by at least 90 percent of the electorate. In April 1992, a month after formal promulgation of the new Burundi Constitution, Buyoya gave up the post of defense minister and appointed Hutus to 15 of the cabinet's 25 posts.

In a presidential election on June 1, 1993, Buyoya ran against Melchior Ndadaye, a Hutu, and was defeated, gaining only 32.4 percent of the vote compared with 64.8 percent for Ndadaye. Buyoya relinquished the presidency peacefully, but Ndadaye was assassinated by Tutsi soldiers in October 1993. Ndadaye was succeeded by Cyprien Ntaryamira who died in the infamous plane crash that launched the genocide in Rwanda in April 1994 and was succeeded by Sylvestre Ntibantunganya. Over the next two years, ethnic tensions intensified, with Hutu extremists and Tutsi soldiers alike carrying out massacres of civilians. The army seized power on July 25, 1996, naming Buyoya as head of state.

In the following years, Buyoya presided over repeated unsuccessful attempts to end the country's long-running civil war. Nelson Mandela agreed to mediate in the conflict in December 1999, but it was several years before negotiations bore fruit. In April 2001, Buyoya thwarted an attempted coup by junior army officers dissatisfied with his stalled efforts to negotiate peace. In July, he and most of Burundi's political parties signed a power-sharing agreement, establishing a transitional government in which he would remain head of state for 18 months, after which a Hutu would assume the office. Buyoya also agreed to 11 conditions stipulated by the mediation team, including the return of refugees, release of political prisoners, and integration of rebel groups into the army. However, the country's two main rebel groups continued to reject the agreement, and fighting intensified just days after the transitional government was sworn in in November 2001.

Buyoya complied with the power-sharing agreement by stepping down and turning the presidency over to Hutu leader Domitien Ndayizeye on April 30, 2003. Although Buyoya subsequently worked in senior diplomatic positions for the African Union (AU) in Chad and Mali, a Burundian court convicted him in absentia for the 1993 murder of Ndadaye and sentenced him to life imprisonment. In December 2020, Buyoya contracted COVID-19 in Mali and died shortly after arriving in France for treatment.

ABC-CLIO

See also: Burundi, Civil War and Genocide; Congo Wars; Coups and Military Regimes in Africa; Hutu Power Movements.

Further Reading

Marineau, Josiah. "Securing Peace in Burundi: External Interventions to End the Civil War, 1993–2006." In *Securing Africa: Local Crises and Foreign Interventions*, edited by Toyin Falola and Charles Thomas, 229–248. New York: Routledge, 2014.

Mwakikagile, Godfrey. *Burundi; The Hutu and the Tutsi: Cauldron of Conflict and Quest for Dynamic Compromise*. Dar es Salaam: New Africa Press, 2012.

Watt, Nigel. *Burundi: The Biography of a Small African Country*. London: Hurst, 2008.

Cabindan Insurgency

Cabinda is a tiny exclave of 2,800 square miles, home to several hundred thousand people. It is separated from the rest of Angola by a 37-mile-wide strip of the Democratic Republic of the Congo. About 60 percent of the Angolan government's oil revenues come from offshore fields in Cabinda. Since the 1960s, an armed independence movement has fought against the central government, first the Portuguese colonial regime and then the Popular Movement for the Liberation of Angola (MPLA). Independence appears to have widespread support in Cabinda.

The Front for the Liberation of the Cabinda Enclave (FLEC) is the main movement, with several smaller groups splintering off over the years. FLEC's persistent factionalism has hurt its ability to confront the much larger and much better-equipped Angolan Armed Forces (FAA). The combined forces of the rebels in the 1990s were estimated to number approximately 2,000 troops.

In January 1993 the FAA moved 15,000 troops into Cabinda, reigniting the fighting after an eight-year cease-fire. Widespread displacement and indiscriminate abuse by the soldiers made life very difficult for civilians, although conditions were not as severe as in the rest of Angola. The renewed conflict internally displaced some 25,000 people and forced 3,100 refugees into the Congo Republic and the Democratic Republic of the Congo. In an effort to win hearts and minds, the government of Angola agreed in 1996 to give Cabinda 10 percent of the taxes paid by the oil companies that operate in the exclave. Cabinda's underdevelopment and high cost of living—supplies are transported to Cabinda from the capital of Luanda—are a persistent complaint of the population.

Following the defeat of the National Union for the Total Independence of Angola (UNITA) in the Angolan Civil War, the government of Angola sent 30,000 troops to Cabinda, determined to defeat the rebel factions once and for all. In October 2002 the FAA destroyed FLEC's main base of operation since 1979. By mid-2003, FLEC had been reduced to small bands of fighters without permanent bases. According to a 2004 Human Rights Watch report, the FAA committed serious and widespread human rights abuses against Cabinda's civilian population, acting "with almost complete impunity."

With FLEC's military capacity all but gone, its army chief and a half dozen other high-ranking officials surrendered to the government in June 2003. The government then extended a reintegration program to FLEC soldiers who laid down their arms in return for food, agricultural tools, and other benefits. By April 2004 roughly 2,000 FLEC ex-combatants and their families had registered. Although the military situation seems to be firmly in hand, the government of Angola still faces a population that has steadfastly fought for independence. Although some separatist leaders agreed to a cease-fire with the government in 2006, violence continued, including a 2010 insurgent attack on the visiting Togo national football team.

Beth K. Dougherty

See also: Angolan Armed Forces (FAPLA and FAA); Angolan Conflicts; National Union for the Total Independence of Angola (UNITA); Popular Movement for the Liberation of Angola (MPLA); Portuguese Africa, Independence Wars (Angola, Mozambique, and Guinea-Bissau).

Further Reading

Hodges, Tony. *Angola: From Afro-Stalinism to Petro-Diamond Capitalism*. Bloomington: Indiana University Press, 2001.

Human Rights Watch. *Angola: Between War and Peace in Cabinda*. New York: Human Rights Watch.

Cabral, Amílcar (1924–1973)

Agronomist and leader of the insurgency in Guinea against Portuguese rule, Amílcar Cabral was born to Cape Verde parents in Bafatá, Portuguese Guinea, on September 12, 1924. Following studies in Guinea and Cape Verde, Cabral attended the Instituto Superior de Agronomia in Lisbon, where he also founded student movements dedicated to the independence of Portugal's African colonies.

Returning to Guinea, in 1956 Cabral formed the Partido Africano da Independência da Guiné e Cabo Verde (PAIGC, African Party for the Independence of Guinea and Cape Verde). Following the failure of political efforts to secure independence, he established training camps in the neighboring Republic of Guinea (Guinea-Conakry) and in Senegal, both of which had just received their independence from France, and in January 1963 he initiated a military campaign against Portuguese rule.

Widely regarded as a brilliant revolutionary theorist and tactician, Cabral was certainly the most effective of the insurgent leaders fighting the Portuguese in Africa. Taking advantage of the fact that much of Portuguese Guinea was low-lying or underwater, Cabral adopted some of the revolutionary theories of Mao Zedong (Mao Tse-tung) in China to establish so-called liberated zones. Cabral sought to win the hearts and minds of the people by employing his training as an agronomist to increase crop yields and insisting that his men assist farmers in their fields when not actually fighting the Portuguese. He also set up a trade-and-barter bazaar system to get goods to the local population at lower cost than those available through colonial merchants, and he arranged for local hospitals and triage stations to aid his own forces but also to bring about improved local medical care.

With some 6,000–7,000 men under arms by 1971 and aided by arms from the Soviet Union, Cabral claimed to control some 80 percent of the territory of Portuguese Guinea. He established a government-in-exile in Conakry, Republic of Guinea, and in 1972 began to plan for a popular assembly and a proclamation of independence. Before he could realize these, he was assassinated in Conakry on January 30, 1973, by a rival, Inocêncio Kani, with the possible assistance of Portuguese authorities.

Guinea-Bissau was granted independence on September 10, 1974. Amílcar Cabral's half brother, Luis Cabral, became the new state's first president.

Spencer C. Tucker

See also: Cold War in Africa; Portuguese Africa, Independence Wars (Angola, Mozambique, and Guinea-Bissau); Soviet Military Involvement in Africa.

Further Reading

Cabral, Amílcar. *Revolution in Guinea: Selected Texts*. New York: Monthly Review Press, 1970.

Chabal, Patrick. *Amilcar Cabral: Revolutionary Leadership and People's War*. New York: Cambridge University Press, 1983.

Cameroon Conflicts (1955–)

Cameroon has had, and continues to be plagued by, different forms of conflict since 1955—a date that marked the beginning of violence attendant with decolonization in the former French colony. In chronological order, the three major conflicts that have afflicted the polity since 1955 include the Union of the Peoples of Cameroon (UPC) uprising, the Anglophone-Cameroon conflict, and the Boko Haram conflict. While there have been minor disturbances over land and boundaries in different parts of Cameroon, these three conflicts involved higher levels of violent engagement.

UPC UPRISING

The UPC was established in 1948 as an opposition political party by a group of nationalists led by the charismatic trade unionizer, Reuben Um Nyobè. It was created to contend power in Cameroon by challenging French colonial authorities; unable to control French meddling/influence in Cameroon politics after 1955, it resorted to terrorism that targeted French colonial machinery and French-backed Cameroonian authorities in parts of Cameroon until 1971. It recruited fighters and received support mainly from the Bamileke and Bassa ethnic groups in present-day West and Littoral regions, respectively, and launched attacks from the forests of those regions.

In the early 1950s, French colonial authorities set out to repress the UPC. Its activities were outlawed in 1954 by Governor Pré; Um Nyobè and his followers were harassed by the police, and in 1955 the UPC was banned (Davidson, 129). During the 1950s, UPC's terrorism targeted only French establishments in Cameroon. Its strategy changed in 1960; its new target was the independent government of President Ahidjo, put in place by French authorities. The UPC rebellion was finally contained in 1971 by a joint Cameroonian/French military force. The rebellion was progressively destabilized through targeted killings of its supporters/fighters; the arrest, trial, and execution of some; while others fled into exile. Emergency orders targeting supporters and fighters of the UPC continued to be effective until 1973.

The UPC's struggle to liberate Cameroon from French colonial and later on neocolonial control failed because of tribal disunity, the resolve of French colonial authorities, and later on, repression from Cameroon authorities. When Um Nyobè and his successor, Félix Moumié, were killed in 1958 and 1960, respectively, the UPC lost the type of personal leadership that had propelled it forward.

THE ANGLOPHONE-CAMEROON CONFLICT

In October 2016, lawyers, teachers, and students from the two Anglophone regions of Cameroon—northwest and southwest—that make up one-fifth of the population of Cameroon, launched peaceful protests in their regional capitals of Bamenda and Buea, respectively, calling on the government to stop marginalizing Anglophones and respect their political and cultural rights, which have been neglected since independence and reunification in 1960/61. Such marginalization, they argue, is seen in the law courts and schools in Anglophone regions that were increasingly being staffed by Francophones who neither spoke English nor comprehended Anglophone culture.

The government's response to the protest was rapid, massive, and brutal: some protesters were killed by the military; Anglophone university students were brutalized, arrested, and detained. When such abuses were exposed on social media, the government "shut down" the internet and banned civil society groups in Anglophone regions. The government's attempts to crack down on new separatist groups have resulted in more arrests/detentions of sympathizers and perceived secessionists, burning of Anglophone villages, countless extrajudicial killings, and other abuses. On their part, Anglophone separatists have also tortured/killed/ kidnapped government soldiers/loyalists and have destabilized schools in Anglophone regions. Hundreds of Anglophones, many of them innocent, are being detained by the government at specialized detention centers. The indiscriminate burning of villages by government soldiers has displaced millions of Anglophones from their homes. The government's response only heightened the resolve of Anglophones, and the armed conflict between government forces and newly formed separatist groups—who have advocated for secession of the Anglophone regions under a Federal Republic of Ambazonia—continues to escalate.

Despite the national dialogue promised by President Paul Biya in September 2019, it is obvious that the crisis cannot be unilaterally resolved. The African Union and the United Nations (UN) Security Council have done little to address the unfolding security and humanitarian crisis. Recently (May/June 2019), some members of the UN met informally to discuss the humanitarian crisis but faced opposition from African members who feared that such action may open the door to Western military intervention in Africa. Rights groups have noted that a civil war is brewing and the humanitarian crisis would worsen if not checked immediately.

CAMEROON AND THE BOKO HARAM CONFLICT

Boko Haram (BH) is a terrorist group that was founded in Maiduguri—Northern Nigeria—in the 1990s by Mohammed Yusuf, an Islamic extremist. Initially the group was nonviolent and preoccupied with issues of poverty, identity and religion, but because it was also anti-government and anti-Western education, it was targeted by the government of Nigeria. The killing of Yusuf with 800 of his supporters by the Nigerian Army in 2009 helped popularize the group, which then became violent. When Abubakar Shekau became its leader following the death of Yusuf, BH started targeting groups indiscriminately, sometimes employing women for suicide-bombing missions, thereby killing thousands of people and displacing many in northeastern Nigeria; Nigerian military forces fighting BH have also killed thousands—including civilians—making it possible for local people to sympathize with, and join, the movement.

From 2011, BH operations extended into neighboring states such as Cameroon, bringing her into the conflict. BH has ethnic/religious sympathizers/followers in Northern Cameroon and regularly moves in and out of the territory. Thus, the killings, abductions/kidnappings and rampages by BH and the brutal retaliation by Cameroon military forces are recurrent in Northern Cameroon. Unable to control BH activities on its territory, Cameroon has requested and received foreign military assistance from some Western countries, but BH still remains an elusive enemy.

Emmanuel M. Mbah

See also: Boko Haram; French Military Involvement in Postcolonial Africa; Genocide in Africa.

Further Reading

Atangana, Martin. *The End of French Rule in Cameroon.* New York: University Press of America, 2010.

Global Security. "Union of the Peoples of Cameroon (Union des Populations du Cameroun, UPC)." *GlobalSecurity.org.* Accessed July 1, 2019, p. 1. http://www.globalsecurity.org/military/world/para/upc-cameroon.htm

O'Grady, Siobhān. "Africa's Next Civil War Could Be in Cameroon." *Washington Post.* World Views Analysis. Accessed April 5, 2019, p. 1. https://www.washingtonpost.com/news/worldviews/wp/2018/05/30/africas-next-civil-war-could-be-in-cameroon/

Searcey, Dionne. "As Cameroon English Speakers Fight to Break Away, Tension Mounts." *New York Times,* June 28, 2018. https://www.nytimes.com/2018/06/28/world/africa/cameroon-secession.html

Segun, Mausi. "Africa Should Not Fail Cameroon." *Human Rights Watch* (HRW), June 28, 2019. https://www.hrw.org/print/331675

Canadian Military Involvement in Africa

Canada rarely jumps to mind as a significant external military actor in Africa. However, the continent has regularly drawn expeditionary forces from Canada since nearly 400 Nile Voyageurs attempted, but failed, to help General Wolseley navigate British colonial forces up the Nile to save Governor Gordon at Khartoum (1884–1885). Wolseley specifically asked for Canadian rivermen due to his service in Canada leading the Red River expedition against Métis leader Louis Riel in 1870. Nearly a century later, it was this role, as multinational force enabler, that would characterize most Canadian military operations in support of UN missions across Africa, from Suez (1950s), Congo (1960s), and Namibia (1989–1990) through to Mali in 2018–2019.

However, there are examples of Canadians fighting in Africa too. Just over a decade after the fall of Khartoum, 8,000 Canadian volunteers served with British military and police forces during and after the South African War (1899–1902). Sudan and South Africa signaled that Canada would likely play a role in African conflicts despite its lack of direct imperial or national interests. While Canada deployed almost no military power to the continent during either world war, from 1954 to 1970 Africa became a surprisingly active theater of operations for the Canadian Armed Forces (CAF), but in substantially new roles. These included brief training for the Royal Canadian Air Force squadrons based in Germany (in French-ruled Morocco), humanitarian and disaster assistance (including to Zambia and Morocco), various UN observation and peacekeeping missions (with Canadian lieutenant general E. L. M. Burns the initial commander of UNEF in Egypt), and support for foreign military training outside NATO (Ghana, Nigeria, and Tanzania, most notably).

Africa was an experimental laboratory for these latter two taskings: peacekeeping and military training. From the early 1960s, Canadians for the first time served alongside, under (e.g., Nigerian major general Ironsi in the Congo), or trained African troops. On more than one occasion, Ghanaian contingents rescued Canadian signalers mistaken for Belgians in the Congo. Due to expeditionary capabilities designed to support NATO commitments in Europe and UN operations in Korea after 1950, Canada could contribute to these new tasks in Africa. During the 1970s, Canada's military presence on the continent diminished as the government's focus shifted toward foreign aid, while the CAF faced severe budget cuts (e.g., its last aircraft carrier was decommissioned in 1970).

From 1989 to 1994, however, the thawing of the Cold War unleashed an activist Security Council that approved 20 new operations, including many in Africa. Canada committed heavily to UN operations in ex-Yugoslavia, but also supported, at least on a token basis, every mission in Africa, including Namibia, Angola, Mozambique, and most notoriously, Rwanda. There, Brigadier General Romeo Dallaire took command of UNAMIR in October 1993 but had minimal Canadian personnel in support until well after the genocide had begun in April 1994. In Somalia, in late 1992, Canada shifted its initial commitment from the UN mission (UNOSOM I) to the American-led UNITAF humanitarian mission that had more robust rules of engagement. There, the Canadian Airborne Regiment fulfilled its security and food distribution objectives centered around Beledweyne, but a cover-up of extrajudicial killings and torture led to a public inquiry, and, in 1995 the regiment was disbanded.

The Somalia and Rwandan operations had a major influence on Canadian military and political attitudes toward UN-authorized missions in Africa. Canada subsequently remained mostly on the sidelines. It briefly deployed a mechanized company for six months after the Eritrean-Ethiopian War in 2000 (UNMEE) but soon found itself embroiled in Afghanistan (2001–2014) and then Iraq (2014–2021). Canada closed its Pearson Peacekeeping Centre in 2013. Since the turn of the millennium, Canada rarely had more than a handful of military and police personnel deployed to large, hazardous UN missions across Africa.

Canadian combat aircraft and frigates did, however, participate in NATO operations authorized by UN Security Council Resolution 1973 against Muammar Gaddafi in 2011, with NATO's Operation Unified Protector commanded by Canadian lieutenant general Charles Bouchard. Additionally, Canadian frigates and patrol aircraft intermittently deployed to the Indian Ocean from 2009 as part of CTF 151, the multinational naval task force combating piracy near Somalia.

Canada temporarily returned to UN peacekeeping in Africa with the deployment of a helicopter task force to conduct medevac and logistics support to UN forces in Mali (MINUMSA) during 2018–2019. Canada, despite admonishments from its NATO allies and African partners, remains a token troop contributor compared to many European middle powers and much smaller African militaries in support of peace and security operations across the continent.

Chris W. J. Roberts

See also: African Armed Forces; Congo Crisis; Libyan Civil War, First; Peacekeeping in Africa; Rwanda, Civil War and Genocide; Somalia Civil War.

Further Reading

Dawson, Grant. *"Here Is Hell": Canada's Engagement in Somalia*. Vancouver: UBC Press, 2007.

Kilford, Christopher R. *The Other Cold War: Canada's Military Assistance to the Developing World, 1945–1975*. Kingston, ON: Canadian Defence Academy Press, 2010.

Moloney, Sean. *Canada and UN Peacekeeping: Cold War by Other Means, 1945–1970*. St. Catharines, ON: Vanwell Publishing, 2002.

Roberts, Chris W. J. "Op Presence–Mali: Continuity over Change in Canada's 'Return to Peacekeeping' in Africa." Policy Paper. Canadian Global Affairs Institute, October 2018. https://www.cgai.ca/op_presence_mali_continuity_over_change_in_canadas_return_to_peacekeeping_in_africa

Spooner, Kevin A. *Canada, the Congo Crisis, and UN Peacekeeping, 1960–1964*. Vancouver: UBC Press, 2010.

Casamance Separatism

Casamance is the southwestern region of Senegal, and its location between the Gambia and Guinea-Bissau largely separates it from the rest of the country. Starting in 1982, the Casamance conflict is West Africa's longest-running civil conflict. The conflict opposes the separatist Mouvement des forces démocratiques de la Casamance (MFDC) to the Senegalese State.

Casamance is ethnically diverse, although the Diola are a majority in the Lower Casamance, the westernmost area that has been most affected by the conflict. Further east, Mandinka and Peul (Fulani) are the predominant ethnic groups. In contrast to other societies in Senegal, the Diola are considered a singular group due to their decentralized or acephalous political organization. Furthermore, whereas the population's main religion in Senegal is Islam, in the Lower Casamance, there are significant minorities of Christians and followers of traditional religions. This represents a major divergence from the overwhelming Muslim national religious landscape. In fact, the Diola are the largest community of followers of an African traditional religion in Senegambia. In the north of Senegal, the marabouts (Muslim religious leaders) have great economic and political influence. According to political scientists, the state has been functioning through an islamo-wólof system, which stresses the relationship between Muslim leaderships and the Wolof people, a northern ethnic group whose language is nowadays the lingua franca of Senegal. However, religious aspects of the conflict have been exaggerated: both the composition and the leaderships of the MFDC reflect Casamance's mixed Muslim, Catholic, and Awasena (Diola traditional religion) population. Rather than religion, what is important is the regional identity expressed among the people of Casamance, particularly the Diola, in which they distinguish themselves from nordistes (northern Senegalese) and that also forms part of the separatists' discourse.

During the colonial period, the French struggled to establish their administrative structures in the Lower Casamance. This led to phases where Casamance was governed directly by the governor of French West Africa, a particularity later used by separatists to support their cause. Difficulties did not end with the colonial era. Throughout the first decade of independence, few Casamançais politicians took part in the Senegalese government. From 1970 onward, there were no ministers from the south. The 1970s saw protests in the Lower Casamance against what were perceived as injustices by the Senegalese administration. Casamance, was said, suffered the political and economic inattention of the government. Progressively, the idea that the French colonization was succeeded by the Senegalese one crystallized in the separatist milieu. The fact that Senegalese northerners arrived at Casamance in the nineteenth century accompanying the French helped to create this idea. This contributed to the growing regionalist sentiment. Local intellectuals shaped separatism on the grounds of discontent with government from Dakar, perceived underdevelopment of Casamance, cultural differences from northerners, and the disputed claim that Casamance had full political autonomy during colonial times.

The conflict started on December 26, 1982, when the MFDC organized a protest march in Ziguinchor, claiming for the independence of Casamance. The Senegalese regime reacted with political oppression and military interventions that resulted in several casualties, a number of injured, and the detention of MFDC leaders and people suspected of being favorable to them. However, the conflict only became fully "militarized" in 1990 with the mobilization of MFDC guerrillas, led by the creation of an armed wing known as "Atika" ("warrior" in the Diola language), and the large-scale deployment of Senegalese military forces in response. Throughout the 1990s a combination of military, political, and diplomatic efforts failed to resolve the conflict as the MFDC split into various factions. The differences between factions caused the failing of all cease-fires. In the 1990s, Amnesty International reported the harsh Senegalese repression and the use of antipersonnel mines by the MFDC, which also pillaged local populations.

Tensions abated during the 2000s, and a peace agreement was signed in 2004. However, the death in 2007 of Abbé Augustin Diamacoune Senghor, the most charismatic leader of the MFDC, resulted in the movement splitting into three major armed factions. Violence returned sporadically. On May 1, 2014, Salif Sadio, leader of one of the factions, sued for peace and declared a unilateral cease-fire after secret talks at the Vatican between him and the Government of Senegal.

Today, peace talks are still in progress, but the divisions inside the separatist movement make it difficult to attain a complete peace. While relatively small compared with wars elsewhere in Africa, the humanitarian impacts of the conflict have been remarkable within Casamance and in neighboring countries. An estimated 3,000–5,000 people have died, and many more have been displaced. According to a 1998 census, a total of 62,638 people have been internally displaced or turned into refugees.

Eric Garcia-Moral

See also: French Military Involvement in Postcolonial Africa; Refugees in Postcolonial Africa.

Further Reading

"Contested Casamance/Discordante Casamance." *Canadian Journal of African Studies/ Revue canadienne des études africaines* 39, no. 2 (2005): 213–445.

Evans, Martin. "Senegal: Mouvement des Forces Démocratiques de la Casamance (MFDC)." December 2004. http://www.adh-geneve.ch/RULAC/pdf_state/Martin-Evans.pdf

Foucher, Vincent. "The Mouvement Des Forces Démocratiques de Casamance: The Illusion of Separatism in Senegal?" In *Secessionism in African Politics Aspiration, Grievance, Performance, Disenchantment*, edited by Lotje de Vries, Pierre Englebert, and Mareike Schomerus, 265–292. Cham: Palgrave Macmillan, 2019.

Lambert, Michael C. "Violence and the War of Words: Ethnicity v. Nationalism in the Casamance." *Africa* 68, no. 4 (1998): 585–602.

Marut, Jean-Claude. *Le conflit de Casamance. Ce que disent les armes*. Paris: Karthala, 2010.

Central African Republic (CAR), Conflict in

From the point it gained independence from France in 1960, the Central African Republic (CAR) government comprised leaders from the country's southern riverine region while people in the northern savannah remained marginalized, including a Muslim minority in the northeast. The megalomaniac military dictator Jean-Bédel Bokassa ruled CAR from 1965 to 1979. The French military overthrew Bokassa, who had himself crowned emperor in 1977 and warmed to Libya's anti-Western strongman Muammar Gaddafi; Paris then reinstated CAR's original president, David Dacko. Following a disputed 1981 election, General Andre Kolingba established a military regime supported by France, which used CAR as a launching pad for military operations and interventions across Francophone Africa during the 1980s and 1990s. Relying on ethnic loyalties, Kolingba manipulated the composition of the CAR military so that soldiers from his own southern Yakoma ethnic group comprised 70 percent of the force while they represented just 5 percent of the population. This strongly politicized the CAR military. In the context of post–Cold War political reforms and democratization supported by France, Ange-Félix Patassé won the 1993 election, becoming CAR's first head of state from the north. Subsequently, and repeating the pattern of his predecessor, Patassé replaced Yakoma military personnel with people from his own Sara-Kaba ethnicity. In the late 1990s members of the politicized military staged a series of violent mutinies that were put down by French troops. This inspired a fearful Patassé to expand his presidential guard so he did not have to rely on the army, and he supplemented this by recruiting militias from his northern region. In 1998 French forces based in CAR joined the United Nations Mission in the Central African Republic (MINURCA), providing security for next year's elections, which Patassé won. Its mission complete, MINURCA peacekeepers departed CAR in 2000, and during the following year, CAR experienced general strikes and attempted military coups.

Fought in the neighboring Democratic Republic of the Congo (DRC), the Second Congo War or "Africa's World War" of 1998–2002 significantly influenced the brewing conflict in CAR. Supported by allies Chad and the Kabila regime in DRC, exiled general François Bozizé orchestrated a violent insurgency in CAR in 2002. Although born in Gabon during colonial times, Bozizé served as a prominent officer in the CAR military during the Bokassa and Kolingba periods. Responding to the rebellion, Patassé's state embarked on a brutal counterinsurgency campaign, assisted by Gaddafi's Libya and that involved fighters from Jean-Pierre Bemba's Movement for the Liberation of Congo (MLC) from the DRC. Seizing the CAR capital, Bangui, in March 2003, Bozizé declared himself president backed by a force of mostly Chadian fighters. Patassé fled the country after the French refused his plea for help. After the 2005 elections confirmed Bozizé's position, rebellions erupted in the north, including among supporters of the ousted Patassé, but other communities as well. Bozizé's CAR responded with extreme violence toward residents of the north. Given French military intervention in CAR in support of Bozizé's government, some northern rebel groups signed a peace deal in 2008 and began a protracted and contested demobilization process. Once again, the UN dispatched international peacekeepers from 2008 to 2010, stabilizing parts of the country for the January 2011 elections, which handed Bozizé a second presidential term.

Disillusioned with the CAR government's failure to honor the peace agreement, an alliance of northern rebel groups calling itself Seleka (union) suddenly captured most northern towns including the diamond-mining center of Bria in December 2012 and advanced on Bangui. With Bozizé's calls for assistance ignored by France and the United States, the Economic Community of Central African States (ECCAS) sent an international force that stopped the Seleka rebels 70 kilometers from the capital. While the rebels dropped their demand for Bozizé's resignation and accepted a transitional government, they refused to relinquish control of their occupied areas. In March 2013, with the breakdown of a cease-fire, the Seleka rebels resumed the offensive, engaging in a running battle with South African troops present in support of ECCAS and then seizing Bangui. Bozizé left CAR, and rebel leader Michel Djotodia declared himself president, becoming the first Muslim to hold this position. In turn, forces loyal to Bozizé continued to resist the northern Seleka, and southern Christian civilians formed the "anti-balaka" (a reference to a traditional protection charm) militia and began massacres of CAR's Muslim minority, many of whom fled the country. "Anti-balaka" fighters destroyed mosques and forced Muslims to convert to Christianity. At the close of 2013, the UN warned that CAR risked "spiraling into genocide," and the French foreign minister stated that the country was "on the verge of genocide." Widely reported in international media, these concerns prompted the UN to deploy the International Support Mission to the CAR (MISCA), consisting mostly of troops from African states augmented by French forces. The next year MISCA transformed and expanded into the 10,000-strong United Nations Multidimensional Integrated Stabilization Mission in the Central African Republic (MINUSCA), specifically focusing on the protection of civilians. In January 2014 Djotodia resigned and was replaced by the nonpartisan leader and former Bangui mayor Catherine Samba-Panza. As Seleka leaders left the capital, violence reduced but did not end. This episode of extreme violence in CAR resulted in at least 6,000 deaths and displaced around 800,000, including 400, 000 who became refugees in neighboring countries. Many Muslims left the country, and some towns were completely cleared of their Muslim inhabitants. In turn, Seleka leaders began to demand the permanent division of CAR into a Christian south and Muslim north. At the end of 2015, the Seleka rebels declared the Republic of Logone as an autonomous region in the north of CAR, though the government refused to recognize it.

Talks held in Brazzaville, Republic of the Congo, in July 2014, resulted in an uncertain cease-fire, and a conference in Bangui in May 2014 produced a peace agreement accepted by most rebel factions and which established a legal process to prosecute those involved in atrocities. In February 2016 a mostly peaceful election resulted in Faustin-Archange Touadera, an academic and prime minster under Bozizé, emerging as president, leading a new government that continued the unsteady peace process. With the power of the national government mostly limited to the capital, CAR became divided into fiefdoms ruled by various ethnoreligious armed groups, some of whom engaged in illegal mining, and separated from each other by UN peacekeepers. Since France terminated its military operation in the country at the close of 2016, a resurgent Russia took an interest in mineral-rich CAR, providing instructors and weapons for a new national military. Sponsored by Sudan, another CAR peace agreement in February 2019 led to the appointment of factional leaders, all with a recent history of human rights abuses, as military advisers to the president, guiding the establishment of new integrated security force representing the various armed groups.

Timothy J. Stapleton

See also: Bokassa, Jean-Bédel; Bozizé, François; Congo Wars; Coups and Military Regimes in Africa; French Military Involvement in Postcolonial Africa; Genocide in Africa; Peacekeeping in Africa.

Further Reading

Bradshaw, Richard, and Juan Fandos-Ruis. *Historical Dictionary of the Central African Republic.* Lanham, MD: Rowman & Littlefield, 2016.

Carayannis, T., and L. Lombard, eds. *Making Sense of the Central African Republic.* London: Zed Books, 2015.

Dwyer, Maggie. *Soldiers in Revolt: Army Mutinies in Africa.* Oxford: Oxford University Press, 2017.

Kalck, Pierre. *Historical Dictionary of the Central African Republic.* Lanham, MD: Scarecrow Press, 2005.

Lombard, Louisa. *State of Rebellion: Violence and Intervention in the Central African Republic.* London: Zed Books, 2016.

Chad, Conflict in (1960–)

In postcolonial Chad, a civil war expanded into a complex interstate conflict with international Cold War dimensions that pitted France against a Soviet-supplied Libya. Independent from 1960, the former French colony of Chad experienced regionalism related to a comparatively prosperous and mostly Christian south and a poor and mainly Muslim north. In 1968, the National Liberation Front of Chad (FROLINAT) initiated a rebellion in the northern region and ultimately received weapons from Eastern Bloc–aligned North African countries Egypt, Algeria, and Libya. Chad's southern-based administration of President François Tombalbaye was bolstered by 3,000 French troops on the ground as well as military support from Western-aligned Zaire, Israel, and the United States. In 1973 Muammar Gaddafi's Libya annexed the Aouzou Strip, allegedly rich in uranium, on the other side of his southern border in Chad and built an air base there. Tombalbaye tolerated the Libyan action, but he was overthrown and killed in a 1975 coup that put General Felix Malloum in power. Since Malloum expressed hostility to the Libyans, Gaddafi dispatched troops into Chad in support of the northern rebels of FROLINAT. At that time the French military presence in Chad comprised several hundred advisers who sometimes engaged in combat and protected Malloum from possible coups. The Libyan intervention incited a split in FROLINAT with the anti-Libyan minority founding the Armed Forces of the North (FAN) under Hissène Habré and the pro-Libyan majority establishing the People's Armed Forces (FAP) led by Goukouni Oueddei. In 1977 FAP, with Libyan-supplied weapons, mounted an offensive that expelled Chadian state forces from most northern towns except Ounianga Kebir where the French held firm. With the start of 1978, after Malloum and FAN's Habré agreed to establish a unity government, FAP and the Libyans launched another offensive that occupied northern government strongholds including Ounianga Kebir and Faya-Largeau. The Libyans contributed armor, artillery, and air support for rebel foot soldiers. In February 1978 France embarked on Operation Tacaud, sending 2,500 troops with helicopter gunships and ground attack jets to Chad to secure the capital of N'Djamena. In May and June Chadian and French troops repelled another FAP offensive, sending the rebels back northward. Since Libyan pilots refused to engage French aircraft and Gaddafi supported a failed attempt to overthrow Oueddei as FAP leader, the rebels ejected Libyan troops from northern Chad.

In February 1979, the FAN of Habré and the FAP of Oueddei joined forces and chased Malloum's state military out of N'Djamena with 2,000–5,000 people killed and 70,000 displaced. The French did nothing. In turn, the Chadian rebel groups established a Transitional Government of National Unity (GUNT) led by Oueddei as president. Following a cross-border raid by 2,500 Libyan troops repelled by Chadian and French forces, GUNT further broadened by including some pro-Libyan factions. In March 1980 Oueddei's FAP and Habré's FAN clashed in the capital, and the latter took over Faya-Largeau in the north. This compelled Oueddei, still president of GUNT, to revive his relationship with Libya and sign a treaty allowing Libyan forces to enter Chad. With the Aouzou Strip as their staging area, Libyan and FAP forces including tanks and artillery recaptured Faya-Largeau and then pushed 1,000 kilometers south to capture N'Djamena in December. The remnants of Habré's FAN withdrew east to the border with Sudan's Darfur region where they received military assistance from Egypt, Sudan, and the United States. Despite Oueddei's agreement to merge Chad with Libya in pursuit of Gaddafi's vision of a greater Saharan nation, the leaders fell out when the latter started supporting the Volcan Army comprising Arab rebels from northern Chad. In late 1981 Oueddei requested that the 14,000 Libyan soldiers in Chad leave the country, and Gaddafi surprisingly agreed as a way of trying to gain influence in the Organisation of African Unity (OAU). With the departure of the Libyans, a 3,300-strong OAU Inter-African Force with troops mostly from Zaire, Nigeria, and Senegal arrived in Chad, representing the first attempt by an African international organization to deploy peacekeepers.

The withdrawal of the Libyans from Chad provided an opportunity for Habré's FAN to mount an offensive from Sudan. In June 1982 Habré's fighters routed GUNT forces in a battle 80 kilometers north of N'Djamena, which they occupied without resistance. Subsequently, Habré's FAN rooted out elements of the old Chadian armed forces to the south and secured control over most of the country. The Inter-African Force did nothing, and Gaddafi rejected the defeated Oueddei's appeals for assistance. Reestablishing the GUNT in northern Chad, Oueddei assembled 3,000–4,000 fighters from various militias, and in December 1982 and January 1983, they repelled attacks by Habré's FAN. Changing his mind once again, Gaddafi decided to back Oueddei, whose fighters, along with Libyan forces, seized Faya-Largeau and other northern towns in June. This Libyan intervention in Chad prompted the French to supply Habré's forces as Zaire sent him 250 paratroopers and the United States provided food. In July Habré's fighters, with the new name of Chadian National Armed Forces (FANT), advanced north and exacted a spectacular defeat on the GUNT/Libyan Army south of Abeche, which led to the recapture of many northern towns including Faya-Largeau. As a result, the Libyan Air Force bombarded Faya-Largeau, and a contingent of some 11,000 Libyan troops assembled nearby. In August some 3,000–4,000 of Oueddei's GUNT troops, supported by Libyan armor, artillery, and air power, expelled Habré's troops from Faya-Largeau. France then mounted Operation Manta with 2,700 French troops, supported by ground attack jets securing N'Djamena. With France unwilling to help Habré recapture the north and Gaddafi hesitant to take on the French military, Chad became partitioned, with the south ruled by Habré backed by French forces and the north under Oueddei bolstered by Libyan troops. In November 1984, with an agreement between France and Libya to mutually withdraw their troops, French forces departed Chad, but Gaddafi reneged, leaving 3,000 Libyans in the north.

In the mid-1980s the Libyans built an air base at Ouadi Doum in northern Chad, increasing their force in the country to 7,000 troops, 300 tanks, and 60 aircraft. As a result, the hawkish American Reagan administration stepped up its support for the Habré regime. In February 1986 Gaddafi reignited the war with an offensive by 5,000 Libyan and 5,000 GUNT troops that attacked Habré's FANT along the 16th parallel, which divided Chad in two. Supplied with new equipment from France, FANT forces counterattacked and pushed the Libyans and GUNT fighters back from where they came. Quickly, French president François Mitterrand, trying to project a strong image ahead of French legislative elections, enacted Operation Epervier (Sparrow Hawk) transporting 1,200 French troops and ground attack aircraft to N'Djamena. Based in Bangui in the CAR, French jets bombed the Libyan air base at Ouadi Doum, and Gaddafi retaliated by dispatching a bomber from Aouzou to fly 1,000 kilometers under French radar to raid N'Djamena airport. In August the uncertain alliance between the Libyans and Oueddei's GUNT again collapsed, and in the ensuing violence, the latter gained support from Habré's FANT, which sent units north, and the French who parachuted in supplies.

The latest Habré-Oueddei alliance unified most Chadians against the Libyan invasion. The Chadian forces numbered around 10,000 men mounted on Toyota pickup trucks equipped with French anti-tank missiles, and the 8,000 Libyan troops and their 300 tanks in northern Chad were confined to their desert outposts without local allies. Commencing in January 1987, the "Toyota War" saw Chadian forces led by General Hassan Djamous and augmented by French air power execute a series of rapid pincer maneuvers, overwhelming many Libyan positions and compelling them to evacuate northern Chad. In August a Chadian effort to take the Aouzou Strip was defeated by the Libyans because the French refused to supply the former with air support that close to the border. In early September a mobile column of 2,000 Chadian troops commanded by Djamous attacked Maaten al-Sarra air base 90 kilometers inside Libya, killing 1,700 of the 2,500 defenders, capturing 300 prisoners and destroying 70 tanks, 26 aircraft, surface-to-air missiles, and radar. The Chadians lost 65 men. As the raid derived the Libyans of air support in the area, the Chadians planned another attempt to secure the Aouzou Strip, but this was aborted over French concerns about potentially expanding the war. An OAU-brokered cease-fire ended the conflict later in September. During the "Toyota War," Libya suffered 7,500 deaths and Gaddafi lost $1.5 billion worth of arms including 800 armored vehicles. About 1,000 Chadians were killed. Blaming his defeat on the Americans and French, Gaddafi authorized the terrorist bombing of an American airliner downed over Scotland in December 1988 and a French airliner destroyed over Niger in September 1989. Libya and Chad normalized diplomatic relations in 1989 with the Aouzou Strip dispute submitted to the International Court of Justice that eventually ruled in favor of Chad's claim.

In 1989, given that Habré had General Djamous killed over coup plot suspicions, Chadian military commander Idriss Déby escaped to Sudan where he founded the rebel Patriotic Salvation Movement (MPS) with support from Khartoum and Tripoli. An MPS invasion of Chad in March 1990 was aborted because of French intervention. In November 1991 the MPS again pressed into Chad, and this time the French forces in the country did nothing, as the brutality of Habré's regime had become an international embarrassment. Some 2,000 MPS fighters occupied N'Djamena, Habré fled to exile, and Déby became an elected but authoritarian president. Starting in 2003, Déby's administration was challenged by numerous rebel groups in eastern Chad armed by Sudan in retaliation for Chad's sponsorship of insurgents in Darfur. The presence of several hundred thousand Sudanese and Chadian refugees along the border complicated this military situation. Rebel incursions into Chad in April 2006 and February 2008 failed to capture N'Djamena, where the Déby regime was bolstered by French forces. From 2008 to 2010, international peacekeepers, initially from the European Union but ultimately from the United Nations Mission in the Central African Republic and Chad (MINURCAT), deployed to eastern Chad and northeastern CAR to protect and provide humanitarian assistance for around 200,000 refugees from Darfur. In 2010 the governments of Chad and Sudan agreed to stop backing rebels from each other's countries, which led to a reopening of their borders. In 2016 a court in Senegal convicted the exiled Habré of murder, rape, and sexual slavery relating to his time in power in Chad, sentencing him to life in prison, marking the first instance when a national court convicted a former head of state of another country of human rights violations. Deby was killed in combat in April 2021 while leading state forces against a new northern rebel group called the Front for Change and Concord in Chad (FACT). The late president was instantly succeeded by his son, military general Mahamat ibn Idriss Déby Itno.

Timothy J. Stapleton

See also: Cold War in Africa; Darfur Genocide; Déby, Idriss; French Military Involvement in Postcolonial Africa; Gaddafi, Muammar; Habré, Hissène; Peacekeeping in Africa.

Further Reading

Azevedo, Mario J. *Roots of Violence: A History of War in Chad*. New York: Routledge, 1998.

Clayton, Anthony. *Frontiersmen: Warfare in Africa since 1950*. London: Routledge, 2004.

Mays, Terry M. *Africa's First Peacekeeping Operation: The OAU in Chad 1981–82*. Westport, CT: Praeger, 2002.

Nolutshungu, Sam. *The Limits of Anarchy: Intervention and State Formation in Chad*. Charlottesville: University of Virginia Press, 1995.

Pollack, Kenneth. *Arabs at War: Military Effectiveness, 1948–1991*. Lincoln: University of Nebraska Press, 2002.

Child Soldiers in Africa

The employment of children as combatants became associated with the spate of civil wars fought in post–Cold War Africa during the 1990s and early 2000s. In reality, though, child soldiers participated in very many wars stretching back over centuries and fought in places outside Africa. For instance, tens of thousands of British teenagers, including some as young as 13 or 14, enlisted in the British Army during World War I. With regard to postcolonial African conflicts, it remains unclear if the use of child soldiers increased proportionally during the 1990s or if a new sensibility in the Western world highlighted the issue or if more wars meant more child soldiers. After all, children served as combatants in Cold

War–era African conflicts such as the Nigerian Civil War (1967–1970) and Zimbabwe's War of Independence (1965–1979) when the matter lacked the same emotional impact as today. Children played an important role in guerrilla warfare with, for instance, young boys called mujibas helping Zimbabwe nationalist insurgents to elude Rhodesian security forces.

A number of factors informed and still informs the employment of child soldiers in postcolonial Africa. Many African cultural understandings of childhood are different from that of Western countries, and the common use of child labor in many parts of Africa, which also stems from poverty, has some relation to child soldiering. Demographically, Africa's population is very young, and this influences the average age of fighters within armed groups. Yet another factor relates to large populations of internally displaced people or refugees from which many child soldiers emerge. Furthermore, children are more susceptible to military indoctrination, and many accounts attest to their commitment and courage in battle. Relating to the post–Cold War era, the demise of ideologically driven superpower sponsorship meant that armed factions in Africa increasingly turned to economic ventures such as resource extraction to support their activities, including buying weapons and paying fighters. In this neoliberal context of African warfare, low-paid or unpaid child soldiers represent a cost-effective solution to building and maintaining a fighting force. The popular idea that modern small arms, made out of light plastic material and easy to use, facilitated the greater mobilization of children for combat is largely a myth. In modern African conflicts, child soldiers and other fighters primarily used and still use decades-old variants of the Soviet-designed AK-47 assault rifle that weighs just as much or more than World War II–era rifles or submachine guns.

During the 1990s, the employment of child soldiers became synonymous with civil wars in Liberia, Sierra Leone, Angola, and the Democratic Republic of the Congo (DRC). In northern Uganda, around the same time, the Lord's Resistance Army (LRA) became notorious for kidnapping children for use as fighters, porters, and sexual slaves. In the Great Lakes conflicts of the 1990s and early 2000s, child soldiers became widely known as Kadogo or "little one" in Kiswahili. The military effectiveness of child soldiers varied considerably during the 1990s with, for example, the Sudan People's Liberation Army (SPLA) raising trained and effective young soldiers, while the "Small Boy Units" of Sierra Leone's Revolutionary United Front (RUF) comprised undisciplined youth motivated by drugs to commit atrocities.

A series of international agreements prohibiting the use of child soldiers emerged in the post–Cold War era. These included the 1989 UN Convention on the Rights of the Child, requiring parties to a conflict to avoid the participation of children under 15 and the 1999 African Charter on the Rights and Welfare of the Child and the 2002 UN Optional Protocol on the Involvement of Children in Armed Conflict, both restricting military service for those under 18. In 2012, Thomas Lubanga, leader of a Hema military group in the northeastern DRC during the 2000s, became the first person convicted by the International Criminal Court, with charges against him including the conscription and enlistment of child soldiers. Western international concern over the use of child soldiers in African conflicts manifested through the publication of books, including memoirs; speaking tours; films; documentaries; and websites. As a result, a series of demobilization and reintegration programs for former child soldiers emerged in some postconflict countries in Africa. Despite the heightened sensitivity over this issue, and potential international prosecution for leaders of armed factions, child soldiers continue to participate in recent African conflicts, including in South Sudan and the Central African Republic.

Timothy J. Stapleton

See also: Congo Wars; Democratic Republic of the Congo (DRC), Continuing Violence in; Liberian Civil Wars; Lord's Resistance Army (LRA); Nigerian Civil War; Revolutionary United Front (RUF); Sierra Leone Civil War; Sudan Civil War, Second; Sudan People's Liberation Movement/Army (SPLM/A); Uganda, Insurgency in the North; Zimbabwe Independence War.

Further Reading

Beah, Ismael. *A Long Way Gone: Memoirs of a Boy Soldier*. New York: Sarah Crichton Books, 2007.

Bogner, Artur, and Gabriele Rosenthal. *Child Soldiers in Context: Biographies, Familial and Collective Trajectories in Northern Uganda*. Göttingen: Göttingen University Press, 2020.

Dallaire, Romeo. *They Fight Like Soldiers, They Die Like Children: The Global Quest to Eradicate the Use of Child Soldiers*. Toronto: Random House Canada, 2010.

Honwana, Alcinda. *Child Soldiers in Africa*. Philadelphia: University of Pennsylvania Press, 2006.

Rosen, David. *Armies of the Young: Child Soldiers in War and Terrorism*. New Brunswick, NJ: Rutgers University Press, 2005.

Singer, P. W. *Children at War*. New York: Pantheon Books, 2005.

Wessells, Michael. *Child Soldiers: From Violence to Protection*. Cambridge, MA: Harvard University Press, 2006.

Christmas War (1985)

After independence from France in 1960, both Mali and Upper Volta (now Burkina Faso) claimed the natural gas and minerals of the Agacher Strip along their common border. In 1974 and 1975, border skirmishes between Mali and Upper Volta resulted in mediation by the Organisation of African Unity (OAU), which recommended a neutral technical commission to study the boundary, and this was accepted by both countries. In 1983 Captain Thomas Sankara, a veteran of the earlier frontier fighting, who saw himself as a Marxist revolutionary along the lines of Che Guevara, took power in Upper Volta, renaming the country Burkina Faso (Land of Upright Men) in anticipation of a national rebirth including the rejection of French influence. Sankara's government rejected foreign assistance, disavowed debts incurred by previous authoritarian regimes, and tried to eliminate the influence of Western-dominated international economic institutions like the International Monetary Fund (IMF) and World Bank. The radical regime of Sankara and the conservative French-backed military state of Moussa Traore in Mali initially cooperated and forwarded the Agacher Stip issue to the International Court of Justice (ICJ), but they fell out while the legal case was still under consideration. Accusing Burkinabe census takers, accompanied by soldiers, of violating its territory and forcing Malian citizens to accept Burkina Faso identity cards, Mali's government launched attacks on Burkina Faso border posts and police stations on Christmas Day 1985. While the Burkina Faso forces counterattacked, the more capable Malian military captured several villages and conducted an air strike on the Burkinabe town of Ouahigouya, inflicting civilian casualties. Neighboring states Libya and Nigeria made separate attempts to sponsor negotiations and reach a cease-fire, but these failed. Finally, through the mediation of Côte d'Ivoire's president Felix Houphouet-Boigny, the combatants declared a cease-fire on December 30, ending what has become known as the "Christmas War." Between 60 and 300 people were killed in the brief conflict that demonstrated the military weakness of Sankara's revolutionary state. In 1986 Mali and Burkina Faso accepted an ICJ decision that divided the Agachar Strip almost equally between them. Subsequently, Sankara was killed in a 1987 coup led by military officer Blaise Compaoré, who restored Burkina Faso's relations with France and the Western world. Compaoré remained in power until 2014 when he was removed by popular protest.

Timothy J. Stapleton

See also: Cold War in Africa; Coups and Military Regimes in Africa; French Military Involvement in Postcolonial Africa; Sankara, Thomas.

Further Reading

Englebert, Pierre. *Burkina Faso: Unsteady Statehood in West Africa*. New York: Routledge, 2018.

Harsch, Ernest. *Thomas Sankara: An African Revolutionary*. Athens: Ohio University Press, 2014.

Kongo, Jean-Claude, and Leo Zeilig. *Thomas Sankara*. Cape Town: National Institute for the Humanities and Social Sciences, 2017.

Peterson, Brian. *Thomas Sankara: A Revolutionary in Cold War Africa*. Bloomington: Indiana University Press, 2021.

Cold War in Africa

The term "Cold War" describes the international tensions between the American-led Western capitalist powers and the Soviet-led Eastern socialist bloc from around the late 1940s to 1990. Since the two superpowers—that is, the United States and Soviet Union—possessed nuclear weapons and direct conflict between them threatened global annihilation, the "Cold War" influenced smaller conflicts in Latin America, Asia, and Africa. When the "Cold War" started, almost all of Africa comprised colonial territories ruled by Western European powers allied with the United States. The few autonomous African countries positioned themselves on the Western side of the global conflict. Liberia enjoyed historic close relations with the United States, and imperial Ethiopia and apartheid South Africa both dispatched forces in support of the Americans during the Korean War

(1950–1953). Therefore, in the late 1940s and early to middle-1950s, the Soviet Union and its eastern allies had very little influence in Africa, lacking state partners on the continent. Communist parties with ties to Moscow existed in a few parts of Africa, particularly in South Africa, but were marginalized. At the same time, British, French and other colonial rulers tended to attribute rising African nationalist movements to imagined communist influence rather than grievances over colonial oppression.

The Cold War began to impact Africa from the late 1950s and 1960s as African colonies transformed into independent states capable of exercising their own foreign policies. The Suez Crisis of 1956 represented one of the first serious examples of Cold War tensions influencing a conflict in Africa as Western allies Britain, France, and Israel invaded Egypt but were forced to back down, given Cairo's support by the Soviet Union. Algeria's Independence War (1954–1962) also involved the Soviets supplying insurgents fighting French colonial rule. The decolonization of Africa took place during the height of the Cold War corresponding with events such as the 1962 Cuban Missile Crisis. As the European colonial powers withdrew, the United States and Soviet Union vied to establish relations with the newly independent African countries, some of which possessed important natural resources or were key strategic locations. However, during the 1960s, the Americans and their allies enjoyed significant advantages in Africa with a strong foothold in many former colonies, while the Soviets struggled to catch up. For example, during the Congo Crisis of the early 1960s, Prime Minister Patrice Lumumba famously sparked Western outrage that ultimately led to his death, by calling for Soviet assistance, which never amounted to very much. Subsequently, Eastern Bloc support for leftist rebels in the eastern Congo in 1964–1965 proved limited and could not compete with direct military intervention by Belgium and the United States. The African states that retained close relations with their former colonial masters, such as Kenya with Britain and Côte d'Ivoire with France, and continued a capitalist economic system tended to orient themselves toward the Western side of the Cold War. On the other hand, and also during the 1960s, a few newly independent African states with socialist agendas such as former French colonies Guinea and Mali developed early contacts with the Soviet Union and other Eastern Bloc powers, including revolutionary Cuba. By the mid-1970s, superpower-sponsored dictatorships became well established in Africa such as the American-backed regime of Mobutu Sese Seko in Zaire (now the Democratic Republic of the Congo or DRC) and the Soviet-supported regime of Mengistu Haile Mariam in Ethiopia. At the same time, however, the rhetoric of international nonalignment appealed to most African governments with some trying to balance relations between both sides of the Cold War.

As in Latin America and Asia, Cold War superpowers supported different sides in African conflicts. Despite gaining the label of "proxy wars," these African conflicts always originated in local issues, though foreign involvement often increased their lethality and scope. The Cold War strongly superimposed itself on the conflicts between Africa's stubborn colonial and settler regimes and militant African liberation movements. From around 1960 to 1974, Portugal fought counterinsurgency wars in its African colonies of Angola, Mozambique, and

Guinea-Bissau, aided by its membership in the American-led North Atlantic Treaty Organization (NATO). Although subject to increasing international sanctions, white minority–ruled Rhodesia and apartheid South Africa portrayed themselves as anti-communist bastions, gaining military and diplomatic support from the Western side of the Cold War. On the other side of these conflicts, African nationalist insurgent groups received backing from the Eastern Bloc and adopted revolutionary socialist doctrine and rhetoric. The Sino-Soviet rivalry sometimes also influenced events in Africa as, in the case of the movements fighting against Rhodesia in the 1970s, the Zimbabwe People's Revolutionary Army (ZIPRA) received sponsorship and Leninist ideology from the Soviet Union and the Zimbabwe African Nationalist Liberation Army (ZANLA) received support and Maoist guerrilla warfare strategy from China.

In 1974, with the independence of Portuguese territories and the overthrow of Ethiopian Emperor Haile Selassie, the Soviet Union gained robust partners in Africa, which accelerated Cold War competition on the continent. Ironically, this intensification of Cold War rivalry in Africa began around the same time as the relaxation of direct tensions or détente between the superpowers. During the Angolan Civil War of the late 1970s and 1980s, the Soviet Union and Cuba rigorously backed the Angolan state and the South West Africa People's Organization (SWAPO), which used Angola as a staging area to fight South African occupation of adjacent South West Africa (now Namibia). The United States supported apartheid South Africa that mounted military incursions into southern Angola in pursuit of SWAPO but that clashed with Angolan government forces, and Washington also backed the Angolan rebels of the National Union for the Total Independence of Angola (UNITA). In the late 1980s, even as reforms began within the Soviet Union that would lead to its withdrawal from Angola and the eventual end of the Cold War, Soviet generals planned an Angolan state offensive against UNITA in southeastern Angola that prompted a final South African cross-border operation and a series of climatic conventional battles. Conflict in the Horn of Africa initially involved American-backed imperial Ethiopia versus Soviet-backed and newly independent Somalia that sought to expand to unite the region's Somali people. However, revolution in Ethiopia prompted the superpowers to change sides in the regional conflict with the Soviet Union and Cuba assisting Ethiopia to successfully defend itself against the 1978 invasion by Somalia that scrambled to secure some American assistance. In Angola and the Horn of Africa, the Soviet Union and Cuba deployed conventional forces and imported massive amounts of weaponry, including armored vehicles and attack helicopters otherwise out of the reach of local combatants. Other examples of Cold War involvement in African conflicts include Soviet support for Egypt during its wars with American-backed Israel in 1967 and 1973 and the 1980s conflict between French and American-backed Chad and Libya that used oil money to purchase Soviet arms. Of course, not all conflicts in postcolonial Africa involved superpowers or Cold War alliances backing opposing sides. During the Nigerian Civil War (1967–1970), Britain and the Soviet Union supported the federal military government, while France sponsored separatist Biafra.

From 1990, the end of the Cold War substantially impacted Africa. The collapse of the Soviet Union meant the end of its support for client regimes, and absent a communist threat, the United States lost interest in its African allies. With the collapse of previously superpower-backed dictatorships such as Mengistu in Ethiopia and Mobutu in Zaire during the 1990s, a wave of democratization movements swept across much of Africa, and in many places, power vacuums led to civil wars. In South Africa, loss of superpower support for both the apartheid state and the liberation movements, contributed to a negotiated transition to democracy. Economically, former Soviet allies such as the governments of Angola and Mozambique abandoned socialist policies, leading to the dominance of a neoliberal economic order across Africa. Unable to gain foreign military support by appealing to ideology, armed groups in Africa sustained themselves by relying more on the extraction and export of valuable resources.

Timothy J. Stapleton

See also: Angolan Conflicts; Arab-Israeli Wars; Chad, Conflict in; Congo Crisis; Cuba and Africa; Ethiopia: Insurgency and Interstate War; Namibia Independence War; Nigerian Civil War; Ogaden War; Portuguese Africa, Independence Wars (Angola, Mozambique, and Guinea-Bissau); Soviet Military Involvement in Africa; U.S. Military Involvement in Africa.

Further Reading

Namikas, Lise. *Battleground Africa: Cold War in the Congo, 1960–65*. Washington, DC: Woodrow Wilson Center Press, 2013.

Nwaubani, Ebere. *The United States and Decolonization in West Africa*. Rochester, NY: University of Rochester Press, 2001.

Schmidt, Elizabeth. *Foreign Intervention in Africa: From the Cold War to the War on Terror*. Cambridge: Cambridge University Press, 2013.

Shubin, Vladimir. *The Hot "Cold War": The USSR in Southern Africa*. London: Pluto Press, 2008.

Villafana, Frank. *Cold War in the Congo: The Confrontation of Cuban Military Forces, 1960–67*. London: Transaction Publishers, 2012.

Yordanov, Radoslav. *The Soviet Union and the Horn of Africa during the Cold War: Between Ideology and Pragmatism*. Lanham, MD: Lexington Books, 2016.

Congo Crisis (1960–1967)

During the colonial era of the late nineteenth and early twentieth century, the Belgian Congo experienced horrific exploitation and violence, and the Belgian colonial state did almost nothing to provide local Africans with administrative experience or Western education. Indeed, during the era of decolonization in the 1950s, Belgium did not want to give up its large resource-rich territory and failed to undertake any significant preparations for self-rule in the Congo. In 1959 Brussels, responding to protest within the Congo and international pressure, provided the Congo with six months' notice of independence, hoping that the unprepared new state would remain dependent upon assistance from Belgium. Mirroring the decentralized nature of Belgian colonial rule, Congolese political parties emerged along ethnoregional lines. At the end of June 1960, the first independent government comprised Prime Minister Patrice Lumumba, a Pan-Africanist of the Congolese National Movement (MNC) based in the northeast region around Stanleyville (now Kisangani), and President Joseph Kasavubu of the Bakongo Alliance (ABAKO) centered in the west around the capital of Leopoldville (now Kinshasa) and sought to reunite the Bakongo ethnic group split between Belgian, French, and Portuguese colonies. In July Congolese soldiers mutinied against the continued authority of Belgian officers, leading to wider attacks on Belgian civilians. Attempting to reassert control over the military, the Congolese government changed its title from the colonial name of Force Publique to the Congolese National Army (ANC); rapidly promoted Africans, including former journalist Colonel Joseph Mobutu, replaced Belgians, and all troops received a promotion.

Regional separatists, supported by Western and South African mining interests, took advantage of the army mutiny. Albert Kalonji proclaimed a self-governing state in diamond-rich South Kasai. Moise Tshombe declared the independence of the southern province of Katanga, which was home to the Congo's largest mining industry. With support from Belgium and France, Tshombe formed a Katanga military with mercenaries recruited from Rhodesia, South Africa, France, and Belgium. When Belgian troops arrived in the rest of the Congo to protect Belgian civilians, Lumumba accused Brussels of trying to recolonize the country, and he demanded their withdrawal. While Lumumba requested UN assistance, the United Nations Operation in the Congo (ONUC) troops who arrived protected Western interests and refused to suppress the Katanga secession. As a result, a disappointed Lumumba called for Soviet military support, which prompted American and Belgian plots to assassinate him. Accusing Lumumba of orchestrating a genocidal campaign to crush the breakaway state in South Kasai, President Kasavubu dismissed the prime minister, who then tried to dismiss the president. The power struggle was decided by Colonel Mobutu who used the Congolese military to detain Lumumba. After Lumumba tried to escape but was recaptured, Mobutu had the deposed prime minister flown to Katanga in January 1961, and it was there that he was executed on the orders of Tshombe.

The UN Security Council, in February 1961, authorized ONUC to use force against the Katanga secession. Bolstered by the arrival of an Indian brigade, ONUC conducted Operation Rum Punch in August, which resulted in the arrest and deportation of some foreign mercenaries working in Katanga. The Katangese siege of 150 Irish UN peacekeepers at Jadotville, which was bombed by Katanga's French-supplied aircraft, incited further UN action. In September, the now 20,000-strong ONUC mounted Operation Morthor, in which they attempted but failed to take Elisabethville (today's Lubumbashi), Katanga's capital. The ANC also launched a failed incursion into Katanga the next month. Although Tshombe's state enjoyed military success on the ground, the United States began to shift away from the anti-communist separatist regime, favoring the creation of a friendly government for the whole Congo. Countering Katanga's air superiority, ONUC assembled a UN air force in the Congo, with jet fighters and bombers from Ethiopia, Sweden, and India. After a long but failed negotiation, ONUC initiated

Operation Grand Slam in December 1962 with air operations that eliminated Katanga aircraft and a ground offensive by Indian and Swedish troops that ended the separatist state.

ONUC's 1964 withdrawal from the Congo provided an opportunity for rebellion in other parts of the country. Following Lumumba's murder, many of his supporters fled to newly independent Congo-Brazzaville and Burundi, where they founded the National Liberation Council (NLC) and acquired Eastern Bloc military assistance. A new phase of the Congo Crisis began in January 1964 when fighters led by Pierre Mulele launched a rebellion in the western region of Kwilu. In May "Simba" (lion) rebels under Gaston Soumialot, including many exiled Rwandan Tutsi fighters, began taking over towns in the eastern Congo, and in August they captured Stanleyville. The rebels proclaimed the People's Republic of the Congo with official recognition from the Soviet Union, China, and Cuba. Sponsored by the United States and Belgium, the Congolese government of former separatist prime minister Moise Tshombe assembled an air force with Cuban exile pilots and supplemented ANC ground forces with foreign white mercenaries, many of whom had recently worked for secessionist Katanga as well as by recalling exiled Katangese troops. The ANC reestablished control over Kwilu in April, but fighting there continued until December. In late 1964 mercenary and ANC forces began to reclaim towns in the eastern Congo. In late November, during Operation Dragon Rouge, a mercenary-ANC mechanized ground column and Belgian paratroopers dropped from American aircraft seized Stanleyville and rescued expatriate hostages. A few days later a similar operation, Dragon Noire, retook the town of Paulis (Isiro). Although two other planned Dragon operations were canceled given international outcry against Western intervention in Africa, Rouge and Noire liberated almost 2,000 hostages and killed 10,000 rebels with minimal ANC-Belgian losses. With the departure of Belgian forces from the Congo, South African mercenary leader Mike Hoare led Operation White Giant, which blocked rebel supply lines from Uganda and Sudan, and occupied the northeast town of Bunia in December. In June 1965 Hoare and French mercenary leader Bob Denard led Operation Violettes Imperiales, which secured the Congo's northern border with the Central African Republic. The arrival of several hundred revolutionary Cubans led by Ernesto "Che" Guevara could not salvage the insurgency, which shrank to several isolated and remote pockets. In late 1965 Tanzanian support for the eastern Congo rebels was disrupted by the arrival of American-supplied gunboats with Cuban exile crews on Lake Tanganyika and mercenary-ANC amphibious landings along the western lake shore finally brought the insurgency to a close. The American-sponsored Mobutu, the real power in the Congo since 1961, overthrew President Kasavubu in November 1965 and dismissed Prime Minister Tshombe, who fled the country. Eventually renaming the country Zaire, Mobutu established an anti-communist dictatorship that persisted for 30 years and became infamous for corruption and oppression. A 1966 mutiny by Katangese troops in the east was suppressed by mercenaries and other ANC forces. Given that Mobutu refused to renew their contracts, white mercenaries in the eastern Congo also rebelled the following year, though their plot to reinstate the exiled Tshombe was thwarted by the American Central Intelligence Agency (CIA). With the arrival of overwhelming ANC forces, some transported in United States aircraft, the mercenaries fled into Rwanda, from where they were repatriated.

Timothy J. Stapleton

See also: Air Power in Postcolonial African Wars; Belgian Military Intervention in Africa; Canadian Military Involvement in Africa; Cold War in Africa; Cuba and Africa; Mercenaries in African Conflicts; Mobutu Sese Seko; Peacekeeping in Africa; Shaba, Zaire: Rebel Incursions and Foreign Intervention; Soviet Military Involvement in Africa; U.S. Military Involvement in Africa.

Further Reading

De Witte, Ludo. *The Assassination of Patrice Lumumba.* London: Verso, 2002.

Kennes, Erik, and Miles Larmer. *The Katangese Gendarmes: Fighting Their Way Home.* Bloomington: Indiana University Press, 2016.

Namikas, Lise. *Battleground Africa: Cold War in the Congo, 1960–65.* Stanford: Stanford University Press, 2015.

Odom, Thomas. "Dragon Operations: Hostage Rescues in the Congo, 1964–65." Fort Leavenworth, KS: Combat Studies Institute, 1988.

Othen, Christopher. *Katanga, 1960–63: Mercenaries, Spies and the African Nation That Waged War on the World.* Stroud: History Press, 2015.

Villafana, Frank. *Cold War in the Congo: The Confrontation of Cuban Military Forces, 1960–67.* New Brunswick, NJ: Transaction Publishers, 2012.

Williams, Susan. *Who Killed Dag Hammarskjold? The UN, the Cold War and White Supremacy in Africa.* Oxford: Oxford University Press, 2014.

Congo Wars (1996–2002)

Losing his longtime American support with the end of the Cold War, the Zairean dictator Mobutu Sese Seko clung to power by dragging out negotiations over political reforms during the first half of the 1990s. In the context of economic collapse, violence erupted in the North and South Kivu provinces of eastern Zaire between communities who thought of themselves as indigenous and others perceived as foreign, given historic links to Rwanda. The influx of nearly a million Hutu refugees, soldiers, and militia from Rwanda at the end of the 1994 genocide gravely worsened tensions in eastern Zaire. At the same time, people of Rwandan Tutsi origin, including many long resident in eastern Zaire, such as the Banyamulenge, sought refuge in Rwanda. Lacking pay from the troubled state, units of the Armed Forces of Zaire (FAZ) sent to stabilize the country's eastern region ultimately sided with local factions that offered them money. In early 1995 exiled Hutu Power fighters who had conducted the genocide in Rwanda and were now based in refugee camps in eastern Zaire began to infiltrate their adjacent home country of Rwanda where they raided schools and ambushed buses. This security threat plus the victimization of the Banyamulenge by the Zairean Army and numerous militias promoted the predominantly Tutsi Rwandan Patriotic Front (RPF) government in Rwanda to send its military across the border to neutralize the Hutu Power groups. In August 1996 the Rwandan Patriotic Army (RPA), Rwanda's military, began infiltrating eastern Zaire via Burundi, and in October the Mobutu regime accused Rwanda and Burundi of invading its country. As the RPA and allied Banyamulenge fighters advanced to seize the towns of Uvira and Bukavu in the South Kivu province at the end of October, the demoralized and incompetent FAZ withdrew. In early November the RPA moved into the North Kivu province to capture the border town of Goma; later in the month it took Masisi and Butembo, and in early December, it occupied the important Bukavu-Goma road junction. Around the same time, the Tutsi-led military government in Burundi briefly dispatched forces into South Kivu to destroy camps used by the exiled Burundian Hutu rebels of the National Council for the Defense of Democracy-Forces for the Defense of Democracy (CNDD-FDD). To the north, the Uganda People's Defence Force (UPDF) advanced into Zaire at the end of November, and on Christmas Day, they helped local insurgents capture the town of Bunia in the Orientale province's Ituri region. The Ugandan government justified its invasion of Zaire as a pursuit of western Ugandan rebels from the Allied Democratic Forces (ADF) who constituted a threat to their home country. To portray their invasion as a domestic Zairean uprising, the Rwandan and Ugandan states arranged the establishment of the Alliance of Democratic Forces for the Liberation of Congo (AFDL), comprising a coalition of anti-Mobutu groups with a core of Banyamulenge and headed by longtime exile and rebel Laurent Kabila.

In November 1996, given international discussions about dispatching a United Nations (UN) peacekeeping force to the Great Lakes region, the RPA forcefully disbanded refugee camps in North and South Kivu, including Mugunga, which accommodated 600,000 people. Hundreds of thousands of refugees returned to Rwanda, but others fled west, undertaking an epic march across the vast territory of Zaire with the RPA and AFDL in pursuit. In May 1997 the AFDL, led by RPA officers, slaughtered hundreds of Rwandan Hutu civilians near the Zairean town of Mbandaka where they gathered to cross the Congo River into the Republic of the Congo. The Rwandan government's claim that these operations in Zaire were important for the security of their country made little sense, as Mbandaka is located about 1,200 kilometers from Rwanda. The next year a team of UN investigators warned that massacres of Rwandan Hutu in Zaire, with 230,000 of them disappearing in 1996 and 1997, might correspond with the international legal definition of genocide.

Joining Rwanda and Uganda, Angola invaded Zaire to prevent the Angolan rebels of the National Union for the Total Independence of Angola (UNITA) from using Mobutu's state as a channel for smuggling diamonds to fund their struggle. In February 1997 Angola flew 2,000–3,000 exiled Zairean Katanga rebels called "Tigres," who had been involved in conflicts in southern Zaire in the 1960s and late 1970s and were then incorporated into the Angolan military, to Rwanda, from where they moved into eastern Zaire. Within a few weeks, the "Tigres" helped the AFDL capture the city of Kisangani, and in April they participated in the AFDL occupation of Shaba (Katanga) province, with some transiting Zambian territory to do so. At the close of April, Angolan military forces moved into southern Zaire to seize Tshikapa and Kikwit on their way toward the capital of Kinshasa. Simultaneously, Rwandan and Ugandan soldiers along with AFDL rebels, wearing their characteristic rubber boots, advanced on Kinshasa from the east.

Mobutu's efforts to defend his regime proved farcical. Using money from longtime ally France and from Kuwait, which Zaire had supported during the First Gulf War, Mobutu attempted to rally his military by paying troops for the first time in months, purchasing new equipment, and hiring French and Serbian mercenaries. However, the Zairean forces usually avoided fighting, sold their weapons to the enemy, and abandoned towns. The war's final battle took place in early May at Kenge where UNITA rebels from Angola failed to stop the advance of the Angolan Army toward nearby Kinshasa. Consequently, an ill Mobutu escaped to Morocco, where he died shortly thereafter, and Kabila entered Kinshasa on May 20, declaring himself president and changing the country's name from Zaire to the Democratic Republic of the Congo (DRC). The 1996 and 1997 conflict that toppled the 30-year old Mobutu regime is often labeled the "First Congo War."

The DRC's new Kabila administration quickly fell out with Rwanda and Uganda, its principal external sponsors. The weak government in Kinshasa in the west could do little to stop exiled Rwandan and Ugandan insurgents from using parts of the faraway eastern DRC as a staging area for incursions into their original countries. In the eastern DRC, these foreign militants included the Army for the Liberation of Rwanda (ALIR), comprising Hutu Power fighters associated with the 1994 genocide and ADF fighters from western Uganda. Local eastern Congolese militias called Mai Mai also became engaged in this complicated web of conflicts and armed groups. Responding to domestic criticism about his regime's dependence on foreign troops, Kabila dismissed Rwandan officer James Kabarebe as chief of staff of the newly formed Congolese Armed Forces (FAC), and in late July 1998, he ordered all foreign military forces out of the DRC including 600 Rwandan soldiers flown from Kinshasa to Kigali. In turn, in early August FAC troops in the eastern DRC towns of Goma and Bukavu rebelled against the Kabila state with the assistance of Rwanda and Uganda. The Katangan "Tigres" went back to Angola after Rwanda forces killed some of them who opposed the rebellion. Adopting the name Rally for Congolese Democracy (RCD), the new rebels in the eastern DRC received strong support from Rwanda, which was itself backed by the United States, given the Clinton administration's guilt over failing to intervene in Rwanda during the 1994 genocide against the Tutsi. On the opposite side of the DRC, Kabila's FAC troops massacred remaining Banyamulenge and Rwandan soldiers at military camps near Kinshasa. In early August, a 1,200-strong expedition of Rwandan troops under Kabarebe hijacked civil airlines from Goma airport in the eastern DRC and flew to Kitona in the west, where they assembled former Mobutu soldiers to bolster their numbers and distracted FAC forces from the rebellion in the east.

Having recently joined the Southern African Development Community (SADC), the beleaguered Kabila requested military support from the regional organization, which maintained a mutual defense pact. However, SADC members Botswana, South Africa, and Zambia balked at defending an unelected regime and disliked the idea of fighting fellow American allies Rwanda and Uganda. Nevertheless, Zimbabwe wanted to secure its new investments in Kabila's DRC; Angola expressed worry about UNITA's warming relations with Rwanda and Uganda; and Namibia supported Angola, which had assisted its recently successful liberation struggle.

An Angolan expeditionary force with armored vehicles and helicopters assembled in Angola's Cabinda enclave and pushed into the western DRC, where it overwhelmed the lightly armed Rwandan troops and seized Kitona toward the end of August. Concurrently, the Zimbabwe Air Force flew 2,800 Zimbabwean soldiers to Kinshasa, where they engaged in a three-day battle to defend the airport as Zimbabwean warplanes intercepted and eliminated a motorized column of rebels on its way to the capital.

Rwandan and Ugandan troops and Congolese RCD rebels controlled most of the eastern Congo including Kisangani by early September 1998. With the capture of strategically important Kindu in October, Kabila's forces could no longer airlift soldiers to the east. This capture also opened up an RCD/Rwandan route to the Congo's diamond-rich Kasai region and a possible connection with UNITA rebels in nearby Angola. In November, in the Equateur province of the northern DRC, the Ugandan Army facilitated the creation of a new insurgent group called the Movement for the Liberation of Congo (MLC) headed by Jean-Pierre Bemba. Some members of this group possessed past associations with the former Mobutu regime that had enjoyed support in this northern area. Since Uganda backed the Sudan People's Liberation Army (SPLA) rebellion in southern Sudan, Khartoum arranged a Libyan airlift of 1,000 Chadian troops to the northern Congo to support the Kabila regime. Sudan's government also recruited exiled Rwandan and Ugandan rebels to join Kabila's forces and dispatched its own bombers to the DRC. Zimbabwe recruited exiled Burundian Hutu fighters from camps in Tanzania, trained them, and sent them to fight on behalf of Kabila in the southern Congo. With so many African countries participating directly and indirectly in this "Second Congo War," it gained the nickname "Africa's World War."

During the first six months of 1999, RCD rebels and the Rwandan Army pressed into Kasai and north Katanga, but stubborn Zimbabwean defenders, assisted by exiled Rwandan Hutu fighters, prevented them from capturing the diamond-mining center of Mbuji-Mayi. In the north, the new MLC, with recruits from the Central African Republic (CAR) including child soldiers, as well as Ugandan troops and Angolan UNITA rebels tried but failed to seize Mbandaka, the possession of which was central for any advance down the Ubangi and Congo rivers to Kinshasa. Angolan and Namibian aircraft transported Congolese soldiers to CAR, from where they moved overland into the northern DRC and pushed MLC/Ugandan forces away from the border. The war's only joint rebel offensive kicked off in February 1999. The MLC/Ugandans pushed Kabila's forces back into the CAR and took the town of Gbadolite in July, and the RCD/Rwandans extended their occupation of northern Katanga in mid-March. However, the rebels and their allies lost momentum, and the ambitious objectives of taking Kinshasa and Lubumbashi proved unattainable. Attempting to support the rebel offensive, UNITA forces from Angola advanced toward Mbuji-Mayi from the other direction but withdrew to deal with problems at home.

The war stalemated with a "frontline"; in reality, a series of pockets where enemies faced one another, instead of a continuous war zone, ran from Mbandaka in the northwest though Mbuji-Mayi in the center to Pweto in the southeast. The rebels fared differently as Bemba's MLC gained popularity in the north as people anticipated the return of a friendly regime, but the RCD in the east lacked legitimacy, as it was seen as a Rwandan puppet, and locals suffered continued factional violence. The once strong Rwanda-Uganda alliance, forged in the Ugandan Bush War of the 1980s, deteriorated as their troops and associated rebels fought each other over control of Kisangani in August 1999 and May–June 2000. In addition, war aims in the Congo diverged, as the Ugandan government favored installing a friendly but independent regime in Kinshasa, while Rwanda desired a puppet state. The RCD rebels split into pro-Rwanda RCD-Goma and pro-Uganda RCD-Kisangani factions. All the foreign forces present in the DRC, including those fighting on both sides, intervened or justified their intervention on the basis of security issues, but they all quickly engaged in looting the country's massive natural resources such as minerals related to the growing worldwide electronics industry.

The Lusaka Agreement of July 1999 technically imposed a cease-fire in the DRC to be monitored by the UN Mission in the Democratic Republic of Congo (MONUC). Nevertheless, the continuation of the war delayed the arrival of international peacekeepers. The major Congolese rebel groups and their external partners advanced down different rivers in the direction of Kinshasa: the RCD-Goma/Rwandans on the Tshuapa and the MLC/Ugandans on the Ubangi. In late November 1999, Zimbabwean and Congolese state troops battled their way up the Tshuapa River to relieve a garrison surrounded at Ikela. During the initial six months of 2000, Kabila mounted two offensives up the Ubangi, both of which failed in the face of MLC/Ugandan counterattack. Displaced by the fighting, around 120,000 Congolese civilians sought refuge in the neighboring Republic of the Congo (Congo-Brazzaville). Eventually, the foreign states involved in this Second Congo War tired of its increasing expense and political embarrassment. Kabila's foreign allies became alienated by his continued sabotage of diplomatic efforts to end the conflict, and Rwanda abandoned its objective of installing a subordinate regime in Kinshasa in favor of extracting mineral resources from occupied areas. At the end of the year 2000, the foreign troops in DRC comprised at least 12,000 Zimbabweans, 7,000 Angolans, and 2,000 Namibians who propped up the Kabila administration and 17,000–25,000 Rwandans, along with 10,000 Ugandans.

In January 2001 Kabila was assassinated by his bodyguards, and his son, Joseph Kabila, came to power and revived diplomatic programs to end the war. In addition, the new Bush administration in the United States, free from its predecessor's guilt over the genocide in Rwanda, pressured Rwanda and Uganda to withdraw from the DRC. As a result of negotiations held in 2001 and 2002, and facilitated by Botswana and South Africa, foreign state forces in DRC pulled back from the frontline. In April 2002 Joseph Kabila and the MLC agreed on a united multiparty government and pledged to eventually hold elections. In the Pretoria Accord of July and the Luanda Accord of September, Rwanda and Uganda, respectively, promised to bring their forces home. All external state forces left the DRC by June 2003. In December 2002 all the major internal DRC factions including the Kabila administration, MLC, three different RCD groups, Mai Mai militias, and civil society organizations signed the Global and Inclusive Accord (AGI). This included vows to establish a shared government under a Kabila presidency, integrate armed groups into a new security force structure, and stage elections within two years. The revived MONUC, increasing from 200 peacekeepers in December 2000 to 4,200 at the close of 2002, supervised the withdrawal of foreign troops and oversaw the disarmament and demobilization process for the numerous reluctant foreign rebel factions such as exiled Rwandan Hutu fighters excluded from the AGI. Labeled "negative forces," these groups continued to use the large ungoverned spaces of the eastern DRC as hideouts, engaging in illegal mining and smuggling.

The Second Congo War death toll remains contested. The International Rescue Committee (IRC), an international humanitarian organization that reported on the impact of the conflict, maintained that between August 1998 and November 2002 the war claimed the lives of 3.3 million people, most of whom died from hunger, disease, and displacement related to state collapse. This figure makes "Africa's World War" the world's deadliest conflict since 1945. Subsequently, however, the Canadian-based Human Security Report Project (HSRP) criticized IRC research methodology and assessed the death toll as ranging from several hundred thousand to 800,000 for the longer period between 1998 and 2007. As with regard to other recent African conflicts, human rights advocates face accusations of inflating numbers of deaths to inspire international assistance and intervention.

After the withdrawal of foreign state forces from the DRC in 2002–2003, violence continued in the eastern and northeastern regions of the country. In Ituri province, a new administrative entity in the northeast, fighting commenced between ethnic Hema and Lendu militias, with the former assisted by Rwanda. In the North and South Kivu provinces of the eastern DRC, exiled Hutu militias from Rwanda organized themselves as the Democratic Forces for the Liberation of Rwanda (FDLR), which thereafter provoked further Rwandan military incursions. Additionally, the eastern Congo's Banyamulenge, with the covert sponsorship of Rwanda, rebelled against the Kabila-led DRC administration from 2006 to 2009 under the title of the National Congress for the Defence of the People (CNDP) and from 2012 to 2013 as the March 23 (or M23) movement. During this period, the UN force in the Congo swelled to around 20,000 international troops and tried with mixed results to contend with the various factions. In 2010, MONUC gained the new title of UN Organization Stabilization Mission in the DRC (MONUSCO) to reflect that it now supported an elected government.

Timothy J. Stapleton

See also: Air Power in Postcolonial African Wars; Angolan Conflicts; Burundi, Civil War and Genocide; Central African Republic (CAR), Conflict in; Congo Crisis; Democratic Republic of the Congo (DRC), Continuing Violence in; Diamonds and Conflict in Postcolonial Africa; Genocide in Africa; Hutu Power Movements; Kabila, Joseph; Kabila, Laurent; Kagame, Paul; Mobutu Sese Seko; Museveni, Yoweri; Peacekeeping in Africa; Rwanda, Civil War and Genocide; Rwandan Patriotic Front (RPF); Sudan Civil War, Second; Sudan People's Liberation Movement/Army (SPLM/A); Uganda, Insurgency in the North; Uganda's Civil War: The Bush War.

Further Reading
Prunier, Gerard. *Africa's World War: Congo, the Rwanda Genocide and the Making of a Continental Catastrophe.* Oxford: Oxford University Press, 2009.

Reyntjens, Filip. *The Great African War: Congo and Regional Geopolitics, 1996–2006.* Cambridge: Cambridge University Press, 2009.

Sterns, Jason K. *Dancing in the Glory of Monsters: The Collapse of the Congo and the Great African War.* New York: Public Affairs, 2011.

Turner, Thomas. *The Congo Wars: Conflict, Myth and Reality.* New York: Zed Books, 2007.

Congolese National Liberation Front (FLNC)

See Shaba, Zaire: Rebel Incursions and Foreign Intervention

Côte d'Ivoire Civil War (2002–2011)

Coming to power in the West African country of Côte d'Ivoire after its 1960 independence from France, Felix Houphouet-Boigny maintained close relations with the former colonial power and pursued a free market economic system, continuing the country's reliance on exporting cocoa and coffee. While this approach initially produced favorable economic results, attracting many labor migrants from neighboring countries, the slump of prices for its agricultural goods in the late 1970s and 1980s prompted the state to take on unmanageable international debts that caused economic crisis. The death of Houphouet-Boigny in 1993 precipitated a conflict. By this time about a quarter of Côte d'Ivoire's population, and particularly in the north of the country, comprised first- or second-generation immigrants from poorer states to the north such as Burkina Faso and Mali who had moved south to work in cocoa plantations. Furthermore, and like other West African countries, Côte d'Ivoire was characterized by a predominantly Muslim and relatively marginalized north and a mostly Christian and better-off south, also the location of the economic center of Abidjan. In this post–Cold War period of political reforms in many authoritarian African states, the transition to democracy in Côte d'Ivoire led to controversy over qualifications to vote and hold political office, with popular northern leader Alassane Quattara barred from running for president because of his foreign parentage. This dispute incited xenophobic violence against those considered not "true" Ivoirians.

In September 2002 Côte d'Ivoire's predominantly northern military personnel mutinied, took control of the northern half of the country, and attacked Abidjan, where former military ruler Robert Guei was killed. Taking the name Patriotic Movement of Côte d'Ivoire (MPCI), the northern rebels retained control of their region and established a capital in the city of Bouake. In turn, later in September, France mounted "Operation Unicorn," in which a 4,000-strong French expeditionary force, with UN authorization, moved to separate the northern rebels and supporters of President Laurent Gbagbo in the south. In November two new rebel groups, the Movement of the Ivory Coast of the Great West (MPIGO) and the Movement for Justice and Peace (MJP), occupied the western part of the country. Subsequently, all the rebel groups allied under the banner of the New Forces. In January 2003 representatives of all the factions met in France and agreed to form a unity government, with Gbagbo remaining as president and the rebels assuming ministries of defense and interior. In addition, the agreement stipulated that French troops would maintain a "peace line" between the north and south and that the factions would cooperate to resolve conflicts over citizenship and land rights. In February 2004 the UN established a multinational peacekeeping force called UN Operations in Côte d'Ivoire (ONUCI) to supervise the peace deal. Absorbing regional Economic Community of West African States (ECOWAS) troops already present in Côte d'Ivoire, ONUCI reached a total of around 6,000 personnel by the end of the year and received support from the 4,000 French soldiers of the separate Operation Unicorn.

Delays in implementing the peace process and outbreaks of violence prompted the rebels to withdraw from the unity government by May 2004. Both sides turned against the French. While Gbagbo loyalists criticized them for protecting the rebels and failing to honor previous defense agreements with the Côte d'Ivoire government, the New Forces accused them of preventing their capture of Abidjan. In early November Gbagbo ordered an air strike on the rebel capital of Bouake, but this also hit a French position, killing nine French soldiers and wounding 31. Although Gbagbo claimed this incident had resulted from an accident, French forces seized Yamoussoukro airport and destroyed Gbagbo's air force comprising a few Russian-made ground attack aircraft and helicopter gunships. This immediately incited anti-French riots in Abidjan, with mobs attacking a French school and residential area and erecting roadblocks. Supported by armored vehicles, helicopters, and swift boats positioned at the city's bridges, French troops took control of the city, killing between 20 and 60 people.

The partition of Côte d'Ivoire into northern and southern zones persisted until October–November 2010 when long-delayed elections took place five years after the expiration of Gbagbo's presidential term. Although Quattara obviously won the election and gained international legitimacy, Gbagbo declared himself the victor and refused to leave office, which incited renewed violence in Abidjan. In March 2011 the northern-based New Forces renamed themselves the Republican Forces of Côte d'Ivoire (RFCI) and mounted a major offensive that seized towns and gained a foothold in Abidjan. At the start of April, UN and French helicopters began attacking pro-Gbagbo forces, explaining that this was necessary to protect civilian lives. Given lack of pay resulting from international sanctions, most of Gbagbo's 50,000-strong military deserted, leaving him just 2,000 presidential guards and student supporters to defend the beleaguered presidential palace. During the fighting, it appears that both sides employed mercenaries recruited from neighboring Liberia, which had endured many years of civil war. On April 11, RFCI troops, with military support from the French, stormed Gbagbo's residence and arrested the former president and handed him over to the UN. As a result, Gbagbo was flown to the Hague where he faced International Criminal Court (ICC) charges of crimes against humanity for murder and rape committed by his forces between during late 2010 and early 2011. Seeing this as victor's justice, some claim that supporters of both Quattara and Gbagbo committed massacres during this second phase of Côte d'Ivoire's civil war. In 2019 the ICC dismissed the charges against Gbagbo, given insufficient evidence, and he was released from detention, pending an appeal by the prosecutor. During a peaceful election in 2015, Quattara received strong support for his second presidential term.

Timothy J. Stapleton

See also: ECOWAS Military Interventions; French Military Involvement in Postcolonial Africa; Gbagbo, Laurent.

Further Reading

Collier, Paul. *Wars, Guns and Votes: Democracy in Dangerous Places.* New York: Harper Perennial, 2010.

Hazen, Jennifer. *What Rebels Want: Resources and Supply Networks in Wartime.* Ithaca, NY: Cornell University Press, 2013.

McGovern, Mike. *Making War in Cote d'Ivoire.* Chicago: University of Chicago Press, 2011.

Straus, Scott. *Making and Unmaking Nations: War, Leadership and Genocide in Modern Africa.* Ithaca, NY: Cornell University Press, 2015.

Coups and Military Regimes in Africa

BACKGROUND

Africa's first military coup of the twentieth century occurred in Egypt on July 23, 1952. Gamal Abdel Nasser, an Egyptian military officer, led a contingent of soldiers known as the Free Officers to depose King Farouk. The reason for the coup was to rid Egypt of its royal family and to terminate the British colonial presence there. Four years after Nasser's coup, sub-Saharan Africa (SSA) experienced its first military overthrow of a civilian government on January 13, 1963, in Togo. The coup was conducted by demobilized Togolese soldiers who were once members of the French colonial army. After independence from France in 1960, many of the Togolese French colonial soldiers were denied admission to that country's downsized armed forces. Facing disfranchisement and unemployment, members of this group usurped the government, in the process, murdering President Sylvanus Olympio.

Since postcolonial independence in Africa, there have been more than 80 successful coups d'état and in excess of 108 failed attempts. While these occurrences have manifested themselves continent wide, West Africa has been particularly prone to corporatist military activism, leading to soldiers usurping the state from civilian rule. Of the successful military coups conducted on the African continent to date, more than 40 were conducted in West Africa, with the majority occurring in Ghana and Nigeria. In the early twenty-first century, Africa and particularly West Africa have witnessed a revival of military coups such as in Zimbabwe in 2017; Mali in 2012, 2020, and 2021; Republic of Guinea in 2021; and Burkina Faso in 2022.

THEORY

There are two prevailing thoughts on the reasons why African soldiers were predisposed to intervene in the political affairs of the state.

The first reason promoted by Samuel Huntington, known as a "man on horseback," states that the military reluctantly took control of the country to save it from incompetent and corrupt civilian politicians. Viewing postcolonial African armies as paradigms of "Western" soldierly indoctrination, theorists who ascribed to the "man on horseback" believed that sub-Saharan African armies were cohesive, unselfish national entities, guided by the military discipline of the colonial armies of which they were once a part. As they were agents of perceived virtue and austerity, they could not remain idle while the politicians ruined the country. This argument should have been valid because many of the high-ranking African officers, post colonialism, were indoctrinated into the military traditions of the metropolitan state. African officers attended European military academies, where they learned and copied the style of their instructors. While it is a reality that postcolonial African civilian governments faced many challenges, under scrutiny, the "man on horseback" concept proved to be in contravention of its stated meaning.

The second theory explaining why soldiers were predisposed to activism is that many postcolonial African soldiers were pursuing their own corporatist agenda, stemming from significant structural imbalances in the military and the lack of civil-military relations. The structural imbalance was due to the lack of ethnic diversity in the armies of many African armed forces. At the time of independence in 1960, only one-third of all African armies were ethnically balanced. In other instances, the data regarding the ethnic makeup of the officer corps versus the enlisted ranks were very profound, "resembling data drawn from different countries." This led to a counterproductive situation, creating an atmosphere where soldiers subdivided themselves ethnically within the military, owing their allegiance to senior officers of their ethnicity. This laid the foundation for the theory that is contrary to the "man on horseback" proposition, which states that in most coups in Africa, the military acted out of its corporatist self-interest, due to ethnic rivalries among the officers, self-enrichment, personal motivation, and the army's need for self-preservation as was the case with SSA's first military coup.

To summarize, in order "to understand why there was a disconnect between civilian authority and the defense forces in sub-Saharan African countries, the traditions and postcolonial realities inherited by the military from its role as a colonial army need to be understood—mainly, that they were oriented inward and second, that in most instances postcolonial sub-Saharan African armies were not included in the democratization process at independence. In some instances, the military was not released from the colonial authority until the day of independence. Consequently, the army was not integrated into the national strategy. As a result, two opposing locales of power were manifested in postcolonial African states, the army and the government. Given that the role of the army was not defined and, furthermore, that it was not included in the democratization process, the army followed its own corporatist agenda."

In the aggregate, not every military takeover had an African origin. Some were planned by external entities, and in one rare case—Operation Barracuda—the takeover was conducted by a foreign nation. In the case of the Central African Republic in "Operation Barracuda," the French-led military action that deposed Jean-Bédel Bokassa from power; he himself had come to power through a military coup.

MILITARY REGIMES

There are four types of African military regimes. Their characterizations are usurpers in uniform, caretakers, reformers and redeemers, and praetorian Marxist.

Usurpers, known as personal dictatorships, are recognized by the "personal rule" style of the leader. Idi Amin's military dictatorship in Uganda and Jean-Bédel Bokassa's regime of the Central African Republic are examples of this rule. Caretaker regimes are those in which the military leadership usurped power from the civilian government with the intention of returning the state back to civilian control after they had achieved certain objectives. In some instances, caretakers became reformer and redeemer regimes. These usurpers were determined to stay in power if they deemed their rule necessary to "correct" the state, irrespective of the motivations for overthrowing the government. The Gowon regime in Nigeria progressed from its goal of fighting an anti-secessionist war—the Biafran War—to economic reform, only to itself become embroiled in its own financial catastrophe, brought on by its fiscally irresponsible spending. Praetorian Marxist regimes, by their designation, are those in which usurpers based the reason for their coup on Marxist principles. Just like their counterparts, however, their claim to ideology was derived after the coup. From the first Marxist military regime of Congo-Brazzaville in 1963, to Colonel Nimeiry's Revolutionary Council that came to power in Sudan in 1969 and the Derg that overthrew the monarchy in Ethiopia in 1974, each created their own version of socialism. In Congo-Brazzaville, Captain Ngouabi proclaimed scientific socialism, while in Sudan, Nimeiry embraced Sudanese socialism. In Ethiopia, the Derg evolved from Ethiopia Tikdem—a nationalist identity—to Ethiopian socialism, before orienting toward Marxism-Leninism. All three regimes are characterized by their brutal crackdown of opposition socialist parties. In Ethiopia, Mengistu went so far as to call his Ethiopian People's Revolutionary Party's, EPRP, assault on the left "red terror."

Jacien Carr

See also: Amin, Idi; Bokassa, Jean-Bédel; Barre, Mohamed Siad; Burundi, Civil War and Genocide; Buyoya, Pierre; Central African Republic (CAR), Conflict in; Doe, Samuel; Ethiopia: Insurgency and Interstate War; "Five Majors" Coup, Nigeria; French Military Involvement in Postcolonial Africa; Gaddafi, Muammar; Gowon, Yakubu "Jack" Dan-Yumma; Habyarimana, Juvénal; Mengistu Haile Mariam; Micombero, Michel; Nigerian Civil War; Nasser, Gamal Abdel; Sankara, Thomas.

Further Reading

Decalo, Samuel. *Coups and Army Rule in Africa: Studies in Military Style*. New Haven, CT: Yale University Press, 1976.

Ellis, Stephen. *The Mask of Anarchy: The Destruction of Liberia and the Religious Dimension of an African Civil War*. New York: New York University Press, 2001.

McGowen, Patrick. "African Military Coups d'état, 1956–2001: Frequency, Trends and Distribution." *Journal of Modern African Studies* 41, no. 3 (September 2003): 339–370.

Siollun, Max. *Oil, Politics and Violence: Nigeria's Military Coup Culture (1966–76)*. New York: Algora Publishing, 2009.

Cuba and Africa

After Fidel Castro came to power in 1959, Cuba began to identify with radical African regimes, especially those in Egypt, Ghana, and Guinea in West Africa.

Africans began to go to Cuba to study and for military training. Until the mid-1960s, however, Cuba's interest in Africa was relatively minor. It was only in 1964 that Cuba's attention began to shift from Latin America to Africa, which was now seen as the continent most ripe for revolution. Castro's close associate Ernesto "Che" Guevara began a three-month visit to eight African countries at the end of 1964, and in Congo-Brazzaville, he met with leaders of the Movimento Popular de Libertação de Angola (Popular Movement for the Liberation of Angola, MPLA). Soon afterward, the first Cubans joined the MPLA guerrillas fighting the Portuguese, and a Cuban force fought in the eastern Congo (Zaire/Democratic Republic of the Congo) in support of rebels opposing the government of Moise Tshombe, who was supported by the United States. To the Cubans, Congo seemed the most ripe for revolution and was significant because of its geographical position at the center of the continent. But Cuba began to lose men in the Congo, and by the end of 1966, the small Cuban force had been withdrawn.

For nearly a decade, the only Cuban military presence was in Guinea-Bissau in West Africa, where from 1965 the Cubans worked closely with the Partido Africano da Independência da Guiné e Cabo Verde (PAIGC) in its struggle against the Portuguese. Cuba sent doctors, nurses, and other volunteers to half a dozen other African countries and gave financial assistance, most notably to Tanzania, in the interests of solidarity with the developing world and spreading anti-Western revolution.

It was the collapse of Portuguese rule in Africa in 1974 that led to the most important Cuban intervention on the continent. As the United States and South Africa intervened in Angola on the side of the opponents of the MPLA in late 1975, Castro responded when the MPLA asked for military assistance and sent thousands of Cuban troops, whose intervention saved the MPLA from defeat. The Cuban leader did not act on Soviet orders, but rather, moved independently, although the Soviet Union supported the decision. The Cuban forces halted the South African advance on Luanda in November 1975 and then remained in the country after the MPLA had taken power.

This dramatic and successful Cuban intervention shocked the United States, which for a time feared that Cuba might also intervene in the guerrilla war then being fought in Rhodesia. The Cuban intervention in Angola therefore pushed the Americans into trying to resolve other African conflicts to head off further Cuban interventions.

The next major Cuban military intervention was not in southern Africa but far to the northeast, in Ethiopia, where the regime of Mengistu Haile Mariam, which proclaimed itself Marxist and revolutionary, was being threatened by neighboring Somalia, which was backed by the United States. This time the Cubans did coordinate their actions with the Soviet Union. In 1978 some 16,000 Cuban combat troops helped the Ethiopians beat back the invading Somali army in the Ogaden and consolidated Mengistu's hold on power. Although Cuban forces in Ethiopia then withdrew, those stationed in Angola remained and were augmented by an additional 15,000 men in 1987, bringing the total of Cubans there to more than 50,000.

From 1981, President Ronald Reagan maintained as a major goal the total withdrawal of Cuban forces from Angola although, ironically, some of the Cuban forces were deployed to protect American oil interests in the Cabinda enclave. Reagan's assistant secretary for African affairs, Chester Crocker, advocated linking a Cuban withdrawal from Angola to a South African withdrawal from Namibia. For many years Angola and Cuba refused to link the two issues and insisted that the Cuban presence in Angola was a matter solely for the two countries.

It was when Castro escalated the Cuban presence in Angola in late 1987, in response to a South African incursion, that Cuban forces, fighting alongside their Angolan allies, prevented the South African Army from capturing Cuito Cuanavale and at the same time moved south, close to the Namibian border. By building new airfields there, the Cubans ensured that the South Africans lost air superiority in the border area. This military pressure helped force the South Africans to the negotiating table, and in December 1988, after lengthy negotiations, the South Africans agreed to withdraw from Namibia in return for the withdrawal of all Cuban forces from Angola. This was seen as a major victory for the United States in the waning years of the Cold War.

Cuba then helped supervise the withdrawal of South African forces from Namibia by serving on a joint commission along with the United States and the Soviet Union. A United Nations mission monitored the withdrawal of Cuban troops from Angola, and the last contingent left Africa in 1991. After that, Cuba's role on the continent was chiefly diplomatic, although it continued to supply medical and other personnel to a number of African countries.

Christopher Saunders

See also: Angolan Conflicts; Cabindan Insurgency; Cold War in Africa; Congo Crisis; Cuito Cuanavale, Battle of; Ethiopia: Insurgency and Interstate War; Mengistu Haile Mariam; Namibia Independence War; National Union for the Total Independence of Angola (UNITA); Ogaden War; Popular Movement for the Liberation of Angola (MPLA); Portuguese Africa, Independence Wars (Angola, Mozambique, and Guinea-Bissau); Quifangondo, Battle of; Soviet Military Involvement in Africa; U.S. Military Involvement in Africa.

Further Reading

Dominguez, Jorge. *To Make a World Safe for Revolution: Cuba's Foreign Policy.* Cambridge, MA: Harvard University Press, 1989.

Gleijeses, Piero. *Conflicting Missions: Havana, Washington, and Africa, 1959–1976.* Chapel Hill: University of North Carolina Press, 2003.

Gleijeses, Piero. *Visions of Freedom: Havana, Washington, Pretoria, and the Struggle for Southern Africa, 1976–1991.* Chapel Hill: University of North Carolina Press, 2013.

Hatzky, Christine. *Cubans in Angola: South-South Cooperation and the Transfer of Knowledge, 1976–1991.* Madison: University of Wisconsin Press, 2015.

Polack, Peter. *The Last Hot Battle of the Cold War: South Africa vs. Cuba in the Angolan Civil War.* Oxford: Casemate, 2013.

Cuito Cuanavale, Battle of (1988)

Cuito Cuanavale is a small town in southern Angola at the confluence of the Cuito and Cuanavale Rivers. Heavy fighting took place near what was then merely a village during the latter period of active foreign intervention in the Angolan Civil War—a conflict running to a large extent concurrently with what in white South Africa was known as the Border War. Between August 1987 and April 1988, two multinational forces fought a series of engagements from the Lomba River in southeastern Angola back to the Cuito Cuanavale area to the northwest of the region.

The opposing sides: During the fighting around Cuito Cuanavale in late 1987 and early 1988, although those forces on the offensive toward the village were nominally headed by UNITA (*União Nacional para a Independência Total de Angola* or National Union for the Total Independence of Angola), on the ground, they were spearheaded by the South African Defence Force (SADF), which had intervened in the fighting in the region in order to prevent the collapse of their UNITA allies. UNITA and the SADF were covertly backed by the United States and equipped with a mix of South African–manufactured, captured Soviet, and U.S.-supplied weapons, along with those from a variety of sources in the South African inventory, for which new equipment was limited by international sanctions. Opposing them were the forces of Angola's MPLA (*Movimento Popular de Libertação de Angola* or Popular Movement for the Liberation of Angola) government, whose armed forces were known by the abbreviation FAPLA (*Forças Armadas Populares de Libertação de Angola* or People's Armed Forces for the Liberation of Angola). FAPLA was supported by a significant contingent of Soviet "advisers"—to be joined later by sizeable Cuban forces—along with elements of SWAPO (South West Africa People's Organization), all equipped predominately with Soviet weapons. The African National Congress's military organization, *Umkhonto we Sizwe*, played little part in the conventional fighting in southern Angola during this period, but stood to gain from the defeat of UNITA in the sense of subsequently being in a stronger position to strike at South African territory. In the white South African historiography dominated by former members of the SADF, the Angolan government side in the fighting is typically associated with communism, although increasingly self-identified as forces for Black "national liberation" with at least some socialist credentials—provided with strong backing from the Soviet-backed international socialist camp. Conversely, although self-identifying as anti-communist forces, the SADF-UNITA alliance was increasingly associated by opponents with the maintenance of apartheid in South Africa and its extension into South African–occupied Namibia.

The Battle: Advocates for both sides agree that the fighting that is typically encompassed by "the Battle for Cuito Cuanavale" began in earnest in August with the blunting of a Soviet-backed FAPLA offensive toward the town of Mavinga in southeastern Angola that had begun in July 1987—Operation *Saudando Outubro*. This operation was undertaken with a view to subsequently pushing on to Jamba and destroying UNITA in Angola. As FAPLA forces made progress toward their objective, UNITA alone was unable to offer sufficient resistance to bring the offensive to a halt. Consequently, South African and South African-backed Namibian territorial troops—that soon made up a brigade-strength force—were launched in Operation Moduler to intervene in support of their UNITA allies. As multiple FAPLA brigades attempted to cross the Lomba River, they were successfully engaged and indeed one brigade routed by what was nominally a joint SADF and UNITA effort. Subsequently, badly mauled FAPLA forces began falling back to the northwest on the village of Cuito Cuanavale with its important airfield. The SADF, supported by UNITA, pressed home its advantage in what had now become Operation Hooper—apparently intent on capturing Cuito Cuanavale, not per se, but as an inevitable consequence of or requirement for routing FAPLA in the area. With the threat of a FAPLA collapse in the region, Fidel Castro's Cuba made the decision to commit significant forces to the battle in November 1987 as part of Operation *Maniobra XXXI Anniversario*. Castro's decision seems to have at least initially been made without Soviet sanction. Cuban operations soon, however, received Soviet backing despite Mikhail Gorbachev's "new thinking" in Soviet foreign policy that entailed a de-escalation of Cold War proxy conflicts between the superpowers. In addition to advisers, translators, and specialists on the ground in Angola, the Soviet Union proved willing to rapidly provide Cuba with significant quantities of arms to replace those being sent to Angola and that were deemed to be required for the defense of Cuba from possible U.S. action. The further commitment of Cuban forces to Angola took the total number of Cuban troops in the country from about 38,000 in November 1987 to 55,000 in August 1988, along with the best of the equipment then available to Cuban forces. In the face of dug-in combined Cuban-FAPLA forces, the SADF and its allies were unable to make further progress and either gain significant ground or destroy the enemy forces. South African qualitative superiority in long-range artillery and armor was to a considerable extent countered by FAPLA/Cuban numbers and the liberal use of mines. In the air neither side could claim sustained air superiority, although the close proximity of Cuban-FAPLA air resources at Menongue (with the airfield at Cuito Cuanavale unusable due to South African artillery) gave them an advantage in terms of being able to acquire air superiority. This Cuban-FAPLA advantage did not, however, translate into significant damage to the SADF forces even if this airpower was at times a constraint on SADF activity. South African airpower was hampered by the fielding of considerable and up-to-date antiaircraft assets by Cuban-FAPLA forces. Ultimately, after a further short-lived South African operation—Operation Packer—the bulk of SADF forces were pulled back into Namibia from the end of April 1988. By this time Cuban forces had for the first time taken up positions close to the Namibian border in the west and threatened to intervene to the south in support of SWAPO.

Outcomes: This commitment of Cuban forces not only prevented the SADF and UNITA from destroying FAPLA forces in the area around Cuito Cuanavale, but also saw a Cuban offensive further to the west push on to the border of South African–controlled Namibia. Whether the intention of SADF forces had been to take Cuito Cuanavale or not—a claim denied by SADF sources despite evidence to the contrary—the South African operational objective after the defeat of FAPLA forces on the Lomba to press home their advantage and effectively route FAPLA in the region was not achieved, although the initial goal for intervention—to prevent the collapse of UNITA in southern Angola—had been. On the FAPLA side, while the offensive toward Mavinga and Jamba intended to crush UNITA in southern Angola had failed, the introduction of Cuban forces had ensured that the SADF and its ally UNITA could not exploit an initially favorable situation in order to strengthen UNITA's position in the region. Heavy fighting in the region of Cuito Cuanavale saw both sides get bogged down in what was by the standards of warfare in the region particularly conventional in nature. Both sides in the fighting suffered heavy casualties but particularly FAPLA with thousands of killed and wounded. While some SADF commanders might have hoped to continue their operations in the Cuito Cuanavale region beyond April, doing so would not only have increased the number of politically sensitive white South African casualties, but also left the SADF with the issue of what to do about Cuban forces to the west. Despite having been in Angola since 1975, this was the first time that Cuban forces had threatened to cross the Namibian border. There are unsubstantiated claims in the white South African literature on the war that fear of South African nuclear weapons constrained Cuban forces on the Namibian border, where the Soviet Union also sought to reign in Cuban forces that had achieved the objective of preventing a FAPLA collapse.

Longer-term consequences: The significance of the fighting around Cuito Cuanavale is heavily contested in the literature. Opponents of the apartheid regime in South Africa and its Angolan UNITA allies such as Nelson Mandela and Fidel Castro subsequently hailed the battle as a turning point in the struggle not only for Angolan security and Namibian independence through the December 1988 "New York Accords," but also for an end to apartheid in South Africa. SADF veterans have, however, tended to see the battle both as a victory for South African arms and as instrumental in forcing the withdrawal of Cuban forces from Angola and hence bringing an end to the threat of communist expansion in the region. Despite the exit of both Cubans and South African forces from Angola, the failure of the MPLA and UNITA to settle their differences after subsequent internationally brokered elections in Angola in 1992 would see the extension of the Angolan Civil War until the death of UNITA's leader, Jonas Savimbi, at the hands of government forces in 2002.

Alexander Hill

See also: Angolan Armed Forces (FAPLA and FAA); Angolan Conflicts; Cold War in Africa; Cuba and Africa; Namibia Independence War; National Union for the Total Independence of Angola (UNITA); Popular Movement for the Liberation of Angola (MPLA); South Africa's Border War; Soviet Military Involvement in Africa.

Further Reading

Baines, Gary. *South Africa's "Border War": Contested Narratives and Conflicting Memories*. London: Bloomsbury, 2014.

Gleijeses, Piero. *Visions of Freedom: Havana, Washington, Pretoria, and the Struggle for Southern Africa, 1976–1991*. Chapel Hill: University of South Carolina Press, 2013.

Kasrils, Ronnie. "Cuito Cuanavale, Angola: 25th Anniversary of a Historic African Battle." *Monthly Review: An Independent Socialist Magazine* (April 2013): 44–51.

Oosthuizen, Gerhard. "The South African Defence Force and Operation Hooper, Southeast Angola, December 1987 to March 1988." *Scientia Militaria: South African Journal of Military Studies* 42 (2014): 84–116.

Scholtz, Leopold. "The South African Strategic and Operational Objectives in Angola, 1987–88." *Scientia Militaria: South African Journal of Military Studies* 38, no. 1 (2010): 68–98.

Shubin, Vladimir. *The Hot "Cold War": The USSR in Southern Africa.* London: Pluto Press, 2008.

Velthuizen, Andreas. "The Significance of the Battle for Cuito Cuanavale: Long-Term Foresight of the Current Strategic Landscape." *Scientia Militaria: South African Journal of Military Studies* 37, no. 2 (2009): 107–123.

Darfur Genocide

In the first years of the twenty-first century, the Sudanese government, aided by Arab militias known as the Janjaweed, carried out a campaign of terror, economic destruction, rape, and murder against the non-Arab "Black Africans" of Sudan's Darfur region. Although labeling the Sudanese government's actions as genocide has proved highly controversial, it is clear that Darfur was and continues to be a hotspot of human rights violations.

Darfur, a region roughly the size of France, is located in the western part of Sudan, bordering Libya, Chad, and the Central African Republic. Prior to the outbreak of violence in 2003, Darfur's population was approximately six million people, consisting of between 40 and 90 different tribal groups, of which 39 percent were considered "Arab" and 61 percent were considered "non-Arab" or "Black African." Due to intermarriage, the distinction between "Arabs" and "non-Arabs" or "Black Africans" owes more to lifestyle differences and cultural affiliation than race. Darfuri Arabs tend to lead nomadic lives, herding cattle and camels throughout the region, while non-Arabs tend to be sedentary farmers. One exception is the Zaghawa, a non-Arab tribe that herds camels.

In late February 2003, conflict erupted in Darfur when two Darfuri rebel movements—the Sudan Liberation Army (SLA) and the Justice and Equality Movement (JEM)—attacked government military installations in Gulu, the capital of the Jebel Marrah province. The SLA and JEM were rising up against the Sudanese government's economic, political, and social marginalization of populations living in the peripheries of Sudan. In response, Sudan's regular armed forces, inclusive of the Popular Defense Force (PDF) and the intelligence services, and government-backed Arab militias, namely the Janjaweed, launched a brutal campaign targeting non-Arab Darfuri tribes suspected of supporting the rebels.

Notably, while many point to February 2003 as the beginning of the conflict that bore the genocide in Darfur, the region had been gripped by violence prior to that date. Indeed, government attacks against non-Arab communities around Darfur were on the rise beginning as early as 2001. Prior to that, in the late 1980s, a coalition of Arab nomads initiated attacks against Fur sedentary farmers after the latter began fencing in land, hindering nomadic migrations. These early conflicts galvanized Darfur's population across tribal lines, pitting Arab nomads against non-Arabs. The Sudanese government capitalized on this division in its campaign to eradicate non-Arab support to Darfuri rebel groups during the genocide.

The victims of the Darfur genocide are primarily from three non-Arab ethnic groups: the Fur, the Zaghawa, and the Massaliet. Eyewitness accounts describe how Sudanese government forces and Janjaweed militias swept into Fur, Zaghawa, and Massaliet villages on horse- or camelback, wielding automatic weapons and firing indiscriminately at civilians. Homes, grain stores, and crops were destroyed, while women, children, and the elderly were whipped, raped, tortured, and, in some instances, ultimately murdered. These tactics were designed to terrorize victims, forcing them to flee their homelands for displaced persons camps within Darfur or refugee camps in neighboring Chad. Once gone, Arab populations would resettle the land, effectively eradicating the rebels' power base.

Initial reaction to the conflict in Darfur was inadequate, as bystanders such as the United Nations (UN), the United States, and the European Union (EU) chose to prioritize other foreign policy issues over the escalating crisis in Darfur—in particular, the ongoing negotiation process between the government of Sudan and southern Sudan's Sudan People's Liberation Movement/Army (SPLM/A). It was not until late 2004 that the international response became more pointed against the government of Sudan. However, by that time, genocide had already occurred and, perhaps, was still ongoing in Darfur.

Not all bystanders to the conflict were inactive. Indeed, throughout the Darfur conflict, the governments of Russia and China provided support to the Sudanese government in the form of arms sales, investment, and the purchase of Sudanese oil. Meanwhile, Darfuri rebel groups sought, and largely won, the support of Chadian president Idriss Déby Itno and the SPLM/A.

Some observers, most prominently the U.S. government, called the Sudanese government's violent and targeted campaign against non-Arab Darfuris a "genocide," while others, including the UN, have refrained from using that term to describe the conflict in Darfur. Regardless, the conflict has had and continues to have devastating consequences for the Darfuri people. By 2008, the UN estimated that between 200,000 and 300,000 people had died in Darfur, and 2.7 million more were displaced. As of late June 2012, 1.7 million people lived in internally displaced persons (IDP) camps in Darfur, and an additional 264,000 resided in refugee camps in Chad. The United Nations High Commissioner for Refugees (UNHCR) reports that the majority of these refugees are reluctant to return to Darfur due to instability in the region.

The suffering of the Darfuri people, coupled with the U.S. government's declaration that genocide had occurred in Darfur, galvanized U.S.-based advocacy organizations, such as the Save Darfur network and the Enough Project, cofounded by John Prendergast, which initiated vociferous and largely effective campaigns designed to raise awareness of the situation in Darfur and encourage individuals and corporations to divest their assets from Sudan. There were, as well, calls for the U.S. government to enhance its existing sanctions against the government of Sudan. In May 2007, President George W. Bush imposed sanctions on Sudanese citizens implicated in the Darfur conflict and Sudanese government–owned or controlled companies.

The UN Security Council, in three successive resolutions passed between 2004 and 2010, has imposed a sanctions regime that precludes UN member states from supplying arms, technical training, or assistance to any actor operating in Darfur. On March 31, 2005, the UN Security Council adopted Resolution 1593, which referred the situation in Darfur, since July 1, 2002, to the prosecutor of the

International Criminal Court (ICC). The referral permitted the ICC prosecutor to initiate investigations into whether Sudanese government officials, rebel leaders, and other actors had committed war crimes, crimes against humanity, crimes of aggression, and genocide.

Since April 2007, the ICC has issued arrest warrants for four current and former Sudanese government officials for their alleged involvement in crimes committed against the people of Darfur: Ahmad Muhammad Harun, Ali Muhammad Ali Abd-Al-Rahman (Ali Kushayb), Omar Hassan Ahmad al-Bashir, and Abdel Raheem Muhammad Hussein. Notably, three of these officials, Bashir, Harun, and Hussein continue to hold prominent positions within the Sudanese government and are suspected of committing further atrocities against Sudanese civilians of the Nuba tribe in the Nuba Mountains within the context of an ongoing conflict with the Sudan Revolutionary Front (SRF), which began in June 2011.

While the fighting and atrocities committed against civilian populations reached their highest levels in the period from 2003 to 2006, insecurity within Darfur continues today, despite the presence of a hybrid UN-African Union peacekeeping force (UNAMID) and the conclusion of two, largely unimplemented, peace agreements. Violence has continued in Darfur despite the fall of the Al-Bashir regime in 2019.

Jennifer Christian

See also: Al-Bashir, Omar (Umar) Hassan Ahmad; Chad, Conflict in; Genocide in Africa; Janjaweed; Justice and Equality Movement (JEM); Peacekeeping in Africa; Sudan Civil War, Second; Sudan Liberation Army (SLA); Sudan People's Liberation Movement/Army (SPLM/A).

Further Reading
Flint, Julie, and Alex de Waal. *Darfur: A Short History of a Long War.* London: Zed Books, 2006.
Hamilton, Rebecca. *Fighting for Darfur: Public Action and the Struggle to Stop Genocide.* London: Palgrave Macmillan, 2011.
Mamdani, Mahmood. *Survivors and Saviors: Darfur, Politics and the War on Terror.* New York: Double Day, 2009.
Prunier, Gerard. *Darfur: The Ambiguous Genocide.* Ithaca, NY: Cornell University Press, 2005.

Déby, Idriss (1952-2021)

A former military commander under Hissène Habré, Idriss Déby and his Patriotic Salvation Movement (MPS) toppled Habré's government in Chad in December 1990 with the help of Libyan leader Muammar Gaddafi. Déby, who became president, has since faced continual opposition from forces loyal to Habré.

The son of a shepherd, Déby was born in the country's northeastern Fada region in 1952. He is a member of the Zaghawa ethnic group. After earning an undergraduate degree, Déby attended N'Djamena's school of officers, completing the officer cadet course in 1975. The following year he was sent to France for fighter pilot training. He returned to Chad shortly thereafter and joined Habré's guerilla movement.

Habré, an enemy of Libya who was backed by France and other opponents of Gaddafi, first took power in 1982. During Habré's presidency, Déby served first as the commander in chief of the army and later as an adviser. In April 1989, Déby was accused of taking part in a plot to overthrow Habré. Before he could be arrested, however, he fled to Sudan, eventually ending up in Libya. There he organized a rebel group that called itself Action du 1 Avril (April 1 Action). This group then merged with others opposed to Habré to form a group that later became Déby's MPS. Déby and the MPS attacked Chad in March 1990, though at first, French backing for Habré thwarted their efforts. In December 1991, the MPS finally forced Habré to flee to Senegal.

After taking power, Déby and the MPS accused Habré of human rights violations and promised to improve the situation in Chad. The MPS suspended the constitution put in place under Habré and adopted a new transitional national charter on March 1, 1991, under which Déby became president three days later. But soon after coming to power, Déby faced opposition from supporters of Habré, who attacked military garrisons in the north in September. At the same time, relations with Libya became strained, and human rights organizations began to accuse Déby's regime of abuses. In April 1993, a sovereign national conference adopted a transitional charter and set the groundwork for an interim legislature. Under the terms of the charter, Déby was to continue as head of state until the holding of multiparty elections. Déby emerged victorious in the July 1996 second round of presidential balloting. The vote was boycotted by much of the opposition, however, and Déby's government remained widely unpopular. Amid claims of electoral fraud by opposition leaders, Déby was reelected president in May 2001 and again in May 2006, April 2011, and April 2016.

Since 2005, the rebel alliance the United Front for Democratic Change posed the greatest challenge to Déby's hold on power, intermittently taking control of Chadian villages and allegedly staging a coup attempt in March 2006. The United Nations has supported Déby's claims that the rebel alliance receives backing from the Sudanese government in an attempt to overthrow his administration. Sudan has denied that it provides the rebels with support. In April 2010, in a positive development for relations between the countries, the Sudan-Chad border reopened after negotiations between Déby and Sudanese leader Omar al-Bashir. In April 2021, Deby was killed in action while leading troops against northern rebels from the Front for Change and Concord in Chad (FACT).

ABC-CLIO

See also: Al-Bashir, Omar (Umar) Hassan Ahmad; Chad, Conflict in; Darfur Genocide; French Military Involvement in Postcolonial Africa; Gaddafi, Muammar; Habré, Hissène.

Further Reading

Azevedo, Mario J., and Emmanuel U. Nnadozie. *Chad: A Nation in Search of Its Future.* New York: Routledge, 2018.

Azevedo, Mario J., and Samuel Decalo. *Historical Dictionary of Chad.* Lanham, MD: Rowman & Littlefield, 2018.

Democratic Forces for the Liberation of Rwanda (FDLR)

See Congo Wars; Democratic Republic of the Congo (DRC), Continuing Violence in; Hutu Power Movements

Democratic Republic of the Congo (DRC), Continuing Violence in (2002–2020)

Although "Africa's World War" or the "Second Congo War" ended in 2002–2003 with the withdrawal of foreign forces and the engagement of the main domestic factions in a peace process, violence continued in the eastern Democratic Republic of the Congo (DRC). The years of foreign occupation created a deadly legacy in parts of the DRC. In 1999, the Ugandan military occupying Congo's northeastern Orientale province founded a separate local administration for the eastern part of this area, which became the new Ituri province. In this area, the earlier Belgian colonial state and Mobutu's dictatorship favored the pastoral Hema people over the Lendu farmers, turning the former into a local administrative and economic elite. During the 1998–2002 war, the Ugandan Army occupying the area also appeared to favor the Hema community, thereby exacerbating existing tensions. In 2001, in Ituri, the eastern Congolese rebel faction known as the Rally for Congolese Democracy-Kisangani (RCD-K) divided into a supposedly pro-Hema RCD-ML (Liberation Movement) and the allegedly pro-Lendu rump of RCD-K. Although both sides accused each other of harboring genocidal intensions, control of the province's valuable mineral resources such as gold provided a strong motivation for conflict. Around 2002, given the upcoming departure of their Ugandan sponsors, Hema militias accepted military assistance from Rwanda, which wanted to access Ituri's mineral wealth and counter Ugandan influence in the area. Rwanda and Uganda invaded the DRC as allies in 1998 but quickly fell out over division of the spoils of war. Hema leaders compared their people to Rwanda's Tutsi, a similarly historic pastoral identity and the victims of genocide in 1994, and their local Lendu enemies to Rwanda's Hutu Power movement that had perpetrated genocide. Conversely, Lendu militias accused Uganda and Rwanda of trying to impose a Tutsi-Hema empire on the region and seeking to exterminate other people.

The withdrawal of the Ugandan military from the Ituri province in the first half of 2003 resulted in increased violence between Hema and Lendu militias. Around the same time, representatives of the historically marginalized Mbuti Twa (pygmy) minority reported to the United Nations that their community had become subject to genocide and cannibalism by various Congolese factions, including the Movement for the Liberation of Congo (MLC) and local Ituri militias. In April 2003, the United Nations Organization Mission in the Democratic Republic of the Congo (MONUC) deployed a Uruguayan battalion in Bunia, but it proved insufficient to stop the fighting. In June, around Bunia, Lendu militias and the Hema-oriented Union of Congolese Patriots (UPC) led by Thomas Lubanga Dyilo, a former Ugandan ally now sponsored by Rwanda, fought each other, causing thousands of civilians to flee to the local MONUC headquarters and airport. Hema and Lendu militias massacred civilians of the other ethnicity. With UN officials warning of impending genocide in Ituri, the European Union mounted its first autonomous military operation (Operation Artemis) outside Europe. Approved by the UN, the Interim Emergency Multinational Force (IEMF), comprising mostly French troops arrived in Bunia and secured the town but did not disarm the militias. While MONUC's new Ituri Brigade replaced the IEMF in September and declared Bunia a "weapons-free" zone, violence resumed in October and continued into the next year. In 2005 MONUC embarked on aggressive cordon-and-search operations against the Ituri factions, resulting in the disarming of 15,600 out of about 20,000 fighters. In February 2007, the Lendu-oriented Nationalist and Integrationist Front (FNI) became the last Ituri militia to start surrendering weapons to UN officials. Nevertheless, in subsequent years, new armed factions involved in mineral smuggling clashed with DRC government forces trying to control the province. In March 2005, the UPC's Lubanga Dyilo became the first person ever arrested on an International Criminal Court (ICC) warrant. Sent to the Hague in the Netherlands, the Hema militia leader was convicted of conscripting child soldiers and served a 14-year prison sentence. Germain Katanga and Mathieu Ngudjolo Chui, pro-Lendu militia leaders, were handed over to the ICC by DRC authorities in 2007 and 2008, respectively, and charged with crimes against humanity and war crimes for the 2003 massacres of Hema. The ICC released Chui in 2012 given lack of evidence, and Katanga was convicted two years later.

The 2002 Pretoria Agreement, in which the DRC government promised to stop supporting exiled Rwandan rebels and the Rwanda government withdrew its forces from DRC, failed to end conflict between the predominantly Tutsi state in Rwanda and exiled Rwandan Hutu groups based in the South Kivu and North Kivu provinces of the eastern Congo. While Rwanda's military had defeated the exiled Hutu movement called the Army for the Liberation of Rwanda (ALIR) during its 1998 invasion of the DRC, the 2001–2002 peace process provided an opportunity for the Hutu fighters who had been mobilized by the Kabila regime during the war to reestablish themselves as the Democratic Forces for the Liberation of Rwanda (FDLR). After the DRC government stopped official support for the FDLR as part of the 2002 peace deal, these Hutu rebels acquired weapons and ammunition from the local Mai Mai militia and corrupt Congolese military officers. The Rwanda Defence Forces (RDF) officially evacuated DRC in September 2002 but left behind a small covert element to combat exiled Hutu militants and continue the acquisition of the Congo's valuable resources. In addition, the Rwanda government convinced some senior officers of the FDLR to leave their organization and join the RDF, and between 2003 and 2007, some 7,000 Hutu fighters returned home as part of a reconciliation project. However, the continued presence of around 5,000 FDLR rebels in the eastern DRC provided the Rwandan state with an ongoing excuse to engage in cross-border operations.

Some Congolese Tutsi (often called Banyamulenge) officers from RCD-Goma, a client of Rwanda during the 1998–2002 war and now encouraged by Kigali, refused integration into the Congo's new military and claimed to defend local Tutsi civilians from the genocidal FDLR. In May 2003 General Laurent Nkunda, a Congolese Tutsi veteran of the Rwandan Patriotic Front (RPF) campaign in

Rwanda that stopped the 1994 genocide and secured control of that state, led mutinous Congolese Tutsi troops from Goma in North Kivu to Bukavu in South Kivu where they killed soldiers and civilians and raped and looted, as MONUC peacekeepers did nothing. After Nkunda's forces left Bukavu, a result of UN, American, and British diplomatic pressure on Rwanda, the returning Congolese troops took revenge on local Banyamulenge, with 3,000 escaping to Rwanda. In late 2004, the Rwandan military crossed the border to attack the FDLR and supplied weapons to Nkunda's fighters, enabling them to repel a Congolese Army offensive, with over 100,000 civilians displaced by the fighting. Around the 10th anniversary of the Rwanda genocide, Nkunda told the international media that he wanted to prevent a similar genocide of the Tutsi in the DRC. In 2005 and 2006, UN and Congolese forces mounted offensive operations against the FDLR, but the rebels survived by moving deeper into the forest. Enlarging their territory in North Kivu, Nkunda's Banyamulenge mutineers sought legitimacy by establishing the National Congress for the Defence of the People (CNDP), which claimed to protect minorities in the eastern DRC.

Following his group's defeat of another Congolese military offensive in 2008, Nkunda signed a peace deal, including a cease-fire, the return of civilians to their homes, and amnesty for combatants. However, the issue of FDLR disarmament remained unresolved. Nkunda's peace treaty with the Congolese government did not last long, as in late October 2008 the CNDP renewed hostilities by seizing a military camp near the Virunga National Park and using it as a staging area for a southward advance toward the city of Goma. Congolese and UN soldiers ran away, leaving local Mai Mai militia and FDLR to defend the area, and 100,000 people fled their homes. The CNDP split in January 2009 with General Bosco "The Terminator" Ntaganda, a Congolese Tutsi and veteran of the early 1990s RPF, leading a faction that agreed to merge into the Congolese military and transform their organization into a political party. Incapable of defeating the CNDP militarily, the DRC's Joseph Kabila administration made a deal with Rwanda to allow its soldiers to cross the border to engage the exiled Hutu FDLR if they also removed Nkunda. Subsequently, in early 2009, a combined Congolese Army-RDF operation that cleared rebels, including FDLR from the border area, defeated Nkunda's remaining forces. Fleeing into Rwanda, the fugitive general was arrested and never seen again. In the eastern DRC, the Hutu fighters of FDLR regrouped, attacked villages, and fought the Congolese Army in South Kivu.

In April 2012, given rumors of their transfer out of their home province of North Kivu and of impending ICC charges, Ntaganda and several hundred former CNDP fighters mutinied from the Congolese Army. Naming themselves the March 23 Movement, or M23, in commemoration of the day in 2009 when they joined the political process, the mutineers assembled in the Virunga National Park under the military leadership of Colonel Sultani Makenga and then captured several towns near Goma. In November 2012 M23 fighters temporarily seized Goma, suddenly abandoned by Congolese and UN troops, where they captured heavy weapons and ammunition. The Rwandan government denied international accusations that it was supplying M23, and this soured Kigali's relations with the UN and the United States. Facing dissent within his movement and loss of support from Rwanda, Ntaganda surrendered himself to the American embassy in Kigali in March 2013, and he was eventually transported to the ICC to face charges related to earlier violence. In November 2013, a UN special intervention brigade comprising South African, Tanzanian, and Malawian troops together with Congolese forces mounted an offensive that routed the M23 movement, with many of its fighters fleeing into nearby Uganda. Convicted of war crimes by the ICC in 2019, Ntaganda became the first person convicted of the crime of sexual slavery, and his 30-year prison term represented the longest sentence imposed by the court.

Continuing to operate in parts of the eastern DRC, the FDLR engaged in illegal mining, charcoal production, and smuggling, facilitated by Congolese military personnel. At the start of 2009, the armed forces of the DRC and Rwanda conducted the joint Operation Umoja Wetu (Our Unity) against the FDLR, but this failed to make much of an impact. By the late 2000s, the ordinary FDLR fighters mostly comprised displaced and impoverished youth with no history of involvement in the 1994 genocide in Rwanda. Nevertheless, FDLR military commander General Sylvestre Mudacumura served as deputy commander of the Rwandan presidential guard during the 1994 genocide, assisted the Kabila regime during the "Second Congo War" of 1998–2002, and became the subject of a 2012 international warrant for war crimes committed in the eastern DRC. Some of the FDLR's European-based political leaders faced prosecution for crimes committed in the DRC. Arrested in Germany in 2009, FDLR leaders Ignace Murwanashyaka and Straton Musoni were eventually convicted of crimes against humanity and war crimes by a German court and sentenced to 13 and 8 years imprisonment, respectively. In 2011 Callixte Mbarushimana, FDLR secretary, was arrested in France and sent to the ICC in the Hague to answer similar charges, but these were dropped because of insufficient evidence. In late February 2015, given a demand by international regional leaders for the FDLR to disarm, the Congolese Armed Forces mounted an offensive against the Hutu group, though UN support was withheld over the alleged involvement of some Congolese commanders in atrocities. In subsequent years, FDLR continued to engage in violence in the eastern Congo such as in 2019 when the Hutu rebels ambushed and killed rangers in Virunga National Park and engagements with the Congolese Army, which resulted in the death of Mudacumura.

Exiled rebels from Uganda also sought sanctuary in the vast and underdeveloped region of the eastern DRC. During the 1990s, rebel groups from northern Uganda such as the Lord's Resistance Army (LRA) and the West Nile Bank Front (WNBF) used parts of eastern Zaire (now DRC) as staging areas where they received support from the Sudan government and mounted attacks inside Uganda. Sudan backed these fighters, given the Uganda state's sponsorship of rebels in southern Sudan. In 1996, Sudanese agents in Zaire facilitated the creation of the Allied Democratic Forces (ADF) from three different groups of Ugandan dissidents: alienated Ugandan Muslims, right-wing Baganda monarchists, and long-term rebels from the Ruwenzori Mountains of western Uganda. The activities of these groups prompted the Ugandan military interventions in eastern Zaire/DRC in 1996–1997 and 1998–2003. While the WNBF did not survive the "Second

Congo War," the ADF evolved into an illegal mining operation based in DRC's North Kivu province and occasionally conducted raids and bombings inside Uganda. From the mid-2000s into the 2010s, repeated operations by the Congolese Armed Forces, supported by the UN and sometimes the Ugandan military, inflicted casualties on the ADF but failed to eliminate it. From around 2016 and 2017, ADF appeared to step up the violence, including a massacre in the town of Beni and an attack on UN peacekeepers from Tanzania. Uganda's government links ADF with the international Islamist extremism, including groups like Somalia's Al-Shabaab and Al-Qaeda, but the evidence for this is far from conclusive. Despite the continued UN presence, conflict in the eastern DRC involving groups like FDLR and ADF hampered the international medical response to an Ebola outbreak in that region in 2018–2019.

Timothy J. Stapleton

See also: Child Soldiers in Africa; Congo Crisis; Congo Wars; French Military Involvement in Postcolonial Africa; Genocide in Africa; Hutu Power Movements; Kabila, Joseph; Lord's Resistance Army (LRA); Museveni, Yoweri; Peacekeeping in Africa; Uganda, Insurgency in the North.

Further Reading
Autesserre, Séverine. *The Trouble with Congo: Local Violence and the Failure of International Peacebuilding.* Cambridge: Cambridge University Press, 2010.
Beloff, Jonathan. *Foreign Policy in Post-Genocide Rwanda: Elite Perceptions of Global Engagement.* New York: Routledge, 2021.
Mills, Kurt. *International Responses to Mass Atrocities in Africa: Responsibility to Protect, Prosecute and Palliate.* Philadelphia: University of Pennsylvania Press, 2015.
Rhoads, Emily Paddon. *Taking Sides in Peacekeeping: Impartiality and the Future of the United Nations.* Oxford: Oxford University Press, 2017.
Veit, Alex. *Intervention as Indirect Rule: Civil War and State-Building in the Democratic Republic of Congo.* Frankfurt: Campus Verlag, 2010.

Diamonds and Conflict in Postcolonial Africa

The extraction and harnessing of diamond resources in postcolonial West and Central Africa and, to a lesser extent, southern Africa sustained conflict and resulted in limited development for alluvial diamond-producing nations. African countries endowed with alluvial diamonds include Sierra Leone, the Democratic Republic of the Congo (DRC), Angola, and Zimbabwe. Botswana and South Africa possess deeply buried Kimberlite diamonds that are easy to regulate, compared to alluvial diamonds found close to the earth's surface and difficult to monitor. Between the 1990s and early 2000s, the extraction and harnessing of diamond resources resulted in the loss of lives due to civil conflicts, destruction of infrastructure, shocking rights abuses, endemic corruption, decimation of livelihoods, and forced displacements. Rebel groups in Sierra Leone, the DRC, and Angola controlled diamond resources and used the proceeds to fund their war efforts against both legitimate governments and civilians. Consequently, the terms "conflict diamonds," "blood diamonds," and "war diamonds" were coined around the middle of 2000 to identify the nexus between diamonds and wars in Africa and global consumer markets. For Botswana and Zimbabwe, governments, not rebels, became the major perpetrators of violence connected to diamonds in the twenty-first century.

The end of the global Cold War in the late 1980s had far-reaching implications on postcolonial Africa. Rebel groups across the continent were left without superpower sponsorship to wage wars. In Sierra Leone, Angola, and the DRC, local resources, notably diamonds, became the backbone of the war economies. The Revolutionary United Front (RUF), the National Union for the Total Independence of Angola (UNITA), and various rebel groups such as the Alliance of Democratic Forces for the liberation of Congo (AFDL), the Movement for the Liberation of Congo (MLC), and factions of the Rally for Congolese Democracy (RCD) controlled the countries' diamond production at different times between the late 1990s and early 2000s and used the proceeds to fund their war efforts against both governments and civilians. In these three countries, resource abundance did not cause civil wars; diamonds entered the story after the conflicts began and played an essential role as a source of funding—sustaining and prolonging conflicts that would otherwise have ended without such funding.

In Sierra Leone diamond resources were used to sustain a brutal intrastate war that decimated the social and economic facets of the country. The conflict began in March 1991 when RUF rebels, led by Foday Sankoh, then army corporal, and supported with much-needed weaponry by Charles Taylor, invaded east Sierra Leone from Liberia and waged a war with an aim to topple President Joseph Momoh, whom they accused for being kleptocratic and inefficient in economic management. Throughout the conflict, RUF rebels used forced labor to extract diamonds and smuggled them through neighboring Liberia where they sold them on the black market for arms purchase. Charles Taylor, a rebel and who later became the president of Liberia from August 1997 to August 2007, was involved with the RUF in 1991 and supported the conflict by supplying the rebels with weapons. The conflict had a profoundly destructive impact in Sierra Leone. The rebels were involved in the perpetration of horrific rights abuses to frighten and force civilians away from diamond-bearing areas. Approximately 75,000 lives were lost between 1991 and 2002.

During the Cold War proxy conflict in Angola (1975–1991), UNITA controlled the most important diamond-producing areas in the Cuango Valley. However, it received material and financial support from the United States, China, and South Africa, while the Marxist Popular Movement for the Liberation of Angola (MPLA) was funded by the Soviet Union and Cuba. With the end of the Cold War, material and financial backing from the superpowers vanished. Both the ruling MPLA and UNITA were faced with a challenge of support. Diamonds and oil became the major source of funding that sustained a ten-year-long brutal civil war (1992–2002) that resulted in the loss of 500,000 lives, with thousands more internally displaced and maimed due to land mines. While UNITA rebels and their leader Jonas Savimbi largely relied on the proceeds from diamonds as the principal source of income throughout the 1990s, the MPLA relied on oil revenues.

In the DRC, the abundant diamond resources enriched the political and military elites in the countries involved in the First and Second Congo war at the expense of the majority of the Congolese people. Natural resources: gold, coltan, cassiterite, and above all, diamonds were at the center of the Second Congo War or Africa's World War (1998–2003). The conflict was between the rebel groups created and supported by Rwanda and Uganda on the one hand and Laurent Kabila's government on the other. Several complex rebel groups and African countries were involved in the conflict and benefited from the Congo's mineral resources, while the majority of Congolese citizens did not benefit in any meaningful way from the natural resources in their country.

In Zimbabwe, the harnessing of diamond resources did not bring meaningful development either in the Marange community where the gems were discovered or to the nation. The Zimbabwean story epitomizes the new dynamics of conflict linked to Africa's alluvial diamonds in the twenty-first century—where diamonds posed a challenge to the government from inside. There was no war linked to diamonds in Zimbabwe. However, the government itself, along with the diamond firms, was the main perpetrator of violence, killings, and gross rights abuses. Between 2006 and 2016, diamonds were linked to horrific rights abuse and killings by both state security forces and diamond firms' security guards. This period witnessed unprecedented plundering and smuggling of the national resource by the military and political elites.

Botswana's management of diamond resources have been cited as an anomaly among other African countries abounding with natural resources. For this reason, the country has gained a reputation as the "miracle of Africa." Contrary to the cases of Sierra Leone, Angola, the DRC, and Zimbabwe, diamond resources have fostered economic growth in Botswana. Diamonds have largely been a blessing—an engine of sustainable development. Most citizens have benefited from diamond resources through the provision of infrastructure like hospitals, schools, and other social services provided by the government. However, Botswana's credentials as the provider of "conflict-free" diamonds came under attack by NGOs in the early 2000s. This was after the government of Botswana evicted the indigenous San people, pejoratively called *Basarwa*, from their home in the Central Kalahari Game Reserve (CKGR) between 1997 and 2002 over issues allegedly linked to the extraction of diamond resources.

Mathew Ruguwa

See also: Angolan Conflicts; Congo Wars; Kabila, Laurent; Liberian Civil Wars; National Union for the Total Independence of Angola (UNITA); Popular Movement for the Liberation of Angola (MPLA); Revolutionary United Front (RUF); Sierra Leone Civil War; Taylor, Charles McArthur Ghankay.

Further Reading

Ballentine, K., and J. Sherman, eds. *The Political Economy of Armed Conflict: Beyond Greed and Grievance*. Boulder, CO: Lynne Rienner, 2003.

Bieri, F. *From Blood Diamonds to the Kimberly Process: How NGOs Cleaned Up the Global Diamond Industry*. Farnham: Ashgate, 2010.

Good, K. *Diamonds, Dispossession, and Democracy in Botswana*. Johannesburg: Jacana Media, 2008.

Reyntjens, F. *The Great African War: Congo and Regional Geopolitics, 1996–2006*. New York: Cambridge University Press, 2009.

Saunders, R., and T. Nyamunda, eds. *Facets of Power: Politics, Profits and People in the Making of Zimbabwe's Blood Diamonds*. Harare: Weaver Press, 2016.

Doe, Samuel (1951–1990)

A career soldier who seized power in a bloody coup in 1980, Samuel Doe was president of Liberia until his murder in 1990 by rebel forces.

Samuel Kanyon Doe was born on May 6, 1951, in eastern Liberia and grew up as a member of the Krahn ethnic group, one of many indigenous groups separate from the Americo-Liberian ruling minority. (Americo-Liberians are descendants of freed U.S. slaves who founded the West African colony in 1822.) Doe entered the army in 1969 and was promoted to first sergeant in 1979 before being recommended for a U.S. Special Forces training program.

Resentful that the highest officer positions were reserved for Americo-Liberians, Doe aligned himself with several left-wing movements emerging at the time, including the Progressive Alliance of Liberia, which sought to abolish the socioeconomic barriers that divided the two cultural groups. After some leftist leaders were jailed in 1980, Doe led an assault on President William Tolbert's executive mansion, killing him and his guards in a short firefight.

Doe quickly formed a cabinet consisting of an assortment of freed leftist leaders and Americo-Liberians, but real authority rested with the People's Redemption Council, composed mainly of soldiers loyal to Doe. Within days of his rise to power, Doe ordered the execution of 13 prominent officials of the former Tolbert government, including a highly regarded diplomat and Supreme Court chief justice, which had the effect of alienating Liberia from other African nations. With his popularity high, Doe imposed a state of martial law, claiming he needed time to remedy the weak national economy.

The flight of professionals and businesses during the first year of Doe's takeover worsened the economic situation in Liberia. The United States became Doe's biggest lender, eventually supplying his regime with $500 million, in order, some analysts believe, to prevent the contingency of a communist-backed Liberia in alliance with Libya. Even so, by 1985, shortly after a failed coup attempt, the International Monetary Fund and the World Bank ceased loans to Liberia, and the United States sharply reduced its support as the depth of the Doe regime's corruption and repression became apparent.

Doe was killed on September 9, 1990, amid a three-way civil war involving two rival rebel leaders, Prince Yormie Johnson and Charles Taylor and Doe loyalists.

ABC-CLIO

See also: Cold War in Africa; Coups and Military Regimes in Africa; Liberian Civil Wars; Taylor, Charles McArthur Ghankay.

Further Reading

Ellis, Stephen. *The Mask of Anarchy: The Destruction of Liberia and the Religious Dimension of an African Civil War*. New York: New York University Press, 2001.

Givens, Willie A., ed. *Liberia: The Road to Democracy under the Leadership of Samuel Kanyon Doe*. Bourne End: Kensal Press, 1986.

Omonijo, Mobolade. *Doe: The Liberian Tragedy*. Ikeja: Sahel, 1990.

Dos Santos, Jose Eduardo (1942–)

Jose Eduardo dos Santos served as president of Angola and leader of the ruling Popular Movement for the Liberation of Angola (MPLA) from the country's first years of independence in 1979 to 2017.

Dos Santos was born on August 28, 1942, in what is now the capital, Luanda. After attending the city's Salvador Correia high school, he joined the Soviet-backed MPLA—then a resistance movement opposing Portuguese rule—in 1961 and was a founding member of the MPLA youth group. In 1963, the MPLA sent dos Santos to Moscow, where he studied petroleum engineering, graduating in 1969 from the Institute of Oil and Gas in Baku. He also earned a telecommunications degree while in the Soviet Union.

Dos Santos returned to Angola in 1970, participating in the fight for independence during the next four years and rapidly ascending in the ranks of the MPLA. He became a member of the party's central committee by late 1974 and in 1975 was named MPLA chairperson. The same year, following independence, he was appointed foreign affairs minister and then vice prime minister. Although those offices were abolished in 1978, he stayed on in the government as the public planning minister. The MPLA named him president of Angola in September 1979 following the death of president and MPLA leader Dr. Agostinho Neto. Dos Santos later won the disputed presidential elections of 1992 against National Union for the Total Independence of Angola (UNITA) rebel leader Jonas Savimbi, who resumed his group's armed struggle after the elections.

In the first 10 years of dos Santos's presidency, his main challenge was the civil war between the government and UNITA. For many years, the United States supported the UNITA rebellion because of the government's Marxist leanings and its Soviet backing, but in 1993 U.S. president Bill Clinton reversed the decades-long American policy, and the U.S. declared its support for dos Santos. Numerous cease-fire accords between the two sides failed until Savimbi was killed in February 2002. Government and rebel leaders began making peace gestures almost immediately after the rebel leader's death, and the two sides signed a peace agreement in April 2002, ending a 27-year civil war that killed nearly a million people.

In the years following the war, dos Santos faced the prospect of repairing the divisions in his country as well as damaged roads and other infrastructure. Rebuilding efforts were helped by the lifting in December 2002 of nine years of United Nations sanctions that resulted from UNITA's trade in illegal diamonds to buy arms. The integration of former UNITA soldiers into society and government and the return of displaced people have further taxed government resources, as has endemic corruption. Though increases in diamond and oil production led to double-digit economic growth from 2004 to 2007, two-thirds of Angolans live on less than two dollars a day, and the International Monetary Fund has criticized a lack of transparency in state-run oil and diamond companies.

In 2008, Angola held its first parliamentary elections in 16 years, with the MPLA receiving more than 80 percent of the vote. Presidential elections to be held in 2009 were delayed pending the completion of a new constitution, and the resulting document, approved by the national assembly in January 2010, abolished direct presidential elections in favor of appointment of the president by the majority party following legislative elections. With the MPLA holding 81 percent of the seats in the national assembly, the new constitution was widely seen as a move to solidify dos Santos's hold. The constitution also replaced the prime minister with a vice president to be appointed by the president. UNITA legislators boycotted the vote on the new constitution, and it passed unanimously. MPLA proponents said a stronger presidency would benefit continued stability.

In the following legislative elections, the MPLA again dominated in balloting deemed free and fair by African Union observers. That was more than enough for the national assembly to reelect dos Santos to a five-year term; however, ahead of the 2017 elections, dos Santos announced that he would step down from the presidency. When the ballots were cast, the MPLA once again secured a comfortable majority of seats in the national assembly, and dos Santos was succeeded by João Lourenço, his former defense minister.

Lynn Jurgensen

See also: Angolan Armed Forces (FAPLA and FAA); Angolan Conflicts; Cold War in Africa; Diamonds and Conflict in Postcolonial Africa; National Union for the Total Independence of Angola (UNITA); Neto, António Agostinho; Popular Movement for the Liberation of Angola (MPLA); Portuguese Africa, Independence Wars (Angola, Mozambique, and Guinea-Bissau); Savimbi, Jonas; Soviet Military Involvement in Africa; U.S. Military Involvement in Africa.

Further Reading

James, W. Martin. *Historical Dictionary of Angola*. Lanham, MD: Scarecrow Press, 2011.

Weigert, Stephen. *Angola: A Modern Military History, 1961–2002*. New York: Palgrave Macmillan, 2011.

East African Mutiny (January 19–27, 1964)

The East African Mutiny was a near-simultaneous mutiny of the militaries of the East African countries of Tanganyika, Kenya, and Uganda. While the military disobedience was not coordinated, the common origin, parallel situations, and close proximity of the forces led them to all mutiny at the same time. While all three militaries were pacified in short order, the mutinies would have far-reaching effects on the states that had needed to endure them.

The roots of the mutinies lay in the British colonial military construct of the three East African countries, the King's African Rifles (KAR). Decolonization caught these military formations flat-footed. While the former KAR formations hoped that independence would mean a continuation of their colonial privileges and professional advancement into officer ranks, this was not to be. The process of educating and commissioning African officers had barely begun even as Tanganyika declared itself independent in 1961, with Uganda and Kenya set to follow in 1962 and 1963, respectively. In addition, the newly independent countries were in no position to pay their militaries more, much less afford them privileges beyond those of other citizens. This meant that with the exception of a few African officers promoted from stereotypical non-martial groups, military service following independence looked much the same as it had before decolonization.

While the grievances of the soldiers were already in evidence, the proximate event setting off the mutinies was the eruption of a bloody revolution in Zanzibar, the archipelago state located off the coast of mainland Tanganyika. To help reimpose order on the islands, President Julius Nyerere of Tanganyika sent his Police Field Force units from Dar es Salaam to the islands, leaving a battalion of the Tanganyika Rifles as the sole security force around the capital. This prompted a group of long-service enlisted soldiers to finally strike on the night of January 19, seizing key points in the city and arresting their officers. The following day the second battalion mutinied, although their commanding officer managed to keep them in their barracks. Meanwhile, the civilian administration of Tanganyika was nowhere to be found, with Nyerere and his cabinet largely having gone into hiding.

In the meanwhile, the unrest spread to Uganda, with the men of the Uganda Rifles organizing themselves on the 22nd and ignoring orders to return to duty on the 23rd. Meanwhile the 11 Kenya Rifles, following a period of disgruntlement, mutinied against their leadership on the 24th, with a minor shoot-out occurring. By the morning of the 25th, all three militaries were ignoring their chain of command in protest. However, at this critical juncture, all three states accepted British aid to quell the mutinies, and the provision of British troops in all three cases broke the mutinies within 48 hours.

For all three countries, these mutinies proved to be stern tests of the new governments. Kenya would be the least affected but still require British troops and partnerships into the future. Uganda would see continued challenges with military loyalty. Finally, Tanganyika would effectively dismantle its old military and build an entirely new military formation.

Charles G. Thomas

See also: African Armed Forces; British Military Involvement in Postcolonial Africa; Nyerere, Julius.

Further Reading

Laurence, Tony, and Christopher MacRae. *The Dar Mutiny of 1964: And the Armed Intervention That Ended It.* Bloomington, IN: AuthorHouse, 2010.

Parsons, Timothy. *The 1964 Army Mutinies and the Making of Modern East Africa.* Westport, CT: Praeger Press, 2003.

Tanzania People's Defence Forces. *Tanganyika Rifles Mutiny, January 1964.* Dar es Salaam: Dar es Salaam University Press, 1998.

Thomas, Charles G. "'Disgraceful Disturbances': TANU, The Tanganyika Rifles, and the 1964 Mutinies." In *Protest, Dissent, and Internal Disputes in Africa*, edited by Emmanuel Mbah and Toyin Falola. New York: Routledge Press, 2016.

ECOWAS Military Interventions

In 1967 the newly independent states of West Africa agree to form a regional intergovernmental organization with a view to creating a common market, but this plan became delayed by the Nigerian Civil War (1967–1970). With the 1975 Treaty of Lagos, the Economic Community of West African States (ECOWAS) emerged to facilitate regional economic cooperation and development among its 16 member states. ECOWAS sought to remove customs duties, trade restrictions, and regulations on the movement of people around the West African region; to synchronize economic policies; and to manage a fund to support development projects. The regional grouping became divided between Anglophone countries, led by Nigeria as the region's primary economic and military power, and Francophone countries closely aligned to France, with their own common currency tied to the French franc. Recognizing the relation between security and economic cooperation, ECOWAS established a Protocol on Non-Aggression in 1978 and a Protocol on Mutual Assistance on Defence in 1981. These agreements prompted the creation of an ECOWAS Defence Committee and Council and raised the likelihood of establishing a West African Allied armed force. While these initial security protocols and arrangements arose in a Cold War context involving a possible external threat to the region or conflicts between member states, the post–Cold War situation threw up new regional challenges with the collapse of authoritarian regimes and a series of civil wars.

In 1990, ECOWAS established a non-standing multinational military force called ECOWAS Monitoring Group (ECOMOG) to intervene in the First Liberian Civil War (1989–1996). A significant step, this intervention marked the first time a regional international body embarked on a military operation to end a conflict without UN authorization, and it represented the first attempt by an African regional organization to end a conflict using its own resources, personnel, and funds. However, the arrival of ECOMOG in Liberia raised questions about whether ECOWAS possessed the legal right to intervene and if unelected military regimes such as existed in Nigeria at the time could justifiably promote peace and democracy. Since the majority of its personnel and resources, and usually its commander, originated from Nigeria, ECOMOG in Liberia was opposed by the governments of Burkina Faso and Côte d'Ivoire, who supported Liberian rebel leader Charles Taylor. In 1992, 1,200 Senegalese troops, funded by the United States as a reward for Senegal breaking with all other sub-Saharan African states to join the First Gulf War (1990–1991), arrived in Liberia in an attempt to encourage more Francophone participation in ECOMOG. However, the plan backfired, as the killing of six Senegalese soldiers by Taylor's rebels prompted Dakar to withdraw its contingent from Liberia in 1993. Likewise, the arrival of allied Organisation of African Unity (OAU) contingents from Tanzania and Uganda in 1994 seemed a promising way of concealing Nigerian dominance in ECOMOG, but the East Africans quickly withdrew, given the lack of resources and support. Although West Africa experienced Africa's largest number of post–Cold War civil conflicts during the 1990s and early 2000s, it was the most pro-active region in terms of mounting armed interventions attempting to restore peace. After the First Liberian Civil War, ECOWAS intervened in Sierra Leone in 1997, Guinea-Bissau in 1999, Liberia in 2003, and Côte d'Ivoire in 2004. Arguably, within West Africa of the 1990s and 2000s, ECOWAS filled a gap created by the UN Security Council's reluctance to act vigorously in Africa and the OAU's lack of capability due to limited resources. Indeed, ECOWAS interventions in Liberia and Sierra Leone paved the way for the eventual arrival of UN peacekeepers, some of whom were also from West African militaries. Although ECOWAS interventions were (and are) called "peacekeeping," they usually involved forceful military action to separate hostile factions or bolster an established government. ECOMOG troops have been criticized for brutality and large-scale theft, especially during the Liberian and Sierra Leonean civil wars of the 1990s. As such, Liberians referred to ECOMOG as "Every Car or Moveable Object Gone."

During the 2010s, the number of ECOWAS military interventions declined, and the organization proved less outgoing in responding to Islamist insurgency in the hinterland of Sahel, related to terrorist attacks in coastal West African countries, preferring to leave the problem to UN or French forces. A complication of the ECOWAS engagement with the Sahelian crisis is the involvement of neighboring non-ECOWAS members such as Cameroon, Chad, and Mauritania. Nevertheless, ECOWAS military operations continue in small coastal countries. In 2017, ECOWAS forces from Senegal, Nigeria, Ghana, Mali, and Togo intervened in the Gambia to remove the dictator Yahya Jammeh after he refused to accept electoral defeat.

Timothy J. Stapleton

See also: Côte d'Ivoire Civil War; Liberian Civil Wars; Peacekeeping in Africa; Sierra Leone Civil War; Taylor, Charles McArthur Ghankay.

Further Reading

Adebajo, Adekeye. *Liberia's Civil War: Nigeria, ECOMOG and Regional Security in West Africa.* Boulder, CO: Lynne Rienner, 2002.

Jaye, Thomas, Dauda Garuba, and Stella Amadi, eds. *ECOWAS: The Dynamics of Conflict and Peace-Building.* Dakar: CODESRIA, 2011.

Kabia, John. *Humanitarian Intervention and Conflict Resolution in West Africa: From ECOMOG to ECOMIL.* Farnham: Ashgate, 2009.

Magyar, Karl, and Earl Conteh-Morgan, eds. *Peacekeeping in Africa: ECOMOG in Liberia.* Basingstoke: Palgrave MacMillan, 1998.

Wilen, Nina. *Justifying Interventions in Africa: (De) Stabilizing Sovereignty in Liberia, Burundi and the Congo.* Basingstoke: Palgrave Macmillan, 2012.

Eritrea-Ethiopia War (1998–2000)

In 1991, after a long war, a coalition of rebel forces overthrew the Ethiopian regime of Mengistu Haile Mariam. One of the most important rebel groups was the Eritrean People's Liberation Front (EPLF), which fought for the independence of Eritrea that had been absorbed by Ethiopia in the 1950s. In April 1993, in a referendum supervised by the United Nations, Eritreans overwhelmingly voted for independence, which became a reality just a few days later. Already in power as a provisional government since 1991, the EPLF continued to rule independent Eritrea, with President Isaias Afewerki renaming his group the Peoples' Front for Democracy and Justice (PFDJ) and developing a highly authoritarian one-party state. In Ethiopia, the former rebel coalition of the Ethiopian Peoples' Revolutionary Democratic Front (EPRDF), with a core from the Tigray People's Liberation Front (TPLF), formed a transitional government under Meles Zenawi, who renounced socialism and cultivated good relations with Western powers. Under a new constitution that created a multiparty democracy, Zenawi was elected as substantive prime minister in 1995 and presided over an increasingly authoritarian government. As such, insurgencies continued in parts of Ethiopia such as the Ogaden region.

Following Eritrea's secession from Ethiopia, the two states disagreed over ownership of the Badme border area, which fell under the Ethiopian region of Tigray. In early May 1998, after some border clashes, two Eritrean infantry brigades along with tanks and artillery invaded Badme and drove away Ethiopian militia and police. The Eritreans also occupied the Ethiopian border town of Zalembessa that was not in the disputed zone. Assembling its forces within a week, Ethiopia counterattacked, which led to four weeks of heavy combat along the frontier, including tank and artillery engagements. In early June, the war escalated, with the Ethiopian Air Force bombing the Eritrean capital of Asmara and Eritrean aircraft retaliating against the city of Mekele, capital of Ethiopia's Tigray region. The conflict stalemated with both sides reinforcing and entrenching their units along the 1,000 kilometer border. Both countries mobilized hundreds of thousands of troops and spent hundreds of millions of dollars on new weapons systems such as fighter jets from former Soviet republics and Eastern Europe. When Eritrea rejected a U.S.-Rwanda-sponsored peace plan in February 1999, Ethiopia mounted a massive offensive that penetrated Eritrean fortifications, recaptured Badme, and advanced 10 kilometers into Eritrea after just five days. At the end of February, Eritrea accepted an Organisation of African Unity (OAU) peace plan, requiring both sides to pull back their forces to prewar positions, but neither followed through. In mid-March Ethiopian forces advanced south of Asmara, but entrenched Eritrean soldiers held them off, killing hundreds of attackers and destroying around 20 tanks.

When negotiations collapsed in mid-May 2000, Ethiopian forces traversed the mountains, enabling them to break through Eritrean defenses, cross the Mereb River, and cut the Barentu-Mandefera road, which served as the main supply line for Eritrean troops in the area. Turning east, the Ethiopians moved behind Eritrean lines at Zalambessa, coming within 100 kilometers of Asmara and threatening the port of Assab, and Ethiopian aircraft bombed near the port of Massawa. Defeated, the Eritrean government accepted an OAU peace plan that included the withdrawal of Ethiopian forces, now occupying a quarter of Eritrea, to prewar positions, therefore giving them control of the disputed Badme. During the conflict Ethiopia deported over 75,000 Eritreans and Ethiopian citizens of Eritrean origin. The war's death toll amounted to between 70,000 and 100,000 people, and almost a million more experienced displacement. As a result of the conflict, Eritrea began supporting the Somalia-based Ogaden Liberation Front (OLF) fighting for the independence of their region from Ethiopia and Islamists inside Somalia resisting Ethiopian intervention. The United Nations Mission in Ethiopia and Eritrea (UNMEE), numbering 4,000 international troops, patrolled a 25 kilometer wide strip along the Eritrean side of the border from 2000 to 2008. Although an international border commission eventually decided that Badme belonged to Eritrea, Ethiopian forces did not relinquish it, and tensions between the two countries continued for many years. In 2018, the new Ethiopian government of Prime Minister Abiy Ahmed, which had come to power amid widespread protests by the country's marginalized Oromo majority, declared its acceptance of the border commission and formalized peace with Eritrea. Prime Minister Ahmed attended a peace summit in Asmara, and Eritrean president Afewerki then visited Ethiopia, and the two countries resumed normal diplomatic and economic relations, including opening borders and resuming civilian air travel. In 2020, Eritrean forces crossed into Ethiopia's Tigray province in the context of a rebellion there by the Tigray People's Liberation Front (TPLF).

Timothy J. Stapleton

See also: Afwerki, Isaias; Eritrean People's Liberation Front (EPLF); Eritrean War of Independence; Ethiopia: Insurgency and Interstate War; Peacekeeping in Africa; Tigray People's Liberation Front (TPLF), Zenawi, Meles.

Further Reading
Lata, Leenco. "The Ethiopia-Eritrea War." *Review of African Political Economy* 30 (September 2003): 369–388.
Negash, Tekaste, and Kjetil Tronvoll. *Brothers at War: Making Sense of the Eritrean-Ethiopian War.* Oxford: James Currey, 2000.
Reid, Richard. *Frontiers of Violence in North-East Africa: Genealogies of Conflict since 1800.* Oxford: Oxford University Press, 2011.

Reid, Richard. *Shallow Graves: A Memoir of the Ethiopia-Eritrea War*. Oxford: Oxford University Press, 2020.

Eritrean Liberation Front (ELF) (1961–1987)

The Eritrean Liberation Front (ELF) was the first of major armed groups that resisted the Ethiopian government in the war for Eritrean independence. For at least the first decade of the struggle, they were the primary armed liberation front and even following the emergence of their rivals, the Eritrean People's Liberation from (EPLF), remained a credible force within the broader war. However, due to organizational struggles and a flawed military strategy, the ELF would be fatally weakened following the Ethiopian offensives of 1978–1979, and they would finally be eliminated as an organization in 1987, with their remnants being absorbed by the rival EPLF.

Following World War II, there were significant questions of what to do with the former Italian colony of Eritrea. While the Eritreans themselves asked for independence, the United Nations eventually acceded to Ethiopian demands that the colony be placed in federation with the restored Ethiopian Empire in 1950. However, Ethiopia immediately began efforts to dismantle the federal structure, attempting to absorb the former colony. Efforts to resist Ethiopian control began with organized political efforts fostered by the Eritrean Liberation Movement (ELM) in 1958, but with these failing, an armed struggle was organized by Idris Muhammad Adam and other prominent exiles in 1960 under the auspices of the new Eritrean Liberation Front.

The ELF began its armed struggle against Ethiopia in 1961, pursuing a guerrilla strategy against the larger and better-equipped Ethiopian military. While they achieved some successes, the division of Eritrea into five operational "zones" led to infighting within the varying ELF military commands even as more radical leftist elements demanded the ELF push for a social as well as a political revolution. By 1970, these dissenters had split off and formed their own armed group, the Eritrean People's Liberation Front (EPLF). These two fronts would continue as rivals, although they would occasionally form a united front against the hated Ethiopians.

The ELF would reach its greatest success following the 1974 Derg revolution that overthrew Haile Selassie. With Ethiopia in chaos, the ELF expanded its territorial control over large swathes of Eritrea and managed to fight effectively alongside the EPLF. However, by this point, the EPLF and its more radical social programs were beginning to eclipse the more conservative ELF, and the former splinter group now was obviously the stronger partner in the struggle. Even worse was to follow, as the new communist Derg government received significant aid from the Soviet Union, and their reinvigorated and reorganized military took square aim at the Eritrean rebel groups. Where the EPLF retreated in the face of the renewed Ethiopian offensives, the ELF tried to hold their new territorial gains. The ELF took severe losses against the 1977–1978 Ethiopian offensives and finally was forced to withdraw.

The ELF would never recover from the losses they had taken in 1978–1979, and although they found some safe havens, they were a ghost of what they had been five years before. By 1980, they had been completely overshadowed by the EPLF, and while some remainders claimed leadership of the struggle in Eritrea from the Sudan, they were effectively absorbed by the EPLF in 1987.

Charles G. Thomas

See also: Afwerki, Isaias; Eritrean People's Liberation Front (EPLF); Eritrean War of Independence; Ethiopia: Insurgency and Interstate War; Soviet Military Involvement in Africa.

Further Reading

Connell, Dan. *Against All Odds: A Chronicle of the Eritrean Revolution.* Lawrenceville, NJ: Red Sea Press, 1997.

Pool, David. *From Guerrillas to Government: The Eritrean People's Liberation Front.* Athens: Ohio University Press, 2001.

Sherman, Richard. *Eritrea, the Unfinished Revolution.* New York: Praeger, 1980.

Tareke, Gebru. *The Ethiopian Revolution: War in the Horn of Africa.* New Haven, CT: Yale University Press, 2009.

Eritrean People's Liberation Front (EPLF) (1970–1994)

The Eritrean People's Liberation Front (EPLF) was the primary armed liberation front against the Ethiopian military during the Eritrean War of Independence. The EPLF was initially a splinter organization of the Eritrean Liberation Front that felt that the leadership of the struggle was both too conservative and too splintered to effectively pursue the conflict with Ethiopia. The EPLF would both pursue a more radical social program and create a centralized and disciplined military structure that would allow them to wage and win a protracted struggle against the Ethiopian state, effectively winning Eritrean independence.

In the wake of the Second World War, Eritrea requested independence on the basis of its former colonizer, Italy, renouncing its colonial possessions. However, the emperor of Ethiopia, Haile Selassie, claimed Eritrea as a historic part of his own possessions that had been illegally seized by the Italians. Ultimately, in 1950 the United Nations placed Eritrea as an autonomous territory federated within Selassie's empire, a status that was rife with contradictions. In protest to the immediate efforts of Ethiopia to absorb Eritrea, the Eritreans immediately organized political and eventually military resistance in the form of the Eritrean Liberation Movement (ELM) and the Eritrean Liberation Front (ELF), respectively, with formal hostilities beginning in 1961.

Due to the massive men and material advantage of Ethiopia, the ELF waged a largely guerrilla struggle, depending on politically motivated recruits and donations of arms. However, many of the youths who made up the struggle resented the conservative and often fractious leadership. Rifts began appearing in the various groups of fighters who made up the EPLF by the late 1960s, and by 1970 the organized dissidents declared their own liberation front, the Eritrean People's Liberation Front. Where the ELF had been solely looking for political independence, the EPLF espoused a radical socialist vision for Eritrean society and set about organizing its "liberated zones" along its espoused ideals of equal land ownership, social service provision, and universal education.

This reordering of society was to pay dividends as the struggle turned against the Eritrean fronts. As EPLF fighters retreated, their former areas remained supportive of the struggle, and the constant guerrilla warfare weakened the resurgent Ethiopians. Even following the major Ethiopian offensives of 1982–1987, the main EPLF force was in the field and maintained significant support from its old liberated areas. These punishing campaigns eventually fatally weakened the Ethiopian forces, leading to their crushing defeat at Afabet in 1988. As the EPLF advanced, their formerly liberated zones provided continued strength and organization, and they would prove to be one of the more potent members of the larger alliance of anti-Derg Ethiopian insurgencies.

Ultimately, the EPLF would be at the head of the insurgent alliance that entered Addis Ababa and overthrew the Ethiopian government in 1991. This would mark the formal transition of the EPLF from an armed force to a political party, and it was as a party that they would oversee Eritrean's plebiscite to separate formally from Ethiopia and rule that independent state. In 1994, the EPLF would have its Third Congress, where it would formally vote to change its name to the People's Front for Democracy and Justice.

Charles G. Thomas

See also: Afabet, Battle of; Afwerki, Isaias; Eritrean Liberation Front (ELF); Eritrean War of Independence; Ethiopia: Insurgency and Interstate War; Women and War in Africa.

Further Reading

Connell, Dan. *Against All Odds: A Chronicle of the Eritrean Revolution.* Lawrenceville, NJ: Red Sea Press, 1997.

Pool, David. *From Guerrillas to Government: The Eritrean People's Liberation Front.* Athens: Ohio University Press, 2001.

Sherman, Richard. *Eritrea, the Unfinished Revolution.* New York: Praeger, 1980.

Tareke, Gebru. *The Ethiopian Revolution: War in the Horn of Africa.* New Haven: Yale University Press, 2009.

Eritrean War of Independence (1961–1991)

The East African nation of Eritrea was an Italian colony during 1889–1941 and was under British-administered control during 1941–1952. Eritrea became federated with Ethiopia in September 1952 but lost all autonomy in 1962, when it was reduced to province status. Several armed groups ideologically committed to the communist bloc fought for independence from 1962 until the fall of Addis Ababa and Asmara in 1991. An Eritrean provisional government was then established until 1993, when a referendum granted the country official independence.

Disagreement over the 1945 United Nations provisions for Eritrean sovereignty and a desire for independence resulted in the creation of the Muslim League in 1946. The Muslim League was replaced by the Eritrean Liberation Front (ELF), formed in 1961, and the Eritrean Liberation Movement, a secular movement founded in 1958 by activists in neighboring Sudan.

From the beginning of ELF, Osman Solih Sabbe was a key figure in the organization. He secured financial assistance from states hostile to Ethiopia. To drum up support, ELF emphasized Ethiopia's links to the United States and subsequently to Israel. This strategy resulted in the perceived association of Eritrean nationalism with Islam.

A 1974 coup in Ethiopia overthrew the pro-Western Emperor Haile Selassie. Replacing Selassie's government was a nominally Socialist-oriented military junta called the Derg (Committee), chaired by Colonel Mengistu Haile Mariam. This also meant a change of policy for Sudan, which had supported Ethiopia since the 1972 Addis Ababa Agreement (leading to a period of peace in Sudan).

Following this radical change in regimes, the Tigray People's Liberation Front (TPLF) was established in 1975 in the province of Tigray in northern Ethiopia, while by 1974 the Eritrean People's Liberation Front (EPLF) emerged from the disenchanted members of ELF. Disagreements between existing armed groups led to a civil war in 1972–1973 and eventually, by 1981, to expulsion of ELF from Eritrea, making the EPLF the dominant military and political force there. Both TPLF and EPLF were Marxist in orientation and opposed the Mengistu regime, but while the EPLF favored independence, the TPLF remained undecided between independence and a role within Ethiopia.

Organizational and leadership differences eventually led to a three-year breach between the two organizations in 1985, when the TPLF began supporting Eritrean opposition movements against the ELPF's perceived hegemony. Disagreements escalated after the creation of the Derg and as the result of Soviet support for Ethiopian military offensives against the Eritrean independence groups, especially during 1977–1979. In this period, the EPLF carried out a strategic withdrawal from central and southern Eritrea into the northern province of Sahel, while the TPLF continued to fight the Ethiopian Army, despite the latter's initial victories.

From the beginning, the TPLF was more sympathetic to an Albanian model of self-reliant communism, whereas the EPLF continued to regard Soviet-style communism with favor. In addition, the TPLF interpreted the independence struggle within a neo-Marxist-Leninist framework, with differences based not on class but rather on ethnicity. The TPLF also favored an ethnic federal system, which the EPLF sought to avoid.

From 1978 onward, the EPLF consolidated its position until in 1980 it drove back Ethiopian forces on all fronts. Finally, in March 1988 the EPLF defeated Ethiopian forces at Afabat. Within a year the Ethiopian Army had evacuated the Tigray province. The EPLF conquered the northwestern part of Eritrea and then took the port of Massawa in 1990 and entered Asmara in May 1991. The same year, the Ethiopian People's Revolutionary Democratic Front (EPRDF), an umbrella organization founded in 1989 that gathered all anti-Derg movements, captured the Ethiopian capital of Addis Ababa, imposing its rule and forcing Mengistu to flee the country.

In May 1991, a conference was held in London to resolve the situation and was chaired by the United States, which held out the promise of aid. The conference was successful and formally ended the war. In July, another conference, at Addis Ababa, led to the establishment of an Ethiopian provisional government, and Eritrea was granted the right to hold a referendum on independence, with the

EPLF as the provisional government. In 1993, 99.8 percent of the population voted for Eritrean independence, whereupon the EPLF transformed itself into the People's Front for Democracy and Justice and became the sole legal and ruling party of Eritrea.

Abel Polese

See also: Afwerki, Isaias; Cold War in Africa; Eritrean Liberation Front (ELF); Eritrean People's Liberation Front (EPLF); Ethiopia: Insurgency and Interstate Conflict; Mengistu Haile Mariam; Tigray People's Liberation Front (TPLF).

Further Reading

Pool, David. *From Guerrillas to Government: The Eritrean People's Liberation Front.* Oxford: James Currey, 2001.

Tekeste, Negash, and Kjetil Tronvoll. *Brothers at War: Making Sense of the Ethiopian-Eritrean War.* Athens: Ohio University Press, 2001.

Tekle, Amare, ed. *Eritrea and Ethiopia: From Conflict to Cooperation.* Lawrenceville, NJ: Red Sea, 1994.

Ethiopia: Insurgency and Interstate War (1960–2020)

With its history as a regional imperial power, Ethiopia experienced a series of interrelated insurgencies, secessionist movements, and interstate wars from the 1960s onward. As a Christian monarchy reinstated by the British during World War II, Emperor Haile Selassie's regime cultivated strong relations with the Western side of the Cold War, which helped expand and modernize the Ethiopian military from the 1950s to the early 1970s. The unification of former Italian and British colonies as the independent Republic of Somalia in 1960, as well as the rise of pan-Somalism, which sought to unite East Africa's Somali people, and Somalia's acceptance of Soviet military support, provided the context for the rise of several ethnic Somali separatist movements in Ethiopia's Ogaden region. These groups included the Ogaden Liberation Front (OLF) that was established in 1963 but was destroyed by Ethiopian forces the following year and the Western Somali Liberation Front (WSLF) that was founded at the end of the 1960s and fought a guerrilla war until the end of the 1980s. In the early 1950s the United Nations federated the former Italian colony of Eritrea to neighboring Ethiopia, therefore giving the latter control of a strategically important stretch of the Red Sea coastline. As a result, the Eritrea Liberation Front (ELF), supported by Muslim Arab countries in the Middle East, initiated a guerrilla struggle against Ethiopian occupation in the early 1960s. The imperial Ethiopian state responded with a vicious counterinsurgency campaign that alienated most Eritreans. In 1973 the ELF split with Christian and secular elements, forming the Eritrean People's Liberation Front (EPLF) that pursued a revolutionary socialist agenda and began to fight a conventional war to expel Ethiopian forces.

In 1974, a military coup overthrew the pro-Western Emperor Haile Selassie and installed what eventually became a Soviet-backed military regime called the Derg led by Colonel Mengistu Haile Mariam. During its 1977 "Red Terror" campaign, the Derg violently eliminated political opposition within Ethiopia, killing from

30,000 to 100,000 people, including many intellectuals and students. While Mengistu's regime inherited Ethiopia's ongoing regional insurgencies and tensions with Somalia, the Derg's brutality stimulated more internal conflict. Attempting to exploit the chaos within Ethiopia, Somalia invaded in 1977, prompting a formal shift in regional Cold War alliances, with the Soviets backing the Derg and abandoning Somalia, and Somalia seeking help from the United States. With Soviet arms and the arrival of a Cuban intervention force, Ethiopia repelled the Somali invaders and emerged victorious in the Ogaden War (1977–1978). In turn, the emboldened Derg launched a series of aggressive campaigns against insurgents within Ethiopia and Eritrea. Between 1978 and 1983, the Mengistu regime mounted at least seven separate military offensives against Eritrean rebels that drove them into Eritrea's mountainous north, eliminated the ELF, and caused the deaths of around 30,000 Eritreans and 50,000 Ethiopians. Representing the most ambitious Ethiopian state offensive in Eritrea, the Red Star campaign began in 1982 and involved around 180,000 Ethiopian troops, mostly conscripts, but completely failed to dislodge the EPLF, which regained lost territory in a successful counterattack. During the late 1970s, insurgency developed in Ethiopia's northern Tigray province, rooted in the area's marginalization and Derg oppression. By the early 1980s, the feuding rebel groups in Tigray merged into the Tigray People's Liberation Front (TPLF), which fought a guerrilla war aimed at gaining self-determination for all of Ethiopia's people. In Tigray, the Derg regime further alienated civilians by imposing unpopular land reform, compulsorily resettling peasants away from rebel areas, terrorizing urban elites, and persecuting the Ethiopian Christian Church. Creating a catastrophic famine in the 1980s, Mengistu's counterinsurgency program in Tigray involved destroying crops and denying people international food aid. On the other hand, the TPLF gained international and local legitimacy by coordinating humanitarian assistance from neighboring Sudan. Although the TPLF and the EPLF formed a shaky alliance, they pursued different military strategies, with the former fighting a guerrilla war and the later a conventional one, to hold territory. At the same time, insurgencies continued or broke out in other parts of Ethiopia. In the Ogaden region, after the defeat of the Somali invasion, the WSLF persisted with the support of Somalia and the Ogaden National Liberation Front (ONLF), emerged in 1984. Based on initiatives in the late 1960s, the Oromo Liberation Front (OLF) fought the Derg during the late 1970s and 1980s, claiming to represent the interests of Ethiopia's marginalized Oromo majority, living mostly in the central and southern parts of the country. In the 1980s, violence flared in the western Gambella region between Anuak communities and people from other parts of Ethiopia moved there by the Mengistu regime and between the Anuak people and ethnic Nuer, many of whom had fled into Ethiopia from adjacent southern Sudan to escape civil war. In 1985 the predominantly Anuak Gambella People's Liberation Movement (GPLM) launched a guerrilla war against the Ethiopian state.

In the late 1980s, given the processes that would lead to the collapse of the Soviet Union and the end of the Cold War, the reduction of Ethiopia's hitherto massive Soviet military assistance fatally weakened Mengistu's state. At the same time, Ethiopia's Derg regime ended its long conflict with Somalia, with both states halting support for each other's rebel groups, enabling the Ethiopian military to redeploy troops from the border and utilize them against internal rebellions. At the end of 1986, the EPLF embarked on an offensive in Eritrea, eventually leading to its decisive victory over Ethiopian forces at the March 1988 Battle of Afabet. In turn, the TPLF broke the existing military stalemate in Tigray by mounting its own offensive, but this prompted a massive counterattack from the Mengistu regime, which recaptured Tigrayan towns and massacred civilians. In early 1989 EPLF forces advanced into Tigray to assist the TPLF, which transformed into a conventional army, and they expelled Ethiopian state forces from the area. Shortly thereafter, the TPLF and other insurgent groups such as the Oromo People's Democratic Organization (OPDO), comprising mostly captured government troops, formed a broad coalition called the Ethiopian Peoples' Revolutionary Democratic Front (EPRDF). During the first half of 1991, the EPRDF and EPLF drove Mengistu's forces out of the Gondar, Gojjam, and Wollo provinces, and the EPLF continued to seize control of Eritrea. In May 1991, Mengistu fled the country. Later that month the EPLF captured Asmara, the capital of Eritrea, and EPRDF and EPLF forces took the national capital of Addis Ababa. The EPRDF and OLF formed a transitional government under TPLF chairman Meles Zenawi and drafted a new constitution that created a multiparty democracy. The EPLF formed a provincial government in Eritrea in May 1991 and a UN-supervised referendum, held in April 1993, resulted almost immediately in independence. As such, Eritrea represented postcolonial Africa's first successful secessionist state. Renaming itself the Peoples' Front for Democracy and Justice (PFDJ), the EPLF, led by Isaias Afwerki, established a repressive single-party state in Eritrea.

Within Ethiopia, though technically remaining a democracy, the EPRDF cultivated an authoritarian state, with Prime Minister Zenawi confirmed in the elections of 1995 and 2005. Despite regime change in Addis Ababa, a number of rebellions continued in parts of Ethiopia. In 1992, violence broke out between the OLF and the OPDO, both claiming to represent the interests of Ethiopia's Oromo people, leading to the former's departure from the transitional government and the renewal of its insurgency. The OLF received support from Eritrea, especially from the 1998–2000 Border War between Eritrea and Ethiopia, and sought sanctuary in the border area of northern Kenya and Somalia, where it made common cause with armed Islamist factions. In addition, the ONLF continued its struggle for the independence of the Ogaden region, and during the 2000s, activists in Gambella accused the Ethiopian government of committing genocide against the area's Anuak people. While Ethiopian forces pursued rebels across the border into Somalia and assisted armed groups inside Somalia during the late 1990s, the 2001 terrorist attacks on the United States turned Ethiopia into a major American ally in the "War on Terror" and provided the context for increased Ethiopian military intervention in Ethiopia. In December 2006, in support of the beleaguered Somali Transitional Government (TNG), Ethiopia launched a major military invasion of Somalia, pushing back the forces of the Islamic Courts Union (ICU) and installed the TNG in Mogadishu. American desire to prevent Somalia from becoming a haven for radical Islamists informed the Ethiopian intervention, but so did factors such as Eritrea's support for Somali Islamists who also threatened Ethiopia. Over the next two years, Ethiopian forces and the newly established African Union Mission in Somalia (AMISOM), assisted by the United States, which staged aerial drones out of Ethiopia, fought Islamist insurgents in Somalia, helping to expand the authority of the TNG. Accused of brutalizing Somali civilians, Ethiopian forces withdrew from Somalia in January 2009 after the TNG absorbed the moderate faction of the ICU, though the radical branch, called Al-Shabaab, continued the war. Nevertheless, the Ethiopian military conducted cross-border incursions into Somalia in the early 2010s in support of TNG and in pursuit of rebels from Ethiopia. The 2018 emergence of a reformist government in Ethiopia under Prime Minister Abiy Ahmed led to peace agreements with a number of insurgent groups such as the OLF and the ONLF and the reestablishment of formal ties with Eritrea. However, the same political changes within Ethiopia led to the decline of the TPLF in central government, prompting that movement to stage a rebellion in its home province of Tigray in 2020. Although the TPLF seemed to advance on Addis Ababa in 2021, Prime Minister Ahmed personally went to the front claiming to lead the counteroffensive that drove the rebels back to Tigray.

Timothy J. Stapleton

See also: Afabet, Battle of; Afwerki, Isaias; Eritrean Liberation Front (ELF); Eritrean People's Liberation Front (EPLF); Eritrean War of Independence; Famine in Postcolonial African Conflicts; Mengistu Haile Mariam; Ogaden War; Refugees in Postcolonial Africa; Tigray People's Liberation Front (TPLF); Zenawi, Meles.

Further Reading

Ayele, Fantahun. *The Ethiopian Army from Victory to Collapse, 1977–1991*. Evanston, IL: Northwestern University Press, 2014.

Berhe, Aregawi. *A Political History of the Tigray People's Liberation Front (1975–1991) Revolt, Ideology and Mobilisation in Ethiopia*. Los Angeles: Tsehai, 2009.

Berhe, Mulugeta Gebrehiwot. *Laying the Past to Rest: The EPRDF and the Challenges of Ethiopian State Building*. London: Hurst, 2020.

Pankhurst, Richard. *The Ethiopians: A History*. Oxford: Blackwell Publishing, 2001.

Reid, Richard. *Frontiers of Violence in North-East Africa: Genealogies of Conflict since c.1800*.Oxford: Oxford University Press, 2011.

Tareke, Gebru. *The Ethiopian Revolution: War in the Horn of Africa*. New Haven, CT: Yale University Press, 2009.

Woldemariam, Michel. *Insurgent Fragmentation in the Horn of Africa: Rebellion and Its Discontents*. Cambridge: Cambridge University Press, 2018.

Zewde, Bahru. *A History of Modern Ethiopia, 1855–1991*. Oxford: James Currey, 2009.

Famine in Postcolonial African Conflicts

The independence of many African countries in the mid-1950s ushered in a new era of sociopolitical and economic challenges in the continent. In countries such as Nigeria, Sudan, Angola, Mozambique, and Ethiopia, interethnic rivalry, strife for natural resources, irredentism, and marginalization of ethnic groups were some of the causes of civil wars. Consequently, the four horsemen of the apocalypse: famine, war, pestilence, and death plagued the victims of this situation. In particular, famine crises often prolonged these civil wars through the restrictions on food aid into certain areas, requisition of food aid by government forces and rebel groups, and the destruction of fertile lands during the war.

For instance, during the Nigerian Civil War (1967–1970) the belligerents, the federal government and Biafran forces exploited the famine that emerged from this situation. The justification for starvation by hardliners within the federal army was based on the opinion that an effective blockade of food aid to the Biafrans would expedite the ending of the civil war. While the Biafran forces, on the other hand, used the restrictions on food aid to advance the claim that federal forces were committing genocide. In particular, Biafran forces commandeered the resources provided by relief agencies during the famine crisis to meet the needs of their troops.

In comparison with the famine crisis during the Nigerian Civil War, that of the First Sudanese Civil War (1955–1972) was caused by both natural and human factors. In the first half of 1961, an incessant drought eventually led to a prevalent famine throughout the Bor District. Although people living close to the Nile River had access to water, those in the interior regions died of thirst. The Khartoum government's lackluster response to this situation increased the number of victims afflicted by the famine. Consequently, this incident aggravated the grievances of the southern Sudanese against the Sudanese government, which exacerbated the sociopolitical and economic causes of the First Sudanese Civil War.

The impacts of famine on sociopolitical upheavals in sub-Saharan countries were more pronounced and prevalent in the 1980s. Countries such as Ethiopia, Sudan, Angola, and Mozambique were embroiled in civil wars during this period. Some of the causes of famine during the civil wars in these countries had some differences and similarities. For instance, in Ethiopia, within the context of the Cold War era, the land reform and collectivization policies of the Mengistu regime coupled with its counterinsurgency tactics against the Tigray People's Liberation Front (TPLF) and the Eritrean People's Liberation Front (EPLF) led to the bombing of markets and the manipulation of food aid, which exacerbated Ethiopia's famine crisis. Similarly, the Sudanese government used food as a weapon against the Sudan People's Liberation Army (SPLA) during the Second Sudanese Civil War (1983–2005).

During the Second Sudanese Civil War, "Operation Rainbow" was initiated by Khartoum to manipulate relief aid by providing access to food only to civilians in government-held towns of southern Sudan, mainly in Juba. This situation enabled the Sudanese government to tighten its control over the operations of relief agencies in southern Sudan and deprived SPLA loyalists of access to food aid. However, in contrast with Ethiopia's famine, inflation was another factor that worsened the famine crisis in Sudan. Despite Khartoum's control over relief aid, the SPLA still exploited the food aid provided by humanitarian agencies to facilitate its insurgent activities. For instance, the SPLA initiated reprisal measures that prevented food relief from reaching government-beleaguered towns, which also initiated a famine crisis.

However, after the inception of Operation Lifeline Sudan (OLS), the SPLA rescinded its food blockage strategies by allowing airlift of food aid and supporting OLS operations in southern Sudan. This strategy enabled the SPLA to gradually gain recognition from Western donors. Also, food aid provided by humanitarian agencies encouraged the return of the displaced population to southern Sudan. This situation provided the SPLA with the opportunity to consolidate its suzerainty over different regions in the south by providing food to returnees and displaced victims of the civil war.

While the SPLA used food aid to reinforce its control over southern Sudan, UNITA rebels, on the other hand, used food relief to instigate pressure on government-controlled cities during the Angolan Civil War (1975–2002). UNITA rebels used food as a war weapon by forcing farmers off their lands. About one million victims of this situation were herded by UNITA forces into government-controlled cities, where food aid provided by the World Food Programme was earmarked for only 800,000 people. In particular, ambushes, land mines, and traps were used by UNITA forces, which made the countryside impassable. In particular, rebel forces aimed to use starvation to prod the population to rebel against the government.

In addition, relief aid provided by nongovernmental organizations unwittingly aggravated food insecurity and prolonged the duration of the civil wars in Africa. For instance, during the Mozambique Civil War (1976–1992), inadequate needs assessment by the United Nations, budgetary constraints of donor countries, and inconsistent provision of food aid in different parts of the country compromised the efficacy of relief aid provided by humanitarian organizations to those afflicted by the scourges of war. Conflict of interest over the accessibility to relief aid was a major cause of the internal rivalry and split within the SPLA during the Second Sudanese Civil War. This incident also prolonged the civil war in southern Sudan with about two million people dying as a result of famine and disease during the conflict. Famine crises also instigate refugee movement across borders in Africa.

Yusuf Sholeye

See also: Angolan Conflicts; Eritrean People's Liberation Front (EPLF); Ethiopia: Insurgency and Interstate War; Mozambique Civil War; National Union for the Total

Independence of Angola (UNITA); Nigerian Civil War; Refugees in Postcolonial Africa; Sudan Civil War, First; Sudan Civil War, Second; Sudan People's Liberation Movement/Army (SPLM/A); Tigray People's Liberation Front (TPLF).

Further Reading

De Waal, Alex. *Famine Crimes: Politics and the Disaster Relief Industry in Africa*. London: African Rights, 1999.

De Waal, Alex. *Food and Power in Sudan: A Critique of Humanitarianism*. London: African Rights, 1997.

Keen, David. *Benefits of Famine: A Political Economy of Famine and Relief in South-West Sudan*. Oxford: Oxford University Press, 1991.

"Five Majors" Coup, Nigeria (January 15, 1966)

In the early morning hours of January 15, 1966, just three days after Lagos hosted a Commonwealth Prime Minister's Conference on the Rhodesia crisis, various units of the Nigerian Army fanned out from their bases on what were planned as nighttime training exercises around Kaduna, Ibadan, and Lagos. As the exhaustive Nigerian Police Report released in August 1966 pointed out, most of the lower-ranking officers and other ranks had no idea what they were about to do. By daybreak, the federal prime minister (Sir Abubakar Balewa) and finance minister (Chief Festus Okotie-Eboh), two regional premiers (the powerful Sardauna of Sokoto, Sir Ahmadu Bello, in the north, and Samuel Akintola in the west), and a handful of other Nigerian politicians and military leaders were dead. The ceremonial President, Nnamdi Azikiwe, was out of the country on holiday, one of the many circumstances that would later fuel notions of an "Igbo coup." However, it was only months later that the coup itself began to be described publicly in ethnic terms.

Nigeria's first coup triggered a series of events including a decree to remake Nigeria as a unitary state (May 1966), a countercoup (July 1966), large-scale ethnic persecution leading to the secession of Biafra, and a horrific civil war. Nevertheless, on that January night, the leaders of the coup, all officers of major or captain rank, were motivated by revolutionary and nationalist aims, not ethnic grievances. Majors Ifeajuna, Nzeogwu, Anuforo, Ademoyega, and others convinced or cajoled (and sometimes threatened) others to join them to take out many of the senior political and military elites. They shared a concern that Nigeria's political class had plunged the country into political and economic crisis, with an unbalanced regionalism that gave the north too much power at the root of the problem. It is mostly forgotten that in the immediate aftermath of the coup, many ordinary Nigerians, including northerners and westerners, celebrated in the streets.

That most of the young officers were of Igbo extraction, and none of the dead politicians or officers were, reflected historical trends in terms of the composition of the Nigerian Army officer corps in 1966. Some of the young officers were more attuned to the vision of Nigeria promoted by imprisoned Action Group leader Chief Obafemi Awolowo, sentenced to 10 years in prison in September 1963 on trumped-up charges of plotting his own coup. Awolowo's falling out with his previous ally, Akintola, caused a constitutional crisis over control of the western region and a realignment of parties during 1962–1963. Schisms were also emerging within the Nigerian Army itself as it deployed for internal security operations in the western region and middle belt. Subsequently, the federal election of late 1964 and regional elections of October 1965 were marred by violence and boycotts. Where some of the putschists aspired toward a social democratic federalism following Awolowo's vision, others considered federalism part of the problem. They all agreed, however, that some key members of the current political class had to go.

Military operations in Kaduna and Ibadan mostly went according to plan, but confusion in Lagos defeated the detachments sent there. The head of the Nigerian Army, Major General Johnson Aguiyi Ironsi, was never secured, and he drove around the city sending various detachments back to their barracks. Without Lagos and Ironsi, the coup fell apart. Within days all the plotters had been arrested, and Ironsi was handed the reins of power by the remaining political elites. Those arrested by Ironsi were kept in prison until the start of the Nigerian Civil War 18 months later. However, the fact they were not immediately court-martialed or otherwise tried for rebellion added fuel to the conspiracy that Ironsi, also of Igbo ethnicity, had been in on the game from the start. The Unification Decree of May 24, 1966, sealed Ironsi's fate, and within two months, Nigeria experienced its first military countercoup by northern officers, bringing Lt. Col. Yakubu Gowon to power until 1975.

Chris W. J. Roberts

See also: Coups and Military Regimes in Africa; Gowon, Yakubu "Jack" Dan-Yumma; Nigerian Civil War.

Further Reading

Ademoyega, Adewale. *Why We Struck: The Story of the First Nigerian Coup*. Lagos: Evans Brothers, 1981.

Gbulie, Ben. *Nigeria's Five Majors: Coup d'etat of 15th January 1966*. Onitsha: African Educational Publishers, 1981.

Siollun, Max. *Oil, Politics and Violence: Nigeria's Military Coup Culture 1966–1976*. New York: Algora Publishing, 2009.

Sklar, Richard. "Nigerian Politics in Perspective." *Government and Opposition* 2, no. 4 (July–October 1967): 524–539.

French Military Involvement in Postcolonial Africa

Most French colonies in Africa became independent in 1960, remaining tied to the former colonial ruler through a series of economic, technical, and military agreements. As such, France pursued a remarkably consistent policy of robust military intervention in postcolonial African states, which continues up to today. From the 1960s, France signed defense agreements with the governments of many of its former African colonies and extended this network to include Francophone former Belgian territories like Zaire and Rwanda in the 1970s. Since around 1960, the French military maintained long-term garrisons in parts of Francophone

Africa, French military personnel trained and advised African armed forces, African officers attended courses in France, and a French air mobile intervention force on the island of Corsica stood ready for deployment to Africa. While French troops sometimes protected postcolonial African leaders allied to France, Paris also engaged in covert and overt actions to depose African rulers who no longer supported French interests or who had become an embarrassment. For instance, in September 1979, during Operation Barracuda, French troops landed by aircraft in Bangui, capital of the Central African Republic, where they deposed the megalomaniac "Emperor" Jean-Bédel Bokassa, replacing him with the previous President David Dacko. In addition, French troops and aircraft engaged in combat operations in support of allied African states. While some French military interventions in African conflicts comprised sudden actions with quick departures, others amounted to protracted campaigns that lasted many years. In May 1978 French paratroopers conducted Operation Leopard, in which they intervened in Zaire's southern province of Shaba (Katanga) to defeat exiled rebels who had invaded from Angola and therefore stabilize the regime of Mobutu Sese Seko. In this case, French forces departed rapidly after the completion of their mission though French military instructors and advisers remained in Zaire. In Cameroon, French counterinsurgency operations in the southwest began in the 1950s during the last years of colonial rule and were renewed in 1960 with authorization from the government of the newly independent country that remained a French client. From the 1960s to the 1980s, French troops supported a series of regimes in Chad against northern-based rebels and eventually their Libyan allies, and during the early 1990s, French forces directly supported Rwanda's Hutu-majoritarian regime of Juvénal Habyarimana against primarily Tutsi rebels who invaded from Uganda. French military operations in Africa benefited from a chain of French military bases in parts of Francophone Africa such as in Gabon, the Central African Republic, and Chad. At times, these interventions also included small contingents of soldiers from allied former French colonies in Africa such as Senegal, Gabon, and Togo. Furthermore, and usually prompted by access to resources, France provided indirect military support to some secessionist movements such as mineral-rich Katanga during the Congo Crisis of the early 1960s and oil-rich Biafra during the Nigerian Civil War of 1967–1970. Several French military interventions in Rwanda during the 1994 genocide against the Tutsi severely damaged France's international reputation. While April's Operation Amaryllis involved a French air mobile extraction of French citizens and Rwandan government allies from Kigali, June's Operation Turquoise saw French troops create a supposed safe zone in southwestern Rwanda, where they facilitated the continuation of genocide by fleeing Hutu soldiers and militia. Another aspect of French military relations with postcolonial Africa involved massive arms sales to regimes such as apartheid South Africa during 1960 and the Kingdom of Morocco as it fought to retain control of Western Sahara during the late 1970s and 1980s.

From the late 1990s, partly as a result of the Rwanda debacle but also related to the changing international context after the end of the Cold War, France sought to legitimize military interventions in its informal empire in Africa by partnering with other international actors such as the European Union or United Nations. During 2003's Operation Artemis, the mostly French troops of the Interim Emergency Multinational Force (IEMF) secured the violence-plagued town of Bunia in northeastern Democratic Republic of the Congo (DRC) in the European Union's first autonomous military operation outside Europe that gave the UN time to send in its own brigade. Nevertheless, unilateral French military action continued. In the Central African Republic during 2006–2008, French troops supported the regime of François Bozizé against northern rebels including a March 2007 airborne operation that recaptured the northern town of Birao. After the 2001 Islamist attacks on the United States, and similar subsequent attacks in Europe including France, French military operations in Africa became absorbed into the American-led "War on Terror." In January 2013, with the assistance of American and British airlifts, France mounted Operation Serval, which delivered a mechanized intervention force to Mali, saving the capital Bamako from occupation by advancing Islamist and separatist Tuareg forces, recapturing towns in the north such as historic Timbuktu and pushing the rebels back into remote desert areas. While the United Nations quickly dispatched a large international force to support the weak government of Mali, the French continued their military presence in the area under the separate command of Operation Barkhane, which sought to counter Islamist insurgency in West Africa's Sahel region. The continuing French military presence also prompted resentment among local people and in 2022, in the context of a new military government in Mali that hired Russian mercenaries to counter the Islamist rebellion, French forces withdrew from Mali focusing their efforts on Niger. On the other side of the continent, the small but strategically located East African state of Djibouti hosted a French military and naval presence since its independence in 1977, and from the 1990s and 2000s, the country began to serve as an important staging area for French and eventually American operations in Somalia and the nearby Middle East.

Timothy J. Stapleton

See also: Bokassa, Jean-Bédel; Bozizé, François; Cameroon Conflicts; Central African Republic (CAR), Conflict in; Chad, Conflict in; Congo Crisis; Democratic Republic of the Congo (DRC), Continuing Violence in; Habyarimana, Juvénal; Hutu Power Movements; Mobutu Sese Seko; Nigerian Civil War; Peacekeeping in Africa; Rwanda, Civil War and Genocide; Shaba, Zaire: Rebel Incursions and Foreign Intervention; Somalia Civil War; Tuareg Rebellions since 1960 (Mali and Niger); Western Sahara, Conflict in.

Further Reading

Carbonneau, Bruno. *France and the New Imperialism: Security Police in Sub-Saharan Africa.* Aldershot: Ashgate, 2008.

Powell, Nathaniel. *France's Wars in Chad: Military Intervention and Decolonization in Africa.* Cambridge: Cambridge University Press, 2020.

Recchio, Stephano, and Thierry Tardy. *French Interventions in Africa: Reluctant Multilateralism.* New York: Routledge, 2020.

Rouvez, Alain. *Disconsolate Empires: French, British and Belgian Military Involvement in Post-Colonial Sub-Saharan Africa.* Lanham, MD: University Press of America, 1994.

Wallis, Andrew. *Silent Accomplice: The Untold Story of France's Role in the Rwandan Genocide*. London: I.B. Tauris, 2006.

Front for National Salvation (FRONASA)

See National Resistance Army (NRA)

Front for the Liberation of the Cabinda Enclave (FLEC)

See Cabindan Insurgency; Portuguese Africa, Independence Wars (Angola, Mozambique, and Guinea-Bissau)

G

Gaddafi, Muammar (1942–2011)

Libyan military officer and head of state (1970–2011). Born the youngest child of a nomadic Bedouin family in the al-Nanja community in Fezzan in June 1942, Muammar Gaddafi attended the Sebha preparatory school from 1956 to 1961. He graduated from the University of Libya in 1963, the same year he entered the Military Academy at Benghazi, where he became part of a cabal of young military officers whose plans included the overthrow of Libya's pro-Western monarchy.

Gaddafi and the secret corps of militant Arab-nationalist officers seized power in Libya on September 1, 1969, following a bloodless coup that overthrew King Idris. After a brief internal power struggle that consolidated his rule, Gaddafi renamed the country the Libyan Arab Republic and officially ruled as president of the Revolutionary Command Council (RCC) from 1970 to 1977. He then switched his title to president of the People's General Congress during 1977–1979. In 1979 he renounced all official titles but remained the unrivaled head of Libya.

Gaddafi's domestic policies were based on Libyan nationalism and Islamic socialism. Loosely following the model of his hero, Egyptian president Gamal Abdel Nasser, Gaddafi believed in the cause of Arab unity. He also sought to promote his own development and economic policy, a middle path that was neither communist nor Western. He sought the privatization of major corporations, the creation of a social welfare system, and the establishment of state-sponsored education and health care systems. He outlawed alcohol and gambling. His political and economic ideas are included within his Green Book. Gaddafi's regime encompassed a dark side, however, including the sometimes violent suppression of Libyan dissidents and the sanctioning of state-sponsored assassinations.

In foreign policy, Gaddafi promoted the ideals of Third Worldism, anti-imperialism, and solidarity between Arab and African nations. He was a major proponent of the Organisation for African Unity (OAU) and supported various anti-colonial liberation struggles in sub-Saharan Africa, including those in Mozambique and Angola. He also supported Zimbabwe's Robert Mugabe and was a staunch ally of Nelson Mandela and the African National Congress (ANC) in South Africa, stances that annoyed the United States, which had maintained a certain loyalty to European interests in Africa and viewed the South African apartheid regime as a bulwark against communism.

Gaddafi's policies alienated him from the West. Libya had been deeply impacted by Italian colonization and, later, by European interests in its oil production. Gaddafi wanted no return of Western control. He viewed himself as heir to Nasser, who had, even with the failure of the United Arab Republic, continued to believe that Arab nations should cooperate politically. In 1972 Gaddafi proposed a union of Libya, Egypt, and Syria, and in 1974 he signed a tentative alliance agreement with Tunisia, although neither scheme was implemented. At the same time, he became a strong supporter of the Palestinian liberation movements and is rumored to have been a chief financier of the radical Islamic Black September Organization, which most notoriously engineered the killing of Israeli athletes at the 1972 Munich Olympics. He was also linked to other non-Arab movements such as the Irish Republican Army (IRA) and terrorist attacks, including the December 21, 1988, bombing of Pan Am Flight 103 over Lockerbie, Scotland, that killed 243 passengers and 18 crew.

As with many other Arab nationalists, Gaddafi generally held a visceral hatred for the State of Israel, which he viewed as a tool of Western imperial domination. He made frequent threats of engaging Israel militarily and publicly expressed hopes that the nation could be wiped off the map. He also urged several African states to withdraw support for Israel as a precondition for receiving foreign aid.

Gaddafi's ties to terrorism drove a deep wedge in Libyan-U.S. relations. By the early 1980s, he had marginally allied himself with and received significant weapons supplies from the Soviet Union. Meanwhile, tensions between Libya and the United States reached fever pitch during the presidency of Ronald Reagan. On April 5, 1986, a bomb exploded in the La Belle discotheque in West Berlin, a venue frequented by U.S. service personnel. The blast killed three and wounded some 230 others (two of the dead and 79 of the injured were U.S. servicemen). After the bombing was linked directly to Libya, Reagan authorized a bombing raid on Libya designed to kill Gaddafi. He escaped, but it killed his infant adopted daughter and scores of civilians.

On December 21, 1988, Pan Am Flight 103 was destroyed over Lockerbie, Scotland, by a terrorist bomb. More than 270 people were killed, and subsequent investigations pointed to two Libyans as primary suspects. When the Gaddafi regime refused to extradite them for trial, the UN imposed sanctions on Libya in 1992. American confrontations with Libya continued, and a second incident over the Gulf of Sidra resulted in the destruction of two Libyan MiG-23 fighter planes in January 1989.

The end of the Cold War witnessed an easing of tensions in U.S.-Libyan relations as Gaddafi took a more conciliatory stance toward the West. He publicly apologized for the Lockerbie bombing and offered compensation to victims' families. He also openly condemned the September 11, 2001, terrorist attacks in the United States and took a more moderate line in the Palestinian-Israeli conflict. In February 2004 Libya publicly renounced its weapons of mass destruction (WMDs) program, and in May 2006 the United States and Libya resumed formal and full diplomatic relations. Most economic sanctions against Libya were then lifted, and the U.S. State Department removed Libya from its list of nations supporting terrorism.

Gaddafi, however, continued to provide a radical, if unique, commentary in Arab affairs. In 2008 he called for a one-state solution to the Arab-Israeli issue. Gaddafi also was committed to retaining firm dictatorial control over his country, and in 2006 he exhorted his supporters to kill those who sought political change.

Popular unrest was growing in Libya, however. Opponents protested decades of authoritarianism, corruption, and repression that had produced economic and political dysfunction. The so-called Arab Spring brought the unrest to the forefront with the beginning of peaceful demonstrations in Benghazi in eastern Libya on February 15, 2011. Gaddafi made clear his refusal to yield political power, and the result was civil war. With the civilian death toll rising and Libya descending into chaos, the North Atlantic Treaty Organization, led by France, Britain, and the United States, intervened with air power, and the rebel forces won. Gaddafi, who had vowed to fight to the end in Tripoli, left the capital for his hometown of Sirte, which came under rebel attack in mid-October. Gaddafi was captured while attempting to escape from Sirte and summarily executed on October 20, 2011.

Jeremy Kuzmarov

See also: Arab Spring; Arab-Israeli Wars; Chad, Conflict in; Cold War in Africa; Coups and Military Regimes in Africa; Libya, Conflicts with Egypt and the United States; Libyan Civil War, First; Nasser, Gamal Abdel; U.S. Military Involvement in Africa.

Further Reading

Chorin, Ethan. *Exit the Colonel: The Hidden History of the Libyan Revolution.* New York: Public Affairs, 2012.

Cojean, Annick. *Gaddafi's Harem: The Story of a Young Woman and the Abuses of Power in Libya.* Translated by Marjolijn de Jager. New York: Grove, 2013.

Davis, Brian L. *Qaddafi, Terrorism and the Origins of the U.S. Attack on Libya.* New York: Praeger, 1990.

Gaddafi, Muammar, with Edmond Jouve and Angela Parfitt. *My Vision.* London: John Blanke, 2005.

Lemarchand, Rene. *The Green and the Black: Qadhafi Policies in Africa.* Bloomington: Indiana University Press, 1988.

Lobban, Richard A., Jr., and Christopher H. Dalton. *Libya: History and Revolution.* Santa Barbara, CA: ABC-CLIO, 2014.

Oakes, John. *Libya: The History of Gaddafi's Pariah State.* Stroud: History Press, 2011.

Pargeter, Alison. *Libya: The Rise and Fall of Gaddafi.* New Haven, CT: Yale University Press, 2012.

Vandewalle, Dirk J. *A History of Modern Libya.* Cambridge: Cambridge University Press, 2012.

Garang, John de Mabior (1945–2005)

A Twic Dinka and founder and leader of the Sudan People's Liberation Army/Movement (SPLA/M) from 1983 to 2005, John Garang was born on June 23, 1945. Until his death in July 2005, Garang championed the sociopolitical and economic development of Sudan. After completing his primary school education in southern Sudan, Garang continued his secondary school education at Magamba Secondary School in Tanzania, where he met Yoweri Museveni, the future president of Uganda. After his high school education, he won a scholarship, which provided him with the opportunity to earn his bachelor of arts degree in economics in 1969 from Grinnell College in Iowa.

In 1970, during the First Sudan Civil War (1955–1972), Garang joined the Anya-Nya rebel movement, which was later incorporated into the Sudanese Armed Forces as part of the Addis Ababa Agreement of 1972. During this period, General Joseph Lagu, the major southern leader, appointed the 26-year-old Garang as his chief aide. This situation enabled Garang to join the Sudanese Armed Forces as captain. By 1974 Garang returned to the United States, where he took military courses at Fort Benning. Afterward, he enrolled at the Iowa State University economics department for his PhD from 1977 to 1981. His dissertation focused on the possibilities of economic development in southern Sudan.

Garang's education in the United States shaped his political ideology known as Sudanism, which espoused the possibility of a secular, multiethnic, and united Sudan. Garang's view was influenced by the nature of the free, secular, democratic, and multicultural diversity of U.S. society. Garang believed that this social structure should be integrated into the Sudanese society despite its religious and ethnic diversity. After returning to Sudan in 1982, Garang's unique combination of both formal military and economics training provided him with the opportunity to teach at both the University of Khartoum and the Khartoum military school.

In May 1983 Garang was sent by Sudan's president Jaafar Nimeiry to quell the Bor mutiny, spearheaded by the 105th Battalion and dominated by Dinka officers in the Sudanese Army. However, Garang was also one of the key officers who orchestrated the mutiny, which led to the formation of the SPLM/A on April 6, 1983. Leadership rivalry, ideological differences, and interethnic clashes were some of the problems Garang contended with after the formation of the SPLM/A. In particular, Garang had an instrumental role to play in several peace initiatives that eventually led to the end of the Second Sudanese Civil War through the Comprehensive Peace Agreement (CPA) of 2005. The CPA was an embodiment of Garang's vision of Sudanism. On July 2005, Garang died in a helicopter crash while returning from a meeting with President Yoweri Museveni of Uganda.

Yusuf Sholeye

See also: Anyanya; Lagu, Joseph Yanga; Sudan Civil War, First; Sudan Civil War, Second; Sudan People's Liberation Movement/Army (SPLM/A).

Further Reading

Arnold, Guy. *Historical Dictionary of Civil War in Africa.* Lanham, MD: Scarecrow Press, 2005.

Collins, Robert. *A History of Modern Sudan.* Cambridge: Cambridge University Press, 2005.

Kramer, Robert S., Richard Lobban, and Fluehr Lobban. *Historical Dictionary of Sudan: African Historical Dictionaries.* Lanham: Scarecrow Press, 2013.

Gbagbo, Laurent (1945–)

Laurent Gbagbo became the fourth leader of Côte d'Ivoire following elections and a popular uprising in October 2000 that forced military dictator Robert Guei from office. Gbagbo was in turn forced from power in 2011, after losing an election to longtime rival Alassane Ouattara. Gbagbo refused to accept the election results or leave office, a decision that led to widespread violence, which did not end until militias loyal to Ouattara, aided by French soldiers, captured Gbagbo and arrested him. He awaits trial by the International Criminal Court on war crimes charges.

An academic and veteran opposition figure who had long drawn the wrath of the Democratic Party of Côte d'Ivoire–African Democratic Rally (PDCI-RDA), which ruled the country from independence until a military coup in December 1999, Gbagbo is considered a charismatic leader with a gift for oratory.

Laurent Gbagbo was born on May 31, 1945, in the Christian central-west of Côte d'Ivoire. After attending high school in Abidjan, the city that houses the nation's seat of government, and earning a degree in philosophy in 1965, Gbagbo studied at the University of Lyons in France. After a year abroad, he returned to Côte d'Ivoire, earning a bachelor's degree in history in 1969. Gbagbo then returned to France to study at the Sorbonne, where he earned a master's degree in history in 1970.

Gbagbo returned to Côte d'Ivoire and taught history and geography at the Lycée Classique of Abidjan. His teaching career came to an abrupt halt, however, when on March 31, 1971, he was arrested on political charges related to "subversive teachings." He served two years in prison and, after his release, worked in the government education department. He completed his formal studies in France, where he was awarded a doctorate in history at the Paris VII University.

Gbagbo returned to Côte d'Ivoire and in 1980 was elected director of the Abidjan Institute of History. During the next two years, Gbagbo led unionization efforts among teachers and academics and secretly formed the Ivorian Popular Front (FPI), a political group opposed to the one-party rule of then president Felix Houphouet-Boigny and his PDCI-RDA. In 1982, after leading a pro-democracy protest against Houphouet-Boigny's autocratic regime, Gbagbo was forced to flee the country and was granted asylum in France in 1985. Three years later, Gbagbo returned to Côte d'Ivoire amid growing signs of political openness. Also in 1988, Gbagbo chaired the inaugural congress of the FPI and was elected its secretary general. When opposition political parties became legal in 1990, Gbagbo's political activities increased, and his political profile rose.

In the nation's first contested presidential elections in October 1990, Gbagbo stood as the only candidate opposing Houphouet-Boigny. Though he was trounced, winning only 11 percent of the vote, a year later he earned a seat in the national assembly. Gbagbo was arrested again in February 1992 after FPI-organized demonstrations against government policies degenerated into riots. Although he was sentenced to three years in prison, a presidential pardon freed him six months later.

Houphouet-Boigny died in December 1993 and national assembly speaker Henri Konan Bedie of the PDCI-RDA succeeded him as president. Shortly before the scheduled October 1995 presidential elections, Gbagbo and the FPI, along with other opposition parties, formed an alliance called the Republican Front to boycott elections they alleged would not be fair.

On December 24, 1999, a military uprising forced Konan Bedie from office. General Robert Guei quickly took charge of the country, forming a transitional government that included Gbagbo and the FPI. Three days after presidential elections, on October 25, 2000, when ballot counting indicated Gbagbo had won, Guei disbanded the independent electoral commission and declared himself the winner, arousing the anger of Ivorians tired of 10 months of government mismanagement and chaos. On October 26, masses of Abidjan demonstrators answered Gbagbo's call to flood the streets to protest the "stealing" of the elections. The demonstrations quickly turned into a mass uprising, as much of the military joined the protesters calling for Guei's ouster. Although some of Guei's private guard remained loyal and fired into the crowds, killing several dozen people, Guei was forced to flee, leaving the government to Gbagbo, the election winner.

Following Guei's ouster, the street protests degenerated into battles between Gbagbo's supporters and opposition party supporters, who demanded a new election that would include their candidate, Alassane Ouattara. In the subsequent violence, Muslim Ivorians were targeted by both street gangs and the military, who had aligned themselves with Gbagbo, and several hundred, mainly Muslims, were killed.

Gbagbo refused to consider new elections and aligned his government and himself against Ouattara. Gbagbo ostracized Ouattara, and by extension, many northern Muslims, as not fully Ivorian, setting the stage for another coup attempt in September 2002 that turned into a full-scale civil war. With the support of northern Muslims, the Patriotic Movement of Côte d'Ivoire (MPCI) quickly took control of the northern cocoa-producing towns, splitting the country in half and demanding that Gbagbo step down and hold free and fair elections. Gbagbo eventually reached a power-sharing agreement with the MPCI in January 2003, but his own supporters refused to accept it, leaving Gbagbo in a precarious position as fighting continued.

Eventually a cease-fire held, with sporadic violence since, and promised elections in 2005, 2007, 2008, and 2009 were postponed amid disputes over voter eligibility and other issues. When national elections were finally held on November 28, 2010, pitting Gbagbo against Ouattara, Gbagbo refused to accept the independent electoral commission's declaration that Ouattara had won with 54.1 percent of the vote to Gbagbo's 45.9 percent. Côte d'Ivoire's Constitutional Council, a branch of the Supreme Court, declared that Gbagbo had won with 51 percent of the vote; in the days afterward, both Ouattara and Gbagbo claimed the presidency, held swearing-in ceremonies, and named cabinets. The United Nations (UN), European Union, and African Union (AU), all demanded that Gbagbo step down. As Gbagbo continued to refuse to do so, clashes between militias loyal to the two men threatened to hurtle the country back into civil war, with an estimated 3,000 people killed before Ouattara's militias, aided by French soldiers, arrested Gbagbo at his compound in Abidjan on April 11, 2011. He awaits trial in the International Criminal Court (ICC) on charges related to the 2011 violence, including deliberately shelling a crowd of protesters. The case marked the first time the ICC has charged a former head of state with such crimes. In 2019, the ICC dismissed the charges against Gbagbo because of lack of evidence, and in 2021, he returned to Côte d'Ivoire.

ABC-CLIO

See also: Côte d'Ivoire Civil War; French Military Involvement in Postcolonial Africa.

Further Reading

Frindethie, K. Martial. *From Lumumba to Gbagbo: Africa in the Eddy of the Euro-American Quest for Exceptionalism*. Jefferson, NC: McFarland, 2016.

McGovern, Mike. *Making War in Cote d'Ivoire*. Chicago: University of Chicago Press, 2011.

Genocide in Africa (1960–)

In the wake of World War II and the Holocaust, the United Nations created a new type of crime through the 1948 "Convention on the Prevention and Punishment of the Crime of Genocide." After much debate among UN member states, this international law defined genocide as "acts committed with intent to destroy, in whole or in part, a national, ethnical, racial or religious group." Among the four African UN member states in 1948, Egypt, Liberia, and Ethiopia signed the genocide convention, but white minority–ruled South Africa declined. While Africans under colonial rule had little input in creating the original genocide concept and international law in the 1940s, the term became widely applied to the continent's postcolonial conflicts. After 1960, genocide accusations became increasingly common in Africa, especially in the context of newly independent states suppressing ethnoregional separatist movements. In 1960 UN secretary general Dag Hammarskjöld accused Congo's Prime Minister Patrice Lumumba of pursuing genocide against the Luba people of the secessionist region of South Kasai. Subsequently, the genocide allegation partly served to justify Lumumba's overthrow and transfer to the breakaway region of Katanga, where he was murdered. In 1967 the secessionist state of Biafra highlighted the alleged genocide of its primarily Igbo people in other parts of Nigeria as a basis for declaring independence. During the subsequent Nigerian Civil War (1967–1970), the Biafran leadership hired a Swiss public relations firm to gain international support by spreading the idea that Biafra was under threat of genocide, and within Biafra, radio broadcasts attempted to motivate Biafrans by repeating the same point. Similarly, during the First Sudanese Civil War (1955–1972), predominantly Christian southern Sudanese separatists accused the northern and Muslim-dominated government of orchestrating a genocide in the south. In 1980s Zimbabwe, some activists accused the predominantly Shona regime of Robert Mugabe of pursuing genocide against the Ndebele minority of the country's southwest. Not all genocide accusations in this Cold War period occurred in the context of separatist conflicts. International observers condemned genocide in Rwanda in 1964, where a Hutu-majoritarian government massacred minority Tutsi, and in Burundi in 1972, where a Tutsi-minority military regime tried to eliminate all educated people among the Hutu majority. International revulsion over the 1960 Sharpeville Massacre in South Africa prompted the UN Commission on Human Rights to suggest that apartheid violated aspects of the genocide convention, and this led to the 1973 International Convention on the Suppression and Punishment of the Crime of Apartheid that criminalized racially based domination and oppression. None of these accusations resulted in national or international criminal prosecution for the crime of genocide.

During the 1990s, concern about genocide in Africa gained new traction. While the broader context for this development included the end of the Cold War, the proliferation of civil wars in Africa, and the rise of global media, the horrific events that occurred in Rwanda in 1994 represented the primary factor. From April to July 1994, Hutu soldiers and militia attempted to exterminate Rwanda's Tutsi minority, killing around 800,000 people while international powers failed to act, except France, which facilitated the genocide. Ashamed of its abject failure in Rwanda, the UN renewed its commitment to genocide investigation and prevention, establishing a special court for genocide crimes committed in Rwanda in 1994, and a series of UN committees investigated genocide claims in other parts of Africa, especially the Great Lakes region. The 1998 conviction of Jean-Paul Akajesu, a mayor in Rwanda during the events of 1994, by the International Criminal Tribunal for Rwanda (ICTR) marked the first instance whereby a court enforced the 1948 international genocide convention. A 1996 UN report concluded that 1993 killings of Tutsi in Burundi amounted to genocide, and another 1998 UN report stated that the predominantly Tutsi Rwandan Army perhaps conducted genocide during its pursuit of Rwandan Hutu refugees across Zaire during 1996 and 1997. During the 2000s, Western obsession with genocide, mostly in Africa, gained expression through a flurry of books, films, documentaries, and websites about the 1994 genocide in Rwanda and the rise of the Save Darfur Movement that emerged from Holocaust-education organizations in the United States and gained the attention of American celebrities. International attention focused on the Sudan government's counterinsurgency campaign in the western region of Darfur, which the U.S. government and the European Union described as genocide, though a 2005 UN report fell short of that conclusion. Some Western states began to extend their legal jurisdiction to include genocide and crimes against humanity committed in other countries, enabling them to prosecute Rwandan immigrants for their actions during the 1994 genocide. In 2005 the UN General Assembly adopted the principle of "responsibility to protect" (R2P), theoretically limiting sovereignty by requiring states to defend their citizens from genocide, ethnic cleansing, crimes against humanity, and war crimes and sanctioning international interventions when national governments failed in this regard. However, critics warned that the new policy would apply only to weak countries such as those in Africa and potentially expand and prolong conflicts. Given this context, the number of accusations of genocide related to Africa increased dramatically. The Congolese began to claim that the invasion of the Democratic Republic of the Congo (DRC) by Rwanda and Uganda from 1998 to 2002 represented not only a massive theft of natural resources but also genocide, claiming several million lives. According to this view, the predominantly Tutsi regime of Rwanda exploited international guilt over the 1994 genocide to enable its own crimes in the DRC. Within the DRC, numerous factions engaged in genocide allegations, including Lendu and Hema militias as well as minority Twa communities in the Ituri province and Congolese Tutsi in the Kivu area, who justified their rebellion against the government as necessary to protect themselves from extermination by exiled Rwandan Hutu. Concerns over potential genocide also arose during the Tuareg rebellions in Mali and Niger during 2006–2009 and in Mali in 2012–2013, the 2007 election violence in Kenya, civil wars in the Central African Republic and South Sudan from 2013, and the Anglophone secessionist insurgency in southwestern Cameroon from 2017. Extending the legal definition of genocide to include extermination of political groups, an Ethiopian court convicted former dictator Mengistu Haile Mariam of genocide and other crimes in 2006, though he remains in exile. In 2010 Sudan's Omar al-Bashir became the first serving head of state indicted for genocide by the International Criminal Court, and after his ousting in 2019, the new Sudan government announced that it would send him to the Hague for trial. Increased awareness around genocide also prompted the revival of historic genocide claims such as in southeastern Nigeria relating to events during the Nigerian Civil War of 1967–1970 and environmental destruction by international oil companies and in Namibia where members of the Herero community seek reparations from Germany for a colonial genocide conducted from 1904 to 1907.

Timothy J. Stapleton

See also: Burundi, Civil War and Genocide; Cameroon Conflicts; Central African Republic (CAR), Conflict in; Congo Crisis; Congo Wars; Darfur Genocide; Democratic Republic of the Congo (DRC), Continuing Violence in; Ethiopia: Insurgency and Interstate Wars; Habyarimana, Juvénal; Hutu Power Movements; Kagame, Paul; Mengistu Haile Mariam; Nigerian Civil War; Rwanda, Civil War and Genocide; South Africa, Armed Struggle against Apartheid; South Sudan Civil War; Tuareg Rebellions since 1960 (Mali and Niger); Zimbabwe, Massacres (Gukurahundi).

Further Reading

Des Forges, Alison. *Leave None to Tell the Story: Genocide in Rwanda.* New York: Human Rights Watch, 1999.

Lemarchand, Rene. *Burundi: Ethnic Conflict and Genocide.* Cambridge: Cambridge University Press, 1994.

Mamdani, Mahmood. *Survivors and Saviors: Darfur, Politics and the War on Terror.* New York: Double Day, 2009.

Mamdani, Mahmood. *When Victims Become Killers: Colonialism, Nativism and the Genocide in Rwanda.* Princeton, NJ: Princeton University Press, 2001.

Melvern, Linda. *A People Betrayed: The Role of the West in Rwanda's Genocide.* London: Zed Books, 2005.

Power, Samantha. *A Problem from Hell: America and the Age of Genocide.* New York: New Republic, 2002.

Prunier, Gerard. *Darfur: The Ambiguous Genocide.* Ithaca, NY: Cornell University Press, 2005.

Prunier, Gerard. *The Rwanda Crisis: History of a Genocide.* New York: Columbia University Press, 1995.

Saro-Wiwa, Ken. *Genocide in Nigeria: The Ogoni Tragedy.* Port Harcourt: Saros International Publishers, 1992.

Smith, Karen. *Genocide and the Europeans.* Cambridge: Cambridge University Press, 2010.

Stapleton, Timothy. *A History of Genocide in Africa.* Santa Barbara, CA: Praeger Security International, 2017.

Straus, Scott. *The Order of Genocide: Race, Power, and War in Rwanda.* Ithaca, NY: Cornell University Press, 2007.

Totten, Samuel. *Genocide by Attrition: The Nuba Mountains of Sudan.* London: Transaction Publishers, 2015.

Gowon, Yakubu "Jack" Dan-Yumma (1934–)

After the July 1967 countercoup in Nigeria, Major General Yakubu "Jack" Gowon emerged as the head of the Supreme Military Council. Yakubu became the youngest Nigerian head of state and served as the commander in chief of the armed forces from August 1, 1966, until July 29, 1975, when he was overthrown in a bloodless coup. Under his leadership, the Nigerian armed forces foiled a secessionist attempt made by the Igbos of southeastern Nigeria to create an independent Republic of Biafra.

Born on October 19, 1934, in the Pankshin Division of the Middle Belt, Gowon grew up and was educated in Zaria where his parents served as CMS missionaries. During his final year in high school, Gowon, who was a renowned sportsman, gave up his goal of teaching and decided to join the Nigerian Army. He began his military career in 1954 and rose steadily through the ranks. He did his officer training in Ghana and later attended the Royal Military Academy Sandhurst, United Kingdom, where he received a commission as second lieutenant. He also attended the Staff College, Camberley (1962), and the Joint Staff College, Latimer (1965). Gowon also served as a member of the Nigerian Peacekeeping Force in the Congo.

After the January 15, 1966, coup that ended the First Republic, Gowon served as the army chief of staff of the Aguiyi Ironsi regime until his overthrow in the July 1966 countercoup. Lieutenant Gowon was later chosen as a consensus candidate (due to his ethnic and religious background) and assumed power as the second military head of state. The outbreak of riots and the widespread killing of Igbos in the Northern region after the countercoup resulted in growing threats of secession by the Eastern region. After a failed attempt at peacemaking in Aburi, Gowon decided to split the country into 12 distinct states on May 27, 1967. The dissolution of regions and the creation of states provoked Lieutenant Colonel Chukwuemeka Odumegwu Ojukwu to declare the Republic of Biafra on May 30, 1967. The country was plunged into a 30-month civil war that began on July 6, 1967, and ended on January 15, 1970.

During the postwar year, the Gowon-led government adopted the rhetoric of "No Victor, No Vanquished" in a bid to ensure the reunification of Nigeria. More significantly, his military government also introduced the postwar policy of reconciliation, rehabilitation, and reconstruction. In 1973, the Gowon regime also introduced the National Youth Service Scheme in a bid to rekindle national unity. On October 1, 1974, Gowon reneged on his promise and indefinitely postponed the handover to democratic rule. Amid a government filled with allegations of corruption, Gowon was ousted in a bloodless coup on July 29, 1975, while attending a meeting of African leaders in Kampala, Uganda. Gowon was later implicated in the 1976 assassination of his successor General Murtala Mohammed and stripped of his military rank. Gowon remained in exile in Britain until all charges against him were dropped by the federal government. During this period, he earned a doctoral degree in political science at the University of Warwick in 1983. Upon his return to Nigeria, Gowon worked as a professor of political science at the University of Jos.

Yolanda Osondu

See also: Coups and Military Regimes in Africa; "Five Majors" Coup, Nigeria; Nigerian Civil War.

Further Reading

Clarke, John D. *Yakubu Gowon: Faith in a United Nigeria.* London: Frank Cass, 1987.

De St. Jorre, John. *The Nigerian Civil War.* London: Hodder & Stoughton, 1972.

Elaigwu, J. Isawa. *Gowon: The Biography of a Soldier-Statesman.* London: Adonis & Abbey, 2009.

Habré, Hissène (1942–2021)

Hissène Habré was a former Chadian defense minister who turned against the government in the early 1980s; he ruled Chad as president from 1982 to 1990. A foe of Libya's Muammar Gaddafi, Habré received support from France, the United States, and other African nations, but his human rights abuses contributed to a withdrawal of French support and his subsequent downfall in 1990.

Born on September 13, 1942, Habré studied in France during his youth and later returned to Chad to became a revolutionary fighting against French imperialism. He was one of the rebel leaders who fought against the government in the mid-1970s, but after a successful coup installed Felix Malloum as president, he reached an agreement with the new regime and became its prime minister. Another rebel group under Goukouni Oueddei, however, continued the fight and chased Malloum from the country in 1979. Oueddei became the new president, and Habré served briefly as defense minister before being forced out, and thereafter, he renewed his guerrilla movement.

Habré drove Oueddei out of N'Djamena, the capital, in 1982 and was sworn in as president that same year. He faced his first major challenge as head of state late the next year, when he requested French intervention to defeat Oueddei's Libyan-backed forces. Throughout his presidency, Habré fought internal challenges, rarely exercising control of the entire country, and struggled against Gaddafi's intrigues. Despite reports of human rights abuses in Chad, he continued to receive support from France, the United States, and African enemies of Gaddafi. In 1990 a rebel movement under Idriss Déby launched a major attack on Habré's regime. France, by that time, reluctant to support the embattled president, kept its troops out of engagements with the rebels, and Déby forced Habré out of office in December 1990. Déby's administration, which itself has been accused of serious human rights violations, charged Habré with involvement in 40,000 political killings and 200,000 cases of torture.

Habré moved to exile in Dakar, Senegal. He lived quietly there until a Senegalese court indicted him on February 3, 2000, on charges of torture, stemming from the time he ruled Chad. The indictment marked the first time a former African ruler was charged in another country for human rights abuses, but the case stalled in 2001, when a Senegalese appeals court ruled that the nation's courts did not have the jurisdiction to try Habré. This eventually prompted Belgium to call for the former leader's extradition to stand trial abroad in 2005. At an African Union (AU) summit in 2006, however, the AU assembly approved the formation of the new African Court on Human and People's Rights and decided that Habré would at last stand trial in Senegal. The case had been stalled by myriad legal maneuverings, although a Chadian court in August 2008 sentenced Habré to death in absentia for war crimes and crimes against humanity.

On July 20, 2015, nearly a decade after the AU set up a special court for him and 25 years after he was overthrown from power, Habré went on trial in Senegal to face charges of crimes against humanity, war crimes, and torture. On May 30, 2016, the Extraordinary African Chambers tribunal in Senegal found Habré guilty of sexual slavery, rape, and ordering the execution of some 40,000 people. He was subsequently sentenced to life imprisonment. This marked the first time that an AU-supported court convicted a former African ruler of war crimes and the first time that a tribunal of one country convicted the leader of another country for war crimes and crimes against humanity. Habre contracted COVID-19 and passed away in August 2021.

Alexander Mikaberidze

See also: Chad, Conflict in; Cold War in Africa; Déby, Idriss; French Military Involvement in Postcolonial Africa; Gaddafi, Muammar.

Further Reading

Hicks, Celeste. *The Trial of Hissène Habré: How the People of Chad Brought a Tyrant to Justice.* London: Zed Books, 2018.

Weill, Sharon, Kim Thuy Seelinger, and Kerstin Bree Carlson, eds. *The President on Trial: Prosecuting Hissène Habré.* Oxford: Oxford University Press, 2020.

Habyarimana, Juvénal (1937–1994)

Juvénal Habyarimana was president of Rwanda from 1973 until his death by assassination on April 6, 1994. He was born into an aristocratic Hutu family on March 8, 1937, in Gasiza, Gisenyi, the son of a landowner, Jean-Baptiste Ntibazilikana, and his wife, Suzanne Nyirazuba. He was educated in Zaire and studied medicine before entering Rwanda's Officer Training School in Kigali in 1960. Graduating in 1961, he rose to become chief of staff in the Rwandan military forces (Forces Armées Rwandaises, or FAR) in 1963. In 1965, at the age of 28, he was made minister for the armed forces and police in the government of his cousin, Gregoire Kayibanda. In 1973 he was promoted to major general; then he overthrew Kayibanda in a military coup on July 5, 1973.

Habyarimana's military regime remained in office until 1978, when a referendum established a new constitution. Habyarimana, setting himself up as the only candidate, was elected to a five-year term as president, which was renewed in subsequent sham elections. Under Habyarimana, the quality of life for most Rwandans improved: there was political stability, and the economy recovered to reach unprecedented levels. This "golden age" came at a price, however. Every Rwandan citizen, including babies and the elderly, had to be a member of Habyarimana's political party (the only one permitted), the Mouvement Révolutionnaire National pour le Développement (National Revolutionary Movement for Development, or MRND). This was a party of Hutu exclusivism, and through it,

Habyarimana was able to build what was, in essence, an apartheid-like state in which the Tutsi minority was discriminated against institutionally.

Throughout this time, Habyarimana relied heavily on an inner clique of the MRND, the so-called Akazu (Kinyarwanda, "Little Hut"), a euphemism given to an informal but tightly knit (and highly corrupt) network of Habyarimana's closest family members, friends, and party associates. It was said to be so thoroughly dominated by Habyarimana's wife, Agathe, that, at times, even her husband could be frozen out of the decision-making process. The name Akazu was originally, in precolonial times, a term given to the inner circle of courtiers to the royal family. Under the MRND regime, and particularly during Agathe Habyarimana's dominance, it developed such awesome power that it even instituted its own death squad, recruited from members of the presidential guard. The Akazu was an oligarchy that not only held back any possibility of Rwanda returning to democracy, but also worked hard to promote the interests of northern Rwanda (the Akazu base) over those of the south. This further destabilized the position of the minority Tutsis throughout the country, and, through its extensive network of supporters in the bureaucracy, the financial sector, and society generally, the Akazu skimmed off vast amounts of public money for the greater good of the extended Habyarimana family.

The late 1980s saw Rwanda experience an economic downturn, as world coffee prices—upon which the Rwandan economy relied heavily—dropped sharply. This destabilized Habyarimana's regime, forcing him to introduce an economic austerity program that led to widespread unrest. In hopes of curbing unprecedented anti-government sentiment, he convened a national commission to study how best to implement a multiparty democracy in Rwanda. While army control ensured that he still held the country in an iron grip, forced budget cuts in 1989—accompanied by a drought in 1988–1989 and a plea for financial assistance to the World Bank—saw pressure brought against Habyarimana to begin a process of liberalization for Rwanda's political system.

Despite this, Habyarimana was and remained a Hutu supremacist. While portraying an image of one who would not be averse to a liberalization of his government, in reality he also armed and encouraged the activities of extremist Hutu militias such as the Interahamwe ("those who attack together") and Impuzamugambi ("those with a common purpose").

In late 1990 a large and well-equipped rebel Tutsi army located in nearby Uganda, the Rwandan Patriotic Front (RPF), invaded the country. This *émigré* force engaged the Rwandan Army in heavy fighting that came close to Kigali and threatened Habyarimana's grip. Only the intervention of French paratroopers, units of which stood physically between the RPF and government forces, stopped the invasion. The civil war continued intermittently for another three years, further damaging Rwanda's already vulnerable economy, and led Habyarimana inevitably to the conclusion that he would have to open some form of negotiation process if his administration was to survive. This began in 1992, when the country held its first multiparty elections, and changes in the legislation provided for both a prime minister and a president.

By August 4, 1993, delegates from the RPF met with officials of the Habyarimana administration and representatives of the United States, France, and the Organisation of African Unity to negotiate a settlement. The resulting settlement, signed at Arusha, Tanzania, saw a set of five accords agreed to between the two parties. These ranged over a wide variety of topics: refugee resettlement, power sharing between Hutu and Tutsi, the introduction of an all-embracing democratic regime, the dismantling of Habyarimana's dictatorship, and the encouragement of a transparent rule of law throughout Rwanda. Arusha guaranteed the RPF half the officer corps and 40 percent of the enlisted men in a reorganized Rwandan Army as well as Tutsi representation in key government posts.

In the months that followed, a number of subsequent meetings took place for the purpose of negotiating their implementation. This involved the parties traveling to and from Arusha, sometimes by road and at other times by plane. Some observers considered that Habyarimana purposely allowed these negotiations to drag on in order to buy time and thereby reinforce his position at home, the more so as Hutu extremist elements were becoming increasingly frustrated at Habyarimana's "capitulation" to the rebel forces by even entering negotiations in the first place.

On April 6, 1994, while returning to Kigali from one of the negotiation rounds in Arusha, Habyarimana's Falcon 50 jet, carrying the president as well as the president of Burundi, Cyprien Ntaryamira, the chief of staff of the Rwandan military, and numerous others, was shot down by two missiles fired from just outside the Kigali airport perimeter. The plane crashed into the grounds of the presidential palace, with all on board killed. Within hours, as if the assassination had sounded a war cry to the Hutu extremists in Rwanda, the killing of all Tutsis and the Hutu liberal middle class began.

It has never been proven conclusively who was responsible for the missile attack. A French investigating team blamed the RPF, in particular its leader (and later president of Rwanda), General Paul Kagame. Others have argued that it was Hutu extremists, believing Habyarimana far too moderate, who decided to use his death as a necessary sacrifice to force a final reckoning with the RPF and the Tutsis. Yet others have even suggested that it was members of the Akazu—and thus, Habyarimana's own family—who arranged for the plane to be shot down.

Whatever the case, the assassination certainly served as an opportunity for extremist Hutus to unleash unprecedented ethnic violence in Rwanda. Within hours, the militias, the FAR, the presidential guard, and the Gendarmerie Nationale (the national police force) unleashed wholesale carnage against Rwanda's Tutsis. At least 800,000 people—though by several estimates, nearly a million—were killed over the next three months, in one of the fastest genocides in recorded history.

Three days after the assassination, French forces escorted the slain president's widow, Agathe Habyarimana, out of the country, evacuating her to France. Reports of her living a life of luxury in Paris surfaced frequently over the next several years, rubbing salt into the wounds of the RPF-dominated government that came to power in Rwanda after the genocide. As one of the leading members of the Akazu (also known in some circles as the "Clan de Madame"), Agathe Habyarimana was alleged by the RPF to have been one of the genocide's masterminds. After many years in exile, "Madame Agathe" was denied political asylum in France on January 4, 2007 (though incongruously, she was permitted to remain in the country).

Then, on March 2, 2010, she was arrested by the government of French president Nicolas Sarkozy on suspicion of her involvement in the genocide. The move against her followed a visit to Rwanda by Sarkozy during which he promised that "those responsible for the genocide must be found and punished." She was detained at her home in the southern Paris suburbs by police executing a Rwandan-issued international arrest warrant released in October 2009. The Rwandan government immediately urged Paris to extradite her for trial, though France has yet to fulfill this request. French judges have consistently refused to extradite genocide suspects to Kigali on the grounds that they would not receive a fair trial, and it is certain that Agathe Habyarimana would find it extremely difficult to obtain this.

Paul R. Bartrop

See also: Burundi, Civil War and Genocide; Coups and Military Regimes in Africa; French Military Involvement in Postcolonial Africa; Genocide in Africa; Hutu Power Movements; Rwanda, Civil War and Genocide.

Further Reading

Mamdani, Mahmood. *When Victims Become Killers: Colonialism, Nativism and the Genocide in Rwanda.* Princeton, NJ: Princeton University Press, 2001.

Melvern, Linda. *Conspiracy to Murder: The Rwandan Genocide.* London: Verso, 2006.

Prunier, Gerard. *The Rwanda Crisis: History of a Genocide.* New York: Columbia University Press, 1995.

Haftar, Khalifa Belqasim (c. 1943–)

A Libyan political and military leader who played a driving role in the Libyan Civil War, beginning in 2014. Born in the city of Ajdabiya c. 1943, Khalifa Haftar completed his military education in 1966, graduating from the Benghazi University Military Academy. As a junior officer he joined the Libyan Free Officers Movement led by Muammar Gaddafi and took part in the 1969 Libyan coup d'état that brought down the Senussi monarchy.

Khalifa Haftar held important political and military positions during Gaddafi's rule. As a member of the military junta, he served on the Revolutionary Command Council. He commanded the Libyan contingent in the 1973 Yom Kippur War. He also led Libyan forces in the Chadian-Libyan War (1978–1987). However, Chad defeated the Libyan forces and captured him. Gaddafi held him responsible for the defeat and disowned him. He moved to the United States and tried unsuccessfully to topple Gaddafi in the 1996 uprising. During the 2011 Libyan Revolution, Haftar returned to Libya and joined the opposition military in the eastern section of the country called Cyrenaica. The rebel forces did not readily welcome him due to his past history of working for Gaddafi, not to mention the support he received from the CIA in his plot to overthrow Gaddafi.

On February 14, 2014, he declared the General National Congress (GNC) suspended because it had exceeded its term of office. In May 2014 Islamists were assassinating activists, politicians, journalists, security professionals, and army officers in Benghazi almost every day. Haftar launched an offensive he called Operation Karama (Dignity) on May 16, purportedly to cleanse Libya of terrorism. He built a military force with aid from Egypt, Russia, and the United Arab Emirates. On March 2, 2015, the House of Representatives (HoR) appointed him commander of the Libyan National Army (LNA), with the rank of lieutenant general. In September 2016 the LNA captured the important oil terminals at Sidra and Ras Lanuf. The HoR then promoted him from lieutenant general to field marshal. The LNA lost these areas in March 2017 but regained them in 2018. In December 2016 and January 2017, the LNA captured airfields in the south and by September 2017 finally consolidated control of Benghazi.

In April 2018 he went to Paris for three weeks of medical treatment. During five years of fighting, he has assembled a heterogeneous coalition, gathering prominent secular politicians as well as army officers and militias from Zintan and Benghazi. On April 5, 2019, his forces moved to take control of Tripoli but ultimately failed.

Taylan Paksoy

See also: Arab Spring; Arab-Israeli Wars; Chad, Conflict in; Gaddafi, Muammar; Libyan Civil War, First; Libyan Civil War, Second.

Further Reading

Lacher, Wolfram. "Libya's Local Elites and the Politics of Alliance Building." *Mediterranean Politics* 21, no. 1 (2016): 64–85.

Tawil, Camille. "Operation Dignity: General Haftar's Latest Battle May Decide Libya's Future." *Terrorism Monitor* 12, no. 11 (May 30, 2014): 8–11

Wehrey, Frederic. *Burning Shores: Inside the Battle for the New Libya*. New York: Farrar, Straus and Giroux, 2018.

Holy Spirit Movement (HSM)

See Uganda, Insurgency in the North

Hutu Power Movements

In Rwanda and Burundi, the development of a Belgian colonial state that favored the Tutsi minority, portrayed as racially superior outsiders, eventually prompted the growth of a counter-elite, seeking rights for the Hutu majority perceived as dispossessed indigenous people. From the decolonization period of the late 1950s and early 1960s, Hutu movements in both countries used violence to pursue their objectives, though in different contexts. In 1959, in the context of outgoing Belgian officials losing confidence in the increasingly nationalist Tutsi elite and seeing conservative Hutu leaders as more compliant postcolonial partners, Hutu militias took power in Rwanda, establishing the foundation of a Hutu-majoritarian republic that gained independence in 1962. Concurrent with this transition,

Belgian officers established a military in Rwanda consisting almost entirely of Hutu soldiers, with most of them originating from the northern part of the country, including Juvénal Habyarimana, who became the force's first Rwandan commanding officer in 1963. Lacking any previous traditions of colonial military recruitment in Rwanda, the Belgians created a system called "pignet," which favored recruits of stocky physical build, stereotypical of Hutu men, and rejected tall and slender Tutsi. After Rwanda's Hutu army repelled an incursion by exiled armed Tutsi fighters at the end of 1963, the government of President Gregoire Kayibanda organized Hutu militias that engaged in revenge massacres of Tutsi civilians during 1964 in what could be described as the first genocide in Rwanda. Initially called the National Guard of Rwanda (GNR), the Hutu-dominated state military eventually became the Armed Forces of Rwanda (FAR). In 1973, Habyarimana staged a military coup removing Kayibanda and his predominantly southern Hutu regime and installing himself as head of state with a northern Hutu-dominated administration. Under Habyarimana, Rwanda became part of France's military alliance of Francophone African states. Strongly backed by the French military, the FAR fought the predominantly Tutsi rebels of the Rwandan Patriotic Front (RPF) who invaded Rwanda in 1990. From 1990, Habyarimana's ruling National Revolutionary Movement for Democracy and Development (MRND) organized a Hutu militia called Interahamwe ("those who work together") that engaged in mass violence against Tutsi civilians. In 1992, with the disbanding of Rwanda's one-party system, a new political group representing the most extreme Hutu agenda called the Coalition for the Defence of the Republic (CDR) formed another Hutu militia called Impunzamugambi ("those with a common purpose"). Trying to avoid a power-sharing agreement with the predominantly Tutsi RPF, elements of the FAR along with the Interahamwe and Impunzamugambi militias attempted to exterminate Rwanda's Tutsi minority during the genocide of 1994.

With the 1994 collapse of Rwanda's Hutu Power regime and the RPF takeover, Hutu-armed movements of Rwandan origin began a long period of exile. In 1994 many soldiers from the defeated FAR and associated Hutu militia members retreated across the border to large refugee camps in eastern Zaire, and a significant number fled to Sudan. In eastern Zaire, given the floundering regime of Mobutu Sese Seko, former FAR and Hutu militia fighters collected a war tax from Hutu refugees and bought back their weapons previously seized by corrupt Zairean troops. In early 1995 exiled Hutu fighters based in Zaire began to infiltrate Rwanda's border areas, where they raided schools and ambushed buses. Given this threat, along with the victimization of Zairean Tutsi by exiled Rwandan Hutu, RPF-ruled Rwanda invaded Zaire in 1996–1997 and orchestrated the rise of a local rebel group that overthrew Mobutu and installed Laurent Kabila in a renamed Democratic Republic of the Congo (DRC). During this First Congo War (1996–1997), ex-FAR and Interahamwe fought on the side of Mobutu's forces withdrawing west across Central Africa while some of the Rwandan Hutu fighters hid out in isolated areas in the eastern DRC's South and North Kivu provinces. Immediately following the First Congo War, exiled Hutu fighters in the eastern DRC formed the Army for the Liberation of Rwanda (ALIR) and mounted attacks inside Rwanda in late 1997 and 1998 with the aim of retaking power in their home country. This prompted Rwanda's RPF regime to pursue an aggressive counterinsurgency campaign in its border regions and to undertake military incursions into the eastern DRC, where Kabila's local Congolese Armed Forces (FAC) did nothing about exiled fighters, in pursuit of Hutu rebels and to once again invade that country in July 1998. Subsequently, during the Second Congo War (1998–2002), Kabila's state mobilized former FAR/Interahamwe members, including the ALIR already in the DRC as well as others recruited in Sudan, Central African Republic, and Congo-Brazzaville to fight against Rwandan and Ugandan invaders and Congolese rebels. Around 2000, during the DRC conflict, a number of ALIR factions and other Hutu groups in the DRC merged to form the Democratic Forces for the Liberation of Rwanda (FDLR). Excluded from the peace process that ended the Second Congo War and labeled "negative forces," the FDLR continued to operate in areas of South and North Kivu provinces after 2002 though without support from the DRC government of Joseph Kabila. Although around 7,000 FDLR members, including General Paul Rwarakabije, returned to Rwanda between 2003 and 2007, the continued presence of exiled Hutu fighters in the eastern DRC incited further Rwandan military involvement in the area and the formation of armed groups by Congolese Tutsi. During 2005 and 2006, the United Nations Operation in the DRC (MONUC) and the Armed Forces of the DRC (FARDC) mounted several major operations against FDLR fighters in the eastern Congo, who simply moved deeper into the bush. A joint military operation by the FARDC and Rwandan state forces in 2009 also had little impact on FDLR. While FDLR became increasingly involved in illegal mining and occasionally implicated in attacks on civilians in the DRC, several of its political leaders based in Europe faced charges over war crimes, and military commander General Sylvestre Mudacumura became the subject of an international arrest warrant in 2011 and was killed by the FARDC in 2019.

With the rise of a Tutsi military regime in Burundi shortly after independence in the 1960s, Burundian Hutu rebel movements developed in exile and eventually came to power inside the country. While Rwanda's new military excluded Tutsi, Burundi's armed forces did the opposite, adopting a set of physical requirements that minimized Hutu enlistment. In 1969, the Burundi military's killing of its few Hutu personnel along with Hutu government officials inspired Hutu students to escape to the bush to organize an armed resistance movement, and they recruited from among Burundian refugee camps in neighboring Tanzania. In 1972, an incursion by Tanzanian-based Burundian Hutu rebels into southern Burundi gave the Tutsi military government of Michel Micombero an excuse to exterminate all educated Hutu and Hutu students, prompting even more Hutu to flee the country. During the late 1970s, an exiled Burundian Hutu group called Tabara ("come to my rescue") formed in Belgium, demanding the removal of the Micombero regime. After the Habyarimana government expelled Tabara from Hutu-ruled Rwanda in 1979 on the basis of jeopardizing fragile relations with Burundi, the group moved to Tanzania where it fell apart given leadership disputes. In 1980, in Tanzania, former Tabara leader Remy Gahutu established the Party for the Liberation of the Hutu People (PALIPEHUTU), and a few years later, it founded an armed wing called National Liberation Forces (FNL) to overthrow the Tutsi regime in Burundi. Opening offices in Europe, PALIPEHUTU-FNL developed a populist ideology that appealed to Burundian Hutu residents of refugee camps in Tanzania, portraying the Tutsi as inherently cruel foreign invaders and identifying the 1972 genocide as the moment of Hutu political awakening. The movement lost its leader in 1990 when Gahutu died under mysterious circumstances while detained by Tanzanian authorities. In the early 1990s the failed transition to democracy in Burundi, including the army's assassination of the country's first Hutu president Melchior Ndadaye and a cycle of revenge and counter-revenge massacres of Tutsi and Hutu led to a civil war. In April 1994, with the death of another Burundian president in the same airplane as Rwanda's Habyarimana and the start of the genocide in Rwanda, a Hutu militia called Intagoheka ("those who do not sleep") started attacking the Tutsi-dominated Burundian Army. Otherwise moderate Hutu politicians formed the National Council for the Defense of Democracy (CNDD) with an armed wing called Forces for the Defense of Democracy (FDD) that launched a guerrilla struggle to reform the country. At the same time, the more extremist PALIPEHUTU-FNL began massacres of Tutsi civilians within Burundi. At the start of the First Congo War in 1996, Burundi's new military regime of Pierre Buyoya invaded eastern Zaire, destroying bases of the exiled CNDD-FDD that then moved to Tanzania. As with the exiled Hutu movement from Rwanda, the CNDD-FDD became embroiled in the Second Congo War (1998–2002), fighting on the side of the Kabila regime and receiving training in Zimbabwe that was also involved in the conflict. On the other hand, PALIPEHUTU-FNL operated mostly within Burundi. The end of the war in the Congo prompted further negotiations in Burundi, which led to a peace process and the transition of CNDD-FDD into a political party that eventually won the 2005 elections with FDD leader, Pierre Nkurunziza, becoming president. Led by Agathon Rwasa, PALIPEHUTU-FNL continued its armed struggle until 2006, with a brief resurgence of fighting in 2008, after which it joined the political process.

Timothy J. Stapleton

See also: African Armed Forces; Belgian Military Intervention in Africa; Burundi, Civil War and Genocide; Buyoya, Pierre; Congo Wars; Democratic Republic of the Congo (DRC), Continuing Violence in; French Military Involvement in Postcolonial Africa; Genocide in Africa; Habyarimana, Juvénal; Kabila, Joseph; Kabila, Laurent; Micombero, Michel; Mobutu Sese Seko; Nkurunziza, Pierre; Rwanda, Civil War and Genocide.

Further Reading

Lemarchand, Rene. *Burundi: Ethnic Conflict and Genocide.* Cambridge: Cambridge University Press, 1994.

Mahmood, Mamdani. *When Victims Become Killers: Colonialism, Nativism and the Genocide in Rwanda.* Princeton, NJ: Princeton University Press, 2001.

Malkki, Liisa. *Purity and Exile: Violence, Memory and National Cosmology among Hutu Refugees in Tanzania.* Chicago: University of Chicago Press, 1995.

Prunier, Gerard. *Africa's World War: Congo, the Rwanda Genocide and the Making of a Continental Catastrophe.* Oxford: Oxford University Press, 2009.

Prunier, Gerard. *The Rwanda Crisis: History of a Genocide.* New York: Columbia University Press, 1995.

Sommers, Marc. *Fear in Bongoland: Burundian Refugees in Urban Tanzania.* New York: Berghahn Books, 2001.

Turner, Simon. *Politics of Innocence: Hutu Identity, Conflict and Camp Life.* New York: Berghahn Books, 2010.

Watt, Nigel. *Burundi: The Biography of a Small African Country.* London: Hurst, 2008.

Islamic Salvation Front (FIS)

An Algerian Islamist political organization founded by Abassi Madani on February 18, 1989, the Islamic Salvation Front (FIS) enjoyed official registration status as a political party from September 6, 1989, until March 4, 1992, when a military coup dismantled it and banned it.

To overcome the legacy of 130 years of French colonization, the government leaders promoted Arabization using teachers from Egypt and Syria. Many of these teachers brought a political ideology of Islamism and a strategy for promoting socially conservative values in the population. Islamist activists rapidly expanded their influence through a network of associations across the country, assisting the poor and promoting opposition to the government during Friday prayers. This Islamist movement started to grow rapidly in the 1970s among college students and the unemployed urban population. Although the government crushed an initial Islamist rebellion from 1982 to 1987, it also employed appeasement, instituting a Family Code in 1984 that restricted the rights and freedoms of women.

In 1989, in the first free elections for local, municipal, and regional assemblies, the FIS won a great proportion of the towns and 32 of 48 provinces. Although the leader, Abassi Madani, claimed support for multiparty democracy, cooperation with France and the West, and only gradual employment of Sharia, his running mate, Ali Ben Hadj, engaged in fiery rhetoric against the government and the National Liberation Front (FLN), calling democracy unbelief. However, most of the people who voted for the FIS considered this party their best hope to punish the FLN and the brutal security services. In the national parliamentary elections on December 26, 1991, the FIS won 188 seats out of 231, leaving the ruling FLN Party in third place with 15 seats.

The prospect that the FIS would win enough seats in the parliament to change the constitution, combined with the rhetoric of Ben Hadj, created great fear that an FIS victory would stop democratic progress and force a radical purge of the government. Before the second round of elections could take place, the army compelled President Chadli Benjedid to dissolve the parliament and then resign. The military leaders blocked the elections, imprisoned the FIS leaders, and put thousands of Islamists into prison camps in the Sahara Desert. Upon release, some activists joined militants, organizing in remote places, who started a guerrilla campaign to force the government to return to democracy. In 1994, the FIS acknowledged an armed wing, the Army of Islamic Salvation (AIS), which formed in reaction to the indiscriminate violence of the Armed Islamic Group (GIA).

Madani and Ben Hadj remained in jail until July 2003, when President Abdelaziz Bouteflika released them as part of his bargaining strategy.

Carolina Bracco

See also: Algerian Civil War; Armed Islamic Group (GIA); Army of Islamic Salvation (AIS); Bouteflika, Abdelaziz; National Liberation Front (FLN) Algeria.

Further Reading

Kapil, Arun. "Algeria's Elections Show Islamist Strength." *Middle East Report* 166 (September–October 1990): 31–36.

Roberts, Hugh. "The Islamists, the Democratic Opposition and the Search for a Political Solution in Algeria." *Review of African Political Economy* 22, no. 64 (June 1995): 237–244.

Willis, Michael. *The Islamist Challenge in Algeria: A Political History*. New York: New York University Press, 1996.

J

Janjaweed

Janjaweed is an informal name for the armed militia that was the principal agent of mass murder, rape, and property destruction in the Darfur region of Sudan during the early 2000s. The militia's members hail primarily from a few traditionally nomadic, Arabic-speaking Abbala and Baggara ethnic groups—camel and cattle herders, respectively—and are lighter-skinned than most of Darfur's sedentary population. Despite the Janjaweed's Arab-supremacist ideology, "Arab" is a misleading term in Darfur, where nearly the entire population is Black as well as Muslim, including those identifying themselves as Arab. While popular media has dramatized the conflict in Darfur as a showdown between Arabs and Africans, many Darfurians who identify themselves as Arab do so primarily on the basis of their communities' use of Arabic and on their pastoralist way of life. Many of the communities in Darfur that identify as ethnically Arab are not associated with the Janjaweed.

Known by a colloquial Arabic expression that roughly means "horseman," the Janjaweed militia has become known for riding into African farming settlements after bombing raids by the Sudanese Air Force and massacring the men, raping the women, and stealing anything they can find. This mass slaughter, characterized by some international observers as genocide and by others merely as war crimes, forced millions of Darfurians to flee to refugee camps.

A modern incarnation of the age-old nomadic Arab militia known as Murahilin (nomads), the origins of today's Janjaweed reach back to 1988, after former Chadian president Hissène Habré, aided by French- and U.S.-backed forces, drove Libyan president Colonel Muammar Gaddafi's invading militia out of Chad into Darfur. There they stayed through the 1990s, continuing to espouse their Arab-supremacist ideology and gathering weapons, and their small-scale territorial incursions at the expense of Darfurian farmers were largely ignored by the Sudanese government in Khartoum.

Conflict between Arab and non-Arab Darfurian groups escalated during 1999–2000, when rebels in western and northern Darfur began to demand more rights from Khartoum. In February 2003 rebels stepped up their attacks against government installations, and Khartoum responded with a counterinsurgency campaign that involved recruiting, organizing, and providing weapons to the Janjaweed militia. While the campaign aimed to destroy the Sudan Liberation Army (SLA) and the Justice and Equality Movement (JEM), as part of its strategy, the government also orchestrated the Janjaweed's scorched-earth campaign against unarmed non-Arab civilian populations, particularly those of the Fur, Zaghawa, and Masalit ethnic groups, which were those most associated with the rebel movements. The Sudanese government largely denied its role in this campaign; however, the evidence contradicting these denials, beginning with thousands of eyewitness accounts, is overwhelming.

Following intense international criticism that included the 2004 naming of Musa Hilal, a Darfurian Arab leader, as a prime suspect for genocide by the U.S. State Department, in 2006 much of the Janjaweed was hired on by Khartoum's Sudan Armed Forces. Those remaining continued to be active in Darfur and in neighboring Chad, and smaller-scale attacks continued even as the United Nations (UN) threatened to send a new peacekeeping force to the region in late 2006. In February 2007 the International Criminal Court (ICC) issued an arrest warrant for another suspected militia leader, Ali Kushayb, on 51 charges of war crimes and crimes against humanity, but the Sudanese government refused to cooperate with arranging for his extradition. After 2008 the Janjaweed declined dramatically in size and strength. However, in 2014 Sudan's president Omar Hassan Ahmad al-Bashir began reconstituting elements of the Janjaweed as his personal army. Although al-Bashir fell from power in 2019, Sudan's paramilitary Rapid Support Forces (RSF), which originated with the Janjaweed militia, continues to wield influence.

Melissa Stallings

See also: Al-Bashir, Omar (Umar) Hassan Ahmad; Darfur Genocide; Genocide in Africa; Justice and Equality Movement (JEM); Refugees in Postcolonial Africa; Sudan Liberation Army (SLA).

Further Reading
Deng, Francis Mading. *War of Visions: Conflict of Identities in the Sudan.* Washington, DC: Brookings Institution Press, 1995.
Flint, Julie, and Alex de Waal. *Darfur: A Short History of a Long War.* London: Zed Books, 2006.
Prunier, Gerard. *Darfur: The Ambiguous Genocide.* Ithaca, NY: Cornell University Press, 2005.

Justice and Equality Movement (JEM)

The Justice and Equality Movement (JEM) is one of the principal groups rebelling against the national government in Sudan's western region of Darfur. Operating primarily in northern West Darfur State, the JEM is second in size and influence only to the Sudan Liberation Army (SLA), whose activities are centered in South Darfur State. While sharing many of the same basic founding principles as the SLA, particularly in its demands for greater regional autonomy and economic opportunity, the JEM is distinct from the SLA in having firm roots in Islamist political ideologies. The organization is also notable for having a strong tribal affiliation with the Zaghawa people, whereas the SLA is not dominated by any one tribe but instead draws its ranks from a broad tribal base that includes Fur, Masalit, Zaghawa, and other people.

FORMATION AND EARLY YEARS OF THE JEM

The JEM emerged as a distinct political entity in 2001 under the leadership of medical doctor and former Darfur government minister Khalil Ibrahim. Its formation was intricately tied to a 1999–2000 power struggle between Sudanese president Omar Hassan Ahmad al-Bashir and his former mentor Hassan Turabi, then speaker of the national assembly. During the peak of this dispute, a mysterious diatribe outlining the imbalance of power in Sudan known as *The Black Book* appeared in print in Khartoum, and soon thereafter, Turabi broke from the ruling National Congress (NC) Party to form the opposition Popular Congress Party (PCP). Ibrahim and other non-Arab Darfurian politicians joined Turabi in founding the PCP during this period and then went on to create the JEM, adopting *The Black Book* as their political manifesto. While Turabi denies government claims that he is the puppet master behind the JEM's rebellion, the organization's leadership is intricately linked with him and his PCP.

During early fighting in 2003, when the crisis in Darfur was only beginning to escalate, Ibrahim told reporters that the goal of his movement was not secession but to secure a role in government. The group had strongholds in several large towns in West Darfur State, including Tina and Karnoi. In April the group launched a major joint operation with the SLA against government installations in Darfur's principal cities of Nyala and El Fasher. In a major symbolic victory during the attacks, JEM forces captured Major General Ibrahim Bashra, the head of Sudan's air force.

In October some 1,000 JEM fighters launched another major assault, this time against Kulbus, killing dozens. They followed this in December with a second operation against the town, in coordination with the SLA. The government of Sudan responded to the rapid expansion of rebel-held territory in January 2004, when it launched aerial bombardments against the JEM's urban strongholds, including Tina and Karnoi. Government forces then followed these strikes with ground campaigns. As the government captured these towns, the JEM was driven back into the rural areas of West Darfur.

In April, the JEM and SLA both agreed to a cease-fire, which was violated within days by the government. During this period of tense negotiations, the JEM showed its first signs of fracturing, and by May the first major rift in JEM ranks had occurred, leading to the creation of the rival National Movement for Reform and Development led by Colonel Gibril Abdel-Karim Bari. The Ibrahim-led faction of the JEM, meanwhile, signed an alliance with the Free Lions, a Rashaida Arab rebel movement in eastern Sudan, vowing to continue fighting until the current government was toppled. Soon thereafter, the JEM was implicated in an alleged coup attempt led by Turabi.

THE JEM SINCE 2006

The JEM refused to sign a May 2006 peace deal brokered by the African Union (AU) between the government and one of the two major factions of the SLA. The JEM has refused to back down from its conditions for peace. These include a

Darfurian regional government, a vice presidential post, greater representation at the national level, a share of the national oil revenue, and compensation for victims of government abuse. The JEM's unwillingness to compromise on these points has earned them a reputation as one of the chief barriers to reconciliation, and the United States has placed sanctions against Ibrahim in an effort to curb the group's ongoing violent activities.

Another splinter group, the JEM–Eastern Command, formed around Abdalla Banda Abbaker in July 2007 after he was dismissed by Ibrahim from his position as JEM commander general on the grounds that he discriminated against non-Zaghawa JEM members. The continued disintegration of the JEM into rival factions has earned its leaders a reputation for being unable to control their own forces—an unsurprising condition, considering that the vast majority of the JEM's leadership operates from exile in Europe. (Ibrahim himself commanded the JEM from France until 2007.) Renegade JEM factions have been among the prime culprits in attacks against aid workers and AU peacekeepers in Darfur.

In July 2011 JEM leaders refused to sign the Doha Documents for Peace, which have since proven ineffectual. In April 2013 JEM forces and their rebel allies launched a major offensive against Sudan's government army in a bid to seize control of South Kordofan. By late May of that year, JEM fighters withdrew to permit humanitarian aid into the region. However, the JEM resumed offensive operations and paid little attention to attempts to broker a lasting peace. In 2020, with the overthrow of the Bashir regime the previous year, JEM signed a peace deal with the Transitional Government of Sudan agreeing to participate in the democratic transition.

David Paige

See also: Al-Bashir, Omar (Umar) Hassan Ahmad; Darfur Genocide; Sudan Liberation Army (SLA).

Further Reading

Burr, J. Millard, and Robert O. Collins. *Darfur: The Long Road to Disaster.* Princeton, NJ: Markus Weiner, 2006.

Burr, J. Millard, and Robert O. Collins. *Revolutionary Sudan: Hasan al-Turabi and the Islamist State, 1989–2000.* Boston: Brill Academic Publishers, 2003.

Flint, Julie, and Alex de Waal. *Darfur: A Short History of a Long War.* London: Zed Books, 2006.

Kabila, Joseph (1971–)

Joseph Kabila was democratically elected president of the Democratic Republic of the Congo (DRC) in November 2006. He served as the nation's appointed president from 2001 to 2006, following the assassination of his father, President Laurent Kabila. He had previously served as a military leader under his father.

At the time of his appointment, the younger Kabila was relatively unknown by the Congolese people. He inherited one of the most unstable governments in Africa, along with a civil war. His willingness to negotiate with rebel groups earned him respect early in his presidency. However, following his reelection in 2011, a wave of instability and violence plunged the DRC into yet another crisis. In 2018 Kabila did not run for reelection. However, he stated interest in running again once term limits no longer apply in 2023.

EDUCATION AND MILITARY SERVICE

Joseph Kabila and his political supporters maintain that he was born in 1971 in the eastern region of the DRC, though many of his opponents claim he was born in Tanzania. His father was a supporter of the country's first Prime Minister, Patrice Lumumba. When Lumumba was assassinated in a military coup in 1961, Kabila's father fled the country. As a result, he was raised in exile in Dar es Salaam, the capital of Tanzania.

Kabila was the eldest of 10 children his father had with different women. Many of Kabila's opponents allege that his mother is a Rwandan Tutsi—an unpopular ethnic background in the DRC. (The Congo Wars, involving Ugandan and Rwandan troops, claimed more lives than any conflict since World War II.) Kabila attended school in both English-speaking Tanzania and Uganda and received his military training in Rwanda and Tanzania as well as in China.

Kabila left Tanzania for the eastern DRC in 1996 to join his father's rebel army; there he was made the protégé of Lt. Col. James Kabarebe, a Rwandan military leader who led one of the first rebellions against the government of Joseph Mobutu. Joseph Kabila was a member of the rebel army that invaded the capital, Kinshasa, in 1997 and overthrew Mobutu's government. Kabila's father claimed the presidency and rewarded him with the title of major general and a post at the head of the country's armed forces.

SUCCEEDING HIS FATHER

Laurent Kabila was assassinated by a bodyguard in January 2001. In the midst of a political crisis, Joseph was unanimously chosen by the nation's parliament to succeed his father. Questions regarding the legitimacy of his succession were raised immediately, with rebels calling him an "unacceptable" choice.

Despite the odds against him, Kabila made progress early in his presidency in bringing democracy to the country. In his first few months in office, Kabila was successful in getting foreign troops—backers of his government as well as rebel forces—to partially withdraw from the front lines. By the end of 2002, the last of the foreign troops had left the Congo. In April 2003, Kabila agreed to a peace plan establishing a two-year power-sharing government that included four deputy vice presidents from various rebel factions and one from the government. The plan called for Kabila to step down and allow democratic, multiparty elections at the end of the two-year period.

PRESIDENCY AND NATIONAL CRISIS

In December 2005 voters in the DRC approved a new constitution, establishing a democratic form of government. The constitution also reestablished the position of prime minister. In 2006, Kabila was elected by popular vote to become the nation's first freely elected leader in four decades.

Early in his first term, Kabila faced the threat of ongoing violence at the hands of rebel groups. He quickly earned a reputation as an effective negotiator; in 2009 he granted amnesty to rebels in the eastern DRC, led by the renegade general Laurent Nkunda, in exchange for the signing of a peace agreement. Kabila also focused on renegotiating the DRC's debts. In July 2010, the World Bank approved $8 billion in debt relief for the country. Kabila was reelected to a second term in 2011. However, unlike his previous election, the 2011 election was criticized by international observers, and opposition leaders alleged that the vote had been rigged.

As he began his second term in late 2011, Kabila vowed to increase investments in infrastructure and public services. However, this agenda was soon derailed by renewed conflicts with a rebel splinter group called M23, composed of soldiers unsatisfied with the 2009 amnesty agreement. In 2013, a United Nations panel accused the governments of Rwanda and Uganda of supplying M23 fighters with weapons.

In 2015, a series of proposed changes to the DRC's election laws sparked large-scale protests against Kabila's rule. Both domestic and foreign critics accused him of attempting to remain in power past his constitutionally permitted second term. These fears gained traction in 2016, when Kabila's government signed an agreement with the opposition to push back scheduled elections to 2018. The following year thousands of people were killed in waves of ethnic violence and protests against the government. By the end of 2017, humanitarian agencies reported that the DRC was facing the largest conflict displacement crisis in the world, with 1.7 million people forced to flee their homes that year alone. The escalating instability spelled an uncertain future for the DRC and Kabila's rule. Violence continued into 2018, with displacement estimates climbing even higher. Kabila announced he would step down in December 2018, deciding not to run for reelection. Kabila became a senator for life and continues to wield enormous influence in DRC.

ABC-CLIO

See also: Congo Wars; Democratic Republic of the Congo (DRC), Continuing Violence in; Kabila, Laurent; Mobutu Sese Seko.

Further Reading

Prunier, Gerard. *Africa's World War: Congo, the Rwanda Genocide and the Making of a Continental Catastrophe.* Oxford: Oxford University Press, 2009.

Reyntjens, Filip. *The Great African War: Congo and Regional Geopolitics, 1996–2006.* Cambridge: Cambridge University Press, 2009.

Sterns, Jason K. *Dancing in the Glory of Monsters: The Collapse of the Congo and the Great African War.* New York: Public Affairs, 2011.

Kabila, Laurent (1939–2001)

Laurent Désiré Kabila was the president of the Democratic Republic of the Congo, the name he gave to Zaire after his rebel forces seized control of the country in May 1997.

Kabila was born on November 13, 1939, in the southern Katanga region (now known as Shaba province) in a port town along Lake Tanganyika. He is a member of the Mulubakat, a Luba group. Kabila attended college in France, where he studied political philosophy and became an ardent supporter of Marxism. He returned home just as the country gained independence from Belgium in 1960 and joined a political party supporting nationalist leader Patrice Lumumba, a Marxist with Maoist tendencies who served as the independent nation's first prime minister.

After Lumumba's 1961 assassination following a military coup led by army chief of staff Mobutu Sese Seko, Kabila and other Lumumba supporters fled into the bush and began organizing an insurrection known as the Simba rebellion. The Lumumbists launched three uprisings in 1964, with Kabila and a colleague spearheading the rebellion near the town of Uvira. Although Mobutu, with the aid of foreign mercenaries, crushed all three insurrections, Kabila continued sporadic fighting until late 1965. For several months during that year, he was joined by Argentine revolutionary Che Guevara and some 100 of his guerrillas, but Guevara left after complaining of a lack of commitment on Kabila's part.

In 1967 Kabila and a group of fellow leftists founded the People's Revolutionary Party (PRP). In the 1970s the PRP, led by Kabila, established an independently governed, socialist ministate in eastern Kivu Province, near Uvira. The enclave was funded by gold mining and ivory trading. (Gold-mining interests also helped Kabila acquire considerable personal wealth.) In 1975 the group kidnapped three Stanford University students and a Dutch researcher from the Gombe Stream

Research Center in neighboring Tanzania, where naturalist Jane Goodall began her study of chimpanzee behavior. Kabila's forces released their hostages after a ransom was paid, and the government freed captured PRP members.

In 1977 government troops forced Kabila out of the country. He and his supporters fled to Tanzania, but he continued to launch attacks against the Mobutu government well into the 1980s. During this decade, he developed close ties with Ugandan rebel leader Yoweri Museveni and Rwandan rebel leader Paul Kagame. (Museveni is now Uganda's president, and Kagame is the president of Rwanda.) By the late 1980s, the enclave in eastern Zaire had dissolved, and Kabila appeared to go underground, prompting some rumors that he was dead. He did not reappear in public view until October 1996, when he emerged to join the uprising begun by members of the Banyamulenge ethnic group, ethnic Tutsis originally from Rwanda who had lived in Zaire for more than a century. The Banyamulenge rebellion began in Uvira, the town where years before Kabila had launched his own insurrection. The Banyamulenge, who had already had their citizenship rights taken away in recent years, took up arms after being threatened with expulsion from Zaire.

With apparent backing from the governments of Uganda and Tutsi-led Rwanda and Burundi, Kabila transformed the regional uprising into a full-scale rebellion against the unpopular, dictatorial Mobutu. The rebels met with astonishing success from the very beginning, largely because the poorly motivated, ill-disciplined Zairian Army—whose soldiers went unpaid for months at a time—simply looted and abandoned towns ahead of the rebels' arrival. Local populations usually welcomed the rebels with enthusiasm. By November 1996 the rebels controlled a large chunk of eastern Zaire; by early 1997 they had captured several major cities; and by May only the capital, Kinshasa, remained to be conquered. Mobutu left the capital on May 16, 1997, and the city fell the next day as Kabila declared himself president of the newly named Democratic Republic of the Congo.

Described as easygoing and cheerful, Kabila was also seen as elusive and unpredictable. Following his ascension to power in 1997, he quickly alienated many of his powerful supporters and established an autocratic regime. Most significantly, Kabila turned his former friends, Uganda's Museveni and Rwanda's Kagame, against him. New rivalries, aggravated greatly by the aftereffects of the 1994 Rwandan crisis (mainly a huge refugee crisis as well as the presence in the Congo of thousands of the Hutu Interahamwe militia responsible for the genocide), boiled over into civil war in the east of the country. Rwanda and Uganda threw their support behind the rebel movements seeking the overthrow of Kabila and the destruction of the Interahamwe, while Kabila received support and troops from new allies, including Zimbabwe, Namibia, Angola, and Chad. The battle lines became further entrenched after Kabila recruited former Interahamwe into his army and gave support to the Congo-based Interahamwe terrorizing Uganda's and Rwanda's border areas. While a peace accord signed in July 1999 slowed the pace of the conflict, a true resolution remained elusive.

In somewhat mysterious circumstances, Kabila was assassinated on January 16, 2001. Although there was speculation that the killing was the result of a dispute between Kabila and some top military officers, little is known for certain about the incident. Kabila's government refused even to acknowledge his death for days following the assassination. The 32-year-old son of the slain leader, Joseph Kabila, an army general little known in political circles, was named to succeed his father.

ABC-CLIO

See also: Congo Crisis; Congo Wars; Hutu Power Movements; Kabila, Joseph; Kagame, Paul; Mobutu Sese Seko; Museveni, Yoweri; Rwanda, Civil War and Genocide.

Further Reading

Ngolet, François. *Crisis in the Congo: The Rise and Fall of Laurent Kabila.* New York: Palgrave Macmillan, 2011.

Nzongola-Ntalaja, Georges. *The Congo: From Leopold to Kabila: A People's History.* London: Zed Books, 2013.

Prunier, Gerard. *Africa's World War: Congo, the Rwanda Genocide and the Making of a Continental Catastrophe.* Oxford: Oxford University Press, 2009.

Reyntjens, Filip. *The Great African War: Congo and Regional Geopolitics, 1996–2006.* Cambridge: Cambridge University Press, 2009.

Kagame, Paul (1957–)

Paul Kagame is a Rwandan politician, who, as the leader of the Tutsi-led Rwandan Patriotic Army (RPA), the military arm of the Rwandan Patriotic Front (RPF), defeated Hutu extremist forces to end the 1994 Rwandan Genocide. In 2000 he became president of Rwanda, a position he holds to this day.

A Tutsi, Kagame was born in Gitarama on October 23, 1957, and as a child, became a refugee as his family (among tens of thousands of other Rwandan Tutsis) fled to Uganda in 1960 in the face of Hutu attacks on Tutsis. In 1962 they settled into a Ugandan refugee camp, where Kagame spent the rest of his childhood years. He was educated in the Ugandan education system, was taught in English rather than French (as spoken in Rwanda), and studied for a time at Makerere University in Kampala. For the next 30 years after 1960, he lived his life as an exile.

Determined to resist oppressive regimes, as a young man, Kagame decided on a rebel military career, and he joined with a Ugandan dissident leader, Yoweri Museveni, who had formed his own National Resistance Army (NRA). Together, the two spent five years fighting as guerrillas against the government of Milton Obote. When Museveni took power in 1986, he sent Kagame to Cuba for training with several other intelligence officers then under Kagame's command. Then, in 1989, Museveni sent Kagame on a training course at the U.S. Army Command and Staff College at Fort Leavenworth, Kansas.

In 1985, as a young, English-speaking Tutsi refugee burning to return to Rwanda, Kagame and his best friend, Fred Rwigyema, established the Rwandan Patriotic Front (RPF), a political organization with an armed wing named the Rwandan Patriotic Army composed mostly of Tutsis who had fought in Uganda with Museveni's NRA in the overthrow of President Idi Amin in 1979. By October 1990 the movement was strong enough to launch an invasion of Rwanda from Uganda, supported by Museveni. Rwigyema was killed during the invasion, which failed after a French-led intervention force stopped its advance after an appeal for help from Rwandan president Juvénal Habyarimana. After Rwigyema's death, Kagame became the head of the RPF. Kagame's role in negotiations with the Habyarimana regime throughout the 1990s was important and certainly contributed to the signing of the Arusha Accords, a peace settlement between the RPF and the Rwandan government signed on August 4, 1993. Habyarimana's assassination in a plane crash on April 6, 1994, however, destroyed any possibility that these accords would be implemented.

Controversy has since dogged Kagame over Habyarimana's assassination, with several accusations made against him for his alleged responsibility for having shot down Habyarimana's plane. In January 2000 three Tutsi informants told United Nations investigators that they were part of an elite hit squad that had assassinated Habyarimana. Their confession implicated Kagame in his capacity as overall commander, though nothing was proven, and no official allegations were made. According to Lieutenant Aloys Ruyenzi, a member of the RPA, Kagame was primarily responsible for shooting down the plane, while the French government launched its own investigation, leading to a conclusion that Kagame in fact ordered the shooting. In response, in November 2006, Rwanda severed all diplomatic ties with France and ordered its entire diplomatic staff out of Rwanda within 24 hours. Relations between the two countries remained strained for several years after this. But in an attempt to establish better relations with France, Kagame visited Paris in mid-September 2011, reciprocating a visit to Rwanda by French president Nicolas Sarkozy in February 2010.

All accusations against Kagame have been met consistently with vigorous denials by Kagame and his supporters, who have argued that the plane was shot down by Hutu extremists furious with Habyarimana for arranging a peace settlement with the detested Tutsis and who exploited the events in order to commence the already well-planned genocide. In 2007, the Rwandan government launched a formal investigation into the plane crash. The results were released in 2010, concluding that Hutu extremists were responsible for shooting down the plane in an effort to derail Habyarimana's peace negotiations with Kagame and the Tutsi rebels.

With the onset of the genocide in April 1994, Kagame and the RPF renewed their civil war against the government, and by the end of May, they controlled most of Rwanda. Kigali was captured on July 4, 1994, and the remnants of the extremist Hutu Power government of Jean Kambanda fled. Once the conflict was over, Kagame became vice president and defense minister under Pasteur Bizimungu, but many believed that Kagame was the real power behind the presidency. Bizimungu, who was a deputy commander of the RPF and an ethnic Hutu, eventually came into conflict with Kagame over the direction of postgenocide policy. He resigned in March 2000, and Kagame became caretaker president. He was then elected in a landslide on August 25, 2003, in the first national elections since the genocide. Kagame won 95.5 percent of all votes cast and was sworn in for a seven-year term on September 12, 2003. He was reelected by overwhelming margins in 2010 and again in 2017, although many observers questioned the fairness and accuracy of those contests.

After the genocide, many of the Hutus responsible for the killing fled to neighboring Zaire (later called the Democratic Republic of the Congo, or DRC) using the country as a base from which to continue attacking Rwanda. Kagame sent Rwandan troops into the country in late 1996 in order to pursue these Hutus, in what was a clear violation of the larger country's sovereignty. Kagame now found himself embroiled in a confusing Congolese civil war involving forces either supporting or opposing Zairean president Mobutu Sese Seko and his adversary Laurent Kabila. Into this mix came the Rwandan Hutu exiles and the invading Rwandan forces as well as an army from Museveni's Uganda. Some parts of the DRC were then occupied by Rwandan troops for the next five years. In the course of the war, the Rwandan Army financed its invasion through an illegal trade in the Congo's natural resources.

Kagame's invasion of the DRC has been severely criticized in several quarters, as the army was known to have committed a series of brutal (and often systematic) massacres against fleeing, unarmed Hutus. Also, in order to finance the campaign, the Rwandan military allegedly plundered vast amounts of precious minerals from the areas in the eastern Congo that it occupied. Kagame was known to support the rebel forces in the DRC until 2002, when he signed a peace accord and agreed to remove Rwandan troops in exchange for the disarmament and repatriation of Hutu forces. This notwithstanding, a Rwandan presence—sometimes quite active and violent—remained throughout the next few years, further confusing an already confused and disastrous situation that some estimates claim have cost up to five million lives overall.

In the aftermath of the genocide, a major focus of Kagame's presidency has been to build Rwandan national unity. Accordingly, his preference for postgenocide Rwanda is for the nation's citizens to downplay all references to their separate ethnic identities. During the 2003 presidential campaign, he portrayed himself as a Rwandan rather than a Tutsi and has since made it illegal for any politician or citizen to make statements encouraging ethnic animosity or expressing ethnic solidarity. Some have seen this as the tip of an antidemocratic iceberg that suppresses human rights, and Kagame has been criticized as an authoritarian leader who often disregards and stifles public opinion. The international humanitarian monitoring organization Human Rights Watch has accused Rwandan police of several instances of extrajudicial killings and deaths in custody. Kagame has also been accused of being a ruthless and repressive leader intolerant of criticism. Some have pointed out that he favors Tutsis over Hutus in senior positions.

On the other hand, Kagame's leadership style has enabled him to devote much of his attention to issues of postgenocide justice, peacebuilding, and reconciliation, often without dissent. Other areas of priority have included economic development, good governance, women's empowerment, and advancement of education. Kagame has received international recognition for his leadership of what was a broken country, and he is considered by many to be one of the most dynamic and effective leaders in Africa in the early twenty-first century.

Paul R. Bartrop

See also: Amin, Idi; Congo Wars; Democratic Republic of the Congo (DRC), Continuing Violence in; Genocide in Africa; Habyarimana, Juvénal; Kabila, Laurent; Mobutu Sese

Seko; Museveni, Yoweri; National Resistance Army (NRA); Rwanda, Civil War and Genocide; Rwandan Patriotic Front (RPF); Uganda's Civil War: The Bush War.

Further Reading

Prunier, Gerard. *Africa's World War: Congo, the Rwanda Genocide and the Making of a Continental Catastrophe.* Oxford: Oxford University Press, 2009.

Prunier, Gerard. *The Rwanda Crisis: History of a Genocide.* New York: Columbia University Press, 1995.

Reyntjens, Filip. *The Great African War: Congo and Regional Geopolitics, 1996–2006.* Cambridge: Cambridge University Press, 2009.

Waugh, Colin M. *Paul Kagame and Rwanda: Power, Genocide and the Rwandan Patriotic Front.* Jefferson, NC: McFarland, 2004.

Kagera War (1978–1979)

The Kagera War was a conflict fought between Uganda and Tanzania from October 1978 until June 1979. The war itself was the result of seven years of tensions between the two countries, which had featured numerous cross-border skirmishes and diplomatic wrangling. When war finally erupted, it was not taken seriously by many Western outlets, most of whom dismissed the resolve of the quiet-spoken President Julius Nyerere of Tanzania or simply broadcast the bombastic proclamations of Uganda's President-for-Life Idi Amin. However, the short conflict would not only end decisively after a string of Tanzanian victories, but it would also have numerous second- and third-order effects on the political and economic future in the region.

The genesis of the Kagera War lay in the 1971 coup launched by Colonel Idi Amin of the Ugandan military against his commander in chief, President Milton Obote. Obote had been a close ally of President Julius Nyerere of neighboring Tanzania, and following his overthrow, Obote and a number of his political allies found refuge across the border in Tanzania. Over the following year, Amin would launch a series of purges within Uganda, attempting to root out any further opposition, swelling the ranks of the exiles in Tanzania. Nyerere, who had refused to recognize the government of Amin, gave permission for a group of armed exiles to invade Uganda in 1972 in an attempt to remove the dictator. However, this attempted invasion went disastrously, and the Ugandan exiles fled back across the border, with Amin's forces in hot pursuit. While Amin's forces shelled and bombed across the border, Nyerere agreed to mediation by the OAU. While the mediation was successful, resulting in the Mogadishu Agreement, the leadership of both countries continued to simmer; Nyerere felt Amin was a vicious and unstable dictator, while Amin mocked Nyerere as a weak and cowardly schoolteacher.

While both leaders attempted to abide by the Mogadishu Agreement, the intervening years saw the two states diverge wildly in development. Nyerere continued Tanzania down the path of nonaligned ujamaa socialism, promoting grassroots participation in the development of his country through sometimes forced agricultural projects. While occasionally taking unpopular actions, his state remained stable and relatively unified. In Uganda, Amin began a series of relatively disastrous economic and political programs. Beginning in 1972 he expelled the Asian population of Uganda and seized their property to be distributed among his cronies. This caused the economy to slowly collapse even as purges in the government and military continued. This destabilized the country, as the military and administration became increasingly amateur and factionalized.

While the tensions between the countries were already at a fever pitch by 1978, the proximate cause of the war was this destabilization within Amin's military. Looking for a way to keep an increasingly unhappy military distracted, Amin finally unleashed them upon the Tanzanians on October 25, having them seize a salient of northwestern Tanzania bounded by the Kagera River and claiming it as his own. The Tanzanians were largely caught unawares and had almost no forces in the region; ultimately, they withdrew to the other side of the river and awaited reinforcements. While Amin would characterize this as him repulsing a Tanzanian attack on Ugandan territory, the next two weeks saw a quiet front as Tanzania mobilized its armed forces and moved them to the battlefront.

While Amin's forces were largely factionalized, the Tanzania People's Defense Forces were a unified and professional force, backed by an extensive system of reserve and militia formations. Nyerere quickly called up the reserves and opened recruitment into the TPDF to expand their formations, while the regular army concentrated in the Kagera region. Although the initial counterattack, called Operation Chakaza, was delayed, the now-sighted Tanzanian artillery bombarded the unprepared Ugandans, leading to several units withdrawing from the salient. By November 19 the Tanzanian counterattack was in full swing, with their forces crossing the river and reoccupying their territory with little resistance and following on to the high ground of Mutukula, slightly across the Ugandan border.

At this point, Tanzania had a choice to make. It would largely be against African opinion to invade fully into Uganda and topple Amin; however, a return to the status quo hardly seemed sustainable. To solve this dilemma, Nyerere called upon the Ugandan exile community, which now housed a plethora of political and resistance groups. These groups formed a coalition called the Ugandan National Liberation Front/Army (UNLF/UNLA) and served as the formal belligerents and initial frontline combatants of the next phase of the war. While the Tanzanian military was the driving force behind the renewed invasion, Nyerere could claim innocence, using the UNLF as a fig leaf.

The renewed Tanzanian invasion pressed into Uganda along two axes, with each advance accompanied by a UNLF formation. Each force encountered steady but largely uncoordinated resistance by Amin's forces, with only occasional major confrontations with Amin's more effective formations. However, even these battles at places like Sembabule, Mbarara, and Masaka ended after Tanzanian forces managed to isolate the Ugandan units and eventually drive them from their positions. The only major setback for the Tanzanian forces was at Lukaya, when one of their untried brigades was repelled after stumbling into several units of Amin's army reinforced with a brigade's worth of men and material sent by Amin's ally Muammar Gaddafi. However, even this setback was reversed when the Ugandan-Libyan forces allowed the Tanzanians to withdraw safely and TPDF reinforcements were brought into the area, flanking the now disorganized opposition.

With the fall of Lukaya and the dispersal of Amin's best forces, the road to Kampala was open. The UNLA/TDPF forces first took Entebbe Airfield and then Kampala itself. Amin in turn fled to Libya, leaving his remaining forces to surrender or be defeated piecemeal by the Tanzanian forces. The war itself was declared over following the last few skirmishes in the north of Uganda, and the new unity government of Yusuf Lule was placed in charge of Uganda.

The war would have numerous second- and third-order effects in the region. For Uganda, the Lule government would prove to be an unstable one, leading to a series of increasingly suspect regimes and finally the Ugandan Bush War of 1981–1986 and the ascent of Yoweri Museveni to power. The Tanzanians, despite being triumphant and removing Idi Amin, found themselves in dire financial straits. Already a poor country and often dependent on outside assistance, the cost of the war sidelined many of the development efforts President Nyerere had intended to continue and likely hobbled the continued economic growth of the country for decades.

Charles G. Thomas

See also: Amin, Idi; Coups and Military Regimes in Africa; Gaddafi, Muammar; Museveni, Yoweri; Nyerere, Julius; Uganda's Civil War: The Bush War.

Further Reading

Avirgan, Tony, and Martha Honey. *War in Uganda: The Legacy of Idi Amin.* Dar es Salaam: Tanzania Publishing House, 1983.

Burrows, Noreen. "Tanzania's Intervention in Uganda: Some Legal Aspects." *World Today* 35, no. 7 (1979): 306–310.

Roberts, George. "The Uganda-Tanzania War, the Fall of Idi Amin, and the Failure of African Diplomacy, 1978–1979." *Journal of Eastern African Studies* 8, no. 4 (October 2, 2014): 692–709. https://doi.org/10.1080/17531055.2014.946236

Smith, George Ivan. *Ghosts of Kampala.* London: Weidenfeld & Nicolson, 1980.

Kamajor Militia

See Sierra Leone Civil War

Kenya, Mau Mau Emergency (1952–1960)

Disproportionally impacted by British settler colonialism, many of the Kikuyu people of central Kenya became landless squatters and low-paid workers on European commercial farms of the "White Highlands," and a large number sought employment in the growing city of Nairobi during World War II. At the same time, colonial cash-cropping fostered the development of a relatively prosperous Kikuyu peasantry associated with the colonial state. After the failure of the moderate Kenya African Union (KAU) to end racial discrimination and increase African representation in the territory's legislative council in the 1940s and early 1950s, militant African leaders within the trade unions and among squatters in the White Highlands gained momentum.

In October 1952, with the killing of a European woman and a Kikuyu chief, newly arrived governor Sir Evelyn Baring declared a state of emergency. In turn, during Operation Jock Scott, British security forces arrested 180 suspected insurgent leaders in Nairobi, including KAU president Jomo Kenyatta later convicted of treason despite lack of evidence. Militants fled to the forest, from where they organized more attacks against settlers and the colonial state.

At the start of the emergency, the British force in Kenya comprised 7,000 soldiers, including the 39 Brigade flown in from Egypt, the East African troops of the King's African Rifles (KAR), and the Kenya Regiment's white settler volunteers. Within a few months, the 49 Brigade arrived from Britain, increasing this force to 10,000 soldiers, assisted by an expanded Kenya Police of 21,000 members and the newly formed 25,000-strong Kikuyu "Home Guard."

Calling themselves the Kenya Land and Freedom Army (KLFA), the insurgents formed small units in the forests of the Aberdare Mountains and Mount Kenya, with a passive support wing in nearby African reserves. Though the derivation of the term remains uncertain, the British called the movement Mau Mau. At its height, the KLFA comprised around 12,000 insurgents, including only 10 percent with firearms. Characteristic of their decentralized leadership, the KLFA divided into three zones: the Central and Northern Aberdare Mountains under Dedan Kimathi, the Southern Aberdares headed by Stanley Mathenge, and Mount Kenya led by Waruhiu Itote called "General China." Mathenge and Itote had served in the Second World War, but former colonial soldiers were rare among the rebels. The movement consisted of a series of independent and sometime feuding groups, with attempts at coordination ending in failure. Unlike anti-colonial insurgents of the next decade, the KLFA lacked a foreign sponsor, cross-border sanctuary, and formal revolutionary ideology or strategy. The mostly illiterate or partly literate insurgents, psychologically bound to the movement by a ritual oath, fought with spears or machetes and a few captured or homemade firearms. Rebel groups communicated by messages hidden in trees or under rocks, and they became skilled at moving quickly and secretly through the bush. While British officials in the 1950s viewed Mau Mau as a form of psychological disorder caused by rapid Westernization, historians of the late twentieth century debated whether it represented a Kenyan nationalist movement or a Kikuyu civil war.

In June 1953 General George Erskine took command of British operations in Kenya, focusing on clearing insurgents from specific areas then patrolled by the Kenya Police and Home Guard. Seeking to deprive the insurgents of resources and recruits, Operation Anvil of April 1954 involved some 25,000 British troops and police who cordoned off and systematically searched Nairobi. After detaining and screening all African residents, security forces moved some 20,000 men to a detention camp and evicted 30,000 women and children to the rural reserves. From June 1953 to October 1955, the Royal Air Force (RAF) dropped six million bombs on Kenyan forests, killing around 900 insurgents and forcing some groups to disband or flee. The RAF also flew reconnaissance and propaganda leaflet–dropping missions during the emergency, and the Kenya Police developed a volunteer air wing to search for insurgents.

Within a detention system called the "Pipeline," British officials color-coded Kenyan prisoners. The most compliant detainees were classified "white" and sent back to the reserves. Known as "grey," those who confessed to taking a Mau Mau oath but were cooperative moved "down" the "Pipeline" to local labor camps and eventual release. The most obstinate prisoners, labeled as "black," were sent "up" the "Pipeline" to special high security camps. Camp living conditions were terrible, causing malnutrition and typhoid, and prisoners experienced torture and other forms of abuse. Most prisoners in the "Pipeline" were male, including some young boys, but a few thousand women and girls were also detained.

In June 1954 the British began forcibly resettling over one million Kikuyu into 800 "protected villages" enclosed by barbed wire, trenches with spikes and watchtowers, and secured by the Kikuyu "Home Guard." Similar to their counterinsurgency program in Malaya, the British divided the protected villages in Kenya between those suspected of harboring rebel sympathies who were punished by denial of food and loyalists who received better treatment. General China surrendered in April 1954 and avoided the death penalty by trying to arrange further organized capitulations. In May 1955 when General Sir Gerald Lathbury took command in Kenya, only around 3,000 active insurgents remained in the field, prompting the withdrawal of Britain's 39 Brigade. Phasing out large and usually unproductive forest sweeps by security forces, Lathbury favored patrols by smaller tracker combat teams and "counter gangs" of former Mau Mau who infiltrated and eliminated rebel groups. In early 1956 the insurgents numbered 900, and later in the year, Dedan Kimathi, the final active Mau Mau leader, was captured and ultimately hanged.

To prevent further insurgency, the British initiated reforms in Kenya, providing more land for the Kikuyu, opening profitable coffee production to the African majority, raising wages of urban workers and permitting the direct election of African members in the Legislative Assembly. With far-reaching implications for decolonization in Africa, the Kenya Emergency showed the British government that maintaining colonial rule would involve increasingly expensive and politically embarrassing military force. One of the most contentious incidents of the conflict occurred in March 1959 when 11 prisoners were beaten to death at Hola detention camp. Subsequently, the British ended the emergency in 1960, abandoned the hollow rhetoric of "multiracialism" rule in Kenya, and organized a "one-person one vote" majority-rule political system, leading to independence in December 1963. Under the authoritarian presidency of Jomo Kenyatta, Kenya did little to address the legacy of settler colonialism and maintained a close relationship with Britain, including military cooperation.

Scholars debate the total number of Kenyans who died because of the emergency, with estimates ranging from 50,000 to 300,000. Most of these deaths related to conditions in the detention camps. More precisely, the British hanged 1,090 Kenyans hastily convicted by colonial courts; the insurgents killed at least 1,819 African, 32 European, and 26 Asian civilians; and the security forces sustained 600 fatalities and killed 10,500 rebels. Although often and inaccurately studied as a case of effective "minimum force" counterinsurgency, the British war against the Mau Mau involved a brutal military campaign and rampant abuse of civilians.

Given the role of former colonial loyalists in their administrations, Kenya's Kenyatta and the Daniel arap Moi regime avoided public celebrations of the KLFA as a national liberation movement. Given political change in Kenya since around 2010, the government declared Mau Mau veterans national heroes and publically feted them on "Heroes Day," which is October 20, marking the anniversary of the declaration of the emergency. The rehabilitation of Mau Mau within Kenya and the publication of new research about British atrocities during the conflict prompted legal action against the British government. In 2013 the British government, given an unfavorable ruling by a British court, agreed to pay compensation to 12,000 elderly Kenyans who had endured human rights abuses in the 1950s. This led to a further legal claim by another 40,000 Kenyans.

Timothy J. Stapleton

See also: British Military Involvement in Postcolonial Africa; Women and War in Africa.

Further Reading

Anderson, David. *Histories of the Hanged: The Dirty War in Kenya and the End of Empire.* London: Weidenfeld & Nicolson, 2005.

Bennett, Huw. *Fighting the Mau Mau: The British Army and Counter-Insurgency in the Kenya Emergency.* Cambridge: Cambridge University Press, 2013.

Blacker, John. "The Demography of Mau Mau: Fertility and Mortality in Kenya in the 1950s: A Demographer's Viewpoint." *African Affairs* 106 (2007): 205–227.

Branch, Daniel. *Defeating Mau Mau, Creating Kenya: Counterinsurgency, Civil War and Decolonization.* Cambridge: Cambridge University Press, 2009.

Chappell, Stephen. "Air Power in the Mau Mau Conflict: The Government's Chief Weapon." *RUSI Journal* 156, no. 1 (February–March 2011): 64–70.

Elkins, Caroline. *Imperial Reckoning: The Untold Story of Britain's Gulag in Kenya.* New York: Henry Holt, 2005.

Page, Malcolm. *KAR: A History of the King's African Rifles.* London: Leo Cooper, 1998.

Kiir, Salva Mayardit (1951–)

Kiir was one of the earliest and most loyal followers of John Garang. Born in the Awan-Chan Dinka community in Gogrial District, Kiir was the eighth out of the nine children of his family. During the First Sudanese Civil War (1955–1972), Kiir joined the Anya-Nya, the southern separatist movement that fought against the Sudanese government. By the end of the war, Kiir was one of the Anya-Nya members absorbed into the Sudanese National Army. In subsequent years he was promoted from a low-ranking officer to the position of colonel.

At the beginning of the Second Sudanese Civil War, Kiir was one of the founding members of the Sudan People's Liberation Movement/Army (SPLM/A) together with Garang. However, in the military command structure, Kiir was outranked by Arok Thon Arok. Nevertheless, Kiir held the rank of commander as well as deputy to the SPLA Council. He oversaw both the foreign and domestic policies of the SPLA while he was in these positions. In particular, during the internal split within the SPLM/A in the 1990s and early 2000s, Kiir had an influential role to play in this situation as an indispensable conciliator and negotiator between warring factions.

Kiir served as an important participant in the negotiation process that ended the Second Sudanese Civil War in 2005. After the death of John Garang in August 2005, Kiir succeeded him as the president of southern Sudan and vice president of Sudan. Kiir was reelected as the president of southern Sudan after receiving about 93 percent of votes. Thus, he continued to serve as the vice president of Sudan.

After South Sudan became independent on July 9, 2011, Kiir became the first president of South Sudan. Different sociopolitical and economic issues such as the unresolved internal dissension, inequitable revenue allocation formula, and border security issues were some of the problems President Kiir had to contend with during the initial years of his administration. Despite several attempts to resolve these issues, interethnic conflict between the two main ethnic groups, the Nuer and Dinka, was inevitable. Eventually, these tensions reached a climax on December 15, 2013, as a result of the impending feud between President Kiir and Vice President Riek Machar. The fact that both leaders identified with the Dinka and Nuer ethnic group, respectively, from which they garnered their supporters led to the interethnic violence between both groups during the South Sudan Civil War (2013–2020).

Although international mediations facilitated peace accords between Kiir and Machar in 2014 and 2015, South Sudan remained embroiled in civil war. However, in March 2018 nine opposition groups collectively reached a compromise with Kiir's administration as part of the efforts to end the conflict.

Yusuf Sholeye

See also: Anyanya; Garang, John de Mabior; Machar, Riek Teny Dhurgon; South Sudan Civil War; Sudan Civil War, First; Sudan Civil War, Second; Sudan People's Liberation Movement/Army (SPLM/A).

Further Reading

Kramer, Robert S., Richard Lobban, and Fluehr-Lobban. *Historical Dictionary of Sudan: African Historical Dictionaries.* Lanham: Scarecrow Press, 2013.

L

Lagu, Joseph Yanga (1931–)

A soldier and political leader from southern Sudan, Joseph Lagu was born on November 21, 1931, in the small hamlet of Monokwe in Moli, Madiland, about 80 miles south of Juba. Lagu's father was the chief clerk of the customs post and river port at the Sudan and Uganda border town of Nimule. This situation enabled Lagu to interact with different ethnic groups who traversed through Nimule. Thus, he developed the flair for different southern Sudanese languages at an early age. He attended the CMS Akon Elementary School, where he was baptized. Afterward he proceeded to the CMS Nugent Intermediate School at Loka before completing his secondary school education at the Rumbek Senior Secondary School.

In 1958 Lagu was admitted into the Sudan Military College. By 1960 Lagu became a commissioned cadet and was posted to the 10th Battalion of the Northern Command. The prevalent discrimination and dehumanization against southerners during the Abbud regime led to Lagu's resignation from the army in 1963. Thereafter, together with the members of the Sudan African National Union in Kampala (SANU), he founded the Anya-Nya on August 19, 1963. After joining the guerrilla group, Lagu was appointed as the defense minister. However, interethnic rivalry, political intrigues, and squabbling among the Anya-Nya leaders evoked Lagu's misgivings about the guerrilla group.

Lagu's aloofness from this internecine conflict reinforced his charisma among the southerners. This situation facilitated Lagu's advancement in the military and also led to his relationship with the Israeli military. From January 1968 to June 1969, the Israelis trained Lagu and also provided him with arms and ammunition in order to facilitate the insurgency in southern Sudan. Eventually, Lagu became the leader of the Southern Sudan Liberation Movement (SSLM). SSLM was a motley of insurgent groups that consisted of former Anya-Nya members and other ethnic factions in southern Sudan. Consequently, Lagu became the main southern leader, representing the interests of the southerners during the Addis Ababa Agreement of 1972.

After the First Sudanese Civil War, Lagu became the inspector general of the Sudanese Armed Forces, and in 1974 he was appointed as the commanding officer of the Sudanese Armed Forces in Southern Region. After his dismissal from the army in 1978, Lagu was elected as the president of the High Executive Council of the Southern Sudan Autonomous Region from 1979 until 1981 when he was forced to relinquish this position. Thereafter, Lagu kept a discreet political profile. However, he occasionally participated in political activities. He was a member of the National Defense Council during the vehement opposition to the Islamization policy in southern Sudan. From 1990 to 1992, Lagu was appointed as the Sudanese ambassador to the United Nations by President al-Bashir. After declining the appointment of presidential adviser in 1998, Lagu requested to be relieved of all official duties.

Yusuf Sholeye

See also: Al-Bashir, Omar (Umar) Hassan Ahmad; Anyanya; Sudan Civil War, First.

Further Reading

Collins, Robert O. *A History of Modern Sudan.* Cambridge: Cambridge University Press, 2008.

Poggo, Scopas. *The First Sudanese Civil War: Africans, Arabs, and Israelis in the Southern Sudan, 1955–1972.* New York: Palgrave Macmillan, 2009.

Liberian Civil Wars (1989–1997 and 1999–2003)
FIRST LIBERIAN CIVIL WAR, 1989–1997

The First Liberian Civil War began on Christmas Eve, 1989, when the National Patriotic Front of Liberia (NPFL) insurgents entered Liberia from the Ivory Coast to oust President Samuel Doe. The immediate cause of the war was the feud between Doe and General Thomas Quiwonkpa. Both men were once leaders of the 1980 coup d'état that deposed President William Tolbert. In November 1985 Quiwonkpa mounted an unsuccessful coup d'état against Doe. At the time Doe had made the transition from military ruler to president of Liberia. This was in contravention of the stated objective of the People's Redemption Council, which saw itself as a caretaker regime; instead, Doe had solidified his role as a usurper. Following Quiwonpka's failed attempt to unseat Doe, the Armed Forces of Liberia (AFL) were dispatched to Nimba Country, an ethnic homeland of the Gio and Mano, with whom Quiwonkpa shared a kinship. At the time of the AFL attack on the citizens of Nimba, it comprised mostly ethnic Krahn soldiers who were of the same ethnicity as Doe. The assault on the population was indiscriminate, resulting in the deaths of hundreds of citizens. This created the narrative that would later haunt the civil war, an ethnic conflict between the Gio and the Krahn that engulfed the country.

It is not a coincidence, therefore, that the NPFL led by Charles Taylor chose Nimba as an entry point from which to begin their insurgency. In Nimba, they encountered a population willing to join in their effort to unseat Doe. Seeking to legitimize the insurgency, Taylor claimed that the NPFL was a continuation of the Quiwonkpa movement against Doe.

The war was marked by periods of intense violence that included the St. Peter's Lutheran Church Massacre conducted by the AFL in 1990 and the savage assault on Monrovia by the NPFL during its "Operation Octopus." The civil war was also characterized by the influence of cultural associations and religious practices such as the use of masks to fortify the combatants spiritually.

To end the violence, the Economic Community of West Africa (ECOWAS) created the Economic Community of West Africa Monitoring Group (ECOMOG) in

1990. ECOMOG was a military alliance comprising soldiers from Ghana, Nigeria, and other West African countries. ECOWAS's intent for ECOMOG was for it to be a neutral arbiter in the conflict, creating the space for the warring groups to enter into a cease-fire, thus paving the way for peace. As the fighting persisted, ECOMOG lost its neutrality when it began offensive military action against the NPFL. This scenario led to Doe's capture, while he was visiting ECOMOG's headquarters in Monrovia, by Independent National Patriotic Front of Liberia (INPFL) fighters. The INPFL was a breakaway faction of the NPFL under the command of Prince Johnson who was also a Quiwonkpa loyalist. Once captured, Doe was tortured and murdered.

Doe's demise did not end the war, as remnants of the AFL, NPFL, and INPFL continued to battle for supremacy. They were joined in the conflict by insurgents from the United Liberation Movement of Liberia for Democracy (ULIMO) in 1991. In 1994 ULIMO broke into two factions based on ethnic bonds. One of the factions comprised mainly Liberia's Muslim citizens. This group was known as ULIMO-K and was led by Alhaji Kromah. The other faction, known as ULIMO-J, was commanded by former AFL officer Roosevelt Johnson and was predominantly Krahn.

There were several unsuccessful attempts to achieve a political solution to end the conflict through peace mediations. These attempts also included establishing a short-lived Government of National Unity in 1991, led by Dr. Amos Sawyer. A cease-fire agreement brokered by former Ghanaian leader Jerry Rawlings in 1995 collapsed the next year.

The war ended at the Abuja II Accords in Nigeria in 1996. According to the peace agreement, all factions decided that they would disarm their combatants by 1997. In addition, the leaders of the various insurgencies elected Ruth Sando Perry as the chairwoman of the ruling council, making Perry the first female leader of a postindependence African country. Later that year in July, Charles Taylor was elected as the president of Liberia.

It is estimated that between 150,000 and 200,000 Liberians were killed during the conflict. The war displaced an estimated 1.2 million Liberians, who sought refuge in neighboring countries. Two years later, the Second Liberian Civil War would begin, this time to oust Charles Taylor.

SECOND LIBERIAN CIVIL WAR, 1999–2003

The Second Liberian Civil War began on April 21, 1999, when Liberians United for Reconciliation and Democracy (LURD) insurgents mounted armed incursions into northwest Liberia from Guinea. There are several reasons why Liberia erupted into a civil war a few years after the previous conflict had ended. The main reason is that the First Liberian Civil War had ended in a stalemate. While there was a formal peace agreement resulting in a commitment that all sides would cease hostilities, disarm, and adhere to democratic free and fair elections, the distrust amongst the leadership of the warring factions prevented a postconflict resolution. Taylor's election made a questionable situation perilous. Taylor had demonstrated that he was not a partner to be trusted. He had violated every peace agreement before the Abuja II Accords, and it was generally believed that he would dishonor the Abuja II as well. For this reason, the warring factions cheated the disarmament process, their leaders fearing that, as president, Taylor would become a maximum leader. As an absolute president they were certain that Taylor would use the apparatus of state security against them. Their fears were not unjustified since Taylor was accustomed to eliminating allies he perceived as his future competition.

This was compounded by the fact that disarmament, demobilization, rehabilitation, and the reintegration of the ex-combatants (DDRR) initiative enacted by international, regional, and local actors was significantly inadequate, nullifying its intended objective of transitioning combatants from war to civilian life. This dysfunctional situation was exacerbated by Taylor's despotic rule and his ethnic "scapegoating" of the Mandingo and Krahn ethnic groups. These actions were combined with his systematic deployment of state resources to subvert every democratic process and institution in Liberia. The conditions set by the peace accord demanded that the Liberian government diversify the armed forces and security sector. Instead, Taylor transformed the AFL into an extension of his NPFL by filling its ranks with its fighters. By 2003 Taylor had transformed Liberia into a "garrison state."

Under these conditions many of the surviving leaders of rival insurgent groups fled to neighboring countries from where they planned to launch an insurgency to oust Taylor. LURD was conceived in this manner and began its assault on Taylor's forces on April 21, 1999. It comprised Krahn and Mandingo militiamen. In March 2003 LURD created the Movement for Democracy in Liberia (MODEL). MODEL was an allied insurgency comprising Krahn fighters. With MODEL, a second front against Taylor was established, adding other dimensions to the war.

Like the conflict before it, the Second Liberian Civil War was marked by periods of indiscriminate violence. By July 2003 Monrovia was under siege by LURD and MODEL. Unable to overrun Monrovia and end the bloodshed, LURD agreed to a cease-fire, which provided the space for an advanced deployment of Nigerian peacekeeping soldiers at the end of July. On August 11, Taylor resigned as president and sought sanctuary in Nigeria. The war came to its conclusion with the Accra Comprehensive Agreement, following Taylor's resignation. On August 14, a contingent of U.S. forces and a Nigerian-led West African peacekeeping contingent entered Monrovia to establish security.

Jacien Carr

See also: Child Soldiers in Africa; Coups and Military Regimes in Africa; Doe, Samuel; ECOWAS Military Interventions; Liberians United for Reconciliation and Democracy (LURD); National Patriotic Front of Liberia (NPFL); Peacekeeping in Africa; Sierra Leone Civil War; Taylor, Charles McArthur Ghankay; Women and War in Africa.

Further Reading

Ellis, Stephen. *The Mask of Anarchy: The Destruction of Liberia and the Religious Dimension of an African Civil War.* New York: New York University Press, 2001.

Hazen, Jennifer. *What Rebels Want: Resources and Supply Networks in Wartime.* Ithaca, NY: Cornell University Press, 2013.

Hoffman, Danny. *The War Machines: Young Men and Violence in Sierra Leone and Liberia*. Durham: Duke University Press, 2011.

Huband, Mark. *The Liberian Civil War*. New York: Frank Cass, 1998.

Wai, Zubairu. *Epistemologies of African Conflicts: Violence, Evolutionism, and the War in Sierra Leone*. Basingstoke: Palgrave Macmillan, 2012.

Waugh, Colin. *Charles Taylor and Liberia: Ambition and Atrocity in Africa's Lone Star State*. London: Zed Books, 2011.

Zack-Williams, Tunde. *When the State Fails: Studies on Intervention in the Sierra Leone Civil War*. London: Pluto Press, 2012.

Liberians United for Reconciliation and Democracy (LURD)

Liberians United for Reconciliation and Democracy (LURD) was Liberia's main rebel group during the country's second civil war (1999–2003). During the struggle, LURD gained control of more than half the country, and in August 2003, it achieved its single objective: to remove President Charles Taylor from power. LURD leaders declared their war with the government over on August 11, 2003, when Taylor left the country to live in exile in Nigeria. After the war, LURD fragmented as various leaders sought to gain the spoils of victory.

With its own constitution and both a military and a political arm, LURD was more organized than many West African rebel groups, and on August 18, 2003, it signed a peace deal with the government and the Movement for Democracy in Liberia (MODEL), a splinter group, agreeing to share power for two years in a transitional government. After this period passed and Ellen Johnson Sirleaf was elected in 2005's momentous democratic vote, LURD leader Sekou Conneh demanded full amnesty for himself and his fellow rebel fighters. A reconciliation commission was formed to confront the crimes and atrocities committed during the nation's civil strife.

Formed in July 1999 by refugees of Liberia's civil war in neighboring Sierra Leone and Guinea, LURD attempted to be inclusive and present a united front against Taylor. In an effort to distance itself from the factional fighting of the country's previous civil war (1989–1997), LURD barred all warlords involved in that war from its membership. In addition, although it was dominated by the northern Mandingo and Krahn ethnic groups, LURD actively encouraged other ethnic groups to join its ranks. The group cut had some difficulty recruiting members from the nation's southern ethnic groups, which traditionally have mistrusted the Mandingos and Krahns. Still, it cut slowly made inroads with these groups, building both its political and fighting forces.

LURD's funding sources remain unclear: its leaders claimed that they were funded solely by exiled Liberians, mainly in the United States, but Taylor repeatedly accused the Guinean and Sierra Leonean governments of providing financial assistance to the rebels. Although during the fighting they were outnumbered by troops loyal to Taylor, LURD rebels—together with the smaller MODEL, which split from LURD in April 2003—controlled about two-thirds of Liberia, with LURD holding the vast majority of that territory.

Conditions in former LURD-held areas, already devastated by the previous civil war, rapidly deteriorated. More than 20 percent of the population was displaced; there were almost no functioning medical facilities and just one school, in Voinjama; roads were all but impassable; and there was no electricity or running water. Until conditions improved in 2005, humanitarian groups had all but left Liberia, saying it was impossible to work under such violent conditions. Three aid workers were killed in March 2003, others were kidnapped, and LURD rebels routinely stole food meant for refugees. The United Nations (UN), the European Union, and the United States all suspended aid shipments to Liberia in April 2003.

In addition, internal divisions cut plagued LURD despite their military gains. The group's military command, based in the northern Liberian town of Voinjama, and its political division, based in the Guinean capital, Conkary, were increasingly at odds. Many of LURD's military leaders cut accused its political representatives of financial mismanagement, corruption, and questionable diplomatic maneuverings. In an effort to ease these conflicts, LURD appointed a former civil servant, Sekou Conneh, as its national chairperson and commander in chief in December 2001, placing him in the Voinjama headquarters. However, this created further problems as senior military adviser General Joe Wylie, a founding member of LURD, accused Conneh and the ethnic Mandingo of turning away from LURD's inclusive principles and rejecting the membership of some southern Liberian ethnic groups. Wylie's calls for Conneh's removal in April 2003 went unheeded, as LURD soldiers moved in on the nation's capital, Monrovia, to depose Taylor.

Emboldened by the UN's June 5, 2003, indictment of Taylor on war crimes charges for supporting Sierra Leonean rebels who committed atrocities in that country's civil war, LURD moved to take control of Monrovia the following day. The rebels made several unsuccessful attempts at this objective before entering into UN-sponsored talks with Taylor's government—a sharp turn from their previous policy of no negotiations with Taylor. On June 17 LURD leaders signed a cease-fire with Taylor's government on the condition that Taylor step down and allow democratic elections to be held. However, Taylor soon reneged on this provision, and on June 25 LURD rebels stormed the capital, resulting in hundreds of deaths and calls for international peacekeepers to intervene. LURD pounded the capital for three weeks, taking over the main port and cutting off supplies to both residents and the government.

West African peacekeepers arrived in Liberia in August 2003, and under growing pressure both from the rebels and from the international community, Taylor left the country just a few days later, on August 11, 2003. He handed over power to his vice president, Moses Blah. Once Taylor had left the country for exile in Nigeria, LURD leaders proudly declared an end to the fighting and laid down their arms. One week later, LURD, MODEL, and Blah's government signed a peace agreement that laid out the framework for a transitional power-sharing government. Under the deal, Blah served until 2003, when a transitional government was formed from among the members of LURD, MODEL, the government, civil society, and political groups, headed by President Gyude Bryant. After a two-year transition period that saw LURD turn over much of its arsenal to a UN peacekeeping force, former Taylor opponent Ellen Johnson Sirleaf won the momentous 2005 presidential election.

Terri Nichols

See also: Liberian Civil Wars; Sierra Leone Civil War; Taylor, Charles McArthur Ghankay; Women and War in Africa.

Further Reading

Gerdes, Felix. *Civil War and State Formation: The Political Economy of War and Peace in Liberia.* Frankfurt/New York: Campus Verlag & University of Chicago Press, 2013.

Hazen, Jennifer. *What Rebels Want: Resources and Supply Networks in Wartime.* Ithaca, NY: Cornell University Press, 2013.

Käihkö, Ilmari. "Bush Generals and Small Boy Battalions: Military Cohesion in Liberia and Beyond." PhD thesis, Uppsala University, 2016.

Libya, Conflicts with Egypt and the United States (1977–1989)

Libya, an Italian colony occupied by the British during and after World War II, gained independence in 1951 under King Idris, who favored his home region of Cyrenaica in the east. In the Cold War context of the 1950s and 1960s, the Kingdom of Libya received military support from Britain and the United States, and the discovery of oil provided the hitherto impoverished country with great wealth. In 1969 a group of Libyan military officers led by Captain Muammar Gaddafi and inspired by Nasser's revolution in Egypt, overthrew King Idris, accusing him of squandering the country's oil wealth and failing to support the Arab struggle against Israel. With its oil revenue and Soviet assistance, Gaddafi's Libya built a strong military to pursue the goals of Arab unification, the elimination of Israel, and the defeat of Western imperialism. Furthermore, Gaddafi founded the Islamic Arab Legion, recruited from foreign migrant workers in Libya, to fight for his ambition of creating a large Islamic State of the Sahel. From 1973, with Egypt's defeat in the October War and its defection from the wider Arab anti-Israeli cause, Gaddafi dramatically expanded the Libyan military, buying billions of dollars' worth of Soviet armored vehicles and aircraft, although Libya lacked enough trained personnel to operate all of them. As such, Gaddafi imported thousands of Soviet, Cuban, Pakistani, Syrian, and North Korean military personnel to work as pilots and technicians. A paranoid dictator, Gaddafi undermined Libyan military effectiveness by killing or imprisoning senior officers accused of coup plotting, frequently transferring officers to disrupt supposed conspiracies and establishing a network of political commissars.

Given Gaddafi's accusations that Egypt's president Anwar Sadat had betrayed the Arab world after the 1973 war with Israel, Egypt deployed two mechanized army divisions and 80 aircraft along its western frontier with Libya. In turn, Gaddafi sent several thousand troops and 150 tanks to the border and founded training camps for Egyptian Islamist militants who raided Egypt. In 1977 Libyan and Egyptian forces fought periodic skirmishes and artillery duels along the border. On July 21, 1977, sustained fighting began when Egyptian forces ambushed and inflicted heavy losses on a Libyan tank column that ventured across the border. While Egyptian aircraft bombed Libyan airfields on the other side of the border, an Egyptian mechanized division advanced 15 kilometers into Libya where it devastated Libyan armor and then withdrew into Egypt. Over the next several days, both sides exchanged artillery fire and launched air raids across the border, and Egyptian commandos stormed Libyan radar facilities, training camps, and a major air base. Attempts by the Palestinian Liberation Organization (PLO) and the government of Algeria to mediate the conflict came to nothing. Under pressure from his new American allies who did not want to see Egypt destabilized through a protracted war with Libya, Sadat suddenly declared a cease-fire on July 24. This short Border War cost Libya 400 troops, 70 armored vehicles, and 20 jet aircraft, while Egypt lost 100 men and perhaps four aircraft. Undeterred by the conflict with Egypt, Gaddafi continued Libyan military operations south in Chad and intervened unsuccessfully in the Uganda-Tanzania War (Kagera War) of 1978–1979.

Gaddafi's support for international terrorist organizations led to conflict with the United States during the 1980s. The Libyan claim to the entire Gulf of Sirte (also called the Gulf of Sidra), spanning 500 kilometers from Tripoli to Benghazi, contradicted international law and inspired the United States to send its navy to the area to enforce freedom of navigation. Entering the Gulf of Sirte in August 1981, the United States' Sixth Fleet shot down two Libyan jet fighters without any American losses. In March 1986, because of Libya's involvement in more international terrorist attacks, U.S. naval forces again ventured into the Gulf of Sirte, sinking several Libyan patrol boats and destroying Libya's air defense system. Gaddafi responded by orchestrating terrorist attacks in Europe, which prompted the United States to conduct an aerial bombing of Libya in April 1986. Since Gaddafi's Libya began producing chemical weapons, the U.S. Navy sent a carrier group to the region in January 1989 shooting down two Libyan fighter jets.

At the start of the 1990s, with the collapse of his Soviet sponsor, Gaddafi improved his relations with Western states by admitting responsibility for the terrorist bombing of a civilian airliner over Scotland, handing over two operatives who were involved, and compensating victims' families. Eager to access Libyan oil and gain Libyan assistance against international Islamist extremists after the 2001 attacks on the United States, the United States and Britain lifted sanctions against Gaddafi's regime, and the dictator publically abandoned attempts to create weapons of mass destruction. However, in the context of the "Arab Spring" across North Africa and the Middle East, Gaddafi faced a popular uprising within Libya in 2011. During this First Libyan Civil War, Western states turned on Gaddafi with the North Atlantic Treaty Organization (NATO) providing air support and military assistance to the rebels who overthrew and killed the dictator.

Timothy J. Stapleton

See also: Arab-Israeli Wars; Chad, Conflict in; Gaddafi, Muammar; Kagera War; Libyan Civil War, Second; Nasser, Gamal Abdel; Soviet Military Involvement in Africa; U.S. Military Involvement in Africa.

Further Reading

Oyeniyi, Bukola. *The History of Libya.* Santa Barbara, CA: Greenwood, 2019.

Pollack, Kenneth. *Arabs at War: Military Effectiveness, 1948–1991.* Lincoln: University of Nebraska Press, 2002.

Wright, John. *A History of Libya.* London: Hurst, 2012.

Libyan Civil War, First (2011)

The Libyan Civil War (also known as the Libyan Revolution and the Libyan Insurgency) was but one uprising during the 2011 tumultuous Arab Spring. Muammar Gaddafi had ruled Libya for 42 years and was the focal point of popular unrest, which was strongest in the eastern region of Libya but also manifested in parts of the western and southern provinces. Opponents protested decades of authoritarianism, corruption, and repression that had produced economic and political dysfunction. Libyans tired of the Gaddafi regime sought to ride the Arab Spring to oust the long-ruling dictator and replace him with a transitional government.

The situation in Libya had been tense since the ousting of Tunisian leader Ben Ali in January, and Libyans abroad who made up the preponderance of organized opposition to the Gaddafi regime began mobilizing prior to the beginning of peaceful demonstrations in Benghazi in eastern Libya on February 15, 2011, protesting the arrest of a human rights lawyer. Two days later the demonstrations escalated, and Libyan security forces opened fire on the crowds. During several days, some 150 people were killed. Protesters overwhelmed the Libyan security forces, which withdrew from Benghazi on February 18. Violence also erupted in al-Bayda, Derna, and Tobruk, and Libyan rebels advanced across the country in makeshift caravans with incredible speed. Gaddafi made clear that he would not yield political power and would rather bring on a civil war.

The opposition in Libya was far more organized than in some other Arab Spring nations. This proved critical in establishing a transitional political movement as well as garnering international support. The opposition leaders formed the Interim Transitional National Council (TNC) on March 5, 2011. It was originally made up of 31 members representing regions of the country as well as the many clans. Local councils from throughout the country selected representatives and charged them with removing Gaddafi and installing democratic rule. The first TNC chairman was Mustafa Mohammad Abdul Jalil, while Mahmoud Jibril chaired the TNC's executive board. The TNC also set up a military committee, led by Omar al-Hariri, although Abdul Fatah Younis Al-Obeidi had actual charge of ground operations.

In the first few days of revolt, Libyan minister of the interior Abdul Fatah Younis Al-Obeidi defected, bolstering rebel support. On February 20, protests reached Tripoli, the nation's capital and Gaddafi's stronghold. By late February Gaddafi had lost control of Cyrenaica, Misrata, Zawiyah, and the Berber areas. Fighting in eastern Libya was intense in February and March, with rebels securing Benghazi and advancing to Brega, site of a major oil and gas refinery. Gaddafi loyalists counterattacked and drove the rebels out of Brega and back to the town of Ajdabiya, a strategic access point to Benghazi. On March 15 Gaddafi mounted a drive on Ajdabiya that ousted the rebels and carried on toward Benghazi.

Meanwhile, the Battle of Misrata raged from February 18 until May 15, as Gaddafi forces laid siege to this city that had been taken by rebels and that in their possession threatened his hold on Tripoli. The rebels quickly organized the Misrata Street and Military Councils, charged with overseeing rebel defenses and continuing public services. Although not as well financed as the TNC, the Military Council, led by General Ramadan Zarmuh, was able to stave off a loyalist onslaught that ultimately reached more than 10,000 men and saw considerable widespread shelling of the city. Misrata was saved thanks to a sealift of rebel weapons, supplies, and manpower from Benghazi.

During the fighting in Cyrenaica, fears abounded that Gaddafi would wreak havoc on Benghazi, resulting in the deaths of countless innocent civilians in what was Libya's second-largest city. Libyan opposition leaders called for international intervention. To avoid the anticipated massacre, on March 17 the United Nations Security Council passed Resolution 1973 calling for a no-fly zone over Libya and permission for member states to take all necessary measures to protect civilians there. The resolution did not authorize foreign ground troops.

The French took the lead, and subsequently their warplanes disrupted Gaddafi's advance on March 19, driving the loyalists back to Ajdabiya. The North Atlantic Treaty Organization (NATO) soon reached agreement on intervention and air strikes, but its aircraft kept the loyalists from massing the forces needed to take Misrata or Benghazi.

INTERNATIONAL INTERVENTION AND GADDAFI'S CAPTURE AND EXECUTION

Such international intervention, led by the United States, Great Britain, and France, drastically altered the conflict. The air campaign, dubbed Operation Odyssey Dawn, ran during March 19–31 and was led by the head of the U.S. Africa Command, General Carter F. Ham. Operation Odyssey Dawn enforced the no-fly zone; destroyed Gaddafi's air force and Libyan air defenses; and mounted air strikes on loyalist armor, artillery, and command-and-control centers. A subsequent NATO operation, Unified Protector, enforced the arms embargo and assumed command of all NATO operations in Libya.

Even with international intervention, the conflict dragged on for months before resolution. The battle for Misrata continued, with Gaddafi seeking to exploit tribal antagonisms to his advantage. He also sought to use his naval forces against the port, with the result that NATO carried out an attack on the Libyan Navy on May 20.

The three-month battle for Misrata ended in an insurgent victory on May 15. The battle had claimed the lives of more than 1,500 rebels and civilians. Meanwhile, Gaddafi's forces employed tanks and artillery against rebel towns in the Nafusa Mountains. This went on for a span of some four months, with rebel forces there in dire straits until several key victories reopened supply lines and NATO air strikes deflected the loyalists.

Another major battle erupted in late February in the port city of Zawiyah, only 30 miles west of Tripoli. More important than its proximity to the capital were its oil refinery and port facilities. Rebel forces under the command of Colonel Hussein Darbouk were unable to hold the city against Gaddafi's onslaught, and Zawiyah remained under loyalist control until August. When the rebels retook Zawiyah, this prompted a drive from the Nafusa Mountains into Tripoli on August 20.

The Tripoli campaign involved rebel elements from the Nafusa Mountains and Misrata as well as from Tripoli itself. The fighting was block by block, with the last government stronghold falling on August 28. Gaddafi, who had vowed to fight to the end in Tripoli, had already departed for his home of Sirte, which was the objective of a rebel attack in mid-October. Gaddafi was captured while attempting to escape from Sirte on October 20 and was executed that same day. Also killed were his son Mutassim Gaddafi and army chief General Abu Bakr Younis. On October 23 the TNC declared victory and set elections to take place 18 months later. The NATO mission ended a week later on October 31.

Larissa Mihalisko

See also: Air Power in Postcolonial African Wars; Ansar al-Sharia in Libya; Arab Spring; Gaddafi, Muammar; Libya, Conflicts with Egypt and the United States; Libyan Civil War, Second; U.S. Military Involvement in Africa.

Further Reading

Lobban, Richard A., Jr., and Christopher H. Dalton. *Libya: History and Revolution.* Santa Barbara, CA: ABC-CLIO, 2014.

Oyeniyi, Bukola. *The History of Libya.* Santa Barbara, CA: Greenwood, 2019.

Pargeter, Alison. *Libya: The Rise and Fall of Qaddafi.* New Haven, CT: Yale University Press, 2012.

St. John, Ronald B. *Libya: From Colony to Revolution.* Oxford: Oneworld, 2012.

Vandewalle, Dirk J. *A History of Modern Libya.* Cambridge: Cambridge University Press, 2012.

Libyan Civil War, Second (2014–2020)

A complex multiparty armed conflict that emerged in Libya in 2014 after the legitimately elected General National Congress (GNC) failed to find a consensus or resolve competing claims by different regions, ethnic groups, tribes, and ideological factions. The elections to the GNC, conducted in freedom and fairness with a large turnout, marked a high point of optimism. However, the GNC could not control the dozens of armed militias, each of which considered themselves entitled to the spoils of war from defeating Gaddafi. Islamist militias threatened and intimidated GNC representatives to exclude prominent liberal politicians and military leaders. In 2014, after its mandate expired, the GNC organized elections for a replacement House of Representatives (HoR), in which liberals gained significant influence. High levels of violence forced the HoR to relocate to Tobruk, in eastern Libya.

The conflict became a full civil war when a rejectionist movement supported by Islamist militias—the Libya Dawn Coalition—captured control of the capital, calling itself a National Salvation Government and claiming the name of the GNC, which most other states did not recognize, aside from Turkey, Sudan, and Qatar. However, this government never gained control over the multitude of militias in Tripoli. Due to the threat of the Islamic State (Daesh), both sides received international support. In addition, many other militias continued to exercise control over their regions and compete for greater resources. This created a general condition of chaos, amplified by international parties taking conflicting sides. Egypt, Russia, and the United Arab Emirates have steadily helped the HoR and Field Marshall Khalifa Haftar's Libyan National Army (LNA).

By 2015 the battle between LNA and the opposing Islamist militias seemed to reach a stalemate. In December 2015 the United Nations persuaded representatives from both sides to sign the Libyan Political Agreement, to form a Government of National Accord (GNA). The UN Security Council then recognized the GNA as Libya's legitimate government. However, the HoR refused to accept the GNA, and parts of the GNC have withdrawn support. In addition to the main competition between the Tobruk government (HoR) versus the GNA and the GNC, other Islamist militias operate against both sides. The Misrata Brigades; the Benghazi Defense Brigades; scattered independent remnants of the Islamic State; and a range of small armed groups with shifting allegiances complete the confusing picture. From 2017 to 2019, Field Marshall Haftar captured substantial areas in the south and had control over the oil fields on the coast, and in April 2019, he moved to take control over Tripoli. Receiving military assistance from Turkey, the Tripoli-based GNA eventually fought off Haftar's LNA, and in October 2020, both sides signed an internationally mediated cease-fire agreement.

Tom Dowling

See also: Ansar al-Sharia in Libya; Gaddafi, Muammar; Haftar, Khalifa Belqasim; Libyan Civil War, First.

Further Reading

Joffé, E. George H. *Insecurity in North Africa and the Mediterranean.* Rome: NATO Defense College, 2017.

Mundy, Jacob. *Libya.* Medford, MA: Polity Press, 2018.

Wehrey, Frederic M. *The Burning Shores: Inside the Battle for the New Libya.* New York: Farrar, Straus and Giroux, 2018.

Libyan National Army (LNA)

See Haftar, Khalifa Belqasim; Libyan Civil War, Second

Lord's Resistance Army (LRA)

The Lord's Resistance Army (LRA) is a rebel group historically active in northern Uganda, the Democratic Republic of the Congo (DRC), the Republic of South Sudan, and the Central African Republic (CAR). The group and its leaders espouse a Christian fundamentalist agenda. Known for its brutal attacks on civilians, the LRA has massacred thousands of civilians and abducted thousands of children and young people, forcing them to serve in its ranks as soldiers. The LRA's violent campaign prompted a top United Nations (UN) official to describe the conditions in northern Uganda in November 2003 as worse than anywhere else in the world.

Formed in 1987 from the remnants of the former Holy Spirit Movement led by Alice Lakwena, the LRA is headed by Joseph Kony, a former faith healer. Kony, who wears white robes, reportedly anoints his fighters with oil, telling them that the oil will protect them from bullets. According to some reports, he seeks to install a government that will rule according to the Ten Commandments. The LRA is also reported to prohibit its members from killing pigs, riding bicycles, or eating chickens with white feathers. Most of the group's soldiers are believed to be members of the northern Acholi ethnic group, which lost much of its dominance when Ugandan president Yoweri Museveni, a southerner from the Ankole ethnic community, came to power in 1986. Before that, most heads of state had come from the north, and the army's ranks were dominated by the Acholi.

The LRA's activities have consisted mostly of violent attacks on villages, the planting of land mines, thievery, and kidnapping. According to former abductees who managed to escape, the group marches children it kidnaps to its camps, where it gives them military training. Anyone who tries to run away or lags behind is killed, and girls are typically handed over as concubines to various LRA commanders. Some human rights groups estimate that the LRA has abducted at least 60,000 children during its decades-long campaign of terror, with other estimates nearing 100,000. Some have escaped, but many more have been killed, sold, traded into South Sudan, or kept in the LRA's fighting ranks. By 2006 more than 1.7 million northern Ugandans, including some 95 percent of the Acholi ethnic group, had been displaced by the fighting.

Initially, the LRA operated almost exclusively in the northern Gulu and Kitgum districts of Uganda, but it soon became active in the DRC, South Sudan, and the CAR. Observers in the Ugandan capital, Kampala, claimed that South Sudan was providing the group with weapons in retaliation for President Museveni's alleged support of the southern rebel group Sudan People's Liberation Movement, which fought South Sudan's northern Muslim government for years. At first, the LRA operated largely out of bases in South Sudan, but a February 2003 agreement between South Sudan and Uganda allowed Ugandan troops to enter South Sudan and attack LRA bases there. This effectively flushed the LRA out of South Sudan for a time, and the Ugandan Army made some gains in fighting the rebels. However, because the LRA was pushed back into northern Uganda, fighting there actually intensified, leaving the region more dangerous than ever.

Numerous international efforts have been applied to stop the fighting instigated by the LRA. In 2006 truce talks held between the LRA and the Ugandan government resulted in a cease-fire signed on August 26. That agreement saw the LRA leave Uganda for the Garamba region of the DRC. In December 2008, however, Ugandan, DRC, and South Sudanese troops launched an offensive against the LRA in Garamba in an attempt to eradicate the group for good. This was accompanied by U.S. logistical and financial assistance, along with 17 U.S. military advisers. The operation forced Kony from his camp and did result in the deaths of a number of LRA members, but it also resulted in horrific retaliatory attacks from scattered LRA fighters, with more than 1,000 people killed or captured in South Sudan and the DRC. Several thousand others became refugees. Kony, meanwhile, remained at large.

The unsuccessful offensive against the LRA brought more violence to civilians, including numerous massacres in the DRC and CAR between December 2008 and summer 2011. During this time, 2,300 civilians were killed, and another 3,000 were abducted. An additional 400,000 people became refugees in the DRC, South Sudan, and CAR. This occurred despite the fact that the LRA had been reduced to just a few hundred soldiers.

Because of the continued violence, in May 2010 U.S. president Barack Obama signed into law legislation that would enable the United States to fight the LRA and end the fighting in Central Africa, in cooperation with the governments of the affected nations. In October 2011 he ordered some 100 military advisers to the region, where they were to gather intelligence and train government soldiers from South Sudan, the DRC, and the CAR. By 2012 U.S. military officials believed that Kony was in hiding in the CAR. In September that year, the African Union joined the fight by offering South Sudan monetary and logistical support to defeat the LRA.

In March 2012 Invisible Children, a nonprofit organization dedicated to the protection of children, produced a 30-minute documentary about Kony and the horrors he had unleashed, especially among children. The film went on to become the most viral video in history, with 112 million views in the first week alone. In addition, in April 2013 the United States announced a $5 million bounty for Kony's capture or killing. These events prompted an escalating manhunt for Kony and his remaining soldiers in the CAR, which in 2015 resulted in the capture of a high-ranking LRA commander, Dominic Ongwen. Ongwen became the first member of the group to appear before the International Criminal Court (ICC) on charges of war crimes and crimes against humanity.

Two years later, however, Kony himself remained in hiding. Despite this failure to accomplish the core objective of the mission, in March 2017 the U.S. military announced it was ending its operations in the CAR. The military claimed that while Kony remained at large, his LRA forces had been "reduced to irrelevance." The next month, the Ugandan military announced it would also be ending operations in the CAR, claiming the situation had been neutralized. While these events have left many hopeful that the long nightmare of the LRA may finally be over, the failure to bring Kony and his commanders to justice has also led some to fear the possibility of the group's resurgence.

Lynn Jurgensen

See also: Central African Republic (CAR), Conflict in; Child Soldiers in Africa; Museveni, Yoweri; Sudan Civil War, Second; Sudan People's Liberation Movement/Army (SPLM/A); Uganda, Insurgency in the North; Uganda's Civil War: The Bush War; U.S. Military Involvement in Africa.

Further Reading

Allen, Tim, and Koen Vlassenroot. *The Lord's Resistance Army: Myth and Reality.* New York: Palgrave Macmillan, 2010.

Axe, David, and Tim Hamilton. *Army of God: Joseph Kony's War in Central Africa.* New York: Public Affairs, 2013.

Cline, Lawrence. *The Lord's Resistance Army.* Santa Barbara, CA: Praeger, 2013.

M23 Rebels
See Democratic Republic of the Congo (DRC), Continuing Violence in

Machar, Riek Teny Dhurgon (1950–)

Machar is a member of the Dok, a subgroup of the Nuer ethnic group. Born in Leer, a town in South Sudan, Machar is a descendant of a prominent Nuer prophet (Teny). After his education at the University of Khartoum, he obtained his PhD in Mechanical Engineering from the University of Bedford in England in 1984. During the Second Sudan Civil War (1983–2005), he was one of the early members of the Sudan People's Liberation Movement/Army (SPLM/A) and was appointed as the regional commander of the Western Upper Nile Province. By 1990 he became the commander of the SPLA forces along the Sudan-Ethiopia borderland from Ayod to Renk.

On August 28, 1991, Machar and two senior commanders instigated the "Nasir coup," aimed at undermining John Garang's leadership within the SPLA. Before this event, Machar had established contact with the Khartoum government, which provided military support for his rebel group. This led to the emergence of the SPLA-Nasir faction. Against the advice of some of his officers, Riek marshaled his forces from Ayod against Garang's troops at Bor on November 15, 1991. This incident led to the infamous "Bor Massacre." During this invasion, about 2,000 Dinka were killed. Consequently, John Garang, commander of the SPLA-Mainstream launched a counterattack, which led to the recapture of Bor from Machar's forces.

Despite the defeat of the SPLA-Nasir forces, Machar became renowned among the Nuer, some of whom proclaimed him as the "Moses of South Sudan" and "Liberator of the Nuer." This belief was based on the recognition of Machar as a descendant of Teny, a revered Nuer prophet. Thus, Riek had privilege to spiritual aid. These beliefs were some of the bases for the interethnic rivalry between Machar and Garang within the SPLA. However, in contrast with Garang's loyalists, those of Machar were often wavering in their allegiance to SPLA-Nasir. This was based on the fact that SPLA-Nasir's pledge to respect human rights was inconsistent with the massacre of southerners by its members. In addition, its promise of independence for South Sudan was irreconcilable with its political relationship with the Khartoum government, which opposed this agenda.

On March 26, 1993, opponents of SPLA-Mainstream joined Machar's SPLA-Nasir. Consequently, SPLA-Nasir transformed into SPLA-United. This situation aggravated the violent conflict between SPLA-Nasir and SPLA-Mainstream from 1993 to 1995. In particular, infighting between these groups stalled the peace initiative intended to resolve the Sudanese civil war. Riek Machar's control over SPLA-United was short-lived as a result of infighting among its members and its inconsistent political objectives. Therefore, Machar's SPLA-United was renamed as the Sudan People's Defence Front (SPDF).

By January 2002, SPDF and SPLA reached a compromise. At the end of the civil war in 2005, Machar became a vice president of southern Sudan. Machar also became the first vice president of South Sudan after its independence in 2011. The South Sudan Civil War broke out in 2013 when Machar was accused of plotting a coup. Machar returned to Juba during negotiations in 2016, but the resumption of fighting meant that he reentered the government as vice president with the end of the conflict in 2020.

Yusuf Sholeye

See also: Garang, John de Mabior; Kiir, Salva Mayardit; South Sudan Civil War; Sudan Civil War, Second; Sudan People's Liberation Movement/Army (SPLM/A).

Further Reading

Collins, Robert O. *A History of Modern Sudan*. Cambridge: Cambridge University Press, 2008.

Johnson, Douglas H. *Nuer Prophets: A History of Prophecy from the Upper Nile in the Nineteenth and Twentieth Centuries*. Oxford: Clarendon Press, 1994.

Mai Mai Militia

See Congo Wars; Democratic Republic of the Congo (DRC), Continuing Violence in

Malloum, Felix

See Chad, Conflict in

Mengistu Haile Mariam (1937–)

Mengistu Haile Mariam (born May 27, 1937) was a military officer, leader of the Provisional Military Administrative Council (also called Derg) from 1977 to 1987, and president of the People's Democratic Republic of Ethiopia from 1987 to 1991. Mengistu fled Ethiopia in 1991 after the collapse of his government and has since remained in exile in Zimbabwe.

There are few confirmed details about Mengistu's early life. Mengistu's mother was a domestic servant who died in childbirth around 1945. Mengistu's father was a soldier, who traveled around the Oromo province during the 1940s and 1950s. In 1960, Mengistu's father became a house guard for Ras Kebede Tessema, who helped Mengistu gain entry to the Holeta Military Academy. Mengistu graduated as a junior ordnance officer in 1966, completed subsequent training in the

United States in the late 1960s, and was a major in the Third Division by June 1974.

There is no substantiated evidence of Mengistu's political views before June 1974. This was typical among the Derg, who lacked a unified political message during the "Creeping Coup," or the five months before Emperor Haile Selassie's overthrow in November 1974. This splintered core meant that multiple factions emerged between 1974 and 1977, although many adopted socialist language previously used in the Soviet Union and the People's Republic of China by 1975. Mengistu began to heavily incorporate Marxist-Leninist rhetoric into his speeches in late 1976 and mostly emphasized the need for land reform and nationalization of private institutions.

Mengistu became the leader of the Derg on February 3, 1977. He soon after launched a campaign of political suppression against other Marxist-Leninist groups in Ethiopia. Observers to this campaign, which they called the Red Terror, estimated that it killed between 32,000 and 150,000 people from mid-1977 to early 1978.

During the early stages of the Red Terror, in June 1977, Somalia invaded Ethiopia to annex the Ogaden province. Somali president Siad Barre believed that the ongoing Red Terror made Ethiopia vulnerable. Mengistu, while initially losing most of the Ogaden province in the summer of 1977, secured an alliance with the Soviet Union and Cuba after they provided military support to him in late 1977 and early 1978. This war ended with an Ethiopian victory and was Mengistu's greatest military success during his reign.

Mengistu lost whatever legitimacy he gained, however, with multiple crises in the 1980s. The largest of these was a famine resulting in 1.2 million dead and over 2.5 million displaced from 1983 to 1985. Scholars attribute this famine to ongoing violence in Ethiopia disrupting harvests and poor management of state-run farms during periods of drought. Ethiopia also launched eight failed offensives against Eritrean nationalist movements from 1978 to 1986, which greatly reduced their control in northeast Ethiopia.

Other anti-government groups became more active, including the Tigray People's Liberation Front, further applied pressure on Mengistu. Finally, the Soviet Union's own weakness meant that it could not provide substantial support to Ethiopia in the late 1980s. Mengistu tried to convert the government into a democratic regime in 1987 and, in a last-ditch effort to remain in power, implemented a mixed-economic system in 1990. These changes came too late and, by 1991, Mengistu fled Ethiopia.

Subsequent Ethiopian governments put major Derg leaders on trial for war crimes and genocide. Mengistu started trial in absentia in 1993, and the Ethiopian High Court convicted him of genocide in December 2006 for his role in the Red Terror and forced migration programs. The high court increased the sentencing from life in prison to the death penalty in 2008 and requested Mengistu's extradition from Zimbabwe. As of August 18, 2019, Mengistu still lives in Zimbabwe, which granted him asylum for his support of the Zimbabwe liberation movement during the country's independence war (1965–1979).

Quentin Holbert

See also: Cold War in Africa; Cuba and Africa; Eritrean Liberation Front (ELF); Eritrean People's Liberation Front (EPLF); Eritrean War of Independence; Ethiopia: Insurgency and Interstate War; Famine in Postcolonial African Conflicts; Genocide in Africa; Ogaden War; Soviet Military Involvement in Africa; Tigray People's Liberation Front (TPLF).

Further Reading

Halliday, Fred, and Maxine Molyneux. *The Ethiopian Revolution.* London: New Left Books, 1981.

Tareke, Gebru. *Ethiopian Revolution: War in the Horn of Africa.* New Haven, CT: Yale University Press, 2009.

Toggia, Pietro. "The Revolutionary Endgame of Political Power: The Genealogy of 'Red Terror' in Ethiopia." *African Identities* 10, no. 3 (2012): 265–280.

Mercenaries in African Conflicts

Although definitions vary and are subject to debate, international law generally defines a mercenary as someone engaged in a conflict for private gain and who is not a national or resident or a member of the armed forces of one of the parties to the conflict. The employment of mercenaries in postcolonial African conflicts comprises two distinct phases: the "golden era" of the 1960s and the "corporatized era" from the 1990s onward. While Europeans and white South Africans represented high-profile mercenaries engaged in modern African wars, most mercenaries who fought in these conflicts were (and still are) much less prominent Black Africans from other countries on the continent.

The golden era of mercenaries in African wars occurred in the 1960s when most newly independent African countries possessed small, poorly trained, and minimally equipped armed forces. These embryonic African militaries often were unprepared to contend with armed insurgencies, including separatist movements backed by neighboring states or one of the Cold War superpowers. In this situation, postcolonial African states sometimes employed foreign mercenaries to compensate for their military weakness. The 1960s Congo Crisis became strongly associated with foreign mercenaries. From 1960 to 1963, and with backing from Western mining interests and France, the separatist state of Katanga employed white mercenaries from France, Belgium, South Africa, and Southern Rhodesia (today's Zimbabwe), who gained the nickname "les affreaux" or "the frightful ones." Subsequently, in 1964 and 1965, many mercenaries who fought for Katanga went to work for the pro-Western government of the Congo, staging a campaign to suppress an armed rebellion in the east of the country that was supported by the Eastern Bloc. Funded by the American Central Intelligence Agency (CIA), the Congolese state hired roughly 1,500 foreign fighters to bolster an offensive by the Congolese National Army (ANC). Wearing ANC uniforms, these mercenary forces comprised five commandos under Mike Hoare, which contained mostly of South Africans and Rhodesians; six commandos led by Bob Denard, comprising mostly French veterans of recent wars in Indochina and Algeria; and Jean "Black Jack" Schramme's 10 commandos made up of Belgians. In addition, the CIA hired Cuban exiles to pilot ground attack aircraft, crew patrol boats on Lake Tanganyika, and supplement ANC ground forces. On the other side of the Congo conflict of the mid-1960s, the ill-fated Simba rebels in the east included foreign fighters such as Tutsi exiles from Rwanda and a contingent of revolutionary Cuban volunteers led by Argentine Ernesto "Che" Guevara. While Hoare and the Anglophone mercenaries departed from the Congo at the end of their contracts, Francophone mercenaries led by Denard and Schramme staged an unsuccessful rebellion in 1967 and withdrew into Rwanda from where they were disarmed and sent home. With strong support from the United States, the recently installed Joseph Mobutu dictatorship built up ANC capabilities using Congolese-Israeli-trained paratroopers transported by American C-130 transport aircraft to defeat the mercenaries.

Both sides of the Nigerian Civil War (1967–1970) employed mercenary fighters. Badly outnumbered and building an army from scratch, secessionist Biafra used its support from France to hire mercenaries as field commanders, including German Rolf Steiner who had served in the French Foreign Legion, the South African Taffy Williams who had fought in the Congo, and Belgian Marc Goossens who was killed in action. In its fledgling air force, Biafra employed mercenary pilots such as German Christian Oppenheim who flew several B-26 raids on Lagos and Swede Carl Gustav Von Rosen who led the "Babies of Biafra" squadron of five light propeller aircraft fitted with rockets. Among the federal forces, Chadian mercenaries fought on the ground, and Egyptian and other foreign pilots flew newly acquired Soviet-made aircraft. Illustrating the eccentric character of some of white mercenaries working in 1960s Africa, Steiner was expelled from Biafra for military incompetence and drunkenness in 1968; he then went to southern Sudan to join separatist rebels but ended up imprisoned in Khartoum in the early 1970s.

Several well-known mercenary leaders staged coups in small African countries. Associated with French activities in Africa, Bob Denard participated in four coup attempts in the Comoros Islands and one in Benin. In 1981, Mike Hoare led a failed coup attempt in the Seychelles Islands, and this resulted in him spending several years in a South African prison. Romanticized in Western popular culture, these white mercenaries became the subject of adventure novels such as Wilbur Smith's *Dark of the Sun* (1965) and Frederick Forsyth's *The Dogs of War* (1974), both of which became films, movies such as *The Wild Geese* (1978) on which Hoare worked as a technical adviser and a 1978 American folk song titled "Roland the Headless Thompson Gunner." With the exception of some anti-communists and racists who joined Rhodesian and South African forces, Western mercenary activity in Africa declined in the 1970s and 1980s as African armed forces improved, and the presence of white foreign fighters became an embarrassment to African states.

A new corporatized era of mercenary work in Africa began from around 1990, with the end of the Cold War leading to the collapse of authoritarian regimes, the proliferation of civil conflicts, and the rise of a neoliberal economic order. British and white South African military veterans formed private military companies or contractors (PMCs) such as Sandline International and Executive Outcomes (EO) offering training, advising, and security and arms procurement services to state clients. In 1995, the government of Sierra Leone hired EO, which provided military advisers and combat troops, primarily white and Black veterans of South

Africa's "Border War," as well as a helicopter gunship that pushed back Revolutionary United Front (RUF) rebels from the country's diamond-producing areas. The next year, however, a new government expelled the EO contingent, which allowed the RUF to recover and the civil war to continue. Around the same time, with the continuation of the decades-long civil war in Angola, the Angolan government used its oil revenues to hire EO to supply South African veterans who deployed against the rebels of the National Union for the Total Independence of Angola (UNITA). As in Sierra Leone, international pressure led to the Angola state canceling its contract with EO. One of the founders of Sandline and EO, former British Army officer Simon Mann, was arrested along with other mercenaries in Zimbabwe in 2004 on their way to attempt a coup in oil-rich Equatorial Guinea, and he spent the next few years in prison in both countries. In 1996–1997, Mobutu attempted to compensate for the weakness of the Armed Forces of Zaire (FAZ) by employing some French and Serbian mercenaries to counter an invasion by Rwanda, Uganda, and Angola, but this failed, and his regime fell.

The September 2001 terrorist attacks on the United States and the subsequent American invasions of Afghanistan and Iraq revolutionized the PMC industry, as the privatization of war offered lucrative economic opportunities. This development also attracted considerable criticism, as mercenaries lacked accountability and became involved in human rights abuses. A significant number of South African veterans of the "Border War," despite their country's strong anti-mercenary legislation, worked with international PMCs in Afghanistan and Iraq. As these wars dragged on and the contracts became less profitable, PMCs began employing lower-paid personnel from postconflict countries such as Uganda and Sierra Leone, including former child soldiers. In addition, PMCs became involved in some African countries such as in Somalia, where piracy and civil war led to the employment of private security contractors on cargo ships. Around 2015 a frustrated Nigerian government hired South African mercenaries in an ultimately failed attempt to thwart the mounting Islamist insurgency of Boko Haram in the country's northeast. During the 2000s and into the 2010s, Western-based groups like Aegis and Frontier Services Group with strong links to the PMC industry provided security and security training and procured arms for some African states and international businesses involved in Africa. In general, and given the controversies surrounding mercenary work, these Western-based companies have tended to minimize their direct involvement in war fighting in Africa. Since the mid-2010s, the international reemergence of Russia prompted the involvement of Russian PMC Wagner Group in some African countries such as the Central African Republic and Libya.

Despite the contentious involvement of foreign PMCs in some African conflicts, most mercenaries present in these situations comprised low-profile fighters from other African countries with no apparent links to the corporate world. African states and armed factions involved in conflict often looked to allies or contacts in nearby countries to supply military personnel, and poor economic conditions facilitated recruiting. For example, foreign fighters from Burkina Faso, Guinea, and the Gambia fought in civil wars in neighboring Liberia (1989–1996 and 1999–2003) and Sierra Leone (1991–2002); Liberians and Sierra Leoneans fought in each other's internal conflicts; and mercenaries from Burkina Faso joined both sides of the civil war in Côte d'Ivoire (2002–2011). Similarly, mercenaries from Chad and the Darfur region of western Sudan became embroiled in conflicts in each other's countries and neighbors such as Libya. Although seemingly motivated by religion and not financial gain, transnationalist Islamist insurgent forces active in West Africa's Sahel countries such as Mali and also in Somalia include foreign fighters arguably defined as mercenaries.

Timothy J. Stapleton

See also: Angolan Conflicts; Boko Haram; Congo Crisis; Congo Wars; Côte d'Ivoire Civil War; Liberian Civil Wars; Nigerian Civil War; Sierra Leone Civil War; Sudan Civil War, First.

Further Reading

Fitzsimmons, Scott. *Mercenaries in Asymmetric Conflicts.* Cambridge: Cambridge University Press, 2013.

Hoare, Mike. *Congo Mercenary.* Boulder, CO: Paladin Press, 2008.

Musah, Abdul-Fatau, and J. Kayode Fayemi, eds. *Mercenaries: An African Security Dilemma.* London: Pluto Press, 2000.

Singer, P. W. *Corporate Warriors: The Rise of the Privatized Military Industry.* Ithaca, NY: Cornell University Press, 2003.

Venter, Al J. *War Dog: Fighting Other Peoples' Wars: The Modern Mercenary in Combat.* New Delhi: Lancer, 2010.

Micombero, Michel (1940–1983)

Michel Micombero was the first president of the central African state of Burundi, serving in that role between 1966 and 1976. A Tutsi, he was born in Rutovu, Bururi province, southern Burundi, in 1940, and educated in local Catholic schools. In 1960 he joined the Belgian colonial army and was sent to Brussels for officer training. In 1962 he returned to Burundi with a commission as captain and took up a position in the armed forces of what had by then become an independent state.

Burundi, at this time, had a population mix dominated by a large Hutu majority (85 percent), with a much smaller Tutsi minority. At independence from Belgium in 1962, the Tutsis, who had been the traditional rulers before and during Belgian colonialism, retained their ascendancy—largely by force of arms and a tightly controlled bureaucracy. Upon his return from Belgium, Micombero joined the Union for National Progress (UPRONA), the ruling party dominated by the Tutsi elite, and rose quickly to become secretary of state for defense (1963). The country, however, was about to enter a period of anarchy. In 1965, legislative elections gave Hutu parties a resounding victory, winning 23 out of 33 seats in the national assembly. This victory was overthrown, however, when the Tutsi *mwaami* (king), Mwambutsa IV, appointed a Tutsi from the royal family as prime minister. Soon thereafter, on October 19, 1965, an attempted coup was suppressed ruthlessly, but this served only to intensify Hutu anger at their second-class status, and in some parts of the country massacres of Tutsis began to take place.

In mid-1966 Micombero conspired with others in arranging for a palace coup that saw the crown prince, Charles Ntare V Ndizeye, take the throne. On July 11, 1966, Micombero formed a government, with himself as prime minister. Then, on November 28, 1966, he overthrew the monarchy, declared Burundi a republic, and placed himself at its head as president.

Micombero now became an advocate of what became known as African socialism. This was a vague ideology asserting that economic resources should be shared in what he called a "traditional African" manner. Within the Cold War context, both the Soviet Union and communist China courted African states professing African socialism, and Micombero's Burundi fell under the patronage of China as a result. Micombero imposed a tight law-and-order regime throughout the country and did all he could to repress any possibility of a Hutu ascendancy. He also cracked down on Hutu militancy.

It was against this background that on April 29, 1972, Hutu radicals in the southern provinces of Burundi launched an uprising against Micombero's military government, massacring several thousand Tutsi civilians. They were supported (and, in some instances, organized) by Hutu refugees outside Burundi itself. This was viewed as a final challenge for supremacy by many Tutsi leaders, in particular Micombero. On the same day as the Hutu rising, he dissolved the government.

It was now that the country began to descend into disorder. Ethnic hostility between Hutus and Tutsis appeared more overtly than beforehand, and regional factionalism between Tutsi politicians and other members of the elite started to divide the government. Micombero adopted harsh measures to bring the country to heel, beginning with the brutal repression of Hutu suspects in Bururi, the physical elimination of all Hutu troops in the army, and the transformation of regionally based measures into countrywide repression. A number of public sector purges were also carried out. Hutu hopes looked to the now exiled ex-king Ntare to return and overthrow Micombero; he did return but was killed soon thereafter while in government custody. It is widely believed that it was Micombero himself who personally ordered Ntare's assassination.

Micombero was now unchallenged in the measures he could adopt to suppress the Hutus, and he began to institute a series of deliberately targeted campaigns that can only be described as genocide. The intention of these killings was the elimination of all Hutu political aspirations, once and for all. A series of deliberate campaigns took place against specific categories of Hutus, such as those in government employment, intellectuals (which could include any Hutu with a university education, whether completed or current; secondary school students; and teachers), and the Hutu middle and upper classes. Estimates of the number killed between April and October 1972 vary, but most settle at somewhere between 100,000 and 150,000. Hundreds of thousands more fled abroad, with Micombero unquestionably playing a leading role in the campaign.

The overall impact of these events took a personal toll on Micombero. Although he could claim to have saved the country (or at least, the Tutsi ascendancy within it), it was reported that he began drinking heavily and slipped into a psychological nether world, paranoid and delusional. His administration henceforth became increasingly corrupt and inefficient. By November 1976, some members of the army, anxious to restore order to Burundi (though without necessarily seeking to come to the aid of the Hutus), staged a coup led by the chief of staff (and Micombero's distant cousin and clan member), Jean-Baptiste Bagaza. Micombero was arrested. After a short period of imprisonment in the capital, Bujumbura, he went into exile in Somalia, where he died of a heart attack in 1983.

The killing, however, did not end there. Subsequent large-scale massacres of Hutus by Tutsi government forces took place in 1988 and by Hutus against Tutsis in 1993. Accompanying these savage assaults was the wholesale exodus of scores of thousands of refugees to neighboring countries, leading to an intensifying destabilization of the Great Lakes region, which culminated in the Rwandan Genocide of April–July 1994. Until the early 1990s, however, successive Burundian governments refused to acknowledge that genocide had even taken place in the country—a situation with which many in the international community seemed content to follow.

Paul R. Bartrop

See also: Belgian Military Intervention in Africa; Burundi, Civil War and Genocide; Coups and Military Regimes in Africa; Hutu Power Movements.

Further Reading

Jennings, Christian. *Across the Red River: Rwanda, Burundi and the Heart of Darkness.* London: Phoenix, 2000.

Lemarchand, Rene. *Burundi: Ethnic Conflict and Genocide.* Cambridge: Cambridge University Press, 1994.

Scherrer, P. Christian. *Genocide and Crisis in Central Africa: Conflict Roots, Mass Violence, and Regional War.* Westport, CT: Praeger, 2002.

Watt, Nigel. *Burundi: The Biography of a Small African Country.* London: Hurst, 2008.

Mobutu Sese Seko (1930–1997)

This Congolese politician and dictator (1965–1997) was born Joseph Désiré Mobutu on October 14, 1930, in Lisala in the former Belgian colony of the Congo (Zaire). Mobutu Sese Seko was educated in Belgian missionary schools. Expelled from school in 1950, he served in the colonial army during 1950–1956. After he left the service, he became a journalist for the *L'Avenir* news journal.

Mobutu was appointed army chief of staff by the Congo's first prime minister, Patrice Lumumba, in 1960. On September 14, 1960, after a showdown between Lumumba and President Joseph Kasavubu, Mobutu announced that he was neutralizing both leaders by launching a coup. Not yet strong enough to form his own government, he grudgingly accepted Kasavubu as president. Relations between Mobutu and Lumumba steadily worsened, however, and Mobutu was among those who plotted the assassination of Lumumba in January 1961.

Following Lumumba's murder, Mobutu remained out of the political limelight for several years while consolidating his power base behind the scenes. On November 25, 1965, he staged a second coup, bringing him to sole power. He formed his own political party, the Mouvement Populaire de la Révolution (MPR, Popular Movement of the Revolution); outlawed all other political parties; and dealt harshly with opponents.

As part of his national authenticity movement, Mobutu changed the name of the Congo to Zaire in 1971 and changed his own name to Mobutu Sese Seko the following year. In a bid to rid Zaire of colonial influences, he mandated that all citizens drop their Christian names in favor of Africanized ones. As head of state, Mobutu promised stability and order. And although there was little internal dissent during his repressive reign, rebellions in the Shaba province during 1977–1978, which were brutally repressed, demonstrated that serious opposition to his rule existed.

Only those loyal to Mobutu served in the civil administration. Most were susceptible to bribery, cronyism, and corruption. Nevertheless, Western aid, especially from the United States and Belgium, filled Mobutu's coffers, and he obliged with strong pro-Western, anti-Soviet policies. But he also had an independent streak. He shrewdly catered to the West by taking advantage of Cold War rivalries while maintaining his own cult of personality at home.

Mobutu ruled for 32 years as an iron-fisted autocrat. These years have become known as the kleptocracy based on evidence that he stole billions of dollars from his own people. Under the guise of "Zairianization," Mobutu nationalized between 1,500 and 2,000 foreign-owned industries. He then channeled the profits from these to his own personal accounts. Not surprisingly, rural areas and the nation's vast peasantry remained wholly neglected.

After the Cold War wound down in the early 1990s, the United States tried to push Mobutu to accept political and economic reforms. He was reluctant to do so and found himself alone facing the rebel forces of Laurent Kabila. In the meantime, the country's economy was in shambles, and Mobutu was powerless to reverse the economic slide. In May 1997 he was forced to relinquish power and was expelled from the country by Kabila's forces. Mobutu died in Rabat, Morocco, on September 7, 1997.

Lise Namikas

See also: Belgian Military Intervention in Africa; Cold War in Africa; Congo Crisis; Congo Wars; French Military Involvement in Postcolonial Africa; Kabila, Laurent; Mercenaries in African Conflicts; Shaba, Zaire: Rebel Incursions and Foreign Intervention; U.S. Military Involvement in Africa.

Further Reading

Kelly, Sean. *America's Tyrant: The CIA and Mobutu and Zaire.* Washington, DC: American University Press, 1993.

Nzongola-Ntalaja, Georges. *The Congo: From Leopold to Kabila: A People's History.* London: Zed Books, 2013.

Prunier, Gerard. *Africa's World War: Congo, the Rwanda Genocide and the Making of a Continental Catastrophe.* Oxford: Oxford University Press, 2009.

Mogadishu, Battle of (1993)

The Battle of Mogadishu was a bloody conflict brought on by U.S. efforts to stabilize Somalia and capture and disarm those leaders seen as most threatening to the peace.

The operation that led to the Battle of Mogadishu, famously referred to as *Black Hawk Down* due to the events of the battle and book chronicling the events by Mark Bowden, was an effort to capture Mohammed Farrah Aidid. Aidid was a former military officer and one of several leaders whose efforts had helped topple the former Siad Barre regime. In the aftermath of independence, Somalia as thrown into flux as several of the factions vied for control of the country and began taking designated humanitarian aid as a means of political and social support for their political cause. In reaction, the international community, specifically the United States and the United Nations, attempted to bring him and others to heel.

The planning for the operation led to difficulties, as the United States wished to bring about peace in Somalia but only with a very low commitment in resources and little to no loss of life. The focus on limited commitment, as well as political demands for success in Mogadishu, may have inadvertently led to the battle and the doomed outcome of U.S. involvement. Despite committing "Task Force Ranger," along with special operations and Delta Force operatives, the United States had been unable to capture Aidid, as they never possessed enough actionable intelligence in time. For over six weeks, the forces proved unable to capture him while also standing up, and down, on several occasions. On October 3, 1993, they finally received enough reliable intelligence to go forward with a military operation. The problem was that while previous operations had played to the strengths of U.S. forces, specifically striking at night when night-vision goggles and the capabilities of U.S. Special Forces were maximized, the engagement on October 3 involved attacking a position in Mogadishu, where Aidid and his lieutenants were meeting, but doing so in the middle of the day. Thus, there was a much greater increase of risk but without an equal commitment of resources. Because of the demands by Washington to avoid an incident, the hope for greater air cover, in the form of large gunships, was denied to prevent a "high-profile" event. What resulted was a very complex operation, involving many parts that ran squarely into the friction of war.

The operation was intended to utilize Ranger and Special Forces units dropped by helicopter onto the building for the quick capture of Aidid and his lieutenants. They would be met on the ground by a ground force driven by Humvees to meet them, collect the prisoners, and return to base. The problems, however, started early with the serious injury of Private Todd Blackburn who fell from his helicopter 70 feet to the ground. Further problems were caused as the convoy attempted to make it back to base but were repeatedly rerouted through the city and suffered attacks nearly the whole way.

The operation went from bad to worse when Aidid's fighters were able to down two of the Black Hawk helicopters providing cover for the operation. This further stretched the resources of the military forces, as it gave them two new areas they needed to attempt to protect. What ensued was a battle in which the isolated forces attempted to protect their positions as well as eventually receive support to return to a safe area. The battle occurred over the course of the day and night and led to 90 U.S. military casualties, with estimates of Somali casualties suggested as 800–1,000 killed and as many as 4,000 wounded.

It also involved great sacrifice, famously in the form of snipers Master Sergeant Gary Gordon and Sergeant First Class Randy Shughart. In order to protect the second crash site, they requested being put on the ground in order to protect pilot Michael Durant who had been wounded in the crash. Both Gordon and Shughart were eventually killed, and Durant was captured by Somali fighters. Their efforts led to both receiving a posthumous medal of honor. Unfortunately, upon their deaths, their bodies were dragged through the streets of Mogadishu. Such images soured the Clinton administration on the operation in Somalia and led to a drawdown of U.S. commitment to the region. Such actions had grave repercussions when Osama bin Laden saw it as proof of the weakness of the United States, which he believed could be brought to heel by acts of terror.

Robert H. Clemm

See also: Barre, Mohamed Siad; Operation Restore Hope; Somalia Civil War; U.S. Military Involvement in Africa.

Further Reading

Bowden, Mark. *Black Hawk Down: A Story of Modern War.* Berkeley: Atlantic Monthly Press, 1999.

Rutherford, Kenneth. *Humanitarianism under Fire: The US and UN Intervention in Somalia.* Sterling, VA: Kumarian Press, 2008.

Mokhtar Belmokhtar (1972–)

There are terrorists, and then there are terrorists. Mokhtar Belmokhtar is the latter, a larger-than-life character who founded and led several terrorist groups in the Sahara, gaining notoriety for his smuggling and kidnapping operations. In the words of the late professor Stephen Ellis: "He is one of the best-known warlords of the Sahara." Born in Ghardaïa, Algeria, on June 1, 1972, Belmokhtar grew up in a Saharan desert environment in a city famed for its founding by an Islamic sect of Berbers, known as the Ibadis, who sought refuge in the Saharan desert. Mokhtar Belmokhtar is actually a nom de guerre deriving from the Arabic *mukhtar*, meaning the chosen one, and is a term often denoting a leader for a local group or town. Belmokhtar moved to Afghanistan in the early 1990s to fight with the Islamist mujahedeen against the Soviet-sponsored government in Kabul, losing an eye in the process—thus gaining one of his many warrior-monikers: "one-eyed." Along with other Algerian-born veterans from Afghanistan, Belmokhtar helped establish a violent extremist organization named the Armed Islamic Group (GIA) after the 1992 military coup in Algeria, which overthrew the Islamic Salvation Front government, then the largest political opposition party to the National Liberation Front (FLN) in Algeria. The GIA grew into a notoriously violent organization renowned for torturing and indiscriminately killing Muslims and civilians. The GIA rebranded itself the Salafist Group for Preaching and Combat (GSPC) in 1998. It is likely that Belmokhtar had moved his terrorist group, which had to be self-sustaining due to lack of external support, into the Saharan desert of northern Mali due to Algerian counterinsurgency operations. In early 2007 the GSPC changed its name to Al-Qaeda in the Islamic Maghreb (AQIM), drawing Belmokhtar and other Saharan terrorists back closer to Osama bin Laden, the Al-Qaeda franchise, and the conflict in Afghanistan. The funds and support AQIM likely expected from bin Laden and the financiers of global jihad apparently never materialized, and Belmokhtar continued his for-profit activities, largely cigarette smuggling, which earned him the nickname "Mr. Marlboro," later turning to more profitable schemes such as cocaine smuggling and kidnap-for-ransom. His group famously kidnapped the Canadian ambassador Robert Fowler in 2009 in Niger and held him and his colleague Louis Guay hostage at various camps across northern Mali for six months, which demonstrated Belmokhtar's operational reach as well as negotiation skills. The 2012 civil war in Mali offered Belmokhtar and other AQIM groups the possibility to form alliances with Tuareg rebels with grievances against the government in Bamako. Before the French intervention in early 2013, however, Belmokhtar broke ties with AQIM—most notably that of Abu Zeid in Mali—recorded in several letters condemning Belmokhtar's independence and freedom of action by AQIM leadership. Belmokhtar then formed the Islamist al-Mulathameen (Masked) Brigade, or al-Mua'qi'oon Biddam ("Those who sign with blood") Brigade and seized the In Aménas gas facility in Southern Algeria, taking more than 800 hostages but was defeated by an Algerian military hostage rescue operation. His group is also considered responsible for a May 2013 attack on a French-owned uranium mine in Arlit, Niger, as well as the November 2015 attack on the Radisson Blue hotel in Bamako. There have been numerous reports about the targeted killing of Belmokhar, leading to the nickname "the uncatchable," but it appears he was killed in an airstrike in Southern Libya in June 2015 or November 2016.

Joseph Guido

See also: Algerian Civil War; Al-Qaeda in the Islamic Maghreb (AQIM); Tuareg Rebellions since 1960 (Mali and Niger).

Further Reading

Fowler, Robert. *A Season in Hell: My 130 Days in the Sahara with Al Qaeda*. New York: HarperCollins, 2011.

Guido, Joseph. *Terrorist Sanctuary in the Sahara: A Case Study*. Carlisle Barracks, PA: Strategic Studies Institute/US Army War College, 2017.

Mokeddem, Mohamed. *Al Qaida Au Maghreb Islamique: Contrebande Au Nom De L'islam* (Al-Qaeda in the Islamic Maghreb: Smuggling in the Name of Islam). Algiers: Casbah-Editions, 2010.

Scheele, Judith. *Smugglers and Saints of the Sahara: Regional Connectivity in the Twentieth Century*. Cambridge: Cambridge University Press, 2012.

Mondlane, Eduardo (1920–1969)

Eduardo Mondale was the founder of the Front for the Liberation of Mozambique (FRELIMO) that led the insurgency against Portuguese rule in Mozambique.

Born in Manjacaze, Gaza Province, in Portuguese Mozambique on June 20, 1920, Eduardo Mondlane was one of 16 sons of a chief of the Bantu-speaking Tsonga ethnic group. Educated at Presbyterian missionary schools in Mozambique and in the Transvaal, South Africa, Mondlane was awarded a scholarship to

Witwatersrand University but left within a year with the rise of apartheid. In 1950 he entered the University of Lisbon but secured a scholarship from Oberlin College, Ohio, in the United States, earning a degree in anthropology and sociology there in 1953. He then earned a doctorate in sociology at Northwestern University.

Following a year's study at Harvard University, in 1957 Mondlane joined the United Nations (UN) as a researcher in the Trusteeship Department but resigned within a year to undertake political activities not permitted in the UN position. He joined the faculty of Syracuse University as an assistant professor of anthropology and helped develop its East African studies program.

In 1962 Mondlane resigned from Syracuse and moved to Tanzania. At Dar es Salaam there that September he was elected the president of FRELIMO, formed of four organizations working for the independence of Mozambique. Enjoying support from a number of African states and the Soviet Union, in 1964 FRELIMO commenced military operations against Portugal in Mozambique.

Throughout, FRELIMO was subject to considerable internal divisions, and Mondlane was assassinated in Dar es Salaam by a parcel bomb on February 3, 1969. Some have attributed the deed to the Portuguese intelligence services. Mondlane's successor, Samora Machel, aligned FRELIMO more closely with the Soviet Union.

Spencer C. Tucker

See also: Cold War in Africa; Portuguese Africa, Independence Wars (Angola, Mozambique, and Guinea-Bissau).

Further Reading
Mondlane, Eduardo. *The Struggle for Mozambique*. Baltimore: Penguin, 1969.
Newitt, Malyn. *A History of Mozambique*. London: Hurst, 1995.
Newitt, Marlyn. *Portugal in Africa: The Last 100 Years*. London: Longman, 1981.

Movement for Democracy in Liberia (MODEL)
See Liberian Civil Wars

Movement for the Liberation of Congo (MLC)
See Central African Republic (CAR), Conflict in; Congo Wars

Mozambique Civil War (1976–1992)

In 1975 Mozambique gained independence after a long war between Portuguese colonial forces and nationalist insurgents from the Front for the Liberation of Mozambique (FRELIMO). Immediately, FRELIMO founded a one-party Marxist-Leninist state, eliminated political opponents, and embarked on a socialist development agenda. FRELIMO improved education, health, and women's rights, but its autocratic manner, focus on industrialization, collective agriculture, and hostility to traditional leaders alienated some rural communities. Furthering revolution in neighboring white minority–ruled states, FRELIMO allowed the insurgents of the Zimbabwe African National Liberation Army (ZANLA) to use Mozambique as a staging area for the infiltration of Rhodesia and hosted the exiled African National Congress (ANC) agents fighting apartheid South Africa. In turn, around 1976, Rhodesian intelligence agents organized former Portuguese colonial troops and dissidents into the Mozambique National Resistance (RENAMO) that embarked on guerrilla warfare to destabilize the FRELIMO state. In 1980, with the demise of Rhodesia and the independence of majority-ruled Zimbabwe, South African assumed sponsorship of RENAMO, founding a new training and logistical base in Phalaborwa in northeastern South Africa. At the time, RENAMO comprised about 2,000 rebels in Mozambique. In June 1980 FRELIMO forces captured RENAMO's Mozambican base at Gorongoza in the mountains north of the Zimbabwe-Beira road, where it discovered evidence of South African assistance such as ammunition containers and parachutes. By February 1981 RENAMO had grown to 10,000 armed fighters inside Mozambique and recaptured Gorongoza.

During the 1980s, South African Special Forces trained, advised, and supplied RENAMO and staged their own military operations against targets in Mozambique. Initially, South African agents and supplies arrived in Mozambique by helicopter or parachute drop from airplanes, but from 1981, when RENAMO extended its activities to Inhambane province, the South African Navy began landing large quantities of equipment on the coast. South African officers played a central role in planning RENAMO operations meant to damage Mozambique's economy to maintain its economic dependence on South Africa and possibly overthrow the FRELIMO government. From a regional perspective, South Africa wanted to undermine attacks by anti-apartheid frontline states to reduce their economic dependence on South Africa by redirecting export and import to Mozambican ports. South African Special Forces operations in Mozambique included a January 1981 raid on ANC houses in Maputo, a November 1981 attack on two bridges near Beira and Beira harbor, a December 1982 bombing of Zimbabwe's oil storage facilities in Beira, and an October 1983 bombing in Maputo. In May 1983 South African warplanes attacked an ANC facility at Maputo, inflicting serious casualties.

In October 1981, Zimbabwe's ruling Zimbabwe African National Union-Patriotic Front (ZANU-PF) under Prime Minister Robert Mugabe and Mozambique's FRELIMO led by President Samora Machel signed a security pact to counter South African destabilization in southern Africa. Consequently, in 1982, 600 Zimbabwean troops arrived in Mozambique to help fight RENAMO. Since ZANU-PF's former armed wing of ZANLA had worked with FRELIMO during the Zimbabwe Independence War of the 1970s, this move represented a continuation of the ZANLA-FRELIMO alliance and an effort by Mugabe to take a prominent role among the frontline states. During the 1980s, RENAMO threatened the transport corridor from the port of Beira in Mozambique to the Zimbabwean border through which Harare's oil supplies arrived without passing through South Africa. Nevertheless, RENAMO's insurgency pressured Mozambique's FRELIMO government into signing the 1984 Nkomati Accord in which it agreed to expel the exiled ANC, and South Africa vowed to abandon RENAMO. FRELIMO lived up to the deal by expelling ANC members from Mozambique, but Pretoria continued to provide RENAMO with covert assistance, often through Malawi. In October 1986, on his return from a meeting in Zambia, Mozambique's president Machel died in an airplane crash in South Africa that many suspected had been orchestrated by the apartheid state.

The Mozambique Civil War continued to the early 1990s. In June 1985 the leaders of Zimbabwe and Tanzania promised to support the Mozambique government against RENAMO. Initially guarding the Biera corridor, the Zimbabwe Defence Forces (ZDF) expanded operations by mounting aggressive search-and-destroy missions in Mozambique. In August 1985, Zimbabwean troops captured a large RENAMO base and discovered evidence of continued South African assistance. Around the same time, Zimbabwe, Mozambique, and Malawi entered a joint security agreement that resulted in the ZDF securing the road from northeast Zimbabwe to southern Malawi that transits Mozambique's Tete province where an important bridge crosses the Zambezi River at the town of Tete. This road had been plagued by RENAMO ambushes. The conservative regime of Dr. Hastings Kamuzu Banda in Malawi played a double game, with the Malawian Army conducting joint patrols with FRELIMO while the Malawi Young Pioneers facilitated South African sponsorship of RENAMO. This almost led to conflict between Malawi and the allied governments of Zimbabwe and Mozambique. In 1986 and 1987 Zimbabwe, Tanzanian, and Mozambican state forces frustrated a RENAMO offensive aimed at cutting the FRELIMO-controlled part of the country in half. In 1987 Zimbabwean, Tanzanian, and Mozambican troops captured five towns in northern Mozambique from RENAMO, prompting the rebels to shift their activities south. At the end of the 1980s, 15,000 ZDF personnel were operating in Mozambique with eight Zimbabwean battalions protecting roads and railways. Within Zimbabwe, as a result, involvement in the Mozambique Civil War became unpopular, with criticisms about cost, casualties, and military corruption. In addition, RENAMO launched revenge attacks inside Zimbabwe's border regions.

During the early 1990s, the end of the Cold War as well as the rise of democracy in South Africa and Malawi compelled FRELIMO to adopt multiparty democracy and a capitalist economy and led to negotiations between FRELIMO and RENAMO. In Mozambique, a massive reconstruction program involved the demobilization of 92,000 combatants, clearance of land mines, infrastructure repair, and the resettlement of almost four million internally displaced people and refugees. Established in 1994, a new Armed Forces for the Defence of Mozambique (FADM) comprised 10,000 personnel from both FRELIMO and RENAMO. In April 1993, the ZDF withdrew from Mozambique, making way for the 6,600 international peacekeepers of the United Nations Operation in Mozambique (UNUMOZ). Initially assigned to protect the strategically important Beira Corridor, 1,000 Italian troops eventually withdrew over a scandal related to their employment of child prostitutes. In the rest of Mozambique, a battalion from Botswana secured the Tete Corridor, Zambian troops protected Maputo, a Uruguayan force occupied Inhambane, and soldiers from Bangladesh garrisoned the northern region. Under the leadership of Joaquim Chissano, FRELIMO won Mozambique's first democratic elections in

1994, though Afonso Dhlakama's RENAMO emerged as a strong parliamentary opposition. UNUMOZ disbanded the following year. After losing several disputed elections, RENAMO attempted to relaunch its insurgency in 2013, though violence remained limited. With the 2018 death of Dhlakama, RENAMO and the FRELIMO government signed a peace deal in August 2019.

Timothy J. Stapleton

See also: Mozambique National Resistance (RENAMO); Portuguese Africa, Independence Wars (Angola, Mozambique, and Guinea-Bissau); South Africa, Armed Struggle against Apartheid; Zimbabwe Independence War.

Further Reading

Emerson, Stephen. *The Battle for Mozambique: The FRELIMO-RENAMO Struggle, 1977–1992.* Solihull: Helion, 2014.

Minter, William. *Apartheid's Contras: An Inquiry into the Roots of War in Angola and Mozambique.* London: Zed Books, 1994.

Newitt, Malyn. *A History of Mozambique.* London: Hurst, 1995.

Mozambique National Resistance (RENAMO)

The Mozambique National Resistance (Resistencia Nacional Mocambicana, or RENAMO) was originally founded in the 1970s to serve as an intelligence network within Mozambique for the white-minority government of Rhodesia (now Zimbabwe). Based in Lisbon, Portugal, it became active in Mozambique in 1976.

When Zimbabwe attained its independence in 1980, it transformed into an insurgent group opposing Mozambique's ruling party, the Mozambique Liberation Front (Frente de Libertação de Moçambique, or FRELIMO). The RENAMO movement was widely condemned for its terrorist tactics during the Mozambique Civil War. As part of the deal to achieve peace in Mozambique, RENAMO was rechristened as a political party.

RENAMO's membership is primarily drawn from defectors from FRELIMO, members of the Shona-speaking Ndau ethnic group, and mercenaries from Portugal and elsewhere. Until the dismantling of apartheid in neighboring South Africa in the early 1990s, RENAMO received most of its funding from the Pretoria government and was effectively controlled by the South African military.

In June 1989 the RENAMO Congress established a 10-member national council, with one member from each province, and a four-member leadership cabinet. At the same time the group declared that it no longer sought to overthrow the Mozambican government but preferred to operate as a legal political force and participate in free elections. The Mozambican government agreed to RENAMO's request in 1990, and a cease-fire was established at the end of that year, although RENAMO continued its guerrilla activities. Sporadic peace talks over the next two years led to the signing of a peace treaty in October 1992.

Although the peace process to end lingering hostilities in the countryside, including the demobilization of troops on both sides, proceeded more slowly than anticipated, multiparty elections were finally held in October 1994. RENAMO gained 112 seats in the new 250-member Assembly of the Republic, and its leader,

Afonso Dhlakama, came in second in the presidential vote, losing to incumbent president Joaquim Chissano. In the country's second multiparty democratic elections in December 1999, RENAMO was again edged out by FRELIMO, as was Dhlakama, again RENAMO's presidential candidate. RENAMO leaders declared the results fraudulent and boycotted the assembly for nearly a year until returning to the legislature in October 2000.

In July 2002 Dhlakama fired the party's secretary general, Joaquim Vaz, and dissolved its national political commission. He also removed two former secretaries general from the party leadership. Dhlakama then announced that he would take over the secretary general's position and also oversee the day-to-day running of the party (formerly the commission's job) for the foreseeable future. However, he did appoint a new national political commission. Dhlakama accused FRELIMO of trying to create divisions within RENAMO for political gain.

In December 2004 presidential and legislative elections, Dhlakama ran against FRELIMO candidate Armando Guebuza, a wealthy businessperson handpicked by outgoing president, Chissano. Dhlakama lost, and he and his party refused to take the 90 legislative seats RENAMO won. In addition, the party's request for a revote was denied. In January 2005, however, Dhlakama and RENAMO conceded defeat and decided to take their 90 elected seats. In 2014, citing election irregularities, RENAMO relaunched its insurgency but agreed to a series of cease-fires with the government in 2015 and 2019.

ABC-CLIO

See also: Mozambique Civil War.

Further Reading

Minter, William. *Apartheid's Contras: An Inquiry into the Roots of War in Angola and Mozambique.* London: Zed Books, 1994.

Newitt, Malyn. *A History of Mozambique.* London: Hurst, 1995.

Mugabe, Robert (1924–2019)

Robert Mugabe was an African nationalist, prime minister (1980–1987), and executive president of Zimbabwe (1987–2017). At the time of his death in 2019, Mugabe's legacy was one of controversy. Although the beginning of his rule was marked by racial reconciliation and an economic boom, racial mistrust began to grow, and constitutional reform gave Mugabe a strong hold over the government and the economy. Increasing corruption and land seizures led to major economic decline, widespread poverty, and social unrest.

Mugabe was born on February 21, 1924, at Kutama Mission in the Zvimba District of Southern Rhodesia (now Zimbabwe). He earned a BA degree from Fort Hare University in South Africa in 1951. He then pursued additional studies in education and worked as a teacher in Ghana during 1958–1960.

Mugabe returned to Southern Rhodesia in 1960 a Marxist and joined Joshua Nkomo's National Democratic Party (NDP). In December 1961 the NDP was banned. Mugabe became secretary general of its successor, the exiled Zimbabwean

African People's Union (ZAPU). Deepening personal and ideological differences with ZAPU led Mugabe to leave the party in 1963. He immediately joined, as secretary general, the newly formed Zimbabwean African National Union (ZANU). He returned to Rhodesia in 1964 and was imprisoned until 1974 when he was released as part of an ultimately unsuccessful negotiation.

From 1965, when white minority–ruled Rhodesia unilaterally declared independence from Britain, both ZAPU and ZANU launched armed liberation struggles for majority rule and independence. Mozambique's independence in 1975 provided ZANU with a secure base in a neighboring country from where it expanded the guerrilla war inside Rhodesia. Since the original ZANU leader Ndabaningi Sithole allegedly renounced the armed struggle while in prison, Mugabe emerged as the political head of the organization. Mugabe quickly developed a close relationship with Mozambican president Samora Machel. Supported by the People's Republic of China (PRC), ZANU became the leading guerrilla force in Zimbabwe forming the Zimbabwe African National Liberation Army (ZANLA). The escalating war gave rise to sustained regional and international attempts to secure a negotiated settlement between the Smith regime and the two main nationalist groups, ZANU and the Zambia-based ZAPU.

During the September 1979 Lancaster House talks, which led to the end of white rule in Rhodesia, Mugabe was persuaded to accept the terms of a political settlement. ZANU was unable to resolve long-standing differences with Nkomo who still led ZAPU. Mugabe's party ran as an independent party (ZANU-Patriotic Front or ZANU-PF) in the February 1980 elections. On April 18, 1980, Zimbabwe declared its independence, with Mugabe as prime minister.

In late 1987, after the violent elimination of ZAPU as a political opposition, Mugabe's position of prime minister was substituted for that of executive president. This combined the posts of head of state and head of government. Mugabe thus gained more power. Pressured by veterans of the liberation war, Mugabe's attempts to introduce land reform brought disaster at the start of the 2000s. Farm productivity plummeted, resulting in widespread food shortages. His regime also grew more repressive and corrupt, drawing the ire of Zimbabweans and regional leaders alike. The economy was in a virtual free fall by the mid-2000s. The nation was gripped by hyperinflation and growing shortages. In 2013, Mugabe won a seventh term as president, amid allegations of electoral fraud. By August 2016, however, there were myriad signs that even some of Mugabe's staunchest supporters were beginning to lose faith. Zimbabwe's war veterans had already begun to turn against Mugabe, claiming that his policies were never carried out effectively and that land reform benefited government elites. Mugabe had attempted to first placate and then silence the veterans, but neither attempt worked. Meanwhile, as Mugabe and his henchmen were purging the ZANU-PF of alleged dissidents, spontaneous protests against the government became more numerous in late 2016.

On November 14, 2017, Zimbabwe's military launched a coup against Mugabe's government. On November 21, President Mugabe reluctantly agreed to resign his post. He was succeeded by recently dismissed first vice president Emmerson

Damdudzo Mnangagwa. Mugabe began receiving treatment for an unknown condition at a hospital in Singapore in April 2019. He died aged 95 on September 6, 2019.

Peter Vale

See also: Nkomo, Joshua; Zimbabwe, Massacres (Gukurahundi); Zimbabwe African National Union (ZANU); Zimbabwe African People's Union (ZAPU); Zimbabwe Independence War.

Further Reading

Chan, Stephen. *Mugabe: A Life of Power and Violence.* London: I.B. Tauris, 2019.

Meredith, Martin. *Robert Mugabe: Power, Plunder and Tyranny in Zimbabwe.* Johannesburg: Jonathan Ball, 2002.

Ndlovu-Gatsheni, Sabelo J., ed. *Mugabeism? History, Politics and Power in Zimbabwe.* New York: Palgrave Macmillan, 2015.

Museveni, Yoweri (1944–)

Yoweri Museveni is the president of Uganda. He led his National Resistance Army (NRA)—the military wing of his National Resistance Movement (NRM)—into the Ugandan capital of Kampala in early 1986 and overthrew military leader Tito Okello. Museveni won praise at home and abroad for beginning the long process of rebuilding his nation after 16 years of war. However, his continuing hold on power over five presidential terms has led some to accuse him of corruption and abuse of power.

RESISTANCE LEADER

Yoweri Kaguta Museveni was born in 1944 in the Ankole district of southwestern Uganda and was educated in the district capital, Mbarara. He went on to receive a bachelor's degree in economics and political science at Dar es Salaam University in Tanzania and returned to Uganda in 1970, taking a job with President Milton Obote's intelligence group. When Idi Amin overthrew Obote the next year, Museveni fled to Tanzania with other Obote supporters. He took part in Obote's failed invasion of Uganda in 1972 and thereafter distanced himself from the former president, helping to form a separate guerrilla movement, the Front for National Salvation (FRONASA). In 1978 he led this group when it helped the Tanzanian Army push back an invasion by Amin.

The 1978 war ended when the Tanzanian Army and Ugandan exile forces marched on Kampala and overthrew Amin, installing an interim government with Museveni as defense minister. Museveni went on to participate in the ouster of interim presidents in 1979 and 1980. He ran for president himself in 1981 as the candidate of the Ugandan Patriotic Movement, but he lost to Obote. Unwilling to accept what he said were fraudulent results, he established the NRM and began a new guerrilla campaign. Meanwhile, Obote's regime lost popularity, and a split in the army resulted in a 1985 coup that brought Okello to power. Museveni and Okello negotiated a peace late that year, but Museveni soon charged that Okello broke the agreement when his troops continued to terrorize citizens. The NRA continued the war and marched into Kampala in January 1986, with Museveni installing himself as president.

REGIONAL INFLUENCE

Despite the warfare that marked his path to power, Museveni had considerable popular support along the way and won the support of the West and international aid organizations for ultimately stabilizing the situation in Uganda. Though the country remains poor after years of civil war, Museveni started it on the road to recovery. His measures to cut the bureaucracy, remove price controls, abolish state monopolies, and reduce the budget deficit brought modest improvement.

Museveni was first elected by popular vote in 1996, and his first term would come to be characterized by regional conflicts and feuds. In 1996–1997, Museveni sent Ugandan forces into Zaire, joining the military campaign that deposed dictator Mobutu Sese Seko. In 1998 Uganda, along with Rwanda, committed troops to eastern Democratic Republic of the Congo (formerly Zaire) in support of rebel groups fighting to oust Laurent Kabila, a former Museveni ally. Kabila's assassination in January 2001 and the subsequent installation of his son, Joseph Kabila, as president of the DRC gave new life to peace negotiations in the region. In May 2001, amid continuing efforts to end the DRC's civil war, Museveni announced the withdrawal of most of the Ugandan troops from that country. Unfortunately, the rise of the Lord's Resistance Army (LRA) rebel group in the 1990s and 2000s extended Uganda's involvement in the DRC. Ugandan troops maintained a heavy presence fighting LRA rebels in the region until 2009. In 2012, the United Nations issued a report accusing Uganda of providing military support to rebel fighters of the March 23 Movement (M23) in the eastern DRC.

CONTROVERSIAL GRIP ON POWER

The Ugandan Parliament voted in August 2005 to abolish the constitutional restrictions that placed limits on the number of terms Museveni could serve as president. His seeming desire to become president for life has caused growing concern in the international community, while Museveni has argued that consistency is essential to the ongoing effort to rebuild and strengthen Uganda. Throughout his tenure in office, he has maintained that his principle goal is to elevate the socioeconomic status of Uganda to that of a First World country.

However, following his election to a fifth presidential term in 2016, Museveni further stoked fears that he was moving Uganda toward autocratic rule by sharply criticizing the International Criminal Court (ICC) during his inauguration speech. The remarks prompted attendees from the United States, Canada, and the European Union to walk out of the inauguration in protest. Museveni has also been sharply criticized in the international community for his signing in 2014 of a national anti-gay law, which provides a maximum sentence of life imprisonment for "homosexual acts." The president's once praised initiative to combat the spread of HIV/AIDS in Uganda has also fallen under scrutiny in recent years, as the administration, under the influence of a strong evangelical lobby, has started to promote abstinence over the use of contraception.

ABC-CLIO

See also: Congo Wars; Democratic Republic of the Congo (DRC), Continuing Violence in; Kagera War; Lord's Resistance Army (LRA); National Resistance Army (NRA); Uganda, Insurgency in the North; Uganda's Civil War: The Bush War.

Further Reading

Brockman, Norbert C. *An African Biographical Dictionary.* Santa Barbara, CA: ABC-CLIO, 1994.

Museveni, Yoweri K. *Sowing the Mustard Seed: The Struggle for Freedom and Democracy in Uganda.* London: Macmillan Education Ltd., 1997.

Pirouet, M. Louise. *Historical Dictionary of Uganda.* 1995.

Namibia Independence War (1966–1989)

Following World War I, the League of Nations gave the Union of South Africa a mandate to administer the adjacent former German colony of South West Africa (SWA), but Pretoria considered the territory as the spoils of war and governed it as another province. In 1946, as a result, South Africa refused to transfer the mandate to the newly established United Nations, triggering a long diplomatic dispute over the territory's status. After 1948, with the rise of the Nationalist Party government, Pretoria extended its strict racially segregationist apartheid policies to SWA, leading to the same type of forced removals that were taking place within South Africa and prompting a 1959 police massacre of 11 protesters in Windhoek. At a time when African nationalists were forming governments in newly independent African countries, those from the South West Africa National Union (SWANU) and South West Africa People's Organization (SWAPO), the latter led by Sam Nujoma, demanded UN trusteeship and eventual independence for their territory. In 1962, around the same time that the anti-apartheid armed struggle began in South Africa, exiled SWAPO activists established an armed wing called the People's Liberation Army of Namibia (PLAN) to fight South African occupation. Based in newly independent Tanzania and Zambia, PLAN fighters received support from the Soviet Union. On the other hand, SWANU eventually dissolved, given hesitance to engage in armed struggle, and lack of consequent international support from the Eastern Bloc, Organisation of African Unity (OAU), or the UN.

During the 1960s and early 1970s, PLAN encountered problems infiltrating insurgents into SWA, as most adjacent territories remained hostile to its agenda. The Portuguese colonial regime in Angola was fighting its own war against African nationalists and therefore cooperated with South African security forces, and recently independent Botswana, impoverished and without its own defense force, became vulnerable to economic and military pressure from Pretoria. In this early phase of the conflict, PLAN's staging areas in Zambia were a long distance away from its main area of popular support in northern SWA's Ovamboland region. Additionally, insurgents traveling from Zambia had to traverse the enemy territory of Portuguese Angola or SWA's narrow Caprivi Strip, heavily guarded by the South African Defence Force (SADF). SWA's independence war began in August 1966 with the destruction of a PLAN camp at Omgulumbashe in Ovamboland by South African paratroopers and police. Given its many problems, PLAN's early operations focused mostly on Caprivi, involving planting land mines on roads and killing headmen who worked with the South African administration. Since PLAN stepped up its activities from around 1972, given labor unrest in SWA, South Africa deployed more security personnel to the territory.

The sudden independence of Angola in 1975 transformed the insurgency in SWA. As the new government of Angola, the Popular Movement for the Liberation of Angola (MPLA) began to host SWAPO/PLAN camps, which resulted in greater insurgent infiltration and the dramatic expansion of the war across the border in northern SWA. After the failure of South Africa's 1975 intervention in Angola, the insurgency in SWA became closely linked to the events of the Angolan Civil War and prompted many South African military incursions into southern Angola in pursue of PLAN fighters and/or to destroy their infrastructure there. During the late 1970s, PLAN experienced great success establishing liberated zones in parts of Ovamboland and periodically sending insurgents south into the white farming areas of SWA. However, a number of developments once again limited insurgent activities during the 1980s. South African incursions into southern Angola pushed SWAPO/PLAN camps farther away from the border, and the presence of South African–backed National Union for the Total Independence of Angola (UNITA) rebels in southeastern Angola prevented PLAN access to that area and hence to adjacent northeastern SWA. This funneled PLAN fighters into Ovamboland, enabling South African security forces to focus on that area, therefore containing the insurgency. Significantly, the South Africans founded aggressive mechanized counterinsurgency reaction forces like the police's Koevoet (crowbar) and the army's 101 Battalion, both recruited from the local Ovambo communities, which performed well in the environment of northern SWA and inflicted stunning losses on PLAN. Although the South Africans in SWA departed from other counterinsurgency programs by not herding rural people into "protected villages" to separate them from the rebels, attempts to win "hearts and minds" were largely abandoned as the conflict unfolded. Within Angola, SWAPO/PLAN fighters became increasingly integrated with MPLA, Cuban, and Soviet forces and were involved in operations against UNITA. With the continued insurgency in SWA mostly confined to Ovamboland, the political fate of the territory was determined by the large conventional battles fought by the SADF/UNITA alliance against the MPLA and allied Cuban forces in southern Angola in the late 1980s. A plan for SWA to achieve independence came as a result of American-sponsored negotiations between South Africa, Angola, and Cuba. In April 1989 the last South African combat operation took place within SWA with around 1,500 PLAN insurgents crossing from Angola to establish a military presence before the territory's upcoming November elections. Given that this represented a SWAPO/PLAN violation of an internationally negotiated cease-fire with the anticipated UN peacekeeping force yet to arrive, UN officials authorized the departing South African forces to intercept the insurgents, who suffered heavy casualties and retreated into Angola. Eventually, SWAPO won the UN-monitored elections and formed the first government of Namibia, the new name of SWA, which became independent in 1990 under President Nujoma. For the apartheid state, withdrawal from SWA/Namibia represented a major defeat and contributed to a negotiated transition to democracy in South Africa.

Timothy J. Stapleton

See also: Angolan Conflicts; Cold War in Africa; Cuito Cuanavale, Battle of; National Union for the Total Independence of Angola (UNITA); Nujoma, Sam; Peacekeeping in Africa; Popular Movement for the Liberation of Angola (MPLA); Portuguese Africa, Independence Wars (Angola, Mozambique, and Guinea-Bissau); South Africa, Armed Struggle against Apartheid; South West Africa People's Organization (SWAPO); Soviet Military Involvement in Africa.

Further Reading

Esterhuyse, Abel, and Evert Jordaan. "The South African Defence Force and Counterinsurgency, 1966–1990." In *South Africa and Contemporary Counterinsurgency; Roots, Practises and Prospects*, edited by Deane-Peter Baker and Evert Jordaan, 104–127. Claremount: International Publishers, 2010.

Leys, Colin, and John Saul. *Namibia's Liberation Struggle: The Two Edged Sword*. London: James Currey, 1995.

Namakalu, Oswin. *Armed Liberation Struggle: Some Accounts of PLAN's Combat Operations*. Windhoek: Gamsberg MacMillan, 2004.

Scholtz, Leopold. *The SADF in the Border War, 1966–1989*. Cape Town: Tafelberg, 2013.

Stiff, Peter. *The Covert War: Koevoet Operations Namibia, 1979–89*. Alberton: Galago, 2004.

Udogu, E. Ike. *Liberation Namibia: The Long Diplomatic Struggle between the United Nations and South Africa*. Jefferson, NC: McFarland, 2012.

Wallace, Marion. *A History of Namibia: From the Beginning to 1990*. New York: Columbia University Press, 2011.

Nasser, Gamal Abdel (1918–1970)

Egyptian nationalist politician, vice president (1953–1954), premier (1954–1956), and president (1956–1970). Born in Beni Mor, Egypt, on January 16, 1918, the son of a civil servant, Gamal Abdel Nasser at an early age developed great antipathy toward Britain's rule over Egypt, setting the stage for his later championing of Egyptian nationalism and Pan-Arabism. Settling on a military career, Nasser graduated from the Egyptian Royal Military Academy in 1936 and was commissioned a second lieutenant. While stationed at a post in the Sudan, he met and became friends with future Egyptian president Anwar Sadat. Based on their mutual dislike of the British, they eventually formed the foundation for a secret anti-British organization that came to be called the Free Officers.

The Free Officers recruited Egyptian military officers who wished to bring about an end to British colonial rule and to oust King Farouk II. After months of painstaking planning, the Free Officers fomented a revolt against Farouk's government on July 23, 1952. Three days later, the king abdicated and fled Egypt. The British withdrew from Egypt in early 1956. Upon Farouk's abdication, a Revolutionary Command Council (RCC) was established under the leadership of Major General Mohammad Naguib, with Nasser working behind the scenes. When the council declared Egypt a republic in June 1953, Naguib became its first president, with Nasser as vice president. Beginning in winter 1954, a political power struggle ensued between Nasser and Naguib. Within months, Nasser took de facto control as president of the Revolutionary Command Council, while Naguib was allowed to continue as president of Egypt, although the latter was in reality little more than a figurehead position.

Nasser and his faction consolidated their hold on power, and after the October 1954 attempt on Nasser's life, which Nasser blamed on Naguib, Nasser ordered Naguib arrested. Using the assassination attempt to solidify his power base, Nasser became the premier of Egypt on February 25, 1955. Seven months later he also took on the title of provisional president.

Nasser quickly moved to centralize his authority, creating a tightly controlled police state in which political opponents were imprisoned, intellectuals and elites disenfranchised, and industries nationalized. In June 1956 a national election was held in which Nasser was the sole candidate for the presidency; thus, he "officially" became Egypt's second president.

In addition to seeking land reform and following quasi-socialist economic policies, Nasser sought to modernize Egyptian infrastructure. His public works projects included the building of a massive dam at Aswan, Egypt, for which he received promises of financial support from the United States as well as Great Britain. Nasser also approached the Americans about purchasing arms, ostensibly to be used against Israel. When the United States refused this request, Nasser turned to the Soviet Union. The Soviets saw a chance to increase their influence in the region and began negotiating an arms deal with Nasser, whereupon the United States and Britain withdrew their support for the Aswan Dam project in early July 1956. Seeing an additional opportunity to gain more influence with the Egyptians and to establish a foothold in the Middle East, the Soviet Union quickly offered to help Nasser with the Aswan Dam.

Nasser used the loss of Western financial support as a pretext to nationalize the Suez Canal on July 26, 1956. This action provoked joint French/British/Israeli military action against Egypt, beginning the Suez Crisis. Thus, on October 29, 1956, Israeli forces attacked Egypt, and French and British forces attacked by air two days later. On November 5, French and British forces landed at Port Said, further escalating the conflict. The United States, not privy to the attack, put great pressure on the Israelis as well as the French and British to withdraw, which they did on November 7.

Far from being defeated, Nasser was vindicated by the Suez Crisis, and he shrewdly used this "victory" to further consolidate his rule at home and to promote Pan-Arabism throughout the Middle East. The Suez Crisis turned Nasser into a hero of Middle East nationalism.

In pursuit of his pan-Arab vision, Nasser established the United Arab Republic (UAR) on February 22, 1958. Consisting of only Egypt and Syria, however, the UAR fell apart when Syria withdrew on September 28, 1961. Nevertheless, Nasser continued to promote Arab nationalism and his vision of a pan-Arab union.

Nasser's strong-arm rule began to work against him as the years progressed. Losing some of his popular appeal at home, Nasser attempted to reform the government, which was corrupt and riddled with cronyism. Instead, he was forced to crack down on his opponents who tried to aggrandize their power during the attempted reorganization. Turning his sights to foreign affairs, in an effort to play up Arab resentment toward Israel, Nasser signed a defense pact with Syria in

November 1966. In early 1967 Nasser began provoking the Israelis through a number of different actions, including having the UN Peacekeepers removed from the border between Egypt and Israel, blockading the Gulf of Aqaba, and moving troops in to the Sinai. In retaliation, on June 5, 1967, the Israelis attacked Egypt, Syria, and Jordan. The war lasted only until June 9 and proved to be a humiliating defeat for Nasser.

Nasser's miscalculation further eroded his support in Egypt and blemished his reputation throughout the Middle East. In March 1969 he launched the War of Attrition against Israel, which resulted in many more Egyptian than Israeli casualties. In July 1970 Nasser agreed to a cease-fire arrangement put forward by U.S. secretary of state William Rogers to end the so-called War of Attrition. Now in deteriorating health, Nasser died on September 28, 1970, in Cairo.

Dallas W. Unger Jr.

See also: Arab-Israeli Wars; British Military Involvement in Postcolonial Africa; Cold War in Africa; Gaddafi, Muammar; Soviet Military Involvement in Africa; Suez Crisis.

Further Reading

Aburish, Abdelmalek. *Nasser: The Last Arab.* New York: Saint Martin's Press, 2004.

DuBius, Shirley Graham. *Gamal Abdel Nasser, Son of the Nile.* New York: Third Press, 1972.

Jankowski, James. *Nasser's Egypt, Arab Nationalism and the United Arab Republic.* Boulder, CO: Lynne Rienner, 2001.

Lacouture, Jean. *Nasser, A Biography.* New York: Knopf, 1973.

McGregor, Andrew. *A Military History of Modern Egypt; from the Ottoman Conquest to the Ramadan War.* Westport, CT: Praeger Security International, 2006.

Nutting, Anthony. *Nasser.* New York: E.P. Dutton, 1972.

National Front for the Liberation of Angola (FNLA)

The National Front for the Liberation of Angola (FNLA) was one of the earliest independence movements in Angola. The FNLA waged a guerrilla war against Portugal for 14 years and then fought against other Angolan groups for control of the newly independent country. After being defeated in the Angolan Civil Wars, the FNLA was transformed into a political party that tried unsuccessfully to win the first election in Angola.

The Portuguese first colonized the Kongo Empire in the fifteenth century. While other European countries were moving toward decolonization in Africa after World War II, Portugal sought to strengthen its control of Angola. Nonetheless, the growing independence movement took hold among the people. One of the most important ethnic groups was the Kikongo, which included people living in both Angola and the neighboring Belgian Congo. In 1957 the Union of the Peoples of Northern Angola (UPNA) was formed by members of the Kikongo. The group was rural based, and its leadership consisted largely of small commercial farmers and small-time urban entrepreneurs. The group adopted a strong ideology of anticommunism, and its leader was Holden Roberto. When Belgium abruptly granted independence to the Democratic Republic of the Congo in 1960, that country was torn apart by the Congolese Civil War. The Kikongo enclaves, however, provided bases for the UPNA. By 1961 the UPNA became the FNLA.

In February that year, colonial authorities killed hundreds of Black Angolans after a riot had freed many Black militants. In March, the FNLA led an uprising in northern Angola. The Portuguese military ruthlessly suppressed the FNLA, killing more than 20,000 Black Angolans. It forced the FNLA to retreat to sanctuaries in the Congo, from which the Angolans mounted ineffectual border raids.

The FNLA also fought the other major independence movement, the Popular Movement for the Liberation of Angola (MPLA). The MPLA was more urban based and followed Marxism. The MPLA attracted recruits from many ethnic groups and grew to be the bigger organization by the end of the 1960s. The FNLA was weakened in 1966, when Jonas Savimbi left it to form a new independence movement, the National Union for the Total Independence of Angola (UNITA). Roberto proved to be a poor guerrilla leader and rarely left the comfort of his headquarters in the Congo during the 1960s.

The strain of a guerrilla war was too much for the Portuguese economy. In 1974 the government was overthrown in a bloodless coup, and the left-wing officers who seized control proclaimed their intention to grant independence to Portugal's remaining colonies. The different rebel groups jockeyed for control of the new government in Angola. The FNLA immediately received arms and funds from both China and the United States, both of whom had suspicions about the Soviet-backed and armed MPLA. In November 1974 representatives of all three rebel groups met with Portuguese officials in Alvor, Portugal. They agreed on elections to follow Angola's formal independence on November 11, 1975. The interim government was composed of members of all three groups.

The new government took office on January 31, 1975, and fighting between MPLA and FNLA followers broke out the next day. Roberto invaded Angola with about 15,000 well-equipped FNLA soldiers from their bases in Zaire (formerly the Congo). The MPLA controlled the Angolan capital of Luanda and started to receive massive arms shipments from the Soviet Union as well as support from Cuban advisers. Fighting escalated through summer 1975. In September the MPLA routed Roberto's FNLA forces. Roberto's American advisers from the U.S. Central Intelligence Agency advised him to retreat and regroup, but he insisted on continuing his march on Luanda. By November 1975 FNLA forces were in the outskirts of Luanda, but they were again defeated by MPLA soldiers, and the survivors fell back into Zaire. The FNLA disintegrated and ceased to be a military force, especially after the U.S. Congress voted to cut off its funding.

Fighting continued between the MPLA and UNITA for another 15 years. Roberto remained in exile in Zaire until 1991. A peace deal was brokered in that year, which called for elections. The FNLA participated in the elections as one of the parties but received only a small part of the vote. Roberto remained among the opposition to the MPLA government, which won the election.

Tim Watts

See also: Angolan Conflicts; Cold War in Africa; Congo Crisis; Cuba and Africa; Mobutu Sese Seko; National Union for the Total Independence of Angola (UNITA); Popular

Movement for the Liberation of Angola (MPLA); Portuguese Africa, Independence Wars (Angola, Mozambique, and Guinea-Bissau); Quifangondo, Battle of; Roberto, Holden Álverto; Soviet Military Involvement in Africa; U.S. Military Involvement in Africa.

Further Reading

Maier, Karl. *Angola: Promises and Lies*. London: Serif, 2013.

James, W. Martin. *A Political History of the War in Angola, 1974–1990*. London: Transaction Publishers, 2011.

Stockwell, John. *In Search of Enemies: A CIA Story*. New York: W. W. Norton, 1978.

National Liberation Front (FLN) Algeria

The Front de Libération Nationale or FLN was the primary force of nationalism and resistance to French rule in Algeria. Formed in 1954, after the weakness of the French state was exposed in Indochina at Dien Bien Phu, the FLN served as the primary vehicle for armed resistance and political action, which would lead to the independence of Algeria in 1962.

The military wing of the FLN, the National Liberation Army, served largely as a guerilla force in Algeria in an attempt to pressure the French *pied noir* and French government to give up their hold on the colony. Additionally, they used violence as a means to attract, or frighten, Algerians to their side in the conflict. Their guerilla efforts in the *casbah* area of Algiers gave the Algerian conflict its distinctive nature, which was heavily popularized in the movie *The Battle of Algiers*.

As a guerilla organization, the FLN relied on terror as a tactical and strategic means of success. Recognizing that much of Algeria was nonaligned in a fight between them and the French, the FLN sought to use terror to achieve popular support. They did this through harsh acts of terror, which they knew would prompt an overwhelming, and indiscriminate, French response. Such an example is the Philippeville Massacre, in which the brutal acts of violence by the FLN against French and Algerian civilians, which killed 70 civilians, ultimately led to a French retaliatory actions that killed roughly 1,200 people. Such reactions by the French ensured that the counterinsurgency campaign was invariably bloody and drew more and more Algerians onto the side of the FLN.

The FLN was organized in guerilla "cells," with the goal being to provide their fighters with a 24-hour window in which they had to resist any interrogation. After such a capture, the organization would shuffle the cells around to negate the need for their fighters to hold out any longer, as their information would no longer be valuable. This defensive measure, paradoxically, became one of the most offensively strategic measures of FLN success. In attempting to quash the FLN cells, and dealing with this 24-hour window, the French began to liberally use harsh means, including torture, to get actionable intelligence in time. This very effort began to sap the political and moral will of the French to continue the fight, let alone the loss of face internationally, and ultimately led to their defeat.

The FLN, as a political organization, also sought to use its position, and the new organization of the United Nations to its advantage in the anti-colonial struggle. In this, the FLN prefigured many of the future decolonization and resistance efforts in that they sought to gain media attention and garner international support. While the French consistently argued that they were fighting a domestic terror and the conflict was, thus, a wholly internal French affair, the FLN popularized the struggle and their suffering in the news media and United Nations in order to gain international support with which to pressure the French to relent.

Robert H. Clemm

See also: Algerian War of Independence; French Military Involvement in Postcolonial Africa.

Further Reading

Evans, Martin. *Algeria: France's Undeclared War.* Oxford: Oxford University Press, 2012.

Horne, Alistair. *A Savage War of Peace: Algeria, 1954–1962.* New York: Viking, 1977.

Talbott, John. *The War without a Name: France in Algeria, 1954–1962.* New York: Knopf, 1980.

National Liberation Front of Chad (FROLINAT)

See Chad, Conflict in

National Movement for the Liberation of Azawad (MNLA)

See Tuareg Rebellions since 1960 (Mali and Niger)

National Patriotic Front of Liberia (NPFL)

The National Patriotic Front of Liberia (NPFL) was an insurgent group during the First Liberian Civil War (1989–1996). The NPFL gained control of most of Liberia in the early 1990s, helping to bring an end to the government of Samuel Doe. Partly because of the presence of the Economic Community of West African States Monitoring Group (ECOMOG) in Monrovia, the capital, the NPFL never established control over the entire nation. After a peace accord was signed in August 1996, the NPFL was transformed into a political party called the National Patriotic Party (NPP). Its leader, Charles Taylor, became Liberia's president in 1997 but was forced to step down amid a new civil war in 2003.

The NPFL was formed by exiled Liberians in the mid-1980s. Charles Taylor joined the group soon after its founding, and under his leadership the NPFL seriously threatened the Doe government in 1989. Supported by Gaddafi's regime in Libya, the NPFL comprised fighters from the Gio and Mano ethnic groups that had been victimized by Doe's forces. The NPFL had taken control of most the country by the time ECOMOG sent a 4,000-member force to Monrovia in August 1990. The war continued between the NPFL and the new ECOMOG-sponsored government, but a cease-fire was arranged in July 1993.

A five-member transitional government, including an NPFL representative, was installed in August 1993, and a transitional parliament with NPFL representatives was established in October. However, the five-member body did not assume real authority until March 1994, and pockets of renewed fighting continued to hamper the peace process. A new accord was signed in August 1995, and NPFL leader Taylor was named to a new six-member Council of State inaugurated in September 1995. In April 1996 Taylor attempted to arrest a rival militia leader, triggering fierce new fighting that plunged Monrovia into chaos. The fighting continued unabated for a number of weeks, despite several attempts at a cease-fire. A tentative peace accord was agreed upon in May 1996, and a concrete peace plan signed in August. Elections were finally held in July 1997, and front-runner Taylor won the presidential balloting. Some political analysts said voters may have decided to support Taylor simply because they did not want him to plunge the country back into bloodshed if he did not gain the leadership post he had been seeking for so long. In preparation for the election, the NPFL reconstituted itself as a political party called NPP, with Taylor as its leader.

As a result of the Second Liberian Civil War (1999–2003), Taylor was forced to step down and leave the country for exile in Nigeria on August 11, 2003. He had been under increasing pressure from a new group of rebel forces, including the Liberians United for Reconciliation and Democracy (LURD), which by August 2003 had taken over half the capital, but growing international criticism also played a role in his departure. Three months earlier Taylor had been indicted by a United Nations court on war crimes charges for his role in supporting and financing rebels in neighboring Sierra Leone, and many African and international leaders were pushing for his resignation. The NPP performed very poorly in Liberia's 2005 election. Based on a request from the new Liberian government of President Ellen Johnson Sirleaf, Nigeria sent Taylor to the International Criminal Court (ICC) in the Netherlands in 2006, and he was convicted of war crimes and crimes against humanity, receiving a 50-year prison term.

ABC-CLIO

See also: ECOWAS Military Interventions; Gaddafi, Muammar; Liberian Civil Wars; Liberians United for Reconciliation and Democracy (LURD); Taylor, Charles McArthur Ghankay.

Further Reading

Ellis, Stephen. *The Mask of Anarchy: The Destruction of Liberia and the Religious Dimension of an African Civil War.* New York: New York University Press, 2001.

Waugh, Colin. *Charles Taylor and Liberia: Ambition and Atrocity in Africa's Lone Star State.* London: Zed Books, 2011.

National Resistance Army (NRA)

Staging one of the most successful insurgencies in modern African history, the National Resistance Army (NRA) took power in Uganda in 1986 and transformed into the state military. In 1979 the exiled Ugandans of the Front for National Salvation (FRONASA), led by Yoweri Museveni, participated in the Tanzanian invasion of Uganda that toppled dictator Idi Amin. With the sidelining of FRONASA members in the creation of a new Ugandan military and the election of former president Milton Obote in December 1980, Museveni founded another rebel group in Tanzania called the NRA. In February 1981 Museveni personally led a small NRA unit into southern Uganda where it attacked a military police academy and launched a guerrilla war. Over the next year, Museveni's force focused on building support among rural people and recruiting former FRONASA members and university students. As the NRA expanded, it established districts defended by zonal units, and in 1983, it established a mobile force, taking the offensive against government troops. Ensuring that every fighter understood the reasons for the war, the NRA stressed discipline, imposing harsh punishment including death for rebels who abused civilians. Well organized, the NRA maintained a council that consisted of all unit commanders and that dealt with administration and command structure. Every NRA unit organized a policy and administrative committee comprising the commanding officer and all officers and department heads that held meetings twice a month to assist the commander. Each unit also maintained separate committees for food, finance, health, and internal discipline. Furthermore, a network of political commissars from platoon to battalion level educated the insurgents and sympathizers and reported to the NRA chief political commissar who held the post of minister of local government. While the NRA received a few weapons from Muammar Gaddafi's Libya, the rebels mostly armed and equipped themselves by capturing resources from the Ugandan state military. As the NRA gained control of more territory, the rebels arranged the election of local councils to handle administration and formed part-time local militias to provide intelligence and military support. Although the NRA initially experienced some internal tensions between the mostly Baganda rank-and-file who originated from the operational area of the Luwero Triangle in southern Uganda and the leadership who primarily came from the southwest, including Rwandan exiles, these problems faded as members of the former group gained experience and seniority. Contrasting starkly to the disciplined NRA, Ugandan state soldiers largely originated from the north and behaved as an oppressive and murderous army of occupation in southern Uganda, driving the people toward the insurgents. During the mid-1980s, the NRA defeated several government offensives and took the initiative, attacking army barracks to capture weapons and extending operations to western Uganda's Ruwenzori Mountains. By this time, the NRA included around 3,000 child soldiers. The movement's success resulted in significant deliveries of weapons and ammunition from the governments of Libya and Tanzania. In January 1986 around 10,000 NRA fighters led by Salim Saleh, Museveni's brother, mounted a well-planned and successful assault on Kampala, taking the capital as the deposed government forces retreated north. Under Museveni's new government, the NRA transformed into the state military and contended with a series of rebellions in the north including by the religiously inspired Holy Spirit Movement and Lord's Resistance Army (LRA) as well as secular groups representing troops from previously ousted regimes. Since Museveni's government supported Sudan People's Liberation Army (SPLA) rebels in southern Sudan, the Sudan government backed insurgents in northern Uganda. In 1990, several thousand Rwandan exiles deserted the NRA, identifying themselves as the Rwandan Patriotic Front (RPF) and invading Rwanda. In 1995 the NRA took the new name Uganda

People's Defence Force (UPDF) reflecting a new Ugandan constitution and the evolution of the force into a conventional military including the acquisition of air power. Given the operation of rebels from western and northern Uganda across the border in Zaire/Democratic Republic of the Congo (DRC), the UPDF invaded that country during the First Congo War of 1996–1997 and the Second Congo War of 1998–2002. The UPDF withdrew from the northeastern DRC in 2003. After the departure of the LRA from northern Uganda in 2006, Ugandan forces conducted operations against these rebels in the DRC and Central African Republic during the 2010s. Since its founding in 2007, the African Union Mission in Somalia (AMISOM) relied heavily on contingents from the UPDF to pursue the war against the Islamist forces of Al-Shabaab.

Timothy J. Stapleton

See also: Al-Shabaab; Child Soldiers in Africa; Congo Wars; Gaddafi, Muammar; Lord's Resistance Army (LRA); Peacekeeping in Africa; Rwanda, Civil War and Genocide; Somalia Civil War; Uganda, Insurgency in the North; Uganda's Civil War: The Bush War.

Further Reading

Kainerugaba, Muhoozi. *Battles of the Ugandan Resistance: A Tradition of Maneuver.* Kampala: Fountain Publishers, 2010.

Ngoga, Pascal. "Uganda: The National Resistance Army." In *African Guerrillas*, edited by Christopher Clapham, 91–106. Oxford: James Currey, 1998.

National Union for the Total Independence of Angola (UNITA)

The National Union for the Total Independence of Angola (UNITA) came into existence during the Angolan struggle for independence from Portugal. Once the Portuguese withdrew, however, the organization was drawn into civil war with other liberationist groups. UNITA lost in the civil war, but the government has never been able to completely eradicate this guerrilla group.

UNITA was the last of the three major liberation forces to organize during the 1960s. Both the Popular Movement for the Liberation of Angola (MPLA), a Marxist group, and the Union of the Peoples of Angola (UPA), led by Holden Roberto, had existed since 1961. UNITA split off from the UPA in 1966 as Jonas Savimbi organized a new guerrilla movement among the Ovimbundu people of south and central Angola. These three groups, while unable to defeat the Portuguese Army, maintained guerrilla actions and hit-and-run ambushes that forced Portugal to constantly devote more money and soldiers in order to maintain control. As similar situations developed in other Portuguese colonies such as Mozambique and Guinea, the army turned on the government in April 1974, taking power in a coup d'état and committing to the liberation of all colonial holdings.

As they withdrew their armed forces from Angola, the Portuguese encouraged the three national movements to combine their ideas in a coalition government. Two efforts at collaboration collapsed before civil war broke out in 1975. At first, the MPLA appeared to be the weakest of the three organizations, and UNITA's Savimbi was easily the most charismatic of the national leaders. The infusion of disciplined Cuban troops along with Soviet technicians and arms, however, soon turned the tide in the MPLA's favor.

UNITA had already come under attack for seeking to ally with Portuguese forces, and once these were gone, it solicited and accepted financial and military aid from South Africa, which was then still deeply committed to its apartheid policy. During the civil war, UNITA also began to receive aid from the U.S. government, which sought to prevent the spread of communism in Africa. In spite of that assistance, UNITA and the UPA were soundly defeated by the MPLA.

Though the MPLA took firm control of the government, it was not able to eradicate UNITA, which survived and periodically controlled large sections of the country. After the election of U.S. president Ronald Reagan, the U.S. government renewed its commitment to supporting Savimbi and UNITA. By the late 1980s, however, both superpowers were losing interest in the continued fight for Angola, even as the MPLA elected a more flexible leader, Jose Eduardo dos Santos, who was willing to negotiate.

As Cuban and South African troops withdrew from the conflict, the two Angolan groups signed a peace treaty in 1992. UNITA became a recognized legal party with headquarters in Luanda. At the same time, however, Savimbi used the transition period to reorganize his guerrilla force into an organized army. In United Nations–monitored legislative elections in September 1992, UNITA captured only 70 seats, while the MPLA won 129. The loss prompted Savimbi to accuse the government of vote rigging and renew UNITA's war against the government in Luanda. Its reputation as a legitimate political entity was further eroded by allegations from former UNITA officials that the group was extensively involved in torture and a number of other human rights abuses. The group boycotted a number of reconciliation meetings staged by the government and proceeded to seize about 60 percent of the country. In 1993, the United States reversed its decades-long policy of supporting UNITA and officially recognized the MPLA government.

Also in 1993, the MPLA started a new military campaign in response to continuing UNITA aggression, during which 1,000 people died as government troops overran three UNITA positions. UNITA incursions occurred despite its total withdrawal from several areas as part of a December 1992 peace agreement with the MPLA. In September 1993, United Nations secretary general Boutros Boutros-Ghali said the fighting in Angola and its effects were causing 1,000 deaths per day, the highest mortality rate among all world conflicts. After several more unsuccessful cease-fire attempts, the government and UNITA signed a new peace accord on November 20, 1994, with a cease-fire going into effect two days later. Shortly thereafter, the two sides accused one another of violating the cease-fire.

Since then, international opinion has gone increasingly against the rebel forces. In 1998 a dissident force from within UNITA split off and accused the group of repeatedly thwarting the peace process. In June that year, the United Nations voted unanimously in favor of sanctions against the UNITA forces, which were intended to make it more difficult for UNITA to finance its operations through the sale of diamonds mined in the Angolan territories it still holds.

On February 22, 2002, government troops killed Savimbi in Moxico province during an attack on UNITA forces. The death of Savimbi, the only leader the organization had ever known, threw the group into disarray, and it quickly agreed a ceasefire with the government. It then became a legitimate political party in Angola regularly engaging in elections and serving as opposition to the ruling MPLA.

ABC-CLIO

See also: Angolan Conflicts; Cold War in Africa; Congo Wars; Cuba and Africa; Diamonds and Conflict in Postcolonial Africa; Dos Santos, Jose Eduardo; National Front for the Liberation of Angola (FNLA); Popular Movement for the Liberation of Angola (MPLA); Portuguese Africa, Independence Wars (Angola, Mozambique, and Guinea-Bissau); Roberto, Holden Álverto; Savimbi, Jonas; South Africa's Border War; U.S. Military Involvement in Africa.

Further Reading

Bridgland, Fred. *Jonas Savimbi: A Key to Africa*. New York: Paragon House, 1987.
James, W. Martin. *A Political History of the Civil War in Angola, 1974–1990*. New Brunswick, NJ: Transaction Publishers, 1992.
Weigert, Stephen. *Angola: A Modern Military History, 1961–2002*. New York: Palgrave Macmillan, 2011.

Navies in Postcolonial Africa

Aside from North Africa, most of Africa lacks a rich naval history. With regard to North Africa, ancient Egypt built the world's first navy to facilitate conquest in neighboring regions; Carthage fought naval campaigns against Republican Rome during the Punic Wars; and Byzantine and Arab navies vied for control of North Africa's Mediterranean coast during the early medieval period. Subsequently, early modern Ottoman corsairs based in North African ports harassed shipping in the Mediterranean and occasionally ventured out into the Atlantic until they were suppressed by European and American naval forces in the early nineteenth century. In the context of its nineteenth-century modernization, Egypt built a fleet that supported the Ottomans during the Greek War of Independence (1821–1830) and fought the Ottomans to achieve Egyptian autonomy, but Egyptian naval power was thwarted by the increasing dominance of European powers in the region. However, south of the Sahara, precolonial African kingdoms and empires focused on developing armies and controlling territory as their oceanic trade connections were dominated by external sea powers. While European and colonial American mariners engaged in the successive Atlantic slave and raw materials trades with West Africa, Arab and eventually European seafarers carried East African goods across the Indian Ocean to the Middle East and Asia. Along the East African coast, the separate Swahili city-states developed seafaring capabilities used in commerce but neglected naval power, which facilitated Portuguese conquest in the 1500s. By the late nineteenth century, the continent's lack of naval capability made it vulnerable to the European invasion and conquest known as the "Scramble for Africa."

During Africa's colonial era (c. 1880–1960), the continent's European rulers founded locally recruited armies to control their territories and supply manpower for overseas conflicts, but they did not create African-based navies. European imperial navies patrolled the coastlines of the African colonies and protected shipping in these waters, and in some places, such as coastal Nigeria, small locally based marine departments provided port security. During World War I, one factor that prompted the British and French invasions of Germany's African colonies was fear that German naval raiders would hide in African ports. During World War II, the importance of African ports like Freetown, Cape Town, and Durban to Allied shipping in the face of German submarine operations led to the establishment of locally based small naval elements in some coastal colonies. The Union of South Africa, a self-governing British dominion, attempted to form a navy during the interwar era but abandoned the project given the Great Depression, yet continued to maintain the South African Royal Navy Volunteer Reserve. In 1940, given the challenges of the Second World War, South Africa formed the Seaward Defence force (SDF) to take over the protection of local waters from Royal Navy ships needed elsewhere. In 1942 the SDF changed its name to the South African Naval Force (SANF), reflecting the transfer of larger ships from Britain. During the Second World War, South African naval vessels conducted operations such as convoy escort and anti-submarine actions in the Mediterranean, Atlantic, and Pacific theaters. In 1946 the SANF became part of South Africa's Union Defence Force (UDF), later renamed South African Defence Force (SADF).

Most modern African navies originated during the decolonization era of the 1950s and 1960s as newly independent African states gained responsibility for their coastal waters and naval vessels became symbols of national power. During Nigeria's staged transition to independence, nationalist politicians who wanted their country to possess a strong navy pressured the outgoing British to create the nucleus of a naval force. As a result, in 1956 the British renamed the Nigerian Marine Department, with its 250 personnel and 11 vessels, as the Nigerian Naval Force (NNF), and over the next two years, it was again renamed the Naval Defence Force of Nigeria and then the Royal Nigerian Navy. Nigeria became independent in 1960, and with its declaration as a republic in 1963, the Nigerian Navy dropped its "royal" designation. With naval bases in Lagos and Calabar, the Nigeria Navy purchased its first capital ship, the Dutch-built frigate *NNS Nigeria* that was renamed *NNS Obuma* in 1965. During the Nigerian Civil War (1967–1970), the Nigerian Navy imposed a federal blockade on secessionist Biafra, which lacked a significant navy, and landed federal troops on the coast of the breakaway republic. As West Africa's main regional power, Nigeria desired to maintain its "blue water" naval capability and therefore commissioned the West German–built frigate *NNS Aradu* in the early 1980s. During the 1990s, the Nigerian Navy supported the deployment of Nigerian troops as part of the Economic Community of West African States (ECOWAS) intervention in the Liberian and Sierra Leonean civil wars. The advent of insurgency in the oil-producing Niger Delta and broader problems with piracy in the 2000s prompted the Nigerian Navy to create a special forces component known as the Special Boat Service and rejuvenate its fleet with two long-range cutters donated by the United States; the purchase of a variety of patrol boats from Israel, China, Sri Lanka, and France; and the local construction of several seaward defense boats.

In 1958 newly independent Ghana established a navy with Israeli assistance as Britain, the former colonial power, was against the idea. The founding commander of the Ghanaian Navy was a British officer, but in 1961 Rear Admiral David Hansen became the force's first Ghanaian commander, transferring from the army like many of the early generation of African senior naval officers. By 1967, given Ghanaian president Kwame Nkrumah's desire to build a powerful military that could challenge remaining colonial regimes, the Ghanaian Navy consisted of two 600 ton corvettes, two armed coastal defense vessels, two coastal minesweepers, one training ship, a maintenance craft, and around 630 personnel. In addition, two Soviet-made fast boats, rumored to be crewed by Russians, delivered weapons to insurgent groups in neighboring territories, particularly in Portuguese Guinea. The Ghanaian Navy developed as an anti-submarine and minesweeping force with secondary duties involving anti-smuggling, and search and rescue. In a project that became much more costly than anticipated, Nkrumah's administration contracted a company from Yugoslavia to construct a naval base at Sekondi. Despite coups and economic crises, the 2,000-strong Ghanian Navy purchased two West German–made Achimota-class fast attack craft at the start of the 1980s, putting them to use in fisheries protection. After years of neglect, and with piracy rising in West African waters and the need to protect a new offshore oil industry, the Ghanaian Navy embarked on a refurbishment program in the 2010s, acquiring used patrol boats from the United States, Germany, and South Korea and a few new ones from China and starting construction of a new naval base at Ezilinbo in western Ghana.

Maintaining close ties with former colonial power France, including defense agreements that sometimes included the hosting of French military personnel, most West African Francophone countries such as Senegal and Côte d'Ivoire developed tiny navies focused on coastal security. In the early 1960s, the Senegalese Navy consisted of two units of small patrol boats and two larger patrol vessels (one acquired from the United States and the other from France), entirely dependent on French officers and technicians. Representing an exception to this pattern, Guinea rejected continued association with France in 1958 and then moved toward alignment with the Eastern Bloc. As such, Sékou Touré's government founded a small navy in 1967 consisting of 200 sailors operating Soviet- and Chinese-made torpedo boats, patrol boats, and landing craft and trained mostly by Chinese advisers. Tensions between Touré's Guinea and Portugal rose over the former's support for nationalist insurgents fighting the colonial Portuguese regime in neighboring Guinea-Bissau. In 1970, as a result, the Portuguese staged an amphibious raid on Conakry called "Operation Green Sea" that destroyed some of Guinea's naval vessels, and this led to the Soviet Navy deploying vessels to Guinea to protect it from further Portuguese attacks. In the 2010s, with the rise of piracy and smuggling in the region and the country's hopes for developing offshore oil and gas, Senegal embarked on naval expansion, receiving several patrol boats donated by the United States and ordering half a dozen offshore patrol vessels including three armed with anti-ship and antiaircraft missiles from French companies.

With its acquisition of Eritrea in the early 1950s, hitherto landlocked imperial Ethiopia gained a coastline and therefore formed a navy based at the strategically important Red Sea port of Massawa. With the country's pro-Western Cold War orientation, Ethiopia's embryonic navy received instructors from Norway and eventually the United States and American patrol boats. At the start of the 1970s, the Ethiopian Navy consisted of 750 personnel operating one 1,800 ton training vessel, formerly an American Second World War–era seaplane tender, five missile-equipped patrol boats, four torpedo boats, one coastal minesweeper, four port defense craft, and four landing craft. Symbolizing Ethiopia's status as an East African regional power, the small navy was commanded by Rear Admiral Iskendar Desta, who was Emperor Haile Selassie's grandson. Following the overthrow of Selassie in 1974, Ethiopia's military regime switched Cold War alliances to the Soviet Union and expanded its navy in response to mounting rebellion in Eritrea. Supporting ground forces in Eritrea, the now 4,750-strong Ethiopian Navy transported 61,000 men, 2,000 armored vehicles, 6,000 tons of weapons and supplies, and 36,000 tons of drinking water between 1975 and 1981. During the early and mid-1970s, Somalia, Ethiopia's regional rival, focused on building an army to pursue territorial expansion, acquired Soviet support by allowing Moscow to build a naval base at the strategic port of Berbera. The Soviets eventually abandoned Berbera after changing sides by backing the new regime in Ethiopia. During its rebellion against Ethiopia in the 1970s and 1980s, the Eritrean People's Liberation Front (EPLF) used a fleet of small craft to conduct hit-and-run attacks along the Red Sea coast. With its independence in 1991, Eritrea created its own navy by taking possession of vessels from the defunct Ethiopian Navy, and within a few years, it developed a fleet of 45 vessels charged with preventing illegal fishing in Eritrean waters.

Other East African states established small navies. Reflecting British ambitions to federate their East African colonial territories, London established the East African Naval Force in 1950, and this was renamed Royal East African Navy (REAN) in 1953. Based in Mombasa, the REAN operated several vessels on loan from the Royal Navy and drew personnel from Kenya, Tanganyika, and Uganda. Nevertheless, the granting of independence to these territories as separate states in the early 1960s led to the disbanding of REAN and the founding of navies by the newly independent states that possessed coastlines. Retaining close military ties with its former British colonial rulers, independent Kenya created a navy in 1964 with 1,000 sailors manning a former British training ship and two patrol craft. British officers commanded the Kenyan Navy until 1972 when Lieutenant Colonel J. C. J. Kimaro became the first Kenyan to take that position. By the early 2000s, the Kenyan Navy operated four missile boats, four patrol craft, two amphibious landing vessels, and one support ship. Departing from the British model and creating a consciously politicized military to support African liberation, Tanzania's government looked to China to help it develop a naval element for the Tanzanian People's Defence Force (TPDF) in 1965. In addition to training personnel and building a naval facility at Dar es Salaam, China provided Tanzania with four patrol boats in 1966 and 10 torpedo/patrol boats in 1971, and later in the 1970s, the TPDF acquired another seven patrol craft from the Soviet Union.

In North Africa, Libya and Tunisia gained independence in the 1950s and created small navies in the early 1960s. In 1963 newly independent Algeria founded a navy with two British-built minesweepers and three torpedo boats, and several year later, it acquired a few missile boats from the Soviet Union. The 1968 handover of the Mers el-Kebir naval base by former colonial power France enhanced Algeria's naval capabilities. During the 1970s and 1980s, and in the context of tensions with neighboring Morocco, Algeria used its oil revenue to purchase billions of dollars of weapons, including naval vessels, from the Soviet Union. Creating the ability to project power out into the Mediterranean, the Algerian Navy acquired Soviet missile boats, six submarines, three frigates, and three corvettes, all equipped with missiles, and an amphibious landing vessel in this period. Around the same time, to reduce dependence on the Soviets, Algeria also purchased a dozen fast attack craft and two amphibious landing ships from Britain, with the later vessels enabling Algeria to form several battalions of marine infantry. In the 2000s, with the end of the Algerian Civil War and better relations with its neighbors, the Algerian government rebuilt its conventional military forces with major weapons purchases from Russia including two "Improved Kilo" class submarines. During the 2010s, Algeria maintained its status as the largest African naval power in the Mediterranean by modernizing its older Soviet-made frigates and submarines and buying new surface vessels from Germany, Italy, and Russia. Although its protracted conflict in Western Sahara and related tensions with Algeria influenced Morocco to build up a large army and air force with the help of France and the United States, the kingdom created a small navy in 1960, which was modernized in the 1990s by the purchase of four missile frigates from Spain and two missile corvettes from Italy.

After its election in 1948, South Africa's Nationalist Party government imposed a strict system of racial segregation called apartheid and built up its military capabilities including its navy. In the early 1950s, South Africa bought two World War II–era destroyers from Britain. In the 1955 Simonstown Agreement, Britain passed control of its Cape naval facilities to Pretoria, which agreed to let the Royal Navy continue use of the port. Furthermore, London agreed to sell South Africa £18 million pounds worth of naval assets over the following eight years, and this amounted to two destroyers, four frigates, 10 minesweepers, and seven coastal patrol aircraft. While South African purchased three submarines from France in the early 1970s, international sanctions against the apartheid regime scuttled the acquisition of more French submarines and corvettes later in the decade. In the late 1970s, in the context of the arms embargo, South Africa covertly acquired nine Israeli missile boats, some built in Israel, and some in South Africa. With the expansion of South Africa's war in Angola during the late 1970s and 1980s, the South African Navy reduced its deep water capabilities and focused on coastal operations, falling victim to budget cuts as more resources were allocated to the army and air force. After the transition to democracy in 1994, the South African government sought to refurbish its conventional military by purchasing almost $5 billion worth of weapons systems, including four corvettes with helicopters as well as three submarines from European countries, but the project became embroiled in corruption.

Postcolonial Africa's experience of naval warfare has involved "brown water" or "green water" operations. At the same time, foreign navies have also conducted operations in African waters. The Arab-Israeli Wars of 1967 and 1973 involved actions by the Egyptian Navy, which focused on trying to blockade Israeli ports like Eilat in the Straits of Tiran and laying mines. In 1967 an Egyptian fast attack craft used anti-ship missiles to sink an Israeli destroyer, becoming the first to demonstrate the effectiveness of this new weapons system. During the late 1970s and 1980s, South Africa's apartheid regime used its superior naval assets to support a campaign of destabilization against neighboring Black-ruled states to discourage them from supporting exiled South African activists. These South African naval operations included launching commando raids against port facilities, as happened in Dar es Salaam in 1972, Beira in Mozambique in 1982, and Namibe in southern Angola in 1986, and landing supplies for the rebel Mozambique National Resistance (RENAMO) in the 1980s. During the 1980s, the U.S. Navy's Sixth Fleet entered the Gulf of Sidra to counter the Libyan regime of Muammar Gaddafi that was supporting international terrorist groups and buying massive amounts of weaponry from the Soviet Union. In 1986 several Libyan patrol boats armed with outdated missiles tried to challenge the U.S. fleet, but these were destroyed by American aircraft launched from aircraft carriers. During the 2000s, Somali piracy against international shipping in the strategic Gulf of Aden increased, given civil war and lack of state control in Somalia, proliferation of small arms in the area, and the collapse of the local fishing industry. Consequently, in 2008 a multinational anti-piracy naval fleet including American, Canadian, European Union, Russian, Pakistani, Indian, and Chinese ships deployed to the region. Reflecting the growing economic and military power of China, this operation represented the first deployment of the People's Liberation Army Navy (PLAN) outside Asia-Pacific waters in modern times and led to the establishment of China's first overseas naval base at Djibouti in 2017. Concerns over piracy also informed the re-creation of the Somali Navy by the Somali Transitional Government in 2009 and the formation of a Maritime Police Force by the autonomous state of Puntland in 2010, both of which received support from the United Arab Emirates and the former from Turkey. Furthermore, the growth of piracy in the region as well as the American-led "War on Terror" led to the expansion of other East African navies. In the early 2010s, the United States donated two defender-class boats and a communications system to the Tanzanian Naval Command, and the Kenya Navy received an offshore patrol vessel donated by France and took delivery of the long-delayed Spanish-built *KNS Jasiri*, which became the largest ship in its small fleet. With its enhanced naval capability, Kenya intervened vigorously in the Somali Civil War, landing troops at the Somali port of Kismayo in 2012, seizing it from the Islamist forces of Al-Shabaab.

Timothy J. Stapleton

See also: Algerian Civil War; Al-Shabaab; Angolan Conflicts; Arab-Israeli Wars; ECOWAS Military Interventions; French Military Involvement in Postcolonial Africa; Mozambique Civil War; Somalia Civil War; Soviet Military Involvement in Africa; U.S. Military Involvement in Africa.

Further Reading

Baynham, Simon. *The Military and Politics in Nkrumah's Ghana.* Boulder, CO: Westview Press, 1988.

Siebels, Dirk. *Maritime Security in East and West Africa: A Tale of Two Regions.* Basingstoke: Palgrave Macmillan, 2019.

Tareke, Gebru. *The Ethiopian Revolution: War in the Horn of Africa.* New Haven: Yale University Press, 2009.

US Army Handbook for Senegal. Washington, DC: Department of the Army, 1963.

Wessels, Andre. "The South African Navy and its Predecessors, 1910–2010: A Century of Interaction with Commonwealth Navies." *Scientia Militaria: South African Journal of Military Studies* 38, no. 2 (2010): 109–130.

Neto, António Agostinho (1922–1979)

António Agostinho Neto was an Angolan insurgent leader and the first president of independent Angola.

Born the son of a Methodist minister on September 17, 1922, in Ícolo de Bengo, Bengo Province, Angola, António Agostinho Neto studied medicine at the Universities of Coimbra and Lisbon in Portugal. Arrested in 1951 for his Angolan separatist activities, he was imprisoned by the Portuguese government. Released in 1958, he completed his medical studies and returned to Angola in 1959. In 1956 the Partido Comunista de Angola (Angolan Communist Party) had merged with the Partido da Luta Unida dos Africanos de Angola (Party of the United Struggle for Africans in Angola) to form the Movimento Popular de Libertação de Angola (MPLA, Popular Movement for the Liberation of Angola), with Neto as president.

On June 8, 1960, Neto was again arrested by the Portuguese. His political supporters and patients marched to demand his release, and Portuguese soldiers opened fire on them, killing 30 and wounding 200 in what became known as the Massacre of Ícolo de Bengo. Neto was exiled to Cape Verde and then sent to Lisbon, where he was imprisoned. Following international protests, the Portuguese government of António de Oliveira Salazar released Neto from prison and placed him under house arrest. Neto escaped and made his way to Zaire (present-day Democratic Republic of the Congo).

In January 1961 the MPLA launched a guerrilla war against Portugal in Angola, and the next year Neto traveled to the United States to request aid from the U.S. government but was turned down by the John F. Kennedy administration, which chose to support the anti-communist Frente Nacional de Libertação de Angola (FNLA, National Front for the Liberation of Angola), headed by Holden Roberto, which was also fighting the Portuguese. Neto then met with and secured the support of Cuban leader Fidel Castro.

Following the April 1974 Carnation Revolution in Portugal, the new Portuguese government agreed to grant its colonies independence. The FNLA and the third Angolan insurgent movement, the União Nacional para a Independência Total de Angola (UNITA, National Union for the Total Independence of Angola), headed by Jonas Savimbi, then joined forces. Supported by military forces from Zaire, they attempted to keep the Marxist MPLA from taking power but were defeated by Cuban troops airlifted into Luanda by the Soviet Union.

Although Angola received independence on November 11, 1975, with Neto as president, a bloody and protracted civil war followed that pitted the MPLA and Cuban forces, supported by the Soviet Union, against UNITA and the FLNA, supported by the United States, Zaire, and South Africa. Although Marxist-Leninism was the official MPLA doctrine, in practice, Neto tended to favor a socialist, not communist, model for Angola. In 1977 he violently suppressed an attempted coup by the Organização dos Communistas de Angola (OCA, Communist Organization of Angola), with some 18,000 OCA supporters killed during a two-year span. President Neto died in Moscow on September 10, 1979, while undergoing cancer surgery. His birthday is celebrated as National Heroes Day, a public holiday in Angola.

Spencer C. Tucker

See also: Angolan Conflicts; Cold War in Africa; Cuba and Africa; Dos Santos, Jose Eduardo; National Front for the Liberation of Angola (FNLA); National Union for the Total Independence of Angola (UNITA); Popular Movement for the Liberation of Angola (MPLA); Portuguese Africa, Independence Wars (Angola, Mozambique, and Guinea-Bissau); Roberto, Holden Álverto; Soviet Military Involvement in Africa; U.S. Military Involvement in Africa.

Further Reading

George, Edward. *The Cuban Intervention in Angola, 1965–1991: From Che Guevara to Cuito Cuanavale*. London: Frank Cass, 2005.

Gleijeses, Piero. *Conflicting Missions: Havana, Washington and Africa, 1959–1976*. Chapel Hill: University of North Carolina Press, 2002.

Gleijeses, Piero. *Visions of Freedom: Havana, Washington, Pretoria and the Struggle for Southern Africa, 1976–91*. Chapel Hill: University of North Carolina Press, 2013.

James, W. Martin. *Historical Dictionary of Angola*. Lanham, MD: Scarecrow Press, 2011.

James, W. Martin. *A Political History of the War in Angola, 1974–1990*. London: Transaction Publishers, 2011.

Weigert, Stephen. *Angola: A Modern Military History, 1961–2002*. New York: Palgrave Macmillan, 2011.

New Forces

See Côte d'Ivoire Civil War

Nigerian Civil War (1967–1970)

The granting of independence to Nigeria by Britain on October 1, 1960, was received with mixed reactions among the multiethnic society. Barely seven years after, the former British colony was plunged into a civil war that began on July 6, 1967, and lasted until January 15, 1970. The Nigerian Civil War, also referred to as the Biafran Civil War, was fought to halt the secession of the Eastern region from Nigeria. Although the Igbos were not the first Nigerian ethnic group to agitate for secession, the resultant civil war made this attempt by the Igbos more renowned. The underlying causes of civil war can be traced to the legacies of colonialism, which resulted in ethnoreligious conflicts and economic disparities between the northern and southern regions. Moreover, the flamboyant and corrupt lifestyles of politicians, electoral fraud, and the intensification of political violence made more evident the extent of political decay in the country. Additionally, the discovery of oil in the Eastern region fueled the conflict. It is estimated that about a million individuals lost their lives, with higher casualty figures from the Eastern region.

The journey to secession, which triggered the Nigerian Civil War, can be traced to a series of military coups that occurred in January and July 1966. On January 15, 1966, a group of soldiers led by Major Kaduna Nzeogwu deposed the government of Prime Minister Sir Abubakar Tafawa Balewa in a bloody coup. The coup also resulted in the death of important politicians such as the Northern premier Sir Ahmadu Bello, Western premier Ladoke Akintola, and the finance minister Festus Okotie-Eboh amid other casualties. Inevitably, the death of only one soldier of Igbo heritage, and the succession of Major Aguiyi Ironsi (another easterner) as the head of state aroused ethnic suspicion. Moreover, Ironsi's failure to immediately punish the coup-plotters and his promulgation of Unification Decree 34, which abolished the federal system, unified the public services, and centralized the government, accentuated the suspicion of an Igbo plot to dominate Nigeria. As a consequence, a countercoup or the "July rematch" dominated by Northern soldiers was staged on July 29, 1966, which led to the death of Major Aguiyi Ironsi, Lieutenant Colonel Adekunle Fajuyi, and other officers who were mostly of Igbo heritage. The coup-plotters immediately reconstituted another military regime and appointed Lieutenant Colonel Yakubu Gowon as the head of state.

However, Lieutenant Colonel Odumegwu Ojukwu, the military governor of the Eastern region refused to recognize the legitimacy of the newly constituted government. Moreover, he condemned the massacre of Igbos in Northern Nigeria and appealed to Igbos to return to their homeland. The mass exodus of Igbos to the Eastern region deepened the antagonism between the Ojukwu-led Eastern regional government and the Nigerian government. In an effort to douse the tension, peace talks were convened in Aburi, Ghana, in 1967, between representatives of the Nigerian government and representatives from the Eastern region. Although both parties reached a consensus at Aburi, differing interpretation of the agreement and the division of Nigeria into 12 states on May 27, 1967, resulted in Ojukwu's declaration of the Republic of Biafra on May 30, 1967.

The discovery of oil in the Eastern region in 1956 made secession economically feasible. However, the Nigeria government was intent on preventing any disintegration of the state and therefore launched an offensive attack on Biafra. The government also blockaded and imposed economic sanctions on the Eastern region, which resulted in widespread starvation and malnutrition. During the war, the penetration and attack of the Midwest and almost an advance into Lagos by Biafran soldiers was considered a threat by the Nigerian forces. This resulted in retaliatory attacks by federal troops, who annihilated thousands of Midwestern Igbos in Asaba. The invasion of the Midwest marked a decisive moment in the war as the federal government launched a War of Attrition against the Biafrans.

Possessing superior weapons and well-organized troops, the port city of Calabar was captured during Operation Tiger-Claw. Other Biafran enclaves soon fell to advancing Nigerian troops. Between January 7 and 12, 1970, Nigerian troops launched their final offensive (Operation Tail-wind), which resulted in the capture of Biafra's strategically important towns of Owerri and Uli. The fall of these cities and the capitulation of Biafra on January 13, 1970, signaled the final moments of the war.

Throughout the war, the Biafran government employed mass media as an effective means of propaganda to influence public opinion, rekindle the declining morale of soldiers, and win humanitarian support. Responding to these appeals, nongovernmental organizations such as the Red Cross, Doctors without Borders (Medicines Sans Frontiers), Oxfam, and Save the Children Funds coordinated relief materials, and airlifted food and medical supplies to the civilian population. Similarly, religious organizations such as Protestant World Council of Churches and Caritas Internationalis supported the relief efforts and donated materials to the Biafrans. Additionally, there was public condemnation of the war and the outpouring of sympathy by churches who painted the war as an outright determination of Northern Muslims to purge the country of Christians. Moreover, the Biafran government used its propaganda machine to try to win diplomatic recognition and support from Western powers, the Soviet Union, and other African nations. However, the Organisation of African Unity, keeping with its principle of recognizing colonial boundaries, refused to recognize the new state while at the same time making attempts to mediate between the warring parties. In the end, Biafra was only formally recognized by Ivory Coast, Haiti, Gabon, Zambia, and Tanzania. However, various countries provided their direct and indirect support to the war. In a bid to protect its economic interest, Britain supported the Nigerian government, while the USSR also remained an ally of the Nigerian government, supporting her with airplanes and ammunition. Although France did not officially recognize Biafra, the French government provided ammunition to Biafran soldiers, while Israel also provided ammunitions and financial assistance. Both warring parties employed mercenaries during the war. Indeed, mercenaries such as Rolf Steiner, Marc Goossens, Taffy Williams, and "Kamikaze Braun" served alongside Biafran soldiers.

On January 15, 1970, Major General Phillip Effiong, the chief of staff of the Biafran government, formally announced the surrender of Biafran troops to the Nigerian government. The Nigerian head of state, General Yakubu "Jack" Gowon issued an amnesty to Biafran troops and declared his government's support to rebuild eastern states.

Yolanda Osondu

See also: Coups and Military Regimes in Africa; Famine in Postcolonial African Conflicts; "Five Majors" Coup, Nigeria; French Military Involvement in Postcolonial Africa; Genocide in Africa; Gowon, Yakubu "Jack" Dan-Yumma; Mercenaries in African Conflicts; Ojukwu, Chukwuemeka Odumegwu.

Further Reading
De St. Jorre, John. *The Nigerian Civil War*. London: Hodder and Stoughton, 1972.

Ekwe-Ekwe, Herbert. *The Biafra War: Nigeria and the Aftermath*. New York: Mellen Press, 1990.

Gould, Michael, and Frederick Forsyth. *The Biafran War: The Struggle for Modern Nigeria*. London: I.B. Tarius, 2012.

Siollun, Max. *Oil, Politics and Violence: Nigeria's Military Coup Culture (1966–1976)*. New York: Algora Publishing, 2009.

Nkomo, Joshua (1917–1999)

After many years of armed struggle against the white-minority regime in Rhodesia, Joshua Nkomo's dream of an independent, Black majority–ruled nation of Zimbabwe was realized on April 18, 1980. Nkomo went on to serve as national vice president from 1990 to 1999. He died in July 1999.

Joshua Mqabuko Nyongolo Nkomo was born on June 19, 1917, in Matabeleland, Southern Rhodesia, the son of a teacher and a member of the Karanga ethnic group. After early schooling in Rhodesia, Nkomo continued his education in South Africa and returned home in 1945 to work for Rhodesian Railways. While working for the railroad, Nkomo became increasingly political and was soon known as an outspoken advocate for the rights of Black rail workers. Nkomo became president of their labor union in 1951, the same year he obtained a BA degree from the University of South Africa, Johannesburg.

During the 1950s, Nkomo became well known as an outspoken opponent of colonialism and was elected president of the Southern Rhodesian African National Congress (ANC), the territory's major Black nationalist organization, in 1957. Following the banning of the ANC in 1959, Nkomo fled to England but returned to Rhodesia in 1960. Subsequently, he founded the National Democratic Party (NDP), which was banned, and then the Zimbabwe African People's Union (ZAPU), which became one of the leading forces in the struggle against the white-minority rule of Ian Smith, who had declared Rhodesia's independence in November 1965. The Rhodesian government held Nkomo in detention from 1964 to 1974, but upon his release, he became one of the leaders of the guerrilla uprising against white rule, which had begun in the early 1970s. Based in Zambia, ZAPU formed a military wing called the Zimbabwe People's Revolutionary Army (ZIPRA) and accepted support from the Soviet Union. The Zimbabwe African National Union (ZANU), led by Robert Mugabe, played a greater role in the conflict, primarily because it shifted military operations to Mozambique and gained support among the majority Shona ethnic group. Relations between ZAPU and ZANU were often strained, although the two groups did coalesce as the short-lived Patriotic Front (PF) in 1976 to effect a more unified strategy.

After majority rule and independence was achieved, ZANU-PF performed much better than ZAPU in the elections of 1980, leading to Mugabe becoming Zimbabwe's first prime minister. Nkomo became a member of President Robert Mugabe's cabinet, but he was dismissed in 1982 and accused of plotting an armed takeover. Nkomo fled the country in the context of Mugabe's violent suppression of ZAPU and general reign of terror in that group's political stronghold of southwestern Zimbabwe. After the 1987 Unity Accord in which ZANU absorbed ZAPU, Nkomo became Zimbabwe's vice president in 1990, following the general elections in which Mugabe won the presidential vote. A second national vice president was appointed shortly thereafter.

Nkomo spent much of 1998 in poor health, prompting his withdrawal from active political life. He died on July 1, 1999. Politically rehabilitated by Mugabe, the late Nkomo became known as "Father Zimbabwe," given his foundational role in the liberation struggle.

ABC-CLIO

See also: Cold War in Africa; Mugabe, Robert; Soviet Military Involvement in Africa; Zimbabwe, Massacres (Gukurahundi); Zimbabwe African National Union (ZANU); Zimbabwe African People's Union (ZAPU); Zimbabwe Independence War.

Further Reading
Nkomo, Joshua. *The Story of My Life*. London: Methuen, 1984.
Sibanda, Eliakim. *The Zimbabwe African People's Union, 1961–1987, A Political History of Insurgency in Southern Rhodesia*. Trenton: Africa World Press, 2005.

Nkunda, Laurent

See Democratic Republic of the Congo (DRC), Continuing Violence in

Nkurunziza, Pierre (1963–2020)

Pierre Nkurunziza was sworn in as president of Burundi on August 26, 2005. During Burundi's civil war from 1993 to 2005, he served as a rebel soldier and deputy secretary general of the Forces for the Defense of Democracy (FDD) Hutu rebel group.

As president, Nkurunziza has pledged to end ethnic violence in Burundi. However, he has provoked concern and criticism from human rights groups for claiming that his rule is the will of God. In 2015 protests erupted in Burundi over his election to a third term, which was prohibited by the nation's constitution.

Pierre Nkurunziza was born on December 18, 1963, in Burundi's capital, Bujumbura. He was one of seven children born to a Hutu father and a Tutsi mother. Nkurunziza's father served in Burundi's legislature and was also a provincial governor. He was murdered in front of Nkurunziza during a wave of ethnic violence in 1972. Nkurunziza graduated from the University of Burundi in 1990 with a degree in physical education and sports. He converted to Protestantism and played and coached for the Burundi soccer team New Sporting Club.

During the late 1980s, tensions in Burundi escalated between the majority Hutus and the minority Tutsis, who controlled the Burundian Army and the government. In 1993 the assassination of Burundi's first democratically elected president, Melchior Ndadaye (a Hutu), initiated a 12-year civil war that would claim the lives of at least 200,000 Burundians, including five of Nkurunziza's siblings. Nkurunziza was working as a lecturer at the University of Burundi in 1995 when a Tutsi army attacked the campus.

Nkurunziza fled Bujumbura and joined the Hutu rebel group FDD as a soldier. The FDD was the largest of several rebel groups fighting the Tutsi government. In 1998 Nkurunziza was promoted to deputy secretary general of the FDD and put in charge of coordinating the political and military wings of the party. That year, he was sentenced to death in absentia (without being in custody) by a Burundian court for laying land mines. In 1999 he was seriously wounded in battle but survived after recuperating for four months without medical care. In 2001 he ousted rebel leader Jean-Bosco Ndayingekurukiye to become chairperson of the FDD; he was reelected to the post in 2004.

Peace talks to end Burundi's civil war began in 1995 and were completed in 2000 with the signing of the Arusha Accords. In November 2001 a three-year transitional government was put into place under the leadership of Pierre Buyoya. The FDD did not sign on to the Arusha Accords and join the government until November 2003, when Nkurunziza negotiated a cease-fire. He was named minister of state for good governance in March 2004. Included in the cease-fire agreement was a commutation of his earlier death sentence.

Burundi held a national referendum on a posttransitional constitution in February 2005. Voters overwhelmingly approved the new constitution, which guaranteed majority rule and minority rights and required political parties to have both Tutsi and Hutu members. It also guaranteed that the national assembly would be 60 percent Hutu and 40 percent Tutsi.

After the constitution was approved, elections were scheduled for June and July 2005. The FDD won a majority of seats in the national assembly and the senate, giving the party the power to choose Burundi's president. Nkurunziza was elected president by a joint session of the new parliament on August 19 and inaugurated on August 26.

Leading a multiethnic, multiparty government presented Nkurunziza with many challenges. He remained relatively popular during his first term in office, negotiating a cease-fire with the Hutu National Liberation Forces (FNL) in 2008 and securing a cancelation of $134 million in foreign debt in 2009. However, Nkurunziza's reelection in 2010 was overshadowed by accusations of vote rigging. Major opposition parties boycotted the election.

In his second term, Nkurunziza grew increasingly controversial. His government was accused of widespread censorship and politically motivated killings. In 2013 Nkurunziza signed a law prohibiting reporting on topics that could damage national security or the economy. Critics argued this was effectively a media censorship law. His subsequent decision to run for a third term—which appeared to violate the two-term limit outlined in the nation's constitution—provoked protests and violence.

In April 2014 a United Nations (UN) report claimed that the government was providing arms to the Imbonerakure, a radical youth group allied with Nkurunziza, ahead of the upcoming election. In June 2015 Nkurunziza was reelected amid opposition protests and boycotts. Over the next year more than 260,000 people fled the country to escape a wave of protests and violent government suppression. In October 2017 Nkurunziza withdrew Burundi from the International Criminal Court, making it the first country to leave the organization. By the end of the year, human rights groups reported that more than 1,200 people had died in protests and unrest since the president's most recent election. In June 2020 shortly after announcing that he would not stand for upcoming elections and endorsing a presidential candidate, Nkurunziza passed away possibly from COVID-19.

Melissa Stallings

See also: Burundi, Civil War and Genocide; Congo Wars; Genocide in Africa; Hutu Power Movements.

Further Reading

Mwakikagile, Godfrey. *Burundi; The Hutu and the Tutsi: Cauldron of Conflict and Quest for Dynamic Compromise.* Dar es Salaam: New Africa Press, 2012.

Watt, Nigel. *Burundi: The Biography of a Small African Country.* London: Hurst, 2008.

Ntaganda, Bosco

See Democratic Republic of the Congo (DRC), Continuing Violence in

Nujoma, Sam (1929–)

Sam Nujoma led the South West Africa People's Organization (SWAPO) in its struggle for Namibian independence from South Africa. He became the nation's first president in March 1990 and held the position for 15 years. He stepped down in 2005, replaced by his handpicked successor, Hifikepunye Pohamba.

Samuel Daniel Nujoma is a member of Namibia's largest ethnic group, the Ovambo. He was born on April 12, 1929, to a peasant family in the village of Etunda in Ovamboland, in the northern part of what was then South West Africa. He received a minimal formal education at a primary school run by Finnish Lutheran missionaries and continued his education through a correspondence school in Johannesburg. He eventually moved to Windhoek with an uncle and in the late 1940s became a janitor and messenger for South African Railways. There he worked to organize Black workers, for which he was fired in 1957. With Herman Toivo ja Toivo, he formed the Ovamboland People's Organization (OPO) in 1959 and continued to promote the welfare of Black workers. That year Nujoma was arrested for participating in a protest that ended when police fired on the demonstrators, killing 12 of them. After a brief imprisonment, he fled the country and began a 30-year exile in Tanzania, Zambia, and Angola.

When the OPO changed its name to SWAPO in 1960, Nujoma became its president. In 1966 he launched a guerrilla war against South African occupation under SWAPO's military wing, the People's Liberation Army of Namibia (PLAN). While the war dragged on, Nujoma took to the diplomatic front, winning a 1971 World Court ruling declaring the South African occupation of Namibia illegal and in 1976 gaining the United Nations General Assembly's recognition of SWAPO as the legitimate representative of the Namibian people. He also participated in an unsuccessful peace conference with South African representatives in 1981.

In 1988 South Africa, Angola, and Namibia agreed to a cease-fire, and Nujoma returned home the next year. During the ensuing negotiations over the terms of independence, opponents criticized Nujoma for his intolerance of dissent within his own organization and portrayed him as uninformed and incapable of running the country. Nonetheless, his party won a majority in the Constituent Assembly in the November 1989 elections, and he was chosen as president, taking office in March 1990.

During his years in office, Nujoma became known for his conservative stances and his denouncement of foreign values being imposed on traditional Namibian cultures. He denounced gay men and lesbians as a product of "foreign influences," ordering police to arrest and imprison them, and in 2002 he banned the showing of foreign television shows. Despite the country's continuing problems with unemployment, illiteracy, and a sluggish economy, Nujoma easily won reelection bids in 1994 and 1999. In March 2004, however, he announced to the national assembly that he would retire from office at the end of his term in March 2005. In the November 2004 presidential and legislative elections, SWAPO secretary general Hifikepunye Pohamba won the presidency. Nujoma stepped down as president of SWAPO in 2007 but has remained active in politics, campaigning for the party on occasion.

ABC-CLIO

See also: Angolan Conflicts; Namibia Independence War; South West Africa People's Organization (SWAPO).

Further Reading

Leys, Colin, and John Saul. *Namibia's Liberation Struggle: The Two Edged Sword.* London: James Currey, 1995.

Udogu, E. Ike. *Liberation Namibia: The Long Diplomatic Struggle between the United Nations and South Africa.* Jefferson, NC: McFarland, 2012.

Nyerere, Julius (1922–1999)

Julius Nyerere was a pivotal figure in the history of Tanzania, East Africa, and the broader Pan-African movement from the 1950s through to his death in 1999. He was the chairman of the Tanganyikan African National Union political party and its successor the Chama Cha Mapinduzi (Party of the Revolution); the first prime minister of independent Tanganyika; and the President of the United Republic of Tanzania. He oversaw the transition of his nation to independence; its attempts at a transformative African form of socialism based on ujamaa principles; and, following his voluntary relinquishment of power in 1985, its passage into multiparty democracy. Beyond this, he also oversaw multiple efforts to build and maintain an overall Pan-African coalition to liberate the still colonized states of Africa, efforts that came to a successful conclusion in 1994 with the fall of apartheid South Africa.

Julius Nyerere was raised as the son of the paramount chieftain of the Zanaki people in Northern Tanzania. He took quickly to Western education, winning places at Makerere College in Uganda and then Edinburgh University in Scotland. While he was employed as a schoolteacher in Tanganyika, he became politically active, helping construct the Tanganyikan African National Union (TANU) party and agitate for decolonization for his home state. These efforts eventually proved successful, with Tanganyika gaining its independence in 1961 with Nyerere as prime minister. By 1964 he had overseen the transition of the government to a republic and its union with the archipelago of Zanzibar, creating the United Republic of Tanzania. From this position he pursued a series of socialist and Pan-Africanist programs on the continent.

A central part of Nyerere's foreign policy was the liberation of the remainder of the continent. As early as 1963, Nyerere hosted the Organization for African Unity's Liberation Committee in his capital of Dar es Salaam and used Tanzania as a hub for the training and equipping of the liberation fronts working toward decolonization of Portuguese Africa, Rhodesia, and South Africa. These ideas were carried out by his military, who constructed a series of guarded camps for the various guerrilla fronts across Tanzania. In addition, under his direction, the Tanzanian military created a special unit that cataloged, stored, and transported the equipment across the continent to the various fronts that needed it, essentially creating the necessary logistics networks to sustain the liberation struggles through the 1960s and 1970s.

Despite his actions as a leader of the coalition who supported these liberation struggles, Nyerere managed to avoid the direct invasion of Tanzania by colonial powers. However, he had to mobilize his nation for a conventional war when Ugandan forces seized the Tanzanian territory in the Kagera region in late 1978, sparking what became known as the Kagera War. This war was a decisive Tanzanian victory, resulting in the overthrow of Idi Amin and his regime. With only this exception, Nyerere managed to lead his country through to the end of his administration without serious domestic incident. Following his relinquishing of power in 1985, he continued to speak out about African issues and serve as a father to his nation until his death in 1999.

Charles G. Thomas

See also: Amin, Idi; Kagera War; Portuguese Africa, Independence Wars (Angola, Mozambique, and Guinea-Bissau); South Africa, Armed Struggle against Apartheid; Zimbabwe Independence War.

Further Reading

Bjerk, Paul. *Building a Peaceful Nation: Julius Nyerere and the Establishment of Sovereignty in Tanzania, 1960–1964*. Rochester, NY: University of Rochester Press, 2018.

Bjerk, Paul. *Julius Nyerere*. Athens: Ohio University Press, 2017.

Fouere, Marie-Aude. *Remembering Julius Nyerere in Tanzania: History, Memory, Legacy*. Dar es Salaam: Mkuki na Nyota Publishers Ltd., 2016.

Liundi, Christopher C. *Quotable Quotes of Mwalimu Julius K. Nyerere Collected from Speeches and Writings*. Dar es Salaam: Mkuki Na Nyota Publishers Ltd., 2012.

Ogaden War (1977–1978)

The Ogaden War was the conflict between Somalia and Ethiopia over control of the Ogaden region of modern-day Ethiopia from July 1977 to March 1978. This war is significant for inverting Cold War alliances in the Horn of Africa and for its role in the destabilization of Somalia.

There were multiple wars between Ethiopia and neighboring states for control of the Ogaden since the thirteenth century. After World War II, Britain initially planned to rejoin the Ogaden with British and Italian Somaliland to create "Somali-weyn," or "Greater Somalia," which many members of the Somali ethnic group greatly desired. Britain ultimately agreed to give the Ogaden to Ethiopia in 1948, which angered many Somali nationalists. From its independence in 1960, Somalia repeatedly pushed for the creation of a Pan-Somali state including ethnic Somali people living in neighboring countries like Ethiopia and Kenya. This led to the rise of the Western Somali Liberation Front's guerrilla campaign in the Ogaden region of Ethiopia, which Somalia supported militarily. The Ethiopian Revolution also began in 1974, with the Derg overthrowing Haile Selassie's imperial government. Military officer Haile Mariam Mengistu consolidated control of the Derg in early 1977, but most of Ethiopia was still engulfed in war. The United States of America, which did not approve of the new Marxist-Leninist regime, pulled all support from Ethiopia by early 1977.

Somali president Siad Barre, seeing Ethiopia's weakened state, launched an invasion on July 13, 1977. His primary objective was to capture the Ogaden to create Greater Somalia. The Somali force, which included 70,000 soldiers equipped with 250 tanks, 350 armored personnel carriers, 600 artillery, 40 fighter planes, comprised most of Somalia's standing army in 1977. Their attack relied on a combination of surprise assaults with high-speed mechanized units mixed with artillery bombardment of secure defensive positions. His plan was to quickly crush Ethiopia's eastern garrisons and gain control of the region with the help of local Somali insurgents.

The Somali invasion was initially successful. In July and August, Somalia captured up to 60 percent of the Ogaden. The Ethiopian garrison was poorly equipped to combat a mechanized assault and, by September, only controlled 10 percent of the Ogaden. Siad relied on a quick victory, however, and was unprepared for a sustained campaign. Somalia lost momentum during the Battle of Dire Dawa, which lasted from August 17 to 19. Dire Dawa housed both Ethiopia's second-largest airbase and their major rail lines to the Red Sea, making this a strategic point. There was intense fighting along the entire Ethiopian-Somali front, but relatively few gains on either side. Barre launched his invasion with the goal to conquer Ethiopia quickly because he did not have the armaments or manpower for attritional warfare. By December, the Somali military has depleted most of their heavy equipment and needed to regroup before resuming offensive operations. The Somali military sustained heavy casualties and contended with overexerted supply lines, which made offensive operations impractical.

While Somalia's manpower and supply situation worsened in late 1977, Ethiopia's situation grew substantially better with military support from the Soviet Union. The Soviet Union previously attempted to avert an Ethiopian-Somali conflict because they enjoyed an alliance with both sides after 1974.

The Soviet Union, plus their Cuban allies, tried to support a merger of Ethiopia and Somalia into one Marxist state in February–March 1977. These plans failed, and subsequent negotiations fell apart. Following Somalia's invasion, the Soviet Union initially attempted to broker a peace but failed. The Soviets decided to align with Ethiopia because they saw Ethiopia as a more valuable ally in the Horn of Africa. The Soviets supplied weapons and advisers, while Cuba supplied soldiers. By January 1978 there were approximately 11,000 Cuban soldiers in Ethiopia.

Barre subsequently cut off all diplomatic ties with the Soviet Union. This severance from the Soviets caused the United States of America to provide financial support to Somalia, which turned the Ogaden War into a proxy war between the Soviets and Americans. The United States turned directly against their former ally because it allowed them to then be fighting against the Soviet Union. The Soviets tried to broker a peace between their two allies until they were forced to choose one to support. The American-Ethiopian and Soviet-Somali alliance from the early 1970s flipped by 1978.

Ethiopia, with fresh Cuban soldiers and Soviet weapons and officers, launched two counterattacks in February–March 1978. Barre ordered a full withdrawal on March 9, 1978. The war ended with an Ethiopian victory. While the Somali advance was initially effective, they lacked sufficient resources for a sustained campaign. Once the Ethiopian forces stopped the Somali advance in the highlands, they were able to mount a counterattack with Soviet-Cuban forces. The Ethiopians sustained approximately 20,000 casualties and Somalia 9,000.

Mengistu's regime gained more legitimacy within Ethiopia because of the successful repulsion of a Somali invasion. The Soviet Union continued to militarily support Ethiopia until 1989. Somalia lost much of its equipment and trained soldiers in a major military failure. Barre also lost the confidence of other Somali leaders, and his failure in the Ogaden War directly caused the formation of the Somali Salvation Democratic Front, which was the first substantial opposition party to Barre's regime. The United States of America maintained diplomatic ties with Somalia until the Somali Rebellion in 1991–1992.

Quentin Holbert

See also: Barre, Mohamed Siad; Cold War in Africa; Cuba and Africa; Ethiopia: Insurgency and Interstate War; Mengistu Haile Mariam; Somalia Civil War; Soviet Military Involvement in Africa; U.S. Military Involvement in Africa.

Further Reading

Haile, Getatchew. "The Unity and Territorial Integrity of Ethiopia." *Journal of Modern African Studies* 24, no. 3 (1986): 465–487.

Nkaisserry, Joseph K. *The Ogaden War: An Analysis of Its Causes and Its Impact on Regional Peace on the Horn of Africa.* Carlisle Barracks, PA: U.S. Army War College, 1997.

Tareke, Gebru. "The Ethiopia-Somalia War of 1977 Revisited." *International Journal of African Historical Studies* 33, no. 3 (2000): 635–667.

Weiss, Kenneth G. *The Soviet Involvement in the Ogaden War.* Professional Paper 269 (February). Alexandria, VA: Center for Naval Analyses, 1980.

Ojukwu, Chukwuemeka Odumegwu (1933–2011)

Chukwuemeka Odumegwu Ojukwu was the leader of the secessionist state of Biafra from May 30, 1967, until its dissolution on January 13, 1970. Although of Igbo origin, Ojukwu was born in Zungeru, Northern Nigeria, in November 1933. The son of a wealthy entrepreneur, his privileged upbringing afforded him the opportunity to study at the prestigious King's College, Lagos. He continued his education at Epsom College, Surrey, and later earned a degree in history at Lincoln College, Oxford, in 1955.

By the 1950s the process toward decolonizing Nigeria had resulted in rapid changes in various sectors of the British administration. It was during this period that Ojukwu returned to Nigeria in 1956 and joined the Eastern Nigerian Civil Service as an administrative officer. After a brief stint at the civil service, Ojukwu adamantly refused to join his father's business but rather decided to serve in the Nigerian Army. He emerged as one of the few educated soldiers in the Nigerian Army and steadily rose through its ranks. After undergoing military training at the Royal West African Frontier Force (RWAFF) Training School in Teshie, Ghana, and officer cadet school, Eaton Hall, Ojukwu was commissioned as a second lieutenant. Upon his return to Nigeria, Ojukwu was assigned to the Fifth Battalion, where he would later emerge as the commanding officer. Ojukwu also served as a member of the United Nations peacekeeping force in the Congo.

By the late 1960s, ethnic strife among various groups in Nigeria became more evident after the coup of January 15, 1966. Ojukwu frustrated the plans of the coup-plotters in Kano and was later appointed as the military governor of the Eastern region. The aftermath of the countercoup in July 1966 resulted in a strained relationship between Ojukwu and the Northern-dominated government led by General Yakubu Gowon. Moreover, Ojukwu vehemently denounced the widespread killing of the Igbos in Northern Nigeria, and his appeal for their return to the Eastern region widened the brewing tension between both regions. The failure of both sides to reach a compromise resulted in the declaration of the Republic of Biafra on May 30, 1967. Famous for his oratory skills and charismatic leadership, Ojukwu led the Biafran Army into a 30-month armed struggle with the Nigerian government. On January 13, 1970, the Biafrans surrendered, and the state ceased to exist. Ojukwu fled into exile to Ivory Coast, where he remained until he was granted a presidential pardon by Alhaji Shehu Shagari in 1982.

Upon his return, Ojukwu continued to actively engage in politics but was imprisoned with other politicians after the coup of December 31, 1983. During the 2003 and 2007 elections, Ojukwu unsuccessfully contested as the presidential candidate of the All Progressive Grand Alliance. Ojukwu died after a brief illness on November 26, 2011.

Yolanda Osondu

See also: Coups and Military Regimes in Africa; Nigerian Civil War.

Further Reading
De St Jorre, John. *The Nigerian Civil War.* London: Hodder & Stoughton, 1972.
Forsyth, Frederick. *Emeka.* Oxford: Spectrum Books, 1991.

Operation Boleas: The SADC's Military Intervention into Lesotho (1998)

As the sun rose on the horizon on the morning of September 22, 1998, elements of a South African National Defence Force (SANDF) armored column crossed the bridge over the Mohokare River, which marked the border between South Africa and Lesotho. SANDF was to operate as part of a supposedly larger Southern African Development Community (SADC) peace enforcement mission (along with a small contingent of soldiers from the Botswana Defence Force (BDF)) at the request of the prime minister of Lesotho, Pakalitha Mosisili, following weeks of violent unrest within the country after a disputed national election in May that year. But within 48 hours, the intervention had left several SANDF soldiers killed and an estimated 100 dead civilians. Many questions and criticisms followed as to the performance and the purpose of the mission of the then infant SANDF.

After the end of apartheid in South Africa, the push to remove racial barriers at all levels of society was made a priority of the new government. Negotiations began in the early 1990s on the process for integrating the various "Bantustan" or "homeland" armies and other so-called nonstatutory forces, such as the African National Congress' Umkhonto we Sizwe (MK) and the Pan-Africanist Congress' Azanian People's Liberation Army (APLA). Ultimately, eight different military organizations would have to be integrated into the former white-dominated South African Defence Force (SADF). This process was far from complete as the troubles in Lesotho began.

Lesotho has had a long and troubled history of autocratic governments, coups, and contentious elections since independence was achieved in 1966. The national election in May 1998 was little different. In this national election the Lesotho Congress for Democracy (LCD) party had won the election. But the validity of the election was immediately questioned by the opposition parties—particularly, by the formerly ruling Basutoland Congress Party (BCP). Neighboring South Africa was asked to step in to mediate the growing dispute, and Deputy President Thabo Mbeki assigned South African High Court judge, Justice Pius Langa, to lead a multicountry team to assess the election results.

However, the Langa Commission's final report did not alleviate tensions and only created more confusion and criticism.

The crisis in Lesotho would only build from there and culminated in the army revolt led by junior officers of the Lesotho Defense Force (LDF) on September 11 and the removal and arrest of senior military officers. This action led to rumors of a potential coup against the government, and this drove the prime minister to make direct appeals to several SADC countries—including South Africa—to intervene militarily in Lesotho. It was up to the decision of the then acting state president Mangosuthu Buthelezi (President Mandela and Deputy President Mbeki were both out of the country at the time) to give the order that SANDF troops should respond to this call.

The high command within the SANDF decided that the most appropriate force available for this mission were soldiers from the 43rd Mechanized Brigade based in nearby Bloemfontein. It was felt that an armored force would be best equipped to handle this type of operation—even though the SANDF had no previous experience in peacekeeping or peace enforcement. To this force was added a company of paratroopers from the 44th Parachute Brigade. All in all a force of approximately 600 SANDF soldiers would participate in the initial phase of the mission. To this total would be added approximately 200 BDF soldiers of a mechanized infantry company, which would enter Lesotho later in the day after the SANDF's entry. While this was supposedly a SADC-sponsored mission, there was little doubt in the minds of many that this was a South African-led operation.

The primary objectives of the intervention force were to secure and protect the following: the Royal Palace, the Katse Dam (as part of the regionally strategic Highlands Water Project), and the two LDF barracks near Maseru. Intelligence was generally poor prior to the intervention. The element that was to secure the palace mistakenly went to the Hilton Hotel in Maseru. Later when the mistake was corrected and the force did locate the palace, the failure to secure all the palace exits led to demonstrators who were within the compound to escape and begin large-scale looting of foreign businesses in Maseru.

Lack of intelligence may have contributed to the belief that resistance to the SANDF incursion would be light or nonexistent. Instead, resistance from the LDF was much stronger than anticipated at certain points during the operation. For instance, at the Katse Dam, which was the responsibility of the SANDF paratroop force, LDF troops guarding the dam opened fire, killing and wounding several paratroopers before they were finally suppressed. At the LDF barracks, the SANDF armored force was pinned down for some time before overcoming resistance.

By September 24, Colonel Robbie Hartslief, commander of the SADC intervention force, would declare that all military objectives were secured but acknowledged that large numbers of rebel LDF troops and various armed youth still remained at large. This potential threat and the lack of forces available led South Africa to increase their force level to 3,500 troops in early October. The SADC intervention then evolved into, what was perceived by many, an occupation of Lesotho, which would last until May the following year.

Patrick Whang

See also: Azanian People's Liberation Army (APLA); Coups and Military Regimes in Africa; South Africa, Armed Struggle against Apartheid; Umkhonto we Sizwe (MK).

Further Reading

Licklider, Roy. "South Africa." In *New Armies from Old: Merging Competing Military Forces after Civil War*, edited by Roy Licklider, 119–133. Washington, DC: Georgetown University Press, 2014.

Neethling, Theo. "Southern African Military Interventions in the 1990s: The Case of the SADC in Lesotho." In *Managing African Conflicts: The Challenge of Military Interventions*, edited by L. du Plessis and M. Hough, 287–331. Pretoria: HSRC Publishers, 2000.

Southall, Roger. "SADC's Intervention into Lesotho: An Illegal Defense of Democracy?" In *African Interventionist States*, edited by Oliver Furley and Roy May, 153–171. Burlington: Ashgate, 2001.

Operation Restore Hope (1992–1993)

Operation Restore Hope was the initial operation designed to bring international aid and support to the troubled country of Somalia.

Somalia was in dire straits after the collapse of the Barre regime, which led the UN to attempt to engage in order to provide humanitarian relief. Somalia was the subject of six Security Council resolutions during 1992, as the humanitarian crisis, with nearly 20,000 killed during the civil war and more than 600,000 refugees, was profound, while NGOs fled out of fear for safety.

The first effort to bring help to Somalia was in the UNITAF phase (United Task Force), which was from December 1992 to May of 1993. It was an attempt to blend traditional peacekeeping operations alongside military operations. Given that it was a new attempt, it was helped by the close and fluid relationship established between Lieutenant General Robert Johnson and Robert Oakley (ambassador to Somalia from 1982 to 1984). Upon arrival they helped create a cease-fire in Mogadishu and committed to a "Seven Point Agreement" whose ultimate goal was the creation of a benign security environment to enable the UN and NGOs to work in peace. Their efforts spanned the spectrum from direct security efforts to creating their own paper (*Rajo* or "Hope"), of which they distributed nearly 18,000 copies per day in order to build bridges with the people themselves. The military also helped with logistical efforts to enable the NGOs to work, building and repairing nearly 2,500 kilometers of roads, nine airfields, and 85 helicopter pads. The military also dug wells and assisted in a UNICEF inoculation program.

While such efforts proceeded, it did not mean there wasn't violence or problems, as clashes between Somali groups led to anti-UNITAF demonstrations. Mohammad Aidid, specifically, was upset with how the UNITAF policy of empowering local leaders meant that his larger organization's (United Somali Congress) power was being undercut. But the consistent meetings not only among UNITAF members but also with Somali leaders ensured that order was eventually restored and the NGO work could continue. By January 1993 it seemed stabilization was truly possible with UNITAF forces even staging a soccer championship with some local care and support.

Problems, however, arose from what to do next. While UNITAF was quite successful in its operation, it was an operation with a very limited scope. The real issue is that the UN wanted to come into the country but only wanted to do so after the warring factions were disarmed. The issue was that UNITAF did not have the mandate, the NGOs did not have the resources, and the Somalis were resistant due to fear. All this was made worse by miscommunication between the United Nations and the United States. The United States wanted the limited scope and commitment of UNITAF, which would be overtaken by a larger UN force. The UN, in contrast, wanted UNITAF to seize major weapons stores and "clear the way" for the UN forces to enter a more peaceful situation. This confusion meant that the next stage, disarmament, was left to UNOSOM II, which had little consultation and agreement between its different components as to its role or the precise rules of engagement. Ultimately, it was this new goal, and the tensions it unleashed, which would lead to conflict and the events that would lead to the Battle of Mogadishu.

Robert H. Clemm

See also: Mogadishu, Battle of; Peacekeeping in Africa; Somalia Civil War; U.S. Military Involvement in Africa.

Further Reading

Njoku, Raphael C. *The History of Somalia.* Santa Barbara, CA: Greenwood, 2013.

Rutherford, Kenneth. *Humanitarianism under Fire: The US and UN Intervention in Somalia.* Sterling, VA: Kumarian Press, 2008.

Patriotic Salvation Movement (MPS)
See Chad, Conflict in

Peacekeeping in Africa

In terms of what the global community understands today as peacekeeping or peace support operations (PSOs), Africa stands as the launch point, the experimental proving ground, and the main theater of operations. During the early decades of the Cold War, the UN Security Council "permanent five" were explicitly excluded from putting boots on the ground in PSOs. African militaries quickly emerged as the main supplier of uniformed personnel for UN and later regional, multilateral PSOs, starting with the United Nations Operation in the Congo (ONUC) in 1960. During the 2010s, Africa surpassed South Asia as the main troop-contributing region. It is impossible to consider conflict in postcolonial Africa without understanding the salience and evolution of peacekeeping on the continent as well as the contributions of African armed forces to these multilateral operations.

While peacekeeping and PSOs cover a broad spectrum of operations, including use of force to achieve specific aims of a mandate, what is not included in this discussion are UN authorizations for collective security interventions similar to Korea 1950 or Kuwait 1990. Thus, in Africa's case, peacekeeping does not include Libya 2011 or UNSC Resolution 2359 that expressed support for the *Force conjointe du G5 Sahel* in 2017, a five-nation effort to combat terrorism and transnational crime in the Sahel.

Nigeria, South Africa, Egypt, and Tanzania have regularly taken regional leadership roles in support of multilateral security operations, often taking on greater risks and responsibilities. In some cases, states that once hosted PSOs later became major troop contributors to other missions, including Burundi, Chad, Ethiopia, and Rwanda. In other cases, countries such as Botswana, Ghana, Senegal, and Tunisia established global reputations for their military professionalism and ongoing commitment to PSOs around the world.

For individual soldiers and officers, PSO deployments can be both professionally and financially rewarding. Depending on the nature of the mission, however, the risks for deployed personnel can be high, while the room for effective action can be highly constrained by mission mandates, rules of engagement, home country caveats, or mundane logistical constraints. Of the 4,027 fatalities across all UN PSOs (up to November 2020), African troop-contributing countries accounted for nearly 1,700, or 42 percent. In comparison, the big three South Asian contributors

(Bangladesh, India, and Pakistan) suffered 482 fatalities, or 12 percent. And these figures do not count the regional missions such as ECOMOG in Liberia or AMISOM in Somalia, where fatalities were not systematically reported. For instance, in AMISOM during 2007–2018, total fatalities were estimated between 1,500 and 1,900 personnel, which means that AMISOM alone potentially led to more deaths for African contingents than 60 years of global UN operations.

Motivations for contributing troops to different missions can range from broad foreign policy impulses in support of the UN or African Union (AU—formerly the Organisation of African Unity or OAU) to military desires to conduct operations abroad and political desires to keep the troops busy. Of course, regional security interests and geopolitical rivalry are often involved as well as direct and indirect financial incentives that benefit contributing governments. Thus, there are various, often multiple, motivations for African politicians to commit troops to UN, OAU/AU, or regional missions, and sometimes withdraw them.

Some of those regional organizations—such as the OAU in Chad in 1981 and ECOWAS in Liberia in 1990—were not initially designed to mobilize and deploy ad hoc multilateral military forces, but much like the UN in the 1950s, necessity overcame legal, political, and logistical challenges. Peacekeeping, as UN secretary general Dag Hammarskjöld explained, was not expressly provided for in the UN Charter: it straddled Chapters VI and VII, what he referred to as "Chapter VI and a half."

After decades of ad hoc planning, the AU and five regional organizations have tried to institutionalize regional and continental military preparedness within the African Standby Force (ASF) arrangement as part of Africa's Peace and Security Architecture. While the first exercises were conducted in 2015 in South Africa, the five regional organizations vary widely in terms of their political will to mobilize and deploy as well as in their military capabilities if they did. Compare, for instance, Economic Community of West African States (ECOWAS) with Nigeria leading missions from ECOMOG in the 1990s (Liberia and Sierra Leone) and ECOMIG in 2017 (to ensure a peaceful transfer of power after elections in Gambia) to Economic Community of Central African States (ECCAS), which has no similar track record. Still, the ASF should improve the ability for regions to mobilize more quickly in response to regional and continental threats to peace and security, without waiting for a UN Security Council authorization. But the subsidiarity principle also means that the UN and even the AU will not act until a regional organization does. This puts the decision-making about what constitutes a threat to regional security (e.g., a coup, an insurgency or civil war, state-sponsored violence, or a president manipulating elections or the constitution to stay in power indefinitely) back into the hands of those regional leaders. For instance, despite expectations that the ECCAS or AU would address the worsening violence in Cameroon since 2017, which might then lead to at least a debate at the UN, the ECCAS remains silent, as it is dominated by Cameroonian president Paul Biya. Without the ECCAS or AU acknowledging a serious crisis in Cameroon, the international community's hands are tied.

There is a misconception that peacekeeping evolved from the earliest unarmed observer missions in the 1940s and lightly armed "interposition" role after a negotiated cease-fire (both authorized under Chapter VI of the UN Charter) during the Cold War to the later complex, robust Chapter VII mandates common in "peacemaking" or "peace enforcement" missions in internal conflicts in places such as DR Congo, Mali, Somalia, or South Sudan. Sometimes that progress is conceptualized as phases or generations, but it is important to identify the continuities and complexities over time that a simple conceptual chronology obscures.

That first generation, beginning with the United Nations Emergency Force (UNEF) for Suez in 1956–1957, established five core peacekeeping principles that mostly fit under the UN Charter's Chapter VI, "The Pacific Settlement of Disputes": (1) universal consent of the parties involved, (2) nonuse of force (except in self-defense), (3) neutrality (which for decades precluded Security Council permanent members from direct participation in missions), (4) impartiality (in terms of supporting the mission mandate), and (5) legitimacy (authorized by the Security Council or, later, a regional organization). Most UN missions during the Cold War followed these principles that emerged during the frantic negotiations to prevent the Suez Crisis in 1956 from escalating to a broader war between the East and West. Some missions after the Cold War, including after the Ethiopia-Eritrea War in 2000, followed this model too. But the challenges faced by a decolonizing Africa from 1960 well into the 2000s required significant alterations to the basic goals of multilateral missions to deal with state breakdown and humanitarian crises, civil war and its aftermath, and transitions to independence.

The Congo mission of 1960–1964, which began with a Chapter VI mandate and those principles in mind, quickly challenged those notions of peacekeeping as conceived in 1956. The ONUC grew to be over three times larger than UNEF, with a more diverse (and often shifting) array of national contingents, including a large number of African units. By the end of 1960, there were over 17,000 UN troops in the country. A year later, ONUC forces were deployed in an African/Asian Brigade and a European Brigade, purportedly to generate a sense of competition. Combat operations against local militias and regional separatists supported by mercenaries ensured that by 1962–1963 the ONUC looked nothing like UNEF. The ONUC was at times conducting conventional military operations, with infantry, armor, artillery, and combat aircraft at its disposal. The future of PSOs was revealed in the Congo, but UNEF and later Cyprus remained the idealized standard of peacekeeping for many Western countries that only played a marginal role in the Congo. The kinetic and political complexities of the ONUC were unfortunately forgotten when it mattered most by the end of the Cold War.

After peacekeepers won the Nobel Peace Prize in 1988, the end of the Cold War unleashed a range of opportunities for a more activist Security Council. Twenty UN missions launched from 1989 to 1994, including many in Africa. The initial success of a multidimensional UNTAG mission in Namibia (1989–1990) that finalized its long road to independence would not prepare the institution of peacekeeping for the crises of Somalia, Rwanda, and the attempt to ensure peace in Angola. In addition, ECOWAS had to fill a void in West Africa as violence spread in Liberia and then Sierra Leone while the international community was focused on the First Gulf War and other crises. This era is often referred to as the second generation of peacekeeping, as it took on a multidimensional flavor that included postconflict peacebuilding. However, missions in Rwanda, Somalia, and Liberia more closely resembled the struggles of the original Congo mission, and UN-led, American-led, and ECOWAS-led efforts, respectively, floundered, shattering confidence in peacekeeping, particularly across Western capitals.

UN-authorized (if possible) but not UN-led coalitions became the preferred security mechanism for Western great and middle powers by the late 1990s. Kosovo, Afghanistan, Iraq, and later, the French intervention in Mali (2013) solidified this pattern. That meant that when the next wave of complex, dangerous missions began to spring up on the continent in the early 2000s, funding and some logistical support would be available, but most of the troops would have to come from Africa or South Asia (with China emerging as the most active great power troop contributor during the 2010s). By 2009, there were 16 UN peacekeeping missions around the globe with around 90,000 troops and police deployed. By 2020, there were still 14 active missions and 82,000 uniformed personnel, with African troops and police the largest regional component. The largest, most complex, and most dangerous UN missions remained in Africa, including Mali (MINUSMA), Central African Republic (MINUSCA), DR Congo (MONUSCO), and South Sudan (UNMISS). The UN and AU created a hybrid mission in Darfur, Sudan (UNAMID) in 2007, the same year the AU launched AMISOM in Somalia, though with considerable financial assistance from the European Union and other funders. Each mission now has a complex mandate, renewed annually, that can run for pages outlining objectives related to stabilization and peacebuilding, development, security sector reform, protection of civilians, use of force, and other specific goals. The Kigali Principles, launched in 2015, provide a framework to improve the planning and performance of peacekeepers to meet the challenge of protecting civilians from violence, including gendered violence, in volatile security environments.

In 2013, the UN authorized a "Force Intervention Brigade" for MONUSCO in DR Congo, initially calling upon South African, Tanzanian, and Malawi battalions to undertake offensive operations in the east against various non-state armed groups (including M23 and the ADF). A look back at the ONUC in the early 1960s shows the continuities between that original complex, internal peacekeeping mission and those that dominate across the continent decades later. This parallel makes it difficult to draw a neat line from first- to third-generation peacekeeping over time, at least on the African continent. Nevertheless, what this brief review of peacekeeping in Africa reveals is that the global community is increasingly dependent on African women and men in uniform to undertake some of the most difficult multilateral missions, usually under tight budgets, without sufficient mobility, medical, and logistics assets, and often under various political and bureaucratic constraints.

Chris W. J. Roberts

See also: Arab-Israeli Wars; Burundi, Civil War and Genocide; Canadian Military Involvement in Africa; Central African Republic (CAR), Conflict in; Chad, Conflict in; Congo Crisis; Congo Wars; Darfur Genocide; Democratic Republic of the Congo (DRC), Continuing Violence in; ECOWAS Military Interventions; Eritrea-Ethiopia War; French Military Involvement in Postcolonial Africa; Liberian Civil Wars; Namibia Independence

War; Refugees in Postcolonial Africa; Rwanda, Civil War and Genocide; Sierra Leone Civil War; Somalia Civil War; South Sudan Civil War; Suez Crisis.

Further Reading

Adebajo, Adekeye. *UN Peacekeeping in Africa: From the Suez Crisis to the Sudan Conflicts.* Boulder, CO: Lynne Rienner, 2011.

Autesserre, Séverine. *The Trouble with the Congo: Local Violence and the Failure of International Peacebuilding.* Cambridge: Cambridge University Press, 2010.

Darka, Linda. "The African Standby Force: The Africa Union's Tool for the Maintenance of Peace and Security." *Contemporary Security Policy* 38, no. 3 (2017): 471–482.

Doss, Alan. *A Peacekeeper in Africa: Learning from UN Interventions in Other People's Wars.* Boulder, CO: Lynne Rienner, 2019.

Kabia, John M. *Humanitarian Intervention and Conflict Resolution in West Africa: From ECOMOG to ECOMIL.* Farnham: Ashgate, 2002.

Koops, Joachim, Norrie MacQueen, Thierry Tardy, and Paul D. Williams, eds. *The Oxford Handbook of United Nations Peacekeeping Operations.* Oxford: Oxford University Press, 2015.

Kotia, Emmanuel Wekem. *Ghana Armed Forces in Lebanon and Liberia Peace Operations.* New York: Rowman & Littlefield, 2015.

Macqueen, Norrie. *United Nations Peacekeeping in Africa since 1960.* London: Routledge, 2002.

Williams, Paul D. *Fighting for Peace in Somalia: A History and Analysis of the African Union Mission (AMISOM), 2007–2017.* Oxford: Oxford University Press, 2018.

People's Liberation Army of Namibia (PLAN)

See Namibia Independence War

Popular Front for the Liberation of Saguia el Hamra and Rio de Oro (POLISARIO)

See Western Sahara, Conflict in

Popular Movement for the Liberation of Angola (MPLA)

The Popular Movement for the Liberation of Angola–Labor Party (Movimento Popular de Libertação de Angola MPLA) instituted a Marxist system in Angola after taking over the government in 1975 and fought during the Angolan Civil Wars against the National Union for the Total Independence of Angola (UNITA).

Agostinho Neto founded the MPLA in Luanda, the capital of the Portuguese colony of Angola, in December 1956. The group was formed to fight against Portuguese colonialism, and its leadership was dominated by *mesticos* (those of mixed-race) like Viriato da Cruz and *assimilados* (assimilated Africans) like Neto. Most had been educated by missionaries either from the Methodist Church or the Catholic Church. The MPLA drew its rank-and-file support, however, from the Mbundu tribe, whose traditional territory surrounded Luanda. As in other nationalist movements in the Portuguese colonies, there were splits in the MPLA. Neto emerged as undisputed leader only in 1963, and there were internal conflicts in 1972 and 1974.

The MPLA's first 350 guerrilla fighters were trained in Algeria during the Algerian War of Independence; thereafter, recruits were also trained in Bulgaria, Czechoslovakia, and the Soviet Union. The MPLA rose in revolt in early 1961, but its early efforts were unsuccessful. A more sustained military campaign was begun by infiltrating the Cabinda enclave from the neighboring Congo Republic in 1963. However, the MPLA was soon forced to move its bases to Zambia through its failure to raise local support in Cabinda. The MPLA opened an "eastern front" in the Moxico and Bié regions during 1966–1967, but its efforts there were badly damaged by the Portuguese Army. By 1974, the MPLA had retired once more to the Congo Republic and was reduced to long-range bombardment of Portuguese targets with mortars and rockets. The MPLA's claim that it controlled 50 percent of Angola at the campaign's peak in the east was false, and it is doubtful if more than a small proportion of its estimated 3,000–5,000 guerrillas ever operated permanently in Portuguese territory.

The MPLA proclaimed the People's Republic of Angola in Luanda in November 1975, while the National Front for the Liberation of Angola (FNLA) and UNITA proclaimed the formation of another government in Huambo, which led to civil war even before the Portuguese withdrew in November 1975. South Africa and the United States did provide some limited assistance to FNLA and UNITA, but the course of the civil war was determined by a massive Soviet airlift of Cuban troops to Angola between October 1975 and January 1976 to aid the MPLA. In 1977, the party restructured itself along Soviet lines. The MPLA controlled the oil of the Cabinda enclave, which supported the group while the economy collapsed.

As a Marxist-Leninist party during the 1980s, the MPLA sought to end tribal, regional, and racial division and unify the nation. The party also proclaimed itself nonaligned in international affairs, but it maintained good relations with the Soviet bloc nations of Eastern Europe. At the same time, relations with the United States and South Africa were poor. However, in the late 1980s, the MPLA instituted economic reforms and sought Western financial assistance. President Jose Eduardo dos Santos announced that, among other measures, industries that had been nationalized would be returned to the private sector.

After the collapse of the Soviet Union, the Cubans finally withdrew in 1991. The MPLA abandoned Marxism and won 129 of 220 seats in the September 1992 election. However, UNITA leader Jonas Savimbi refused to accept the results and resumed the war. In 1993, U.S. president Bill Clinton officially recognized the MPLA government and condemned UNITA for renewing hostilities. Hostilities continued until Savimbi was killed in fighting in February 2002. The MPLA declared the conflict over in March 2002. Winning regular elections since the end of the war, the MPLA continues to serve as the government of Angola.

ABC-CLIO

See also: Angolan Conflicts; Cabindan Insurgency; Cold War in Africa; Cuba and Africa; Dos Santos, Jose Eduardo; National Front for the Liberation of Angola (FNLA); National Union for the Total Independence of Angola (UNITA); Neto, António Agostinho; Portuguese Africa, Independence Wars (Angola, Mozambique, and Guinea-Bissau); Roberto,

Holden Álverto; Savimbi, Jonas; Soviet Military Involvement in Africa; U.S. Military Involvement in Africa.

Further Reading

George, Edward. *The Cuban Intervention in Angola, 1965–1991: From Che Guevara to Cuito Cuanavale*. London: Frank Cass, 2005.

Gleijeses, Piero. *Conflicting Missions: Havana, Washington and Africa, 1959–1976*. Chapel Hill: University of North Carolina Press, 2002.

Gleijeses, Piero. *Visions of Freedom: Havana, Washington, Pretoria and the Struggle for Southern Africa, 1976–91*. Chapel Hill: University of North Carolina Press, 2013.

James, W. Martin. *A Political History of the Civil War in Angola, 1974–1990*. New Brunswick, NJ: Transaction Publishers, 1992.

Weigert, Stephen. *Angola: A Modern Military History, 1961–2002*. New York: Palgrave Macmillan, 2011.

Portuguese Africa, Independence Wars (Angola, Mozambique, and Guinea-Bissau) (1960–1974)

During the 1960s and early 1970s, Portugal clung to its colonial empire in Africa. Unlike most European powers that granted independence to their African colonies through a process of negotiation in the late 1950s and 1960s, the dictatorial regime of Antonio Salazar in Lisbon asserted that its African territories of Angola, Mozambique, and Guinea-Bissau represented integral parts of Portugal. Nevertheless, Portuguese colonial rule in these colonies had been particularly oppressive, and frustrated African nationalists decided to fight for independence. The global Cold War influenced all three independence wars in Portuguese Africa. Portugal held membership in the North Atlantic Treaty Organization (NATO) and therefore received support from Western powers as well as from affiliated white-minority regimes in South Africa and Rhodesia, leaving the independence movements to look to the socialist Eastern Bloc.

A series of rebellions against tyrannical Portuguese rule broke out in Angola in 1961. In January a dissident Christian movement destroyed European crops and property on Angola's central plateau and was brutally repressed by the Portuguese Army. In February the Popular Movement for the Liberation of Angola (MPLA) hijacked a Portuguese cruise liner and attacked a police headquarters and a prison in Luanda. In the north, a more serious rebellion erupted among the Bakongo people related to grievances over land and Portuguese interference in the appointment of their traditional king. As a result, the Union of Peoples of Angola (UPA), based across the border in newly independent Congo, infiltrated small groups of insurgents into northern Angola. UPA leader Holden Roberto obtained arms from his brother-in-law Joseph Mobutu, head of the new Congolese military, who would eventually take over that country. In mid-March 4,000–5,000 UPA rebels attacked coffee plantations in the north killing 200 Portuguese and many more pro-colonial Africans. The UPA insurgents believed this shocking violence would prompt the Portuguese to quickly leave Angola as the Belgians had in the Congo. Completely unprepared for the insurgency, the Portuguese military in Angola at the start of the 1960s comprised only 3,000 mostly locally recruited soldiers and a few aircraft. With the rainy season delaying the movement of Portuguese colonial troops to northern Angola, the Portuguese Air Force assisted Portuguese farmers and their African allies who fortified plantations and organized militias that burned and massacred villages suspected of sympathizing with the rebels. Portuguese reinforcements began to arrive in Angola in May 1961 and restored colonial control over the north. Although the army stopped settler atrocities, the air force conducted aerial bombing with napalm, and soldiers forced African civilians into concentrated settlements for more efficient supervision. The poorly equipped and untrained rebels conducted guerrilla tactics against Portuguese forces and escaped into the Congo when pursued. In August and September, Portuguese forces seized the main insurgent strongholds after heavy fighting, which led to the decline of the rebellion over the following two years. The fighting claimed the lives of around 2,000 Europeans and 50,000 Africans, and thousands of Angolan refugees fled into the Congo, which was in the midst of its own crisis.

After the initial rebellions, different Angolan nationalist organizations emerged during the early 1960s. In 1962, Roberto's UPA amalgamated with another group to form the National Front for the Liberation of Angola (FNLA), which established an exiled government in Leopoldville (today's Kinshasa) in the Congo with support from Mobutu and the Organisation of African Unity (OAU). Led by Agostinho Neto, the MPLA continued to gain most of its support from around Angola's capital of Luanda. In 1966, Jonas Savimbi founded the National Union for the Total Independence of Angola (UNITA) among the Ovimbundu of the southern region close to the border with South West Africa (now Namibia). Moreover, in 1963 three groups pursuing independence for oil-rich Cabinda, an enclave disconnected from the bulk of Angola, merged into the Front for the Liberation of the Cabinda Enclave (FLEC).

In 1963, the MPLA began planning a Maoist-style guerrilla campaign against the Portuguese colonial state in Angola. Evicted from Congo-Kinshasa because of Mobutu's links with the rival FNLA and rejected by the residents of Cabinda, the MPLA moved to neighboring and newly independent Zambia, where it acquired arms from the Eastern Bloc and launched operations against the Portuguese in southern and eastern Angola in 1966. While the Portuguese considered the 2,000 MPLA fighters their most serious military threat, the MPLA tried to expand its activities across the whole country instead of liberating specific areas. In addition, it took MPLA insurgents six weeks to march from faraway Zambia to operational areas in Angola, and they traveled in large groups of around 250 that were easily located by Portuguese aircraft. In the north, the MPLA faced both the Portuguese Army and the FNLA, and nearby Congo represented a hostile power. While the number of MPLA fighters grew to around 5,000, these problems meant that only a small portion operated within Angola. A late 1971 MPLA offensive mobilizing several thousand fighters to destroy UNITA in the south and attack the Portuguese failed miserably. During the next year combined Portuguese-South African offensives in Angola's Moxico Province drove MPLA insurgents back to their bases in Zambia.

In the early 1970s, the Chinese-armed FNLA comprised around 4,000 combatants based in Zaire (formerly the Belgian Congo and now the Democratic

Republic of the Congo, DRC) who conducted small raids across the border into Angola. Additionally, the FNLA maintained 200–300 fighters in Angola's Dembos Mountains where they tied down a large number of Portuguese troops, and another 300 FNLA rebels deployed along Angola's eastern border countered the MPLA. Initially based in Zambia from where it launched incursions into Angola, the government in Lusaka expelled UNITA in 1967 after a raid on Angola's Benguela railway along which Zambia exported its copper. Lacking a foreign sanctuary or staging area, UNITA remained limited to around 500 insurgents mostly operating in the eastern highlands where Savimbi attempted a Maoist guerrilla war with some Chinese support. Overall, UNITA and FNLA cooperated in their struggles against the MPLA.

In 1970 Portuguese forces in Angola amounted to around 60,000 troops, about one-third of whom comprised local Africans, with most military assets deployed to the north and oil-rich Cabinda. Recruiting captured insurgents who changed sides and among historically marginalized minority Khoisan (Bushmen) communities, Portuguese intelligence formed special small units called Flechas (arrows) who tracked insurgent forces. Portuguese military leaders understood the counterinsurgency theory that emphasized winning the "hearts and minds" of Angolan civilians, but poor training meant that this was not put into practice on the ground. Portugal's unopposed control of the air represented its greatest military advantage in the Angolan war. In the early 1970s, the Portuguese Air Force in Angola comprised 3,000 personnel with 51 ground strike aircraft, 50 reconnaissance aircraft, 16 transport planes, and more than 60 helicopters. These aircraft supplied ground forces, evacuated casualties, destroyed insurgent agricultural production, sprayed defoliant to eliminate bush cover utilized by the rebels, provided combat support, and transported troops. Influenced by French counterinsurgency methods in Algeria, the Portuguese partitioned Angola into grids, each with a garrison and searched areas with airmobile formations. During the early 1970s, the Portuguese confined a million Angolans to protected villages to separate them from the insurgents, and this led to food shortages and further alienation of rural communities. Compared to Lisbon's two other African colonies, Portuguese operations in Angola proved more successful because of the vast size of the country, the deployment of more military resources to protect oil revenue and the divided nationalist organizations.

Mozambique's independence war began in 1960 when Portuguese security forces slaughtered 500 protesters in the northern town of Mueda. In 1962 African nationalist groups from Mozambique, hosted in newly independent and sympathetic Tanganyika (soon renamed Tanzania), formed the Front for the Liberation of Mozambique (FRELIMO), led by Eduardo Mondlane. FRELIMO launched a guerrilla war in northern Mozambique in 1964. Using southern Tanzania as a staging area, FRELIMO received military assistance from the Soviet Union and China, humanitarian aid from Scandinavian countries, and funding and political support from the newly created OAU. In the late 1960s, FRELIMO insurgents established "liberated zones" in northern Mozambique where they provided medical care and education to local people, dispossessed chiefs and landlords, and founded cooperative agricultural projects. Commencing in 1968, FRELIMO expanded the war by moving through friendly Zambia to infiltrate Mozambique's Tete province and, therefore, challenge the Portuguese in the country's central region. With about 8,000 insurgents operating within Mozambique, many small FRELIMO units harried and ambushed Portuguese forces, planted land mines, and acquired supplies and recruits from rural communities. The Cabora Bassa hydroelectric project on the Zambezi River became a focal point for insurgent operations in the late 1960s though they did not attack the dam itself because of its economic importance in building a future independent Mozambique. FRELIMO experienced internal struggled, with African nationalists interested in a local agenda clashing with Marxists who perceived themselves as engaged in a global anti-imperialist and anti-capitalist revolution. After Mondlane's 1969 assassination by the Portuguese who sent him a parcel bomb in Tanzania, the Marxist and pro-Soviet Samora Machel became FRELIMO's top leader.

In 1970, the Portuguese in Mozambique mounted the six-month-long Operation Gordian Knot, comprising an offensive by 35,000 troops with helicopters and artillery led by General Kaulza de Arriaga. The operation aimed to block FRELIMO's infiltration routes from Tanzania, eliminate its Mozambican bases, and pursue insurgents into Tanzania. Although FRELIMO lost with 650 fighters killed and another 1,800 captured, politically worrisome Portuguese casualties and heavy rains limited the operation's impact. During the early 1970s, the Portuguese in Mozambique altered their strategy by Africanizing their security forces, constructing "strategic hamlets" to separate civilians from insurgents, and focusing on small search-and-destroy missions. It was at this point that Portuguese forces in Mozambique began direct cooperation with security forces in adjacent white minority–ruled Rhodesia that also faced an African nationalist insurgency. A FRELIMO offensive in Tete province incited Portuguese reprisals such as the 1972 massacre of several hundred civilians at Wiriyamu. At the same time, FRELIMO mounted operations in southern Mozambique, which caused Portuguese morale to decline. By 1974, FRELIMO controlled one-third of Mozambique and its newly acquired Soviet ground-to-air missiles threatened Portuguese dominance in the sky.

Founded in 1956, the African Party for the Independence of Guinea and Cape Verde (PAIGC) initially embarked on a peaceful political campaign for the independence of these small Portuguese colonies in West Africa. Nevertheless, the 1959 Portuguese massacre of 50 striking dockworkers forced PAIGC leader Amílcar Cabral to flee to the adjacent and recently independent Republic of Guinea, formerly a French colony but now under the Pan-Africanist rule of Sékou Touré, from where he organized an armed struggle for independence. With a broad socialist ideology and seeking to unite mixed-race Cape Verdeans and the Balante people of mainland Guinea-Bissau, PAIGC mobilized rural people within Portuguese territory, and from 1963 it founded "liberated zones" with their own elected local governments. At the same time, PAIGC's military campaign focused on interior rural areas, with insurgents initially politicizing local communities and then conducting guerrilla attacks on Portuguese forces, restricting them to towns. While small groups of rebels attacked Portuguese outposts and economic infrastructure, PAIGC avoided violence against Africans loyal to the colonial state.

The PAIGC armed wing numbered around 6,000 members in 1971. With their staging areas in the Republic of Guinea and eventually Senegal, the insurgents received weapons and training from the Soviet Union, Cuba, and Czechoslovakia. Eventually, PAIGC gained artillery support with Guinean guns firing across the border, and from 1971 the insurgents crewed their own heavy rocket launchers. With a developed medical system, PAIGC fighters wounded in Guinea-Bissau received treatment at field hospitals in neighboring countries, with some evacuated to Eastern Europe.

Although small Guinea-Bissau did not represent an economically profitable Portuguese territory, the regime in Lisbon feared that its loss would undermine control of Angola and Mozambique. The Portuguese military presence in Guinea swelled from a few hundred men in 1963 to 30,000 in 1971 and half of these comprised local people. As insurgent ambushes became common on the territory's roads, Portuguese forces employed the country's many rivers as an alternative transport system. While early Portuguese strategy focused on defending a network of strong points, they reasserted control of major roads and drove rural people into protected villages, which created popular resentment between 1964 and 1968. Unlike the situation in Angola and Mozambique, West Africa contained no allied settler regimes to assist Portuguese forces. In 1968 General Antonio de Spinola, influenced by American counterinsurgency operations in Vietnam, took command of Portuguese forces in Guinea-Bissau and launched a massive development program called "Better Guinea," which included improving roads and constructing schools and hospitals. Participation in the fortified village scheme became voluntary. Simultaneously, Spinola employed newly arrived French-made helicopters to increase the tempo of operations against the insurgents. Although the Portuguese refrained from pursuing insurgents into neighboring states, they mounted a November 1970 amphibious raid called "Operation Green Sea" on Conakry in the Republic of Guinea, rescuing 26 Portuguese prisoners and destroying five PAIGC supply boats. The raid failed in its mission to kill insurgent leaders, generated international diplomatic condemnation, and inspired the Soviet Union to dispatch warships to the coast of the Republic of Guinea to deter future aggression.

In 1973, despite the loss of Cabral to assassination, PAIGC gained the upper hand in the war using Soviet surface-to-air missiles to destroy Portuguese aircraft and Soviet heavy artillery to hammer Portuguese outposts. Portuguese pilots refused to fly, insurgents besieged Portuguese garrisons, and only the capital city and some towns remained under Portuguese control. Spinola resigned as Portuguese military commander in Guinea-Bissau when Lisbon rejected his advice to engage in a peace process started by Senegal's president Leopold Senghor. In September 1973, PAIGC declared the independence of Guinea-Bissau, which was quickly recognized by the United Nations. The total death toll in the Guinea-Bissau independence war remains unknown, though Portugal admitted that 1,875 metropolitan troops were killed, and it is likely that around 6,000 to 8,000 African colonial soldiers and 12,000 rebels lost their lives.

Responding to the great unpopularity and expense of the African wars, the Portuguese armed forces staged a coup in Lisbon in April 1974 that overthrew the authoritarian government of Marcello Caetano, the late Salazar's successor. As a result, Portugal suddenly granted independence to its colonies in Africa. Taking power in Angola and Mozambique, the MPLA and FRELIMO, respectively, faced challenges from other groups that led to postindependence civil wars and military involvement by neighboring states.

Timothy J. Stapleton

See also: Angolan Conflicts; Cabral, Amílcar; Cuba and Africa; Mondlane, Eduardo; Mozambique Civil War; National Front for the Liberation of Angola (FNLA); National Union for the Total Independence of Angola (UNITA); Neto, António Agostinho; Popular Movement for the Liberation of Angola (MPLA); Roberto, Holden Alverto; Savimbi, Jonas; Soviet Military Involvement in Africa.

Further Reading

Cann, John P. *Brown Waters of Africa: Portuguese Riverine Warfare, 1961–1974*. St. Petersburg, FL: Hailer Publishing, 2007.

Cann, John P. *Counter-insurgency in Africa: The Portuguese Way of War, 1961–1974*. Westport, CT: Greenwood, 1997.

Jones, Stewart Lloyd, and Antonio Costa-Pinto, eds. *The Last Empire: Thirty Years of Portuguese Decolonization*. Bristol: Intellect Books, 2003.

Newitt, Malyn. *A History of Mozambique*. London: Hurst, 1995.

Van der Waals, W. S. *The Portugal's War in Angola*. Rivonia: Ashanti, 1993.

Venter, Al J. *Portugal's Guerrilla Wars in Africa: Lisbon's Three Wars in Angola, Mozambique and Guinea-Bissau*. Solihull: Helion, 2013.

Quifangondo, Battle of (1975)

Quifangondo is a small settlement approximately 25 km to the northeast of the Angolan capital, Luanda, and a locale in which of one of the most significant military engagements of the Angolan Civil War took place. What is often seen as the Battle of Quifangondo took place on November 10, 1975, but was the culmination of reconnaissance, skirmishes, and small-scale engagements that had taken place to the northeast of the capital since October 23.

The context: The fighting near Quifangondo in late October and early November 1975 took place between the armed forces of two of the three principal Angolan political groups vying for power in an independent Angola—in this instance, Holden Roberto's FNLA (*Frente Nacional de Libertação de Angola* or National Front for the Liberation of Angola) and the MPLA (*Movimento Popular de Libertação de Angola* or Popular Movement for the Liberation of Angola), by this point led by Agostinho Neto. These two groups, along with Jonas Savimbi's UNITA (*União Nacional para a Independência Total de Angola* or National Union for the Total Independence of Angola), had in January 1975, in the shadow of prior internecine strife, agreed to form a coalition government for an independent Angola on Portuguese withdrawal. However, what amounted to a truce between the rival parties did not last long, and renewed fighting between the competing groups had broken out again by late March 1975. All three groups sought to control as much Angolan territory as possible as formal independence approached and, in particular, to control the capital Luanda, which on the eve of independence was in the hands of the MPLA. By October 23 forces of the MPLA with Cuban advisers had—after an unsuccessful attempt at offensive operations against the FNLA northeast of Luanda—taken up defensive positions on higher ground near the settlement of Quifangondo, behind the River Bengo. Most significant of the subsequent encounters in the area prior to November 10 was an attempt on November 7 by the FNLA, supported by white Portuguese "volunteers" equipped with Panhard armored cars, to advance on Quifangondo through the Lake Panguila area, which was halted by heavy fire from FAPLA. Forces of the FNLA subsequently regrouped for what was supposed to be a decisive push through the area in order to move on the capital prior to independence being declared on November 11.

The opposing sides: The armed forces of the Angolan protagonists at Quifangondo—ELNA (*Exército de Libertação Nacional de Angola* or Army of National Liberation of Angola) for the FNLA and FAPLA (*Forças Armadas Populares de Libertação de Angola* or People's Armed Forces for the Liberation of Angola) for the

MPLA—had only recently been formed as conventional forces and lacked the training, organization, and esprit de corps to make them effective fighting forces in intensive or sustained combat. They were, however, supported on both sides by foreign advisers and troops.

By November 10 forces of the MPLA with Cuban allies could field in the region of 1,300 troops in the Quifangondo area, of whom all but around 200 were FAPLA. FAPLA was equipped predominately with Soviet-supplied equipment, much of it recently arrived. During October alone Soviet aircraft had made up to 40 flights into the Congo with arms and equipment destined for FAPLA. At Quifangondo, on November 10, many of the FAPLA troops committed were nominally part of FAPLA's Ninth Brigade, although it is unclear to what extent this designation had meaning in terms of organization and command and control. A contingent of FAPLA cadres had undergone training and instruction in the Soviet Union from March 1975, with the first contingent returning to Angola in September to participate in the formation of the Ninth Brigade. Troops committed with the Ninth Brigade at Quifangondo included female troops—up to 100 female MPLA activists serving in roles such as radio operators and medics.

The formation of FAPLA's Ninth Brigade was taking place with the assistance of Cuban advisers and technical specialists who had arrived in Angola late that summer. In addition to Cuban advisers and technical personnel, the first Cuban combat units were flown into Angola after the Cuban leadership became aware of South African intervention on the side of those forces opposing the MPLA in mid-October. This Cuban introduction of combat units and additional personnel received the operational code name Carlota. By November 10 Cuban troops in the Quifangondo area included a company of Cuban special forces troops who had arrived in Luanda on the evening of November 9 and had taken up positions behind FAPLA forces on the approaches to Luanda from the northeast by next morning. They were joined by a maximum of six recently arrived BM-21 launch systems and their Cuban crews, the former having only recently been flown into the Congo by the Soviet Union and then shipped by sea to Angola. Cuban specialists and advisers were deployed farther forward with a range of Soviet heavy weapons that included three 76 mm ZIS-4 guns, ZPU-4 antiaircraft guns, 82 mm mortars and a battery of six Grad-P portable rocket launchers. These launchers—first used on November 7—are sometimes confused in the literature with the truck-mounted BM-21 launchers that would first be used against the FNLA on November 10.

By November 10, in addition to Soviet material assistance being provided to FAPLA, Soviet military specialists and advisers had also arrived in the theater. On November 1 the first group of Soviet specialists arrived in the Congo in order to train FAPLA and Cuban troops in the use of the Soviet shoulder-launched Strela-2M antiaircraft missile. These advisers would not arrive in Angola itself until November 16, and despite reports in some accounts to the contrary, not a single Soviet adviser seems to have been involved in the fighting at Quifangondo on November 10.

For the United States and South Africa—keen to see one of the other warring parties likely to be more favorably disposed toward the West take control of Angola—at this point in the Angolan Civil War, hopes were focused on the FNLA and ELNA rather than UNITA. Not only were the FNLA and ELNA financed and equipped in part by the CIA, but they were also receiving material assistance and training from China through Zaire. Zaire was not only a conduit for military assistance to ELNA but was also providing some equipment and troops itself to support the FNLA in its operations in northern Angola. In addition, South African forces and advisers were now engaged in Angola both in the south alongside UNITA and also in the north in support of the FNLA, both as part of Operation Savannah—the South African intervention in Angola that had begun in mid-October. Although South African forces were concentrating their efforts in the south of Angola for obvious reasons of geographical convenience for troops operating from Namibia, a South African artillery battery of three BL 5.5″ guns (G-2) with 20 South African crew members was deployed in support of ELNA forces advancing from the north on Luanda as independence approached.

At Quifangondo, on November 10, the ELNA force of up to 1,200 troops was also supported by a force of Zairian "commandos" up to 700 strong, along with a Zairian artillery battery. The latter would make little contribution to the battle after one gun had blown up killing its crew early in the engagement, with the second disabled by a misfire. Although many of the up to 700 Zairian troops had the elite designation "commando," this does not seem to have been reflected in their quality. Apparently more resolute under the at times heavy fire experienced during the battle were the up to 154 white Portuguese "volunteers," many of whom were native Angolans, and a small number of additional South African advisers and CIA personnel operating alongside the ELNA. These forces were equipped with a significant number of armored and light vehicles from the ELNA inventory that included a number of Panhard ANL-90 and -60 armored cars from Zaire and Jeeps with 106 mm recoilless guns. Additional firepower was theoretically provided by a battery of CIA-supplied 120 mm mortars, but their operability was apparently hampered by the absence of among other items their firing pins. Whereas the troops of the FAPLA were willing to operate under the direction of Cuban personnel with some military experience, the FNLA's leader, Holden Roberto, however, purportedly insisted on directing the advance of the ELNA forces on Luanda himself, choosing a direct assault on the FAPLA positions on November 10.

The battle: In preparation for what was supposed to be the decisive assault on FAPLA in the Quifangondo area, FAPLA positions were subjected to artillery bombardment on November 9 and then again during early morning on November 10. FAPLA was also attacked from the air by the South African Air Force. Although three Canberra bombers did apparently drop a total of four bombs over the area, they were flying so high in order to avoid identification from the ground that in less than ideal conditions their bombs did not land anywhere near their intended targets and went largely unnoticed on the ground. Between 6:00 and 7:00 a.m. in the morning, FNLA forces advanced along the road toward Luanda, led by some of the Portuguese "volunteers" in their armored cars, with the remainder in a second and third echelon—the former made up of the Jeeps with recoilless rifles, and the third, infantry that had been trucked in for part of the way. No attempt was made to send any troops by alternative off-road routes because of poor going for vehicles and apparently even a fear of crocodiles. Very soon the ELNA column came under fire and was halted approximately 100 m short of the key bridge over the Bengo River by FAPLA and Cuban fire that included that from the ZIS-3 anti-tanks guns, with a number of the attacking armored cars either knocked out or abandoned. Although the attacking column was initially subjected to fire from the six Grad-P launchers, what seems to have subsequently proven decisive in routing the ELNA forces was, by many accounts, the intervention of the BM-21 launchers on the FAPLA side, which according to Cuban sources fired in the region of 700 rockets that afternoon from about 1400 hours onward and turned a stalled advance into a rout of the bulk of the attacking force.

Outcomes: Most sources commenting on ELNA losses suggest that several hundred ELNA troops were lost during the fighting at Quifangondo, excluding any losses among the Zairians that certainly included a number of artillerymen. On the MPLA side, casualties were light, with a single FAPLA soldier reported killed along with several wounded. In the aftermath of the rout of the FNLA and Zairian forces that afternoon, the South African artillerymen and advisers were evacuated from Angola by helicopter and subsequently by sea. The fighting at Quifangondo on November 10 and subsequent follow-on operations proved to be crucial in allowing the MPLA to consolidate its hold on power in the northern regions of Angola and legitimate its formation of a government for the newly independent country by maintaining control of the capital at the crucial moment of independence.

Longer-term consequences: The defeat of the FNLA at Quifangondo and in follow-on operations effectively spelled the end of the FNLA as a significant force in Angolan politics and led to a shift in attention for the United States from the FNLA to UNITA as the principal opposition group to the Soviet-backed MPLA government. Continued U.S. and South African support for UNITA meant that it would continue to be a potent opposition to the MPLA government through to the end of the Cold War and indeed beyond.

Alexander Hill

See also: Angolan Armed Forces (FAPLA and FAA); Angolan Conflicts; Cold War in Africa; Cuba and Africa; National Front for the Liberation of Angola (FNLA); Neto, António Agostinho; Popular Movement for the Liberation of Angola (MPLA); Portuguese Africa, Independence Wars (Angola, Mozambique, and Guinea-Bissau); Roberto, Holden Álverto; Soviet Military Involvement in Africa.

Further Reading

Garcia, José M. Ortiz. *Angola from the Trenches*. Translated from Spanish by L. Stradalova. Prague: International Organization of Journalists, 1984.

Gleijeses, Piero. *Conflicting Missions: Havana, Washington and Africa, 1959–1976*. Chapel Hill: University of North Carolina Press, 2002.

Kolomnin, Sergei. *Russkii sled pod Kifangondo*. Moscow: Etnika, 2014.

Shubin, Vladimir. *The Hot "Cold War": The USSR in Southern Africa.* London: Pluto Press, 2008.

Steenkamp, Willem. *Borderstrike: South Africa into Angola 1975–1980.* 3rd ed. Durban: Just Done Productions Publishing, 2006.

Stockwell, John. *In Search of Enemies: A CIA Story.* New York: W. W. Norton, 1978.

Westad, Odd Arne. *The Global Cold War.* Cambridge: Cambridge University Press, 2005.

R

Rally for Congolese Democracy (RCD)

See Congo Wars; Democratic Republic of the Congo (DRC), Continuing Violence in

Refugees in Postcolonial Africa

The refugee crisis in Africa escalated in the decolonization years of the 1950s and 1960s. While there had been anti-colonial wars before, recognition of forced migration in Africa came after the establishment of the United Nations High Commissioner for Refugees (UNHCR). Because conflict in Africa was and still is concentrated in sub-Saharan Africa, the region hosts about 26 percent of the world's refugees. This section explores the refugee crisis in Africa from a historical perspective.

WHAT/WHO IS A REFUGEE?

The UNHCR was established in 1950 for Europeans displaced by the Second World War. Article 6 of the 1951 Convention suggests that the refugee phenomenon was viewed as a crisis that would continue to cause concern after World War II, but expectations were that it would be resolved after reconstruction. As per terms of Article 1 of the 1951 UNHCR Convention, a refugee is defined as any individual who flees their country of nationality out of fear of being persecuted for reasons of religion, race, nationality, or membership of a particular social group and/or political opinion.

When the refugee situation did not improve, the international community made revisions to the convention to include the 1967 Protocol on the Status of Refugees. One of its revisions was the elimination of geographic limitations, which allowed the organization to extend its assistance to other regions, including Africa. In 1969, the Organisation of African Unity (OAU) adopted its own refugee convention. It expanded on the UNHCR criteria to add that a refugee is any individual who "owing to external aggression, occupation, foreign domination or events seriously disturbing public order" in their home country are compelled to flee abroad. The main difference between the two definitions is that countries applying the UNHCR 1951 definition require that the individual in question be under threat or "fear of persecution" for reasons stated above while the OAU definition exists as a formality to allow for objective conditions in an individual's country of origin to act as a determining factor for refugee status.

In Africa, refugee crises began with wars of decolonization of the 1950s–1970s. While some Africans gained independence through peaceful negotiations with the former colonial power, others had to fight for it because the imperial power was not willing to give up control. In the refugee crisis, countries that had negotiated independence ended up as safe havens for people fleeing wars of independence in countries where Africans had to fight for liberation.

INTERNALLY DISPLACED PERSONS (IDPS)

Internally displaced persons are another group of people forced to leave their homes due to strenuous political and safety issues. Unlike refugees, these people remain within the borders of their countries but migrate from one region to another. Oftentimes, this group receives less assistance from the UNHCR and other NGOs as compared to refugees in refugee camps. This is mainly because expectations are that IDP home governments will provide for their basic needs and because authoritarian governments often deny international bodies access to their countries. Opening borders to international organizations exposes the tyrant government to international criticism and possible intervention.

TYPES OF REFUGEES

There are two sets of refugees in Africa: rural refugees and urban refugees. In both cases, refugees tend to flee to areas that allow them to continue with their normal economic and social activities as much as possible. Rural refugees, more often than not, cross borders in very large numbers to a neighboring country. They hardly travel long distances, and they usually relocate to an area that has similar environmental characteristics as their homeland. In some cases, rural refugees already have relatives across the border as colonial borders sometimes cut through ethno-linguistic communities. For example, following annexation into Ethiopia in 1962 and the beginning of independence wars shortly after, Eritreans living in the western region fled to the eastern region of Sudan in Kassala. The distance they had to travel was relatively short; they were reunited with their relatives, and a number of them were already seasonal wage laborers in Kassala.

Urban refugees usually flee in small and scattered groups and have some level of intellectual and professional training. They are usually groups who had already disconnected from the rural area even in their country of origin, and they tend to immigrate to urban areas of their host nation. Urban refugees seek opportunities to utilize their professional training to earn a living and maintain a lifestyle similar to one they had in their country. Life in a refugee camp caters less to their needs and lifestyle, and so when fleeing their country, they move to towns and cities. Because cities are usually located in the central parts of a country, urban refugees often travel longer distances compared to rural refugees. Urban refugees stand better chances of assimilation in their country of asylum because of their professional and intellectual training. They are more independent in the sense that they offer a valuable service in return for wages. Rural refugees, on the other hand, are more dependent on aid they receive from the UNHCR, NGOs, and the host country.

NOTABLE EXAMPLES

As noted earlier, decolonization wars created many refugees in Africa. For example, the Algerian War of Independence, which ended in 1962, created about 200,000 refugees who fled to Tunisia and Morocco. Former Portuguese colonies Angola, Mozambique, and Guinea-Bissau created about 56 percent of Africa's 1,018,000 refugees in the early 1970s. Rhodesia (Zimbabwe), the scene of fighting between a white settler–minority regime and African nationalist insurgents, contributed to the refugee crisis in southern Africa. By 1979, about a quarter of a million Zimbabwean refugees had fled to Mozambique, Botswana, and Zambia. They, however, were repatriated in 1980 with the negotiated end of the conflict and the independence of Zimbabwe under a majority-rule government.

In the Horn of Africa, the struggle between Eritrea and the Ethiopian government forced Eritreans into the eastern region of Sudan. Eritrean refugees added to about 200,000 more refugees from Uganda and about 5,000 from Zaire who were already settled in Sudan. War in the Ogaden region created a wave of refugees fleeing to Somalia between July 1977 and March 1978. About 700,000 refugees from the Ogaden lived in 40 camps in the regions of Hiran, Gedo, Lower Shobelle, and the northwest. The Ugandan civil unrest that took place in 1982 in the Mbarara district forced about 44,000 people to flee to southern Sudan, Zaire, and Rwanda. A majority of the "Ugandan" refugees who fled to Rwanda were actually Rwandan nationals who fled to Uganda during the Rwandan Civil War of 1959. The 1972 genocide against Hutu in Burundi forced more than 200,000 Hutu to flee to Tanzania and Rwanda, which had about 18,000 refugees from Burundi.

From 1959 to 1990, Hutu-majoritarian regimes in Rwanda persecuted the Tutsi minority, leading to the departure of around one million refugees to neighboring countries. At the end of the 1994 genocide against the Tutsi in Rwanda, the takeover by the predominantly Tutsi Rwandan Patriotic Front (RPF) led to a mass exodus of two million Hutu, who feared revenge. About 1.2 million people fled to Zaire, 580,000 to Tanzania, 270,000 to Burundi, and about 10,000 to Uganda. The majority of the Hutu hardliners and members of the defeated Rwandan Armed Forces (ex-FAR) sought refuge in camps in Goma, in eastern Zaire, which was close to the Rwandan border.

REFUGEE CAMPS

Refugees dreaded life in a refugee camp, both rural and urban types. In theory, refugee camps represent temporary settlements that house displaced people until they can safely be repatriated or integrated into their host countries. In reality, refugees remain in refugee camps indefinitely because it is either unsafe to return to their country of origin, and/or the host country is reluctant to assimilate them. Economically, a refugee camp offers little opportunity for one to advance up the socioeconomic ladder. As refugees are still considered foreigners, they hardly receive good quality education and employment opportunities. They are forced to rely heavily on aid provided by the UNHCR and other NGOs, which is always in moderation, given the overcrowding situation in most camps.

The security and safety of refugees in camps has been a major concern throughout the years. Most refugee camps are located in border areas, which have made them prone to outside attacks. For example, Ethiopian refugees in the Walda camp in Kenya expressed this fear of attack by Ethiopian forces. The Walda camp was located about 100 kilometers from the southern border of Ethiopia. A well-equipped Ethiopian force could effortlessly raid the camp to kill the refugees. UNHCR efforts to intervene were minimal and came in the form of creating a fortressed compound in the middle of the camp, surrounded by barbed wire and sandbags. Refugees were still murdered by mysterious killers until the Kenyan government relocated them to the newly established Kakuma camp in 1993.

In other cases, liberation fighters used refugee camps as militarization zones. Refugees have launched cross-border attacks using weapons they smuggled in because of relaxed screening procedures. Tutsi refugees, who fled to Burundi in the early 1960s, were militarized upon arrival and staged failed cross-border attacks into Rwanda. After the genocide and victory of the RPF in 1994, Hutu refugees fled to Zaire and began to militarize from across the border. Between 1994 and 1996, refugee camps in Zaire that accommodated Hutu refugees became training zones of the defeated Rwandan Army and militias. Their activities created a major security problem for the nations involved and the refugees themselves, and this in turn created a difficult dilemma for the UNHCR. The camps in Zaire only demilitarized following cross-border attacks from RPF troops from Rwanda.

CONCLUSION

The refugee crisis in Africa began with the continent's decolonization wars. In the postindependence era, refugees have been generated by new conflicts as well as economic and ecological issues, but the dynamics and movement patterns remain the same. Most countries that had to fight for independence became authoritarian regimes that were corrupt and oppressive on civilian society. The looting of government resources by politicians in power intensified the suffering of ordinary civilians, making fleeing to a slightly better country the only option. A number of refugees who flee to seemingly worse-off countries are usually attracted by the structures of the host country that support the resettlement of refugees in a third country. A majority of Eritrean refugees fled to Sudan because the Sudanese government worked well with UNHCR and other aid agencies that accommodated the needs of refugees. For as long as civil unrest continues in Africa, the refugee crisis will always exist. The only way to fix it is to tackle the underlying causes of forced displacement.

Gorata Sello

See also: Congo Wars; Eritrean War of Independence; Ethiopia: Insurgency and Interstate War; Famine in Postcolonial African Conflicts; Portuguese Africa, Independence Wars (Angola, Mozambique, and Guinea-Bissau); Rwanda, Civil War and Genocide.

Further Reading
Hamrell, Sven, ed. *Refugee Problems in Africa*. New York: Africana Publishing Company, 1981.

Hollenbach, David, ed. *Refugee Rights: Ethics, Advocacy, and Africa.* Washington, DC: Georgetown University Press, 2008.

Muggah, Robert, ed. *No Refuge: The Crisis of Refugee Militarization in Africa.* London: Zed Books, 2006.

United Nations High Commissioner for Refugees. *The State of the World's Refugees 2000: Fifty Years of Humanitarian Action.* Oxford: Oxford University Press, 2000.

Revolutionary United Front (RUF)

The Revolutionary United Front (RUF) first emerged as a dedicated entity in 1991. The group waged a 11-year civil war against the government of Sierra Leone that resulted in tens of thousands of deaths and the displacement of more than two million people. With the help of the United Nations (UN), the RUF was disarmed and demobilized in 2002.

The RUF was founded as a rebel group by former army corporal Foday Sankoh in response to one-party rule in Sierra Leone. It began an active insurgency in Sierra Leone in March 1991, not long after guerrilla leader Charles Taylor started a civil war in neighboring Liberia in late 1989. Sankoh is believed to have received training in Libya along with Taylor, who himself is believed to have supported the RUF as a proxy to gain control over Sierra Leone's diamond trade. Huge quantities of arms eventually made their way across the Liberian border into Sierra Leone, giving the RUF the firepower to fight its insurgency.

Although it clashed frequently with government troops, the RUF's methods of operation consisted primarily of attacks on villages and other civilian targets. The group is thought to have killed thousands during its operational life in addition to displacing millions of others, and it became infamous for its use of child soldiers and the trademark of severing the hands, feet, and limbs of its victims. Although the RUF never clearly enunciated its objectives, witnesses who lived among the group's members say they were characterized by a hybrid ideology mixing agrarian democracy with revolutionary socialism.

In early 1995 the RUF rejected calls by the Organisation of African Unity (OAU), the UN, and the British Commonwealth to hold a peace summit with the government of President Valentine Strasser. In early 1996, however, shortly after Strasser's ouster in a military coup, the rebels announced a unilateral one-week cease-fire and declared their willingness to open talks with the new administration of Julius Maada Bio. Negotiations were held during February 25–March 3, 1996, but amounted to nothing. In reaction, the RUF commenced a campaign of intimidation to disrupt the nation's first-ever multiparty elections, declaring that all balloting should be postponed until after a peace agreement was reached. It was at this time, during the run-up to the second round of elections in mid-March, that the RUF began its infamous practice of dismemberment, ostensibly as a way of terrorizing people into not voting.

Despite this intimidation, elections proceeded in April, and former UN diplomat Ahmed Tejan Kabbah returned as president. In May 1997, however, Kabbah was ousted in a coup led by Major Johnny Paul Koroma, reportedly because he had failed to establish a lasting peace with the RUF. Sankoh declared the overthrow a victory for Sierra Leone and announced that he would work with the new army regime to "make a revolution." His group subsequently joined forces with Koroma, and together they fought Nigerian troops that had been deployed in an effort to reverse the coup. As a reward, Sankoh and the RUF were invited to join in a "broad-based government of national unity."

In February 1998 a Nigerian-led contingent of Economic Community of West African States (ECOWAS) forces successfully managed to restore Kabbah to power, and the RUF returned to guerrilla war tactics. After a year of increasingly brutal and bloody conflict, the Sierra Leone government and RUF leaders reached a peace settlement that provided an amnesty for all former rebel fighters and guaranteed the group four seats in the cabinet. A UN peacekeeping mission to Sierra Leone was established (UN Mission in Sierra Leone, or UNAMSIL) to oversee the accord, and in November 1999 the RUF registered as an official political party.

Despite this ostensible progress, however, the RUF refused to disarm or relinquish control of the diamond-mining centers that financed the rebel movement and enriched its leaders (both of which were required as part of the peace agreement). Tensions were exacerbated as a result of clashes between UNAMSIL forces and RUF fighters that led to the deaths of several UN troops and the capture of hundreds more. Matters came to a head in May 2000 when Sankoh was arrested along with other senior rebel commanders for failing to abide by the terms of the November 1999 accord; all were removed from their cabinet posts.

By the end of May 2000, with Sankoh arrested and detained in a secret location, the RUF returned to full-scale war against the Sierra Leonean Army. A cease-fire was signed in Abuja in November 2000 but had little consequence. Another settlement was concluded in May 2001, and this one gradually took hold. President Kabbah declared the civil war officially over in January 2002, after which some 72,000 rebel combatants were disarmed and demobilized. The political arm of the RUF participated in legislative elections four months later but failed to win a single seat.

Following the end of the conflict, the UN set up a special court to try the rebel commanders who bore the greatest responsibility for inflicting crimes against humanity and engaging in other serious violations of international law. Indictments were duly issued against Sankoh and another senior RUF member, Sam "Mosquito" Bockarie, in March 2003. The latter fled to Liberia, where he was assassinated in May; the former died in prison of a heart attack in July that same year. The withdrawal of UNAMSIL forces from Sierra Leone was completed in 2005.

Edward F. Mickolus

See also: British Military Involvement in Postcolonial Africa; Child Soldiers in Africa; Diamonds and Conflict in Postcolonial Africa; ECOWAS Military Interventions; Liberian Civil Wars; Peacekeeping in Africa; Sankoh, Foday Saybana; Sierra Leone Civil War; Taylor, Charles McArthur Ghankay.

Further Reading

Denon, Myriam. *Child Soldiers: Sierra Leone's Revolutionary United Front*. Cambridge: Cambridge University Press, 2010.

Gberie, Lansana. *A Dirty War in West Africa: The RUF and the Destruction of Sierra Leone*. London: Hurst, 2005.

Hoffman, Danny. *The War Machines: Young Men and Violence in Sierra Leone and Liberia*. Durham: Duke University Press, 2011.

Surhone, Lam, ed. *Sierra Leone Civil War: Revolutionary United Front, Foday Sankoh, Joseph Mamoh, Recreational Drugs, Child Soldiers*. Beau Bassin: Betascript, 2010.

Roberto, Holden Álverto (1923–2007)

Holden Álverto Roberto was an Angolan insurgent leader and founder of the Frente Nacional de Libertação de Angola (FNLA, National Front for the Liberation of Angola).

Holden Álverto Roberto was born on January 12, 1923, in São Salvador, Angola, then a Portuguese colony. He moved with his family to Leopoldville (now Kinhasa) in the Belgium Congo (present-day Democratic Republic of the Congo) and in 1940 graduated from a Baptist missionary school. For the next eight years, Roberto worked for the Belgian Finance Ministry in the Congo. In 1951, he visited Angola, where he witnessed the mistreatment of an old man by the Portuguese authorities, which Roberto said aroused him politically.

In July 1956 Roberto and Barros Necaca founded the Union of Peoples of Northern Angola, subsequently renamed the Union of Peoples of Angola. In December 1958, Roberto represented Angola at the Ghana-sponsored All-African People's Congress, where he also met a number of future African leaders. In the 1950s, the U.S. government paid Roberto a small stipend for intelligence collection.

António Agostinho Neto's Movimento Popular de Libertação de Angola (MPLA, Popular Movement for the Liberation of Angola) initiated the Angolan Insurgency in January 1961. That March, having organized militants among the Bakongo ethnic group of northern Angola, Roberto led some 4,000–5,000 men from Kinshasa during attacks against Portuguese border posts and farms in Angola, killing all the Portuguese they encountered. In March 1962 Roberto formed the FNLA. Jonas Savimbi, who had joined Roberto's movement the year before, became foreign minister in Roberto's self-proclaimed Revolutionary Government of Angola in Exile. Roberto received the support of the president of Zaire (now the Democratic Republic of the Congo) Mobutu Sese Seko, when he divorced his wife and then married a woman from Mobuto's wife's village. Roberto also received some aid from Israel.

In 1964, Savimbi broke with Roberto when the latter refused to expand his movement beyond the Bakongo. Savimbi founded the União Nacional para a Independência Total de Angola (UNITA, the National Union for the Total Independence of Angola). Thus, there were three groups—the MPLA, the FNLA, and UNITA—fighting the Portuguese in Angola. The FNLA largely operated from bases in Zaire into Angola and claimed to have some 10,000 men in 1972.

On the eve of Angolan independence in 1975, the FNLA and UNITA formed an alliance, and Mobuto sent Zairean forces into the country in a bid to block the leftist MPLA from taking power. He hoped thereby to establish a pro-Kinshasa government. This bid failed thanks to a Soviet airlift of Cuban troops, who defeated the FNLA, UNITA, and Zairean forces.

A Cold War proxy battle ensued between the Marxist MPLA government of Angola, which enjoyed the support of the Soviet Union and Cuba, and the allegedly anti-communist FNLA and UNITA received assistance from the United States, Zaire, and China. In 1991 both UNITA and FNLA agreed to the Bicesse Accords, which allowed Roberto to return to Angola and permitted him to run for president, but he received only 2 percent of the vote. Roberto died in Luanda on August 2, 2007. Upon his death, the Angolan government recognized him as one of the leaders of the "national liberation struggle."

Spencer C. Tucker

See also: Angolan Conflicts; Cold War in Africa; Congo Crisis; Cuba and Africa; Mobutu Sese Seko; National Front for the Liberation of Angola (FNLA); National Union for the Total Independence of Angola (UNITA); Neto, António Agostinho; Popular Movement for the Liberation of Angola (MPLA); Portuguese Africa, Independence Wars (Angola, Mozambique, and Guinea-Bissau); Quifangondo, Battle of; Soviet Military Involvement in Africa; U.S. Military Involvement in Africa.

Further Reading

James, W. Martin. *Historical Dictionary of Angola*. Lanham, MD: Scarecrow Press, 2011.

James, W. Martin. *A Political History of the War in Angola, 1974–1990*. London: Transaction Publishers, 2011.

Weigert, Stephen. *Angola: A Modern Military History, 1961–2002*. New York: Palgrave Macmillan, 2011.

Rwanda, Civil War and Genocide (1990–1994)

While Rwanda's Belgian colonial rulers favored the Tutsi minority, whom they considered a superior race, a Hutu counter-elite took power in 1959 in the context of decolonization and established a majoritarian republic that gained independence in 1962. With Tutsi-educated elites turning to African nationalism and socialism in the 1950s, the Belgians began to see the conservative and anti-communist Hutu leaders as more compliant postcolonial partners. In the early 1960s an exiled Rwandan Tutsi insurgent movement developed in neighboring countries, particularly in Burundi, where local Tutsi retained power over the Hutu majority, and acquired some support from communist China. However, the Belgian-led Rwandan Hutu military repelled armed incursions by exiled Tutsi fighters, and this incited 1964 revenge massacres of Tutsi inside Rwanda, which many described as genocide. Although hundreds of thousands of Rwandan Tutsi fled the country, given massacres and discrimination from the 1960s to 1980s, the exiled Tutsi movement remained in disarray. A new generation of Rwandan Tutsi refugees in Uganda joined Yoweri Museveni's National Resistance Army (NRA) in the early 1980s, fighting an insurgency in southern Uganda and then continued into the Ugandan state military after Museveni's 1986 takeover. Facing xenophobia in Uganda, including demotion from senior military positions, these Rwandan-Ugandan soldiers formed the exiled Rwandan Patriotic Front (RPF) and decided to use their military skills and resources to seize control of their home country.

In early October 1990, around 2,500 exiled Rwandan Tutsi soldiers commanded by Major General Fred Rwigyema deserted the Ugandan Army with their weapons and equipment and invaded neighboring Rwanda. The 5,200-strong Rwanda Armed Forces (FAR) possessed better equipment such as armored vehicles and helicopters but lacked combat experience and was surprised by the incursion. As such, the RPF force rapidly advanced 60 kilometers south into Rwanda but was slowed by extended supply lines, roads choked by refugees, and the murder of Rwigyema by two fellow officers during an argument over strategy. The entirely Hutu FAR staged a fake rebel attack on Kigali to justify its apprehension and murder of Tutsi civilians. Given its defense agreement with the Rwandan regime of President Juvénal Habyarimana, France sent weapons to the FAR and mounted Operation Noroit in which 500 French paratroopers arrived to secure Kigali and assist Rwandan government troops. In addition, Zaire's dictator Mobutu Sese Seko dispatched 1,000 soldiers to assist his ally Habyarimana, but they were quickly sent back home after abusing Rwandan civilians.

Assisted by the French military, the FAR launched a counteroffensive in early October, driving the RPF to Akagera National Park in northeast Rwanda. Hastily returning from military training in the United States, Paul Kagame assumed command of the RPF and led it into the Virunga Mountains, where it reorganized and started a hit-and-run war against the Rwandan state that responded by murdering more Tutsi civilians. With recruits from the Rwandan Tutsi diaspora flocking to the RPF, the rebel force grew from 5,000 in early 1991 to 12,000 in late 1992 to 25,000 in April 1994. The RPF acquired supplies from Ugandan military officers, who sympathized with their former colleagues, and bought weapons from bankrupt former Soviet republics with money raised by the Rwandan Tutsi diaspora. Conscripting Hutu peasants and unemployed urban youth, the FAR swelled from 5,200 in October 1990 to 30,000 in late 1991 to 50,000 by the middle of 1992. The minimal training provided to FAR troops meant that French military advisers played an active role in combat operations. A series of negotiations and cease-fires failed as the FAR remained confident in French military assistance, and the RPF hid safely in its Virunga stronghold. While a shaky cease-fire came into effect in July 1992, a massacre of 300 Tutsi inspired the RPF to go on the offensive in February 1993, doubling the size of the territory it controlled. RPF units approached within 23 kilometers of Kigali but stopped, as they did not want direct conflict with French forces in the city.

In April 1993 both sides resumed talks in Arusha, Tanzania, where they eventually reached an agreement. While the Rwandan state was militarily exhausted and pressured by the UN to end the conflict, the RPF worried about its perceived legitimacy, as their occupied territory was almost uninhabited, given the departure of terrified Hutu civilians. In the Arusha Accords of August 1993, the Habyarimana government, moderate Rwandan opposition parties, and the rebel RPF promised to form a combined transitional government and a new integrated state security force and to permit almost one million Tutsi exiles to return home.

The United Nations Assistance Mission in Rwanda (UNAMIR), a 2,500-strong international force, but with only two combat-capable battalions, arrived in Rwanda to monitor the peace process. Nevertheless, Hutu extremists decried the deal and spread anti-Tutsi hatred through newspapers and radio. In early April 1994 Habyarimana's presidential aircraft was shot down while approaching Kigali airport, and FAR elements and Hutu militias such as the Interahamwe ("those who work together") and Impunzamugambi ("those with a common goal") embarked on the extermination of the Tutsi minority so as to avoid sharing power. The subsequent 100 days of mass violence resulted in the deaths of 800,000 people in what represented the world's deadliest genocide since 1945. During the initial days of the genocide, France mounted Operation Amaryllis and the European Union mounted Operation Silverback that flew their citizens out of Kigali. The murder of 10 Belgian peacekeepers by FAR soldiers prompted Belgium to withdraw from UNAMIR, further weakening the force. One of the few countries with the capability to intervene to stop the genocide, the United States vacillated, given its recent military disaster in Somalia and Rwanda's lack of strategic position or valuable resources. With UNAMIR incapable of stopping the slaughter, Kagame's RPF very quickly mounted an aggressive three-pronged offensive that drove back the FAR and took control of the entire country by the end of July. During Operation Turquoise, the French military briefly established an occupied zone in southwestern Rwanda officially meant to given the UN time to prepare a new force and provide safety to civilians. In reality, however, the French were not a neutral power, and the Turquoise zone served as an escape route for retreating elements of the FAR and Hutu militias who killed Tutsi on their way into eastern Zaire. The RPF seized power in Rwanda, and its fighters formed the new national army. The presence of exiled Rwandan Hutu fighters in eastern Zaire/Democratic Republic of the Congo (DRC) provided context for two RPF invasions of that country in the late 1990s during which stolen minerals fueled Rwanda's economic miracle. Initially serving as the deputy president and defense minister of Rwanda's new government, Kagame became president in 2000, presiding over an authoritarian RPF state in which political opposition leaders were imprisoned for harboring alleged genocide ideology or simply killed, or they fled the country.

Timothy J. Stapleton

See also: Belgian Military Intervention in Africa; Canadian Military Involvement in Africa; Congo Wars; French Military Involvement in Postcolonial Africa; Genocide in Africa; Habyarimana, Juvénal; Hutu Power Movements; Kagame, Paul; Mobutu Sese Seko; Peacekeeping in Africa; Refugees in Postcolonial Africa; Rwandan Patriotic Front (RPF); Uganda's Civil War: The Bush War.

Further Reading

Des Forges, Alison. *Leave None to Tell the Story: Genocide in Rwanda*. New York: Human Rights Watch, 1999.

Guichaoua, Andre. *From War to Genocide: Criminal Politics in Rwanda, 1990–94*. Madison: University of Wisconsin Press, 2015.

Mamdani, Mahmood. *When Victims Become Killers: Colonialism, Nativism and the Genocide in Rwanda*. Princeton, NJ: Princeton University Press, 2001.

Melvern, Linda. *Conspiracy to Murder: The Rwanda Genocide*. London: Verso, 2006.

Prunier, Gerard. *The Rwanda Crisis: History of a Genocide*. New York: Columbia University Press, 1995.
Wallis, Andrew. *Silent Accomplice: The Untold Story of France's Role in the Rwandan Genocide*. London: I.B. Tauris, 2006.

Rwandan Patriotic Front (RPF)

With the 1959 takeover by Hutu Power leaders in Rwanda, members of the Tutsi minority began leaving the country, with some forming armed groups in neighboring states such as Burundi, Tanganyika (Tanzania from 1964), Uganda, and the Belgian Congo (independent Congo from 1960). During the early 1960s, the Rwandan Tutsi exiled movement remained divided among monarchists, socialists, and apolitical militants, with China providing some military training and weapons. A series of armed incursions into Rwanda by these Tutsi fighters, including a major invasion attempt in December 1963 from Burundi, Uganda, and the Congo, experienced decisive defeat at the hands of the Belgian-led Rwandan Army and incited revenge massacres of Tutsi civilians inside the country, including the first genocide against the Tutsi in 1964. Although the Tutsi exiles conducted a few raids into Rwanda in 1966, the movement collapsed, given leadership disputes and its involvement in the failed uprising in the eastern Congo. With the Tutsi continuing to leave Rwanda, the number of exiles amounted to 360,000 in 1964 and at least 500,000 in the 1980s. In Uganda, the xenophobia encountered by Rwandan Tutsi exiles prompted some to join the Ugandan exile movement in Tanzania led by Yoweri Museveni and that joined with the 1979 Tanzanian People's Defence Force (TPDF) invasion of Uganda that toppled Idi Amin. In 1979, after the fall of Amin, Rwandan exiles in Uganda formed a self-help group called the Rwandese Refugee Welfare Association (RRWA), and the next year the group changed its name to the Rwandese Alliance for National Unity (RANU), reflecting a more militant stance, including an eventual return to Rwanda. The return to power of Ugandan president Milton Obote at the end of 1980 prompted RANU to relocate to Nairobi, Kenya, and recruit Tutsi exiles for Museveni's new movement called the National Resistance Army (NRA) that launched an insurgency in southern Uganda. Famously, the small NRA unit that opened the war in 1981 by raiding a police station included Museveni and Rwandans Fred Rwigyema and Paul Kagame, who went on to become prominent leaders within the NRA. When the NRA seized power in Uganda in 1986, its total of 14,000 fighters included 4,000 Rwandans, representing some of the force's most experienced soldiers. Subsequently, these Rwandan troops became members of the Ugandan military, with many holding high positions such as Major General Rwigyema as deputy army commander and deputy defense minister. In 1987, RANU moved its headquarters back to Uganda and eventually changed its name to the Rwandan Patriotic Front (RPF), with Rwigyema as president. A 1988 conference of Rwandan exiles held in Washington, DC, resolved to demand the "right of return" to their motherland.

Given continued xenophobia in Uganda that motivated the Museveni government to sideline Rwandan exiles, Rwigyema-led 2,500 Rwandan exiled soldiers deserted the Ugandan Army, taking their weapons and equipment, and invaded

Rwanda in September 1990. Rwigyema's force constituted itself as the RPF and took the Kinyarwanda name "Inkotanyi," meaning "those who struggle together." Despite a stunningly successful initial advance into Rwanda, the invasion ground to a halt, given Rwigyema's murder by some of his own officers over an argument about strategy and a French military intervention to bolster the Armed Forces of Rwanda (FAR.) The RPF retreated to the mountainous Virunga National Park in northern Rwanda, and Kagame returned from a training course in the United States, where he had been sent as a Ugandan officer, to take command of the rebel army. After the war stalemated, the RPF entered negotiations that resulted in the 1993 Arusha Accord that aimed to create a national unity government. With the peace plan aborted by the start of the genocide against the Tutsi in April 1994, and the lack of action by United Nations peacekeepers and the international community, Kagame's RPF quickly went on the offensive, driving back the FAR and Hutu militias and occupying the entire country by July. In the wake of genocide, the RPF and several moderate Rwandan political parties formed a government with Hutu RPF member Pasteur Bizimungu as president. Nevertheless, the RPF emerged as the dominant faction, with Kagame as defense minister and vice president, and his former rebels transformed into state military called the Rwandan Patriotic Army (RPA). In 2000, after the resignation and assassination of some government officials who criticized RPF violence, Kagame assumed the presidency, with the resignation of Bizimungu who formed an opposition party and then was imprisoned. Under an authoritarian RPF regime, Rwanda created strict anti-genocide ideology laws used to imprison critics of the government, with Kagame continually reelected as president with an unrealistically high 95 percent or more of the popular vote. During the late 1990s, the RPA invaded neighboring Zaire/Democratic Republic of the Congo (DRC), pursuing exiled Hutu Power fighters but also extracting valuable resources used to fuel Rwandan economic success.

Timothy J. Stapleton

See also: Congo Wars; Kagame, Paul; Museveni, Yoweri; National Resistance Army (NRA); Rwanda, Civil War and Genocide; Uganda's Civil War: The Bush War.

Further Reading

Mamdani, Mahmood. *When Victims Become Killers: Colonialism, Nativism and the Genocide in Rwanda*. Princeton, NJ: Princeton University Press, 2001.

Prunier, Gerard. *Africa's World War: Congo, the Rwanda Genocide and the Making of a Continental Catastrophe*. Oxford: Oxford University Press, 2009.

Prunier, Gerard. *The Rwanda Crisis: History of a Genocide*. New York: Columbia University Press, 1995.

S

Sankara, Thomas (1949–1987)

On October 15, 1987, Blaise Compaoré—founder of Burkina Faso's Congress for Democracy and Progress—staged a coup d'état against President Thomas Sankara. After shooting him to death, with a dozen other government officials, the assassins dismembered Sankara's corpse and buried the remains in in an unmarked grave. Sankara's widow and two children fled the country, and Compaoré installed himself as president holding that position until overthrown by a popular uprising in 2014. Observer Ulises Estrada, former colleague of South American revolutionary Che Guevara, expressed his conviction that "the hand of [Sankara's] assassins was guided by imperialism, which could not allow a man with the ideas and actions of Sankara to lead a country on a continent so exploited for hundreds of years by international imperialism, colonialism, and neocolonial governments that do their bidding."

Thomas Sankara was born on December 21, 1949, at Yako, French Upper Volta, a colony of French West Africa. His parents were Roman Catholics of the Silmi-Mossi ethnic group, considered lower-class members of the tribal caste system, chiefly farmers, smiths, and leatherworkers. Sankara's father, a gendarme who fought with the Free French in World War II and was captured by Nazis, urged his son to train for the priesthood after graduating from high school in Bobo-Dioulasso, but Thomas joined the army instead, enlisting at age 19. A year later, he was dispatched for officer's training at Antisrabe, Madagascar. There, Sankara witnessed mass demonstrations against the state, forcing President Philibert Tsiranana's resignation in October 1972. At the same time, Sankara was exposed for the first time to works by Karl Marx, Friedrich Engels, and Vladimir Lenin.

Their message sank in, but Sankara still required further impetus to break with the establishment of his homeland. Upper Volta had achieved autonomy as a self-governing colony within the French Community in December 1958, followed by full independence from France in August 1960. Soon after Sankara returned from training in Madagascar, he was thrown into a Border War with the neighboring Republic of Mali, formerly part of French Sudan. Though decorated for his valor in that conflict, Sankara regarded the war as "useless and unjust." Still, he remained in uniform, rising by 1976 to direct the elite Commando Training Center at Pô, in Nahouri Province. That same year, during advanced training in Morocco, he met and befriended another native officer, 25-year-old Blaise Compaoré.

Politics at home remained unstable. Major General Aboubakar Sangoulé Lamizana claimed the presidency of Upper Volta in January 1966, after mass strikes and demonstrations unseated predecessor Maurice Yaméogo. Lamizana led a "provisional military government" until a new constitution was ratified in June 1970 and then served as president until November 25, 1980, when Colonel Saye Zerbo ousted him at gunpoint, suspended the constitution, and ruled in the name of a Military Committee of Recovery for National Progress. Quickly dissatisfied with Zerbo and his junta, Sankara and Compaoré organized a cover *Regroupement des officiers communistes* (Communist Officers' Group) within the army, plotting the dictator's downfall.

Before they could strike at Zerbo, he was replaced by Major Jean-Baptiste Ouédraogo in November 1982. Their coup d'état proceeded, with a new target, on August 4, 1983, unseating Ouédraogo and installing Sankara as president at age 33. His stated goal was to eradicate corruption and to cast aside the remnants of French colonial domination. To symbolize that sweeping change, he renamed Upper Volta as Burkina Faso ("Land of Upright Men") on August 4, 1984. The new nation shunned foreign aid, nationalized all land and mineral wealth, vaccinated 2.5 million children against deadly diseases, and planted more than 10 million trees to halt the spread of the Sahara Desert, while severing connections to the World Bank and International Monetary Fund (IMF). Expanding into social issues, Sankara outlawed forced marriage, polygamy, and female circumcision, appointed women to government posts, and encouraged them to stay in school if pregnant. Sankara's reforms—coupled with his penchant for guitar playing and motorcycle riding—soon earned him the nickname of "Africa's Che Guevara."

Inevitably, Sankara's new programs made enemies. They included quasi-feudal landlords stripped of property, tribal chiefs deprived of tribute payments and obligatory labor, corrupt officials driven from their public offices, and "lazy workers" held for trial before local revolutionary tribunals. An admirer of both Che Guevara and Fidel Castro, Sankara also challenged established military authority by creating and arming Cuban-style Committees for the Defense of the Revolution. Conscious of his adversaries, Sankara gave a public address six days before his slaying—on the 20th anniversary of Che Guevara's assassination—declaring that "while revolutionaries as individuals can be murdered, you cannot kill ideas."

It was all too much for Blaise Compaoré, who justified his October 1987 coup as a bid to "rectify" Burkina Faso's revolution. Compaoré instantly reversed the nationalization of land and natural resources, welcomed new investment from the IMF and World Bank to assist the country's "shattered" economy, and generally scrapped the bulk of Sankara's reforms. Compaoré initially ruled as one of a triumvirate, including cohorts Henri Zongo and Jean-Baptiste Boukary Lingani and then had both arrested and shot in September 1989 on charges of conspiring to overthrow the government. Subsequently, Compaoré was elected president in 1991 (with only 25 percent of the electorate voting) and then won reelection in 1998. A constitutional amendment, passed in 2000, limited the president to a five-year term, but Compaoré was exempted from the rule on grounds of his incumbency. Reelected once again in November 2005, Compaoré survived an army mutiny in April 2011 but was overthrown during a popular revolution in 2014. In 2015, Sankara's body was exhumed, confirming that he had been shot over a dozen times. In 2021, the government of Burkina Faso charged Compaoré, who was in exile, with the murder of Sankara.

Michael Newton

See also: Christmas War; Cold War in Africa; Coups and Military Regimes in Africa; Cuba and Africa.

Further Reading

Cudjoe, Alfred. *Who Killed Sankara?* Berkeley: University of California Press, 1988.

Englebert, Pierre. *Burkina Faso: Unsteady Statehood in West Africa*. New York: Routledge, 2018.

Harsch, Ernest. *Thomas Sankara: An African Revolutionary*. Athens: Ohio University Press, 2014.

Kongo, Jean-Claude, and Leo Zeilig. *Thomas Sankara*. Cape Town: National Institute for the Humanities and Social Sciences, 2017.

Manson, Katrina, and James Knight. *Burkina Faso*. Guilford, CT: Pequot Press, 2006.

Peterson, Brian. *Thomas Sankara: A Revolutionary in Cold War Africa*. Bloomington: Indiana University Press, 2021.

Sankara, Thomas. *Thomas Sankara Speaks: The Burkina Faso Revolution: 1983–87*. New York: Pathfinder, 2007.

Sankoh, Foday Saybana (1937–2003)

Foday Sankoh was born in Masang Mayoso in the Tonkolili District of Sierra Leone on October 17, 1937. By all accounts, his childhood was not unlike those of his peers. He joined the Sierra Leonean Army in 1956, five years before Sierra Leone's independence from Great Britain. His only promotion was to corporal, which he earned in 1962. In 1963 Sankoh was a part of Sierra Leone's military contingent sent to the Congo. This was a volatile time in the Congo's history, as it had just gained independence from Belgium in 1960, and its first prime minister, Patrice Lumumba, had been murdered in 1961. Sankoh would soon become disillusioned with the UN mission and the role of foreign entities operating in the Congo due to what he perceived as neocolonialism.

Disillusionment followed Sankoh upon his return to Sierra Leone. He attempted to enter politics but was unsuccessful due to the incestuous nature of Sierra Leone's political parties, which favored the ruling party. In 1971 he was arrested for his role in an attempted overthrow of President Siaka Stevens. He received a six-year sentence, which he served at the Pedamba Road Prison in Freetown. His revolutionary zeal was hardened in prison. While incarcerated, Sankoh read Mao Tse-tung's ideology extensively, in the process developing his own philosophy on governance. Accordingly, he rejected Sierra Leone's version of civilian rule and military dictatorship. In time, Sankoh began to recruit disaffected Sierra Leoneans to his cause, a "people's" overthrow of the existing political order. He also established his revolutionary headquarters in Bo, Sierra Leone's provincial capital city, in the country's southern region.

Sankoh's opportunity to realize his insurgency began when he forged a partnership with Libya's leader Colonel Muammar Gaddafi. Gaddafi was an avid supporter of anti-colonial and anti-Western insurgencies. He had established training camps in Libya to train revolutionary cadres and erstwhile fellow travelers. Sankoh and his group of Sierra Leonean revolutionaries were welcomed in Libya where they began combat training and instructions on anti-Western revolutionary ideology in 1988. It was also in Libya that Sankoh met Charles Taylor, who would become the leader of the National Patriotic Front of Liberia (NPFL). In Libya, both men recognized their shared political ideals and mutual goal, which was to topple their respective governments. Their acquaintance would lead to an alliance that would eventually lead to their demise.

Sankoh and the Revolutionary United Front (RUF) launched their insurgency from northwest Liberia into southeast Sierra Leone on March 23, 1991. The war in Sierra Leone exhibited many of the same violent characteristics as the conflict in Liberia, which began with the NPFL incursion into Liberia from the Ivory Coast on Christmas Eve, 1989. Like the war in Liberia, it was interspersed with periods of political intrigue. As the war lulled, Sankoh was offered a cabinet-level position, equivalent to the country's vice president, as Sierra Leone's minister of natural resources in 1997.

Whatever harmony existed between Sankoh and the government was undermined by Sankoh when he refused the government's decision to allow the deployment of UN soldiers into Sierra Leone in 1999. The RUF also rejected the plan. Soon after, an arrest warrant was issued for Sankoh, after which a group of angry citizens apprehended him with the assistance of Nigerian soldiers. He was handed over to a UN tribunal and indicted on various war crimes charges. Sankoh died on July 29, 2003 while in custody awaiting his trial.

Jacien Carr

See also: Child Soldiers in Africa; Diamonds and Conflict in Postcolonial Africa; ECOWAS Military Interventions; Gaddafi, Muammar; Liberian Civil Wars; Peacekeeping in Africa; Sierra Leone Civil War; Taylor, Charles McArthur Ghankay.

Further Reading

Ellis, Stephen. *The Mask of Anarchy: The Destruction of Liberia and the Religious Dimension of an African Civil War.* New York: New York University Press, 2001.

Hoffman, Danny. *The War Machines: Young Men and Violence in Sierra Leone and Liberia.* Durham: Duke University Press, 2011.

Waugh, Colin. *Charles Taylor and Liberia: Ambition and Atrocity in Africa's Lone Star State.* London: Zed Books, 2011.

Zack-Williams, Tunde. *When the State Fails: Studies on Intervention in the Sierra Leone Civil War.* London: Pluto Press, 2012.

Savimbi, Jonas (1934–2002)

Jonas Savimbi was president of the National Union for the Total Independence of Angola (*Uniao Nacional para a Independencia Total de Angola*—UNITA), the rebel group–turned–political party that fought a long civil war against the Angolan government. Savimbi was killed in an engagement with government forces in February 2002.

Born in 1934, Jonas Malheiro Savimbi went to Protestant missionary schools and later received a scholarship to continue his education in Lisbon, Portugal, where he studied political science and law. He was expelled from Portugal in 1959 after speaking out against colonial rule and afterward spent a short time in China studying guerrilla warfare. Savimbi received his higher education at Switzerland's University of Fribourg and University of Lausanne, receiving an honors degree in political science from the latter institution in 1965. His involvement in politics led him to become foreign minister in the Revolutionary Government of Angola in Exile from 1962 to 1964. In November 1974 he was named president of an unrecognized self-proclaimed nation, the People's Democratic Republic of Angola, but finding that his political agenda was generally being ignored, he turned to guerrilla warfare.

Savimbi founded UNITA in 1966 and led the group almost single-handedly from its origin as an anti-Portuguese insurgent organization to its recognition as a legitimate political force in Angola in 1992. Upon Angola's independence from Portugal in 1975, Savimbi cooperated with invading South African forces in a failed attempt to seize power. During the late 1970s and 1980s, Savimbi's movement remained in southern Angola where it received South African and American assistance in its war against the ruling Popular Movement for the Liberation of Angola (MPLA) backed by Cuba and the Soviet Union. In 1986, in the context of the Cold War, he met with U.S. president Ronald Reagan in Washington, DC, in a highly publicized visit during which he was treated as a top-level foreign dignitary. The meeting resulted in a U.S. promise to provide covert military assistance for UNITA's continuing fight against the Luanda government, apparently based on Washington's view of Savimbi as a "freedom fighter" against the Marxist MPLA.

With the end of the Cold War phase of Angola's civil war, Savimbi and the government of President Jose Eduardo dos Santos came to terms that allowed for United Nations–supervised elections to be held September 29–30, 1992. Nevertheless, more than 300,000 people had died in the country's civil war, and some two million others had been forced to leave their homes. Upon final declaration of the election results in October of that year, which confirmed the MPLA's victory by a wide margin, Savimbi raised charges of election fraud, and his troops returned to armed insurrection. In May 1993, U.S. president Bill Clinton, in a reversal of the policies of former U.S. administrations, officially recognized the dos Santos government and condemned UNITA for its resumption of hostilities.

After a series of failed cease-fire accords in 1993 and 1994, the two sides signed a new peace agreement in November 1994. Savimbi did not attend the signing ceremony, saying his life would be in danger from government troops, but he endorsed the new pact shortly afterward. In May 1995, Savimbi and dos Santos met for the first time in three years, spending an hour in discussions aimed at cementing the November accord. Despite the talks, the peace plan languished, and in December 1998 it completely fell apart when UNITA returned to the battlefield. Lacking the external support he enjoyed in the Cold War years, Savimbi's movement maintained its struggle by smuggling Angolan diamonds through Zaire/Democratic Republic of the Congo (DRC). Prospects for peace changed dramatically in February 2002, however, when government troops killed Savimbi in a military attack on UNITA forces in the southeastern part of the country. Two months later, UNITA and the Angolan government signed a peace accord, ending their long civil war.

ABC-CLIO

See also: Angolan Conflicts; Diamonds and Conflict in Postcolonial Africa; Dos Santos, Jose Eduardo; National Union for the Total Independence of Angola (UNITA); Popular Movement for the Liberation of Angola (MPLA); Portuguese Africa, Independence Wars (Angola, Mozambique, and Guinea-Bissau).

Further Reading
Van der Waals, W. S. *The Portugal's War in Angola*. Rivonia: Ashanti, 1993.
Venter, Al J. *Portugal's Guerrilla Wars in Africa: Lisbon's Three Wars in Angola, Mozambique and Guinea-Bissau*. Solihull: Helion, 2013.
Weigert, Stephen. *Angola: A Modern Military History, 1961–2002*. New York: Palgrave Macmillan, 2011.

Seleka Rebels
See Central African Republic (CAR), Conflict in

Shaba, Zaire: Rebel Incursions and Foreign Intervention (1977–1978)

During the Congo Crisis of the 1960s, fighters from the southern province of Katanga initially supported the secessionist state of Moise Tshombe and then fought for the Congo government against a rebellion in the east. After a failed mutiny against the Congo's new Joseph Mobutu regime in 1966, many Katanga soldiers moved to Portuguese-ruled Angola where they established the Congolese National Liberation Front (FLNC) under Nathaniel Mbumba. Given Mobutu's support for his brother-in-law Holden Roberto's National Front for the Liberation of Angola (FNLA), the Portuguese enlisted Katangese fighters against African nationalist insurgents. With Portugal's sudden departure from Africa in 1974–1975, Mobutu dispatched Zairian (Congolese) troops into Angola to support the FNLA's attempt to take power in the brewing civil war. However, the FNLA, also backed by the United States and apartheid South Africa, was quickly eliminated in Angola and the Popular Movement for the Liberation of Angola (MPLA), sponsored by the Soviet Union and Cuba, took power and began assisting the Katangese FLNC exiles in their struggle against the Mobutu regime in Zaire. Katangese fighters supported the MPLA at the crucial 1975 battles at Quifangondo against the FNLA, Zairians, and Portuguese mercenaries and Benguela against the National Union for the Total Independence of Angola (UNITA) and South African forces. Despite the official normalization of Angolan-Zairean relations through the Brazzaville Accords of February 1976, Mobutu continued backing exiled Angolan rebel groups such as UNITA, and Angola continued sponsorship of the Katangese FLNC. The Cold War context also persisted, with Zaire backed by

Western powers like the United States and France, and Angola directly supported by the Soviet and Cuban forces present in that country.

During the late 1970s, the Angola-based Katangese rebels staged a series of incursions into southern Zaire. In early March 1977, 2,000 FLNC fighters riding bicycles crossed from Angola into the Zaire's Shaba province (formerly Katanga) and captured several towns, including the manganese mining center of Kisenge and advanced to within 30 kilometers of Kolwezi. The invaders' goal was not the secession of Shaba but the overthrow of Mobutu's regime, and many unpaid soldiers from the Armed Forces of Zaire (FAZ) deserted or ran away when fighting started. Mobutu flew two battalions of the new Kaymanyola Division to Shaba to join paratroopers already in the area, but the composite force collapsed during its first engagement with the Katangese FLNC. Subsequently, Zairian units fought a series of separate and failed counterattacks. Mobutu dismissed army chief of staff Colonel Mampa Ngakwe Salamayi, whom he had sent to take charge in Shaba along with his entire staff and took a personal role in directing operations. Although Mobutu dispatched further reinforcements, including a brigade from the Kaymanyola Division and two paratrooper battalions to Shaba, a stalemate developed as the Zairian forces failed to displace the rebels who could not advance.

Portraying his regime as under communist attack, Mobutu appealed to his allies, but Belgium was displeased with him for nationalizing some businesses, and the American Carter administration's human rights agenda made it hesitant to help an oppressive state. Nevertheless, the anti-communist king of Morocco dispatched a 1,500-strong parachute brigade in French aircraft to Shaba, Egypt provided pilots and mechanics for Zaire's French-built Mirage jets, Saudi Arabia gave money, and the Belgians and Americans donated supplies. From mid-April to the end of May, Zairian and Moroccan troops with artillery, armor, and air support mounted an offensive that slowly pushed the FLNC fighters back into Angola. Although the Shaba civilian population had not rebelled in support of the rebels, Mobutu's forces undertook brutal reprisals, particularly against the Lunda ethnic group associated with the FLNC, and about 200,000 people escaped across the border. Given the near disaster of "Shaba I," also called the "Eighty Day War," Mobutu purged his officers; reorganized and streamlined the FAZ; stationed the entire Kaymanyola Division in Shaba; engaged French instructors to train a new parachute unit; and imported French, Belgian, and American military advisers. The Sino-Soviet rivalry became relevant as Mobutu gained sympathy from China against the Soviet-Cuban backed FLNC, prompting the Americans and Belgians to renew their relationship with Zaire. At the same time, the FLNC in Angola recruited from recently arrived Zairean refugees, growing from 2,000 to 5,000 combatants.

Inside Shaba, FLNC agents prepared for another incursion, politicizing the oppressed population and recruiting 500 militiamen who established caches of weapons smuggled from Zambia. Given that most of the 8,000 FAZ soldiers in Shaba defended the border with Angola, some 3,000–4,000 FLNC fighters crossed into the Congo from Zambia in May 1978, intending to rapidly seize key mining centers such as Kolwezi and Lubumbashi (formerly Elisabethville). At Kolwezi, the FLNC surprised a brigade of the Kaymanyola Division, which collapsed allowing the rebels to capture the airfield, destroy Zairian military aircraft, and occupy the town that was home to 2,500 Europeans and 89 Americans mostly working in the mining industry. Pressured by French officials, Mobutu immediately airlifted two infantry battalions to Lubumbashi by Zairian C-130 transport aircraft and civilian planes. As ordered by Mobutu, a company of FAZ paratroopers jumped onto the Kolwezi airfield but were hopelessly outnumbered and slaughtered before two other companies arrived in the area and took control of the airfield the next day. The surviving pockets of FAZ defenders fled Kolwezi as the FLNC rebels began murdering Europeans. French instructor pilots took charge of Zaire's Mirage fighter jets and conducted air strikes against the rebels around Kolwezi.

The U.S. Carter administration put its 82nd Airborne Division on alert for possible deployment to Zaire but then canceled the mission, given the departure of American construction workers from Kolwezi. On May 19 and 20, France enacted Operation Leopard with 700 paratroopers of the French Second Foreign Parachute Regiment (2 REP) dropped directly on Kolwezi from overloaded Zairian transport aircraft. In their regiment's first combat jump since the 1954 Battle of Dien Bien Phu in Indochina, the legionnaires rescued hostages and killed about 100 rebels. In the separate Operation Red Bean, on May 20, two Belgian parachute battalions totaling 1,180 men and carried in Belgian C-130s landed at the Kolwezi airfield. While the Belgians initially planned a parachute jump, the Belgian commander ordered a combat landing at the last minute upon learning that French troops were on the ground, as this would allow more time for hostage rescue. Advancing into the town, the Belgians narrowly avoided "friendly fire" from the French. The two uncoordinated airborne expeditions pursued different objectives as the French 2 REP supported Mobutu's regime by evicting the FLNCs from Kolwezi and the Belgians evacuated Europeans. Other countries assisted the operation such as the Americans who flew fuel into the staging areas at Kamina and Lubumbashi, the British who dispatched a flying hospital to Zaire, and the Italians who sent a C-130 with spare parts for the Belgian aircraft. Within a day, the French overcame most resistance in Kolwezi, the Belgians evacuated 2,000 expatriates, and the FLNC retreated toward the border.

Using light vehicles to Kolwezi by aircraft, the French paratroopers pursued the rebels in the last days of May and flew back to Corsica in early June. During their operation, 2 REP killed 252 rebels, captured 163, and seized a large number of weapons at a cost of five dead and 25 wounded. During "Shaba II," as this brief conflict came to be known, several hundred Congolese civilians and 160 foreign residents were killed. Suffering no casualties in the operation, one Belgian battalion flew home within two days while the other remained in Shaba for two months as an interim security force though banned from assisting Zairean forces in combat. Replacing the Belgians, a Western-backed Inter-African Force comprising 1,500 Moroccan troops and smaller contingents from former French colonies such as Senegal and Togo arrived in Shaba, transported by the U.S. Air Force. The Inter-African Force defended Shaba for 15 months while Mobutu rebuilt his discredited military with assistance from France and Belgium. While Mobutu and Carter blamed the Cubans for instigating the Shaba incursion, Fidel Castro had tried to derail it as Cuban forces in Angola had been weakened by the departure of

5,000 troops for Ethiopia where they intervened in the Ogaden War, and the crisis in Zaire took international attention away from the South African airborne assault on Cassinga in southern Angola. With his mining economy in a shambles given the violence, Mobutu bowed to demands from his Western allies to release some political prisoners and place his economy more closely under Western supervision. Under pressure from their external sponsors, Zaire and Angola tried to end the Shaba conflict through a nonaggression pact in which they promised to stop supporting each other's exiled rebels. Assisted by Cuban troops, Angola repatriated some FLNC insurgents and incorporated others into the Angolan military, and Zaire halted support for Angolan rebels, which caused the final collapse of Roberto's FNLA. Two decades later, during the First Congo War of 1996–1997, Angola deployed exiled Katangese fighters to Zaire to overthrow Mobutu's faltering regime.

Timothy J. Stapleton

See also: Air Power in Postcolonial African Wars; Angolan Conflicts; Belgian Military Intervention in Africa; Congo Crisis; Congo Wars; Cuba and Africa; French Military Involvement in Postcolonial Africa; Mobutu Sese Seko; National Front for the Liberation of Angola (FNLA); National Union for the Total Independence of Angola (UNITA); Ogaden War; Popular Movement for the Liberation of Angola (MPLA); Portuguese Africa, Independence Wars (Angola, Mozambique, and Guinea-Bissau); Roberto, Holden Álverto; Soviet Military Involvement in Africa; U.S. Military Involvement in Africa.

Further Reading

Kennes, Erik, and Miles Larmer. *The Katangese Gendarmes: Fighting Their Way Home.* Bloomington: Indiana University Press, 2016.

Odom, Thomas P. *Shaba II: The French and Belgian Intervention in Zaire in 1978.* Fort Leavenworth, KS: U.S. Army Command and General Staff College, Combat Studies Institute, 1993.

Sierra Leone Civil War (1991–2002)

On March 23, 1991, Revolutionary United Front (RUF) insurgents launched attacks from Liberia into Sierra Leone. Their first target was the border town of Bomaru. After their assault, they retreated to Voinjama across the border in Liberia. The attack killed several civilians and soldiers from the Sierra Leonean armed forces. The government in Sierra Leone downplayed the attack, attributing the incursion to banditry. Several days later, on March 27, the RUF attacked the border town of Buedu followed by Koindu two days later, on March 29. The RUF executed another attack on March 28, expanding the war front south with attacks on the Pujehun District and the Mano River Bridge. In April, Foday Sankoh, a former Sierra Leonean Army corporal and now the leader of the RUF, announced from a satellite phone in Libera that the "father of all wars" had begun. His acknowledgment made on the BBC "Focus on Africa" program also revealed the nexus between the RUF and the National Patriotic Front of Liberia (NPFL). Many of the fighters who formed the RUF raiding force were Liberian NPFL fighters.

While the proximate cause of the conflict was the RUF's assault on Bomaru, Sierra Leone's decades-long postindependence political dysfunction was the conflict's catalyst. The RUF's objective was to topple Prime Minister Joseph Momoh and the ruling All People's Congress (APC). After a brief period of multiparty political participation following independence in 1961, Sierra Leone was transformed into a one-party state under Siaka Stevens by 1970. The election of Stevens of the APC in 1967 changed the nascent political fabric of Sierra Leone's postindependence government. The previous Sierra Leone People's Party (SLPP) government under the leadership of Prime Minister Milton Margai had mismanaged their mandate. The corrupt and nepotistic rule they established created the conditions for Steven's election as prime minister. The political situation under the APC did not improve and worsened over time. Decades of APC one-party state rule solidified corruption while stifling political descent. By 1990 the APC had bankrupted the country. The RUF's initial assault, while met with trepidation, did engender hope among the citizenry that the insurgency would improve Sierra Leone's political situation. Any goodwill that the insurgents enjoyed, however, was quickly dashed due to the brutality they visited on the civilians.

The Sierra Leonean armed forces were not prepared to fight the RUF. After years of neglect, mismanagement, and mistrust of the military by the civilian leadership, the army lacked the training and materials to mount a counteroffensive against the RUF. Unable to defend the homeland, the government appealed to the Guinean government for military support. In addition, the Sierra Leonean administration launched an initiative to organize dissenting Liberians who had fled the war in Liberia into a counterinsurgency force. This group, initially known as the Liberian United Defense Force (LUDF) in 1991, became the United Liberation Movement of Liberia for Democracy (ULIMO).

The combined Guinean and dissident Liberian forces were able to retake territory from the RUF, and by 1992 the war was at a stalemate. Overall, the pause proved detrimental for the country. The stalemate made for restless army soldiers, some of whom began to plot to overthrow the government. On April 29, 1992, Sierra Leone was thrown into further chaos when soldiers executed a successful coup. The dissident soldiers called their junta the National Provincial Ruling Council (NPRC) and named Captain Valentine Strasser their leader. The NPRC rejected a RUF offer for a cease-fire and renewed attacks on the insurgent group. After substantial military victories against the RUF, the tide turned against the army when the RUF changed their tactic to a full-fledged guerrilla war, abandoning the conventional posture that they had previously assumed. The shift in tactics was effective, and soon the RUF was regaining territory while putting the army on the defensive. Under pressure, the NPRC contracted foreign mercenary organizations to repel the RUF advance. This did not ease the anxiety felt by the population, and the NPRC was forced to return the country to civilian rule. Elections were set for February 1996. In the interim, however, the NPRC removed Strasser as their leader in 1995 after he appeared to want to contest the elections. Further complicating an already serious situation, the RUF objected to the elections and launched a terror campaign to discourage the citizenry from voting. Their methods involved dismembering people's hands and forearms as a punishment for voting.

On March 15, 1996, Ahmed Tejan Kabbah (SLPP), was elected the president of Sierra Leone. The new government was able to achieve a peace agreement with the RUF on November 30, 1996; however, when the plan's implementation stalled, Kabbah tried to get rid of Sankoh. In March 1997 Sankoh was arrested in Nigeria on firearms violations charges and placed under house arrest. Meanwhile a dissident RUF faction briefly assumed command of the RUF before being dislodged by RUF commander Sam "Mosquito" Bockarie and other Sankoh loyalists.

Another armed faction adding to the complexities of the conflict was the Kamajor militia, which by 1997 was a credible fighting force. Tired of the abuse suffered at the hands of both the Sierra Leonean Army and the RUF, Mende communities organized themselves into a self-defense force based on the traditions of the Poro society. Once allies in fighting the RUF, Kamajor militia's distrust of the army, due to opportunism by soldiers to collaborate with the RUF for financial gain, soured the relations between them and the armed forces. The combination of soldier and RUF rebel hybridity was known as "sobel."

On May 27, 1997, mutinous soldiers conducted another coup, usurping the state from civilian rule. Kabbah fled to neighboring Guinea from where he began to organize a resistance to the junta. The junta called the Armed Forces Revolutionary Council (AFRC) was led by Major Johnny Paul Koroma. The AFRC came immediately under international and West African pressure to restore Sierra Leone to civilian rule. After a peace agreement that meant to restore Kabbah as the president failed, the junta was militarily dislodged with the help of combined ECOMOG, Western, and local forces such as the Kamajor. Following the removal of the AFRC, Kabbah was returned to power on March 10, 1998.

To bring the conflict to an end, another peace accord was signed on July 7, 1999, in which Sankoh was given a cabinet-level position equal in seniority to the vice president with a portfolio giving him authority over Sierra Leone's natural resources. Later that year in October, the UN Security Council established the United Nations Mission in Sierra Leone (UNAMIL) to assist with stability operations and postwar reconstruction. At the time UNAMIL numbered almost 20,000 soldiers, making it the largest UN peacekeeping force. The RUF rejected the deployment of UNAMIL and decided to wage a harassment operation against the UN force. As the threat to peace increased and with the situation on the ground reaching a critical mass, the UK deployed 800 paratroopers to Freetown under "Operation Palliver." Shortly after, an arrest warrant was then issued for Sankoh, and he was captured by citizens eager to rid Sierra Leone of the RUF menace.

In August 2000 another insurgent group comprising former AFRC members now calling themselves the West Side Boys took up arms and began terrorizing the citizenry. They eventually kidnapped 11 British soldiers. In response, the British command in Sierra Leone launched "Operation Barrass" to subdue the West Side Boys. With the West Side Boys as the only remaining insurgent group neutralized, further stability operations were initiated. On January 12, 2002, , with the disarmament of over 40,000 former fighters, President Kabbah declared the end of the war.

Jacien Carr

See also: British Military Involvement in Postcolonial Africa; Child Soldiers in Africa; Diamonds and Conflict in Postcolonial Africa; ECOWAS Military Interventions; Liberian Civil Wars; Peacekeeping in Africa; Revolutionary United Front (RUF); Sankoh, Foday Saybana; Taylor, Charles McArthur Ghankay.

Further Reading

Bellman, Beryl L. *The Language of Secrecy: Symbols and Metaphors in Poro Ritual.* New Brunswick, NJ: Rutgers University Press, 1984.

Denon, Myriam. *Child Soldiers: Sierra Leone's Revolutionary United Front.* Cambridge: Cambridge University Press, 2010.

Gberie, Lansana. *A Dirty War in West Africa: The RUF and the Destruction of Sierra Leone.* London: Hurst, 2005.

Hazen, Jennifer. *What Rebels Want: Resources and Supply Networks in Wartime.* Ithaca, NY: Cornell University Press, 2013.

Hoffman, Danny. *The War Machines: Young Men and Violence in Sierra Leone and Liberia.* Durham: Duke University Press, 2011.

Wai, Zubairu. *Epistemologies of African Conflicts: Violence, Evolutionism, and the War in Sierra Leone.* Basingstoke: Palgrave Macmillan, 2012.

Waugh, Colin. *Charles Taylor and Liberia: Ambition and Atrocity in Africa's Lone Star State.* London: Zed Books, 2011.

Zack-Williams, Tunde. *When the State Fails: Studies on Intervention in the Sierra Leone Civil War.* London: Pluto Press, 2012.

Simba Rebels

See Congo Crisis

Sirte, Battle of (2016)

A major, bloody battle for the control of Sirte between the forces of the Government of National Accord (GNA) and the Islamic State (Daesh). The battle took place from May 12 to December 6, 2016. In 2014, the conflict between the Operation Dignity coalition forces of the east versus the Libya Dawn forces from around Tripoli created a gap in security and governance in Sirte, which had suffered extensive damage in the battle of 2011 and did not receive help to recover afterward. The Islamic State began sending fighters to Libya in 2014, where they competed with the Ansar al-Sharia. Local resistance forces expelled the Islamic State fighters from their first stronghold in Derna, and they began infiltrating Sirte. By the spring of 2015, Daesh fighters defeated the coalition of Ansar al-Sharia, Libya Dawn, and the Libyan National Army that controlled the city and then began using it to launch raids on many other towns. International supporters of Libyan independence did not want to help only one militia defeat Daesh, but rather pushed hard to persuade Operation Dignity to join with the Libya Dawn forces to form a Government of National Accord, as a condition for military support. The Libyan Political Agreement of December 17, 2015, established the conditions for international support, although the Operation Dignity forces later backed out.

On May 5 and 6, 2016, Daesh fighters attacked the Misratan Military Council with suicide bombers, which provoked a counterattack in the name of the GNA, an operation called "Al-Bunyan Al-Marsoos" (Solid Structure-BM) in mid-May 2016. Between May and July 2016, suicide bombers, booby traps, and heavy sniper fire prevented BM forces from achieving meaningful gains in Sirte. During this period, the Libyan Navy helped secure Sirte's coast, thus blocking Daesh fighters from escaping by sea. On July 25, 2016, the BM forces asked the Presidential Council to call for U.S. airstrikes. On August 1, in response to a request by Prime Minister Fayez al-Serraj, AFRICOM launched Operation Odyssey Lightning with air strikes by the U.S. Air Force and Marine Corps forces targeting Daesh fighters and their heavy equipment. Air strikes continued off and on from August until December 2016, giving priority to avoiding civilian casualties. AFRICOM reported that U.S. forces conducted 495 precision air strikes during this period, in addition to the air strikes and intense artillery shelling by the GNA.

During the remaining three months (September–December 2016), the GNA fought a slow and bloody offensive to retake the last remaining Daesh-held areas in Sirte. Daesh forces used civilians as human shields, as well as booby traps and mines, which delayed the advancing GNA forces. By December 2016 Daesh fighters controlled only an area with 50 buildings. Several women pretending to surrender blew themselves up to kill and wound GNA forces. On December 6, 2016, GNA forces completed their capture of Sirte after heavy fighting against the last Daesh fighters, who surrendered at night.

Steven A. Quillman

See also: Ansar al-Sharia in Libya; Libyan Civil War, Second; U.S. Africa Command; U.S. Military Involvement in Africa.

Further Reading

Chivvis, Christopher S. "Countering the Islamic State in Libya." *Survival* 58, no. 4 (August–September 2016): 113–130.

Pack, Jason, Rhiannon Smith, and Karim Mezran. *The Origins and Evolution of ISIS in Libya*. Washington, DC: Atlantic Council, June 2017.

Somalia Civil War (1981–)

In 1960 the Republic of Somalia became independent as an amalgamation of the former British and Italian colonies of Somaliland. Coming to power in a military coup in 1969, Siad Barre created a military regime in Somalia that attempted to minimize historic clan affiliations and pursued an aggressive Pan-Somali ideology that involved uniting Somalis living in separate East African states. In return for permitting the Soviet Union to establish a naval base at the strategically important Berbera on the Red Sea, Barre's government gained substantial Soviet assistance in creating a large Somali military. Nevertheless, Somalia's defeat by Ethiopia during the 1977–1978 Ogaden War as well as the loss of Soviet support at the same time significantly weakened Barre's regime. Since the now American-backed Somalia continued to sponsor ethnic Somali rebels in Ethiopia's Ogaden region, the Soviet-sponsored Mengistu regime in Ethiopia supported clan-based insurgent groups that developed in Somalia during the late 1970s and 1980s. At the end of the 1970s, some dissatisfied Somali military officers, mostly from the northeastern Majeerteen clan, failed in an attempt to oust Barre and escaped to Ethiopia where they established the Somali Salvation Democratic Front (SSDF) that launched an insurgency within Somalia. Although SSDF and Ethiopian forces captured towns in central Somalia in 1982, the rebellion failed within a few years given American military support for the Barre government and internal conflicts among the insurgents. In 1981 the Somali National Movement (SNM) emerged from among the Isaaq clan of northern Somalia and launched a rebellion by raiding a prison near Berbera. During the mid-1980s, SNM attacks continued, and Barre's state forces responded by executing civilians and attempting to block rebel escape routes into neighboring Djibouti. In 1987 the civil war expanded to the south when exiled members of the southern Hawiye clan, previously occupying senior government positions but then persecuted by Barre, founded the United Somali Congress (USC). The USC split between factions associated with the Abgal subclan from Mogadishu and the Habar Gidir subclan under former general Mohamed Farrah Aidid. Both facing escalating internal rebellions and diminishing superpower support, given the winding up of the Cold War, Barre and Mengistu agreed to stop backing insurgents in each other's countries in 1988 and redeployed their forces from the Somalia-Ethiopia border to counterinsurgency operations. Now expelled from Ethiopia, SNM rebels invaded Somalia, taking control of the north and capturing weapons and vehicles from Barre's Army. As a result, half a million people from northern Somalia escaped into adjacent Ethiopia and Djibouti. In January 1991, Barre fled Mogadishu after his order to bombard Hawiye-clan neighborhoods incited a widespread uprising. The Somalia state military dissolved, with soldiers joining various clan-based armed factions. With Aidid's USC forces in pursuit, Barre retreated to the southwest, where he attempted to rally his Marrehan clansmen as the Somali National Front (SNF), but this failed, and he moved into Kenya in May and never returned to Somalia. In July, the Abgal and Habar Gidir USC factions suspended their battle over Mogadishu and agreed to form an interim government. With southern Somalia, including the capital of Mogadishu in chaos, parts of the comparatively stable north seceded from the Republic of Somalia, with the SNM declaring the Somaliland Republic in the northwest in May 1991 and Puntland founded in the northeast in 1998. These breakaway states survived despite lack of formal recognition by other countries.

In September 1991 fighting resumed between the USC factions in Mogadishu. By August 1992 the civil war resulted in a refugee crisis with hundreds of thousands of Somalis fleeing to other countries, including 500,000 in Ethiopia, 300,000 in Kenya, 65,000 in Yemen, 15,000 in Djibouti and 100,000 in Europe. Furthermore, the UN warned that famine caused by war and drought would shortly claim the lives of 1.5 million Somalis. In Mogadishu and other southern ports like Kismayo, leaders of the many armed factions blocked the delivery of international food aid, and Aidid demanded the withdrawal of the small United Nations Operation in Somalia (UNOSOM) founded in April 1992 to supervise an ultimately aborted cease-fire. In early December 1992, the United States mounted Operation

Restore Hope (also dubbed United Task Force or UNITAF) as an American-led and UN-authorized international intervention to create a safe zone in southern Somalia to facilitate humanitarian assistance. With 37,000 troops, including 25,000 Americans, UNITAF occupied Mogadishu harbor and airport and the port of Kismayo. UNITAF distributed food to Somali civilians but neglected to disarm the Somali factions. During this operation, Belgian, Italian, and Canadian peacekeepers abused and killed some Somali civilians, inciting international criticism and triggering scandals in their home countries. In May 1993 UNITAF was replaced by the 22,000-strong UNOSOM II, which planned to disarm militias and establish a new government with the support of a U.S. quick reaction force and U.S. Navy ships off the coast of Somalia. After Aidid's fighters attacked UN forces, the American Clinton administration orchestrated a U.S. Special Forces raid to arrest him, but the operation backfired, with two helicopters shot down and 18 American troops killed in what is now called the "Black Hawk Down" incident. This disaster prompted the Americans to abandon their search for Aidid, and American ground forces departed Somalia in March 1994. With the failure of international peacekeeping in Somalia, the UN Security Council voted in November 1993 to withdraw UNOSOM II and its last elements left via U.S. naval vessels in March 1995. This debacle contributed to the "Somalia Syndrome," whereby Western states, including the United States became hesitant to stage military interventions for humanitarian reasons, which profoundly influenced events in Rwanda in April 1994.

The quintessential "failed state" of the 1990s and 2000s, Somalia lacked an effective government and experienced continued factional violence. After the 2001 Islamist terrorist attacks on the United States, Washington began to militarily support secular Somali warlords against the rising Islamic Courts Union (ICU) that had begun to stabilize parts of the war-torn south through the imposition of Sharia law. During the first half of 2006, an alliance of U.S.-backed Somali warlords lost control of Mogadishu to the ICU, which brought peace to the city for the first time in 15 years. Concerned that southern Somalia might become a sanctuary for international Islamist terrorists, the United States encouraged Ethiopia to invade in December 2006 in support of the hitherto powerless and beleaguered Somali Transitional National Government (TNG). Ethiopia's involvement was further informed by the support that its rival Eritrea provided to Somali Islamists. Pushed out of Mogadishu, Kismayo, and other towns by the Ethiopian offensive, the ICU continued a guerrilla war against the TNG supported by Ethiopia and the African Union Mission in Somalia (AMISOM) that arrived during 2007 and 2008. Ethiopian forces withdrew in 2009 leaving the American- and European-funded AMISOM, consisting mostly of Ugandan and Burundian troops, and TNG forces now constituted as the Somali National Army (SNA) to fight the ICU. While some moderate ICU members joined the TNG in 2009, a radical ICU youth wing called Al-Shabaab renewed the struggle, which included fighting in Mogadishu. The United States contributed to the war against ICU and then Al-Shabaab by providing, for example, air strikes by drones based in Ethiopia and Djibouti and special forces operations. Based in its former colony of Djibouti, France also provided military support for the fight against Al-Shabaab, now broadly explained as part of the international "War on Terror." From 2008 to 2010, around 22,000 people died in the fighting in Somalia, over one million Somalis experienced displacement, and 475,000 sought refuge in other countries. From 2011, Al-Shabaab terrorist acts in Kenya prompted Kenyan military and naval intervention in southern Somalia, with Kenyan troops eventually joining AMISOM, raising the force's total strength from 9,000 to 18,000. Around the same time, some Somalis turned to piracy in the Red Sea, given the absence of state control, the proliferation of small arms, and the collapse of the local fishery as well as opportunities presented by the passage of many undefended but highly insured large cargo vessels on their way to or from the Suez Canal. In 2008, as a result, a multinational anti-piracy naval fleet, including ships from the United States, Canada, the European Union, Russia, Pakistan, and India formed off the Horn of Africa. The inclusion of Chinese vessels in the anti-piracy operations represented China's first naval deployment outside its home waters since the 1400s. In addition, the TNG recreated the Somali Navy, defunct since 1991, and Puntland founded a Maritime Police Force. As a result of these actions, piracy off the coast of Somalia has declined in recent years.

Timothy J. Stapleton

See also: Al-Shabaab; Barre, Mohamed Siad; Canadian Military Involvement in Africa; Cold War in Africa; Ethiopia: Insurgency and Interstate War; Famine in Postcolonial African Conflicts; Mengistu Haile Mariam; Mogadishu, Battle of; Navies in Postcolonial Africa; Ogaden War; Operation Restore Hope; Peacekeeping in Africa; Rwanda, Civil War and Genocide; Soviet Military Involvement in Africa; U.S. Africa Command; U.S. Military Involvement in Africa.

Further Reading

Hansen, Stig Jarle. *Al Shabaab in Somalia: The History and Ideology of a Militant Islamist Group, 2005–2012.* Oxford: Oxford University Press, 2013.

Lewis, Ioan. *Understanding Somalia and Somaliland.* New York: Columbia University Press, 2008.

Njoku, Raphael C. *The History of Somalia.* Santa Barbara, CA: Greenwood, 2013.

Rutherford, Kenneth. *Humanitarianism under Fire: The US and UN Intervention in Somalia.* Sterling, VA: Kumarian Press, 2008.

Williams, Paul. *Fighting for Peace in Somalia: A History and Analysis of the African Union Mission in Somalia (AMISOM), 2007–2017.* Oxford: Oxford University Press, 2018.

Woldemariam, Michel. *Insurgent Fragmentation in the Horn of Africa: Rebellion and Its Discontents.* Cambridge: Cambridge University Press, 2018.

South Africa, Armed Struggle against Apartheid (1961–1994)

In 1910, in the wake of Britain's conquest of the Boer (Afrikaner) republics during the South African War (1899–1902), the British government combined colonial territories in southern Africa to create the white settler minority–ruled Union of South Africa. With a large mining economy subsidized by low-paid Black labor, South Africa became a major power in the southern Africa region and became functionally independent in 1931 just as the British Empire's other white settler dominions, including Canada and Australia. Elected as the government of South Africa in 1948, the extreme white supremacist Afrikaner group called the Nationalist Party (NP) implemented a series of laws that imposed a strict racially segregationist policy called apartheid.

While anti-apartheid protest initially took the form of passive resistance, the March 1960 Sharpeville massacre, in which South African Police shot into a crowd of Black demonstrators, killing 69, prompted the transition to armed struggle to overturn white minority rule. South Africa's NP government banned anti-apartheid movements such as the long-established African National Congress (ANC) and the new Pan-Africanist Congress (PAC). In July 1961 members of the South African Communist Party (SACP) and the ANC, including Nelson Mandela, founded a military organization called Umkhonto we Sizwe (Spear of the Nation or MK) to pursue limited violence against the apartheid state. At that time, MK represented a technically separate organization from the ANC, as some of the group's leaders remained committed to a nonviolent strategy. At the end of 1961, MK operatives launched a bombing campaign across South African urban areas that lasted for about a year and published a manifesto declaring war on the apartheid regime and their aim of establishing democratic government. Some MK fighters covertly left South Africa for military training in Algeria and Ethiopia. In October 1962 the ANC officially recognized MK at a meeting in the British colony of Bechuanaland (independent Botswana from 1966). In 1963 South African security forces arrested most MK leaders, including Mandela, subsequently convicted them of treason, and sentenced them to long prison terms. Other ANC and MK leaders escaped to re-create the movement in exile.

Splitting from the ANC in 1959, the more radical PAC engaged in less controlled violence. Following the Sharpeville massacre, the PAC planned a South African–wide mass uprising for 1963 and organized armed groups generally referred to as "Poqo" (meaning alone in the Xhosa language). In 1962 and 1963, mostly in the Cape province, Poqo formations armed with axes and machetes attacked police, whites, and African traditional leaders who worked for the state. A crackdown by South African Police and a British colonial police raid on PAC offices in British Basutoland (Lesotho) ended the PAC armed campaign. The PAC's anticipated 1963 uprising never happened, and the movement's leaders were imprisoned or went into exile.

After 1964, and given the Cold War context in which apartheid South Africa positioned itself as a Western ally, the exiled ANC/MK received military training in the Soviet Union and established camps in Tanzania. In this period, South Africa enjoyed protection by a ring of allies such as the Portuguese colonies of Angola and Mozambique and white minority–ruled Rhodesia and economically dependent African states such as Botswana and Swaziland. Since MK lacked staging areas from where it could infiltrate South Africa to conduct insurgent operations, the insurgents joined with the Zimbabwe African People's Union (ZAPU) in the ultimately disastrous Wankie and Sipolilo campaigns, whereby they attempted to cross into Rhodesia from Zambia. Some MK fighters called these operations a suicide mission. In 1969 at the Morogoro conference in Tanzania, the ANC decided to increase integration of political and military issues and build popular support within South Africa as a basis for revolutionary war.

The 1976 Soweto Uprising, a South African–wide rebellion by Black youth, inspired by the Black Consciousness movement, revitalized the ANC/MK, with many Black youth fleeing the country to join the exiled movement. In the late 1970s, MK founded camps in newly independent Angola where members received military training from Soviet instructors, and during the 1980s, in the context of the Angolan Civil War, MK combatants deployed against South African and American-backed rebels from the National Union for the Total Independence of Angola (UNITA). In some MK camps in Angola, fighters mutinied over poor living conditions and disappointment related to lack of direct action against apartheid South Africa. The independence of the Portuguese territories, especially Mozambique, along with the strengthening of Botswana and the 1980 independence of Zimbabwe (formerly Rhodesia) weakened South Africa's regional protective ring. During the late 1970s and early 1980s, as a result, MK operatives infiltrated South Africa to develop covert networks and carry out limited military actions called "armed propaganda," which targeted police stations and other state institutions to inspire mass action. This campaign also included high-profile attacks such as the bombing of an oil refinery in 1980, a nuclear facility in 1982, and a rocket attack on a military base in 1981.

The region's changing strategic situation in the late 1970s prompted the apartheid regime to implement a "total strategy" to mobilize its combined economic, political, and military resources against what it described as a Soviet orchestrated "total onslaught." In addition to its military operations in southern Angola, the South African government used conventional and covert military means to destabilize neighboring Black-ruled states and therefore discourage their support for the anti-apartheid movement. For example, South Africa's sponsorship of the rebels of the Mozambique National Resistance (RENAMO) forced the Mozambique government to sign the 1984 Nkomati Accords that led to the expulsion of the ANC from that country.

During the mid- to late 1980s, given increased popular protest among Black South Africans and the apartheid government's declaration of state of emergency, MK expanded its armed operations and widened its definition of legitimate military targets. Within South Africa, MK planted land mines in rural areas to kill white farmers active in the part-time security forces; insurgents conducted bombings and mortar attacks, and occasionally killed white civilians in shopping centers and restaurants. Launched in 1986, the ANC's "Operation Vula" (Open) involved smuggling weapons into South Africa, planting covert operatives within South African security forces, and organizing a military coup in the self-governing Transkei homeland with the territory then used as a sanctuary.

The exiled PAC fought its own war against the apartheid state. In the late 1960s, after the failure of its initial rebellion within South Africa, the PAC embraced Maoist guerrilla warfare strategy and dispatched some fighters for training in the People's Republic of China. Around that time, the PAC officially renamed its armed wing the Azanian People's Liberation Army (APLA), establishing camps in Zambia and Tanzania. The Zambian government expelled PAC/APLA operatives on several occasions, given their poor discipline and pressure from South Africa through which Zambia exports its copper. During the 1970s and 1980s, violent conflict between PAC factions, comprising African nationalists, Black Consciousness followers, Leninists, and Maoists limited the movement's ability to conduct military operations against South Africa. In addition, the absence of Soviet support meant that PAC/APLA did not participate in the war in Angola. Without powerful sponsors, APLA combatants trained in pariah states such as Gaddafi's Libya, Idi Amin's Uganda, and Pol Pot's Cambodia. APLA mounted its first operations in South Africa in 1986, and it became well established across the country by the end of the decade. The APLA military campaign of the late 1980s included attacks on police stations and white farmers as well as a "robbery unit" that secured funds. During South Africa's transition to democracy in the early 1990s, the PAC refused to enter negotiations with the NP government and continued its violent struggle, including attacks on white civilians.

By 1990, crippling international sanctions, massive internal protest, military defeat in Angola, withdrawal from Namibia, and the end of the Cold War combined to render South Africa's apartheid system untenable. A change of leadership within the governing NP resulted in the unbanning of the anti-apartheid movements and the release of political prisoners like Nelson Mandela. Negotiations between the ANC and the NP state during the early 1990s produced a nonracial constitution despite violent resistance from disenchanted groups like extremist right-wing Afrikaners, rogue security force agents, Zulu nationalists, and the PAC/APLA. South Africa's first democratic election, held in April 1994, produced an ANC-led government of national unity, with Mandela as the country's first Black president. Within this transition, members of the old South African Defence Force (SADF), homeland armies, and MK and APLA merged to form the new South African National Defence Force (SANDF).

Timothy J. Stapleton

See also: Angolan Conflicts; Azanian People's Liberation Army (APLA); Cold War in Africa; Mozambique Civil War; Mozambique National Resistance (RENAMO); Umkhonto we Sizwe (MK); Zimbabwe Independence War.

Further Reading

Cherry, Janet. *Spear of the Nation; Umkhonto we Sizwe, South Africa's Liberation Army, 1960s-90s*. Athens: Ohio University Press, 2012.

Lodge, Tom. "Soldiers of the Storm: A Profile of the Azanian People's Liberation Army." In *About Turn: The Transformation of the South African Military and Intelligence*, edited by Jakkie Cilliers and Markus Reichardt, 105–117. Halfway House: IDP, 1995.

Maaba, Brown Bavusile. "The PAC's War against the State, 1960–63." In *The Road to Democracy in South Africa Vol. 1 (1960–70)*, 257–297. South African Democracy Education Trust. Cape Town: Zebra Press, 2004.

Magubane, Bernard, Philip Bonner, Jabulani Sithole, Peter Delius, Janet Cherry, Pat Gibbs, and Thomzama April. "The Turn to Armed Struggle." In *The Road to Democracy in South Africa Vol. 1 (1960–70)*, 53–145. South African Democracy Education Trust. Cape Town: Zebra Press, 2004.

Shubin, Vladimir. *The Hot Cold War: The USSR in Southern Africa.* London: Pluto Press, 2008.

Simpson, Thula. *Umkhonto we Sizwe: The ANC's Armed Struggle.* Cape Town: Penguin, 2016.

Williams, Rocky. "The Other Armies: A Brief Historical Overview of Umkhonto we Sizwe (MK) 1961–1994." *South African Military History Journal* 11, no. 5 (June 2000).

South Africa's Border War (1966–1989)

The South African Border War was in fact two separate but intertwined conflicts that raged over a vast stretch of southern African geography. The first conflict revolves around the quest for independence for the indigenous peoples of Namibia from South African administration, while the second part involves South Africa's involvement within Angolan internal affairs.

ORIGINS

At the outbreak of World War I in 1914, South Africa's Union Defence Force (UDF) invaded and captured the German colony of South West Africa (hereafter called Namibia) because powerful radio masts located within the colony allowed Berlin direct communication with its naval forces operating in the southern oceans. After the war, the United Nations granted the territory to South Africa as a trustee territory to administer. In the 1950s opposition to South African administration resulted in the formation of the South West Africa People's Organization (SWAPO). In 1965 SWAPO launched its first armed incursions into Namibia from Kongwa, Tanzania, with the first clashes occurring between SWAPO's PLAN (People's Liberation Army of Namibia) and the SAP (South African Police) and SADF (South African Defence Force) the following year.

OPERATION SAVANNAH

On April 25, 1974, a military coup in Lisbon, Portugal, overthrew the authoritarian Estado Novo regime. On January 15, 1975, the new leaders of Portugal signed the Alvor Agreement with three leading Angolan liberation organizations: the Popular Movement for the Liberation of Angola (MPLA), National Front for the Liberation of Angola (FNLA), and National Union for the Total Independence of Angola (UNITA). According to the agreement, the organization that controlled the most territory and support by November 11, 1975, would inherit the country.

All three groups immediately began seeking international support in their ensuing battles for control. The FNLA, UNITA, and the RDL (the Eastern Revolt)—an MPLA breakaway group—approached the South African authorities for military support. The SADF, fearing a victory for the communistically aligned MPLA, who would then grant SWAPO access to Angolan territory, decided to assist all the organizations. This initial assistance quickly escalated, when Cuba, an ally of the MPLA, began deploying its armed forces in the conflict. By November 11, 1975, the SADF had five combat groups (Zulu, Foxbat, X Ray, Orange, and Beaver) operating inside Angola. After heavy fighting between SADF and Cuban units, the SADF was forced to withdraw back to Namibia, due to sustained international pressure.

CROSS-BORDER RAIDS

The assumption of political power in Angola by the MPLA changed the dynamics of the conflict. As predicted, SWAPO was allowed to build military camps within Angola from which to launch its attacks into Namibia. In retaliation, the SADF would launch brigade-size cross-border raids targeting these camps. Often, this involved direct clashes between the SADF and the newly established People's Armed Forces for the Liberation of Angola (FAPLA) along with its Cuban and Soviet military advisers.

The first major raid, Operation Reindeer (1978), consisted of a three-pronged assault into Angola. The first prong consisted of an assault by Second South African Infantry Battalion on two SWAPO base complexes, Chetequera and Dombondola, near to the Namibian/Angola border. The second, an assault by the elite 32nd Battalion on SWAPO's Omepepa-Namuidi-Henhombe base complex around 20 kilometers east of Chetequera, and finally, a controversial airborne assault by paratroopers on Cassinga, a refugee camp and SWAPO's regional headquarters, 260 kilometers inside Angola.

Three years later the SADF launched Operation Protea (1981), a heavy, mechanized assault into Angola. Task Force Alpha was tasked with the destruction of SWAPO's command and training center at Xangongo and its logistic bases at Xangongo and Ongiva. In three weeks of heavy fighting, the SADF cleared SWAPO from the Angolan province of Cunene for the loss of 10 dead and 64 wounded. SWAPO and FAPLA suffered over 800 dead, but more importantly, nine Soviet military advisers were also killed and one captured, Warrant Officer Second Class Nikolai Feodorovich Pestretsov.

In order to prevent a large-scale infiltration by PLAN fighters planned for 1984, the SADF launched Operation Askari (1983). Askari consisted out of an aerial assault by the South African Air Force (SAAF) on a PLAN training base outside the Angolan town of Lubango, followed by a ground offensive on SWAPO camps located near the towns of Cahama, Mulondo, and Cuvelai. While SWAPO/FAPLA suffered almost 500 killed, including five Cuban military advisers, the SADF also suffered, with 25 dead and 94 soldiers wounded.

This greater-than-expected loss of life prompted both sides to sign the Lusaka Accords (1984), which declared a cease-fire between the two countries, agreed to a withdrawal of South African troops from Angola, and established a commission to oversee the treaty's implementation.

UNITA AND CUITO CUANAVALE

UNITA, after losing to the MPLA in 1975, had withdrawn into its stronghold of southeastern Angola to recover. By the mid-1980s, UNITA guerrillas were attacking targets all over Angola. In response, the MPLA launched a huge eight brigade assault supported by numerous T-55 tanks from its main base at Cuito Cuanavale against the UNITA capital located at Jamba.

Faced with imminent destruction, UNITA requested urgent South African assistance. The SADF, not wishing to see UNITA destroyed, as it would open up their areas to SWAPO infiltration, decided to once again intervene within Angola. Mobilizing, the SADF deployed into Angola a brigade-size force consisting of mechanized and motorized units. However, faced with large numbers of FAPLA tanks, the SADF was forced to deploy its own tanks in response. Over four months of heavy fighting, the combined UNITA-SADF forces stopped the FAPLA advance, destroying two brigades and mauling the remaining two, with the survivors retreating over the Cuito River back into Cuito Cuanavale.

In 1988, the SADF and UNITA launched three assaults on the city, but resolute defense by the Angolans, assisted by their Cuban allies, kept them out. Realizing that the capture of the city would require far greater force levels than was currently deployed, the SADF decided to destroy the bridge over the Cuito River using a laser-guided smart bomb launched from an SAAF fighter-bomber. Additionally, SADF sappers constructed an extensive minefield to protect Jamba from further assaults.

While the fighting was raging around Cuito Cuanavale, Fidel Castro the Cuban president, decided to deploy to Angola the crack 50th Cuban Division, including its T-62 tanks. The arrival of the division in Angola went unnoticed by South African Military Intelligence, and it was only picked up when it was already deployed and marching southward toward the Namibian border. South Africa reacted by mobilising its national reserve and deploying them to northern Namibia. The stage was set for an all-out conventional warfare.

However, both sides realized that negotiations were better than war. Between May and September 1988, the various parties met for several rounds of talks in Cairo, New York, Geneva, and Brazzaville, but remained deadlocked on various issues. The Cubans demanded that South Africa withdraw its forces from Angola, while the South Africans demanded that Cuba withdraw its forces from Angola, while SWAPO demanded that South Africa grant Namibia its independence.

NAMIBIAN INDEPENDENCE

On December 20, 1988, United Nations Security Council Resolution 626 was passed, creating the United Nations Angola Verification Mission (UNAVEM) to verify the redeployment northward and subsequent withdrawal of Cuban forces from Angola. In February 1989 the United Nations Transition Assistance Group (UNTAG) was formed to monitor the withdrawal of SADF forces from Namibia and the implementation of the Namibian independence process.

General elections under a universal franchise were held in the territory between November 7 and 11, 1989, returning 57 percent of the popular vote for SWAPO. This gave the party 41 seats in the territory's constituent assembly, but not a two-thirds majority, which would have enabled it to impose a unilateral constitution on the other parties represented. The territory formally obtained independence as the Republic of Namibia on March 21, 1990.

Jean Pierre Scherman

See also: Angolan Armed Forces (FAPLA and FAA); Angolan Conflicts Cuba and Africa; Cuito Cuanavale, Battle of; Namibia Independence War; National Front for the Liberation of Angola (FNLA); National Union for the Total Independence of Angola (UNITA); Peacekeeping in Africa; Popular Movement for the Liberation of Angola (MPLA); Portuguese Africa, Independence Wars (Angola, Mozambique, and Guinea-Bissau); South West Africa People's Organization (SWAPO).

Further Reading

Breytenbach, Jan. *The Buffalo Soldiers: The Story of South Africa's 32-Battalion, 1975–1993*. Alberton: Galago, 2002.

Bridgland, Fred. *The War for Africa: Twelve Months That Transformed a Continent.* Oxford: Casemate Publishers, 2017.

Hooper, Jim. *Koevoet: Experiencing South Africa's Deadly Bush War*. Solihull: Helion, 2013.

Scholtz, Leopold. *The SADF in the Border War, 1966–1989*. Cape Town: Tafelberg, 2013.

Steenkamp, Willem. *South Africa's Border War, 1966–89*. Solihull: Helion, 2014.

Stiff, Peter. *The Covert War: Koevoet Operations in Namibia, 1979–1989*. Alberton: Galago, 2004.

Stiff, Peter. *The Silent War: South African Recce Operations 1969–1994*. Alberton: Galago, 2001.

Venter, Al J. *Battle for Angola: The End of the Cold War in Africa c 1975–89*. Solihull: Helion, 2017.

South Sudan Civil War (2013–2020)

The 2011 independence of South Sudan from Sudan resulted from two protracted insurgencies known as the First Sudan Civil War (1955–1972) and Second Sudan Civil War (1983–2005). After gaining independence from Britain in 1956, Sudan became the scene of civil conflict between a series of northern-based Muslim regimes that tried to Islamize and Arabize the extremely marginalized and predominantly Christian and traditionalist south. Foreshadowing later events, the Second Sudan Civil War included violence within the rebel South Sudan People's Liberation Movement/Army (SPLM/A) during the 1990s between a predominantly Dinka group led by John Garang and mostly Nuer fighters led by Riek Machar. In the early 2000s, Sudan's government of Omar al-Bashir engaged in negotiations to end the Second Sudan Civil War, given its desire to emerge from international isolation so that it could market the products of a newly developed oil industry. The al-Bashir government agreed to hold a referendum on self-determination in southern Sudan while the rebel SPLM accepted Islamic law in the north. After a delay related to the outbreak of another insurgency in western Sudan's Darfur region, the 2005 signing of the Comprehensive Peace Agreement (CPA) between the Khartoum government and SPLM resulted in self-government for southern Sudan within Sudan. Shortly after becoming president of the autonomous Government of

South Sudan (GOSS) and vice president of Sudan's national government, SPLM leader John Garang died in a helicopter crash and was replaced by the SPLM's Salva Kiir Mayardit. With the end of the Second Sudan Civil War, the oil industry expanded in southern Sudan, leading to competition among leaders of local armed factions over control and distribution of oil revenues. During 2010 and 2011, several armed factions claiming to represent the disaffected Murle and Shilluk ethnic groups formed the South Sudan Democratic Movement/Army (SSDM/A) and staged rebellions against Kiir's GOSS, seen as favoring the Dinka ethnicity.

The southern Sudanese voted overwhelmingly for independence in a January 2011 referendum, and in July South Sudan became Africa's newest sovereign state with Salva Kiir as president. The United States supported the independence of South Sudan, removing sanctions that applied to Sudan. Around the same time, an interstate war broke out between Sudan and newly independent South Sudan, as the former tried to seize the oil-producing area of Abyei on the border, with a cease-fire brokered by the African Union (AU) in March 2012. The South Sudan Civil War began in December 2013 when President Salva Kiir accused Vice President Machar of plotting a coup and dispatched Dinka soldiers to disarm their Nuer colleagues, and this led to violence against Nuer civilians in the capital of Juba. In turn, Nuer soldiers and militia retaliated against the Dinka in other parts of the country. As a result, Machar broke with the ruling SPLM, forming the Nuer-oriented Sudan People's Liberation Movement-In Opposition (SPLM-IO). In addition, violence broke out in Upper Nile state between pro-government Dinka militia and the Shilluk people over access to resources and the manipulation of internal political boundaries. While the United Nations Mission in South Sudan (UNMISS) had been established around the time of the country's independence, the UN force stayed out of the violence, sheltering thousands of fearful civilians at its compounds and helping arrange the evacuation of foreigners. The UN Security Council then increased UNMISS from 7,600 peacekeepers to around 14,000. While Sudan possibly supplied weapons to the rebel factions to destabilize South Sudan, Uganda deployed troops across the border, assisting its longtime SPLM ally to retake major towns from the rebels. Although international diplomats and UN officials warned of the conflict in South Sudan escalating to genocide, a 2014 AU commission highlighted the organized nature of the violence against civilians but concluded that there was no evidence that genocide had occurred. While the civil war began with elites vying for control over oil revenue, it descended into a lower-level conflict, with local leaders engaged in struggles over land and cattle and cycles of revenge and counter-revenge. A host of international arms dealers and manufacturers, including from China and the United States sold weapons and ammunition to the various factions in South Sudan. Throughout 2014 and into 2015, negotiations sponsored by the East African regional organizational known as the Intergovernmental Authority on Development (IGAD) produced a series of cease-fire agreements, all of which dissolved within days. The factions signed a tentative peace deal in August 2015, leading to the return of Machar to Juba in April 2016.

Heavy fighting broke out again in Juba in July 2016 just as Kiir and Machar were meeting, and UN peacekeepers failed to protect civilians. With the resumption of the war, Machar fled Juba and eventually went to exile in the DRC, Sudan, and South Africa. Machar's Nuer SPLM-IO along with the Shilluk SSDM and National Democratic Movement (NDM) continued their war against Kiir's SPLM government. Further fragmentation took place with new groups hiving off from both Kiir's and Machar's forces. Despite objections from President Kiir, the UN dispatched a 4,000-strong Regional Protection Force to Juba to bolster its capabilities. In February 2018 nine rebel groups, including Machar's SPLM-IO formed the South Sudan Opposition Alliance (SSOA) to present a common front at negotiations with the Kiir government, but the group broke up and reformed several times. Kiir and other South Sudan leaders came under pressure to conclude a negotiated settlement as the UN imposed an arms embargo on the country in July 2018, and Khartoum tired of the war, as it interrupted the northward flow of oil from which Sudan benefited. In September 2018 Kiir and Machar signed a peace agreement that included the latter's reinstatement as vice president, though he delayed returning to Juba over security concerns. Facilitated by an element of the Catholic Church, Kiir's government signed a January 2020 peace deal with the SSOA, confirmed by Machar's SPLM-IO. In February 2020 after Kiir agreed to return to an administrative framework that reduced the number of South Sudan's states from 23 to 10, a new unity government formed in Juba with Machar sworn in as first vice president. From 2013 to 2018, the South Sudan Civil War claimed the lives of around 380,000 people and displaced 4.5 million, half of whom became refugees in neighboring countries.

Timothy J. Stapleton

See also: Genocide in Africa; Kiir, Salva Mayardit; Machar, Riek Teny Dhurgon; Peacekeeping in Africa; Sudan Civil War, First; Sudan Civil War, Second; Sudan People's Liberation Movement/Army (SPLM/A).

Further Reading

Knopf, Katie Almquist. *Ending South Sudan's Civil War*. New York: Council on Foreign Relations, 2016.

Martell, Peter. *First Raise the Flag: How South Sudan Won the Longest War but Lost the Peace*. Oxford: Oxford University Press, 2019.

Pinaud, Clemence. *War and Genocide in South Sudan*. Ithaca, NY: Cornell University Press, 2021.

Rolandsen, Oystein, and M. W. Daly. *A History of South Sudan: From Slavery to Independence*. Cambridge: Cambridge University Press, 2016.

Young, John. *South Sudan's Civil War: Violence, Insurgency and Failed Peacemaking*. London: Zed Books, 2019.

South West Africa People's Organization (SWAPO)

Originating from the Ovamboland People's Congress, a group representing South West African (Namibian) contract workers in the late 1950s, the South West Africa People's Organization (SWAPO) was founded in 1960, with Sam Nujoma at its helm. It began a guerrilla war against South African occupation in 1966, forming a military wing called the People's Liberation Army of Namibia (PLAN).

During the late 1960s and early 1970s, SWAPO/PLAN received military support from the Eastern Bloc and used Zambia as an operational base from which to infiltrate South West Africa's Caprivi Strip where it planted land mines and attacked low-level state officials. In 1972 the United Nations recognized SWAPO as the "sole legitimate representative of the Namibian people." With the 1975 independence of Angola under a sympathetic Popular Movement for the Liberation of Angola (MPLA) government, SWAPO/PLAN began using southern Angola as a staging area from where it conducted insurgent operations in northern South West Africa, particularly Ovamboland, during the late 1970s and 1980s. Given South African incursions into southern Angola in pursuit of SWAPO insurgents, the group developed a close military relationship with Cuban and Angolan state military forces in that area. By the late 1980s, SWAPO forces included conventional mechanized units in southern Angola as well as guerrillas conducting operations inside northern South West Africa. With the 1989 South African withdrawal from South West Africa and the territory's independence as Namibia the next year, SWAPO transformed into a political party.

During the 1989 legislative elections, SWAPO won 41 of 72 seats and 57.3 percent of the popular vote, leading to Nujoma becoming Namibia's first president. Abandoning its hard-line Marxist ideology with the end of the Cold War, SWAPO's transition from guerrilla movement to ruling party was relatively smooth. Without the two-thirds majority needed to dictate policy in building a new nation, SWAPO followed a conciliatory approach, choosing a number of white cabinet members and giving sub-cabinet positions to minority parties. In subsequent elections, however, SWAPO secured a two-thirds majority in the legislature. Despite independence, the country still faces problems regarding unemployment, economic revitalization, housing, education, and dissatisfied minority political groups.

SWAPO consists mainly of members representing the Ovambo people of northern Namibia, the largest population group in the country. Since independence and the subsequent elections, the party has worked to build a platform to deal with the many problems linked to the transition from South African protectorate to independent nation. At a December 1991 congress, SWAPO held elections for major party posts and issued a series of policy statements emphasizing educational reform, the curbing of crime, the enlargement of the army, and the creation of a navy.

Since Namibia's independence, SWAPO retained political power, winning strong support in regular elections and changing presidential candidates after several terms. In national elections in 1999, SWAPO received 77 percent of the vote, with Nujoma continuing as president. During the November 2004 elections, SWAPO won 75.1 percent of the vote, securing 55 of 72 seats in the national assembly and SWAPO secretary general Hifikepunye Pohamba won 76.4 percent of the vote to become the country's new president the next year. In 2015, long-serving SWAPO official Hage Geingob became president of Namibia with a strong electoral mandate.

ABC-CLIO

See also: Angolan Armed Forces (FAPLA and FAA); Angolan Conflicts; Cuba and Africa; Namibia Independence War; Nujoma, Sam; Popular Movement for the Liberation of Angola (MPLA); South Africa's Border War; Soviet Military Involvement in Africa.

Further Reading
Leys, Colin, and John Saul. *Namibia's Liberation Struggle: The Two Edged Sword.* London: James Currey, 1995.

Udogu, E. Ike. *Liberation Namibia: The Long Diplomatic Struggle between the United Nations and South Africa.* Jefferson, NC: McFarland, 2012.

Wallace, Marion. *A History of Namibia: From the Beginning to 1990.* New York: Columbia University Press, 2011.

Southern Sudan Liberation Movement (SSLM)

See Sudan Civil War, First

Soviet Military Involvement in Africa

The Soviet Union did not become meaningfully involved in Africa until after the death of Joseph Stalin in 1953. This lack of previous engagement was not only because there were practical impediments to intervention, but also because there wasn't the ideological justification for the Soviet Union to put great effort into doing so. Despite Vladimir Lenin's hostility toward imperialism, in the absence of the appropriate development of productive forces and the class system in African colonies, there was deemed to be little hope for socialist revolution without bourgeois revolution first. Hence, for Lenin, the first requirement for African nations under an imperial yoke in progression toward socialism—and ultimately communism—was to achieve "bourgeois-democratic liberation" from imperial power, a process in which the proletariat of the imperial power itself was expected to be the driving force. There were certainly few signs of revolutionary potential in the colonies themselves. A short-lived flurry of excitement within the white-dominated Communist Party of South Africa and Comintern over workers' unrest at the end of the World War I ended up highlighting the differences and divisions between white and Black workers more than proletarian class consciousness. Given such issues, Soviet involvement in Africa itself was neither a particular priority, nor was it practical, given relative Soviet economic and military weakness and concerns closer to home.

While during the late 1920s and 1930s under Stalin the Soviet Union was growing in strength, the theoretical need for African nations to undergo bourgeois-democratic revolution as a prerequisite for any move toward socialism remained. In this context, for example, very limited Soviet attempts to keep Ethiopia independent made theoretical sense—despite it being a monarchy—even if the complex international situation in the mid-1930s meant that meaningful assistance to prevent Italian takeover was neither viable nor diplomatically pragmatic. From the mid-1930s to 1945, the Soviet leadership was increasingly preoccupied with threats to the Soviet Union on the Eurasian landmass.

After Soviet victory in the Great Patriotic War, where Stalin did subsequently come to depart from Lenin in his approach toward Africa was in that there was an acceptance that indigenous communists could fight for and indeed should lead struggles for national liberation and where a subsequent transition to state socialism need not be protracted and could take place without a bourgeois-democratic interregnum. It was in fact deemed that genuine national liberation could only come about through revolution led by communists. That such ideas might practically be applied at the time to former Western colonies might have seemed unlikely in 1945—and particularly in favorable circumstances where colonial powers chose to relinquish authority over their colonies. When India was given independence in 1947, and there were multiple communist-led insurrections in Asia by the late 1940s, the same trend did not follow immediately in Africa. Indeed, only by 1960, was the "wind of change" blowing through much of Africa, by which point the Soviet Union had already involved itself in African affairs and national liberation struggles north of the Sahara and was starting to involve itself to the south.

The Soviet Union was the first to become involved on the African continent in Egypt. The Soviet supply of weapons to Egypt—under Gamal Nasser, now seen as an important anti-imperial ally in the region—had already begun in 1955 and would ultimately see more than 50,000 Soviet military personnel serve in Egypt in advisory, training, and de facto combat roles as "specialists." The Soviet decision to support the Aswan Dam project in the face of Western vacillation in 1958 is seen as an important marker in increasing Soviet commitments in Egypt. In light of Egypt's convenient and strategically valuable location, the Soviet Union would continue to provide considerable material and financial support to Egypt despite turbulent relations through to the expulsion of a significant number of Soviet personnel in 1972 and an end to treaty relations between the two states in 1976. Additional early Soviet involvement on the African continent came further west. Soviet commitments to the Algerian struggle for "liberation" from colonialism began prior to the independence achieved in 1962, although practical support was much greater and far more obvious after independence. In addition to the supply of arms and provision of training to the new state, the Soviet Union played a significant role in the removal of mines that were vestiges of the French counterinsurgency. Despite political turbulence within it, Soviet involvement in Algeria extended all the way to 1991. From 1962 to 1991, more than 10,000 Soviet military personnel served in a variety of capacities in Algeria, with the Algerian armed forces being a major recipient of Soviet military equipment. This equipment was paid for, as was the norm for Soviet arms deliveries on the continent, through loans that typically remained unpaid or at best partially paid off by the collapse of the Soviet Union. Local raw materials, often oil, increased the likelihood of at least some return on loans. At times lucrative for the Soviet Union was its later relationship with nearby Libya after a coup in 1969 led to Muammar Gaddafi's leadership of the new Libyan republic. Considerable purchases of military equipment and wider Soviet support soon followed, which included Soviet assistance in Libya's brief war with Egypt in 1977. Substantial Soviet arms deliveries from 1973 were initially paid for through oil revenues, but Gaddafi's erratic foreign policy and failure to pay growing debt to the Soviet Union were both factors in declining Soviet enthusiasm for support to the regime.

Under the premiership of Nikita Khrushchev in the late 1950s and early 1960s—as national liberation became a viable pursuit for the people of many African nations—the Soviet Union started to show increased and wider interest in Africa and particularly in sub-Saharan Africa. Only in 1958 had the Communist Party in the Soviet Union started in earnest to establish the organizational capacity for engagement with Africa through the international department of the central committee of the Communist Party (CPSU) and an Africa department in the ministry for foreign affairs, for example. The foundation of the People's Friendship University in Moscow in 1960, although open to students from other continents, was closely linked to increasing Soviet interest in Africa and would in 1961 be renamed in honor of the fallen first leader of an independent Congo, Patrice Lumumba. Undoubtedly, Soviet ambitions on a global scale were one factor fueling Soviet interest in Africa in which there was certainly opportunity as part of the global challenge to imperialism and capitalism. Other factors were undoubtedly the interest in acquiring allies and bases for future expansion of Soviet interests. The leaders of African liberation movements also, however, seem to have played an important role in bringing the Soviet Union into sub-Saharan Africa in their requests for Soviet assistance. At this time Soviet assistance to African liberation movements was in the first instance still geared toward the achievement or maintenance of national liberation as a precursor to socialist revolution in many cases, meaning that strong socialist credentials were not necessarily a prerequisite for Soviet assistance. Certainly, strong Marxist-Leninist or socialist credentials had not been in evidence among the leaders of either Egypt or Algeria. In July 1960, and in response to requests for assistance, the Soviet Union beat the West to providing support to Ghana led by Kwame Nkrumah, whose regime claimed to be neutral in the Great Power struggles of the Cold War. Nkrumah's government was nonetheless willing to orientate itself more toward the Soviet Union, where as an early focal point for African liberation movements after gaining independence in 1957, it faced Western unwillingness to provide support. Soviet military specialists would arrive in Ghana in 1962, and Ghana was a gateway for limited Soviet support for the newly independent Congo. A military coup in Ghana in 1966 would, however, lead to a reorientation of the country toward the West and a souring of, even if not a break in, relations with the Soviet Union.

A limiting factor in Soviet involvement in Africa was undoubtedly the relative weakness of the Soviet navy for power projection into African waters. Soviet premier Nikita Khrushchev was opposed to the necessary expenditure required for the Soviet Navy to be able to back up Soviet intervention in much of Africa with the sort of naval power that had clearly been lacking off Cuba in 1962 and that was increasingly available in the Mediterranean as the 1960s progressed. By 1969 the Soviet Union was in a position to send a small naval detachment to distant Ghana to intervene in a dispute over the seizure of two Soviet trawlers the previous year, where Soviet involvement in nearby Dahomey (later, the People's Republic of Benin), Guinea-Bissau, and early and very short-lived involvement in Guinea made the region something of a focal point for Soviet interests but with little long-term return.

Under Leonid Brezhnev, during the 1970s, the necessary investment in the Soviet Navy as a means of power projection and more determined intervention in sub-Saharan Africa would be forthcoming. Soviet intervention was also made easier by the fact that by this point many African states had either broken free from their former colonial masters or were in the process of doing so. When Russia had been a fledgling bourgeois-democratic state, Lenin had argued back in 1917 that Russia was sufficiently advanced for the state in the hands of the proletariat and its allies to be the vehicle for Russian development toward socialism and on to communism—despite evident Russian "backwardness." This idea could now be applied to recently or newly decolonized African states and states that were in the throes of decolonization and for which there was now considerable momentum on the continent. Increasingly, at least a veneer of socialism was a requirement for Soviet assistance for particular groups, where assistance to Kwame Nkrumah and Ghana and Ahmed Sékou Touré in Guinea under Khrushchev had highlighted the possibility of poor returns for international communism in assuming that a group's opposition to colonial rule made that country a sustainable Soviet ally. Soviet intent was that revolution in Africa would ideally follow the Soviet model applicable across the globe, where it would be led by urban elites and, in Africa, an inevitably small proletariat. That African states typically lacked a significant proletariat was acknowledged in later Soviet theoretical justifications for intervention in Africa, as, for example, in the work of theorist of the international department of the CPSU Karel Brutents. For Brutents, national liberation movements of the mid-1970s were contributing to the cause of international revolution not because they were close to achieving socialism themselves, but because they were contributing to "progressive" forces destabilizing capitalism. Given that the Soviet Union was there to guide and support national liberation movements, they might, however, advance more quickly down their road to socialism than would otherwise have been the case, even if that road was a long one. The Soviet model contrasted with that of the Chinese—now a rival in Africa after the Sino-Soviet split of the early 1960s—that stressed that the peasantry could with the appropriate cultural outlook be a driver for revolutionary change. Understandably, the Chinese model had the potential for wider appeal on a continent that by and large had seen only limited urbanization and industrialization. However, arguably, the Chinese lack of power projection capabilities at this time weakened the scope for Chinese intervention.

By the late 1970s, Soviet commitments south of the Sahara had become far more substantial than they had been a decade before. Soviet support for the MPLA government in Angola from 1974 was not limited to material assistance, but also saw just under 11,000 personnel serve in Angola in varying capacities, including as military advisers and specialists alongside Cuban allies against the rival FNLA and UNITA. Almost 7,000 Angolans were trained in Soviet and Russian military educational institutions up to the beginning of 1995. While the FNLA was effectively destroyed in the late 1970s, rival UNITA's sustained backing from South Africa that included active support from the South African military—itself supported by the United States—fueled a protracted war that only came to an end after the collapse of the Soviet Union. Soviet support for SWAPO's struggle in Namibia, the ANC's struggle in South Africa, FRELIMO in Mozambique, and ZAPU in Zimbabwe are all additional examples of Soviet support for leftward leaning national liberation movements during this period, representing a considerable commitment to southern Africa.

During the 1970s the Horn of Africa saw considerable Soviet investment, although this did not lead to stable return in terms of providing reliable and respectable allies as was arguably by now the norm. Soviet commitments in Somalia from the early 1960s had grown after a coup there in 1969 led to a more Soviet orientation. From 1972 Somalia hosted Soviet naval facilities established in part with a view to Soviet penetration of the Indian Ocean. Soviet assistance to neighboring Ethiopia after 1974—with Soviet commitments becoming significant in 1976–1977 after Soviet wariness over support for Mengistu Haile Mariam's fledgling regime had been sufficiently overcome—would, however, prove unpopular with a Somalian regime keen to gain control over the Ogaden region, claimed by both Ethiopia and Somalia. Despite Soviet attempts at mediation between what, for a brief period, were two Soviet allies, after invading the Ethiopian-controlled Ogaden, in 1977, Somalia went as far as to break treaty relations with a Soviet Union that was also supporting Ethiopia. Soon, with U.S. backing for the now anti-Soviet Somalia, the stage was set for heavy fighting between Ethiopia and Somalia, with Ethiopia also receiving Soviet support in its war against rebels in Eritrea, whose territory provided Ethiopia's access to the sea.

By the early 1980s Soviet enthusiasm for African intervention was waning, given both the expense and the increased tension with the West. Certainly, Soviet support for Mengistu's Ethiopian regime had played a meaningful part in the deterioration of the fledgling Soviet-U.S. détente that would be further accelerated by the Soviet invasion of Afghanistan at the end of 1979. Nonetheless, the Soviet Union proved unwilling to abandon its African allies even after Brezhnev's death due, a large extent, to the political capital it had invested on the continent and the prestige at stake.

Under Mikhail Gorbachev, from 1985, Soviet involvement in Africa would continue despite the financial constraints now dogging Soviet foreign policy and even as in the context of Gorbachev's policy of glasnost or "openness," the Soviet Union started to lose control over the Eastern Bloc closer to home. While, to a large extent, diminishing enthusiasm for intervention under Gorbachev was for financial reasons, as to some extent had been the case under Brezhnev, rapprochement with the West on moral grounds was also a factor in Gorbachev's "new thinking" in the late 1980s that meant much more than the notion of détente that increasingly only nominally existed under Brezhnev. This "new thinking" was particularly apparent after a metamorphosis of Gorbachev's perestroika or "restructuring" of the Soviet Union by 1989. By 1990 Soviet military support for African regimes that were not paying for their military support in hard currency was increasingly meagre and especially where—as in Ethiopia in particular—the Soviet client regime's conduct did not fit in with Gorbachev's "new thinking" morality.

The waning of Soviet enthusiasm for intervention in Africa was not mirrored in Fidel Castro's Cuba, which clung to its support of socialist revolution in Africa beyond the collapse of the Soviet Union, even if with increasingly meagre resources. Cuban forces played particularly key roles in Angola and Ethiopia.

Soviet involvement in Africa did not lead not long-lived socialist governments on the continent where Cold War allies were frequently quick to change political colors in the face of declining Soviet power and ultimately the collapse of the Soviet Union. Soviet involvement in Africa had undoubtedly contributed to considerable and prolonged bloodshed as African conflicts became Cold War ones by proxy through local alliances with Cold War powers. The Soviet Union—and in particular through its independently minded Cuban allies—can, however, be argued to have played a meaningful supporting role for groups that were able to successfully push for the independence of Namibia (in 1990) from South Africa and those seeking an end of apartheid in the latter—both coming to fruition after the superpowers had all but withdrawn from these conflicts and Cold War allies on both sides were left floundering.

More recently, Russia, under Vladimir Putin, has shown signs of seeking influence on the African continent, where the Soviet Union left off, both in North Africa—in Egypt, and in Algeria with which ties were never severed—and indeed south of the Sahara. Russian motives for involvement on the African continent are numerous but include the exploitation of raw materials and exports as well as prestige.

Alexander Hill

See also: Angolan Armed Forces (FAPLA and FAA); Angolan Conflicts; Arab-Israeli Wars; Cuba and Africa; Ethiopia: Insurgency and Interstate War; Gaddafi, Muammar; Libya, Conflicts with Egypt and the United States; Mengistu Haile Mariam; Namibia Independence War; Nasser, Gamal Abdel; Ogaden War; Portuguese Africa, Independence Wars (Angola, Mozambique, and Guinea-Bissau); Somalia Civil War; South Africa, Armed Struggle against Apartheid; Zimbabwe African People's Union (ZAPU); Zimbabwe Independence War.

Further Reading

Ginor, Isabella, and Gideon Remez. *The Soviet-Israeli War 1967–1973: The USSR's Military Intervention in the Egyptian-Israeli Conflict*. Oxford: Oxford University Press, 2017.

Okorokov, Aleksandr V. *Sovetskii soiuz i voini v Afrike*. Moscow: Veche, 2018.

Shubin, Vladimir G. *The Hot "Cold War": The USSR in Southern Africa*. London: Pluto Press, 2008.

Westad, Odd Arne. *The Global Cold War*. Cambridge: Cambridge University Press, 2007.

Yordanov, Radoslav A. *The Soviet Union and the Horn of Africa during the Cold War: Between Ideology and Pragmatism*. Lanham, MD: Lexington Books, 2016.

Sudan Civil War, First (1955–1972)

The First Sudanese Civil War was between the government of Sudan and the Anya-Nya, the rebel group in southern Sudan. The root causes of the conflict were as a result of the sociopolitical and economic differences between northern and southern Sudan. This situation was instigated by the disparity in the British colonial administrative policy in northern and southern Sudan during the Anglo-Egyptian period from 1899 to 1955. In particular, the southern policy of the 1920s prevented any form of sociopolitical interaction between the Muslim Arabs in the North and sub-Saharan Africans in the southern region who were predominantly Christians. After Sudan gained its independence from the British on January 1, 1956, the sociopolitical relationship between both ethnic groups in northern and southern Sudan was filled with uncertainty and suspicion.

The implementation of the southern policy of the 1920s by the British colonial administrators led to the treatment of northern and southern Sudan as two different colonial regions based on the cultural and religious differences between the ethnic groups inhabiting both regions. However, between June 12 and 13, 1947, the Juba Conference was convened in southern Sudan. The main aim of the conference was to facilitate the sociopolitical relationship between northern and southern Sudan in order to foster the unity of Sudan.

However, the Juba Conference reflected how unprepared the southern delegates were for any form of self-government in Sudan compared with their more educated northern counterparts. In addition, ethnic differences and rivalry among the southerners weakened the possibility of unity them among. Conversely, the shared religious identity as Muslims coupled with their ethnic identity as Arabs were some of sociocultural factors that united the northerners at the Juba Conference.

Toward the eve of Sudan's independence in the 1950s, the sociopolitical differences between the north and south were aggravated by the Sudanization policy. This was part of the British plan to prepare the Sudanese for self-government. However, the Sudanization committee was dominated by northerners. Consequently, southern Sudanese soldiers in the Equatorial Corps were marginalized based on the fact that most southerners in the army were not promoted, while their northern counterparts replaced the positions of British and Egyptian officers in the Sudanese Army. In addition, few southern officers in the army were promoted during this period.

As a result of these grievances, the tension between the northern and southern Sudanese came to a climax on August 18, 1955, when the southern soldiers in the No. 2 Company of the Equatoria Corps in Torit mutinied and attacked northern officers. Although the mutiny started in the Equatoria region, the Upper Nile and Bahr-el-Ghazal, the two other regions in southern Sudan, were also affected by these incidents. Consequently, southern Sudan was occupied by northern Sudanese troops, and southerners were arbitrarily intimidated, tortured, and killed.

The sociopolitical climate in southern Sudan worsened after General Ibrahim Abboud's coup overthrew the parliamentary government of Sudan on November 17, 1958. Abboud's discriminative policies and violent actions toward the southerners escalated the civil war. During this period Islamization and Arabization policies were implemented in the south in an attempt to convert Christians and traditionalist to Muslims. By May 15, 1962, the Abboud government promulgated the Missionary Societies Act, which expelled Christian missionary societies from

Sudan. In addition, southern Sudan refugees along the borders of Uganda, Kenya, Ethiopia, and the Congo were attacked by the Sudanese Army.

An aftermath of these events was that on August 19, 1963, southern intellectuals and politicians in exile such as Joseph Lagu, Joseph Oduho, Father Saturnino Lohure, George Akumbek, Julius Moroga, and Severino Fuli instigated the formation of a guerrilla movement known as *Anya-Nya*. The Anya-Nya consisted of different ethnic groups in southern Sudan such as the Azande, Shilluk, Dinka, Nuer, and Madi. Despite their ethnic differences, their desire to secede from northern Sudan united them against the government of Sudan. On September 19, 1963, Anya-Nya launched its first attack on the Sudanese Army from the Eastern Equatoria region.

During the civil war moral and financial support were provided to the Anya-Nya movement through southern Sudanese refugees in neighboring countries. For instance, southern refugees in the Congo served as recruits and also raised funds for the guerrilla group. In addition, the external military aid from Israel provided arms and ammunition for the Anya-Nya. Within the context of the Cold War period, Israeli support was based on the strategy of using southern insurgency to thwart Sudan's military from supporting the Arab states during the Arab-Israeli War of 1967. The Sudanese Army was assisted by Egypt and Syria during the civil war. Both countries had strong diplomatic relations with the Soviet Union just as the United States was Israel's main ally.

The civil war lasted for 17 years and eventually came to end with the signing of the Addis Ababa Agreement on February 27, 1972. The peace agreement was negotiated between the Government of Sudan and the Southern Sudan Liberation Movement (SSLM), which represented the interests of the southern Sudanese. Despite the regional autonomy granted to the southerners, mutual distrust and ethnic rivalry were still prevalent among the ethnic groups in the region. One of the major reasons for this situation was the rivalry among southern politicians based on their ethnic differences. This affected the possibility of peaceful coexistence among them. For instance, the High Executive Council delegated with the responsibility of facilitating sociopolitical development in southern Sudan was headed by Abel Alier, a Southern Dinka. However, the educated Equatorians dominated the civil service in the south, and some of them were disgruntled with Alier's leadership. Thus, the grievances among the southerners were preserved.

Yusuf Sholeye

See also: Anyanya; Arab-Israeli Wars; Cold War in Africa; Coups and Military Regimes in Africa; Lagu, Joseph Yanga.

Further Reading

Beshir, Mohammed Omer. *The Southern Sudan: Background to Conflict*. London: Hurst 1968.

Collins, Robert O. *A History of Modern Sudan*. Cambridge: Cambridge University Press, 2008.

Johnson, Douglas. *The Root Causes of Sudan's Civil Wars*. Kampala: Fountain Publishers, 2011.

Poggo, Scopas. *The First Sudanese Civil War: African, Arabs, and Israelis in the Southern Sudan, 1955–1972*. New York: Palgrave Macmillan, 2009.

Sudan Civil War, Second (1983–2005)

The Second Sudanese Civil War was a conflict between the government of Sudan and the Sudan People's Liberation Movement/Army (SPLM/A). About two million people died during this conflict. Ethnic and religious differences between northern and southern Sudan, the discovery of oil in the southern region, and interethnic rivalry within the SPLA were some of the root causes of the Second Sudanese Civil War. The prevalence of famine and drought in Sudan aggravated the civil war and prolonged it.

Although the Addis Ababa Agreement of 1972 ended the First Sudanese Civil War, the division of the southern region into three regions, Bahr-el-Ghazal, Equatoria, and the Upper Nile compromised the peace agreement. In particular, the discovery of oil in the south by Chevron in 1974, instigated President Jaafar Nimeiry's decision to redraw the boundaries of Sudan in order to control the oilfields. On June 5, 1983, Nimeiry proclaimed Republican Order Number One, imposing Arabization and Islamization policies on the southern Sudanese.

In order to clamp down on any form of uprising from southern officers based on this new policy, Nimeiry ordered that the First Division of the Southern Command transfer to the garrisons in the northern and western parts of Sudan. However, the disgruntled southern officers, most of whom were former Anya-Nya members who had fought in Sudan's First Civil War, used this tense situation to express their grievances. Thus, in May 1983, battalions 104 and 105, which consisted of mainly southern Sudanese soldiers, mutinied in Bor, Pibor, and Ayod. They later sought refuge in Ethiopia, and by July about 2,500 soldiers within the Southern Command defected to the new guerrilla base in Belpam, Ethiopia.

These events led to the emergence of the Sudan People's Liberation Movement/Army (SPLM/A), which was formed by Dr. John Garang in April 1983. The SPLA's guerrilla activities consisted of sporadic attacks on towns in the south and disruption of food aid to the southerners. This situation aggravated the famine and drought crisis in Sudan in the 1980s. Within the context of these events, mounting pressure against Nimeiry's regime became widespread in northern and southern Sudan. By September 1984 Nimeiry rescinded the decision to divide the south into three regions and revoked the application of Sharia laws in the south. However, these moves came too late to stop the war when the SPLA had gained control of most regions in the south.

Eventually, on April 6, 1985, minister for defense General Abdel Rahman Suwar al-Dahab ousted Nimeiry from power. Shortly afterward, elections were held in April 1986, which led to the appointment of Sadiq al-Mahdi as the new prime minister of Sudan. Sadiq and Garang met in Addis Ababa on July 31, 1985, in order to resolve the civil war. However, there was no compromise between them. During this period the refugee crisis in Sudan worsened. From May 1983 to the end of 1987, the number of southern Sudanese refugees in Ethiopia increased from about 40,000 to around 221,000. Also, the SPLA bases and training centers were strategically located in refugee camps in Bilpam, Dima, Bonga, and Zinc in the Gambella region of Ethiopia.

Just as Ethiopia aided the SPLA insurgent activities in southern Sudan so did Sudan support the guerrilla operations of the Eritrean People's Liberation Front (EPLF) in northern Ethiopia. After the collapse of Ethiopia's Mengistu regime in 1991, SPLA support shifted to Uganda. As a result, Khartoum backed rebels in northern Uganda, including the Lord's Resistance Army (LRA). Furthermore, the Baggara Arabs from Darfur and Kordofan regions were commandeered by Sadiq to attack Dinka villages, destroying crops and stealing cattle. Eventually, political instability and social unrest in Sudan instigated the military coup of June 30, 1989, led by Omar al-Bashir. At this point, the government of Sudan had spent about $1 million a day on the war, and by the end of 1989, about 500,000 had died from the war.

Several peace talks such as the Abuja Peace Conference of 1993 were initiated by the international community but were ineffectual. In addition, humanitarian agencies facilitated the delivery of relief aid to southern Sudanese affected by the war. Unfortunately, the appropriation of these aids by both the Sudanese Army and SPLA aggravated the casualties of the war. In particular, disputes over food aid distribution represented a major cause of the internal split within the SPLA into the SPLA-Mainstream and SPLA-Nasir on August 28, 1991.

Despite the division within the guerrilla movement by February 1997, regions such as Rumbek and Wunrok in the Bahr-el-Ghazal region were recaptured by SPLA-Mainstream from the Sudanese Army. However, in an attempt to reverse this situation, the Khartoum government provided rival rebel factions with arms and ammunition in order to compromise SPLA-Mainstream guerrilla activities in southern Sudan. Thus, Riek Machar, Kerubino Kuanyin, and Arok Thon Arok, leaders of rival groups in southern Sudan, were united against John Garang's SPLA-Mainstream. In addition, the discovery of oil in the southern region by Chevron aggravated the civil war. Chevron ended its oil exploration activities by 1984. Soon other multinational companies such as Tailsman were interested in Sudan's oil reserves. This situation instigated the Khartoum government to perpetuate violence among rival ethnic groups in southern Sudan.

Sudan's oil revenue soared from $547 million in 2000 to $805 million in 2001. Most of these revenues were used to purchase military equipment to fight the civil war. The indiscriminate killing, torture, and displacement of southern Sudanese affected by the war galvanized the international community to protest against human rights violations in Sudan. Eventually, given international pressure on Khartoum, the 21-year-long conflict ended with the Comprehensive Peace Agreement of 2005, which was signed by government of Sudan, John Garang, and other international dignitaries.

Yusuf Sholeye

See also: Al-Bashir, Omar (Umar) Hassan Ahmad; Anyanya; Darfur Genocide; Eritrean People's Liberation Front (EPLF); Ethiopia: Insurgency and Interstate War; Famine in Postcolonial African Conflicts; Garang, John de Mabior; Lord's Resistance Army (LRA); Machar, Riek Teny Dhurgon; Refugees in Postcolonial Africa; Sudan Civil War, First;

Sudan People's Liberation Movement/Army (SPLM/A); Uganda, Insurgency in the North.

Further Reading

Collins, Robert O. *A History of Modern Sudan.* Cambridge: Cambridge University Press, 2005.

Johnson, Douglas H. *The Root Causes of Sudan's Civil War.* Kampala: Fountain Publishers, 2003.

Jok Madut Jok. *Sudan: Race, Religion and Violence.* Philadelphia: University of Philadelphia Press, 2001.

Sudan Liberation Army (SLA)

The Sudan Liberation Army (SLA) is a rebel group operating in Sudan's strife-torn western Darfur region. Following a series of internal power struggles that broke out in late 2005, the group is now divided into numerous factions. Unlike the similarly named Sudan People's Liberation Army, which operates in southern Sudan, the SLA states that its goal is a unified Sudan in which Darfur's people are given political autonomy and economic opportunity. Fighting between the SLA and the Sudanese government–sponsored Janjaweed militias has been ongoing since 2003. The SLA draws the core of its membership from three Darfurian ethnic groups: the Fur, Zaghawa, and Masalit.

SLA'S ORIGINS AND EARLY YEARS

The SLA's origins reach back to the 1980s, when young Fur first banded together to protest the Arab domination of the central government in Sudan's capital, Khartoum, and the harassment of their people by local Arabic-speaking nomads. This group of Fur would evolve into what became known as the Darfur Liberation Front (DLF). Largely preoccupied with a decades-long civil war in southern Sudan, Khartoum paid little attention to what was happening in Darfur until 2003. In February that year, the DLF took control of Gulu, the main town in Darfur's central province of Jebel Marrah. Led by Abd al-Wahid Muhammad Ahmad al-Nur, the DLF set up camps in Gulu and began staging attacks against the Sudanese military.

In March 2003, the DLF announced it had changed its name to the SLA. The same day, it released a "political declaration" stating the SLA's goal: to "create a united democratic Sudan." The declaration went on to say: "Armed struggle is one of our means to achieve our legitimate objective" and called for the replacement of Sudan's autocratic government with a "united democratic" regime. A few days after the declaration was released, the SLA entered into a short-lived cease-fire with Khartoum.

The SLA took control of the village of Tine on the border with Chad on March 26, 2003. The conflict between the SLA and government forces intensified, and by the beginning of August, the government had recruited Darfurian Arab militias to help with the fighting. These so-called Janjaweed entered into very few direct battles with the SLA during the next three years, but they carried out a scorched-earth campaign against the mostly unarmed people of Darfur, raping, pillaging, and murdering in village after village. The guerrilla SLA, with far fewer troops than the Janjaweed, had strong popular support. Headquartered in the mountains of central Darfur, the SLA has been supported by villagers who have provided its fighters with food, shelter, and intelligence on its adversaries.

Unsuccessful peace talks were held in Chad in December 2003; thus the conflict continued. In January 2004 Sudan's government filed a complaint with neighboring Eritrea, which it claimed had been helping the SLA. Neither the SLA nor Eritrea has confirmed these claims.

Along with Darfur's other major rebel group, the Justice and Equality Movement (JEM), the SLA signed a cease-fire in Chad in April 2004. The agreement included safe passage for humanitarian aid teams and the disarmament of the Janjaweed, and Sudan's government made plans to return many refugees to the country. In July the SLA, the JEM, and the government began peace talks. Talks fell apart in December, however, because of alleged cease-fire violations. The African Union, which sent 7,000 peacekeeping troops to Darfur, said the cease-fire was frequently violated by all groups involved.

SPLINTERING OF THE SLA

November 2005 marked the beginning of the splintering of the SLA into numerous factions that have competed for territory and fought against one another, a phenomenon that has had drastic consequences for the peace process and increased the complexity of the conflict. The first split within the SLA occurred following the election of Minni Minawi as SLA leader during a conference boycotted by Nur, the heroic leader who had led the DLF during the siege of Gulu. Nur loyalists, primarily of his own Fur ethnicity, did not recognize the election of Minawi, an ethnic Zaghawa, and the two emerging factions soon engaged in bloody fighting in North Darfur.

While the predominantly Fur SLA-Nur and the predominantly Zaghawa SLA-Minawi remain the two largest factions, the extent of these internal power struggles was reflected in the existence of an estimated dozen rival factions. On May 5, 2006, the SLA-Minawi faction signed a peace agreement with the government. For his cooperation, Minawi was made senior assistant to the president. Both the SLA-Nur and the JEM continued to hold out for the government to agree to such demands as greater compensation for Darfur war victims, an SLA role in disarming the Janjaweed and aiding refugees in their return. It is alleged that Minawi, and his branch of the SLA, began raids on Northern Darfur to punish those non-signing rebels.

Shifting alliances and splintering within the SLA created complexity in regards to further peacemaking attempts in Darfur. In 2010 Abdelshafi allied the Juba faction of the SLA with other rebel groups to create the Liberation and Justice Movement (LJM). The LJM signed, in July 2011, the Doha Documents for Peace, though Abdelshafi then distanced himself from the LJM, believing the government was not truly invested in peace. Later in 2011 two major factions of the SLA joined with the JEM and the Sudan People's Liberation Movement–North to continue the resistance. In 2020, after the fall of Sudan's Bashir regime, the SLA entered a peace agreement with the transitional government and joined the democratic process.

ABC-CLIO

See also: Al-Bashir, Omar (Umar) Hassan Ahmad; Darfur Genocide; Janjaweed; Justice and Equality Movement (JEM).

Further Reading

Flint, Julie, and Alex de Waal. *Darfur: A Short History of a Long War.* London: Zed Books, 2006.

Mamdani, Mahmood. *Survivors and Saviors: Darfur, Politics and the War on Terror.* New York: Double Day, 2009.

Prunier, Gerard. *Darfur: The Ambiguous Genocide.* Ithaca, NY: Cornell University Press, 2005.

Sudan People's Liberation Movement/Army (SPLM/A)

The Sudan People's Liberation Army (SPLA) emerged as the military wing of the Sudan People's Liberation Movement (SPLM) that was founded on April 6, 1983. Dr. John Garang was the leader of the SPLM/A, from 1983 to 2005, based on his role in orchestrating the mutiny of southern officers from the Sudanese Army in 1983. The guerrilla group was dominated by the Dinka ethnic group from the Upper Nile and Bahr-el-Ghazal regions. Former members of the Anya-Nya who fought in the First Sudan Civil War (1955–1972) and later known as the Anya-Nya II also joined the SPLA.

The SPLA's military ideology was shaped by its relationship with the Marxist regime of Colonel Mengistu Haile Mariam in Ethiopia. Mengistu's military strategy was based on the Soviet belief in the preponderance of military force and Ethiopia's traditional doctrine of deployment of a mass army. Thus, a massive army, forced conscription, and rudimentary training were some of the main features of the Ethiopian Army that carried over to the SPLA. The creation of southern Sudanese refugee camps and SPLA training centers in the Gambella region in Ethiopia facilitated the relationship between SPLA and Mengistu's regime. By 1989 over 70,000 SPLA troops graduated from training camps in Ethiopia.

Compared with the Anya-Nya's secessionist agenda during the First Sudan Civil War, the SPLA's political aim focused more on the capturing of state power in Khartoum, which would be used to facilitate radical change in Sudanese society. The SPLA's abandonment of secessionism also reflected the views of its main sponsor, Ethiopia, which faced several separatist insurgencies and the failure of prominent secessionist movements in other parts of Africa during the 1960s. The creation of a united socialist Sudan became the SPLA's major objective. This ideal was infused into the recruitment and organizational structure of the movement. Recruits were transferred to training camps in Gambella and then organized into units under a central commander and redeployed for combat in southern Sudan.

The SPLA's guerrilla strategy included the cutting of government supply lines, especially in rural areas, and overrunning small garrisons. Land mines, ambushes, and sabotage of bridges were used to make travel and transportation into southern Sudan difficult. The SPLA also integrated famine into its insurgent strategy. Food convoys were ambushed to prevent them from reaching starving garrison towns. Consequently, severe famine ensued in the Upper Nile region from 1987 to 1988, with 250,000 Sudanese dying from hunger in this period.

Nevertheless, on January 28, 1989, the alliance between the SPLA and Anya-Nya II led to the capture of the strategic town of Nasir in the Upper Nile region. Subsequently, the insurgents gained control over the southern regions of Torit, Akobo, and the north Bahr-el-Ghazal regions. At this point, the SPLA commandeered thousands of men and captured substantial quantities of government equipment such as vehicles, tanks, and heavy artillery. In addition, the SPLA's guerrilla tactics changed from the deployment of mobile units to entrenched sieges of major cities and towns held by state forces. By 1990, this development enabled the SPLA to effectively repulse offensives by the Sudanese Army.

The early 1990s represented a troubled time for the SPLA. In 1991 the SPLA suffered a major blow with the collapse of Ethiopia's Mengistu regime, which had been its major sponsor. Around the same time, the controversy over the beneficiaries of relief aid, ideological differences, and ethnic rivalry between rebel leaders John Garang and Riek Machar led to the internal division of the guerrilla group into SPLA-Mainstream and SPLA-Nasir on August 29, 1991. In terms of ethnic affiliation, Garang's SPLA-Mainstream comprised mostly Dinka while Machar's SPLA-Nasir became a primarily Nuer group. This situation not only compromised SPLA control over conquered regions in southern Sudan but also instigated the emergence of other splinter factions within the guerrilla group. Thus, the SPLA was divided against itself. These internal conflicts led to the Bor Massacre of November 15, 1991, when about 2,000 Dinka civilians were indiscriminately killed by members of the SPLA-Nasir who were led by Riek Machar. This outrageous event instigated vehement reactions both from the southern Sudanese and the international community. Consequently, popular support for SPLA-Nasir gradually declined. This was also caused by the duplicity of Machar's political agenda as the leader of SPLA-Nasir, which transformed into the South Sudan Independence Movement/Army (SSIM/A). Although SSIA clamored for the independence of South Sudan, it also received arms and ammunition from Khartoum, which opposed South Sudan independence.

However, during this period, Garang made pragmatic efforts to reunify splintered factions with the SPLA-Mainstream, despite the criticism against the authoritarian style of his leadership within the movement. During early 1994 the National Convention (NC) of Southern Sudanese was convened at Chukudum in Eastern Equatoria. The main significance of this meeting was that SPLM/A military leaders discussed and decided on different issues with local southern Sudanese. The endorsement of an independent South Sudan was also a landmark achievement of this convention. In addition, the SPLA gained a new external sponsor in the form of Yoweri Museveni's government in Uganda.

By the beginning of 1996, John Garang compromised with factions within the SPLA. This development was facilitated by the vote of confidence for Garang during the NC and the collapse of SSIA, which precipitated massive defection to the

SPLA-Mainstream. Consequently, these events consolidated SPLA's influence in South Sudan. Based on this situation, the government of Sudan (GoS) negotiated with the SPLA on how to end the civil war. Eventually, this situation led to the Comprehensive Peace Agreement, also known as the Navisha Agreement between the GoS and John Garang, which was signed on January 5, 2005.

This agreement enabled the southerners to decide through a referendum if they wanted an independent South Sudan. In addition, members of SPLA were integrated into the Sudanese Army. After the independence of South Sudan on July 11, 2011, the SPLA became South Sudan's government and regular army. Interethnic conflict between the Dinka and Nuer in the army led to South Sudan's own civil war from 2013 to 2020. In August 2017 South Sudan's president Salva Kiir renamed the SPLA the South Sudan People's Defence Force (SSPDF) in an attempt to restructure the army.

Yusuf Sholeye

See also: Anyanya; Ethiopia: Insurgency and Interstate War; Garang, John de Mabior; Kiir, Salva Mayardit; Machar, Riek Teny Dhurgon; Mengistu Haile Mariam; Museveni, Yoweri; South Sudan Civil War; Sudan Civil War, First; Sudan Civil War, Second.

Further Reading

Collins, Robert O. *A History of Modern Sudan*. Cambridge: Cambridge University Press, 2005.

De Waal, Alex. *Food and Power in Sudan: A Critique of Humanitarianism*. n.p.: African Rights, 1997.

Johnson, Douglas H. "The Sudan People's Liberation Army and the Problem of Factionalism." In *African Guerrillas*, edited by Christopher Clapham, 53–72. Oxford: James Currey, 1998.

Jok Madut Jok. *War and Slavery in Sudan*. Pennsylvania: University of Pennsylvania Press, 2001.

Suez Crisis (1956)

The Suez Crisis was one of the major events of both the Cold War and the Arab-Israeli Wars. It ended Britain's pretensions to be a world superpower and fatally weakened Britain's hold on what remained of its empire. It also placed a dangerous strain on U.S.-Soviet relations, strengthened the position of Egyptian leader Gamal Abdel Nasser throughout the Middle East, and distracted world attention from the concurrent Soviet military intervention in the Hungarian Revolution.

The Suez Crisis had its origins in the development plans of Gamal Abdel Nasser. In 1952 a reformist and anti-British coup d'état in Egypt, led by young army officers, toppled the government of King Farouk I. During the months that followed, Nasser emerged as the strongman and ultimately became president of Egypt. Nasser hoped to enhance his prestige and improve the quality of life for his nation's burgeoning population by carrying out long-discussed plans to construct a high dam on the Upper Nile River south of Aswan to provide electric power. To finance the project, Nasser sought assistance from Western powers. But Nasser had also been endeavoring to build up and modernize the Egyptian military.

Toward that end he had sought to acquire modern weapons from the United States and other Western nations. When the U.S. government refused to supply the advanced arms, which it believed might be used against the State of Israel, in 1955 Nasser turned to the communist bloc. In September 1955, with Soviet encouragement, he reached a barter arrangement with Czechoslovakia for substantial quantities of weapons, including jet aircraft and tanks, in return for Egyptian cotton.

This arms deal impacted the Aswan High Dam construction project for which Nasser had sought Western financing. In December 1955 Washington declared its willingness to lend $56 million for financing the dam, while Britain pledged $14 million and the World Bank $200 million. The condition to the aid was that Egypt provides matching funds and that it will not accept Soviet assistance.

Nasser was unhappy with the attached strings. With Nasser expecting a Soviet offer of assistance, the controlled Egyptian press launched an all-out propaganda offensive against the West, especially the United States. But when no Soviet offer was forthcoming, Nasser finally accepted the Western aid package on July 17, 1956. Much to his chagrin, two days later U.S. secretary of state John Foster Dulles announced that it had been withdrawn. Britain immediately followed suit. The official U.S. reasons were that Egypt had failed to reach an agreement with Sudan over the dam (most of the vast lake created by the dam would be in Sudanese territory), and the Egyptian part of the financing for the project had become uncertain. The real reasons were objections from some U.S. congressman, especially Southerners fearful of competition from Egyptian cotton and Dulles's determination to teach Nasser and other neutralists a lesson. Dulles was angry over Nasser's flirtation with the communist bloc to include the arms purchases and was especially upset over Egypt's recent recognition of the People's Republic of China (PRC).

Nasser's response to this humiliating rebuff came a week later on July 26 when he nationalized the Suez Canal. He had contemplated such a move for some time, but the U.S. decision prompted its timing. In 1955 the canal produced net revenues of nearly $100 million, of which Egypt received only $2 million. Seizure of the canal would not only provide additional funding for the Aswan High Dam project, but it would make Nasser a hero in the eyes of many Arab nationalists.

The British government regarded the sea-level Suez Canal, which connected the eastern Mediterranean with the Red Sea across Egyptian territory, its lifeline to Middle Eastern oil and the Far East. Indeed, 60 percent of all oil consumed in Western Europe passed through the canal. The canal, built by a private company headed by Frenchman Ferdinand de Lesseps, had opened to much fanfare in 1869. It quickly altered the trade routes of the world, and two-thirds of the tonnage passing through the canal was British. Khedive Ismail Pasha, who owned 44 percent of the company shares, found himself in dire financial straits, and in 1875 the British government stepped in and purchased his shares. In 1878 Britain acquired the island of Cyprus north of Egypt from the Ottoman Empire, further strengthening its position in the eastern Mediterranean north of Egypt. The British also increased their role in Egyptian financial affairs, and in 1882 they intervened militarily in Egypt, promising to depart once order had been restored. Britain remained in Egypt and in effect controlled its affairs through World War II.

In 1954 Nasser, determined to end British influence in Egypt, succeeded in renegotiating the 1936 treaty with the British to force the withdrawal of British troops from the Suez Canal Zone. The last British forces departed the Canal Zone on June 13, only six weeks before Nasser nationalized the canal.

The British government took the lead in opposing Nasser. London believed that Nasser's growing popularity in the Arab world was encouraging Arab nationalism and threatening to undermine British influence throughout the Middle East. British prime minister Anthony Eden developed a deep and abiding hatred of the Egyptian leader. For Eden, ousting Nasser from power became nothing short of an obsession. In the immediate aftermath of Nasser's nationalization of the canal, the British government called up 200,000 military reservists and dispatched military resources to the eastern Mediterranean.

The French government also had good reason to seek Nasser's removal. Paris sought to protect its own long-standing interests in the Middle East, but more to the point, the French were now engaged in fighting the National Liberation Front (FLN) in Algeria. The Algerian War, which began in November 1954, had greatly expanded and had become an imbroglio for the government, now led by socialist premier Guy Mollet. Nasser was a strong and vocal supporter of the FLN, and there were many in the French government and military who believed that overthrowing him would greatly enhance French chances of winning the Algerian War. This position found considerable support when on October 18, 1956, the French intercepted the Egyptian ship Athos and found it loaded with arms and documents proving Egyptian support for the FLN.

Israel formed the third leg in the triad of powers arrayed against Nasser. Egypt had instituted a blockade of Israeli ships at the Gulf of Aqaba, Israel's outlet to the Indian Ocean. Also, Egypt had never recognized the Jewish state and indeed remained at war with it following the Israeli War of Independence (1948–1949). In 1955 Israel mounted a half dozen cross-border raids, while Egypt carried out its own raids into Israeli territory by fedayeen (guerrilla fighters).

Over the months that followed Egyptian nationalization of the Suez Canal, the community of interest among British, French, and Israeli leaders developed into secret planning for a joint military operation to topple Nasser. The U.S. government was not consulted and indeed opposed the use of force. The British and French governments either did not understand the American attitude or, if they did, believed that Washington would give approval after the fact to policies undertaken by its major allies, which the latter believed to be absolutely necessary.

The British government first tried diplomacy. Two conferences in London attended by the representatives of 24 nations using the canal failed to produce an agreement on a course of action, and Egypt refused to participate. A proposal by Secretary of State Dulles for a canal users' club of nations failed, as did an appeal to the United Nations (UN) Security Council. On October 1 Dulles announced that the United States was disassociating itself from British and French actions in the Middle East and asserted that the United States intended to play a more independent role.

Meanwhile, secret talks were going forward, first between the British and French for joint military action against Egypt. Military representatives of the two governments met in London on August 10 and hammered out the details of a joint military plan known as MUSKETEER that would involve occupation of both Alexandria and Port Said. The French then brought the Israeli government in on the plan, and General Maurice Challe, deputy chief of staff of the French Air Force, undertook a secret trip to the Middle East to meet with Israeli government and military leaders. The Israelis were at first skeptical about British and French support. They also had no intention of moving as far as the canal itself. The Israelis stated that their plan was merely to send light detachments to link up with British and French forces. They also insisted that British and French military intervention occur simultaneously with their own attack.

General André Beaufre, the designated French military commander for the operation, then came up with a new plan. Under it, the Israelis would initiate hostilities against Egypt in order to provide the pretext for military intervention by French and British forces to protect the canal. This action would technically be in accord with the terms of the 1954 treaty between Egypt and Britain that had given Britain the right to send forces to occupy the Suez Canal Zone in the event of an attack against Egypt by a third power.

On October 23 Mollet and French foreign minister Christian Pineau met in the Paris suburbs at Sèvres with Israeli prime minister David Ben-Gurion, defense minister Shimon Peres, and chief of the Israeli general staff Lieutenant General Moshe Dayan. The French agreed to provide additional air cover for Israel. French ships supposedly searching for Egyptian arms shipments to the Algerian rebels would move to the Israeli coast immediately, and French Mystère aircraft flown by French pilots would be repositioned in Israel. That afternoon British foreign secretary Selwyn Lloyd and foreign office undersecretary of state Patrick Dean joined the discussions. The British, while staunchly pro-intervention, were deeply concerned about their position in the Arab world and were not anxious to be seen in collusion with the Israelis. Thus, an Israeli strike toward the canal through the Sinai would enable the British to have it both ways: they could join the French in demanding of Nasser the right to protect the canal. When he refused, as he certainly would, they could join the French in destroying the Egyptian Air Force, eliminating the one possible threat to Israeli success on the ground. All parties agreed to this new plan, dubbed the "Treaty of Sèvres" and signed by Dean, Pineau, and Ben-Gurion.

On October 23, meanwhile, unrest began in Hungary. The next day Soviet tanks entered Budapest to put down what had become the Hungarian Revolution. French and British planners were delighted at this international distraction that seemed to provide them with a degree of freedom of action.

On the afternoon of October 29 Israeli forces began Operation Kadesh, the invasion of the Sinai Peninsula. Sixteen C-47 transports took off from Israeli fields, each with a paratroop platoon. The objective of the 395-man paratroop battalion was the key Mitla Pass, 156 miles from the Israeli border and only 45 miles from the canal. Meanwhile the remainder of Colonel Ariel Sharon's 202nd Parachute Brigade would race for the pass in French-provided trucks, linking up with the paratroopers within 36 hours. This operation was designed to trigger a major

Egyptian response and threaten the canal in order to trigger the planned British-French response.

The announced objective of Operation Kadesh was the eradication of the fedayeen bases, but it was begun so as to appear to the Egyptians as if it was the beginning of an all-out war. Dayan's detailed plan called for nothing less than a weeklong lightning advance that would end with Israeli forces securing the entire Sinai and a total victory over Egypt. The destruction of Nasser's prestige in the Arab world and final Egyptian recognition of the impossibility of an Arab military victory over Israel were the goals rather than destruction of the Egyptian Army or acquisition of its new Soviet equipment.

A day later, October 30, the British and French governments issued an ultimatum, nominally to both the Egyptian and Israeli governments but in reality only to Egypt, expressing the need to separate the combatants and demanding the right to provide for the security of the Suez Canal. The ultimatum called on both sides to withdraw their forces 10 miles from the canal and gave them 12 hours to reply. The Israelis, of course, immediately accepted the ultimatum, while the Egyptians just as promptly rejected it.

At dusk on October 31, British and French aircraft struck Egyptian airfields and military installations from bases on Cyprus and Malta and from aircraft carriers. The aircraft attacked four Egyptian bases that day and nine the next. On November 1, meanwhile, a British and French naval task force sailed from Malta to join with other ships at Cyprus. In all, the allied landing force numbered some 80,000 men: 50,000 British and 30,000 French. There were 100 British and 30 French warships, including seven aircraft carriers (five British) and the French battleship *Jean Bart*, hundreds of landing craft, and some 80 merchant ships carrying 20,000 vehicles and stores. Yet when Eden reported to the House of Commons on the events, he encountered a surprisingly strong negative reaction from the opposition Labour Party.

Also, following the initial British and French military action, the Egyptians immediately sank a number of ships in the canal to make it unusable. The Israelis, meanwhile, swept across the Sinai in only four days against ineffective Egyptian forces. Finally, on November 5, British and French paratroopers carried out a vertical envelopment of Port Said, Egypt, at the Mediterranean terminus of the canal, while at the same time, French and British destroyers carried out a shore bombardment against those targets likely to impede a landing. Early on November 6, British troops began coming ashore at Port Said and the French at Port Fuad. A single day of fighting saw the ports in allied hands. French and British forces then began a virtually unopposed advance southward along the canal.

President Dwight D. Eisenhower had already entered the picture. On October 31 he described the British attack as "taken in error." He was personally furious at Eden over the events and is supposed to have asked when he first telephoned the British leader, "Anthony, have you gone out of your mind?" The United States applied immediate and heavy financial threats, both on a bilateral basis and through the International Monetary Fund, to bring the British government to heel. Eisenhower also refused any further dealings with Eden personally.

The Soviets, preoccupied by Hungary, took some five days to come to the conclusion that the United States was actually opposing the British and French action. On November 5, Moscow threatened to send "volunteers" to Egypt. This proved a further embarrassment for the British government, but it was U.S. pressure that proved decisive. Nonetheless, the world beheld the strange spectacle of the United States cooperating with the Soviet Union to condemn Britain and France in the UN Security Council and call for an end to the use of force. Although Britain and France vetoed the Security Council resolution, the matter was referred to the General Assembly, which demanded a cease-fire and withdrawal.

Israel and Egypt agreed to a cease-fire on November 4. At midnight on November 6, the day of the U.S. presidential election, the British and French governments also accepted a cease-fire, the French only with the greatest reluctance. By the time the cease-fire went into effect, the French and British controlled about half of the canal's length. French and British losses in the operation were 33 dead and 129 wounded. Egyptian losses are unknown.

A 4,000-man United Nations Emergency Force (UNEF) authorized on November 4 and made up of contingents from the Scandinavian countries, Brazil, Colombia, India, and Indonesia then arrived in Egypt to take up positions to keep Israeli and Egyptian forces separated. At the end of November, the British and French governments both agreed to withdraw their forces from Egypt by December 22, and on December 1 Eisenhower announced that he had instructed U.S. oil companies to resume shipping supplies to both Britain and France. Under pressure from both the United States and the UN, Israel withdrew its forces from the Sinai, to include the Gaza Strip, during February 5–March 6, 1957. A UN observer force of 3,500 men then took up station in Gaza, at Sharm al-Sheikh, and along the Sinai border. Although Israel had been assured that Egyptian forces would not return to Gaza, they were there within 48 hours of the Israeli withdrawal.

Nasser and Arab self-confidence were the chief beneficiaries of the crisis. The abysmal performance of Egyptian military forces in the crisis was forgotten in Nasser's ultimate triumph. Nasser found his prestige dramatically increased throughout the Arab world. Israel also benefited. The presence of the UN force guaranteed an end to the fedayeen raids, and Israel had also broken the Egyptian blockade of the Gulf of Aqaba, although its ships could still not transit the Suez Canal. The crisis also enhanced Soviet prestige in the Middle East, and the UN emerged with enhanced prestige, helping to boost world confidence in the organization.

The Suez Crisis ended Eden's political career. Ill and under tremendous criticism in Parliament from the Labour Party, he resigned from office in January 1957. The events also placed a serious, albeit temporary, strain on U.S.-British relations. More importantly, they revealed the serious limitations in British military strength. Indeed, observers are unanimous in declaring 1956 a seminal date in British imperial history that marked the effective end of Britain's tenure as a great power. The events had less impact in France. Mollet left office in May 1957 but not as a result of the Suez intervention. The crisis was costly to both Britain and France in economic terms, for Saudi Arabia had halted oil shipments to both countries.

Finally, the Suez Crisis could not have come at a worse time for the West because the event diverted world attention from the concurrent brutal Soviet military intervention in Hungary. Eisenhower believed, rightly or wrongly, that without the Suez diversion, there would have been far stronger Western reaction to the Soviet invasion of its satellite.

Spencer C. Tucker

See also: Arab-Israeli Wars; British Military Involvement in Postcolonial Africa; Cold War in Africa; French Military Involvement in Postcolonial Africa; Nasser, Gamal Abdel; Peacekeeping in Africa; Soviet Military Involvement in Africa; U.S. Military Involvement in Africa.

Further Reading

Gorst, Anthony, and Lewis Johnman. *The Suez Crisis*. New York: Routledge, 1997.

McGregor, Andrew. *A Military History of Modern Egypt; from the Ottoman Conquest to the Ramadan War*. Westport, CT: Praeger Security International, 2006.

Morris, Benny. *Righteous Victims: A History of the Zionist-Arab Conflict, 1881–2001*. New York: Vintage Books, 2002.

Oren, Michael B. *Six Days of War: June 1967 and the Making of the Modern Middle East*. New York: Oxford University Press, 2002.

Varble, Derek. *The Suez Crisis—1956*. London: Osprey Publishing, 2003.

Zelikow, Philip, and Ernest May. *Suez Deconstructed: An Interactive Study in Crisis, War and Peacemaking*. Washington, DC: Brookings Institute Press, 2018.

T

Taylor, Charles McArthur Ghankay (1948–)

Charles McArthur Ghankay Taylor was born in Arthington, Liberia, on January 28, 1948, the son of Louise Yassa Zoe and Nielsen Philips. As is the case with many Liberians, Taylor shared both African and African American lineage. Juxtaposed his English name is "Ghankay," his Gola name meaning "strong one," which was likely inherited from his mother.

Taylor was born into a humble working-class family, without the benefits of wealth or the social privileges afforded to those associated with political elite families who were the descendants of the African American settler ruling class. Taylor's upbringing was like those of his social strata. At a young age he was sent to live with a more prominent family, which offered him better educational opportunities. Through the generosity of a Lebanese entrepreneur, Taylor received a scholarship to study at the Rick's Institute, a Baptist missionary school. Taylor proved unruly in school and was expelled. His studies eventually led him to the United States where he studied at Bentley College in Waltham, Massachusetts. While in Waltham, he met Enid Bokai, a relative of Thomas Quiwonkpa. Quiwonkpa would later become one of the leaders of the coup that would depose President William Tolbert.

Taylor and Bokai married in 1980 after his return to Liberia. Before returning to Liberia, however, Taylor had become a political activist for social justice causes in Liberia. It is stated that he would sit on the steps of the U.S. Capitol to plead his case to congressmen. On one occasion, he was part of a demonstration that took a mock coffin of President Tolbert to the White House.

After the 1980 coup in Liberia, Taylor was given a position as the chief of the Government Service Agency (GSA). In 1983 the Ministry of Finance became aware of the inconsistent appropriations practices at the GSA. Upon further investigation it was discovered that Taylor's office had over-remunerated a U.S. firm by $22,000 for a total payment of $922,382. Unable to rectify the situation, Taylor was demoted and assigned to the commerce department. As relations between Quiwonkpa and the junta leader Samuel Doe deteriorated, Taylor realized that his days were numbered since his mentor had fallen out of favor with Doe. His opportunity to flee presented itself when his wife boarded a flight to the United States for medical treatment. Taylor forced himself onto the aircraft with his wife and left Liberia. He was later detained in the United States at the request of the Liberian government on embezzlement charges. Doe wanted Taylor extradited to Liberia; however, the Liberian government's request encountered roadblocks, leaving Taylor in legal limbo until 1985 when he escaped prison. From Massachusetts, he made his way to New York before crossing into Mexico and then arriving in Ghana.

For about two years before the start of the First Liberian Civil War, Taylor would traverse West Africa assembling the National Patriotic Front of Liberia (NPFL). His travels eventually led him to Libya where he and his initial NPFL cadre received training at Colonel Muammar Gaddafi's training camps. While in Libya, Taylor met Sierra Leonean revolutionary Foday Sankoh, a fellow traveler who shared similar ambition as Taylor for his native Sierra Leone.

On Christmas Eve 1989, the NPFL launched the First Liberian Civil War when its insurgents entered Liberia from Ivory Coast and attacked an Armed Forces of Liberia (AFL) barracks in Nimba County. Their objective was to oust Doe and his government. The war would last until 1996 and was marked by periods of broken cease-fires and peace agreements. The 1997 Abuja II Peace Accord formally ended the war, paving the way for Taylor's election as Liberia's president in 1997.

Taylor ruled Liberia as a despot. He used Liberia's state security agencies to eliminate his political opponents or anyone he felt was a threat to his rule. Rampant corruption, nepotism, and lawlessness were the order of the day as Taylor transformed Liberia into a gangster state. His tenure was marked by his support for Sankoh's Revolutionary United Front in Sierra Leone's civil war. The beginning of the end of Taylor's rule began on April 21, 1999, when Liberians United for Reconciliation and Democracy (LURD) insurgents launched their campaign to topple Taylor and his regime. The Second Liberian Civil War was brought to its conclusion in August 2001 with the establishment of the Accra Comprehensive Agreement. A few days prior to the resolution, Taylor had resigned as president and been given safe passage to Nigeria, where he was to remain under supervision.

In 2006 Taylor fled his Nigerian compound in Calabar but was apprehended near the Nigerian-Cameroonian border. Following his capture, Taylor was eventually transferred to the International Criminal Court in the Hague to stand trial for his assistance to the RUF. He was sentenced to 50 years imprisonment in May 2012 for crimes against humanity and for supporting the RUF.

Jacien Carr

See also: Child Soldiers in Africa; Coups and Military Regimes in Africa; Doe, Samuel; Diamonds and Conflict in Postcolonial Africa; ECOWAS Military Interventions; Liberian Civil Wars; Liberians United for Reconciliation and Democracy (LURD); National Patriotic Front of Liberia (NPFL); Revolutionary United Front (RUF); Sankoh, Foday Saybana; Sierra Leone Civil War.

Further Reading

Ellis, Stephen. *The Mask of Anarchy: The Destruction of Liberia and the Religious Dimension of an African Civil War.* New York: New York University Press, 2001.

Hoffman, Danny. *The War Machines: Young Men and Violence in Sierra Leone and Liberia.* Durham: Duke University Press, 2011.

Huband, Mark. *The Liberian Civil War.* New York: Frank Cass, 1998.

Wai, Zubairu. *Epistemologies of African Conflicts: Violence, Evolutionism, and the War in Sierra Leone.* Basingstoke: Palgrave Macmillan, 2012.

Waugh, Colin. *Charles Taylor and Liberia: Ambition and Atrocity in Africa's Lone Star State*. London: Zed Books, 2011.

Zack-Williams, Tunde. *When the State Fails: Studies on Intervention in the Sierra Leone Civil War*. London: Pluto Press, 2012.

Tigray People's Liberation Front (TPLF) (1975–)

The Tigray People's Liberation Front (TPLF) was one of the leading ethnically focused armed resistance groups within Ethiopia during the Marxist Derg regime from 1975 until the Derg's fall in 1991. The TPLF, like many of its contemporary organizations, had its roots in nonviolent political movements that were critical of the Derg's repressive political programs. However, following the continued violent responses of the Derg, the TPLF was formed and began a lengthy guerrilla resistance against the regime. During this struggle the TPLF forged a series of pragmatic alliances that allowed for their survival and growth, and the end of the conflict saw the TPLF as the central partner of the larger Ethiopian People's Revolutionary Democratic Front (EPRDF), which would become government of Ethiopia upon the end of the conflict in 1991.

The roots of the Tigray People's Liberation Front lie in the initial political organization of Tigrayan students and intellectuals in the 1960s and 1970s, which protested the marginalization of the Tigrayan people within the larger Ethiopian state. Following the fall of Haile Selassie and the imposition of the Marxist Derg regime in 1974, these protests were met with increasingly violent military oppression, driving the activists to their own violent responses. One of these groups, the Tigrayan National Organization approached the already-militarized Eritrean People's Liberation Front (EPLF) for training and military assistance. The EPLF, looking to broaden its struggle and already finding success against the disorganized Derg forces, accepted the first delegation of fighters from the group that would now call itself the Tigrayan People's Liberation Front.

Upon reorganizing itself and completing the military training offered, the nascent TPLF began a series of small-scale raids against the Ethiopian forces. Despite these limited successes, the armed group grew slowly, largely due to both increasingly organized Ethiopian resistance and the Tigrayan's clashes with the multitude of other armed fronts competing with them. The next several years even saw a rupture with their initial allies, the EPLF, which denied the validity of the TPLF's ethnoregional approach to organization. By 1979, the TPLF was largely marginalized due to Ethiopian resurgence and would spend its time ensuring its own survival and reorganizing for a potential future resurgence.

This resurgence would occur beginning in 1985, when the weakened Ethiopian forces finally failed in their bid to defeat the insurgency in Eritrea and left an opening for local dissident forces to organize. The TPLF established itself as a credible group following their response to the massive famine engulfing their country and followed up their relief work with a 1988 congress intended to help organize the many armed groups operating in Ethiopia. This congress resulted in the creation of the overarching Ethiopian People's Revolutionary Democratic Front, which was an umbrella organization focused on finally toppling the Derg and reforming the overall governance of Ethiopia. The EPRDF coordinated its following offensives with the EPLF, and by 1991 the coalition had defeated the final vestiges of the Derg regime. With the military campaign completed, the EPRDF transitioned into being the head of the multiparty government of Ethiopia, with the TPLF being the central organization of the coalition. As such, and particularly under Prime Minister Meles Zenawi, the TPLF dominated the Ethiopian state for the next three decades. In 2020, given political changes in Ethiopia around the rise of Prime Minister Abiy Ahmed and the alienation of the TPLF from the federal government, the TPLF initiated a rebellion in Tigray region.

Charles G. Thomas

See also: Eritrean People's Liberation Front (EPLF); Ethiopia: Insurgency and Interstate War; Mengistu Haile Mariam; Zenawi, Meles.

Further Reading

Berhe, Aregawi. *A Political History of the Tigray People's Liberation Front (1975–1991) Revolt, Ideology and Mobilisation in Ethiopia.* Los Angeles: Tsehai, 2009.

Tareke, Gebru. *The Ethiopian Revolution: War in the Horn of Africa.* New Haven: Yale University Press, 2016.

Young, John. *Peasant Revolution in Ethiopia: The Tigray People's Liberation Front, 1975–1991.* Cambridge: Cambridge University Press, 2006.

Toyota War (1987)

See Chad, Conflict in

Tuareg Rebellions since 1960 (Mali and Niger)

The Tuareg Rebellions refer to a serious of violent conflicts in Niger and Mali since independence from France after the dissolution of French West Africa in 1960. These rebellions are violent manifestations to create an independent polity in the Sahara based upon the Tuareg ethnic identity. The Tuareg people are groups of seminomadic people who live in the Saharan desert and are largely unified through their common Berber language Tamasheq yet often divided by their highly localized family and clan loyalties. These rebellions have been fueled by proceeds from illicit trade across the Sahara, desires for self-determination exacerbated by grievances with the national government, and external assistance for or against Tuareg insurgents. The Tuareg often portray themselves as independent and fierce desert fighters descended from long lineages of warriors and nobles in highly stratified societies. Conversely, they portray the government as illegitimate if not oppressive.

The First Tuareg Rebellion, or *Alfellaga*, began in Northern Mali in 1962 as an uncoordinated insurrection against the Malian state by armed Tuareg groups but without a clear political platform and lacking popular support. The Malian Army, then equipped by the Soviet Union, militarily destroyed the insurgency in 1964 and placed Northern Mali under military control.

The Second Tuareg Rebellion initially began in Mali in 1990 and triggered another rebellion by Tuaregs in the Aïr Mountain region of Northern Niger. These two separate rebellions had political parties and were led in the field by a panoply of armed insurgent groups; the most significant groups included the Arab Islamic Front of Azawad (FIAA), Popular Movement for the Liberation of Azawad (MPLA), United Movements and Fronts of Azawad (MFUA), Front for the Liberation of Aïr and Azaouak (FLAA), Front for the Liberation of Tamoust (FLT), and coalitions of the Coordinated Armed Resistance (CRA) and Organized Armed Resistance (ORA). Moderates in Mali eventually negotiated a cease-fire in 1995, which maintained the self-governing Region of Kidal but reduced the military presence, included repatriations for displaced Tuaregs, and increased political representation for Malian Tuaregs in the central government as well as Malian military. The Niger conflict ended with the signing of the Ouagadougou Accords in April 1995 and incorporated some former rebels into the Armed Forces of Niger while assisting others in returning to a productive civilian life through a French-sponsored Disarmament, Demobilization, and Reintegration (DDR) program.

The unstable peace in Mali and Niger continued for a decade, but violence erupted in Niger early February 2007, due to Tuareg ex-combatants who were dissatisfied with the slow progress of the promised benefits, lack of functioning democratic institutions, and lack of adequate compensation to local Tuareg communities from increased tourism and mining operations, particularly French extraction of uranium. This rebel force consisted of ex-combatants, some defections from the Niger Army, and militarized youth. They refuted the 1995 Ouagadougou accords and declared the formation the Niger Movement for Justice (MNJ), led by Aghaly ag Alambo, a former member of the FLAA, and Mohamed Acharif, a former captain in the Nigerien Armed Forces who defected to the rebels in May 2007. After several successful raids and attacks, the Niger government declared a state of emergency and passed anti-terror legislation. By summer 2008, the Niger military went on the offensive, which effectively countered MNJ operations and broke apart the alliance. Aghaly Alambo fled from Niger in 2009, and the remainder of the MNJ leadership announced the creation of the Nigerien Patriotic Front (FPN), declaring in their first statement a desire for a cease-fire and peace talks with the government.

In Mali, Tuaregs led by the former leader of the Democratic Alliance for Change (ADC) and a Malian Army officer who had deserted in summer 2007, Ibrahim ag Bahanga, seized a military convoy near the town of Tinsawatene, near the border with Algeria. Bahanga's forces, then called the Tuareg Northern Alliance for Change (ATNMC), successfully attacked and seized numerous garrisons in Northern Mali over 2007 and 2008 as well as conducted political assassinations of Tuareg leaders opposed to the armed insurrection or cooperating with the central Malian government. By early 2009 the Malian Army, with assistance from partners like France and the United States, successfully defeated ATNMC forces and fractured the Tuareg rebel alliances, leading to an armistice by February. Libyan president Muammar Gaddafi, who claims Tuareg ethnic origins, brokered separate peace agreements with both the Malian and Niger governments and rebel factions. These agreements contained many of the provisions from the Second

Tuareg Rebellion, such as increased political representation, demobilization and reintegration of Tuareg fighters, and an increased share of mineral wealth.

The Tuareg Rebellion of 2012 was an insurgency against the Malian government by rebels of the National Movement for the Liberation of Azawad (MNLA). The MNLA was formed by ex-combatants and a significant number of heavily armed Tuaregs who fought in the Libyan Civil War and returned to Northern Mali with extensive combat experience and weapons taken from Libya. The rebellion led to a military coup of the Malian government followed by the unification of MNLA with terrorist organizations in the region such as Ansar Dine and the Movement for Oneness and Jihad in West Africa (MOJWA), which were loosely affiliated with Al-Qaeda in the Islamic Maghreb (AQIM). The combined rebel and terrorist fighting forces seized all of Northern Mali and declared independence in April 2012. However, disagreements and conflicts between the various groups caused violent rifts and a complete breakdown in communication and coordination. The French military intervention in early 2013 ended the rebellion, although small terrorist groups continue to operate in the region.

The Tuareg Rebellions since 1960 are really a modern continuation of traditions of violence in the region based upon identity but also greatly affected by climatic conditions, largely water scarcity. While such identity and resource violence precede the historical record, neighboring states such as Libya have increasingly played roles in these rebellions as well as the various ways these groups fund their operations, such as smuggling. Violence has proven especially likely when rebel groups perceive the central government to be vulnerable and incapable of securing Saharan regions. Importantly, the postcolonial states have always defeated these rebellions through military force and with external assistance to include mediation. It is also significant that terrorism has further blurred the distinctions between Tuareg rebels, smugglers, criminal enterprise, and terrorists, greatly confounding conflict resolution efforts.

Joseph Guido

See also: Al-Qaeda in the Islamic Maghreb (AQIM); French Military Involvement in Postcolonial Africa; Gaddafi, Muammar.

Further Reading

Boilley, Pierre. *Les Touaregs Kel Adagh, Dépendances Et Révoltes: Du Soudan Français Au Mali Contemporain* (Kel Adagh Tuaregs, Dependencies and Revolts: From Colonial French West Africa to Contemporary Mali). Paris: Éditions Karthala, 1999.

Creisson, Pierre, and Thomas Dandois. *En Territoire Interdit* (In Forbidden Territory). Paris: Arthaud, 2008.

Gamawa, Yusuf Ibrahim. *The Tuaregs and the 2012 Rebellion in Mali*. South Africa: Partridge Publishing, 2017.

Keenan, Jeremy. *The Lesser Gods of the Sahara: Social Change and Contested Terrain Amongst the Tuareg of Algeria*. London: Frank Cass Publishers, 2004.

Keita, Kalifa. *Conflict and Conflict Resolution in the Sahel: The Tuareg Insurgency in Mali*. Carlisle Barracks, PA: U.S. Army War College, 1998. https://permanent.access.gpo.gov/lps12312/carlisle-www.army.mil/usassi/ssipubs/pubs98/tuareg/tuareg.pdf

Kokalla Maiga, Choguel, and Issiaka Ahmadou Singaré. *Les Rebellions Au Nord du Mali, des Origines a Nos Jours* (The Rebellions in the North of Mali: From Origins to Today). Bamako: EDIS, 2018.

Saint Girons, Anne. *Les Rébellions Touarègues* (The Tuareg Rebellions). Paris: Ibis Press, 2008.

Uganda, Insurgency in the North (1979–2006)

After the 1979 Tanzanian invasion of Uganda that overthrew the military dictator Idi Amin, northern Uganda experienced a series of insurgencies. During the early 1980s, former members of the Amin regime established rebel groups in Amin's home West Nile District located in the far northwest of Uganda along the Sudan border. Comprising fighters from Amin's Kakwa ethnic group, the Former Uganda National Army (FUNA) quickly retreated into Sudan and Zaire. Led by Brigadier Moses Ali, the Uganda National Rescue Front (UNRF) consisted of ethnic Aringa fighters and gained control of West Nile from 1980 to 1982. However, President Milton Obote's new government sent its army into this area where it slaughtered civilians and drove UNRF into Sudan. Following a long insurgency in southern Uganda, Yoweri Museveni's primarily southern National Resistance Army (NRA) seized power in 1986, prompting an expansion of insurgency in the north, which was the home of previous leaders like Obote and various deposed generals. Defeated by the NRA, the old northern-oriented Ugandan Army withdrew into Sudan in 1986 and formed the Uganda Peoples' Democratic Army (UPDA), and with Khartoum's support, it launched a guerrilla war among the Acholi people of central northern Uganda. Given their movement's ineffective campaign, some frustrated UPDA fighters ultimately joined other northern rebel groups inspired by Christian millenarianism. Around 1986, a Christian prophetic group called the Holy Spirit Movement (HSM), led by spirit medium Alice Auma, arose within Acholi society and formed a military wing called the Holy Spirit Mobile Force (HSMF) that fought the new NRA state. Rejecting guerrilla warfare, the HSMF utilized so-called Holy Spirit Tactics that combined conventional warfare with religious beliefs that holy oil protected fighters from bullets, hurled rocks would turn into grenades, and the most effective battlefield formation resembled the shape of a cross. With 6,000 to 10,000 troops, the HSMF mounted a spectacularly successful offensive that drove the NRA back to the south but was defeated at Jinja, 50 kilometers from Kampala, in October 1987. The defeat of the HSM led to another religiously inspired and much more protracted insurgency in Acholiland. Claiming a family relation to Alice Auma who escaped to Kenya, Joseph Kony led the new Lord's Resistance Army (LRA). While the LRA embraced some of the doctrines and practices of the defunct HSM, Kony waged a guerrilla war against Museveni's NRA state and viciously extorted supplies and recruits, including children, from Acholi communities.

During the 1990s, the war in northern Uganda undermined Museveni's positive international reputation as a new type of ethical and efficient African leader.

Motivated by a World Bank loan conditional on security, Museveni launched the 1991 Operation North in Acholiland that included the arrest of Acholi political leaders and the detention of tens of thousands in an effort to find and eliminate LRA insurgents. The NRA state also conscripted thousands of Acholi men into militias called "Arrow Groups" sending them to fight the better-armed LRA who then took revenge on these people and their families. Subsequently, Museveni's government attempted to negotiate with the LRA, which took advantage of the lull in the fighting to regroup and rearm, assisted by Sudan, which wanted to punish Uganda for its support of Sudan People's Liberation Army (SPLA) insurgents in southern Sudan. As the price of Khartoum's sponsorship, the LRA also fought the SPLA in southern Sudan, which prompted the Ugandan military to conduct cross-border operations. It was around this time that the NRA took the new name Uganda People's Defence Force (UPDF), reflecting its status as the state military. In 1996, in a sadly familiar counterinsurgency strategy, the UPDF began forcibly resettling rural Acholi into "protected villages" near towns where farming was impossible; food was provided by humanitarian organizations and movement strictly controlled. In just two years, 1.5 million people were confined to these squalid rural prisons in northern Uganda. By 2006 a combination of factors drove Kony's LRA out of northern Uganda. Representing one of the most important developments, the end of the Second Sudan Civil War (1983–2005) and Khartoum's desire to market its oil internationally meant that Sudan stopped supporting the LRA. Furthermore, the UPDF launched a series of major offensives in northern Uganda and southern Sudan; the Ugandan government expanded local militias, and the Acholi people rejected the LRA's outrageously brutal behavior. The 2005 International Criminal Court (ICC) indictment of Kony on war crime charges undermined ongoing negotiations between the Ugandan government and the LRA, including offers of amnesty. After 2006, given the untenable nature of its position in northern Uganda, the LRA relocated to the isolated, forested, and ungoverned border region of the Democratic Republic of the Congo (DRC, formerly Zaire) and the Central African Republic (CAR), where it continued to terrorize rural communities and kidnap children to serve as fighters and/or slaves.

Insurgencies developed in other parts of northern and western Uganda from the mid-1990s. Although Museveni's government quieted the situation in West Nile by incorporating UNRF members into the state armed forces, this changed given problems with military integration and the area's continuing marginalization. In 1994 the West Nile Bank Front (WNBF), led by Juma Oris who had been involved in the now defunct FUNA, initiated a guerrilla war against the Ugandan state, but the group's alliance with the LRA led to extreme violence toward civilians, limiting its popular support. From staging areas in Zaire, where it gained assistance from Khartoum in the context of the Second Sudan Civil War, the WNBF disrupted SPLA supply lines from northern Uganda into southern Sudan. In 1996 disgruntled members of West Nile's original UNRF split from the WNBF to form UNRF II, which, also encouraged by Khartoum, pursued a separate war against the Ugandan government. Concurrently, Sudan orchestrated a rebellion by the Allied Democratic Forces (ADF) in western Uganda that capitalized on long-standing tensions in the Ruwenzori Mountains and involved some members of

Uganda's marginalized Muslim minority. The presence of ADF staging areas in neighboring Zaire inspired Museveni's government to join Rwanda's invasion of that country during the First Congo War of 1996–1997. During that conflict, in 1997, a unit of 4,000 WNBF fighters escaped encirclement by Ugandan and Rwandan forces by moving into southern Sudan where they were ambushed and almost annihilated by the SPLA. In 1998, at the start of the Second Congo War (1998–2002), the Ugandan military again intervened in eastern Democratic Republic of the Congo (DRC), attacking WNBF and ADF forces. The WNBF dissolved, and the Ugandan Army mounted an effective counterinsurgency campaign in West Nile that gained the support of local residents and convinced rebels to surrender. In 2002, with the end of the Second Congo War and a decline in Sudanese support, UNRF II entered a peace deal, and its fighters demobilized with some integrated into the Ugandan military. As one of the numerous armed groups in the eastern DRC engaged in illegal mining, the ADF survived the Second Congo War and mounted limited attacks into Uganda as well as a 2010 bombing in Kampala. Around the same time, Ugandan military operations to track down LRA fugitives in CAR became undermined by that country's civil war.

Timothy J. Stapleton

See also: Congo Wars; Lord's Resistance Army (LRA); Museveni, Yoweri; National Resistance Army (NRA); Sudan Civil War, Second; Sudan People's Liberation Movement/Army (SPLM/A); Uganda's Civil War: The Bush War.

Further Reading

Allen, Tim, and Koen Vlassenroot, eds. *The Lord's Resistance Army: Myth and Reality.* London: Zed Books, 2010.

Branch, Adam. *Displacing Human Rights: War and Intervention in Northern Uganda.* Oxford: Oxford University Press, 2011.

Cline, Lawrence. *The Lord's Resistance Army.* Santa Barbara, CA: Praeger Security International, 2013.

Prunier, Gerard. *Africa's World War: Congo, the Rwanda Genocide and the Making of a Continental Catastrophe.* Oxford: Oxford University Press, 2009.

Uganda's Civil War: The Bush War (1981–1986)

The end of the five-year-long civil war in Uganda (otherwise known as the Bush War or Luwero War) was the end to a long string of wars, conflicts, coups, and reigns of terror that had plagued the country since the early years after independence. When the National Resistance Army (NRA) of the National Resistance Movement (NRM) led by Yoweri Museveni marched victoriously into Kampala in January 1986, there were questions as to whether this regime would be any different than previous ones and also whether it would be able to manage the political and tribal rivalries that still existed at the time.

As the historian Thomas P. Ofcansky put it, "Uganda's history has been determined largely by the divisions among its people." It was these divisions—Nilotic- and Bantu-speaking pastoralists and agriculturalists—that had originated in precolonial times and have lasted, to some extent, throughout and beyond the

British colonial period. Today there are 56 different ethnicities as recognized by the modern constitution of Uganda.

It was during British rule that the Buganda Kingdom would become the one most favored by the colonial rulers. The willingness of Buganda tribal leaders to collaborate with the British also ensured that they would be favored by the colonial masters. Often, the British would employ the Buganda to "advise" other tribal chiefs and impart their authority in a system of indirect rule. These actions led to resentment and resistance at times against the Buganda.

However, by the end of World War II, the strong connection between the Buganda and the British had begun to fray. Opposition to a British policy of creating a stronger confederation with neighboring Kenya and Tanganyika grew as the Buganda began to feel they would lose out if there were stronger ties to the larger white settler–dominated Kenyan economy. The rise of a Western-educated youth also contributed to the push for more democratization.

During the colonial period, the first official, indigenous army was the Uganda Rifles, which was formed in 1895. This force was largely made up of Sudanese led by British officers. Eventually they would be supplanted by the creation of the King's African Rifles (KAR) in 1905. The KAR would be the military force that would protect the territories of East Africa for the next several decades. Recruitment into the KAR was often based on perceived tribal differences and values. In this sense, the British focused on groups that exhibited "ideal military qualities." In the Uganda case, they recruited heavily from northern communities, such as the Acholi and Langi. One prominent example of this was the future ruthless dictator Idi Amin, who was once a member of the KAR and originated from northern Uganda's West Nile district.

When independence finally came in 1962, Milton Obote, Uganda's first prime minister utilized strong-arm tactics and tribal divisions to eventually gain complete control of the government and removed the constitutional monarchy of King Mutesa II of Buganda by ordering the army to storm his palace. Mutesa fled into exile in the United Kingdom and would die there a few years later. Obote's tactics came back to haunt him when he himself was removed in a military coup in early 1971 by his own army chief, Idi Amin.

The long reign of terror that swept Uganda under the Amin regime has been well documented by the media and scholars. For all his faults, Amin was able to maintain power throughout most of the 1970s. He might have even been able to remain in office for longer had he not decided to invade the Kagera salient in western Tanzania in October 1978. The military response by Tanzania, along with exiled Ugandan groups, eventually led to the downfall and exile of Idi Amin in 1979.

However, peace was still elusive, as the disparate Ugandan factions competed for control of the country in the vacuum that followed the ousting of Amin's regime. A highly contested election in 1980 brought Milton Obote once more back to power. This led a variety of armed groups to wage their own campaigns for control of various parts of the country. For example, former soldiers of Idi Amin's army banded together into the Former Uganda National Army (FUNA) and the Uganda National Rescue Front (UNRF), while other groups operated under other opposition leaders, such as the Uganda Freedom Movement/Army (UFM/A) and the Federal Democratic Movement of Uganda (FEDEMU) army. All these armed groups vied against Obote's Uganda National Liberation Army (UNLA) and, at times, each other.

But there was some opposition within the Obote government as well. Yoweri Museveni who had led the rebel Front for National Salvation (FRONASA) had joined the government as head of the Ministry of Defense. However, a limited authority given to him to lead the ministry and to integrate former FRONASA fighters into the UNLA was one reason for his decision to break from the government. From there Museveni would form the Popular Resistance Army (PRA) and began a guerilla war based in the area of what would become the Luwero Triangle—encompassing the Luwero district north of Kampala. Later, the PRA would merge with the former interim president Yusuf Lule's Uganda Freedom Fighters (UFF) group to form the National Resistance Army.

Museveni's philosophy on how to fight a successful guerilla war was summarized in his autobiography, *Sowing the Mustard Seed*. Within it, he indicated that guerillas should focus on the following elements: "accurate reconnaissance, surprise, fighting battles of short duration, proper use of terrain to gain cover, and concealment in approach and withdrawal." If a guerilla force could master these concepts and fought "for a just cause, it will eventually win the war." However, this style of warfare against the UNLA would lead to hardships for the NRA and particularly for the civilian population. The eventual cost for this type of campaign would be quite high. After the end of the war in 1986, the International Committee of the Red Cross would estimate that approximately 300,000 people had perished within the Luwero Triangle.

The spillover effects from the Bush War within the broader region would be profound as well. Two NRA veterans, Fred Rwigyema and Paul Kagame, would use their combat experiences to form the Rwandan Patriotic Front (RPF) that would wage a guerilla war against the Hutu-dominated Rwandan government—finally succeeding to power after the 1994 genocide.

Patrick Whang

See also: Amin, Idi; Genocide in Africa; Kagame, Paul; Kagera War; Museveni, Yoweri; National Resistance Army (NRA); Rwanda, Civil War and Genocide; Rwandan Patriotic Front (RPF); Uganda, Insurgency in the North.

Further Reading

Amaza, Ondoga Ori. *Museveni's Long March from Guerilla to Statesman*. Kampala: Fountain Publishers, 1998.

Cooper, Tom, and Adrien Fontanellaz. *Africa @ War 23: Wars and Insurgencies of Uganda, 1971–1994*. West Midlands: Helion, 2015.

Kainerugaba, Muhoozi. *Battles of the Ugandan Resistance: A Tradition of Maneuver*. Kampala: Fountain Publishers, 2010.

Museveni, Yoweri Kaguta. *Sowing the Mustard Seed: The Struggle for Freedom and Democracy in Uganda*. London: Macmillan Education Ltd., 1997.

Ngoga, Pascal. "Uganda: The National Resistance Army." In *African Guerrillas*, edited by Christopher Clapham, 91–106. Oxford: James Currey, 1998.

Ofcansky, Thomas P. *Uganda: Tarnished Pearl of Africa*. Boulder, CO: Westview Press, 1996.

Umkhonto we Sizwe (MK)

The African National Congress's fight against the apartheid-based South African regime became the longest irregular war in modern African history, running from 1961 to 1990. That protracted campaign was waged, in large part, by the ANC's armed wing—Umkhonto we Sizwe (Spear of the Nation)—often referred to simply as "MK." Initially led by a young lawyer-turned revolutionary who ultimately became South Africa's most famous statesman, Nelson Mandela, MK carried on a protracted, episodic, and erratic campaign of attacks against government facilities, and occasionally persons, that supposedly was designed to "bring the government to its senses before it was too late." MK generally sought to achieve its goals while being careful to avoid innocent casualties.

The ANC leadership approved the formation of a military force in mid-1961 after agreeing that its previous commitment to nonviolence was not having any appreciable effect on the government's undemocratic policies. The South African regime most clearly demonstrated its intensifying brutality by the shooting of hundreds of unarmed protesters at Sharpeville in 1960, killing 69. Events like this, and the subsequent banning of the ANC, increasingly convinced a number of ANC leaders that a resort to violence was not only justified, but essential. Having led the charge to secure ANC approval for this monumental shift in policy, Mandela became MK's first commander. Without any previous military experience, Mandela embarked on an extensive program of self-study in military history, theory, and application—examining the writings of Clausewitz and other writers; studying recent campaigns in Cuba, China, and Israel; traveling abroad for military training and to secure international support; and gleaning what he could from men who had military experience in World War II. He also formed a High Command composed of himself, his mentor Walter Sisulu, and the communist lawyer Joe Slovo. In fact, members of the South African Communist Party (SACP) were particularly well represented in MK at all levels, a fact that complicated diplomatic matters during the Cold War. According to Mandela, MK initially was not officially a part of the ANC, but a "separate and independent organ, linked to the ANC and under the overall control of the ANC, but fundamentally autonomous." The ANC dropped this complicated distinction by the end of 1962.

On December 16, 1961, MK conducted its first attacks of sabotage by exploding a number of bombs at government facilities in major cities across the country. At the same time, MK initiated an information campaign by releasing a manifesto that announced its creation as "a new, independent body, formed by Africans," took credit for its attacks, and justified the "new methods which are necessary to complement the actions of the established national liberation movement." Two weeks later, on New Year's Eve, MK conducted a second round of bombings. Over the next 18 months, MK made approximately 200 attacks against police stations, pass offices, electrical infrastructure, and other sites related to apartheid rule. Predictably, the government viewed these operations as acts of terrorism, not an encouragement to negotiate, and it embarked on an energetic campaign to find, arrest, and prosecute those responsible. Mandela was arrested in mid-1962, and Raymond Mhlaba, a longtime communist party member recently returned from military training in the People's Republic of China, took command. The leadership soon decided that episodic sabotage was not likely to have the desired effect and that "mass revolutionary action" was the only answer. They began designing Operation Mayibaye, a plan to initiate full-on guerrilla war. However, in 1963 Mhlaba and a number of other senior MK leaders were arrested at their de facto headquarters at Rivonia Farm. They, along with Mandela, were convicted and given life sentences. The success of the government's response to the initial waves of MK attacks forced a major change in the ANC's approach to the military campaign—it would have to be led, grown, and trained in exile abroad.

Most MK members were spirited to Dar es Salaam, before moving on to training camps assembled in Algeria, Morocco, and Egypt. Top candidates were sent to the Soviet Union or various Eastern Bloc countries. Although MK leaders and recruits expected their time abroad to last just a few years, at most, before returning as part of a revolutionary army that would topple the South African regime, exile proved to be a near-permanent situation for most. In the mid-1960s, MK had four camps in Tanzania alone (though they were ejected by the end of the decade after getting embroiled in Tanzanian political turmoil) as well as camps in Zambia. In Zambia, MK leaders worked with Zimbabwean ZIPRA guerrillas to infiltrate through Rhodesia on their way to South Africa in the Wankie and Sipolilo campaigns, but these efforts were crushed by joint Rhodesian-South African forces. The fall of Portuguese rule in Mozambique and Angola in 1975 removed neighboring regimes hostile to MK's mission and put into place new governments that welcomed MK forces and camps.

Nevertheless, during the long exile experience, large numbers of MK rank-and-file, and even some leaders, succumbed to disappointment, disillusionment, and open dissension that rose to the level of mutiny. Challenging living conditions, exasperating distinctions of rank and position, as well as horrific losses in most operations, made most MK camps hotbeds of frustration and distrust. Even after the numbers of MK forces abroad were swelled by a wave of young volunteers and recruits after the Soweto Uprising of 1976—the so-called June 16 Detachment—serious morale problems continued to plague the organization. The South African regime's remarkable success at infiltrating MK camps with spies and double agents, followed by draconian countermeasures by MK leaders, eventually pushed the organization over the edge. In 1984, as much as 90 percent of the MK troops in Angola were in a state of mutiny—later known as the Mkatashinga—which was only defused after great difficulty and much violence.

Despite these serious challenges, MK attempted to dramatically increase its activities in South Africa throughout the mid-1980s, as they sought to make the country "ungovernable" by the apartheid regime. MK operatives successfully set off bombs at military headquarters, courthouses, power plants, shopping centers, and beachfront bars, but MK leaders have admitted that attrition and casualty rates for infiltrated operatives were well over 90 percent. Government diplomatic initiatives were nearly as successful as their military responses, as agreements with Angola and Mozambique officials forced MK to relocate to Zambia and Uganda, dramatically reducing MK attacks in 1989. But by then, other significant changes, such as economic difficulties and the end of the Cold War, were bringing the National Party government to the negotiating table. By early 1990 the regime released Mandela, as well as other former MK officials, and removed the ban on the ANC, which responded by suspending the armed struggle in August that year.

While many ANC leaders claimed that the armed struggle had finally succeeded in pressuring the government to change its policies, most scholars have credited other forces for bringing about the end of the apartheid system. As a strictly military force, MK was largely ineffective in achieving results at the tactical, operational, and strategic levels of war despite the extraordinary efforts and sacrifices made by its soldiers over the course of three decades.

Mark Grotelueschen

See also: Angolan Conflicts; Cold War in Africa; Portuguese Africa, Independence Wars (Angola, Mozambique, and Guinea-Bissau); South Africa, Armed Struggle against Apartheid; Zimbabwe Independence War.

Further Reading

Cherry, Janet. *Spear of the Nation (Umkhonto Wesizwe): South Africa's Liberation Army, 1960s-1990s*. Athens: Ohio University Press, 2011.

Davis, Stephen R. *The ANC's War against Apartheid: Umkhonto We Sizwe and the Liberation of South Africa*. Bloomington: Indiana University Press, 2018.

Ellis, Stephen. *External Mission: The ANC in Exile, 1960–1990*. New York: Oxford University Press, 2013.

Ellis, Stephen, and Tsepo Sechaba. *Comrades against Apartheid: The ANC & the South African Communist Party in Exile*. London: James Currey, 1992.

Stapleton, Timothy J. *A Military History of South Africa: From the Dutch-Khoi Wars to the End of Apartheid*. Santa Barbara, CA: Praeger, 2010.

Williams, Rocky. "The Other Armies: A Brief Historical Overview of Umkhonto we Sizwe (MK) 1961–1994." *South African Military History Journal* (June 2000).

United Liberation Movement for Democracy (ULIMO)

See Liberian Civil Wars; Sierra Leone Civil War

U.S. Africa Command (2008–)

The U.S. Africa Command, or AFRICOM, is the most recent of five geographic combatant commands created by U.S. armed forces to coordinate military actions and responses on the continent of Africa. AFRICOM is somewhat of an anomaly among the combatant commands, with officially a largely noncombatant mission and housing high-level members of the U.S. Department of State and the United States Agency for International Development (USAID). However, despite AFRICOM's initially stated mission set, it has evolved since its inception and is now seen as having become far more militarized and carrying out more direct combat missions on the continent through its regional and state-specific partnerships.

The United States initially set up its series of geographic combatant commands in the wake of World War II as a way to effectively manage larger regional military issues within the tumultuous Cold War. During this period African issues were not considered sufficiently critical to warrant their own specific command-and-control structure. Until the end of the Cold War, African issues were covered as a subsidiary within the U.S. European Command, or EUCOM, with elements of East Africa being rolled into Central Command, or CENTCOM. However, with the end of the Cold War and the United States' unipolar moment, the need for a specific command to coordinate American military issues within Africa stepped to the fore, and finally, after much deliberation, the George W. Bush administration took the step of directing the creation of a formal Africa Command in 2007.

The planning for Africa Command was fraught with significant lingering issues within U.S.-Africa relations following the Cold War. The command had issues finding an effective location on the continent, with many countries being unwilling to host what was seen as a potentially neoimperial structure. Other countries were denied due to political considerations. Ultimately, the command was placed within Stuttgart, Germany, due to availability, political sensitivity, and relative proximity to the continent. Additionally, the command was conceived as a very different organization than EUCOM or PACOM, both of which coordinated hundreds of thousands of military personnel. Instead, AFRICOM was to emphasize the "Three Ds" of diplomacy, development, and defense, pursuing largely pacifist goals on the continent through partnerships and aid with local partners.

While the structure of the organization, which included high-level members of the Department of State and USAID, was intended to further this mission, events and incentives have largely overtaken this initial approach. Initially seen as a "forgotten command" within the U.S. military, the counterterror missions that took center stage following the fall of Gaddafi's Libya in 2011 generated an influx of funds and personnel. Since then, AFRICOM has faced accusations of increasing militarization, with an ever-increasing number of special forces operations and local bases being placed on the continent. These accusations are often paired with observations of brutality or overaggression among U.S. military partners in Africa, such as the militaries of Chad, Cameroon, and Nigeria. While AFRICOM emphasizes its devotion to its initial mission set, there remains suspicion toward its actions on the continent.

Charles G. Thomas

See also: Cold War in Africa; Gaddafi, Muammar; U.S. Military Involvement in Africa.

Further Reading

Brown, David E. *AFRICOM at 5 Years: The Maturation of a New U.S. Combatant Command*. Carlisle, PA: Strategic Studies Institute, 2014.

Piombo, Jessica, ed. *The US Military in Africa: Enhancing Security and Development?* Boulder, CO: Lynne Reinner, 2015.

Thomas, Charles G. "The U.S. Can't Fight Terrorists in Africa. So Guess What It Does Instead." *Washington Post*, sec. Monkey Cage. February 1, 2016. https://www.washingtonpost.com/news/monkey-cage/wp/2016/02/01/the-u-s-cant-fight-terrorists-in-africa-so-guess-what-it-does-instead/

"United States Africa Command Posture Statement 2018." Accessed August 30, 2019. https://docs.house.gov/meetings/AS/AS00/20180306/106953/HHRG-115-AS00-Wstate-WaldhauserT-20180306.pdf

U.S. Military Involvement in Africa

The United States has a long, though sporadic, history of military involvement in Africa. Rarely using conventional force, most missions focused on piracy, terrorism, and airlift support.

The earliest U.S. military involvement in Africa was the Barbary Wars, a counterpiracy campaign against Algiers, Tripoli, and Tunis. While the navy had its successes, the campaign is most famous for the embarrassing grounding of the *USS Philadelphia* and the subsequent daring raid to burn the ship to deny it as a trophy. The Barbary conflict also included William Eaton's leading of a paramilitary ground force that showed some success and earned a line in the Marine Corps Hymn. By 1819 the navy shifted its focus: the U.S. Navy's Africa Squadron was a small naval, antislavery unit based in Cape Verde and later in Angola. Through 1861 the unit intercepted slave traders off the coast of West Africa, taking the liberated slaves to Liberia regardless of their place of origin.

Prior to World War II, ground force involvement in Africa was limited to small-scale shows of force and consulate security missions such as 1903 Abyssinia (now Ethiopia) and 1904 Tangiers. The large-scale invasion of North Africa in World War II resulted in a long-term U.S. presence at Wheelus Air Base in Libya. Until forced to close in 1970, Wheelus was used for fighter aircraft training, as an air transport hub, and as a forward bomber base for Strategic Air Command. The continued deterioration in U.S.-Libya relations resulted in several skirmishes, including U.S. Navy fighters shooting down two Libyan fighters in 1981 (and again in 1989) over the Gulf of Sidra. In 1983, the United States provided air support to Chad against a Libyan invasion. In 1986 the United States conducted Operational El Dorado Canyon—air strikes in retaliation for state-sponsored terrorist attacks in Europe.

Despite the base in Libya, the majority of U.S. military activity in Africa during the Cold War focused on airlift support to CIA paramilitary operations in the Congo and Angola, allied military forces such as the Belgians in the Congo, and the frequent delivery of peacekeepers to Congo-Zaire (1967, 1978, and 1991), and humanitarian operations. For humanitarian missions, airlifts typically delivered basic requirements such as medicine, food, water, tents, and blankets: Morocco (1960); Nigeria-Biafran refugees (1970); Algeria (1980); Chad (1982); famine relief to Mali, Niger, and Sudan (1983); and Ethiopian refugees in Sudan (1984).

The end of the Cold War brought significant instability across Africa, as numerous regimes suddenly lost their benefactor. To protects its citizens (and often allied citizens), the United States conducted security missions and evacuation operations across the continent: 1992, Sierra Leone; 1994, Rwanda (via Burundi); 1996, Central African Republic and Burundi; 1997, the Congo, Gabon, and Sierra Leone; 1998, Guinea-Bissau; 2002, Côte d'Ivoire; and 2013, South Sudan. Liberia would be a special case on its own, with operations repeated in 1990, 1996, 1998, and 2003. Comparatively, the only major Cold War evacuation was in Egypt during the 1956 Suez Crisis.

Amid the instability, famine in East Africa prompted the commitment of military forces for humanitarian relief operations in *1992–1995:* United Nations

Missions in Somalia and Operation Restore Hope (1992–1993). As warlords began disrupting food relief missions, U.S. forces took a more aggressive posture, culminating in the infamous Battle of Mogadishu (1993). The humiliation deterred involvement in the 1994 Rwandan Civil War except for a belated airlift support to a 1996 UN humanitarian operation for Rwandan refugees in the eastern Congo. With the growth of humanitarian nongovernment organizations, the need for military involvement in humanitarian operations drastically decreased. Now, U.S. military forces are typically the resource of last resort for humanitarian missions such as the West Africa Ebola epidemic in 2014.

In a foreshadowing of the importance of U.S. counterterrorism operations in Africa, Al-Qaeda attacked the U.S. embassies in Kenya and Tanzania in 1998. In addition to providing disaster assistance from the attacks, U.S. forces conducted missile strikes against Al-Qaeda targets in Sudan (and Afghanistan). U.S. strategic concern over Africa spiked after 9/11, resulting in the 2002 establishment of the Combined Joint Task Force–Horn of Africa in Djibouti and the 2007 creation of the U.S. Africa Command. After 2001 the U.S. War on Terror in Africa primarily targeted Al-Qaeda in the Islamic Maghreb (AQIM), Al-Shabaab, Boko Haram, and the Islamic State in Africa. Most of the groups periodically took hostages. U.S. forces conducted several hostage rescue attempts in or off the coast of Somalia. The more famous successful episodes include the 2009 movie-famous Captain Phillips and the 2012 rescue of an American woman and a Danish man.

With the exception of U.S. support to NATO's 2011 intervention in the Libyan civil wars, the U.S. military primarily focused on security cooperation as its primary effort. The United States provided military training and aid to almost every country in Africa. The training varies from preparation for UN peacekeeping missions to counterterrorism operations to building defense institutions to basic infantry training. For example, in a rare mission not related to Islamist extremists, U.S. advisers assisted Uganda in the attempt to find Joseph Kony and defeat his Lord's Resistance Army (LRA).

The year 2012 was an inflexion point in the U.S. approach to Africa. Despite a decade of work, the terrorism problem continued to grow. The 2012 terrorist attack against the U.S. consulate in Benghazi resulted in the military's "New Normal," an increase in military quick response forces to support embassy security. Plus, the collapse of Mali in 2012 ushered in a new era of U.S.-French cooperation in counterterrorism operations. As French ground and air forces deployed to reestablish the territorial integrity of Mali from AQIM, the United States provided intelligence support. While there have been some successes in Africa over the past six years, the strategic picture has changed little. The United States continues to conduct operations against terrorists while developing partner countries' security capabilities.

Michael Fowler

See also: Al-Qaeda in the Islamic Maghreb (AQIM); Al-Shabaab; Angolan Conflicts; Belgian Military Intervention in Africa; Cold War in Africa; Congo Crisis; French Military Involvement in Postcolonial Africa; Libyan Civil War, First; Lord's Resistance Army (LRA); Mogadishu, Battle of; Somalia Civil War; U.S. Africa Command.

Further Reading

Chau, Donovan C. "U.S. Counterterrorism in Sub-Saharan Africa: Understanding Costs, Cultures, and Conflicts." *Strategic Studies Institute* (September 2008). https://ssi.armywarcollege.edu/pubs/display.cfm?pubID=821

Griffiths, Robert J. *U.S. Security Cooperation with Africa: Political and Policy Challenges.* New York: Routledge, 2016.

Kindl, Marin. "African Security Futures: Threats, Partnerships, and International Engagement for the New U.S. Administration." *PRISM* 6, no. 4 (2017): 15–31.

Piombo, Jessica. "US Africa Policy: Rhetoric versus Reality." *Current History* 111, no. 745 (May 2012): 194–197.

Ploch, Lauren. "Africa Command: U.S. Strategic Interests and the Role of the U.S. Military in Africa." *Congressional Research Service* (July 22, 2011): 1–39.

Reveron, Derek S. *Exporting Security: International Engagement, Security Cooperation, and the Changing Face of the U.S. Military.* Washington, DC: Georgetown University Press, 2010.

West Nile Bank Front (WNBF)

See Uganda, Insurgency in the North

Western Sahara, Conflict in (1975–)

Gaining independence from France in 1956, Morocco claimed the adjacent French colony of Mauritania, which became autonomous in 1960 and the colonial territory of Spanish Sahara (now Western Sahara). Formed in 1973, the Popular Front for the Liberation of Saguia el Hamra and Rio de Oro (POLISARIO) fought Spanish colonial rule in Western Sahara and received assistance from neighboring Algeria. Backed by the Soviet Union and Cuba, Algeria harbored concerns about the potential expansion of the pro-Western and conservative Kingdom of Morocco into Western Sahara. Additionally, Algeria and Morocco had fought a brief border war in 1963. In November 1975 Morocco tried to claim Western Sahara by organizing the "Green March" with 350,000 Moroccan civilians and 20,000 soldiers trying to enter the Spanish territory, but they were halted at the border by minefields and 30,000 Spanish troops. Some of the marchers also clashed with POLISARIO fighters.

In 1976 Spain's weakening fascist regime withdrew from its colony of Western Sahara. Based on a secret deal between the two governments, Moroccan forces occupied the northern and central parts of the former Spanish territory, and Mauritanian forces seized the southern portion. At the same time, POLISARIO declared the area's independence as the Sahrawi Arab Democratic Republic (SADR). Based in camps in Algeria, the 10,000 POLISARIO insurgents fought Moroccan and Mauritanian occupation during the late 1970s. POLISARIO received weapons, armored vehicles, and tanks from Algeria, Libya, and the Soviet Union, and in Mauritania, it was assisted by Tuaregs alienated from the country's government. In June 1976 a POLISARIO column attacked the Mauritanian capital of Nouakchott, and in May 1977 the insurgents briefly occupied the Mauritanian mining town of Zouerate. Consequently, the Mauritanian government invited Moroccan troops and French military advisers with French air support into the country to help fight POLISARIO. However, a 1978 military coup in Mauritania, partly incited by the presence of foreign troops, resulted in a ceasefire with POLISARIO and Mauritanian recognition of the SADR. Mauritanian forces abandoned the southern part of Western Sahara, but Moroccan troops replaced them.

In January 1979 POLISARIO mounted an offensive against Moroccan forces in Western Sahara that involved highly mobile insurgent columns each consisting of 400–600 vehicles transporting 2,000–4,000 fighters. As Moroccan troops retreated to besieged garrison towns, Moroccan air superiority was challenged by POLISARIO's Soviet-made surface-to-air missiles. Venturing into southern Morocco, POLISARIO forces attacked the town of Tantan three times in 1979. During the early and mid-1980s, Morocco, with money from Saudi Arabia, constructed a 2,700 km long fortification comprising sand walls, military strong points, and electronic detection equipment southward from the Moroccan border, which protected the economically important mining areas of Western Sahara. This confined POLISARIO to the arid interior of Western Sahara along the Algerian and Mauritanian borders. During the late 1970s and 1980s, Morocco pursued its war in Western Sahara by purchasing in excess of $4 billion worth of arms from France, nearly one billion from the United States, and another billion from Austria, West Germany, Italy, and apartheid South Africa. These arms acquisitions included jet fighters, transport aircraft, command-and-control aircraft, training aircraft, helicopters, tanks, armored personnel carriers, self-propelled artillery, and air defense systems. For Morocco, such sophisticated military equipment was also meant to deter direct intervention in Western Sahara by Soviet-sponsored Algeria. Furthermore, several hundred French military advisers worked in Morocco, the United States dispatched some instructors and counterinsurgency experts, and 1,500 Moroccan troops trained in the United States. While the war in Western Sahara tended to keep the Moroccan military out of politics, the royal family eventually exerted more control over military operations, with Crown Prince Sidi Mohamed (future King Mohammed VI) appointed chief of staff in 1985.

By 1990, 150,000 Moroccan troops with over 300 tanks and 250 artillery pieces occupied Western Sahara, and POLISARIO engaged in periodic raids that occasionally penetrated the Moroccan-defended wall. During the early 1990s, POLISARIO became weak and isolated, given the collapse of the Soviet Union, Algeria's distraction by its own civil war, and the establishment of the Arab Maghreb Union comprising Morocco, Mauritania, Algeria, Tunisia, and Libya. Libyan support for POLISARIO ended in the 1980s when the king of Morocco promised Libya's leader Muammar Gaddafi that they would unite their countries, but this never happened. While POLISARIO agreed to a UN-monitored cease-fire in September 1991, Morocco continually delayed a promised referendum on the political future of Western Sahara. The territory became permanently divided between areas occupied by Morocco and POLISARIO, with the former violently crushing pro-independence protests in 1999, 2005, and 2011. UN-brokered peace talks involving Morocco, Algeria, Mauritania, and POLISARIO resumed in 2018 but achieved nothing to resolve this frozen conflict. With limited international diplomatic recognition, Western Sahara's SADR lacks full membership in the UN but joined the Organisation of African Unity (OAU) (now African Union) in the early 1980s, prompting a long diplomatic dispute with Morocco. Although Moroccan arms purchases from Western powers declined to some extent in the 1990s and 2000s with the de-escalation of the war in Western Sahara, the kingdom remained a strong American ally, stepping up its security cooperation with Washington during the international "War on Terror."

Timothy J. Stapleton

See also: Algerian Civil War; Cold War in Africa; French Military Involvement in Postcolonial Africa; Gaddafi, Muammar; Soviet Military Involvement in Africa; U.S. Military Involvement in Africa.

Further Reading

Jensen, Eric. *Western Sahara: Anatomy of a Stalemate*. London: Lynne Rienner, 2004.

Ojeda-Garcia, Raquel, Irene Fernandez-Molina, and Victoria Veguilla, eds. *Global, Regional and Local Dimensions of Western Sahara's Protracted Decolonization: When Conflicts Get Old*. Basingstoke: Palgrave Macmillan, 2017.

Pennell, C. R. *Morocco: From Empire to Independence*. Oxford: One World, 2009.

Willis, Michael. *Power and Politics in the Maghreb: Algeria, Tunisia and Morocco from Independence to the Arab Spring*. London: Hurst, 2012.

Zunes, Stephen, and Jacob Mundy. *Western Sahara: War, Nationalism and Conflict Irresolution*. Syracuse, NY: Syracuse University Press, 2010.

Women and War in Africa

Historical records provide evidence of wars fought across the African continent from the precolonial to the postcolonial era. Men were often direct participants in these wars as decision-makers and combatants. On the other hand, due to the patriarchal structure of most African societies but, more importantly, as a result of cultural stereotypes, women were often presumed to have no direct involvement in war. However, experiences of war shattered gender stereotypes, reconfigured gender roles, and created some avenues for women to assert their agency. In most cases, war also reinforced social differentiation, as women were more often exploited and their rights violated. During periods of warfare in Africa, female realities differed, and they experienced wars in diverse ways. While a large majority of women constituted the bulk of civilian casualties and the refugee population, some women under compulsion or voluntarily were fully engaged in combatant and noncombatant roles. Women also played mediatory roles in conflict resolution.

Precolonial warfare sometimes began as skirmishes that resulted in the conquest of small states and the expansion and consolidation of larger states. In some cases, such conflicts were triggered by tensions between royal families over succession to the throne, struggles over fertile land and natural resources, and the desire to control and dominate trade. Undoubtedly, women were impacted by wars during the precolonial period and assumed different roles. Oral traditions from across the African continent reveal the roles of female warriors who defended their kingdoms from invasion and expanded their empire. In precolonial Northern Nigeria, Queen Amina of Zazzau was known to be a military strategist and embarked on campaigns that resulted in the subjugation of states such as Nupe and Kwararafa and the expansion of her territories across other Hausa states. Also included in the king's list of the Oyo Empire is the mention of a female warrior king (*Alaafin*) named Orompoto who is renowned for her conquest of Nupe. As in most African cultures, a king whose mother was alive was usually considered a lucky man. In the Buganda kingdom, the queen mother (*Namasole*) and the queen sister (*lubuga*) were important members of the royal court, and in fact, the queen mother was assigned a portion of the war spoils. Oba Esigie (c. 1504–1550) of the Benin Empire was also known to have placed his mother, Queen Idia in an honorary position due to the support services that she provided to him during his wars of expansionism. Princess Moremi of Ile-Ife is also revered for her willingness and courage to infiltrate into enemy territory and gather intelligence that resulted in victory for her people. Women in traditional societies also played important roles in conflict resolution. As messengers, traditional diplomats, and mediators, women sometimes organized peace meetings between warring parties. In some cases, conflicts between former antagonistic communities were resolved through marriage. Traditionally, women also sued for peace by abstaining from sexual relations with their husbands. In some occasions, elderly women protested naked and threatened to curse men when they refused to quickly resolve conflicts. This action by women was quite popular among various African societies.

The trans-Atlantic slave trade deeply intensified internal warfare among African states as prisoners of war were captured and sold as slaves. The nineteenth century also witnessed the arrival and settlement of European explorers and traders, who gradually controlled legitimate commerce and also dominated various African communities. African states continuously opposed colonial rule, which culminated in wars of resistance and, later, wars fought for national independence. Colonial records and oral sources detail the roles assumed by women in some of these wars. In the seventeenth century, Queen Njinga Mbandi (1581–1663), the queen of Ndongo and Matamba, was known as a skillful diplomat and sound military strategist. In 1622 Queen Njinga was sent by her brother King Ngola Mbandi to negotiate with the Portuguese who were gradually penetrating and encroaching on their land. Njinga aptly negotiated a treaty with Correia de Souza, the Portuguese governor. Njinga later assumed the leadership of the Mbundu people and is remembered as a female warrior who successfully led her soldiers to war against the Portuguese and Dutch armies. In West Africa, the queen mother of the Asante Empire Yaa Asantewaa was another renowned female warrior who challenged and resisted colonial rule. In 1900 she remarkably displayed courage by rebelling against British attempts to take possession of the "Golden Stool"—a symbol of Asante sovereignty. As a result of this rebellion, Yaa Asantewaa lost her freedom, and she later died in exile in Seychelles in 1921. Undoubtedly, the most famous female warriors on the continent were the Amazons of Dahomey who engaged in local campaigns against other African states and anti-colonial struggles against France in the late nineteenth century. The courage and fearlessness of these women are well documented in various literature on African history.

Furthermore, the agitation for independence resulted in clashes between colonial officials and African nationalists. African women played active roles in these wars fought for national independence. In Kenya, the Mau Mau Uprising (1952–1960) was an anti-colonial struggle against Britain's rule. Women opposed colonial rule and became members of the movement by swearing oaths of initiation to prove their allegiance to the struggle. Some women played important roles as fighters, while others supported the movement by acting as spies and transporting food and other items to the rebels. Like men, women were arrested, detained, and even sentenced to prison. During the Mozambique War of Independence against the Portuguese colonialists, the *Destacamento Feminino* (female detachment) was established in 1967 by the Front for the Liberation of Mozambique (FRELIMO). This detachment was composed of girls and young women who engaged in gathering intelligence and who played other supportive roles for the guerilla force. Similarly, during the Eritrean War of Independence, women were integrated into the armed struggle as members of the Eritrean People's Liberation Front (EPLF). These rebels were deeply influenced by Marxist ideology and operated a system of gender equality, which enabled women to fight alongside men in mixed units, while other women served in other noncombatant capacities. Likewise, during the Zimbabwean struggle for liberation also known as the second *chimurenga,* women participated in the struggle by providing support services to the fighters. Women such as Teurai Ropa (Joyce Mujuru) and Sally Mugabe played recognizable roles during the struggle for Zimbabwean independence.

As early as the 1960s, independent countries in Africa were ravaged by civil wars. The root of these struggles could be traced back to the legacy of colonial rule, which had unified distinct ethnicities into single states. Irredentist agitations and political tensions sometimes resulted in attempts by some ethnic groups to secede. A classic example was during the Nigerian Civil War (1967–1970), which was fought between soldiers of the Federal Republic of Nigeria and members of Biafran troop. During the war, Biafran women masked their identities and entered into Nigerian territory to trade and buy food (these trades are popularly referred to as *Afia* attack). Women also worked as spies and intelligence gatherers and assisted in the production of local war materials. As men were recruited into fighting forces, women assumed duties that were often carried out by men such as farming.

Furthermore, the struggle over political power and natural resources triggered the outbreak and sustenance of civil wars in Africa, especially during the Cold War and post–Cold War eras. Women were abducted and, in most cases, forced to fight in these wars both in combatant and noncombatant positions. However, a few women willingly became members of guerilla forces as a result of peer pressure, the need for protection and survival, fear, and sometimes, revenge. During the Second Liberian Civil War, the Liberians United for Reconciliation and Democracy (LURD) rebel force established an all-female unit known as the Women Artillery Commando. Although many women were recruited into the fighting forces, one of the most popular female rebel leaders was known as General Black Diamond. Similarly, during the civil war in Sierra Leone, between March 1991 and January 2002, many women were forced to become bush wives and fighters. Female rebels were renowned for their brutality and violence. In recent years, women have been linked to widespread terrorist attacks such as suicide bombings across the continent. Although some women voluntarily engaged in these acts, others succumb to pressure and act as spies and even recruiters. Over the years, women have also served in administrative but, more popularly, nursing positions in the armed forces of various countries across the continent. During armed conflicts, most women were victims of sexual abuse and were often stigmatized in the postconflict era. Rape was a major weapon of war. In a bid to gain respect and acceptance from other rebel members, some women indirectly participated in rape by holding down female victims for their gang members. Women were also randomly tortured and killed during crossfires, while others were sexually abused and became pregnant. Additionally, some women were victims of domestic violence, intimidation, and societal scorn and were even rejected by their families.

African women also played important roles in advocating for peace and criticizing the military during wartime. Female-led organizations organized peace protests and demonstrations. Perhaps, the more famous anti-war campaign was the Leymah Gbowee–led Women of Liberia Mass Action for Peace Campaign. In 2003 Gbowee said that she had received a revelation from God to assemble Liberian women and pray for peace. Her message brought Christian and Muslim women together who demonstrated and openly agitated for peace. They also adopted the age-long African technique used by women during conflicts such as threatening to undress and place curses on male fighters. These threats were usually feared and proved the seriousness of women's demands. The advocacies by Leymah Gbowee and her female associates deeply influenced the signing of the Accra Comprehensive Peace Agreement in October 2003. Leymah Gbowee was later awarded the Nobel Peace Prize in 2011. In Uganda, Betty Bigombe, a peacebuilder was also involved in negotiations between the Lord's Resistance Army and the government of Uganda. In most cases, women were often ignored and excluded from formal peace processes in Africa. However, a few women have continued to participate in local community peacebuilding activities and reconciliation groups.

Yolanda Osondu

See also: Eritrean People's Liberation Front (EPLF); Ethiopia: Insurgency and Interstate War; Kenya, Mau Mau Emergency; Liberian Civil Wars; Liberians United for Reconciliation and Democracy (LURD); Lord's Resistance Army (LRA); Nigerian Civil War; Portuguese Africa, Independence Wars (Angola, Mozambique, and Guinea-Bissau); Taylor, Charles McArthur Ghankay; Uganda, Insurgency in the North; Zimbabwe Independence War.

Further Reading

Coulter, Chris. *Bush Wives and Girl Soldiers: Women's Lives through War and Peace in Sierra Leone*. Ithaca, NY: Cornell University Press, 2009.

Coulter, Chris, Mariam Persson, and Mats Utas. "Young Female Fighters in African Wars: Conflict and Its Consequences." Occasional Study Paper. Uppsala: Nordiska Afrikainstitutet, 2008.

Gbowee, Leymah, with Carol Mithers. *Mighty Be Our Power: How Sisterhood, Prayer and Sex Changed a Nation at War*. New York: Beast Book, 2011.

Lyons, Tanya. *Guns and Guerrilla Girls: Women in the Zimbabwe National Liberation Struggle*. Trenton, NJ: Africa World Press, 2004.

Nhongo-Simbanegavi, J. *For Better or Worse: Women and ZANLA in Zimbabwe's Liberation Struggle*. Harare: Weaver Press, 2000.

Presley, Cora-Ann. *Kikuyu Women, the Mau Mau Rebellion and Social Change in Kenya*. Boulder, CO: Westview Press, 1992.

Z

Zenawi, Meles (1955–2012)

Meles Zenawi was a former communist activist who became president of Ethiopia in July 1991 after he led the ouster of Mengistu Haile Mariam earlier in the year. He was also head of the Tigray People's Liberation Front (TPLF), the dominant group within the ruling Ethiopian People's Revolutionary Democratic Front (EPRDF). In August 1995 Meles was elected prime minister by a newly installed legislature, and the presidency became a largely ceremonial position. Meles died in office on August 20, 2012.

Born on May 8, 1955, as Legesse Zenawi, Meles was raised in a middle-class environment, attending a school structured along the lines of the British education system. He adopted the name Meles as his nom de guerre in recognition of an ordinary soldier who died in the armed struggle against the former Ethiopian regime.

Meles enrolled at Addis Ababa University to study medicine in 1971, but his studies were interrupted by the 1974 coup that ousted Emperor Haile Selassie. During the fighting, Meles fought with the Marxist forces, but in 1975 he lost faith that Mengistu's military regime was committed to the introduction of democracy and turned to armed struggle that pitted him against many of his former allies on the communist side. He fought with the TPLF and then formed the EPRDF in 1989. Although he was widely viewed as a Stalinist and his troops studied Stalinism as part of their rebel training, partly due to their isolation from the rest of society during their insurgency, Meles became increasingly moderate as he moved closer to a position of power.

Meles and his forces succeeded in ousting Mengistu in May 1991. Meles served as acting president until he was formally elected to that post on July 23, 1991. Unlike many leaders who have seized power after a long insurgency, Meles did not adopt a dictatorial approach; soon after he ousted Mengistu, Meles convened a national conference to create a new government. After being formally ensconced in the presidency, he moved to institute further reforms, including one that is uncommon in many African states: permitting demonstrations and freedom of assembly. However, his government also took action against the opposition. In December 1993 authorities arrested seven leading opponents as they arrived in Addis Ababa for a dissident peace conference—a move that was criticized by Western governments.

Ethiopia's first multiparty legislative elections took place in May 1995 following the December 1994 ratification of a new Ethiopian Constitution. Meles's EPRDF swept the balloting, which most of the opposition boycotted; international observers concluded that had more opposition parties contested the seats, some could have won. Several months later the legislature elected a new national president, whose role is largely ceremonial, and Meles was elected prime minister. The EPRDF prevailed in subsequent elections in 2000, 2005, and 2010, keeping Zenawi in power; however, the victories came amid charges of voter intimidation and fraud by both opposition leaders and international observers. In 2005, opposition parties performed better than expected, winning a combined 41 percent of the seats in the House of the People's Representatives; the opposition Coalition for Unity and Democracy, which came in second to the EPRDF with 20 percent of the 547 seats, called for protests believing that opposition gains should have been much higher. In the ensuing riots, 193 protesters and seven police officers were killed.

The EPRDF won a larger landslide in the May 2010 election results that opposition parties rejected and international observers said did not meet international standards of fairness, with some citing intimidation. The U.S. State Department in March 2010 harshly criticized the state of human rights in Ethiopia, citing murders and torture by state security services, among other abuses.

Despite international criticism of his government, Meles remained a key Western ally in a volatile region. He was also prominent on the international stage, often representing the African Union at international conferences. Known as a savvy and articulate diplomat, Meles also managed to resume his academic studies even while serving as prime minister, completing a master of business administration degree from the United Kingdom's Open University in 1995 and a master of science degree in economics from Erasmus University in the Netherlands in 2004.

Meles had been reported to be in failing health through much of 2012, though the government did not release any details. Authorities announced his death, from what is believed to have been liver cancer, on August 20. The deputy prime minister, Haile Mariam Desalegn, was sworn in as Meles's replacement the following day.

Lynn Jurgensen

See also: Eritrea-Ethiopia War; Eritrean People's Liberation Front (EPLF); Ethiopia: Insurgency and Interstate War; Mengistu Haile Mariam; Tigray People's Liberation Front (TPLF).

Further Reading

Berhe, Mulugeta Gebrehiwot. *Laying the Past to Rest: The EPRDF and the Challenges of Ethiopian State Building.* London: Hurst, 2020.

Prunier, Gerard, and Eloi Foicquet, eds. *Understanding Contemporary Ethiopia: Monarchy, Revolution and the Legacy of Meles Zenawi.* London: Hurst, 2015.

Tareke, Gebru. *The Ethiopian Revolution: War in the Horn of Africa.* New Haven: Yale University Press, 2009.

Zimbabwe, Massacres (Gukurahundi) (1981–1987)

In 1965 Southern Rhodesia's white-minority regime, led by Prime Minister Ian Smith, unilaterally declared independence from Britain to avoid granting equal rights to the Black majority. As a result, the country's African nationalists embarked on an armed insurgency in pursuit of majority rule and independence. Previously, in 1964, the exiled African nationalist movement split with the Zimbabwe African People's Union (ZAPU) led by Joshua Nkomo and the Zimbabwe African National Union (ZANU) under Ndabaningi Sithole. Once the independence war began, these organizations developed military wings, with ZAPU establishing the Zimbabwe People's Revolutionary Army (ZIPRA) and ZANU founding the Zimbabwe African National Liberation Army (ZANLA). Although the division of ZAPU and ZANU originated in disagreements over strategy, these groups eventually developed differing ethnic orientations, revolutionary ideologies, and external alliances. Based in Zambia and eventually Botswana, ZAPU-ZIPRA cultivated support among the Ndebele minority of Rhodesia's southwestern Matabeleland region. With Soviet support, ZAPU-ZIPRA adopted a Leninist strategy, forming a conventional army that was meant to invade Rhodesia and seize power at a key moment that would never take place. Hosted in Mozambique, ZANU-ZANLA operated in the eastern half of Rhodesia; therefore, developing support from the country's Shona majority and Chinese sponsorship meant that they pursued peasant mobilization and guerrilla warfare. Several attempts by the Organisation of African Unity (OAU) to unify the Zimbabwe liberation movements failed. At the end of the 1970s, with the collapse of white-ruled Rhodesia in sight, ZIPRA and ZANLA insurgents fought in the country's southwestern region. In 1979, the war ended with the British-sponsored Lancaster House talks that resulted in a universal suffrage constitution and independence under the name Zimbabwe the following year. As part of the peace process, insurgents reported to assembly areas for demobilization or absorption into a new Zimbabwe security force, including elements of the former Rhodesian state forces. In April 1980, given the results of an election, ZANU-PF (ZANU-Patriotic Front) formed the country's first independent government under Prime Minister Robert Mugabe, with Nkomo's ZAPU as the main opposition party.

During the early 1980s, violence flared, given problems related to the amalgamation of the new Zimbabwe Defence Forces (ZDF). In 1981, at Entumbane in Bulawayo, ZIPRA combatants rebelled over delays in the integration process, poor living conditions, favoritism toward ZANLA fighters affiliated with Mugabe's ZANU-PF state and rumors that former ZIPRA personnel disappeared once they joined the ZDF. Former Rhodesian police and military units crushed the Entumbane mutiny. In early 1982, with the government's discovery of arms caches in ZAPU's stronghold of southwestern Matabeleland, ZAPU-ZIPRA leaders were detained and charged with treason or fled the country. Some ZIPRA veterans deserted the ZDF or their integration camps and took to the bush as dissidents attempting to restart the war. Apartheid South Africa's plots to destabilize independent Zimbabwe induced paranoia within Mugabe's new government. South African agents bombed aircraft at a Zimbabwe Air Force base in Gweru in 1982, and Pretoria attempted to establish a counterrevolutionary group called Super-ZAPU in Zimbabwe's Matabeleland, but it failed to attract support. Furthermore, ZDF soldiers became involved in fighting the South African–sponsored Mozambique National Resistance (RENAMO) that was destabilizing Mozambique.

Consequently, the Mugabe ZANU-PF government overreacted to the disturbances in Matabeleland by dispatching a special ZDF formation called Fifth Brigade to suppress a relatively small number of dissidents. Trained by North Korean instructors, the 3,500-strong Fifth Brigade comprised almost entirely former ZANLA combatants from eastern Zimbabwe's Shona ethnicity. Under the command of Colonel Perence Shiri, Fifth Brigade adopted the Shona phrase "Gukurahundi," meaning "the rain that washes away the rubbish," which seemed to refer to the rural people of Matabeleland; Fifth Brigade imposed a reign of terror on rural Matabeleland and parts of Midlands province from 1983 to 1987. During this campaign, the region's Ndebele and Kalanga people were compelled to participate in all-night "pungwes," where they sung Shona songs in praise of ZANU-PF; their crops and houses were destroyed, they were subjected to collective punishment and curfews, and they experienced public beatings and summary executions. State forces disposed of corpses in mass graves or threw them down abandoned mineshafts. Around 20,000 people were killed. The December 1987 Unity Accord ended the violence, with ZAPU leaders such as Nkomo agreeing to the absorption of their group into ZANU-PF and gaining senior government positions under Mugabe who became an executive president. In 1988 Mugabe granted amnesty to the dissidents, who numbered just over 120, and security force personnel for crimes committed during the period of violence in the 1980s that Zimbabweans refer to as "Gukurahundi." In turn, there were no official investigations or charges related to the episode. Although foreign governments knew about the massacres in Matabeleland, including the British who were training ZDF troops and selling arms to Zimbabwe at the time, international media neglected to report on these events and generally portrayed Mugabe in a positive light given his policy of reconciliation with the white minority and his criticism of apartheid South Africa.

At the 1999 funeral of Vice President Nkomo, shortly after Zimbabwe's Catholic Commission on Peace and Justice released a damning report on the 1980s atrocities, Mugabe broke his usual silence over Gukurahundi, regretfully describing it a "moment of madness." While some activists in the 1980s accused the Mugabe regime of engaging in genocide in Matabeleland, these allegations gained more traction in the late 1990s and 2000s as the Zimbabwe state victimized political opponents, embarked on a botched land reform program that destroyed the economy, and fell out with the Western world. Lingering grievances over the massacres of the 1980s meant that Matabeleland became a political stronghold for Zimbabwe's opposition Movement for Democratic Change (MDC) during the 2000s.

Timothy J. Stapleton

See also: Genocide in Africa; Mozambique Civil War; Mozambique National Resistance (RENAMO); Mugabe, Robert; Nkomo, Joshua; Zimbabwe African National Union (ZANU); Zimbabwe African People's Union (ZAPU); Zimbabwe Independence War.

Further Reading

Chan, Stephen. *Mugabe: A Life of Power and Violence.* London: I.B. Tauris, 2019.

Ndlovu-Gatsheni, Sabelo J., ed. *Mugabeism? History, Politics and Power in Zimbabwe.* New York: Palgrave Macmillan, 2015.

"Report on the 1980s Disturbances in Matabeleland and the Midlands." Catholic Commission for Justice and Peace in Zimbabwe. March 1997. http://www.rhodesia.nl/Matabeleland%20Report.pdf

Sibanda, Eliakim. *The Zimbabwe African People's Union, 1961–1987*. Trenton: Africa World Press, 2005.

Tendi, Blessing Miles. *Making History in Mugabe's Zimbabwe: Politics, Intellectuals and the Media*. Berlin: Peter Lang, 2010.

Zimbabwe African National Union (ZANU)

ZANU originated as an African nationalist movement seeking majority rule and independence for the white minority–ruled British colonial territory of Southern Rhodesia. In 1963, while in exile in soon-to-be independent Zambia, members of the established Zimbabwe African People's Union (ZAPU) split off to form ZANU. Disagreeing with ZAPU leader Joshua Nkomo's strategy of remaining in exile to mobilize international sanctions against Southern Rhodesia, the young intellectuals who formed ZANU returned home to lead mass protests against the settler state, resulting in their imprisonment for the next decade. With Rhodesia's unilateral declaration of independence (UDI) from Britain in 1965, both ZAPU and ZANU embarked on armed struggles to liberate their country. Initially based in Zambia along with ZAPU, ZANU formed the Zimbabwe African National Liberation Army (ZANLA) that launched the liberation war in 1966 when a small number of its insurgents clashed with Rhodesian police in the northern town of Sinoia (now Chinhoyi). After the failure of attempts by both nationalist organizations to infiltrate Rhodesia from Zambia, ZANLA, under the military leadership of Josiah Tongogara, moved to Mozambique's Tete province in 1971, allying with the Front for the Liberation of Mozambique (FRELIMO) fighting the Portuguese colonial regime. From Tete, utilizing the forested terrain of the border area, ZANLA insurgents effectively infiltrated adjacent northeastern Rhodesia, where they embarked on a guerrilla campaign. Receiving support from China, ZANLA pursued a Maoist-style insurgency focused on using small cells to gain the support of rural people, from whom they received food and recruits, and avoided direct combat with more powerful Rhodesian security forces. An all-night gathering called a "pungwe" in Shona language represented one of ZANLA's favorite methods for politicizing the peasants and involved singing revolutionary songs and denouncing alleged traitors. To cultivate sympathy among rural people, ZANU also highlighted grievances over previous colonial dispossession of African communities from their land and recruited Shona traditional spirit mediums. While ZANU and ZANLA maintained a relationship through the "dare re chimurenga" (council of the struggle), the overall organization took on an increasingly military character. In 1975, with the independence of Mozambique under a friendly FRELIMO regime, ZANLA expanded its staging areas along the entire border and therefore dramatically escalated the guerrilla war inside Rhodesia. This also increased the association of ZANU/ZANLA with the Shona ethnic majority of that region. ZANU/ZANLA experienced internal conflict during the mid-1970s with a series of mutinies in camps in Mozambique and the assassination of prominent political leader Herbert Chitepo in Zambia. Although it declared its struggle to include gender as well as racial equality, ZANU/ZANLA reinforced traditional women's roles by expecting rural women to cook for insurgents and forcing female fighters to carry supplies and ammunition, and women experienced sexual abuse in ZANLA camps in Mozambique. With the release of nationalist leaders from detention in 1974, Robert Mugabe rose to the head of ZANU as previous leader Ndabaningi Sithole supposedly renounced violence while in prison.

The negotiated end of the conflict resulted in ZANU, renamed ZANU-Patriotic Front or ZANU-PF, winning the country's first democratic election in 1979 and forming a government under Prime Minister Mugabe when Zimbabwe became independent in 1980. Increasingly authoritarian, Mugabe's ZANU-PF state politicized the new Zimbabwe Defence Forces (ZDF), using it to eliminate the opposition ZAPU party and impose a reign of terror on that group's political stronghold among the southwest Ndebele minority during the 1980s. The 1987 Unity Accord saw former ZAPU leaders like Nkomo rehabilitated and absorbed by ZANU-PF and Mugabe transform into a powerful executive president. Although it never officially declared a one-party state, ZANU-PF encountered little effective political opposition during the late 1980s and most of the 1990s. Given its authoritarianism and the country's increasing economic problems, ZANU-PF faced its first serious political challenge at the end of the 1990s with the rise of the Movement for Democratic Change (MDC), representing a coalition of trade unions, civil society groups, and intellectuals. At the same time, ZANU-PF gave into pressure from veterans of the liberation war and embarked on a chaotic and long-delayed land reform program seizing large commercial farms from Zimbabwe's white minority. During the 2000s, as Zimbabwe's economy collapsed with world-record inflation, ZANU-PF used its control of state security forces and organized political violence by its supporters to survive a series of electoral challenges by the MDC, which itself split. After a particularly troubled election in 2008, a ZANU-PF/MDC unity government under Mugabe that lasted from 2009 to 2013 salvaged the economy, leaving ZANU-PF more firmly entrenched in power. In 2017, given continued economic problems and a crisis over the succession of power within ZANU-PF, the ZDF staged a coup to remove the elderly Mugabe and install his recently dismissed vice president and ZANU-PF veteran Emmerson Mnangagwa as president of Zimbabwe.

Timothy J. Stapleton

See also: Mugabe, Robert; Nkomo, Joshua; Women and War in Africa; Zimbabwe, Massacres (Gukurahundi); Zimbabwe African People's Union (ZAPU); Zimbabwe Independence War.

Further Reading

Lan, David. *Guns and Rain: Guerrillas and Spirit Mediums in Zimbabwe*. London: James Currey, 1985.

Martin, D., and P. Johnson. *The Struggle for Zimbabwe*. New York: Monthly Review, 1981.

Moorcroft, P., and P. McLaughlin. *The Rhodesian War: A Military History*. London: Pen and Sword, 2008.

Nhongo-Simbanegavi, J. *For Better or Worse: Women and ZANLA in Zimbabwe's Liberation Struggle*. Harare: Weaver Press, 2000.

Ranger, T., and N. Bhebhe, eds. *Soldiers in Zimbabwe's Liberation War.* London: James Currey, 1995.

Zimbabwe African People's Union (ZAPU)

Founded in 1961, the Zimbabwe African People's Union (ZAPU) represented the continuation of a succession of African nationalist organizations, including the African National Congress (ANC) and National Democratic Party (NDP) banned by the white-minority government during the late 1950s and early 1960s. Led by former trade unionist Joshua Nkomo, ZAPU campaigned for the extension of civil rights to Southern Rhodesia's Black majority and the independence of the country from Britain. Given a crackdown by Rhodesian security forces, ZAPU leaders fled to soon-to-be independent Zambia where the group split in 1963. While Nkomo and others wanted to remain in exile to campaign for international sanctions against Southern Rhodesia, some younger and more radical members formed a new organization called the Zimbabwe African National Union (ZANU) and returned home to lead mass protests against the settler regime. Faced with this rebellion, Nkomo also returned to Southern Rhodesia, where he and other nationalist activists were detained for the next decade. With white-ruled Rhodesia's unilateral declaration of independence (UDI) in 1965, ZAPU and ZANU launched an armed struggle to liberate their country. Based in Zambia, ZAPU formed a military wing called the Zimbabwe People's Revolutionary Army (ZIPRA). During the late 1960s, ZAPU conducted joint operations with the South African African National Congress (ANC), sending combined insurgent units across the Zambian border into Southern Rhodesia. Rhodesian security forces eliminated these ZAPU/ANC forces during engagements around Wankie and Sipolilo in the northern part of Rhodesia. From the early 1970s, and with Soviet support and Leninist revolutionary ideology, ZAPU/ZIPRA developed a conventional mechanized army brigade in Zambia, waiting for an opportune moment to invade Rhodesia and seize the centers of power. This moment never came. In the late 1970s, in response to ZANU's escalation of its guerrilla war along Rhodesia's border with Mozambique, ZAPU/ZIPRA established staging areas in Botswana, from where its insurgents infiltrated southwestern Rhodesia. Unlike ZANU, ZAPU/ZIPRA units inside Rhodesia did not pay much attention to gaining popular support but focused on engaging Rhodesian security forces. In 1978 and 1979, ZAPU/ZIPRA used Soviet-supplied surface-to-air missiles to shoot down two Rhodesian civilian airliners shaking the confidence of the white minority and contributing to further negotiations. Upon Zimbabwe's independence in 1980, ZAPU became an opposition political party, as its main base of support consisted of the Ndebele ethnic minority of the southwest. Although some former ZIPRA fighters integrated into the new Zimbabwe Defence Force (ZDF) during the early 1980s, problems in this process led a few ZAPU veterans to return to the bush to wage an insurgency against the ZANU-PF government of Prime Minister Robert Mugabe. In turn, Mugabe dispatched elements of the ZDF to suppress ZAPU and conduct widespread oppression in southwestern Zimbabwe. Some ZAPU leaders like Nkomo fled the country, and others were arrested and charged with treason. With the 1987 Unity Accord, the governing ZANU-PF party absorbed ZAPU, with former ZAPU leaders gaining state positions such as Nkomo who became vice president.

Timothy J. Stapleton

See also: Mugabe, Robert; Nkomo, Joshua; Soviet Military Involvement in Africa; Zimbabwe, Massacres (Gukurahundi); Zimbabwe African National Union (ZANU); Zimbabwe Independence War.

Further Reading

Martin, D., and P. Johnson. *The Struggle for Zimbabwe.* New York: Monthly Review, 1981.

Moorcroft, P., and P. McLaughlin. *The Rhodesian War: A Military History.* London: Pen and Sword, 2008.

Ranger, T., and N. Bhebhe, eds. *Soldiers in Zimbabwe's Liberation War.* London: James Currey, 1995.

Sibanda, Eliakim. *The Zimbabwe African Peoples' Union, 1961–87: A Political History of Insurgency in Southern Rhodesia.* Trenton, NJ: Africa World Press, 2005.

Zimbabwe Independence War (1965–1979)

In Southern Rhodesia (now Zimbabwe), the small white settler minority gained internal political control in 1923, and after the Second World War, this regime expected Britain to grant the territory dominion status, a form of autonomy, along the lines of Canada or Australia. This ambition approached reality with the 1953 formation of the Central African Federation, which brought together white-dominated Southern Rhodesia with the copper mining economy of Northern Rhodesia and the labor pool of Nyasaland. Britain initially supported the federation as a new regional ally after the 1948 election of the republican-minded Afrikaner Nationalist Party and the consequent imposition of apartheid in South Africa. Since the tiny white minority controlled the federal government, African nationalists in the three territories protested against the federation, which contradicted the emerging continental movement for independence and majority rule. In Southern Rhodesia, in the late 1950s and early 1960s, the settler state banned a series of increasingly radical African nationalist groups comprising the Southern Rhodesian African National Congress (SRANC), National Democratic Party (NDP), and Zimbabwe African People's Union (ZAPU). Mounting nationalist protest and state repression led to the dissolution of the federation in 1963, and the British, now impatient to withdraw from Africa, granted independence to Northern Rhodesia, which became Zambia, and Nyasaland, which became Malawi, in 1964. The majority of the federation's military resources, including aircraft and armored vehicles, supplied by Britain during the 1950s, transferred to Southern Rhodesia, where Ian Smith's Rhodesian Front came to power to protect settler dominance. Arguing over strategy, the African nationalist movement split with ZAPU under Joshua Nkomo, who wanted to mobilize international sanctions, and the Zimbabwe African National Union (ZANU) led by Ndabaningi Sithole, determined to confront the regime more directly. In turn, Rhodesian security forces arrested most of the top nationalist leadership who spent the next decade in prison. At the same time, an impasse emerged between Rhodesia's Smith government that demanded dominion status and Britain that refused to do so unless Smith acknowledged the eventuality of majority rule. In November 1965 the Smith regime issued its illegal Unilateral Declaration of Independence (UDI), which prompted minimal reaction from Britain.

From the mid-1960s, both ZAPU and ZANU established military wings to embark on an armed struggle against minority-ruled Rhodesia. Now located in adjacent and newly independent Zambia, ZAPU created the Zimbabwe People's Revolutionary Army (ZIPRA), and ZANU formed the Zimbabwe African National Liberation Army (ZANLA). Rhodesia received economic, diplomatic, and military support from the Portuguese colonial rulers of neighboring Mozambique, where a similar nationalist insurgency unfolded, and from apartheid South Africa, and limited covert backing from Western powers in a Cold War context, in which Smith's regime was valued as anti-communist. The two Zimbabwe liberation movements gained Eastern Bloc sponsorship and adopted socialist revolutionary rhetoric. During the initial phase of the conflict in the late 1960s, ZIPRA and ZANLA sent armed groups from Zambia into Rhodesia to prepare the African population for revolutionary warfare. However, the obstacle posed by the Zambesi River border, the Zambesi Valley's semi-open environment, and absence of support from rural communities resulted in the pursuit and elimination of all these insurgent units by Rhodesian forces. In April 1966, in what is remembered as the opening battle of Zimbabwe's Liberation War, a group of 21 ZANLA insurgents that had crossed from Zambia into Rhodesia was defeated by Rhodesian security forces at Sinoia (today's Chinhoyi). In the late 1960s, ZAPU conducted joint operations with the anti-apartheid African National Congress (ANC) of South Africa. In 1967 and 1968, combined ZAPU-ANC groups of around 100 insurgents each penetrated Rhodesia but were detected by security forces and disrupted after engagements around the Wankie and Sipolilo areas. ZAPU and the ANC had not previously mobilized rural communities, and people informed the Rhodesian police of their presence; the relatively large insurgent units were easily detected by ground tracking and from the air, and the campaign incited apartheid South Africa to send security personnel to assist Rhodesia.

During the 1970s ZAPU-ZIPRA and ZANU-ZANLA evolved into different types of insurgent organizations. Staying in Zambia, ZAPU-ZIPRA gained Soviet sponsorship, which came with a Leninist strategy to cultivate a compact professional military to invade Rhodesia at some critical point when it was weakened by guerrilla warfare and international sanctions. As a result, ZIPRA established a conventional Soviet-style army brigade in Zambia, including armored vehicles. Nevertheless, the Zambesi River, with few bridges and crossing points, as well as Lake Kariba, represented a major hindrance, and ZIPRA did not coordinate closely with the host Zambian military that avoided the war. From the mid-1970s, given the expansion of the conflict, ZAPU-ZIPRA established staging areas in Botswana, infiltrating adjacent western Rhodesia. Inside Rhodesia, ZIPRA relied on ZAPU's existing political networks and directly engaging and often defeating Rhodesian security forces and creating liberated zones. Most ZIPRA recruits tended to originate from ethnic Ndebele, Karanga, or Sotho communities, and the movement gained popularity in Rhodesia's southwestern Matabeleland region.

In 1969 ZANU founded the "dare re chimurenga" (Shona language for "council of the struggle") to direct the war and ZANLA operations. Initially dominated by politicians, the "dare" transformed into a primarily military body in 1973 with the appointment of Josiah Tongogara as defense secretary. With Chinese sponsorship, ZANU-ZANLA adopted Maoist revolutionary strategy that stressed politicizing rural populations and pursuing a guerrilla conflict that would eventually transform into a conventional war, aimed at seizing centers of power. During the 1970s ZANLA worried less about fighting Rhodesian forces and more about using persuasion and intimidation to garner support from rural communities. Methods of political indoctrination included an all-night meeting called "pungwe," in which insurgents led local people in revolutionary songs and statements and denunciation of collaborators who faced torture and death. Villagers were expected to provide food, information, and recruits to ZANLA fighters or suffer reprisals. Additionally, ZANLA attempted to appeal to rural people by highlighting their grievances over land and enlisting traditional Shona spirit mediums, including the famous Nehanda popularly associated with the 1896–1897 rebellion or "First Chimurenga" (First Struggle for Independence). ZANU-ZANLA portrayed itself as fighting the "Second Chimurenga," therefore claiming historical legitimacy. As a military organization, ZANLA became highly structured and utilized very small insurgent cells that, for security reasons, were ignorant of each others' activities in the field. Although ZANU-ZANLA emphasized women's emancipation as a socialist objective of the struggle, female insurgents performed traditional women's work such as cooking food and carrying supplies, which reinforced established gender roles.

In 1972 the second phase of the conflict began when ZANLA, led by Tongogara, moved to Mozambique's Tete province, where it cultivated an alliance with the Front for the Liberation of Mozambique (FRELIMO) that had been fighting Portuguese colonial forces for 10 years. While the Zambezi River limited the usefulness of staging areas in Zambia, ZANLA insurgents in Tete more easily crossed into the forests and hills of northeast Rhodesia. This change represented the most important strategic development of the war, relaunching and escalating the insurgency. With the sudden departure of the Portuguese from Africa and FRELIMO taking state control in Mozambique in 1975, the war in Rhodesia intensified, with ZANLA expanding its staging areas and infiltrating across the entire eastern border. In turn, ZANLA developed an increasingly Shona ethnic orientation, with recruits coming mostly from the Mashonaland region of eastern Rhodesia. In late 1974 Thomas Nhari, a Soviet-trained senior member of ZANLA's leadership, staged a mutiny in Zambia and Mozambique by those disillusioned with poor camp conditions and lack of supplies and weapons. Ultimately, ZANU-ZANLA crushed the rebellion, with Nhari and many others executed. After the 1975 assassination of ZANU leader Herbert Chitepo in Zambia, which was blamed on internal disputes but was probably conducted by Rhodesian agents, ZANLA transferred totally to Mozambique. With the expanded insurgency, Rhodesian forces orchestrated cross-border raids against ZANLA camps in Mozambique such as at

Nyadzonya in 1976 and Chimoio in 1977. Rhodesian forces also conducted strikes against ZIPRA camps in Zambia and Botswana. Reacting to ZANLA's expanding insurgency in eastern Rhodesia after Mozambique's independence, ZIPRA initiated an offensive in the west from 1976, including the abduction of African children from schools near the border who were brought to camps in Botswana. In 1978 and 1979 ZIPRA, led by Lookout Masuku and intelligence head Dumiso Dabengwa, employed Soviet ground-to-air missiles to down two Rhodesian civilian airliners, severely undermining white Rhodesian morale. In 1979 ZIPRA moved 3,000 fighters into Rhodesia to prepare for a conventional military invasion, which never took place. In response, ZANLA dispatched mostly Shona insurgents into the predominantly Ndebele southwest where they fought Rhodesian and ZIPRA forces.

Losing control of rural areas, Rhodesian security forces deployed counterinsurgency methods based on the 1950s' British campaign in Malaya in which they had participated. Rhodesian forces herded rural people into "protected villages" to prevent them from assisting the guerrillas but where residents were subject to squalid living conditions, a curfew, and abuse by guards. With rural dwellers confined to camps, the state declared large tracts as "free fire zones," where anyone seen was considered an insurgent and killed. In the early 1970s, the Rhodesian military formed the Selous Scouts under Lieutenant Colonel Ron Reid Daly to utilize "turned terrorists" (captured insurgents who switched sides) to locate and infiltrate insurgent groups and then call on airmobile "fire forces" to engage them. In a typical "fire force," a helicopter carrying the commander circled the suspected insurgent position, several small teams landed by helicopter to block enemy escape routes, and a larger unit parachuted from an airplane and then swept toward the target. Communication difficulties between Selous Scouts troops on the ground and "fire force" commanders in the air, as well as the insurgent tactic of fleeing in all directions, meant that these operations often failed to locate the enemy, but occasionally, they trapped and killed many. Initially, "fire forces" consisted of the white Rhodesian Light Infantry (RLI), but as the war expanded, the white-led but primarily Black Rhodesian African Rifles (RAR) also participated as did some South African forces. Furthermore, Rhodesian security forces deployed a number of "dirty tricks," attempting to kill insurgents by circulating poisoned clothing and tinned food as well as transistor radios containing bombs in rural areas. While the Rhodesian approach to counterinsurgency stressed achieving a higher and higher insurgent body count, dramatic cross-border raids that killed many rebels only attracted international condemnation and the brutalizing and killing by mistake of rural people only pushed them toward the nationalist movements. Despite the fact that African soldiers and police comprised the core of the professional Rhodesian forces, Smith's racist government wavered over expanding the use of armed African personnel until the late 1970s by which time the war was lost. Consistently short of personnel, the Rhodesian war effort depended on young white male conscripts and white reservists drawn from the small white minority and called up for increasingly long periods of obligatory service.

After Portugal's withdrawal from Africa, both sides of the Rhodesian war experienced pressure to negotiate from their allies. In late 1974 failed talks led to the release of long imprisoned nationalist leaders such as Nkomo and Sithole. Robert Mugabe was also released from detention and assumed leadership of ZANU as Sithole supposedly renounced the armed struggle in prison. Increasing "call ups" of whites and international sanctions crippled the Rhodesian economy. Within South Africa, which Rhodesia was entirely dependent upon for key imports such as oil and arms, a surge of internal African protest began in 1976 and informed Pretoria's new regional policy of using economic strength to passively dominate its Black-ruled neighbors. The war in Rhodesia threatened to undermine that strategy by pulling South Africa into a wider conflict. In addition, the Organisation of African Unity (OAU) and the Zambian government expressed worry that the war was damaging the Zambian economy dependent upon copper exports through Rhodesia and South Africa and pushed ZAPU and ZANU to end the conflict. In the "internal settlement" of 1978, South Africa and Smith arranged for the installation of a pro-Western government under moderate Black leader Bishop Abel Muzorewa, in which whites retained considerable power in a renamed Zimbabwe-Rhodesia. Nevertheless, the war continued as this new seemingly puppet state proved intolerable to the liberation movements. In 1979, at the British-sponsored Lancaster House talks, the warring sides reached an agreement in which Zimbabwe would formally gain independence the next year with universal adult suffrage. As concessions to the white minority, and for the first decade of independence, the whites would send their own representatives to parliament, and forced land redistribution was delayed, with Britain and the United States promising to fund land redistribution in the country within a free market system. After an abortive attempt to unite ZAPU and ZANU as the Patriotic Front (PF), the latter would be known as ZANU-PF. Under Commonwealth supervision, insurgents collected at assembly areas for planned absorption, together with former Rhodesian personnel, into a new Zimbabwe security force structure. Shortly after Lancaster House, in December 1979, the popular Tongogara died in an automobile accident, inspiring numerous conspiracy theories. As a result of the subsequent elections, ZANU-PF formed a government with Mugabe as the first prime minister of Zimbabwe, which gained independence in April 1980. Within parliament, Nkomo's ZAPU formed the main opposition party, though its relationship with the government soon deteriorated.

Timothy J. Stapleton

See also: Cold War in Africa; Mugabe, Robert; Nkomo, Joshua; Portuguese Africa, Independence Wars (Angola, Mozambique, and Guinea-Bissau); South Africa, Armed Struggle against Apartheid; Soviet Military Involvement in Africa; Women and War in Africa; Zimbabwe, Massacres (Gukurahundi); Zimbabwe African National Union (ZANU); Zimbabwe African People's Union (ZAPU).

Further Reading

Lan, David. *Guns and Rain: Guerrillas and Spirit Mediums in Zimbabwe*. London: James Currey, 1985.

Martin, D., and P. Johnson. *The Struggle for Zimbabwe*. New York: Monthly Review, 1981.

Moorcroft, P., and P. McLaughlin. *The Rhodesian War: A Military History*. London: Pen and Sword, 2008.

Nhongo-Simbanegavi, J. *For Better or Worse: Women and ZANLA in Zimbabwe's Liberation Struggle*. Harare: Weaver Press, 2000.

Ranger, T., and N. Bhebhe, eds. *Society in Zimbabwe's Liberation War*. London: James Currey, 1995.

Ranger, T., and N. Bhebhe, eds. *Soldiers in Zimbabwe's Liberation War*. London: James Currey, 1995.

Sibanda, Eliakim. *The Zimbabwe African Peoples' Union, 1961–87: A Political History of Insurgency in Southern Rhodesia*. Trenton, NJ: Africa World Press, 2005.

Wood, J. R. T. "Countering the Chimurenga: The Rhodesian Counterinsurgency Campaign 1962–80." In *Counterinsurgency in Modern Warfare*, edited by D. Marston and C. Malkasian, 185–202. New York: Osprey Publishing, 2008.

Wood, J. R. T. *Counter-Strike from the Sky: The Rhodesian All-Arms Fireforce in the Bush 1974–1980*. Johannesburg: 30 Degrees South Publishers, 2009.

Bibliography

Aburish, Abdelmalek. *Nasser: The Last Arab.* New York: St. Martin's Press, 2004.
Adan, Avraham. *On the Banks of the Suez: An Israeli General's Personal Account of the Yom Kippur War.* Novato, CA: Presidio Press, 1980.
Adebajo, Adekeye. *Liberia's Civil War: Nigeria, ECOMOG and Regional Security in West Africa.* Boulder, CO: Lynne Rienner, 2002.
Adebajo, Adekeye. *UN Peacekeeping in Africa: From the Suez Crisis to the Sudan Conflicts.* Boulder, CO: Lynne Rienner, 2011.
Ademoyega, Adewale. *Why We Struck: The Story of the First Nigerian Coup.* Lagos: Evans Brothers, 1981.
Aker, Frank. *October 1973: The Arab-Israeli War.* Hamden, CT: N.p., 1985.
Allen, Tim, and Koen Vlassenroot, eds. *The Lord's Resistance Army: Myth and Reality.* London: Zed Books, 2010.
Al-Sumait, Fahed, Nele Lenze, and Michael C. Hudson, eds. *The Arab Uprisings: Catalysts, Dynamics, and Trajectories.* Boulder, CO: Rowman & Littlefield, 2015.
Amaza, Ondoga Ori. *Museveni's Long March from Guerilla to Statesman.* Kampala: Fountain Publishers, 1998.
Amin, Idi, Barbet Schroeder, Jean-Pierre Rassam, Charles-Henri Favrod, Jean-François Chauvel, Nestor Almendros, Denise de Casabianca, et al. *Général Idi Amin Dada: Autoportrait.* 2014. http://ucsb.kanopystreaming.com/node/113004
Anderson, David. *Histories of the Hanged: The Dirty War in Kenya and the End of Empire.* London: Weidenfeld & Nicolson, 2005.
Anugwom, Edlyne Eze. *The Boko Haram Insurgency in Nigeria: Perspectives from Within.* Basingstoke: Palgrave Macmillan, 2019.
Arnold, Guy. *Historical Dictionary of Civil War in Africa.* Lanham, MD: Scarecrow Press, 2005.
Atangana, Martin. *The End of French Rule in Cameroon.* Lanham, MD: University Press of America, 2010.
Autesserre, Severine. *The Trouble with Congo: Local Violence and the Failure of International Peacebuilding.* Cambridge: Cambridge University Press, 2010.
Avirgan, Tony, and Martha Honey. *War in Uganda: The Legacy of Idi Amin.* Dar es Salaam: Tanzania Publishing House, 1983.

Axe, David, and Tim Hamilton. *Army of God: Joseph Kony's War in Central Africa*. New York: Public Affairs, 2013.

Ayele, Fantahun. *The Ethiopian Army from Victory to Collapse, 1977–1991*. Evanston, IL: Northwestern University Press, 2014.

Azevedo, Mario J. *Roots of Violence: A History of War in Chad*. New York: Routledge, 1998.

Azevedo, Mario J., and Samuel Decalo. *Historical Dictionary of Chad*. Lanham, MD: Rowman & Littlefield, 2018.

Azevedo, Mario J., and Emmanuel U. Nnadozie. *Chad: A Nation in Search of Its Future*. New York: Routledge, 2018.

Baines, Gary. *South Africa's "Border War": Contested Narratives and Conflicting Memories*. London: Bloomsbury, 2014.

Baker, Deane-Peter, and Evert Jordaan, eds. *South Africa and Contemporary Counterinsurgency; Roots, Practises and Prospects*. Claremount: International Publishers, 2010.

Ballentine, K., and J. Sherman, eds. *The Political Economy of Armed Conflict: Beyond Greed and Grievance*. Boulder, CO: Lynne Rienner, 2003.

Baynham, Simon. *The Military and Politics in Nkrumah's Ghana*. Boulder, CO: Westview Press, 1988.

Beah, Ismael. *A Long Way Gone: Memoirs of a Boy Soldier*. New York: Sarah Crichton Books, 2007.

Becker, Dave. *On Wings of Eagles: South Africa's Military Aviation History*. Durban: Walker-Ramus, 1991.

Bellman, Beryl L. *The Language of Secrecy: Symbols and Metaphors in Poro Ritual*. New Brunswick, NJ: Rutgers University Press, 1984.

Beloff, Jonathan. *Foreign Policy in Post-Genocide Rwanda: Elite Perceptions of Global Engagement*. New York: Routledge, 2021.

Bennett, Huw. *Fighting the Mau Mau: The British Army and Counter-Insurgency in the Kenya Emergency*. Cambridge: Cambridge University Press, 2013.

Berhe, Aregawi. *A Political History of the Tigray People's Liberation Front (1975–1991) Revolt, Ideology and Mobilisation in Ethiopia*. Los Angeles: Tsehai, 2009.

Berhe, Mulugeta Gebrehiwot. *Laying the Past to Rest: The EPRDF and the Challenges of Ethiopian State Building*. London: Hurst, 2020.

Beshir, Omer Mohamed. *The Southern Sudan Conflict: Background to Conflict*. London: Hurst, 1968.

Bieri, F. *From Blood Diamonds to the Kimberly Process: How NGOs Cleaned Up the Global Diamond Industry*. Farnham: Ashgate, 2010.

Bjerk, Paul. *Building a Peaceful Nation: Julius Nyerere and the Establishment of Sovereignty in Tanzania, 1960–1964*. Rochester, NY: University of Rochester Press, 2018.

Bjerk, Paul. *Julius Nyerere*. Athens: Ohio University Press, 2017.

Bogner, Artur, and Gabriele Rosenthal. *Child Soldiers in Context: Biographies, Familial and Collective Trajectories in Northern Uganda*. Göttingen: Göttingen University Press, 2020.

Boilley, Pierre. *Les Touaregs Kel Adagh, Dépendances Et Révoltes: Du Soudan Français Au Mali Contemporain* (Kel Adagh Tuaregs, Dependencies and Revolts: From Colonial French West Africa to Contemporary Mali). Paris: Éditions Karthala, 1999.

Botha, Anneli. *Terrorism in the Maghreb: The Transnationalisation of Domestic Terrorism.* Pretoria: Institute for Security Studies, 2008.

Bradshaw, Richard, and Juan Fandos-Ruis. *Historical Dictionary of the Central African Republic.* Lanham, MD: Rowman & Littlefield, 2016.

Branch, Adam. *Displacing Human Rights: War and Intervention in Northern Uganda.* Oxford: Oxford University Press, 2011.

Branch, Daniel. *Defeating Mau Mau, Creating Kenya: Counterinsurgency, Civil War and Decolonization.* Cambridge: Cambridge University Press, 2009.

Breytenbach, Jan. *The Buffalo Soldiers: The Story of South Africa's 32-Battalion, 1975–1993.* Alberton: Galago, 2002.

Bridgland, Fred. *The War for Africa: Twelve Months That Transformed a Continent.* Oxford: Casemate, 2017.

Brown, David E. *AFRICOM at 5 Years: The Maturation of a New U.S. Combatant Command.* Carlisle Barracks, PA: Strategic Studies Institute, 2014.

Burr, J. Millard, and Robert O. Collins. *Darfur: The Long Road to Disaster.* Princeton, NJ: Markus Weiner, 2006.

Burr, J. Millard, and Robert O. Collins. *Revolutionary Sudan: Hasan al-Turabi and the Islamist State, 1989–2000.* Boston: Brill Academic Publishers, 2003.

Cabral, Amílcar. *Revolution in Guinea: Selected Texts.* New York: Monthly Review Press, 1970.

Cann, John P. *Brown Waters of Africa: Portuguese Riverine Warfare, 1961–1974.* St. Petersburg, FL: Hailer Publishing, 2007.

Cann, John P. *Counter-insurgency in Africa: The Portuguese Way of War, 1961–1974.* Westport, CT: Greenwood, 1997.

Carayannis, T., and L. Lombard, eds. *Making Sense of the Central African Republic.* London: Zed Books, 2015.

Carbonneau, Bruno. *France and the New Imperialism: Security Police in Sub-Saharan Africa.* Aldershot: Ashgate, 2008.

Chabal, Patrick. *Amilcar Cabral: Revolutionary Leadership and People's War.* New York: Cambridge University Press, 1983.

Chan, Stephen. *Mugabe: A Life of Power and Violence.* London: I.B. Tauris, 2019.

Cheadle, Don, and John Prendergast. *The Enough Moment: Fighting to End Africa's Worst Human Rights Crimes.* New York: Three Rivers Press, 2010.

Cherry, Janet. *Spear of the Nation; Umkhonto we Sizwe, South Africa's Liberation Army, 1960s-90s.* Athens: Ohio University Press, 2012.

Chorin, Ethan. *Exit the Colonel: The Hidden History of the Libyan Revolution.* New York: Public Affairs, 2012.

Chretien, Jean-Pierre, and Jean-François Dupaquier. *Burundi 1972; Au Bord du Genocides.* Paris: Karthala, 2007.

Cilliers, Jakkie, and Markus Reichardt, eds. *About Turn: The Transformation of the South African Military and Intelligence.* Halfway House: IDP, 1995.

Clapham, Christopher, ed. *African Guerrillas*. Oxford: James Currey, 1998.
Clarke, John D. *Yakubu Gowon: Faith in a United Nigeria*. London: Frank Cass, 1987.
Clayton, Anthony. *Frontiersmen: Warfare in Africa since 1950*. London: Routledge, 2004.
Cline, Lawrence. *The Lord's Resistance Army*. Santa Barbara, CA: Praeger Security International, 2013.
Cojean, Annick. *Gaddafi's Harem: The Story of a Young Woman and the Abuses of Power in Libya*. Translated by Marjolijn de Jager. New York: Grove, 2013.
Collier, Paul. *Wars, Guns and Votes: Democracy in Dangerous Places*. New York: Harper Perennial, 2010.
Collins, Robert O. *History of Modern Sudan*. Cambridge: Cambridge University Press, 2008.
Comolli, Virgina. *Boko Haram: Nigeria's Islamist Insurgency*. London: Hurst, 2015.
Connell, Dan. *Against All Odds: A Chronicle of the Eritrean Revolution*. Lawrenceville, NJ: Red Sea Press, 1997.
"Contested Casamance/Discordante Casamance." *Canadian Journal of African Studies/Revue canadienne des études africaines* 39, no. 2 (2005): 213–445.
Cooper, Tom, and Adrien Fontanellaz. *Africa @ War 23: Wars and Insurgencies of Uganda, 1971–1994*. West Midlands: Helion, 2015.
Coulter, Chris. *Bush Wives and Girl Soldiers: Women's Lives through War and Peace in Sierra Leone*. Ithaca, NY: Cornell University Press, 2009.
Creisson, Pierre, and Thomas Dandois. *En Territoire Interdit* (In Forbidden Territory). Paris: Arthaud, 2008.
Cudjoe, Alfred. *Who Killed Sankara?* Berkeley: University of California Press, 1988.
Dallaire, Romeo. *They Fight Like Soldiers, They Die Like Children: The Global Quest to Eradicate the Use of Child Soldiers*. Toronto: Random House Canada, 2010.
David, Ojochenemi J., Lucky E. Asuelime, and Hakeem Onapajo. *Boko Haram: The Socio-economic Drivers*. Cham: Springer International Publishing, 2015.
Davis, Brian L. *Qaddhafi, Terrorism and the Origins of the U.S. Attack on Libya*. New York: Praeger, 1990.
Davis, Stephen R. *The ANC's War against Apartheid: Umkhonto We Sizwe and the Liberation of South Africa*. Bloomington: Indiana University Press, 2018.
Dawson, Grant. *"Here Is Hell": Canada's Engagement in Somalia*. Vancouver: UBC Press, 2007.
De St. Jorre, John. *The Nigerian Civil War*. London: Hodder & Stoughton, 1972.
De Waal, Alex. *Famine Crimes: Politics and the Disaster Relief Industry in Africa*. London: African Rights 1999.
De Waal, Alex. *Food and Power in Sudan: A Critique of Humanitarianism*. London: African Rights, 1997.
De Witte, Ludo. *The Assassination of Patrice Lumumba*. London: Verso, 2002.

Decalo, Samuel. *Coups and Army Rule in Africa: Studies in Military Style.* New Haven, CT: Yale University Press, 1976.
Decker, Alicia. *In Idi Amin's Shadow: Women, Gender and Militarism in Uganda.* Athens: Ohio University Press, 2014.
Deng, Francis Mading. *War of Visions: Conflict of Identities in the Sudan.* Washington, DC: Brookings Institution Press, 1995.
Denon, Myriam. *Child Soldiers: Sierra Leone's Revolutionary United Front.* Cambridge: Cambridge University Press, 2010.
Des Forges, Alison. *Leave None to Tell the Story: Genocide in Rwanda.* New York: Human Rights Watch, 1999.
Dominguez, Jorge. *To Make a World Safe for Revolution: Cuba's Foreign Policy.* Cambridge, MA: Harvard University Press, 1989.
Dorman, Andrew. *Blair's Successful War: British Military Intervention in Sierra Leone.* Farnham: Ashgate, 2009.
Doss, Alan. *A Peacekeeper in Africa: Learning from UN Interventions in Other People's Wars.* Boulder, CO: Lynne Rienner, 2019.
DuBius, Shirley Graham. *Gamal Abdel Nasser, Son of the Nile.* New York: Third Press, 1972.
Dunstan, Simon. *The Yom Kippur War 1973 (I): The Golan Heights and (II): The Sinai.* Oxford: Osprey Publishing, 2003.
Dwyer, Maggie. *Soldiers in Revolt: Army Mutinies in Africa.* Oxford: Oxford University Press, 2017.
Ekwe-Ekwe, Herbert. *The Biafra War: Nigeria and the Aftermath.* New York: Mellen Press, 1990.
Elaigwu, J. Isawa. *Gowon: The Biography of a Soldier-Statesman.* London: Adonis & Abbey, 2009.
Elkins, Caroline. *Imperial Reckoning: The Untold Story of Britain's Gulag in Kenya.* New York: Henry Holt, 2005.
Ellis, Stephen. *External Mission: The ANC in Exile, 1960–1990.* New York: Oxford University Press, 2013.
Ellis, Stephen. *The Mask of Anarchy: The Destruction of Liberia and the Religious Dimension of an African Civil War.* New York: New York University Press, 2001.
Ellis, Stephen, and Tsepo Sechaba. *Comrades against Apartheid: The ANC & the South African Communist Party in Exile.* London: James Currey, 1992.
Emerson, Stephen. *The Battle for Mozambique: The FRELIMO-RENAMO Struggle, 1977–1992.* Solihull: Helion, 2014.
Englebert, Pierre. *Burkina Faso: Unsteady Statehood in West Africa.* New York: Routledge, 2018.
Evans, Martin. *Algeria: France's Undeclared War.* Oxford: Oxford University Press, 2012.
Evans, Martin. *Senegal: Mouvement des Forces Démocratiques de la Casamance (MFDC).* December 2004. http://www.adh-geneve.ch/RULAC/pdf_state/Martin-Evans.pdf
Evans, Martin, and John Phillips. *Algeria: Anger of the Dispossessed.* New Haven, CT: Yale University Press, 2007.

Falola, Toyin, and Charles Thomas, eds. *Securing Africa: Local Crises and Foreign Interventions*. New York: Routledge, 2014.

Fergusson, James. *The World's Most Dangerous Place: Inside the Outlaw State of Somalia*. Boston: Da Capo Press, 2013.

Filiu, Jean Pierre. *From Deep State to Islamic State: The Arab Counter-Revolution and Its Jihadi Legacy*. London: Hurst, 2015.

Fitzsimmons, Scott. *Mercenaries in Asymmetric Conflicts*. Cambridge: Cambridge University Press, 2013.

Flint, Julie, and Alex De Waal. *Darfur: A Short History of a Long War*. London: Zed Books, 2006.

Forsyth, Frederick. *Emeka*. Oxford: Spectrum Books, 1991.

Fouere, Marie-Aude. *Remembering Julius Nyerere in Tanzania: History, Memory, Legacy*. Dar es Salaam: Mkuki na Nyota Publishers Ltd., 2016.

Fowler, Robert. *A Season in Hell: My 130 Days in the Sahara with Al Qaeda*. New York: HarperCollins, 2011.

Frindethie, K. Martial. *From Lumumba to Gbagbo: Africa in the Eddy of the Euro-American Quest for Exceptionalism*. Jefferson, NC: McFarland, 2016.

Gaddafi, Muammar, with Edmond Jouve and Angela Parfitt. *My Vision*. London: John Blanke, 2005.

Gamawa, Yusuf Ibrahim. *The Tuaregs and the 2012 Rebellion in Mali*. South Africa: Partridge Publishing, 2017.

Gberie, Lansana. *A Dirty War in West Africa: The RUF and the Destruction of Sierra Leone*. London: Hurst, 2005.

Gbowee, Leymah, with Carol Mithers. *Mighty Be Our Power: How Sisterhood, Prayer and Sex Changed a Nation at War*. New York: Beast Book, 2011.

Gbulie, Ben. *Nigeria's Five Majors: Coup d'etat of 15th January 1966*. Onitsha: African Educational Publishers, 1981.

George, Edward. *The Cuban Intervention in Angola, 1965–1991: From Che Guevara to Cuito Cuanavale*. London: Frank Cass, 2005.

Gerdes, Felix. *Civil War and State Formation: The Political Economy of War and Peace in Liberia*. Frankfurt/New York: Campus Verlag and University of Chicago Press, 2013.

Ginor, Isabella, and Gideon Remez. *The Soviet-Israeli War 1967–1973: The USSR's Military Intervention in the Egyptian-Israeli Conflict*. Oxford: Oxford University Press, 2017.

Givens, Willie A., ed. *Liberia: The Road to Democracy under the Leadership of Samuel Kanyon Doe*. Bourne End: Kensal Press, 1986.

Gleijeses, Piero. *Conflicting Missions: Havana, Washington and Africa, 1959–1976*. Chapel Hill: University of North Carolina Press, 2002.

Gleijeses, Piero. *Visions of Freedom: Havana, Washington, Pretoria and the Struggle for Southern Africa, 1976–91*. Chapel Hill: University of North Carolina Press, 2013.

Good, K. *Diamonds, Dispossession, and Democracy in Botswana*. Johannesburg: Jacana Media, 2008.

Gorst, Anthony, and Lewis Johnman. *The Suez Crisis*. New York: Routledge, 1997.
Gould, Michael, and Frederick Forsyth. *The Biafran War: The Struggle for Modern Nigeria*. London: I.B Tauris, 2012.
Griffiths, Robert J. *U.S. Security Cooperation with Africa: Political and Policy Challenges*. New York: Routledge, 2016.
Guichaoua, Andre. *From War to Genocide: Criminal Politics in Rwanda*. Madison: University of Wisconsin Press, 2015.
Guido, Joseph. *Terrorist Sanctuary in the Sahara: A Case Study*. Carlisle Barracks, PA: Strategic Studies Institute/U.S. Army War College, 2017.
Gwyn, David, and Ali A. Mazrui. *Idi Amin: Death-Light of Africa*. Boston: Little, Brown, 1977.
Halliday, Fred, and Maxine Molyneux. *The Ethiopian Revolution*. London: New Left Books, 1981.
Hamilton, Rebecca. *Fighting for Darfur: Public Action and the Struggle to Stop Genocide*. London: Palgrave Macmillan, 2011.
Hammer, Joshua. *The Bad-Ass Librarians of Timbuktu and Their Race to Save the World's Most Precious Manuscripts*. New York: Simon & Schuster, 2016.
Hamrell, Sven, ed. *Refugee Problems in Africa*. New York: Africana Publishing Company, 1981.
Hansen, Stig Jarle. *Al-Shabaab in Somalia: The History and Ideology of a Militant Islamist Group*. Oxford: Oxford University Press, 2013.
Harbeson, John, and Donald Rothchild, eds. *Africa in World Politics: Constructing Political and Economic Order*. 6th ed. Boulder, CO: Westview Press, 2017.
Harper, Mary. *Getting Somalia Wrong?: Faith, War and Hope in a Shattered State*. London: Zed Books, 2012.
Harsch, Ernest. *Thomas Sankara: An African Revolutionary*. Athens: Ohio University Press, 2014.
Hatzky, Christine. *Cubans in Angola: South-South Cooperation and the Transfer of Knowledge, 1976–1991*. Madison: University of Wisconsin Press, 2015.
Hazen, Jennifer. *What Rebels Want: Resources and Supply Networks in Wartime*. Ithaca, NY: Cornell University Press, 2013.
Herzog, Chaim. *The Arab-Israeli Wars: War and Peace in the Middle East*. Updated by Shlomo Gazit. New York: Vintage Books, 2004.
Hicks, Celeste. *The Trial of Hissène Habré: How the People of Chad Brought a Tyrant to Justice*. London: Zed Books, 2018.
Hoare, Mike. *Congo Mercenary*. Boulder, CO: Paladin Press, 2008.
Hodges, Tony. *Angola: From Afro-Stalinism to Petro-Diamond Capitalism*. Bloomington: Indiana University Press, 2001.
Hoffman, Danny. *The War Machines: Young Men and Violence in Sierra Leone and Liberia*. Durham: Duke University Press, 2011.
Hollenbach, David, ed. *Refugee Rights: Ethics, Advocacy, and Africa*. Washington, DC: Georgetown University Press, 2008.
Honwana, Alcinda. *Child Soldiers in Africa*. Philadelphia: University of Pennsylvania Press, 2006.

Hooper, Jim. *Koevoet: Experiencing South Africa's Deadly Bush War.* Solihull: Helion, 2013.

Horne, Alistair. *A Savage War of Peace: Algeria, 1954–1962.* New York: Viking, 1977.

Huband, Mark. *The Liberian Civil War.* New York: Frank Cass, 1998.

Human Rights Watch. *Angola: Between War and Peace in Cabinda.* New York: Human Rights Watch.

Iyob, Ruth. *The Eritrean Struggle for Independence: Domination, Resistance, Nationalism, 1941–1993.* Cambridge: Cambridge University Press, 1997.

James, W. Martin. *Historical Dictionary of Angola.* Lanham, MD: Scarecrow Press, 2011.

James, W. Martin. *A Political History of the War in Angola, 1974–1990.* London: Transaction Publishers, 2011.

Jankowski, James. *Nasser's Egypt, Arab Nationalism and the United Arab Republic.* Boulder, CO: Lynne Rienner, 2001.

Jaye, Thomas, Dauda Garuba, and Stella Amadi, eds. *ECOWAS: The Dynamics of Conflict and Peace-Building.* Dakar: CODESRIA, 2011.

Jennings, Christian. *Across the Red River: Rwanda, Burundi and the Heart of Darkness.* London: Phoenix, 2000.

Jensen, Eric. *Western Sahara: Anatomy of a Stalemate.* London: Lynne Rienner, 2004.

Johnson, Douglas H. *Nuer Prophets: A History of Prophecy from the Upper Nile in the Nineteenth and Twentieth Centuries.* Oxford: Clarendon Press, 1994.

Johnson, Douglas H. *The Root Causes of Sudan's Civil Wars.* Kampala: Fountain Publishers, 2011.

Jok Madut Jok. *Sudan: Race, Religion and Violence.* Philadelphia: University of Philadelphia Press, 2001.

Jones, Stewart Lloyd, and Antonio Costa-Pinto, eds. *The Last Empire: Thirty Years of Portuguese Decolonization.* Bristol: Intellect Books, 2003.

Junior, Miguel. *The Formation and Development of the Angolan Armed Forces.* Bloomington, IN: AuthorHouse, 2019.

Junior, Miguel. *Popular Armed Forces for the Liberation of Angola, First National Army and the War (1975–1991).* Bloomington, IN: AuthorHouse, 2015.

Kabia, John. *Humanitarian Intervention and Conflict Resolution in West Africa: From ECOMOG to ECOMIL.* Farnham: Ashgate, 2009.

Kainerugaba, Muhoozi. *Battles of the Ugandan Resistance: A Tradition of Maneuver.* Kampala: Fountain Publishers, 2010.

Kalck, Pierre. *Historical Dictionary of the Central African Republic.* Lanham, MD: Scarecrow Press, 2005.

Keen, David. *Benefits of Famine: A Political Economy of Famine and Relief in South-West Sudan.* Oxford: Oxford University Press, 1991.

Keenan, Jeremy. *The Dark Sahara: America's War on Terror in Africa.* London: Pluto Press, 2009.

Keenan, Jeremy. *The Dying Sahara: US Imperialism and Terror in Africa.* London: Pluto Press, 2013.

Keenan, Jeremy. *The Lesser Gods of the Sahara: Social Change and Contested Terrain Amongst the Tuareg of Algeria*. London: Frank Cass, 2004.

Keita, Kalifa. *Conflict and Conflict Resolution in the Sahel: The Tuareg Insurgency in Mali*. Carlisle Barracks, PA: U.S. Army War College, 1998. https://permanent.access.gpo.gov/lps12312/carlisle-www.army.mil/usassi/ssipubs/pubs98/tuareg/tuareg.pdf

Kelly, Sean. *America's Tyrant: The CIA and Mobutu and Zaire*. Washington, DC: American University Press, 1993.

Kennes, Erik, and Miles Larmer. *The Katangese Gendarmes: Fighting Their Way Home*. Bloomington: Indiana University Press, 2016.

Kettle, Michael. *De Gaulle and Algeria, 1940–1960*. London: Quartet, 1993.

Khatib, Lina, and Ellen Lust, eds. *Taking It to the Streets: The Transformation of Arab Activism*. Baltimore: Johns Hopkins University Press, 2014.

Kibreab, Gaim. *The Eritrean National Service: Servitude for "the Common Good" and the Youth Exodus*. Woodbridge: James Currey, 2017.

Kilford, Christopher R. *The Other Cold War: Canadian Military Assistance in the Developing World*. Kingston: Canadian Defence Academy Press, 2010.

Knopf, Katie Almquist. *Ending South Sudan's Civil War*. New York: Council on Foreign Relations, 2016.

Kokalla Maiga, Choguel, and Issiaka Ahmadou Singaré. *Les Rebellions Au Nord du Mali, des Origines a Nos Jours* (The Rebellions in the North of Mali: From Origins to Today). Bamako: EDIS, 2018.

Kolomnin, Sergei. *Russkii sled pod Kifangondo*. Moscow: Etnika, 2014.

Kondlo, Kwandiwe. *In the Twilight of the Revolution. The Pan Africanist Congress of Azania (South Africa) 1959–1994*. Basel: Basler Afrika Bibliographien, 2009.

Kongo, Jean-Claude, and Leo Zeilig. *Thomas Sankara*. Cape Town: National Institute for the Humanities and Social Sciences, 2017.

Koops, Joachim, Norrie MacQueen, Thierry Tardy, and Paul D. Williams, eds. *The Oxford Handbook of United Nations Peacekeeping Operations*. Oxford: Oxford University Press, 2015.

Kotia, Emmanuel Wekem. *Ghana Armed Forces in Lebanon and Liberia Peace Operations*. New York: Rowman & Littlefield, 2015.

Kramer, Robert S., Richard Lobban, and Fluehr Lobban. *Historical Dictionary of Sudan: African Historical Dictionaries*. Lanham: Scarecrow Press, 2013.

Kyemba, Henry. *A State of Blood: The Inside Story of Idi Amin*. Kampala: Fountain Publishers, 1997.

Lacouture, Jean. *Nasser, A Biography*. New York: Knopf, 1973.

Lan, David. *Guns and Rain: Guerrillas and Spirit Mediums in Zimbabwe*. London: James Currey, 1985.

Laurence, Tony, and Christopher MacRae. *The Dar Mutiny of 1964: And the Armed Intervention That Ended It*. Bloomington, IN: AuthorHouse, 2010.

Le Suer, James D. *Between Terror and Democracy: Algeria since 1989*. New York: Zed Books, 2010.

Lemarchand, Rene. *Burundi: Ethnic Conflict and Genocide*. Cambridge: Cambridge University Press, 1994.

Lemarchand, Rene. *The Dynamics of Violence in Central Africa.* Philadelphia: University of Pennsylvania Press, 2009.

Lemarchand, Rene. *The Green and the Black: Qadhafi Policies in Africa.* Bloomington: Indiana University Press, 1988.

Lewis, Ioan. *Understanding Somalia and Somaliland.* New York: Columbia University Press, 2008.

Leys, Colin, and John Saul. *Namibia's Liberation Struggle: The Two Edged Sword.* London: James Currey, 1995.

Liundi, Christopher C. *Quotable Quotes of Mwalimu Julius K. Nyerere Collected from Speeches and Writings.* Dar es Salaam: Mkuki Na Nyota, 2012.

Lobban, Richard A., Jr., and Christopher H. Dalton. *Libya: History and Revolution.* Santa Barbara, CA: ABC-CLIO, 2014.

Lombard, Louisa. *State of Rebellion: Violence and Intervention in the Central African Republic.* London: Zed Books, 2016.

Lyons, Tanya. *Guns and Guerrilla Girls: Women in the Zimbabwe National Liberation Struggle.* Trenton, NJ: Africa World Press, 2004.

Macqueen, Norrie. *United Nations Peacekeeping in Africa since 1960.* London: Routledge, 2002.

Magyar, Karl, and Earl Conteh-Morgan, eds. *Peacekeeping in Africa: ECOMOG in Liberia.* Basingstoke: Palgrave Macmillan, 1998.

Maier, Karl. *Angola: Promises and Lies.* London: Serif, 2013.

Malkki, Liisa. *Purity and Exile: Violence, Memory and National Cosmology among Hutu Refugees in Tanzania.* Chicago: University of Chicago Press, 1995.

Mamdani, Mahmood. *Survivors and Saviors: Darfur, Politics and the War on Terror.* New York: Double Day, 2009.

Mamdani, Mahmood. *When Victims Become Killers: Colonialism, Nativism and the Genocide in Rwanda.* Princeton, NJ: Princeton University Press, 2001.

Manson, Katrina, and James Knight. *Burkina Faso.* Guilford, CT: Pequot Press, 2006.

Martell, Peter. *First Raise the Flag: How South Sudan Won the Longest War but Lost the Peace.* Oxford: Oxford University Press, 2019.

Martin, D., and P. Johnson. *The Struggle for Zimbabwe.* New York: Monthly Review, 1981.

Martinez, Luis. *The Algerian Civil War 1990–1998.* New York: Columbia University Press, 2000.

Maruf, Harun, and Dan Joseph. *Inside Al-Shabaab: The Secret History of Al Qaeda's Most Powerful Ally.* Bloomington: Indiana University Press, 2018.

Marut, Jean-Claude. *Le conflit de Casamance. Ce que disent les armes.* Paris: Karthala, 2010.

Mays, Terry M. *Africa's First Peacekeeping Operation: The OAU in Chad 1981–82.* Westport, CT: Praeger, 2002.

McDougall, James. *A History of Algeria.* Cambridge: Cambridge University Press, 2017.

McGovern, Mike. *Making War in Cote d'Ivoire.* Chicago: University of Chicago Press, 2011.

McGregor, Andrew. *A Military History of Modern Egypt; from the Ottoman Conquest to the Ramadan War.* Westport, CT: Praeger Security International, 2006.

Melvern, Linda. *Conspiracy to Murder: The Rwanda Genocide.* London: Verso, 2006.

Melvern, Linda. *A People Betrayed: The Role of the West in Rwanda's Genocide.* London: Zed Books, 2005.

Meredith, Martin. *Robert Mugabe: Power, Plunder and Tyranny in Zimbabwe.* Johannesburg: Jonathan Ball, 2002.

Mills, Kurt. *International Responses to Mass Atrocities in Africa: Responsibility to Protect, Prosecute and Palliate.* Philadelphia: University of Pennsylvania Press, 2015.

Minter, William. *Apartheid's Contras: An Inquiry into the Roots of War in Angola and Mozambique.* London: Zed Books, 1994.

Mokeddem, Mohamed. *Al Qaida Au Maghreb Islamique: Contrebande Au Nom De L'islam* (Al-Qaeda in the Islamic Maghreb: Smuggling in the Name of Islam). Algiers: Casbah-Editions, 2010.

Moloney, Sean. *Canada and UN Peacekeeping: Cold War by Other Means, 1945–1970.* St. Catharines, ON: Vanwell Publishing, 2002.

Mondlane, Eduardo. *The Struggle for Mozambique.* Baltimore: Penguin, 1969.

Moorcroft, Paul. *Omar al-Bashir and Africa's Longest War.* Barnsley: Pen and Sword, 2015.

Moorcroft, Paul, and Peter McLaughlin. *The Rhodesian War: A Military History.* London: Pen and Sword, 2008.

Morris, Benny. *Righteous Victims: A History of the Zionist-Arab Conflict, 1881–2001.* New York: Vintage Books, 2002.

Muggah, Robert, ed. *No Refuge: The Crisis of Refugee Militarization in Africa.* London: Zed Books, 2006.

Musah, Abdul-Fatau, and J. Kayode Fayemi, eds. *Mercenaries: An African Security Dilemma.* London: Pluto Press, 2000.

Museveni, Yoweri Kaguta. *Sowing the Mustard Seed: The Struggle for Freedom and Democracy in Uganda.* London: Macmillan Education Ltd., 1997.

Mustapha, Abdul Raufu, ed. *Sects & Social Disorder: Muslim Identities & Conflict in Northern Nigeria.* Woodbridge: Boydell & Brewer, 2014.

Mwakikagile, Godfrey. *Burundi; The Hutu and the Tutsi: Cauldron of Conflict and Quest for Dynamic Compromise.* Dar es Salaam: New Africa Press, 2012.

Namakalu, Oswin. *Armed Liberation Struggle: Some Accounts of PLAN's Combat Operations.* Windhoek: Gamsberg MacMillan, 2004.

Namikas, Lise. *Battleground Africa: Cold War in the Congo, 1960–65.* Washington, DC: Woodrow Wilson Center Press, 2013.

Ndlovu-Gatsheni, Sabelo J., ed. *Mugabeism? History, Politics and Power in Zimbabwe.* New York: Palgrave Macmillan, 2015.

Negash, Tekaste, and Kjetil Tronvoll. *Brothers at War: Making Sense of the Eritrean-Ethiopian War.* Oxford: James Currey, 2000.

Newitt, Malyn. *A History of Mozambique.* London: Hurst, 1995.

Newitt, Malyn. *Portugal in Africa: The Last 100 Years.* London: Longman, 1981.

Ngolet, Francois. *Crisis in the Congo: The Rise and Fall of Laurent Kabila*. New York: Palgrave Macmillan, 2011.

Nhongo-Simbanegavi, J. *For Better or Worse: Women and ZANLA in Zimbabwe's Liberation Struggle*. Harare: Weaver Press, 2000.

Njoku, Raphael C. *The History of Somalia*. Santa Barbara, CA: Greenwood, 2013.

Nkaisserry, Joseph K. *The Ogaden War: An Analysis of Its Causes and Its Impact on Regional Peace on the Horn of Africa*. Carlisle Barracks, PA: United States Army War College, 1997.

Nkomo, Joshua. *The Story of My Life*. London: Methuen, 1984.

Nolutshungu, Sam. *The Limits of Anarchy: Intervention and State Formation in Chad*. Charlottesville: University of Virginia Press, 1995.

Nutting, Anthony. *Nasser*. New York: E. P. Dutton, 1972.

Nwaubani, Ebere. *The United States and Decolonization in West Africa*. Rochester, NY: University of Rochester Press, 2001.

Nzongola-Ntalaja, Georges. *The Congo: From Leopold to Kabila: A People's History*. London: Zed Books, 2013.

Oakes, John. *Libya: The History of Gaddafi's Pariah State*. Stroud: History Press, 2011.

Odom, Thomas. *Dragon Operations: Hostage Rescues in the Congo, 1964–65*. Fort Leavenworth, KS: Combat Studies Institute, 1988.

Odom, Thomas P. *Shaba II: The French and Belgian Intervention in Zaire in 1978*. Fort Leavenworth, KS: U.S. Army Command and General Staff College, Combat Studies Institute, 1993.

Ofcansky, Thomas P. *Uganda: Tarnished Pearl of Africa*. Boulder, CO: Westview Press, 1996.

Ojeda-Garcia, Raquel, Irene Fernandez-Molina, and Victoria Veguilla, eds. *Global, Regional and Local Dimensions of Western Sahara's Protracted Decolonization: When Conflicts Get Old*. Basingstoke: Palgrave Macmillan, 2017.

Okorokov, Aleksandr V. *Sovetskii soiuz i voini v Afrike*. Moscow: Veche, 2018.

Omonijo, Mobolade. *Doe: The Liberian Tragedy*. Ikeja: Sahel, 1990.

Oren, Michael B. *Six Days of War: June 1967 and the Making of the Modern Middle East*. New York: Oxford University Press, 2002.

Othen, Christopher. *Katanga, 1960–63: Mercenaries, Spies and the African Nation That Waged War on the World*. Stroud: History Press, 2015.

Oyeniyi, Bukola. *The History of Libya*. Santa Barbara, CA: Greenwood, 2019.

Page, Malcolm. *KAR: A History of the King's African Rifles*. London: Leo Cooper, 1998.

Pankhurst, Richard. *The Ethiopians: A History*. Oxford: Blackwell Publishing, 2001.

Pargeter, Alison. *Libya: The Rise and Fall of Gaddafi*. New Haven, CT: Yale University Press, 2012.

Parsons, Timothy. *The 1964 Army Mutinies and the Making of Modern East Africa*. Westport, CT: Praeger, 2003.

Pennell, C. R. *Morocco: From Empire to Independence*. Oxford: One World, 2009.

Peters, Jimi. *The Nigerian Military and the State*. London: I.B. Tauris, 1997.

Peterson, Brian. *Thomas Sankara: A Revolutionary in Cold War Africa*. Bloomington: Indiana University Press, 2021.

Pinaud, Clemence. *War and Genocide in South Sudan*. Ithaca, NY: Cornell University Press, 2021.

Piombo, Jessica, ed. *The US Military in Africa: Enhancing Security and Development?* Boulder, CO: Lynne Reinner, 2015.

Poggo, S. Scopas. *The First Sudanese Civil War: Africans, Arabs, and Israelis in Southern Sudan, 1955–1972*. New York: Palgrave Macmillan, 2009.

Pollack, Kenneth. *Arabs at War: Military Effectiveness, 1948–1991*. Lincoln: University of Nebraska Press, 2002.

Pollack, Peter. *The Last Hot Battle of the Cold War: South Africa vs. Cuba in the Angolan Civil War*. Oxford: Casemate, 2013.

Pool, David. *From Guerrillas to Government: The Eritrean People's Liberation Front*. Athens: Ohio University Press, 2001.

Powell, Nathaniel. *France's Wars in Chad: Military Intervention and Decolonization in Africa*. Cambridge: Cambridge University Press, 2020.

Power, Samantha. *A Problem from Hell: America and the Age of Genocide*. New York: New Republic, 2002.

Presley, Cora-Ann. *Kikuyu Women, the Mau Mau Rebellion and Social Change in Kenya*. Boulder, CO: Westview Press, 1992.

Prunier, Gerard. *Africa's World War: Congo, the Rwanda Genocide and the Making of a Continental Catastrophe*. Oxford: Oxford University Press, 2009.

Prunier, Gerard. *Darfur: The Ambiguous Genocide*. Ithaca, NY: Cornell University Press, 2005.

Prunier, Gerard. *The Rwanda Crisis: History of a Genocide*. New York: Columbia University Press, 1995.

Prunier, Gerard, and Eloi Foicquet, eds. *Understanding Contemporary Ethiopia: Monarchy, Revolution and the Legacy of Meles Zenawi*. London: Hurst, 2015.

Ranger, T., and N. Bhebhe, eds. *Society in Zimbabwe's Liberation War*. London: James Currey, 1995.

Ranger, T., and N. Bhebhe, eds. *Soldiers in Zimbabwe's Liberation War*. London: James Currey, 1995.

Recchio, Stephano, and Thierry Tardy. *French Interventions in Africa: Reluctant Multilateralism*. New York: Routledge, 2020.

Reid, Richard. *Frontiers of Violence in North-East Africa: Genealogies of Conflict since c. 1800*. Oxford: Oxford University Press, 2011.

Reid, Richard. *Shallow Graves: A Memoir of the Ethiopia-Eritrea War*. Oxford: Oxford University Press, 2020.

Reid, Richard. *Warfare in African History*. Cambridge: Cambridge University Press, 2012.

Reno, William. *Warfare in Independent Africa*. Cambridge: Cambridge University Press, 2011.

"Report on the 1980s Disturbances in Matabeleland and the Midlands." Catholic Commission for Justice and Peace in Zimbabwe, March 1997. http://www.rhodesia.nl/Matabeleland%20Report.pdf

Reveron, Derek S. *Exporting Security: International Engagement, Security Cooperation, and the Changing Face of the U.S. Military.* Washington, DC: Georgetown University Press, 2010.

Reyntjens, Filip. *The Great African War: Congo and Regional Geopolitics, 1996–2006.* Cambridge: Cambridge University Press, 2009.

Rhoads, Emily Paddon. *Taking Sides in Peacekeeping: Impartiality and the Future of the United Nations.* Oxford: Oxford University Press, 2017.

Rolandsen, Oystein, and M. W. Daly. *A History of South Sudan: From Slavery to Independence.* Cambridge: Cambridge University Press, 2016.

Rosen, David. *Armies of the Young: Child Soldiers in War and Terrorism.* New Brunswick, NJ: Rutgers University Press, 2005.

Rouvez, Alain. *Disconsolate Empires: French, British and Belgian Military Involvement in Post-Colonial Sub-Saharan Africa.* Lanham, MD: University Press of America, 1994.

Rupiya, Martin, ed. *Evolutions and Revolutions: A Contemporary History of Militaries in Southern Africa.* Pretoria: Institute for Security Studies, 2005.

Rusagara, Frank. *Resilience of a Nation: A History of the Military in Rwanda.* Kampala: Fountain Publishers, 2009.

Rutherford, Kenneth. *Humanitarianism under Fire: The US and UN Intervention in Somalia.* Sterling, VA: Kumarian Press, 2008.

Saint Girons, Anne. *Les Rébellions Touarègues* (The Tuareg Rebellions). Paris: Ibis Press, 2008.

Sankara, Thomas. *Thomas Sankara Speaks: The Burkina Faso Revolution: 1983–87.* New York: Pathfinder, 2007.

Saro-Wiwa, Ken. *Genocide in Nigeria: The Ogoni Tragedy.* Port Harcourt: Saros International Publishers, 1992.

Saunders, R., and T. Nyamunda, eds. *Facets of Power: Politics, Profits and People in the Making of Zimbabwe's Blood Diamonds.* Harare: Weaver Press, 2016.

Scheele, Judith. *Smugglers and Saints of the Sahara: Regional Connectivity in the Twentieth Century.* Cambridge: Cambridge University Press, 2012.

Scherrer, P. Christian. *Genocide and Crisis in Central Africa: Conflict Roots, Mass Violence, and Regional War.* Westport, CT: Praeger, 2002.

Schmidt, Elizabeth. *Foreign Intervention in Africa: From the Cold War to the War on Terror.* Cambridge: Cambridge University Press, 2013.

Scholtz, Leopold. *The SADF in the Border War, 1966–1989.* Cape Town: Tafelberg, 2013.

Servan-Schreiber, Jean-Jacques. *Lieutenant in Algeria.* Translated by Ronald Matthews. New York: Knopf, 1957.

Sherman, Richard. *Eritrea, the Unfinished Revolution.* New York: Praeger, 1980.

Shubin, Vladimir. *The Hot "Cold War": The USSR in Southern Africa.* London: Pluto Press, 2008.

Shurkin, Michael. *France's War in Mali: Lessons for an Expeditionary Army.* Santa Monica, CA: RAND, 2014.

Sibanda, Eliakim. *The Zimbabwe African People's Union, 1961–1987, A Political History of Insurgency in Southern Rhodesia.* Trenton, NJ: Africa World Press, 2005.

Siebels, Dirk. *Maritime Security in East and West Africa: A Tale of Two Regions*. Basingstoke: Palgrave Macmillan, 2019.

Simpson, Thula. *Umkhonto we Sizwe: The ANC's Armed Struggle*. Cape Town: Penguin, 2016.

Singer, P. W. *Children at War*. New York: Pantheon Books, 2005.

Singer, P. W. *Corporate Warriors: The Rise of the Privatized Military Industry*. Ithaca, NY: Cornell University Press, 2003.

Siollun, Max. *Oil, Politics and Violence: Nigeria's Military Coup Culture (1966–76)*. New York: Algora Publishing, 2009.

Smith, George Ivan. *Ghosts of Kampala*. London: Weidenfeld & Nicolson, 1980.

Smith, Karen. *Genocide and the Europeans*. Cambridge: Cambridge University Press, 2010.

Sommers, Marc. *Fear in Bongoland: Burundian Refugees in Urban Tanzania*. New York: Berghahn Books, 2001.

Spooner, Kevin A. *Canada, the Congo Crisis, and UN Peacekeeping, 1960–1964*. Vancouver: UBC Press, 2010.

St. John, Ronald B. *Libya: From Colony to Revolution*. Oxford: Oneworld, 2012.

Stapleton, Timothy J. *Africa: War and Conflict in the Twentieth Century*. London: Routledge, 2018.

Stapleton, Timothy J. *A History of Genocide in Africa*. Santa Barbara, CA: Praeger Security International, 2017.

Stapleton, Timothy J. *A Military History of Africa. Vol. 3, The Era of Independence: From the Congo Crisis to Africa's World War, c. 1963–2012*. Santa Barbara, CA: Praeger Security International, 2013.

Stapleton, Timothy J. *A Military History of South Africa: From the Dutch-Khoi Wars to the End of Apartheid*. Santa Barbara, CA: Praeger, 2010.

Steenkamp, Willem. *Borderstrike: South Africa into Angola 1975–1980*. 3rd ed. Durban: Just Done Productions Publishing, 2006.

Steenkamp, Willem. *South Africa's Border War, 1966–89*. Solihull: Helion, 2014.

Sterns, Jason, K. *Dancing in the Glory of Monsters: The Collapse of the Congo and the Great African War*. New York: Public Affairs, 2011.

Stiff, Peter. *The Covert War: Koevoet Operations Namibia, 1979–89*. Alberton: Galago, 2004.

Stiff, Peter. *The Silent War: South African Recce Operations 1969–1994*. Alberton: Galago, 2001.

Stockwell, John. *In Search of Enemies: A CIA Story*. New York: W. W. Norton, 1978.

Straus, Scott. *Making and Unmaking Nations: War, Leadership and Genocide in Modern Africa*. Ithaca, NY: Cornell University Press, 2015.

Straus, Scott. *The Order of Genocide: Race, Power, and War in Rwanda*. Ithaca, NY: Cornell University Press, 2007.

Surhone, Lam, ed. *Sierra Leone Civil War: Revolutionary United Front, Foday Sankoh, Joseph Mamoh, Recreational Drugs, Child Soldiers*. Beau Bassin: Betascript, 2010.

Talbott, John. *The War without a Name: France in Algeria, 1954–1962*. New York: Knopf, 1980.

Tanzania People's Defence Forces. *Tanganyika Rifles Mutiny, January 1964*. Dar es Salaam: Dar es Salaam University Press, 1998.

Tareke, Gebru. *The Ethiopian Revolution: War in the Horn of Africa*. New Haven, CT: Yale University Press, 2009.

Tendi, Blessing Miles. *Making History in Mugabe's Zimbabwe: Politics, Intellectuals and the Media*. Berlin: Peter Lang, 2010.

Thomas, Charles G. "The Tanzanian People's Defence Force: An Exercise in Nation Building." PhD thesis, University of Texas at Austin, 2012.

Thurston, Alexander. *Boko Haram: The History of an African Jihadist Movement*. Princeton, NJ: Princeton University Press, 2018.

Totten, Samuel. *Genocide by Attrition: The Nuba Mountains of Sudan*. London: Transaction Publishers, 2015.

Turner, Simon. *Politics of Innocence: Hutu Identity, Conflict and Camp Life*. New York: Berghahn Books, 2010.

Turner, Thomas. *The Congo Wars: Conflict, Myth and Reality*. New York: Zed Books, 2007.

Udogu, E. Ike. *Liberation Namibia: The Long Diplomatic Struggle between the United Nations and South Africa*. Jefferson, NC: McFarland, 2012.

United Nations High Commissioner for Refugees. *The State of the World's Refugees 2000: Fifty Years of Humanitarian Action*. Oxford: Oxford University Press, 2000.

Van der Waag, Ian. *A Military History of Modern South Africa*. Oxford: Casemate, 2018.

Van der Waals, W. S. *The Portugal's War in Angola*. Rivonia: Ashanti, 1993.

Vandewalle, Dirk J. *A History of Modern Libya*. Cambridge: Cambridge University Press, 2012.

Vanthemsche, Guy. *Belgium and the Congo, 1885–1980*. Cambridge: Cambridge University Press, 2012.

Varble, Derek. *The Suez Crisis—1956*. London: Osprey Publishing, 2003.

Varin, Caroline. *Boko Haram and the War on Terror*. Santa Barbara, CA: Praeger, 2016.

Veit, Alex. *Intervention as Indirect Rule: Civil War and State-Building in the Democratic Republic of Congo*. Frankfurt: Campus Verlag, 2010.

Venter, Al J. *Battle for Angola: The End of the Cold War in Africa c 1975–89*. Solihull: Helion, 2017.

Venter, Al J. *Portugal's Guerrilla Wars in Africa: Lisbon's Three Wars in Angola, Mozambique and Guinea-Bissau*. Solihull: Helion, 2013.

Venter, Al J. *War Dog: Fighting Other Peoples' Wars: The Modern Mercenary in Combat*. New Delhi: Lancer, 2010.

Villafana, Frank. *Cold War in the Congo: The Confrontation of Cuban Military Forces, 1960–67*. London: Transaction Publishers, 2012.

Wai, Zubairu. *Epistemologies of African Conflicts: Violence, Evolutionism, and the War in Sierra Leone*. Basingstoke: Palgrave Macmillan, 2012.

Wallace, Marion. *A History of Namibia: From the Beginning to 1990*. New York: Columbia University Press, 2011.

Wallis, Andrew. *Silent Accomplice: The Untold Story of France's Role in the Rwandan Genocide*. London: I.B. Tauris, 2006.

Watson, William E. *Tricolor and Crescent: France and the Islamic World*. Westport, CT: Praeger, 2003.

Watt, Nigel. *Burundi: The Biography of a Small African Country*. London: Hurst, 2008.

Waugh, Colin. *Charles Taylor and Liberia: Ambition and Atrocity in Africa's Lone Star State*. London: Zed Books, 2011.

Waugh, Colin. *Paul Kagame and Rwanda: Power, Genocide and the Rwandan Patriotic Front*. Jefferson, NC: McFarland, 2004.

Wehrey, Frederic. *Burning Shores: Inside the Battle for the New Libya*. New York: Farrar, Straus and Giroux, 2018.

Weigert, Stephen. *Angola: A Modern Military History, 1961–2002*. New York: Palgrave Macmillan, 2011.

Weill, Sharon, Kim Thuy Seelinger, and Kerstin Bree Carlson, eds. *The President on Trial: Prosecuting Hissène Habré*. Oxford: Oxford University Press, 2020.

Weiss, Kenneth G. *The Soviet Involvement in the Ogaden War*. Professional Paper 269 (February). Alexandria, VA: Center for Naval Analyses, 1980.

Wessells, Michael. *Child Soldiers: From Violence to Protection*. Cambridge, MA: Harvard University Press, 2006.

Westad, Odd Arne. *The Global Cold War*. Cambridge: Cambridge University Press, 2007.

Whitaker, Blake. "The 'New Model' Armies of Africa? The British Military Advisory and Training Team and the Creation of the Zimbabwe National Army." PhD thesis, Texas A&M University, 2014.

Wilen, Nina. *Justifying Interventions in Africa: (De) Stabilizing Sovereignty in Liberia, Burundi and the Congo*. Basingstoke: Palgrave Macmillan, 2012.

Williams, Paul. *Fighting for Peace in Somalia: A History and Analysis of the African Union Mission in Somalia (AMISOM), 2007–2017*. Oxford: Oxford University Press, 2018.

Williams, Paul. *War and Conflict in Africa*. Cambridge: Polity Press, 2011.

Williams, Susan. *Who Killed Dag Hammarskjold? The UN, the Cold War and White Supremacy in Africa*. Oxford: Oxford University Press, 2014.

Willis, Michael. *The Islamist Challenge in Algeria: A Political History*. New York: New York University Press, 1997.

Willis, Michael. *Power and Politics in the Maghreb: Algeria, Tunisia and Morocco from Independence to the Arab Spring*. London: Hurst, 2012.

Woldemariam, Michel. *Insurgent Fragmentation in the Horn of Africa: Rebellion and Its Discontents*. Cambridge: Cambridge University Press, 2018.

Wood, J. R. T. *Counter-Strike from the Sky: The Rhodesian All-Arms Fireforce in the Bush 1974–1980*. Johannesburg: 30 Degrees South Publishers, 2009.

Wright, John. *A History of Libya*. London: Hurst, 2012.

Yordanov, Radoslav. *The Soviet Union and the Horn of Africa during the Cold War: Between Ideology and Pragmatism*. Lanham, MD: Lexington Books, 2016.

Young, John. *Peasant Revolution in Ethiopia: The Tigray People's Liberation Front, 1975–1991*. Cambridge: Cambridge University Press, 2006.

Young, John. *South Sudan's Civil War: Violence, Insurgency and Failed Peacemaking*. London: Zed Books, 2019.

Zack-Williams, Tunde. *When the State Fails: Studies on Intervention in the Sierra Leone Civil War*. London: Pluto Press, 2012.

Zartman, I. William, ed. *Arab Spring: Negotiating in the Shadow of the Intifadat*. Athens: University of Georgia Press, 2015.

Zelikow, Philip, and Ernest May. *Suez Deconstructed: An Interactive Study in Crisis, War and Peacemaking*. Washington, DC: Brookings Institute Press, 2018.

Zewde, Bahru. *A History of Modern Ethiopia, 1855–1991*. Oxford: James Currey, 2009.

Zunes, Stephen, and Jacob Mundy. *Western Sahara: War, Nationalism and Conflict Irresolution*. Syracuse, NY: Syracuse University Press, 2010.

About the Editor and Contributors

EDITOR

Timothy J. Stapleton is professor of African history at the University of Calgary and has taught at Rhodes University and the University of Fort Hare in South Africa. His published works include *Maqoma: Xhosa Resistance to Colonial Advance 1798–1873* (J. Ball, 1994); *No Insignificant Part: The Rhodesia Native Regiment and the East Africa Campaign of the First World War* (Wilfrid Laurier University Press, 2006); *A Military History of South Africa: From the Dutch-Khoi Wars to the End of Apartheid* (Praeger, 2010); *African Police and Soldiers in Colonial Zimbabwe, 1923–1980* (University of Rochester Press, 2011); and *West African Soldiers in Britain's Colonial Army, 1860–1960* (2022).

CONTRIBUTORS

Gershon Adela
University of Calgary
Alberta, Canada

Paul R. Bartrop
Florida Gulf Coast University

Walter Boyne
Independent Scholar

Carolina Bracco
University of Buenos Aires
Argentina

Jacien Carr
SOAS University of London
England

Jennifer Christian
Enough Project

Robert H. Clemm
eSchool of Graduate PME
Air University

Beth K. Dougherty
Beloit College

Tom Dowling
Independent Scholar

Valentina Fedele
Università della
 Calabria
Castrolibero, Italy

Michael Fowler
U.S. Air Force Academy

Eric Garcia-Moral
Universitat Pompeu Fabra
Barcelona, Spain

Mark E. Grotelueschen
U.S. Air Force Academy

Joseph Guido
U.S. Army

Alexander Hill
University of Calgary
Alberta, Canada

Quentin Holbert
University of Calgary
Alberta, Canada

Lynn Jurgensen
University of California

Melvin R. Korsmo
School of Advanced Air & Space Studies
Air University

Jeremy Kuzmarov
University of Tulsa

Emmanuel M. Mbah
CUNY/College of Staten Island

Edward F. Mickolus
Vineyard Software Inc.

Larissa Mihalisko
U.S. Marine Corps

Alexander Mikaberidze
Louisiana State University

Lise Namikas
Louisiana State University

Michael Newton
Independent Scholar

Terri Nichols
Freelance Writer and Researcher

Yolanda Osondu
University of Calgary
Alberta, Canada

David Paige
ABC-CLIO, LLC

Taylan Paksoy
Bilkent University
Anikara, Turkey

Abel Polese
Hanna Arendt Institute
Dresden, Germany

Steven A. Quillman
U.S. Air Force

Chris W. J. Roberts
University of Calgary
Alberta, Canada

Mathew Ruguwa
University of Calgary
Alberta, Canada

Christopher Saunders
University of Cape Town
Rondebosch, South Africa

Jean Pierre Scherman
Stellenbosch University
Saldanha, South Africa

Gorata Sello
University of Calgary
Alberta, Canada

Yusuf Sholeye
University of Calgary
Alberta, Canada

About the Editor and Contributors

Paul J. Springer
Air Command and Staff College
Maxwell Air Force Base

Melissa Stallings
Malibu Library

Charles G. Thomas
Air Command and Staff College
Maxwell Air Force Base

Spencer C. Tucker
Independent Scholar

Dallas W. Unger Jr.
Independent Scholar

Peter Vale
Rhodes University
Grahamstown, South Africa

Richard Warnes
Rand Europe
Cambridge, England

William E. Watson
Immaculata University

Tim Watts
Kansas State University

Patrick Whang
Independent Scholar

Jonathan K. Zartman
Air University

Index

Note: Page numbers in **bold** indicate the location of main entries.

Afabet, Battle of, **1–2**
   aftermath and consequences, 1–2
   battle, 1
   deaths and casualties, 1–2
   Eritrean Liberation Front (ELF) and, 1, 126
   Eritrean victory, 1
   history and origins, 1
African Armed Forces, **2–5**
   Cold War era, 3
   colonial history, 2–3
   postcolonial militaries, 3–4
   praetorian and predatory habits, 4
   precolonial history, 1
   Western models, 3
Afwerki, Isaias, **5–6**
   birth and early career, 5
   conflict in Tigray province (Ethiopia), 6
   criticism and controversy, 5–6
   Eritrean–Ethiopian War, 6
   first president of Eritrea, 5
   founding of EPLF, 5
   independence of Eritrea, 5
   peace agreement with Abiy Ahmed, 6
   statement at OAU opening session, 5
Air power in postcolonial African wars, **6–10**
   "Africa's World War," 9–10
   Biafra Air Force, 9
   colonial history, 6–8
   Command of the Air (Douhet), 6
   decolonization era, 8–10
   Egyptian Air Force, 7–8, 9, 10
   Ethiopian Air Force, 8
   first African air forces, 7–8
   Ghana Air Force, 8
   Israeli Air Force, 10
   Kenyan Air Force, 8
   Nigerian Air Force, 8
   Operation Serval (France), 10
   Royal Air Force, 7
   Royal Moroccan Air Force, 9
   South African Air Force, 7
   Southern Rhodesian Air Force, 7
   Ugandan Air Force, 9
   U.S. Air Force, 9
   World War II, 7
   Zimbabwe Air Force, 10
Al-Bashir, Omar (Umar) Hassan Ahmad, **10–11**
   birth and education, 10
   coup of 1989, 10
   creation of Revolutionary Command Council (RCC) for National Salvation, 10
   ICC arrest warrant for, 11
   support for National Islamic Front (NIF), 10–11
   support for Sharia Law, 11
   war with Sudan People's Liberation Army, 11
Algerian Civil War, **11–14**
   aftermath and consequences, 13
   arms and personnel, 12
   creation of Armed Islamic Group, 12
   creation of Islamic Armed Movement, 12
   deaths and casualties, 13
   destruction of Armed Islamic Group, 13
   end of, 13
   guerrilla warfare, 12
   historical context and origins, 11–12
   start of, 12

Algerian War of Independence, **14–18**
  Algerian independence, 17
  Battle of Algiers, 15–16
  deaths and casualties, 17
  French colonialism, 14–15
  Generals' Putsch, 17
  historical context and origins, 14–15
  start of, 15
Alliance of Democratic Forces for the Liberation of Congo (AFDL), 89, 114
Allied Democratic Forces (ADF)
  Congo Wars and, 89, 90
  creation of, 112
  Democratic Republic of the Congo and, 112–113
  insurgency in northern Uganda and, 336–337
  Namibia Independence War and, 217, 218
  peacekeeping and, 255
Al-Qaeda in the Islamic Maghreb (AQIM), **18–19**
  history of, 18–19
  motives of, 19
  Operation Serval and, 18–19
  operations, 18–19
Al-Shabaab, **19–21**
  allegiance to Al-Qaeda, 20
  command structure, 20
  early domestic attacks, 20
  history and early leadership, 19–20
  international attacks, 20–21
  U.S. bombing of Raso training camp, 21
Amin, Idi, **21–23**
  birth and early military career, 22
  coup of 1971, 22
  exile and death of, 22
  invasion of Tanzania's Kagera region, 22
  regime of, 22
Angolan Armed Forces (FAPLA and FAA), **23–26**
  Battle of Cuito Cuanavale, 24
  creation of FAA, 25
  creation of FAPLA, 23
  FAA personnel, 25
  FAPLA guerrilla units, 23
  FAPLA personnel and training, 24
  Soviet support for, 24–25
Angolan conflicts, **26–33**
  diamond smuggling, 32
  Independence Day massacre (1975), 27
  Operation Askari, 29

Operation Carnation, 28
  Operation Congresso II, 29
  Operation Daisy, 29
  Operation Excite, 31
  Operation Modular, 30
  Operation Packer, 31
  Operation Protea, 28–29
  Operation Reindeer (Cassinga raid), 28
  Operation Saluting, 29–30
  Operation Savannah (SADF invasion of Angola), 26–27
  Operation Sceptic (Smoke Shell), 28
  Operation Wallpaper, 29
Ansar al-Sharia in Libya, **33–34**
  attacks on U.S. diplomatic facilities in Benghazi, 33
  decline and dissolution of, 33
  history and creation of, 33
Anti-balaka militia, 74–75
Anyanya, **34–35**
  history and origins of, 34
  targets of, 34
  training camps of, 34–35
Arab Spring, **35–37**
  aftermath and consequences, 36
  civil wars, 36
  February 20 Revolution (Morocco), 36
  February 17th Revolution (Libya), 35
  governmental suppressions of, 36
  Green March protests (Oman), 35
  history and origins of, 35
  international interventions, 36
  Jasmine Revolution (Tunisia), 35
  Operation Odyssey Dawn, 36
  origins of the term, 36
  Tahrir Square protests (Egypt), 35
Arab-Israeli Wars, **37–41**
  history and origins of, 37
  Israeli War of Independence, 37–38
  Operation Nickel Grass, 40
  post-1973 developments and conflicts, 40–41
  Sinai Campaign, 38
  Six-Day War, 38–39
  War of Attrition, 39
  Yom Kippur War, 39–40
Armed Islamic Group (GIA), **41–42**
  decline and dissolution of, 41–42
  goals of, 41
  history and origins of, 41
  legacy of, 42

Army for the Liberation of Rwanda
    (ALIR)
  Congo Wars and, 90
  Democratic Republic of the Congo
    and, 110
  Hutu power movements and,
    156–157
Army of Islamic Salvation (AIS),
  42–43
  arrests of former militants, 42
  dissolution of, 42
  goals of, 42
  history and founding of, 42
Azanian People's Liberation Army
  (APLA), **43–45**
  history and origins of, 43
  name change from PAC to
    APLA, 44
  "New Road of Revolution," 44
  "One settler, one bullet," 44
  "positive action campaign," 43
  training of, 44

Barre, Mohamed Siad, **46–47**
  birth and early career, 46
  coup of 1969, 46
  exile and death of, 47
  Greater Somalia goal, 46
Belgian Military Intervention in Africa,
  47–49
  Operation Blue Beam, 48
  Operation Dragon Noire, 47
  Operation Dragon Rouge, 47
  Operation Green Apple, 48
  Operation Green Bean, 48
  Operation Red Bean, 48
  Operation Restore Hope, 48
  Operation Silverback, 48
Bokassa, Jean-Bédel, **49–50**
  assumption of presidency, 50
  birth and education, 49
  conviction of, 50
  death of, 50
  erratic behavior of, 50
  role in independence of Central African
    Republic, 49
Boko Haram, **51–54**
  heavy-handed approach toward, 53
  history and origins of, 51–53
  impact of killing of Mohammed Yusuf
    on, 53
  legacy of, 53

Bouteflika, Abdelaziz, **54–55**
  birth and early career of, 54
  presidencies of, 54–55
  resignation of, 55
Bozizé, François, **55–57**
  armed rebellions against, 57
  assumption of presidency, 55
  international arrest warrant for, 57
  regime of, 55–57
British military involvement in
    postcolonial Africa, **57–59**
  British Military Advisory and Training
    Team (BMATT), 58
  in East Africa, 57
  in Nigeria, Kenya, and Malawi,
    57–58
  Operation Barras, 58
  Operation Palliser, 58
  in Sierra Leone, 58
  in Uganda, 57
Burundi, civil war and genocide,
  59–63
  assassination of Melchior Ndadaye, 60
  civil war, 60–62
  genocide against Hutu, 59–60
  Tutsi military regimes, 59–60
Buyoya, Pierre, **63–64**
  birth and early career, 63
  conviction of, 64
  coup of 1987, 63
  coup of 1996, 63
  death of, 64
  electoral defeat of, 63
  rule of, 64

Cabindan insurgency, **65–66**
  aftermath and consequences of,
    65–66
  events of, 65
  Front for the Liberation of the
    Cabinda Enclave (FLEC)
    and, 65
  history and origins of, 65
Cabral, Amílcar, **66–67**
  assassination of, 66
  birth and early career, 66
  tactical success of, 66
Cameroon conflicts, **67–69**
  Anglophone-Cameroon conflict, 68
  Boko Haram, 68–69
  Union of the Peoples of Cameroon
    (UPC) uprising, 67–68

Canadian military involvement in Africa, 69–71
  Canadian Armed Forces (CAF), 70
  NATO missions, 70, 71
  Operation Unified Protector (NATO), 71
  Royal Canadian Air Force, 70
  in Rwanda, 70
  in Somalia, 70
  South African War, 70
  UN missions, 69, 70–71
  UN peacekeeping in Africa, 71
Casamance separatism, 71–73
  colonial period, 72
  history and origins of, 71–72
  onset of conflict, 72
  peace talks, 73
Central African Republic (CAR), conflict in, 73–76
  anti-balaka militia, 74–75
  early leaders and coups, 73–74
  International Support Mission to the CAR (MISCA), 75
  Movement for the Liberation of Congo (MLC) and, 74
  peace talks, 74–75
  Second Congo War ("Africa's World War"), 74
  Seleka rebels, 74–75
Chad, conflict in, 76–79
  civil war, 76, 78
  Habré-Oueddei alliance, 76, 78
  Libyan air base at Ouadi Doum, 77–78
  Libyan intervention, 76
  Malloum, Felix, and, 76
  National Liberation Front of Chad (FROLINAT), 76
  Operation Epervier (France), 78
  Operation Manta (France), 77
  Operation Tacaud, 76
  Patriotic Salvation Movement (MPS) and, 78
  "Toyota War," 78
  withdrawal of Libyans, 77
Child soldiers in Africa, 79–81
  civil wars, 80
  factors informing use of, 80
  history of, 79–80
  prohibition of, 80–81
Christmas War, 81–82
  aftermath and consequences, 82
  deaths and casualties, 82
  events of, 82
  history and onset of, 81–82
Cold War in Africa, 82–85
  Cold War superpowers, 83–84
  collapse of Soviet Union, 85
  Congo Crisis, 83
  Nigerian Civil War, 84
  Soviet support for Egypt, 84
  Suez Crisis, 83
Congo Crisis, 85–88
  deaths and casualties, 87
  ONUC withdrawal, 87
  Operation Dragon Rouge, 87
  Operation Grand Slam (ONUC), 86
  Operation Morthor (ONUC), 86
  Operation Rum Punch (ONUC), 86
  Operation Violettes Imperiales, 87
  Operation White Giant, 87
  Simba rebels, 87
Congo wars, 88–94
  Alliance of Democratic Forces for the Liberation of Congo (AFDL) and, 89
  Allied Democratic Forces (ADF) and, 89, 90
  Army for the Liberation of Rwanda (ALIR) and, 90
  First Congo War, 89–91
  historical context, 88–89
  Lusaka Agreement, 92
  Mai militia and, 90, 92
  Movement for the Liberation of Congo (MLC) and, 91–92
  Rally for Congolese Democracy (RCD) and, 90–92
  Second Congo War ("Africa's World War"), 91–93
  withdrawal of foreign state forces, 93
Congolese National Liberation Front (FLNC), 286–289
Côte d'Ivoire Civil War, 94–96
  events of, 94–95
  historical context, 94
  New Forces and, 94–95
  onset of, 94
  Operation Unicorn (France), 94–95
  partition of Côte d'Ivoire, 95
Coups and military regimes in Africa, 96–98
  background and historical context, 96
  Operation Barracuda (France), 97
  theories of, 96–97
  types of military regimes, 97–98
COVID-19 pandemic, 62, 64, 151, 242
Cuba and Africa, 98–100

Cuban intervention in Angola, 99
Cuban intervention in Ethiopia, 99
Cuban presence in Guinea-Bissau, 99
escalation of Cuban presence in Angola, 100
historical context, 98–99
withdrawal of South African forces from Namibia, 100
Cuito Cuanavale, Battle of, **100–104**
consequences of, 103
events of, 101–102
historical context, 100–101
Operation Hooper (SADF), 102
Operation *Maniobra XXXI Anniversario* (Cuba), 102
Operation Modular, 101–102
Operation Packer (South Africa), 102
Operation *Saudando Outubro,* 101
outcomes of, 102–103

Darfur genocide, **105–107**
historical context, 105
international response of, 106–107
origins of, 105
victims of, 105–106
Déby, Idriss, **107–108**
assumption of power, 108
birth and education, 107–108
death of, 108
regime of, 108
Democratic Forces for the Liberation of Rwanda (FDLR), 93
Democratic Republic of the Congo and, 110–112, 113
Hutu power movements, 157
Democratic Republic of the Congo (DRC), continuing violence in, **109–113**
Allied Democratic Forces (ADF) and, 112–113
Army for the Liberation of Rwanda (ALIR) and, 110
Democratic Forces for the Liberation of Rwanda (FDLR), 110–112, 113
Mai Mai militia and, 110, 111
March 23 Movement (M23), 111–112
Nkunda, Laurent, and, 110–111
Ntaganda, Bosco, and, 111–112
Operation Artemis (European Union), 110
Operation Umoja Wetu (Our Unity), 112
Pretoria Agreement, 110

Rally for Congolese Democracy (RCD) and, 109
Second Congo War, 112–113
Diamonds and conflict in postcolonial Africa, **113–116**
in Angola, 114
in Botswana, 115
in DRC, 114–115
end of Cold War and, 114
historical context, 113–114
in Sierra Leone, 114
in Zimbabwe, 115
Doe, Samuel, **116**
birth and early career, 116
coup of 1980, 116
death of, 116
Dos Santos, Jose Eduardo, **117–118**
assumption of presidency, 117
birth and education, 117
civil war, 117
resignation of, 118

East African Mutiny, **119–120**
aftermath and consequences of, 120
events of, 119–120
history and origins of, 119
inciting factors, 119
ECOWAS military interventions, **120–122**
in Côte d'Ivoire, 121
First Liberian Civil War, 120–121
in Gambia, 121
in Guinea-Bissau, 121
historical context, 120
in Liberia, 121
in Sierra Leone, 121
Eritrea-Ethiopia War, **122–124**
deaths and casualties, 123
events of, 122–123
historical context, 122
onset of, 122
Eritrean Liberation Front (ELF), **124–125**
absorbed by EPLF, 125
Derg revolution (1974), 124
guerrilla strategy in Ethiopia, 124
Eritrean People's Liberation Front (EPLF), **125–126**
Battle of Afabet, 125
guerrilla tactics, 125
history and origins of, 125
name change to People's Front for Democracy and Justice, 126

Eritrean War of Independence, **126–128**
  Battle of Afabet, 1–2, 130
  end of, 126–127
  Eritrean independence, 126–127
  Ethiopian coup of 1974 and, 127
  historical context, 126–127
  Tigray People's Liberation Front (TPLF), 127
Ethiopia: insurgency and interstate war, **128–131**
  Border War, 130
  Cold War and, 128–130
  Derg revolution (1974), 128–129
  historical context, 128
  "War on Terror" and, 130

Famine in postcolonial African conflicts, **132–134**
  Angolan Civil War, 133
  Cold War era, 132–133
  First Sudanese Civil War, 132
  Mozambique Civil War, 133
  Nigerian Civil War, 132
  Operation Lifeline Sudan (OLS), 133
  Operation Rainbow (Khartoum), 133
  Second Sudanese Civil War, 133
"Five Majors" coup, Nigeria, **134–135**
  aftermath and consequences, 134–135
  events of, 134
  historical context, 134
French military involvement in postcolonial Africa, **135–138**
  Operation Amaryllis, 136
  Operation Artemis, 137
  Operation Barkhane, 137
  Operation Barracuda, 136
  Operation Leopard, 136
  Operation Serval, 137
  Operation Turquoise, 136
Front for National Salvation (FRONASA), 214, 225–226, 339
Front for the Liberation of the Cabinda Enclave (FLEC), 65, 259

Gaddafi, Muammar, **139–141**
  Arab-Israeli issue and, 140–141
  birth and education of, 139
  coup of 1969, 139
  death of, 141
  domestic policies, 139
  foreign policies, 139
  terrorism and, 140
Garang, John de Mabior, **141–142**
  birth and education of, 141
  death of, 142
  First Sudan Civil War, 142
  political ideology, 142
Gbagbo, Laurent, **142–145**
  arrests of, 143
  birth and education of, 143
  charges against, 144
  civil war, 144
  coup of 1999 and, 143–144
  early career, 143
Genocide in Africa, **145–147**
  against Hutu people, 146–147
  against Igbo people, 146
  against Luba people, 146
Gowon, Yakubu "Jack" Dan-Yumma, **148–149**
  birth and education of, 148
  coup of 1966 and, 148
  exile of, 149
  "No Victor, No Vanquished," 148
  ousted in coup of 1975, 148–149

Habré, Hissène, **150–151**
  assumption of power, 150
  birth and education of, 150
  death of, 150–151
  exile and indictment of, 150–151
Habyarimana, Juvénal, **151–154**
  birth and education of, 151
  civil war, 152–153
  death of, 153
  as Hutu supremacist, 152
  regime of, 151–152
  widow of, 153–154
Haftar, Khalifa Belqasim, **154–155**
  birth and education of, 154
  Libyan National Army (LNA), 155
  Operation Karama (Dignity), 155
  political positions of, 154–155
Holy Spirit Movement (HSM), 335
Hutu power movements, **155–159**
  Armed Forces of Rwanda (FAR), 156
  Army for the Liberation of Rwanda (ALIR), 156–157
  Army for the Liberation of Rwanda (ALIR) and, 156–157

Index

Democratic Forces for the Liberation of Rwanda (FDLR), 156–157
historical context, 155–156
Party for the Liberation of the Hutu People (PALIPEHUTU), 157–158

Islamic Salvation Front (FIS), **160–161**
Army of Islamic Salvation (armed wing), 160
first free elections and, 160
history and origins of, 160

Janjaweed, **162–163**
history and origins of, 162
influence of, 163
origins of the term, 162
Justice and Equality Movement (JEM), **163–165**
formation and early years, 164
post-2006 years, 164–165

Kabila, Joseph, **166–168**
education and military service, 166
presidency and national crisis, 167–168
succession of, 167
Kabila, Laurent, **168–170**
assassination of, 168–169
birth and education of, 168
regime of, 168
Kagame, Paul, **170–173**
birth and education of, 170
civil war, 171
creation of Rwandan Patriotic Front, 170
criticism and controversy, 171, 172
genocide and, 171–172
Kagera War, **173–175**
aftermath and consequences of, 175
events of, 174–175
historical context, 173
Mogadishu Agreement and, 173
Operation Chakaza, 174
origins of, 173–174
Kamajor militia, 291
Kenya, Mau Emergency, **175–178**
aftermath and consequences of, 177–178
deaths and casualties, 177
events of, 176–177
historical context, 175
Operation Anvil, 176

Operation Jock Scott, 176
origins of, 176
Kiir, Salva Mayardit, **178–179**
birth and early career, 178
first president of South Sudan, 179
Second Sudanese Civil War, 178–179

Lagu, Joseph Yanga, **180–181**
birth and education of, 180
leader of Southern Sudan Liberation Movement, 180
president of the High Executive Council of the Southern Sudan Autonomous Region, 180
Liberian civil wars, **181–184**
First Liberian Civil War, 181–182
Movement for Democracy in Liberia (MODEL) and, 183
Operation Octopus, 181
Second Liberian Civil War, 182–183
United Liberation Movement for Democracy (ULIMO), 182
Liberians United for Reconciliation and Democracy (LURD), **184–186**
creation of, 184
funding sources, 184–185
historical context, 184
internal divisions, 185
peace agreement, 185
Libya, conflicts with Egypt and the United States, **186–188**
Border War, 187
collapse of Soviet Union and, 187
First Libyan Civil War, 187
historical context, 186
Kagera War, 187
terrorism and, 187
Libyan Civil War, First, **188–190**
Arab Spring and, 188
Battle of Misrata, 189
events of, 188–189
Gaddafi's capture and execution, 189–190
historical context, 188
international intervention, 189–190
Operation Odyssey Dawn, 189
Libyan Civil War, Second, **190–191**
events of, 191
historical context, 190
Libyan National Army (LNA), 191
Libyan Political Agreement, 191
Libyan National Army (LNA), 155, 191

Lord's Resistance Army (LRA), **191–194**
   activities of, 192
   creation of, 192
   historical context, 191–192
   international efforts against, 192–193
   Invisible Children and, 193
   Kony, Joseph, and, 192–193

M23 Rebels, 93, 111–112, 167, 215, 255
Machar, Riek Teny Dhurgon, **195–196**
   birth and education of, 195
   Nasir coup, 195
   vice president of southern Sudan, 196
Mai militia, 90, 92, 110, 111
Malloum, Felix, 76, 150
Mengistu Haile Mariam, **196–198**
   birth and education of, 196–197
   conviction of, 197
   criticisms and controversy, 196
   Derg and, 196–197
Mercenaries in African conflicts, **198–201**
   end of Cold War and, 199–200
   "golden era" of, 198–199
   historical context, 198
   Nigerian Civil War, 199
   September 2001 terrorist attacks and, 200
Micombero, Michel, **201–203**
   advocate of African socialism, 202
   birth and education of, 201
   death of, 203
   dissolution of government, 202
   first president of Burundi, 201
   Hutu uprising against, 202
Mobutu Sese Seko, **203–204**
   assumption of power, 203
   birth and education of, 203
   death of, 204
   expulsion of, 204
   national authenticity movement of, 203–204
Mogadishu, Battle of, **204–206**
   aftermath of, 206
   "Black Hawk Down" and, 205
   events of, 205–206
Mokhtar Belmokhtar, **206–207**
   birth and early life of, 206
   death of, 206
   terrorism and, 206–207
Mondlane, Eduardo, **207–208**
   birth and education of, 207–208
   president of FRELIMO, 208
Movement for Democracy in Liberia (MODEL), 183, 184–185
Movement for the Liberation of Congo (MLC), 74, 91–92
Mozambique Civil War, **208–211**
   end of Cold War and, 210
   historical context, 208
   peace deal, 211
   security pact between ZANU-PF and FRELIMO, 209
   South Africa and, 209
Mozambique National Resistance (RENAMO), **211–212**
   elections of October 1994, 211–212
   founding of, 211
   insurgency, 212
   membership, 211
   national council, 211
Mugabe, Robert, **212–214**
   birth and education of, 212
   coup against (2017), 213
   death of, 212, 214
   as executive president, 213
   as prime minister, 213
   resignation of, 213–214
Museveni, Yoweri, **214–216**
   birth and education of, 214
   criticism and controversy, 215–216
   regional influence of, 215
   as resistance leader, 214–215

Namibia Independence War, **217–219**
   Allied Democratic Forces (ADF) and, 217, 218
   historical context, 217
   independence of South West Africa (SWA), 218
   People's Liberation Army of Namibia (PLAN), 217–218
   Popular Movement for the Liberation of Angola (MPLA), 218
Nasser, Gamal Abdel, **219–221**
   assumption of presidency, 220
   birth and education of, 219
   death of, 221
   defense pact with Syria, 220–221
   domestic policy, 220
   early military career, 219–220
   foreign policy, 220
   Six-Day War, 221
   Suez Crisis, 220

National Front for the Liberation of
 Angola (FNLA), **221–223**
 conflict with Popular Movement for the
  Liberation of Angola (MPLA) and, 222
 creation of Union of the Peoples of
  Northern Angola (UPNA), 221
 historical context, 221–222
National Liberation Front (FLN) Algeria,
 223–224
 historical context, 223
 as political organization, 223–224
 terror and guerilla tactics, 223
National Liberation Front of Chad
 (FROLINAT), 60, 76
National Movement for the Liberation of
 Azawad (MNLA), 333
National Patriotic Front of Liberia (NPFL),
 224–225
 creation of, 224
 historical context, 224
 Taylor, Charles, and, 224–225
National Resistance Army (NRA),
 225–227
 child soldiers, 226
 Front for National Salvation
  (FRONASA) and, 225–226
 historical context, 225–226
 impact of, 225–226
 renamed Uganda People's Defence
  Force (UPDF), 226–227
National Union for the Total Independence
 of Angola (UNITA), **227–229**
 civil war and, 227–228
 creation of, 227
 criticism and controversy, 228
 death of Savimbi, 229
 historical context, 227–228
Navies in postcolonial Africa, **229–235**
 Algerian Navy, 233
 colonial era, 230
 decolonization era, 230–233
 Egyptian Navy, 234
 Ethiopian Navy, 232
 Ghanaian Navy, 231
 historical context, 229
 Kenyan Navy, 232, 234
 Nigerian Navy, 230–231
 Operation Green Sea (Portugal), 231
 People's Liberation Army Navy
  (PLAN), 234
 postcolonial era, 234
 Royal East African Navy, 232

Royal Navy, 232, 233
Senegalese Navy, 231
Somali Navy, 234
South African Naval Force (SANF), 230
South African Navy, 233
Soviet Navy, 231
Tanzanian Naval Command, 234
Neto, António Agostinho, **235–236**
 birth and education of, 235
 Carnation Revolution and, 235–236
 death of, 236
 first president of independent Angola,
  235, 236
New Forces, 94–95
Nigerian Civil War, **236–239**
 events of, 237–238
 historical context, 236–237
 oil and, 237
 Operation Tail-wind, 238
 Operation Tiger-Claw, 238
Nkomo, Joshua, **239–240**
 birth and education of, 239
 death of, 240
 early political career, 239
 vice president of Zimbabwe, 239, 240
Nkurunziza, Pierre, **240–242**
 criticism and controversy, 241
 death of, 242
 as president of Burundi, 240–242
Nujoma, Sam, **242–243**
 birth and education of, 242
 first president of independent Namibia,
  242, 306
 views of, 243
Nyerere, Julius, **243–244**
 death of, 244
 early years and education of, 243–244
 foreign policy of, 244
 as prime minister, 244

Ogaden War, **245–247**
 aftermath and consequences of, 246
 Battle of Dire Dawa, 245
 events of, 245–246
 historical context, 245
 onset of, 245
Ojukwu, Chukwuemeka Odumegwu,
 247–248
 birth and education of, 247
 coup against and imprisonment of, 248
 death of, 248
 leader of secessionist state of Biafra, 247

Operation Amaryllis, 136, 278
Operation Anvil, 176
Operation Artemis, 110, 137
Operation Askari, 29, 301
Operation Barkhane, 137
Operation Barracuda, 97, 136
Operation Barras, 58, 291
Operation Blue Beam, 48
Operation Boleas: the SADC's military intervention into Lesotho, **248–250**
   aftermath, 249
   historical context, 248–249
   primary objectives of, 249
Operation Carnation, 28
Operation Chakaza, 174
Operation Congresso II, 29
Operation Daisy, 29
Operation Dignity, 292
Operation Dragon Noire, 47
Operation Dragon Rouge, 47, 87
Operation El Dorado Canyon, 344
Operation Epervier, 78
Operation Excite, 31
Operation Gordian Knot, 261
Operation Grand Slam, 86
Operation Green Apple, 48
Operation Green Bean, 48
Operation Green Sea, 231, 262
Operation Hooper, 102
Operation Jock Scott, 176
Operation Kadesh, 324–325
Operation Karama (Dignity), 155
Operation Leopard, 136, 288
Operation Lifeline Sudan (OLS), 133
Operation *Maniobra XXXI Anniversario*, 102
Operation Manta, 77
Operation Mayibaye, 341
Operation Modular, 30, 101–102
Operation Morthor, 86
Operation Nickel Grass, 40
Operation Noroit, 277
Operation Octopus, 181
Operation Odyssey Dawn, 36, 189
Operation Odyssey Lightning, 293
Operation Packer, 31, 102
Operation Palliser, 58
Operation Palliver, 291
Operation Protea, 28–29, 301
Operation Rainbow, 133
Operation Red Bean, 48, 288
Operation Reindeer, 28, 301

Operation Restore Hope, **250–251**
   aftermath and consequences, 251
   Battle of Mogadishu and, 251
   goals of, 250–251
   historical context, 250
Operation Rum Punch, 86
Operation Saluting, 29–30
Operation *Saudando Outubro*, 101
Operation Savannah, 26–27, 266, 300–301
Operation Sceptic (Smoke Shell), 28
Operation Serval, 10, 18–19, 137
Operation Silverback, 48, 278
Operation Tacaud, 76
Operation Tail-wind, 238
Operation Tiger-Claw, 238
Operation Turquoise, 136, 278
Operation Umoja Wetu (Our Unity), 112
Operation Unicorn, 94–95
Operation Violettes Imperiales, 87
Operation Vula, 298
Operation Wallpaper, 29
Operation White Giant, 87

Patriotic Salvation Movement (MPS), 78, 107–108
Peacekeeping in Africa, **252–256**
   activist UN missions, 254–255
   African Standby Force (ASF), 253
   Allied Democratic Forces (ADF) and, 255
   Congo mission, 254
   exclusions from, 252
   "Force Intervention Brigade" for MONUSCO, 255
   historical context, 252
   misconceptions regarding, 253–254
   motivations for, 253
   PSO deployments, 252–253
   regional organizations, 253
   UN-authorized versus UN-led coalitions, 255
   United Nations Emergency Force (UNEF) for Suez, 254
People's Liberation Army of Namibia (PLAN), 217–218, 242, 300–301, 305–306
Popular Front for the Liberation of Saguia el Hamra and Rio de Oro (POLISARIO), 347–348
Popular Movement for the Liberation of Angola (MPLA), **256–258**
   collapse of Soviet Union and, 257

historical context, 256
history and founding of, 256–257
proclamation of People's Republic of Angola, 257
training of first guerrilla fighters, 257
Portuguese Africa, Independence Wars (Angola, Mozambique, and Guinea-Bissau), **258–263**
African Party for the Independence of Guinea and Cape Verde (PAIGC), 261–262
Angola, 258–260
coup in Lisbon (1974), 262–263
Front for the Liberation of the Cabinda Enclave (FLEC) and, 259
Guinea-Bissau, 262
historical context, 258
Mozambique, 260–261
Operation Gordian Knot, 261
Operation Green Sea, 262

Quifangondo, Battle of, **264–268**
consequences of, 267
events of, 266–267
historical context, 264
Operation Savannah, 266
opposing sides in, 264–266
outcomes of, 267

Rally for Congolese Democracy (RCD), 90–92, 109
Refugees in postcolonial Africa, **269–273**
defining "refugee," 269–270
examples of refugees, 271
internally displaced persons, 270
refugee camps, 271–272
types of refugees, 270
Revolutionary United Front (RUF), **273–275**
diamond mining and, 273, 274
founding of, 273
historical context, 273
methods of operation, 273
Roberto, Holden Álverto, **275–276**
birth and education of, 275
death of, 276
founding of Union of Peoples of Northern Angola (renamed Union of Peoples of Angola), 275
Rwanda, civil war and genocide, **276–279**
civil war, 277–278
genocide, 278

historical context, 276–277
Operation Amaryllis (France), 278
Operation Noroit, 277
Operation Silverback (European Union), 278
Operation Turquoise (France), 278
Rwandan Patriotic Front (RPF), **279–280**
criticism and controversy, 279–280
historical context, 279
name change from Rwandese Alliance for National Unity to, 279

Sankara, Thomas, **281–283**
assumption of presidency, 282
birth and early years, 281
coup against (1987), 281, 282–283
death of, 281, 283
Sankoh, Foday Saybana, **283–284**
arrest of, 284
birth and early years, 283
death of, 284
insurgency, 284
partnership with Gaddafi, 283–284
Savimbi, Jonas, **284–286**
birth and education of, 285
founding of UNITA, 285
president of National Union for the Total Independence of Angola, 284, 285
Seleka rebels, 57, 74–75
Shaba, Zaire: rebel incursions and foreign intervention, **286–289**
Battle of Dien Bien Phu, 288
Congolese National Liberation Front (FLNC) and, 286–289
Operation Leopard (France), 288
Operation Red Bean, 288
Sierra Leone Civil War, **289–292**
historical context, 289
Kamajor militia, 291
Operation Barras (UK), 291
Operation Palliver (UK), 291
origins of, 289–290
United Liberation Movement for Democracy (ULIMO), 290
Simba rebels, 47, 87, 168, 199
Sirte, Battle of, **292–293**
events of, 293
historical context, 292
Operation Dignity, 292
Operation Odyssey Lightning (AFRICOM), 293

Somalia Civil War, **293–296**
   historical context, 293–294
   Operation Restore Hope (U.S.), 294–295
   refugee crisis, 294–295
South Africa, armed struggle against apartheid, **296–300**
   African National Congress (ANC) and, 297
   apartheid regime's "total strategy," 298
   historical context, 296–297
   Mandela, Nelson, and, 297, 299
   Operation Vula (ANC), 298
   Pan-Africanist Congress (PAC) and, 297, 298–299
   passive resistance, 297
   Soweto Uprising, 298
South Africa's Border War, **300–303**
   cross-border raids, 301
   historical context, 300
   Namibian independence, 302–303
   Operation Askari, 301
   Operation Protea, 301
   Operation Reindeer, 301
   Operation Savannah, 300–301
   origins of, 300
   UNITA and Cuito Cuanavale, 301–302
South Sudan Civil War, **303–305**
   historical context, 303–304
   independence of South Sudan, 304
   resumption of the war, 304–305
South West Africa People's Organization (SWAPO), **305–307**
   elections of 1989, 306
   history and origins, 305–306
   membership, 306
   political power of, 306
Southern Sudan Liberation Movement (SSLM), 180, 314
Soviet military involvement in Africa, **307–312**
   Brezhnev era, 310
   Gorbachev era, 311
   Great Patriotic War, 308
   historical context, 307–312
   Khrushchev era, 309
   Putin ear, 312
   Soviet navy and, 309–310
   Stalinist era, 307–308
Sudan Civil War, First, **312–315**
   events of, 314
   historical context, 312–313
   Juba Conference, 313
   onset of, 314
   Southern Sudan Liberation Movement (SSLM) and, 314
Sudan Civil War, Second, **315–317**
   Addis Ababa Agreement, 315
   aftermath and consequences, 316
   deaths and casualties, 315
Sudan Liberation Army (SLA), **317–319**
   origins and early years, 317–318
   splintering of, 318–319
Sudan People's Liberation Movement/Army (SPLM/A), **319–321**
   capture of Nasir, 320
   Comprehensive Peace Agreement (Navisha Agreement), 321
   guerrilla strategy, 319–320
   historical context, 319
   military ideology, 319
Suez Crisis, **321–327**
   cease-fire, 326
   historical context, 321–322
   legacy of, 326–327
   Operation Kadesh (Israel), 324–325

Taylor, Charles McArthur Ghankay, **328–330**
   birth and education of, 328
   First Liberian Civil War and, 329
   president of Liberia, 329
   rule of, 329
   trial of, 329
Tigray People's Liberation Front (TPLF), **330–331**
   creation of, 330
   historical context, 330
   legacy of, 331
"Toyota War," 78
Tuareg rebellions since 1960 (Mali and Niger), **331–334**
   First Tuarge Rebellion, 331
   historical context, 331
   National Movement for the Liberation of Azawad (MNLA) and, 333
   rebellions since 1960, 333
   Second Tuarge Rebellion, 332
   Tuareg Rebellion of 2012, 333

Uganda, insurgency in the North, **335–337**
   allied Democratic Forces (ADF) and, 336–337
   "Arrow Groups," 336

historical context, 335
Holy Spirit Movement (HSM), 335
West Nile Bank Front (WNBF) and, 336–337
Uganda's Civil War: the Bush War, **337–339**
  events of, 338–339
  historical context, 337–338
  legacy of, 339
Umkhonto we Sizwe (MK), **340–342**
  bombings, 340–341
  exile, 341
  historical context, 340
  legacy of, 342
  Operation Mayibaye, 341
United Liberation Movement for Democracy (ULIMO), 182, 290
U.S. Africa Command, **342–343**
  creation of, 342–343
  historical context, 342
  purpose of, 342
  structure of, 343
U.S. military involvement in Africa, **344–346**
  attack on U.S. consulate in Benghazi, 345
  Barbary Wars, 344
  counterterrorism, 345
  humanitarian relief, 344–345
  military training, 345
  Operation El Dorado Canyon, 344
  World War II, 344

West Nile Bank Front (WNBF), 112, 336–337
Western Sahara, conflict in, **347–349**
  arms sales, 348
  historical context, 347
  Popular Front for the Liberation of Saguia el Hamra and Rio de Oro (POLISARIO), 347–348
  "War on Terror" and, 349
Women and war in Africa, **349–353**
  civil wars, 351
  decolonization and, 350–351
  historical context, 349
  peace advocacy, 351
  precolonial warfare, 349–350
  slave trade and, 350

Zenawi, Meles, **354–355**
  birth and education of, 354
  criticism and controversy, 355
  death of, 355
  president of Ethiopia, 354, 355
Zimbabwe, massacres (Gukurahundi), **355–358**
  Catholic Commission on Peace and Justice report on, 357
  historical context and origins of, 355–357
  meaning of "Gukurahundi," 357
Zimbabwe African National Union (ZANU), **358–360**
  coup of 2017, 359
  historical context, 358
  renamed ZANU-Patriotic Front (ZANU-PF), 359
Zimbabwe African People's Union (ZAPU), **360–361**
  founding of, 360
  historical context, 360
  Nkomo, Joshua, and, 360–361
Zimbabwe Independence War, **361–364**
  aftermath and consequences, 365
  end of, 365
  first phase of, 362–363
  historical context, 361–362
  second phase of, 363–364

www.ingramcontent.com/pod-product-compliance
Lightning Source LLC
Chambersburg PA
CBHW082023300426
44117CB00015B/2326